A

TREATISE

ON

OBLIGATIONS,

CONSIDERED IN A

MORAL AND *LEGAL* VIEW.

Translated from the French of POTHIER.

IN TWO VOLUMES.

With a New Introduction

by

Warren M. Billings

Distinguished Professor of History Emeritus University of New Orleans
and Bicentennial Historian of the Supreme Court of Louisiana

THE LAWBOOK EXCHANGE, LTD.
Clark, New Jersey

ISBN 978-1-886363-62-5

Lawbook Exchange edition 1999, 2014

The quality of this reprint is equivalent to the quality of the original work.

The Lawbook Exchange, Ltd.
33 Terminal Avenue
Clark, New Jersey 07066-1321

Please see our website for a selection of our other publications and fine facsimile reprints of classic works of legal history:
www.lawbookexchange.com

Library of Congress Cataloging-in-Publication Data

Pothier, Robert Joseph, 1699-1772.
[Traité des obligations selon les règles tant du for de la conscience que du for extèrieur. English]
A treatise on obligations, considered in a moral and legal view / translated from the French of Pothier.
p. cm.
translated by Francois-Xavier Martin.
Originally published: Newburn, N.C. : Martin & Ogden, 1802.
Includes bibliographical references.
ISBN 1-886363-62-5 (cloth : alk. paper)
1. Contracts—France. 2. Obligations (Law)—France. I. Title.

KJV1668.P6813 1998
346.4402—dc21 98-38360
CIP

Printed in the United States of America on acid-free paper

Introduction

No longer is Robert Joseph Pothier a name that resonates with present-day American attorneys or historians, but that was not always so. In the decades before the Civil War, practitioners and scholars regarded the Frenchman's *Traité des obligations selon les règles tant du for de la conscience que du for extèrieur* (Paris, 1761) as essential reading. David Hoffman, an authority on legal education, recommended it, the Supreme Court of Louisiana required it of would-be lawyers, and Luther S. Cushing, editor of *American Jurist*, declared it a "standard work, without which even a moderately sized law-library would scarcely be considered complete."[1]

Cushing, Hoffman, and the judges of the Louisiana high court knew the *Traité* in the language of its author, but those of their generation who had no command of French relied upon English renderings. François-Xavier Martin, a printer of New Bern, North Carolina, had the distinction of producing the first ever translation, which he issued in 1802 under the title *A Treatise on Obligations, Considered in a Moral and Legal View*. Nevertheless, a rival version, done by William David Evans and published in 1804, quickly

---

[1] David Hoffman, *A Course of Legal Study, Addressed to Students and the Profession Generally* (Baltimore, 1836), 322, 481; Rule of Court, 24 Nov. 1840, in Warren M. Billings, ed., *The Historic Rules of the Supreme Court of Louisiana, 1813–1879*), 10; Cushing, *American Jurist,* 12 (1843): 455. Unless noted otherwise, this and subsequent citations to contemporary legal texts are to the witnesses in the Law Library of Louisiana or in the editor's personal library.

became the preferred choice of American lawyers.[2] Martin's edition fell from fashion, and surviving witnesses eventually wound up on library shelves gathering dust in quiet obscurity. The facsimile that follows brings this important example of early American legal publishing within convenient reach for the first time in nearly two hundred years.

Martin's Pothier is seldom consulted as a work of law nowadays. Its value is thus mainly historical. Consequently, why and how Martin came to offer his translation throws light on the links between books, printers, lawyers, and the spread of legal knowledge during a formative period of American law.

When the Continental Congress proclaimed independence in 1776, it signaled a revolution of law as well as government. Revolutionizing government ended with the adoption the Constitution and the Bill of Rights; revolutionizing law continued well into the nineteenth century. A blooming market economy, in conjunction with technological innovation and territorial expansion, wrought immense sea changes that generated masses of novel laws and required the recasting of older ones. Reform-minded attorneys, judges, legislators, and even plain citizens wrestled with ways to distinguish state and federal law from its English antecedents while educators sought to elevate lawyering from a gentleman's occupation to a profession. Professionalization also went tongue in groove with the founding of law schools and a general drift towards turning law into a "science." Then too, as practitioners labored to

---

[2] William David Evans (1767–1821), a barrister and publisher of law texts, produced this translation, which A[ndrew] Strahan printed for the London bookseller Joseph Butterworth under the title *A Treatise on the Law of Obligations, or Contracts. By M. Pothier*. It became the basis for three subsequent American editions that the Philadelphia printer, Robert H. Small, issued beginning in 1826.

make law more rational, their strivings inspired in some a fondness for codification that in its turn encouraged a keen interest in civil law treatises such as Pothier's.[3] All told, such refinements fueled an already constant need for legal texts, which were as elemental to attorneys as planes and chisels were to cabinetmakers. Industrious entrepreneurs like François-Xavier Martin responded with a steady output of titles that ranged across every conceivable legal subject.[4]

---

[3] J. Louis Telkampf, "On Codification, Or The Systematization of the Law," *American Jurist*, 8 (1841–42): 113–44, 283–329; J. Willard Hurst, *Law and the Conditions of Freedom in the Nineteenth-Century United States* (Madison, 1967); Maxwell J. Bloomfield, "William Sampson and the Codifiers: Roots of American Legal Reform, 1820–1830" *American Journal of Legal History* 11 (1967): 234–252; Gerard W. Gawalt, "Massachusetts Lawyers: A Historical Analysis of the Process of Professionalization, 1760–1840" (Ph.D. diss., Clark University, 1969); Lawrence M. Friedman, *A History of American Law* (New York, 1973), 202–264; William E. Nelson, *The Americanization of the Common Law: The Impact of Legal Change in Massachusetts, 1776–1830* (Cambridge, Mass., 1975); Maxwell J. Bloomfield, *American Lawyers in a Changing Society* (New York, 1976); Charles M. Cook, *The American Codification Movement, A Study in Legal Reform* (Westport, Conn., 1981), 161–184.

[4] Kate Wallach, "The Publication of Legal Treatises in America from 1800 to 1830," *Law Library Journal*, 45 (1942): 136–148; Meira G. Pimsleur, ed., *Checklist of Basic American Legal Publications*, (Hackensack, N.J., 1962); Rollo G. Silver, *The American Printer, 1787–1825* (Charlottesville, 1967), 114–145; Friedman, *A History of American Law*, 282–292; Warren M. Billings, "An American Original: John Bouvier's Law Dictionary," *LH&RB*, Newsletter of the Legal History & Rare Books Special Interest Section of the American Association of Law Libraries, 6 (1996): 8–9; "A Neglected Treatise: Lewis Kerr's *Exposition* and the Making of Criminal Law in Louisiana," *Louisiana History* 38 (1997): 261–287; Florence M. Jumonville, "'The Peoples' Friend—The Tyrant's Foe': Law-Related New Orleans Imprints, 1803–1860," in Warren M. Billings and Mark F. Fernandez, eds., *A Law Unto Itself? Essays in the New Louisiana Legal History* (Baton Rouge, 2001), 40–58.

Martin in many ways typified American law publishers of his era. He and his colleagues catered mainly to local and regional customers, though a fortunate few—situated in Boston, New York, or Philadelphia—hawked their wares nationally. While the production of law books assured a regular income, the returns were not always handsome. Nor did the business necessarily confer high standing, especially in a day when occupation still determined rank to a large extent. Printers commanded a measure of respectability, owing to the skills required of their craft and the services they provided for their communities, but they did not enjoy the social stature of a minister, a teacher, or a lawyer. Writing, setting, binding, and selling legal texts often led individual print shop owners to take up the practice of law. The more successful of those who walked that way then went on to careers at the bar or on the bench. So it was with Martin.

Born in Marseilles into a mercantile family, Martin(1762–1846) trained for the Roman Catholic priesthood as a youth. He disdained holy orders in his twenties, opting instead for a commercial opportunity with an uncle who lived on the island of Martinique in the West Indies. The venture misfired, whereupon Martin sailed to New York, hoping to collect the proceeds from a debt for a fresh start. That plan went awry too. Penniless, he set off south and joined the Continental Army. His military service was ingloriously short. While on picket duty one day, he sounded the alarm, only to discover that the British redcoats his near-sighted eyes perceived were in reality no more menacing than red nightshirts on a washerwoman's clothesline. His embarrassment and the merciless taunts of his comrades sent him over the hill, and he at length alighted in New Bern.[5]

---

[5] Martin has no modern biographer, but aspects of his life and career are discussed in Henry Adams Bullard, *A Discourse on the Life and Character of the Hon. François-Xavier Martin, Late Senior Judge of*

A deserter, broke, and barely fluent in English, he had few visible prospects but lots of ambition. He scrambled for work, taking whatever odd tasks fell his way. A break came when he approached a local printer, variously identified as James Davis or Robert Keith,[6] for work as a typesetter. Martin knew absolutely nothing about the craft, but he fibbed himself into a job nonetheless. He explained his initial ineptitude by saying that French compositors used different methods, and it would be a while before he understood the American system. His employer's indulgence enabled him to develop into a master printer in his own right. Indeed, at the close of the 1790s, Martin's was one of the more prolific printeries in North Carolina; newspapers, broadsides, advertisement, blank forms, sermons, almanacs, novels, school books, and law books fell from his press in ever increasing numbers. Compling and publishing legal texts kindled his interest not only in

---

the Supreme Court (New Orleans, 1847); William Wirt Howe, "Memoir of François-Xavier Martin," in François-Xavier Martin, *The History of Louisiana from the Earliest Period*, ed. by James Gresham (New Orleans, 1882), vii–xxxviii; Edward L. Tinker, "Jurist and Japer: François-Xavier Martin and Jean LeClerc: With a List of Their Publications in This Library and Elsewhere," *Bulletin of the New York Public Library*, 29 (1935): 675–697; R. Don Higginbotham, "François-Xavier Martin's History of North Carolina," in Lawrence H. Leder, ed., *The Colonial Legacy* (New York, 1968), 4: 265–282; Michael Chorazzi, "François-Xavier Martin: Printer, Lawyer, Jurist," *Law Library Journal* 80 (1988); 63–97; Kathy T. Dugas, „An Immigrant's Journey to Wealth and Power: The Story of François-Xavier Martin," *Louisiana History*, 50 (2009): 321–340.

[6] In later life, Martin told his friend and judicial colleague, Henry Adams Bullard, that it was Davis who first hired him as a compositor (Bullard, *Discourse on the Life and Character of the Hon. François Martin*, 5). However, the historian Stephen Weeks pointed out early in the twentieth century that Davis had sold his press to Robert Keith before Martin showed up in New Bern (Weeks, "François Xavier Martin," in Stephen Ashe, ed., *Biographical History of North Carolina* [Raleigh, 1906], 4: 307–308). Thus, it seems that Martin's memory dulled with age or that Bullard misunderstood his friend.

the scholarship of law but in its practice too. So in his spare time, he read law with a well-regarded attorney and future governor, Abner Nash, who taught him sufficiently to gain a barrister's license in 1789.[7]

Thereafter his renown for advocacy and erudition led to an enlarging legal practice. A follower of Thomas Jefferson's politics, Martin sat for a term in the North Carolina assembly before he caught the eye of President James Madison, who named him to a judgeship in the Mississippi territory and then to a seat on the Superior Court for the Territory of Orleans. Martin next became the first attorney general of the Bayou State before Governor William C.C. Claiborne appointed him to the Supreme Court of Louisiana. Martin stayed on that court for thirty-one years (1815–1846), serving as its chief for the last ten. He thus grappled with the intricate task of blending American and civil law into a distinctive, mixed jurisprudence that met the needs of his fellow Louisianians. Together with his colleague and friend, Henry Adams Bullard, he also drafted a plan of study that stood as the basis of legal education in Louisiana for nearly eighty years. However Martin gave up printing once he succeeded to the bench, although he continued to prepare case reports and digests even as he wrote numerous opinions, all of which eventually drove him blind. His blindness allowed him fortuitously to stamp a final mark on Louisiana jurisprudence from the grave. Martin died possessed of an estate that approached half a million dollars in value, all of which he willed to a brother. As state law permitted, he set forth his wishes in an unwitnessed testament that he wrote and signed in his own hand. A challenge to the will in *State* v. *Martin* resulted in his beloved court's holding that

---

[7] Bullard, *Discourse on the Life and Character of the Hon. François Xavier Martin*, 5–6; Chiorazzi, "Francois-Xavier Martin," 85–91.

validated his bequest as it laid down the rule that blind Louisianians were legally capable of executing olographic wills. In short, Martin's long tenure during pivotal times made him the most notable of nineteenth-century Louisiana jurists, and to this day he is revered in the state as one of its pre-eminant legal thinkers.[8]

That Martin the printer translated and published *Traité des obligations* had little to do with his Gallic origins or affinities for things French. He sought instead to introduce his readers to Pothier's work for practical and philosophical reasons. His choice of the *Traité* had a certain logic to it because Pothier (1699–1772), long-time judge of the presidial court in Orléans, wrote prolifically on French contract law throughout his career.[9] Indeed, his countrymen esteemed the erudite jurist as their equivalent of Sir Edward Coke or Sir William Blackstone. Even English legal commentators regarded his writings highly, especially before the availability of works like Sir William Jones's *Essay on the Law of Bailments* (London, 1790 and later) or Joseph Chitty's *A Practical Treatise on the Law of Contracts Not Under Seal; and Upon the Usual Defenses to Action* (London, 1836 and later).[10] To Martin's way of thinking, then, an English version of the *Traité* could be

---

[8] Chorazzi, "Francois-Xavier Martin," 94; Warren M. Billings, "'A Course of Studies': Books That Shaped Louisiana Law," in Billings and Fernandez, eds., *A Law Unto Itself?*, 25–42; Carla Downer Pritchett "Case Law Reporters in Nineteenth-Century Louisiana," ibid., 58–77; 2 La. Ann 667 (1847); Warren M. Billings, "A Judicial Legacy: The Last Will and Testament of François-Xavier Martin," *Louisiana History*, 35 (1984): 277–289.

[9] "Eloge of M. Pothier" in William David Evans, trans., *Treatise on the Law of Obligations*, 1–46; August Frederic Frémont, *Recherches historiques et biographiques sur Pothier* (Orléans, 1859); G.W. Wilton, "Pothier (1699–1772), *Juridical Review*, 59 (1947): 208–226 cover Pothier's life and work in some detail.

[10] E.g. Evans, Introduction, *Treatise on the Law of Obligations*, 47–103, *passim*; Jones, *Essay on the Law of Bailments*, 41.

marketed as a handy reference that would instruct his potential customers in the universal principals of contractual obligations, which even in Anglo-American law had foundations in civilian jurisprudence.

To that extent, Martin anticipated his American contemporaries whose writings would one day rely upon Pothier's authority too.[11] He shared with them a philosophical view of law as the highest expression of ageless wisdom and reason. He, like they, conceived law as diverse gatherings of statutes and opinions, the whole of which ruled all human conduct, albeit in different ways in different times and places. Flowing from manifold wellsprings, law could be channeled into coherent schemes that gave ordered meanings to particular polities. Seen in these terms, common law and civil law complemented rather than rivaled one another, and they could thus be blended into jurisprudence that responded to the distinctly American needs. These were ideas that remained fixed firmly in Martin's understanding for all of his life, and he found ready application for them once he became a judge in Louisiana. And so his publication of *A Treatise on Obligations* provides an early insight into the range of his legal thought.

Loss of his papers and business records precludes identifying which edition of the *Traité* Martin employed for his source text. The possibilities are these. Five printings appeared between 1761 and Pothier's death a decade later; two more came off the press of his Parisian publisher in 1774

---

[11] *E.g.* Hoffman, *A Course of Legal Studies*, 536–41; James Kent, *Commentaries on American Law*, 5th ed. (New York, 1844). 2: 449–613, *passim*; John Bouvier, comp., *A Law Dictionary, Adapted to the Constitution of the United States of America, and of the Several States of the American Union; With References to the Civil and Other Systems of Foreign Law* repr. ed. (New York, 1993, first publ. 1839), 1: 230–33; 2: 199–201.

and 1777 respectively. Some have conjectured that Martin set type from a 1768 issue, though the evidence for that surmise is slim; the only certainty is that he replicated the French format and bound the two-volume work as one.[12]

In doing so, Martin prepared a quarto volume, measuring roughly 8-1/4 by 5-1/4 inches over the boards, which he printed on laid linen paper and encased in sheep skin. A red label on the spine reads "POTHIER ON/OBLIGATIONS" in gold-stamped lettering; beneath that is a black label that says "VOLS. I & II." Both labels are also bordered with gold rules. As for other embellishments, Martin merely employed a blind stamped floral roll to decorate the edges of the boards. Type, page layout, and textual adornments are also of an unfussy, straightforward design. All told, the overall look is of a serviceable rather than an artistic volume—one that could withstand continual handling before its owner cast it aside or wore it out.

There is now no way of calculating the size of the press run. Apparently Martin did a single printing that numbered in the hundreds rather than thousands. That seems a reasonable inference, given that a mere forty-two witnesses have been located. Forty-one rest in academic or public libraries from California to Louisiana and from Virginia to Ontario to England.[13] A forty-second copy, the source of this facsimile, belongs to the editor.[14] Others may be held by individual collectors too, although to date none has ever been identified as such.

Martin forbore any display of intellectual prowess, despite his affinity for scholarship. Apart from reprinting a

---

[12] *Bibliothêque Nationale, Catalogue Général*, 141: 514; Chiorazzi, "Francois Xavier Martin," 92.

[13] I am indebted to Janice Shull formerly of the Law Library of Louisiana who located the forty-one via an OCLC search for me.

[14] The source text is missing its front board, but the remainder of the original binding is intact.

laudatory passage out of Jones' *Essay on the Law of Belmont* as part of the frontmatter, nothing serves to introduce the reader either to Pothier himself or to the subject of the work itself. Moreover, Martin elected to forego the annotations that related the text to contemporary American practice, as others were doing at the time.[15] Evans, by contrast, translated a lengthy obituary sketch that acquainted his readers with Pothier. He followed that with an equally expansive introduction. There he talked of the "science" of law in general, commended Pothier's writings as worthy of contemplation, and related Pothier's treatment of obligations to Anglo-American jurisprudence. Furthermore, he added extensive notes to the body of the text. Those features made his translation quite desirable from the standpoint of utility, which was one reason why readers likely preferred it to Martin's. Besides, Evans's American publisher, Robert H. Small, worked in Philadelphia, and that gave Evans a huge advantage in marketing his rendition to customers throughout the United States. Finally, the fact that Martin appears to have printed only a single run argues that his edition was of limited commercial success. Despite its shortcomings for nineteenth-century practitioners, Martin's Pothier deserves notice as an exemplar of early American legal publishing as well as an insight into the thought of a jurist who significantly influenced the law of his adopted state.

Warren M. Billings
Distinguished Professor of History Emeritus
University of New Orleans and
Bicentennial Historian of the Supreme Court of Louisiana
1999

[15] *E.g.* St. George Tucker, comp., *Blackstone's Commentaries: With Notes and References to the Constitution and Laws of the Federal Government* . . . (Philadelphia, 1803).

A TREATISE ON OBLIGATIONS,

CONSIDERED IN A *MORAL* AND *LEGAL* VIEW.

Translated from the French of POTHIER.

IN TWO VOLUMES.

VOLUME THE FIRST.

NEWBERN, N. C.

MARTIN & OGDEN.

1802.

IT *is imagined, that this Treatiſe will find a ſufficient recommendation in the opinion which Sir* WILLIAM JONES *expreſſes, of the writings of its author.*

"At the time when M. Le Brun wrote, the learned M. POTHIER was compoſing ſome of his admirable *treatiſes* on the different ſpecies of expreſs, or implied, *contracts* : and here I ſeize with pleaſure an opportunity of recommending thoſe treatiſes to the *Engliſh* lawyer, exhorting him to read them again and again ; for, if his great maſter Littleton has given him, as it muſt be preſumed, a taſte for luminous method, appoſite examples, and a clear manly ſtyle, in which nothing is redundant, nothing deficient, he will ſurely be delighted with works, in which all theſe advantages are combined, and the greateſt portion of which is law at *Weſtminſter* as well as at *Orleans* : for my own part, I am ſo charmed with them, that, if my undiſſembled fondneſs for the ſtudy of juriſprudence were never to produce any greater benefit to the public, than barely the introduction of POTHIER to the acquaintance of my countrymen, I ſhould think that I had in ſome meaſure diſcharged the debt, which *every man*, according to lord Coke, *owes to his profeſſion*." LAW OF BAILMENTS, *p.* 41. *Boſt. Edit.*

Newbern, January 22*d,* 1802.

ERRATA.

PAGE.	LINE.	
4,	17,	*for* being, *read* not being.
24,	24,	intereſts, — intereſt.
38,	28,	for, — with.
	29,	obligation, — agreement.
	36,	for, — with.
43,	11,	in, — on.
51,	12,	ſecond, — third.
97,	5,	for — this.
110,	23,	them, — it.
211,	30,	debt, — debt is.
224,	12,	expreſſion, — exception.
229,	37,	are — are not.
276,	25,	ſhare — have.
326,	9,	is — he is.

TABLE.

A

TREATISE

ON

OBLIGATIONS.

PRELIMINARY ARTICLE.

1. THE term *Obligation* has two fignifications.

In its moft extenfive fignification, *lato sensu*, it is fynonymous with the term *duty*, and comprehends *imperfect*, as well as *perfect* obligations.

We call *imperfect* obligations, the obligations for which we are accountable to God alone, and which give to no man the right of requiring the performance of them. Such are the duties of charity, of gratitude. Such is, for example, the obligation of giving alms from our fuperfluities. This is an actual obligation, and the rich fin when they fail to perform it. Yet it is an imperfect obligation, becaufe for the performance of it they are accountable to God alone. When they perform it, the poor, to whom they give alms, do not receive a debt, but a mere benefit. It is fo with regard to the duties of gratitude. He, who has received a fignal benefit, is bound to render his benefactor all the fervices of which he is capable, when he finds the opportunity. He fins and difhonors himfelf, when he fails. Yet his benefactor has no right of requiring thofe fervices from him, and when they are rendered, this benefactor receives in his turn a benefit.

If my benefactor had a right to require from me, that I ſhould render him, on the ſame occaſion, the ſame ſervices which he rendered me, it would no longer be a benefit I had received from him; it would be an actual commerce: and the ſervices I ſhould render him would no longer be *gratitude* on my part; gratitude being eſſentially voluntary.

The term *Obligation*, in a ſenſe more proper and leſs extenſive, comprehends only perfect obligations, which are called alſo *personal engagements*, giving to him, with whom they are contracted, the right of requiring the performance of them: and it is of this kind of obligation, that we mean to ſpeak in this treatiſe.

Juriſts define theſe obligations or perſonal engagements, "a bond of right, binding us to another, to give, do, or refrain from doing, ſomething." *Vinculum juris, quo necessitate adstringimur, alicujus rei solvendae.* Inſtit. tit. de Oblig. *Obligationum substantia consistit ut alium nobis obstringat, ad dandum aliquid, vel faciendum, vel praestandum.* L. 3, ff. *de Oblig.*

Theſe words, *vinculum juris*, are applicable to the civil obligation alone. The mere natural obligation which is *solius aequitatis vinculum*, is alſo, although in a ſenſe leſs proper, a perfect obligation; for it gives, if not a legal, at leaſt a moral right of requiring the performance of it: while the imperfect obligation does not give even that right. See *infra, n.* 197.

We ſhall divide this treatiſe into four parts. We ſhall ſee in the firſt part, what belongs to the eſſence of obligations, and what are their effects.

In the ſecond, the different diviſions and different kinds of obligations.

In the third, the manner in which obligations are extinguiſhed, and the exceptions or pleas, with the preſcriptions againſt the rights which reſult from them.

We ſhall add a fourth part, on the proof as well of obligations, as of the performance of them.

FIRST PART.

Of what belongs to the effence of obligations, and of their effects.

CHAPTER THE FIRST.

Of what belongs to the essence of obligations.

2. IT is of the effence of all obligations, that there be, I. a caufe from which the obligation arifes, II. perfons between whom it is contracted, III. fome thing which is the object of it.

The caufes of obligations are contracts, quafi-contracts, torts and quafi-torts; fometimes the law or equity alone.

We fhall treat, I. of contracts, which are the moft frequent caufes from which obligations arife.

II. Of the other caufes of obligations.

III. Of the perfons between whom they are contracted.

IV. Of the things, which may be the object of them.

SECTION THE FIRST.

Of contracts.

I. We fhall fee what a contract is, in what it differs from a pollicitation; and what things are principally to be confidered in every contract. II. We fhall relate the different divifions of contracts. III. We fhall treat of the different defects which may be found in them. IV. Of the perfons capable or incapable of contracting. V. Of what may be the object of contracts. We fhall fee that it muft be fomething concerning the contracting parties; according to the rule that *one cannot validly stipulate or promise but for himself*, a rule which we fhall endeavour to unfold and explain. VI. We fhall treat of the effects of contracts. VII. We fhall give fome rules for their interpretation. VIII. We fhall fpeak of the oath which the parties fometimes add to their agreements.

Article the First.

What a contract is; in what it differs from a pollicitation: and what things are principally to be considered in every contract.

§. I.

What a contract is.

3. A contract is a kind of agreement. To know what a contract is, it is then previously requisite to know what an agreement is.

An agreement or a pact (for these are synonimous expressions) is the assent of two or more persons, to form an engagement betwen them, or to dissolve or modify one already formed. *Duorum vel plurium in idem placitum consensus. L.* 1, §. 1, *ff. de Pact.* Domat, *p.* 1, *l.* 1, *t.* 1.

The kind of agreement, which has for its object to form some engagement, is what is called a *contract*. The principles of the Roman law, on the different kinds of pacts and the distinction between contracts and simple pacts, being grounded on natural law and being very distant from its simplicity, are not admitted in our jurisprudence. Those who are curious to know them, may consult our work on the Pandects.

Hence it follows, that with us a contract ought not to be defined, as it was by the interpreters of the Roman law, *conventio nomen habens à jure civili vel causam*: but it ought to be defined an agreement, by which both parties promise reciprocally, or only one of them promises and engages to the other, to give, do or refrain from doing, something.

I have said *promise and engage*; for it is only the promises which we make, with an intention of engaging and binding ourselves and of conferring on the other party the right of requiring the performance of them, that constitute a contract or an agreement.

There are other promises, which we make with good faith and with the actual intention to perform them, but without an intention of engaging or binding ourselves and conferring on the party, to whom they are made, the right of requiring their performance. This happens when he, who promises, expressly declares that he does not mean to bind himself, or when this is fairly to be implied and results from the circumstances, or from the relation in which the parties stand to each other. For example; when a father promises to his son, who studies law, to give him money for a jaunt of pleasure during the vacations, if he studies well: it is evident that the father, in making this promise, does not mean to contract, with his son, an engagement properly speaking.

These promises produce indeed an imperfect obligation to perform them, provided nothing happen which, had it been foreseen, would have prevented the making of the promise: but they form no engagement, and therefore no contract.

§. II.

In what a contract differs from a pollicitation.

4. The definition which we have given of a contract points out this difference. A contract includes a concurrence of the will of two persons at least, one of whom makes and the other accepts the promise. A pollicitation is a promise which is not yet accepted by him to whom it is made. *Pollicitatio est solius offerentis promissum*; L. 3, ff. *de Pollicitat.*

The pollicitation, according to the principles of mere natural law, produces no obligation, properly speaking. He who makes this promise, may revoke it, as long as it is unaccepted by him to whom it is made. For there can be no obligation without a right acquired, by the person in whose favour the obligation is contracted, against the person who contracts it. Hence as I cannot, by my own will alone, transfer to another the property of my goods, if his will does not concur in the acquisition of it: so I cannot, by my promise, transfer to another a right on my person, until his will concur in the acquisition of it, by his acceptance of the promise. *Grotius de j. b. & p. l.* 2, *cap.* 11, *v.* 3.

Although the pollicitation be not obligatory, according to the principles of mere natural law, the civil law, adding to the natural, had, among the Romans, rendered obligatory in two cases the pollicitations of a citizen to his city. I. When he had just cause to make them; *puta*, in consideration of some municipal magistracy, conferred on him *ob ho-*

norem. II. When he had begun to carry them into execution. *L.* 1, §. 1 & 2, *ff. d. tit.*

It is ufelefs to enquire now, whether pollicitations are obligatory in our law. For as the ordinance of 1731, *art.* 3, has declared that there fhall be but two ways of difpofing gratuitoufly of one's goods, by donation *inter vivos* and *by testament,* it follows that it rejects the pollicitation.

§. III.

Of the three things which are to be distinguished in every contract.

5. Cujas diftinguifhed in contracts only the things which are of their effence and thofe which are accidental to them. The diftinction made by feveral writers of the feventeenth century is much more correct. They diftinguifh three different things in every contract, thofe which are of the effence of the contract, thofe which are of its nature and thofe which are accidental to it.

6. I. The things, which are of the effence of a contract, are thofe without which it cannot exift. On the abfence of any of them, there is either no contract at all, or a contract of another kind.

For example. It is of the effence of a contract of fale, that there be a thing fold, and a price for which it is fold. Therefore, if I had fold you a thing which we knew not had then ceafed to exift, there would be no contract. L. 57, ff. *de Contr. empt.* For there cannot be a contract of fale, without a thing that is fold. Likewife, if I fell you a thing at the price at which my kinfman, who bequeathed it to me, bought it, and it is found that the thing was not fold but given to him, there will be no contract; becaufe there is not a price, which is of the effence of the contract of fale.

In the above cafes, the abfence of one of the things which are of the effence of the contract, prevents there being any contract: fometimes it only changes the nature of the contract.

For example. It being of the effence of the contract of fale that there be a price, which confifts in a fum of money which the buyer pays or engages to pay to the feller, if it be mentioned in an agreement made with you that I fell you my horfe for a book which you engage to deliver me as the price of the horfe, this agreement will not conftitute a contract of fale, becaufe fuch a contract cannot exift without a price confifting in a fum of money. Yet the agreement is not void; it conftitutes another contract, viz. a contract of exchange.

Likewife, it being of the effence of the contract of fale, not indeed that the feller fhould bind himfelf precifely to transfer to the buyer the property of the thing fold, in cafe he is not the owner of it, but at leaft that he fhould not retain it, if he is; if we agreed that I fhould fell to you a certain piece of land for a fpecified fum and a rent which you engage to pay me, and I agree that you fhall enjoy the premifes under a condition that the property of the land fhall remain with me, this agreement will not contain a contract of fale, for it is contrary to the effence of fuch a contract, that the feller fhould retain the property of the thing fold; but it will contain a contract of leafe. *Labeo, L. 80, §. 3, ff. de Contr. empt. Nemo potest videri rem vendidisse de cujus dominio id agitur, ne ad emptorem transeat; sed hoc aut locatio est, aut aliud genus contractus.*

Likewife, it being of the effence of the contracts of loan, mandate and depofit, that they be gratuitous, if I lend you a thing on condition that you pay me a certain fum for the ufe of it, this will not be a contract of loan, but another kind of contract, viz. a contract of hire. For the fame reafon, if in accepting the power of attorney which you gave me, or the depofit of a thing which you entrufted me with, I have ftipulated for the payment of a fum of money as a compenfation for my care in the management of your concerns or the fafe keeping of the depofit, this contract will not be a contract of mandate or of depofit, but a contract of hire; by which I hire to you my care in the management of your concerns or the keeping of the depofit.

7. II. The things, which are only of the nature of the contract, are thofe which, without being of the effence of the contract, make part of it, although the parties did not

mention them; it being of the nature of the contract that such things be included and implied in it.

These things hold a middle rank between the things which are of the essence of the contract and those which are accidental to the contract; and they differ from both.

They differ from those which are of the essence of the contract in this, that the contract may exist without them and they may be excluded by the agreement of the parties. They differ from the things which are accidental to the contract in this, that they make part of the contract without having been expressly agreed upon. This will be illustrated by examples. In the contract of sale the obligation to warrant, which the seller contracts to the buyer, is of the nature of the contract. Therefore the seller contracts, by the sale, this obligation to the buyer, although the parties do not expressly agree on it, and not a word be said on this subject in the contract. But this obligation being of the nature, and not of the essence of the contract of sale, the contract of sale may exist without this obligation; and if by the contract it be expressly agreed that the seller shall not be bound to warrant the thing sold, the agreement will be valid and the contract will, not the less, be a contract of sale, although the seller is not bound to warrant.

It is also a thing which is of the nature of the contract of sale, that as soon as it has received its perfection, by the assent of the parties, although before the delivery, the thing sold be at the risk of the buyer, and that if it happen to perish, without the fault of the seller, the loss should fall on the buyer, who is not on this account discharged from paying the price. But as this is of the nature only, and not of the essence of the contract of sale, the parties, in making the contract, may agree on the contrary.

It is of the nature of the contract of loan to use, that the borrower be liable for the slightest fault with regard to the thing loaned. He contracts this obligation from the nature of the contract itself, and without its being expressed by the parties, at the time of the contract. But as this obligation is of the nature and not of the essence of the contract of loan to ufe, it may be excluded by a claufe of the contract, and it may be agreed that the borrower fhall only be bound to ufe good faith in the prefervation of the thing and that he fhall not be liable for any accident which may happen through his negligence, but without malice.

It is alfo of the nature of the fame contract, that the lofs of the thing lent, when it happens *vi majore*, from a caufe not within the control of the borrower, fhould fall on the lender. Yet this being of the nature only and not of the effence of the contract, the borrower may, by a fpecial claufe, be charged with this rifk till he reftore the thing.

A number of other examples might be adduced relating to the different kinds of contracts.

8. III. The things which are accidental to the contract are thofe which not being of the nature of the contract, are part of it only, on account of fome fpecial claufe added to the contract.

For example. The time allowed by the contract for the delivery of the thing or the payment of the fum due, the liberty of paying the latter by inftalments, or giving fomething elfe in lieu of it, or of paying to fome other perfon than the creditor and the like, are things accidental to the contract; for they only make part of the contract, inasmuch as they are ftipulated in fome claufe added to the contract.

In the contract of fale of an annuity, the obligation by which the feller makes himfelf anfwerable for the folvency of the debtors, as long as the annuity fhall laft, is a thing accidental to the contract; for the feller does not contract this obligation from the nature of the contract: he only contracts it, by virtue of a fpecial claufe added to the contract: and this claufe, although frequently inferted in contracts of fale of annuities, ought to be expreffed; otherwife the want of it cannot be fupplied by implication or prefumption.

Various other examples might be adduced.

ARTICLE. II.

Division of contracts.

9. The divisions which the Roman law makes of contracts, into named and unnamed contracts, contracts *bonae fidei* and *stricti juris*, do not hold with us.

The divisions admitted by our jurisprudence are I. into contracts synallagmatic, or bilateral, and contracts unilateral.

The synallagmatic or bilateral, are those in which each of the contracting parties binds himself to the other, as in contracts of sale, hire, &c.

Unilateral are those in which one of the parties only binds himself to the other, as in the loan of money.

Among synallagmatic contracts, we distinguish those which are absolutely so, and those which are so, qualifiedly. The contracts, which are perfectly synallagmatic or bilateral, are those in which the obligation, which each party contracts, is equally a principal obligation of the contract; as contracts of sale, hire, partnership, &c. For example. In the contract of sale, the obligation, which the seller contracts to deliver the thing, and that which the buyer contracts to pay the price, are equally principal obligations of the contract. The contracts which are qualifiedly synallagmatic, are those in which the obligation of one party alone is the principal obligation of the contract. Such are the contracts of mandate, deposit, loan to use and pledge. In these contracts, the obligation which the mandatary contracts to account, those contracted by the depositary, borrower or creditor, to restore the thing deposited, lent or pledged, are the only principal obligations of the contract. Those which are contracted by the mandator, depositor or debtor, are but incidental obligations resulting from the contract, from the expences incurred by the other party, in the execution of the mandate, or the preservation of the thing deposited, lent or pledged.

The action which arises from the principal obligation is called *actio directa;* that which arises from the incidental obligation is called *actio contraria.*

10. II. Contracts are divided into those which are formed, by the mere assent of the parties, and are therefore called *consential* contracts, as sale, hire, mandate, &c. and those in which something else is requisite, as contracts for the loan of money or of things to be used, deposit and pledge, which, from the nature of the contract, require the delivery of the thing that is the object of the contract: These are called *real* contracts.

Although the mere assent of the parties suffices for the perfection of consential contracts, yet if the parties in a sale, or hire, or any other kind of bargain, agree to have an instrument respecting it made by a notary, with a view that their bargain be not concluded and perfect, till the instrument shall have received its legal form by the signature of the parties and the notary, the bargain will not be complete until the notarial instrument shall become so; and the parties, although they did perfectly agree to the terms of the bargain, will be at liberty to recant at any time before the notarial instrument is subscribed. *L. Contractus*, 17, *cod. de fid. instr. Instit. tit. de contr. empt.*

But if in this case the instrument is required for the perfection of the contract, it is not from the nature of the contract, which of itself requires nothing but the assent of the parties; it is because the contracting parties have required it, and because it is lawful for the parties to a contract to render their obligations dependent on what condition they please.

It must be observed that an agreement, that a notarial instrument evidencing the bargain shall be drawn, does not of itself render the perfection of the bargain dependent on the instrument. It ought to appear that the intention of the parties was that it should depend on this. Therefore it has been adjudged, in a case reported by *Mornac*, *ad. d. l.* 17. that a party could not recede from a contract of sale, reduced to writing with a clause that there should be a notarial instrument, although no such instrument had been executed: for it could not be concluded from this clause that the parties had intended to render the completion of their bargain dependent on the execution of a notarial inſtrument, which might have been thought of in order to provide a lien on the party's lands, which ſuch an inſtrument procures, or to obviate the danger of loſing a private paper.

But when the agreement is oral, it is eaſier for the party who is preſſed to comply with it, to avoid it by contending that it was an inchoate bargain, which was not to have its perfection before the execution of the notarial inſtrument, which the parties had agreed to procure. For as contracts, the object of which exceed in value the ſum of £.100, cannot be proved by witneſſes, and there being in this caſe no proof of the bargain but this declaration of the party, it muſt be taken *in toto*, as we ſhall ſee in the fourth part of this work, *n.* 799.

When a contract is reduced to writing, without being ſubſcribed by all the parties named in it, ſome refuſing to ſubſcribe, thoſe who have ſubſcribed may retract, and will be believed in their declaration that in cauſing the writing to be drawn, their intention was to render the completion of the bargain, dependent on that of the writing. On this principle, the ſale of an office made by the plaintiff, a widow, as well in her own right as in quality of tutrix of her infant ſon, was adjudged imperfect, in a caſe reported by *Soefve*, *t.* 1. *cent.* 4. *chap.* 75. It was made in writing, and the defendant who had ſubſcribed it, was held not to be bound by it; becauſe the writing was incomplete, not being ſubſcribed by the curator of the infant, who was mentioned in it, although unneceſſarily, as a party on behalf of the infant.

12. The third diviſion of contracts, is into contracts of intereſt on both ſides, contracts of beneficence, and mixt contracts.

Contracts of intereſt on both ſides are thoſe which are made for the reciprocal intereſt and advantage of both parties. Such are contracts of ſale, exchange, hire, annuity, partnerſhip and an infinity of others.

Contracts of beneficence are thoſe which are made only for the advantage of one of the contracting parties.

Such are the loan to ufe, the loan to confume, depofit and mandate.

The contracts by which one of the parties, who confers a benefit on the other, requires from him fomething below the value of what he gives him, are called mixt contracts. Such are gifts made under a charge on the donee.

13. Contracts of intereft on both fides are fubdivided into commutative contracts and aleatory contracts.

Commutative contracts are thofe in which each of the contracting parties gives and receives ordinarily the equivalent of what he gives. Such is the contract of fale. The feller ought to give the thing fold and receive the price, which is the equivalent of it; the buyer ought to give the price and receive the thing fold, which is its equivalent.

They are diftributed into four claffes, *Do ut des*, *Facio ut facias*, *Facio ut des*, *Do ut facias*.

Aleatory contracts are thofe in which one of the parties, without giving any thing on his part, receives fomething from the other not as a liberality, but as the price of a rifk which he runs. All games are contracts of this nature, fo are wagers and contracts of infurance.

14. A fourth divifion of contracts is into principal contracts, and acceffory contracts. Principal contracts are thofe which intervene principally and for themfelves. Acceffory contracts are thofe which intervene to infure the execution of another contract. Such are contracts of fecuritifhip and of pledge.

15. A fifth divifion of contracts is into thofe which are fubjected by the municipal law to certain rules or forms and thofe which are regulated by natural law alone.

Thofe which are fubjected, among us, to certain rules and forms are the contracts of marriage, donation, bill of exchange, annuity. Other agreements are not fubjected, with us, to any particular form or arbitrary rule prefcribed by the municipal law, and provided they contain nothing contrary to law or good morals, and they be entered into by perfons capable of contracting, they are obligatory and give rife to an action. If our laws require that those, the object of which exceeds in value the sum of 100 livres, be reduced to writing, it is only with the view to regulate the manner in which they are to be proved, when their existence is denied. But it is not the intention of the law to make writing the substance of the agreement. The agreement is valid without, and the parties, who do not deny that it intervened, may be compelled to execute it. The decisory oath may be deferred to the party who denies it. The writing is necessary to the proof, but not to the substance of the agreement.

ARTICLE III.

Of the different defects which may happen in contracts.

16. The different defects which may happen in contracts are error, violence, fraud, lesion*, want of consideration and want of obligation. We will treat of these defects in as many distinct paragraphs.

With regard to the defects that result from the inability of some of the contracting parties, or from what is the object of contracts, we shall treat of these in the following articles.

§. I.

Of error.

17. Error is the greatest defect in agreements. For agreements are formed by the assent of the parties and there can be no assent, when the parties have erred as to the object of their agreement. *Non videntur qui errant consentire;* L. 116. §. 2, *de R. Juris;* L. 57, *de Obligat. & Act.*

Therefore, if one means to sell me a thing, and I mean to receive it as a loan or a gift, there will be in this case no sale, no loan, nor gift. If one means to sell or give me a thing and I mean to buy from him another thing, or to accept the gift of another thing, there is neither sale nor gift. If one means to sell me a thing for a certain price, and I mean to buy it for a less price, in all such cases there is no sale. *Sive in ipsa emptione dissentiam, sive in pretio, sive in quo alio, emptio imperfecta est. Si ego me fundum emere putarem*

* See *postea*, §. IV & V.

Cornelianum, tu mihi te vendere Sempronianum putasti; quia in corpore dissensimus, emptio nulla est. L. 9, ff. *de Contr. empt.*

18. Error annuls the agreement, not only when it falls on the thing itſelf, but alſo when it falls on the quality of it which the parties had chiefly in view and which conſtitutes the ſubſtance of the thing. Therefore if, intending to buy a pair of ſilver candleſticks, I buy a pair which you offer me and which I take to be ſilver, while they are only plated copper; although indeed you had no deſign of deceiving me, being yourſelf in the ſame error, the agreement will be null becauſe the error in which I have been deſtroys my aſſent. For the thing which I wiſhed to buy is a pair of ſilver candleſticks; that which you offered me, being a pair of copper candleſticks, cannot be ſaid to be the thing which I intended to buy. *Julian*, L. 41, §. 1, *ff. d. t.* *Ulpian*, L. 14, *ff. d. t.* *Si aes pro auro veneat, non valet.*

It is otherwiſe, when the error falls only on ſome accidental quality of the thing. For example. If I buy, in a bookſeller's ſhop, a certain book, under the falſe perſuaſion that it is excellent, while it is below mediocrity: this error does not deſtroy my aſſent and conſequently not the contract of ſale. The thing, which I wiſhed to buy and which I had in view, is actually the book which the bookſeller ſold to me and not another thing. The error in which I was as to the merit of the book fell only on the motive which induced me to buy it, and does not prevent its being the very book which I wiſhed to buy: and we ſhall ſee ſhortly that error as to the motive does not deſtroy the agreement. It ſuffices that the parties did not err as to the thing which is the object of it, *& in eam rem consenserint.*

19. Does error as to the perſon with whom I contract deſtroy likewiſe the aſſent and annul the agreement? I think that this queſtion ought to be decided by a diſtinction. Whenever the conſideration of the perſon enters into the contract which I wiſh to make, the error as to the perſon deſtroys my aſſent, and conſequently renders the agreement null. Therefore, if wiſhing to give or lend a thing to Peter, I give or lend it to Paul, whom I miſtake for Peter, the gift or loan is null, for want of aſſent

on my part: for I did not wiſh to give or lend this thing to Paul, I only wiſhed to give or lend it to Peter. The conſideration of the perſon of Peter entered into the gift or loan I intended to make.

Likewiſe, if wiſhing to have a painting made by Natoire, I bargain to have it done with James whom I miſtake for Natoire, the bargain is null, for want of aſſent on my part: for I did not wiſh to have a painting made by James, but by Natoire. The conſideration of the perſon of Natoire, and of his reputation, entered into the bargain which I wiſhed to make.

Note, however, that if James, who was ignorant that I was miſtaking him for Natoire, in conſequence of this erroneous agreement made the painting, I ſhall be bound to take it, and to pay what it may be really worth. But it is not, in this caſe, the agreement which thus binds me; for this agreement, which is null, cannot produce any obligation. The cauſe of my obligation in this caſe is equity, which obliges me to indemnify him whom I have, by my imprudence, led into an error. There ariſes from this obligation an action, which is called *actio in factum*.

We have ſeen that error as to the perſon annuls the agreement, whenever the conſideration of the perſon enters into it.

On the contrary, whenever the conſideration of the perſon with whom I thought I was contracting has not entered into the contract, and I would as willingly have contracted with any other perſon, as with the one with whom I did contract, the contract ought to be valid. For example. I bought of a bookſeller a book in ſheets, which he obliged himſelf to deliver to me bound. Although this bookſeller, in ſelling me the book, thought he was dealing with Peter, whom I reſemble, and he called me Peter at the time, and I did not undeceive him; this error in which he was as to the perſon to whom he ſold the book does not annul the agreement, and cannot authoriſe him to refuſe to deliver me the book at the ſtipulated price, if ſince the agreement the price of it has riſen. For although he thought he he was felling his book to Peter, yet as it was indifferent to him to whom he fold his ware, it is not precifely and perfonally to Peter he wifhed to fell this book, but to the perfon who would give the price he afked, whoever he might be. Confequently it is proper to fay that it was to me, who was that perfon, to whom he wifhed to fell his book, and to whom he bound himfelf to deliver it. *L.* 3. *ch.* 6. *n.* 7. *not.* 2.

20. Does error on the motive annul the agreement? Puffendorf, *l.* 3. *ch.* 6. *n.* 7. thinks it does, provided I communicated to the perfon, with whom I contracted, the erroneous motive that induced me to contract; becaufe, according to his opinion, the parties ought, in this cafe, to be prefumed to have intended to render their agreement dependent on the truth of the motive, as on a fort of condition. He ftates, as an example, the cafe in which, on the falfe report of the death of my horfes, I fhould have bought others, communicating in my converfation with the feller the falfe news which I had received. He thinks that in fuch cafe, on receiving advice of the falfity of the report, I might refufe to comply with the agreement, provided it is yet abfolutely executory on both fides, indemnifying the feller for the injury he might fuftain from the inexecution of the agreement.

Barbeyrac demonftrates very clearly the fallacy of this reafoning. For if it were true that we had made our agreement dependent on the truth of the intelligence which I had received; the intelligence happening to be falfe, the agreement would be abfolutely void, *defectu conditionis*, and the feller could not claim damages for its inexecution. Barbeyrac afterwards very properly fays that this error in the motive does not in any way affect the agreement. Indeed, as in legacies the falfity of the motive which the teftator has mentioned, does not affect the legacy and prevent its being valid; becaufe it is not the lefs true that the teftator intended to bequeath, and it cannot be concluded from what he has faid as to the motive that induced him to bequeath, that he intended to make the legacy dependent on the truth of the motive, as on a condition, unlefs this doth otherwife appear: fo, and *a fortiori*, it ought to be held with regard to agreements, that error as to the motive which induced one of the parties to contract, has no influence on the agreement, and does not prevent its validity; becaufe there is much lefs room to prefume that the parties intended to make their agreement dependent on the truth of this motive as on a condition: for agreements ought to be interpreted *prout sonant*, and conditions which can only be annexed to them by the will of both parties, ought to be prefumed with lefs facility than in a teftament.

§. II.

Of the want of freedom.

21. The affent which forms agreements ought to be free. If the affent of one of the contracting parties has been extorted by violence, the contract is defective. However, as the affent, though extorted by violence, is an affent fuch as it is, *voluntas coacta est voluntas* (gloff. ad L. 21. §. 5. ff. *quod met. caus.*) it cannot be faid, as in the cafe of error, that there has been abfolutely no contract. There is one, but it is defective, and he whofe affent has been extorted, or his heirs or affigns, may have it annulled and refcinded, by obtaining letters of refciffion for this purpofe.

But if, fince the violence has ceafed, he has acceded to the contract either exprefsly, or impliedly, by fuffering the time of reftitution (which is ten years fince the violence ceafed) to elapfe, the defect of the contract is cured.

22. When the violence has been exercifed by the perfon with whom I contracted, or when he has participated in it, the agreement is invalid, both according to the municipal law which gives an action to have it refcinded, and according to natural law. For even if it were fuppofed that there refults an obligation on me towards you from the affent which I gave to the contract, although it was extorted by violence; the injuftice you committed towards me, by exercifing this violence, obliges you on your part to indemnify me, for what I fuffer from it; and this indemnification confifts in releafing me from the obligation which you compelled me to contract. Hence it follows that my

obligation, if any be ſuppoſed, cannot be valid according to natural law. *Grotius de Jure belli, lib. 2. cap. 11. n. 7.*

23. When the violence which has been exerciſed againſt me to compel me to contract, has been exerciſed by a third perſon, without the participation of the perſon with whom I contracted, ſtill the municipal law affords me relief, and reſcinds all obligations, cauſed by violence, to be contracted, from what cauſe ſoever the violence may proceed. *L.* 9. §. 1. *ff. Quod met. Prætor generaliter & in* rem *loquitur. Id est personaliter de sola* re; *de sola vi illata, non attendens per quem illata sit, an per ipsum cum quo invitus contraxi, an per alium.* Therefore the Baſiliques have taken out the words *sciente emptore*, which are in the *l.* 5. *Cod. de his quæ vi &c.* it being indifferent whether he to whom I was compelled by violence to ſell, had knowledge or not of this violence.

But Grotius contends that it is only from the municipal law that I hold the reſciſſion of my obligation, which would be valid according to the principles of natural law. According to him, it is only the municipal law that holds my aſſent imperfect on account of the perturbation of mind, which the violence has occaſioned, nearly as it conſiders the aſſent of minors imperfect, when it grants them the reſciſſion of their contracts, *propter infirmitatem judicii.* But, according to this writer, on the principles of mere natural law, my aſſent, although given in the trouble of mind occaſioned by the violence, is no leſs an actual aſſent, ſufficient to produce an obligation, like that of a minor, although he may not have the maturity of underſtanding, which is had at a more advanced age.

Puffendorf and Barbeyrac think, on the contrary, that on the principles of mere natural law, when I am compelled by violence to contract, the contract does not bind me; even when the perſon with whom I contracted had no ſhare in the violence.

Barbeyrac reaſons thus. It is true, ſays he, that an aſſent, though extorted by violence, is ſtill an aſſent, *coacta voluntas est voluntas;* and it ſuffices to render us guilty when we conſent, even by conſtraint, to do what natural law forbids, or to abstain from what it commands. Thus was a christian guilty when he sacrificed to idols, though compelled by the fear of tortures and death. But although an extorted assent be an actual assent, it does not suffice validly to bind us to give or do what we promised; because natural law leaving to our free and spontaneous choice all what it allows, it can only be by a free and spontaneous choice that we may bind ourselves to another, to give or do what natural law allowed us to give or not to give, to do or not to do.

The agreement then, is no less defective, although the person with whom I was compelled to make it, had no share in the violence which was exercised upon me; for although he had no share in it, my assent is not the less imperfect; and it is this imperfection of assent which the law regards, when it discharges me from the obligation which was pretended to result from it: *Neque enim lex adhibenti vim irascitur, sed passo succurrit; & iniquum illi videtur id ratum esse, quod aliquis, non quia voluit, pactus est, sed quia coactus est: nihil autem refert per quem illi necesse fuit; iniquum enim, quod rescinditur, facit persona ejus qui passus est, non persona facientis.* Senec. *controver.* IV. 26.

24. Puffendorf excepts a case in which the obligation, although contracted under an impression of fear caused by the violence which was exercised upon me, is not the less valid. It is the case in which I had promised to a person to give him something to induce him to come to my assistance and deliver me from the violence which another was exercising upon me. For example. If being attacked by robbers, I perceive some one and promise him a sum of money if he will come and rescue me from their hands, this obligation, although contracted under an impression of the fear of death, will be valid. *L.* 9. §. 1. *ff. Quod met. causa. Eleganter Pomponius ait: Si quo magis te de vi hostium vel latronum tuerer, aliquid a te accepero, vel te abligavero, non debere me hoc edicto teneri..... ego enim operæ potius meæ mercedem accepisse videor.*

Neverthelefs, if I had promised an excessive sum, I might have my obligation reduced to the sum, at which the just reward of the service he had rendered me, might be estimated.

25. The violence which vitiates a contract on account of the want of freedom must, according to the principles of the Roman law, be a violence capable of moving a man of firmness; *metus non vani hominis, sed qui in homine constantissimo cadat*; L. 6, ff. *dicto titulo*.

It is requisite that the party who pretends to have been compelled to contract, should have been intimidated by the fear of a great evil, *metu majoris mali*, L. 5, ff. *dicto tit.* either in his own person or that of his children, or some other of his near relations; *nam nihil interest in se quis veritus sit, an in liberis suis*; L. 8, f. 3. ff. *d. tit.* It ought to be an evil which was threatened to be imposed instantaneously, unless he did what was proposed; *metum præsentem, non suspicionem inferendi ejus*; L. 9, ff. *dicto titulo*.

When the menaces which another has made use of to compel me to enter into an engagement to him, are only vague threats of a distant evil, by which I suffered myself to be vainly intimidated, although, according to the principles of the Roman law, the contract be not reputed defective on account of the want of freedom in the assent, it is not to be concluded that such a manœuvre ought to remain unpunished and that the contract ought to stand good. The law, 7 ff. *d. tit.* says, indeed, *Si quis meticulosus rem nullam frustra timuerit,* PER HOC EDICTUM *non restituitur*. But it does not say absolutely *non restituitur*. If the contract does not fail in this case, on account of the absence of what the law judges to be requisite to the freedom of the assent, it is defective on account of the want of good faith, which ought to reign in all contracts.

This manœuvre, of which the person with whom I contracted made use of, is an injustice, which binds him to me for the reparation of the injury which it has occasioned me and this reparation consists in the rescission of the contract. *Grotius, dicto loco.*

If it is by the act of a third person that I suffered myself to be intimidated, and he with whom I contracted had no share it, the contract will be valid: and I shall have the action *de dolo* against him alone, who intimidated me.

All these principles of the Roman law are very just, and drawn from natural law, except that the one, which admits of no fear as sufficient to vitiate a contract on account of the want of freedom, but that which is capable of moving the firmest man, is too rigid and ought not to be literally received with us. In such a case regard ought to be had to the age, sex and condition of the parties and a fear, which should not be deemed sufficient to intimidate a man of ripe age and a soldier, and consequently to have occasioned the rescission of the contract which he had made, may be held sufficient in the case of a woman or an old man. See Bruneman *ad* L. 6, ff. *Quod met. causa*, and the authors he cites.

26. The violence which may give room for the rescission of a contract, ought to be an unjust violence, *adversus bonos mores*; L. 3, §. 1. ff. *d. tit.* Legal means can never pass for a violence of this sort. Therefore a debtor cannot attack a contract, which he has made with a creditor, on the pretence that he was intimidated by the threats of the creditor to exercise the right which he had of imprisoning him; nor even under the pretence that the contract was made in a prison, if the creditor might have lawfully detained him there. The law 22, ff. *Quod met. causa*, which says, *Qui in carcerem quem detrusit ut aliquid ei extorqueret, quicquid ob hanc causam factum est, nullius momenti est*, ought to be understood of an illegal imprisonment. See Wisenbach, *P.* 1, *disp.* 13, *n.* 22.

27. Neither is the fear of displeasing parents, or other persons to whom reverence is due, sufficient to vitiate a contract made under the impression of such fear; L. 22, ff. *de Rit. nupt.* L. 26, §. 1, ff. *de Pign. & Hyp.* Duaren, *ad h. tit.* & Wisenbach, *disp.* 13, *ch.* 13, *&c.* But if a person who has authority over another, uses ill treatment or threats, to induce him to contract, the contract may, according to circumstances, be liable to rescission.

§. III.

Of fraud.

28. We call fraud every ſpecies of artifice uſed to deceive. *Labeo definit dolum, omnem calliditatem, fallaciam, machinationem, ad circumveniendum, fallendum, decipiendum alterum, adhibitam;* L. 1, §. 2, ff. *de Dol.*

29. When one party has been induced to contract by the fraud of the other, the contract is not abſolutely and eſſentially void; becauſe an aſſent, although obtained by ſurpriſe, is ſtill an aſſent; but this contract is defective, and the party who is ſurpriſed may (within ten years) by obtaining letters of reſciſſion, have it reſcinded; becauſe it is contrary to the good faith which ought to reign in all contracts. Add that if my promiſe binds me to you, the fraud you exerciſed upon me in taking this promiſe from me by ſurpriſe, binds you to indemnify me, and conſequently to diſcharge me from my promiſe.

30. In a moral light, we ought to view as contrary to good faith every thing that deviates, in the leaſt, from the moſt exact and ſcrupulous ſincerity. Mere diſſimulation, as to what concerns the thing, which is the object of the contract and which the party with whom I contract has an intereſt to know, is contrary to good faith. For ſince we are commanded to love our neighbour as ourſelves, it cannot be permitted us to conceal from him, what we would not wiſh ſhould be concealed from us, were we in his place. See this matter treated at large in the *Traite du Contrat de Vente, part.* 2, *ch.* 2; *part* 3, *sect.* 2.

But courts of juſtice could not liſten to a party who would complain of ſuch ſlight breaches of good faith of which the perſon he contracted with might have been guilty: otherwiſe there would be too many agreements liable to be reſcinded. It would be a ſource of much litigation and of much obſtruction to commerce. It is only what is openly contrary to good faith, that may be regarded by them, as a fraud ſufficient to give occaſion for the reſciſion of a contract, ſuch as the manœuvres and artifices which one of the parties might have employed, in order to induce the other to contract; and those artifices and manœuvres ought to be fully proved: *Dolum non nisi perspicuis indiciis probari convenit*; L. 6, *Cod. de Dol. mal.*

31. It is only the fraud which has given rise to the contract, that may give occasion for the rescission of it: *viz.* the fraud by which one of the parties has induced the other to contract, who would not have contracted without it. All other frauds, which intervene in contracts, give only a right to damages, as an indemnification for the injury which the party defrauded sustains.

32. It is requisite also, in order that I may claim the rescission of my engagement, that the fraud which has been made use of, in order to induce me to contract, should have been committed by the party with whom I contracted, or at least that he should have participated in it. If it has been committed without his participation, and if I have not besides been enormously injured, my engagement is valid and is not liable to rescission. I have only an action for damages against the party who deceived me.

§. IV.

Of lesion between persons of age.

33. Equity ought to reign in all agreements. Hence it follows that in all contracts of interests in which one of the parties gives or does something in order to receive another thing as the price of what he gives or does, the injury or lesion which one of the parties suffers, although indeed the other party had not recourse to artifice in order to deceive him, is alone sufficient to render the contract defective. For as equity, in matters of commerce, consists in equality, whenever that equality is broken and one of the parties gives more than he receives, the contract is defective, because it is contrary to the equity which ought to reign in it.

Besides the assent of the party injured is imperfect: for he only consented to give what he parted with in the contract, under the false supposition that what he received in its place was equal to what he gave; and he was in the difpofition not to have given it, if he had known that what he received was not worth as much.

But it is to be obferved, 1. that the price of things does not confift in an indivifible point. There is a certain fpace within which the parties are permitted to range. And there is no lefion and confequently no iniquity in a contract, unlefs that which one of the parties has received be above the higheft price of the thing which he gave, or below the loweft. *Traite du Contrat de Vente, n.* 242.

34. II. Although every lefion, whatever it may be, renders contracts iniquitous and confequently defective, and confcience requires the juft price to be fupplied; yet perfons of age are not admitted to attack their agreements in a court of juftice on pretence of lefion, unlefs the lefion be enormous. Which has been wifely eftablifhed for the fafety and freedom of commerce, which requires that agreements may not be eafily fet afide. Otherwife one would not dare to contract, left the perfon he contracted with, imagining himfelf to be injured, fhould fue him.

The lefion is commonly efteemed enormous when it exceeds the juft price by one half. The perfon who has fuffered this lefion, may (within ten years after the contract) by obtaining letters of refciffion, demand to have it annulled. *Traite du Contrat de Vente, part.* 5, *ch.* 2, *sect.* 2.

35. There are however certain agreements in which equality is more particularly required. Such are divifions between co-heirs and co-tenants; *Molin. de Usur. quæst.* 14. *n.* 182.

With regard to thefe agreements, it fuffices that the lefion fhould exceed the juft price by one fourth, to give occafion for reftitution.

This is what practitioners call "lefion from the third to the fourth;" *viz.* that which runs between the third and the fourth, which may not go quite to the third, but which ought at leaft to exceed the fourth. For example. If I have been injured in a divifion in which I ought to have received

12000 livres for my ſhare, it is not requiſite, in order that I may have relief, that the leſion, which I have ſuffered, ſhould amount to 4000 livres, which is the third of what I ought to have had, it ſuffices that it exceeds 3000 livres, the fourth of it. *Imbert. Enchirid.* title *Division & Partage mal fait.*

36. There are certain agreements againſt which perſons of age cannot be relieved on the ſcore of leſion, however enormous it may be.

Such are tranſactions according to the edict of Francis II. in April, 1560. Thus are called the agreements which take place relatively to pretenſions, for which there is a ſuit depending or about to be inſtituted between the parties.

The reaſon of this edict is drawn from the particular nature of theſe agreements. In the other contracts of intereſt, each of the parties has an intention to receive as much as he gives, and to give up nothing that belongs to him; his aſſent then is not entirely perfect when he is injured, ſince in that caſe it proceeds from the error in which he is, that he receives as much as he gives, and it is on the ground of this defect in his aſſent that he is allowed to ſeek to be relieved from his contract. On the contrary, in tranſactions, from the very nature of theſe agreements, the parties have an intention to avoid a ſuit, even at the expence of what belongs to them.

From this principle it follows that the edict is not to be extended to agreements that would determine no conteſtation, and which for example ſhould contain nothing elſe but a diviſion, although the notary might have ſtyled them *transactions.* For it is not the name which the notary gives to the inſtrument, but the nature of it, which ought to regulate its effect.

37. Neither is relief often granted, on the ſcore of leſion, in contracts in which the price of the thing, which is the object of the contract, being very uncertain, it is difficult or almoſt impoſſible to determine its juſt price, and conſequently to judge whether there is leſion beyond one half of the juſt price.

Such is the contract of sale of the right to the estate of a deceased person, for the uncertainty of the debts which may appear, renders the value of such rights very uncertain.

Such are all aleatory contracts: for although the risks which one of the parties takes upon himself, be something appreciable in money, it must be conceded that it is very difficult to determine the just price of them. For this reason relief is seldom granted, on the score of lesion, on contracts of life-annuities, insurance, &c.

38. Nor is the purchaser of an estate at more than one half of its just price, admitted to relief on the score of lesion alone, when what exceeds the intrinsic value is the price of affection. *Traite du Contrat de Vente, part.* 2, *chap.* 2, *art.* 4, §. 2.

39. Neither are contracts which have personal property alone for their object, liable to be set aside on the score of lesion alone, however great it may be. *Coutume d'Orleans, n.* 446.

The reason of this right is perhaps that our ancestors made wealth to consist in real property, and placed little value in moveable things. Hence in our jurisprudence less regard is paid to personal property. Another reason may be drawn from the frequent commerce in this kind of goods, which pass through a number of hands in a short time. This commerce would be obstructed, if contracts relating to it were liable to be rescinded on the score of lesion.

Nor is lesion a cause of relief, in the case of a lease. For a lease includes only a disposition of the profits of an estate, which are personal property.

§. V.

Of lesion with regard to minors.

40. All that has been said before relates to persons of age only. Minors are relieved against their agreements, not only in the case of an enormous lesion, but in the case of any lesion whatever. And this relief is extended to them, even in those cases in which we have said that persons of age are not admitted to be relieved, such as in transactions.

The ordinance of 1539, *art.* 134, has limited the time within which minors are to apply for this relief; it does not permit them to be admitted to it after their thirty-fifth year.

Obferve that the ordinance has not faid *ten years* after coming of age; becaufe there are provinces in which one is of age at twenty, as in Normandy. It has, in this refpect, placed every individual on the fame footing. They are all relievable till the age of thirty-five years completed.

41. There are certain agreements againft which minors capable of contracting, that is to fay emancipated, are not relievable any more than perfons of age, on the fcore of lefion alone. Such are their agreements relative to the alienation or acquifition of perfonal property. *Coutume d'Orleans, art.* 446.

We fhall fay no more on this head, intending to treat of the fubject in a particular treatife.

§. VI.

Of the want of confideration.

42. Every engagement ought to have a lawful confideration. In contracts of intereft, the confideration of the engagement which one of the parties contracts, is what the other gives or engages to give, or the rifk he takes on himfelf. In contracts of beneficence, the liberality which one of the parties defires to exercife towards the other, is a fufficient confideration for the engagement he contracts with him. But when an engagement has no confideration, or which is the fame thing, when the confideration under which it is contracted, is a falfe confideration, the engagement is void and the contract which contains it is null. For example. If falfely believing that I owe you a fum of ten thoufand livres, which were bequeathed to you by the will of my father, that was revoked by a codicil of which I had no knowledge, I engaged to give you a piece of land in lieu of it; this contract is null, becaufe the confideration of my engagement, which was the difcharge of the debt, happens to be falfe: therefore the falfity of the confidera-

tion appearing, not only will you have no action to claim the land from me, but if I had delivered it to you, I should have an action to recover it back. This action is called *condictio sine causa*. See *tit.* ff. *de Cond. sine causa*.

43. When the consideration for which the engagement has been contracted is contrary to justice, good faith or morality, the engagement is null as well as the contract which contains it. This principle serves for the decision of a question which often occurs. A mortgaged estate is sold under a decree; the mortgagor stipulates with the last bidder that he shall give him a certain sum of money, for which the former will surrender to the latter the title deeds. It is asked whether this be a valid agreement? In other words, whether it be contrary to justice? It certainly is. For the title deeds are accessory to an estate, as the keys are to a house; and it is the nature of accessory things to belong to the owner of the principal thing: *accessoria sequuntur jus ac dominium rei principalis*. The title deeds then belong to the last bidder; for the sale, in transferring to him the property of the estate, transferred to him also that of the title deeds. The mortgagor in mortgaging the land consented that, in case of failure of payment, the creditor might obtain a decree for the sale of it: hence he bound himself to surrender it, with the title deeds, to the last bidder, as if he had sold it himself. He cannot then retain them, without injustice. The agreement, by which he exacts money from the last bidder, has a consideration contrary to justice: this renders it null. Therefore, not only is an action denied to the mortgagor to recover the sum which was promised him, but if the last bidder had paid it, he would have an action to recover it back.

Observe that with regard to this action, care ought to be taken to distinguish, whether the consideration for which some thing has been promised, is contrary to justice or morality, on the part of him alone who stipulates, or on that of both parties. An example of the first case is that which we have just given. When the mortgagor requires from the last bidder a sum of money for the delivery of the deeds, it is the mortgagor alone who acts contrary to justice and good morals; the last bidder on his part does nothing contrary to them, in promising the money to obtain the deeds which he wants, and which are refused him without it. It is in such a case, and in similar ones, that there is ground to recover back what has been paid in execution of the agreement.

An example of the second case is when an officer promised a sum of money to a soldier, if he would fight a duel with a soldier of another regiment. The consideration of this agreement is contrary to good morals, on both sides. For the officer has not acted the less contrary to law and to good morals, in making this promise, than the soldier in accepting it. This second case agrees with the first in this, that, as in the first, the engagement is null, being made on a consideration which is contrary to good morals: consequently no action can be grounded on it; and the soldier, who fought the duel, cannot recover the sum, which the officer promised him for it. But, this second case differs from the first in this, that if in execution of the contract, altho it be null, the officer has paid the sum agreed, he will have no right to recover it back, as in the preceding case. For the officer, who has promised the reward, has no less sinned against the laws and good morals than the soldier to whom he promised it. He is unworthy of the assistance of the law to recover it back. This double decision is in the words of the law: *ubi dantis & accipientis turpitudo versatur, non posse repeti dicimus . . . . . . Quoties autem accipientis turpitudo versatur, repeti potest*; L. 3, L. 4, §. 2, ff. *de Condict. ob turp. causa.*

44. It is not to be doubted that, according to what we have just established, if I have promised something to another to commit a crime, *puta*, to beat my enemy, I am not legally bound to keep this promise. There is more difficulty, in a moral view. Grotius (II. XI.) contends that such promises are not indeed obligatory, as long as the crime has not been committed, and that until then, he who made the promise may recall it by a contrary order; but that as soon as the crime has been committed, the promise becomes obligatory, as well in *foro legis* as in *foro conscientiæ.* His reason is that the promise is defective, inasmuch as it is an inducement to a crime, and this defect ceases, when the crime is consummated. The defect of this promise ceasing to ex-

ist, nothing can prevent its having its effect, which is to bind the person who made it to the performance of it. He cites the example of the Patriarch Judah, who performed the promise he had made to Thamar.

Puffendorf thinks, on the contrary, that a promise made to another to induce him to commit a crime, is no less obligatory after it is committed than before. Because the reward of the crime, which the performance of the promise contains, after the crime is committed, is something no less contrary to natural law and good morals than the invitation to a crime. If, after the crime has been committed, the performance of the promise can no longer be an inducement to the commission of it, it may be an inducement to commit others. Besides, every obligation pre-supposes a right in the person to whom it is contracted. When I have promised something to another for committing a crime, his acceptance of the promise is no less criminal on his part, than the promise itself on mine: and can a right be acquired by a crime? Can it be believed that natural law favours criminals so far as to insure to them the salary of their crimes? These reasons determine me for the opinion of Puffendorf.

45. I subscribe likewise to the decision which he afterwards gives; that if I have voluntarily paid, after the commission of the crime, what I had promised to another to induce him to commit it, I have no more right to reclaim it in *foro conscientiæ* than in *foro legis*, although I have paid what I did not owe. It is true, that both the natural and municipal law give a right to reclaim what has been paid, without its being due, when the payment has been made through error. It is supposed then that the payment was made under a sort of condition, that there should be a right to claim back what is paid, if it be afterwards discovered that the thing was not due. Although this condition was not expressed, it is implied. It is conformable to the disposition and will of the person who paid. Equity, which forbids us to avail ourselves of the error of another, in order to enrich ourselves at his expence, implies this condition. But a like supposition cannot be made in the case we are considering. He who pays, does so with a perfect know-

ledge of the cause for which he pays: he cannot consequently retain any right to claim back what he voluntarily parts with, having a perfect knowledge of every circumstance. It is true, it is contrary to natural law that one should be rewarded for a crime, and the repentance which the person who committed it should have, ought to induce him to give up the reward which he received for it: but this forms but an imperfect obligation, of the kind of those we spoke of in the beginning of this treatise, *n.* 1, and which give to no one the right of requiring the performance of them.

46. Has a promise a lawful consideration, when it is made to one to induce him to do or give what he was already bound to do or give? Puffendorf in this case distinguishes very properly the perfect, from the imperfect obligation. When the obligation was only an imperfect obligation, the promise has a lawful consideration and is obligatory. For example, If I have promised something to another, if he would render me a service, although gratitude for benefits he had received from me, bound him to render this service to me gratuitously, yet the promise I made to him has a lawful consideration and is obligatory. For, as I had no right to require this service from him, he might lawfully, though not decently, require that I should promise him something, in exchange for the right, which I had not before, of requiring this service from him.

On the contrary, when the obligation is a perfect obligation, the promise which I make to my debtor to give him something, if he will do what he is bound to do, is a void promise: for it has an unlawful consideration, when he required that I should make the promise. Such is that of which we have spoken before, made by the last bidder to the mortgagor to induce him to give up the title deeds of the estate which was put down to him. For being bound to give them, it is an exaction on his part to require the promise of something for it.

But, although the obligation be a perfect obligation, if the promise which I made to my debtor, if he would do what he was bound to do, is a promise which I made voluntarily without his requiring it; the promise is valid and has a lawful consideration. The consideration being, in such case, the liberality which I wished to exercise towards him.

§. VII.

Of the want of obligation in the person who promises.

47. It is of the essence of agreements which consist in promising something, that they produce in the person who made the promise an obligation that binds him to perform it. Hence it follows that as there is nothing more contrary to the obligation than the absolute freedom which might be left to him, to do or not to do what he promised, the agreement which would leave this entire freedom, would be absolutely void, on account of the want of obligation. If then, for example, I were to agree with you to give you a certain thing, if I please, the agreement would be absolutely void.

The Roman lawyers thought it was otherwise of an agreement by which one should promise to do something *when he pleased.* They thought that these expressions did not leave it to the choice of the person who made the promise, to do or not to do what he promised; that it only left to his choice the time *when* he should do it; and that thus the agreement was valid and bound his heirs, if he died without performing it. *L.* 46. §. 2 & 3. *ff. de verb. oblig.* But there is room to believe that this subtle distinction would not be admitted with us, and that such an agreement would not be more valid than the other.

48. There is an actual obligation when I promise to give you such a thing, *if I judge it reasonable:* for then it is not left to my choice to give or not to give it to you, since I am bound to do it, in case it be reasonable. *L.* 3. §. 7. *Leg.* 3.

Finally, although I have promised a thing, under a potential condition, so that it depends upon my will to perform it or not to perform it; as if I promised you ten pistoles in case I should go to Paris: the agreement is valid. For it is not entirely in my power not to give them, since I cannot dispense with it, without abstaining from going to Paris.

There is then on my part an obligation and an actual engagement. *L.* 3. *ff. de legat.* 2.

ARTICLE IV.

Of the persons who are capable or not of contracting.

49. The effence of the agreement confifting, as we have faid, in the affent, it follows that one muft be able to affent, and confequently have the ufe of reafon to be capable of contracting.

Hence it is evident that neither children, ideots nor lunatics, while they continue fuch, can contract by themfelves: but thefe perfons may contract by the intervention of their tutors or curators, as we fhall fee in the following articles.

It is evident that ebriety, when it is fuch as to take away the ufe of reafon, renders the perfon who is in that condition, while it continues, unable to contract; fince it renders him incapable of affent.

Corporations, as colleges, hofpitals, parifhes, &c. being only civil perfons, cannot contract by themfelves; but they may do it by the intervention of their truftees or other proper officers.

50. There are perfons who, being naturally capable of contracting, are incapacitated to contract by the municipal law. Such are, in the cuftomary provinces, married women when they are not authorifed by their hufbands or the court. For it is a confequence of the marital power, that the wife be incapable of doing any thing except it be dependently on the hufband and by his authority. Hence it follows that, without his authority, fhe is incapable of making any agreement, and that fhe can neither bind herfelf to others, nor bind others to her. We have treated of this matter in the introduction to *tit.* 10. of the Cuftom of Orleans, chap. 8.

It is alfo the municipal law alone which renders perfons interdicted, on account of their prodigality, incapable of binding themfelves by their contracts: for thefe perfons know what they are doing; the affent which they give is an actual affent, which is fufficient to form a contract.

51. Hence arises the difference between persons interdicted for that cause and persons interdicted on account of lunacy. All contracts made with a lunatic, although before his interdiction, are void; if it can be proved that he was a lunatic at the time of the contract. For it is his lunacy which alone and of itself incapacitates him to contract, independently of the judgment of interdiction, which serves only to ascertain the lunacy. On the contrary, contracts made with a prodigal, before his interdiction, are valid, although he was a prodigal before; for it is the judgment of interdiction alone which disables him from contracting.

Nevertheless, if I had contracted with a prodigal, although before his interdiction, in buying a thing from him, or in lending him money, knowing that he sold or borrowed merely to employ immediately in his debaucheries the price of the thing sold or the money borrowed, the contract would be void *in foro conscientiæ*, and I could not keep the thing which he had sold me, nor require from him the sum which I had lent him. For in knowingly supplying him with money, to be wasted in debauchery, I have done him a wrong which binds me to him to repair it, in not requiring of him the sum which he received from me to spend in debauchery, and in restoring to him the thing which he sold me. This is conformable to what is declared in L. 8, ff. *pro empt.* that he ought not to be regarded as a purchaser, *bona fide*, who has purchased a thing from a libertine, knowing that he sold it merely to procure money to bestow on courtezans: *Nisi forte is qui a luxurioso, & protinus scorto daturo pecuniam, servos emit, non usucapiet.*

These decisions are good *in foro conscientiæ*; but in our courts a person of age and not interdicted, would not be allowed to attack his contract for a sale or loan, under the pretence that the person with whom he contracted, knew that he sold or borrowed for the purpose of procuring money to be spent in debauchery.

52. It is also the municipal law alone which invalidates the obligations which minors contract without the authority of their guardians, when at the time of the contract they

are nearly of age, and have a sufficient use of their reason to know the extent of the engagement which they contract. Therefore minors may well, even in a moral light, avail themselves of the benefit of the letters of rescission, which the law grants them, against the contracts in which they have been wronged: natural equity forbidding the person who contracted with them to avail himself of their want of experience. But they cannot honestly avail themselves of the benefit of these letters of rescission, which the municipal law grants them, to avoid restoring money which they have received and wasted, when, at the time they contracted, they had a sufficient use of their reason, provided the person they contracted with made the loan *bona fide*, without knowing that the money was to be wasted in foolish expences. *La Placette*, cited by Barbeyrac, in his notes on Puffendorf.

There remains for us to notice a difference between the incapacity of interdicted persons and minors, and that of *feme coverts*. The latter are absolutely incapable of contracting without being authorised so to do: and they can no more, without authority, bind others to them by their contracts, than bind themselves. They cannot even accept a gift which may be made to them: *Ord.* 1731, *art.* 9. On the contrary, prodigals and minors who begin to have the use of reason, are rather incapable of binding themselves by their contracts, than absolutely incapable to contract. They may, by contracting without the authority of their guardians, bind others to them, although they may not bind themselves to others: *Placuit meliorem conditionem licere eis facere etiam sine tutoris autoritate*; Instit. tit. de Autor. tut. *Is cui bonis interdictum est, stipulando sibi acquirit*; L. 6, ff. *de Verb. oblig.* The reason of this distinction is; that the authority of guardians is established in favor only of minors and interdicted persons. The assistance of guardians is required when these persons contract, for the interest of these persons alone, and in order to prevent their being imposed upon. Therefore it becomes superfluous whenever their condition is bettered. On the contrary, the power of the husband over the wife not being established in favor of the wife, but in favor of the husband; the necessity, she is under, of requiring the authority of the husband in order to contract, not being established for her interest, but as a deference which she owes to her husband: she cannot contract in any manner, either to her advantage or to her disadvantage.

The ordinance of 1731 has in no way altered the principle which we have established, that a minor may better his condition without the authority of his guardian: and it is without reason that Furgole says, that according to the seventh article of that ordinance, minors cannot accept, without the authority of their guardians, the gifts which may be made to them. This article only provides that fathers and mothers, or other ascendants, without being guardians to their children, and consequently without being qualified to manage their affairs, may accept gifts made to their minor children, as validly as guardians may; natural affection supplying in this case the qualification which they have not. But from this ordinance allowing such persons to accept gifts made to their children, it does not follow that it prohibits minors to accept them themselves, when they have the use of their reason. *Introduction au Titre des Donations, de la Coutume d'Orleans, n.* 31.

Article V.

Of what may be the object of contracts. That it can only be something which concerns the parties, according to the rule that one can validly stipulate but for himself.

53. Contracts have for their object, either the things which one of the contracting parties stipulates shall be given to him, and which the other promises to give him; or something which one of the parties stipulates to be done or not to be done, and which the other party promises to do or not to do.

We shall see hereafter, when we come to treat of what may be the object of obligations, what are the things which one of the parties may stipulate to be given him, and which the other party may engage to give; and what are the things which one of the parties may stipulate to be done or not to be done; *chap.* 2, *art.* 2. We refrain from ſpeaking of this here, to avoid repetition.

We will content ourſelves with developing here a principle relating to what may be the object of contracts. This principle is, that it is only what one of the contracting parties ſtipulates, and likewiſe that it is only what the other party promiſes, for himſelf, that may be the object of a contract: *Alteri stipulari nemo potest*; Inſtit. *de inut. Stipul.* §. 18. *Nec paciscendo, nec legem dicendo, nec stipulando, quisquam alteri cavere potest*; L. 73, §. fin. ff. *de R. J.* Verſa vice, *Qui alium facturum promisit, videtur in ea esse causa ut non teneatur, nisi pœnam ipse promiserit*; Inſtit. *d. tit.* §. 20. *Alius pro alio promittens daturum facturumve, non obligatur; nam de se quemque promittere oportet*; L. 83, ff. *de Verb. oblig.*

To develop this principle, we ſhall ſee, in a previous paragraph, what are the reaſons of it. In a ſecond, we ſhall relate ſeveral caſes in which we contract for ourſelves although another perſon be mentioned in the agreement. In a third, we ſhall remark that what concerns a perſon not one of the contracting parties, may be the mode or condition of an agreement, although it may not be the object of it. In a fourth, we ſhall obſerve that one may contract by the intervention of a third perſon, and that this is not to ſtipulate or promiſe for another.

§. I.

What are the reasons of the principle that one cannot stipulate or promise for another.

54. If I ſtipulate ſomething for you in favor of a third perſon, the agreement is void. For by this obligation you contract no obligation to that third perſon nor to me. It is obvious that you contract none to the third perſon. For it is a principle that agreements can have no effect except between the contracting parties: conſequently they cannot acquire any right to a third perſon who is not a party. Neither do you contract any civil obligation to me: for what I ſtipulated for you in favor of a third perſon, being a thing in which I have not an intereſt that is appreciable in money; there can reſult no damages to me from the inexecution of

your promise. You may then disregard it with impunity. Nothing is more contrary to the civil obligation than the power of contravening it with impunity. This is the meaning of Ulpian when he says: *Alteri stipulari nemo potest; inventæ sunt enim obligationes ad hoc, ut unusquisque sibi acquirat quod sua interest; cæterum ut alii detur nihil interest mea;* L. 38. §. 17, ff. *de Verb. obl.*

55. This first part of our principle, that it is only what a party stipulates for himself that may be the object of an agreement, is true only in a legal point of view and with regard to civil obligations. But in *foro conscientiæ*, if I have stipulated with you that you should give something to a third person, or that you should do something in his favor, the agreement is valid. Although the interest, which I take in it, is not appreciable in money, it is still an actual interest: *hominis enim interest, alterum hominem beneficio affici:* and this interest of mere affection for this third person, gives me a sufficient right to require from you in *foro conscientiæ* the performance of your promise in his favor, and to render you guilty if you fail to perform it, when you have it in your power to do so and this third person is willing to accept what you promised to give him. It is true that my interest not being appreciable in money, and being incapable of being the object of an agreement, I shall not be able to recover damages in the municipal tribunals, if you fail in your promise. Yet the liberty in which you are of failing to do it thus with impunity, is an obstacle to the civil obligation, but does not affect the moral obligation. *Grotius, l.* 2, *c.* 11, *n.* 18.

Note that the moral obligation which results from this agreement, by which I have stipulated that you should give something to a third person, is an obligation which is contracted to me and not to this third person, when it is in my name and not in that of this third person that I agreed with you. Therefore I may release you from it, without the consent of this third person. *Grotius, ibid. Puffendorf.*

But if it was in the name of this third person and as acting under his authority, that I stipulated with you that you ſhould give him or do for him ſuch thing, it would be this third perſon who had contracted for you by my intervention, and not I. *Infra*, §. 4.

56. The ſecond part of this principle, that one may promiſe for himſelf alone, is obvious. For when I promiſed that another ſhould give you ſomething or ſhould do ſomething, without pretending to have any authority from him, and without promiſing any thing for myſelf, this agreement can neither bind this third perſon nor me. It cannot bind the third perſon: for it is not in my power to bind a third perſon without his aſſent. Neither does it bind me: for ſince it is ſuppoſed that I promiſed for another perſon and not for myſelf, I intended not to bind myſelf.

But courts will eaſily preſume that he who promiſed that a third perſon ſhould give or do ſomething, did not mean *pure de alio promittere*, but that he meant to promiſe *de se*, i. e. that he would procure it to be done by that perſon, although this be not expreſſed. In ſuch caſe, the agreement is valid and binds the perſon who made the promiſe to pay the damages reſulting from the inexecution of what he promiſed; L. 81, ff. *de Verb. oblig.*

When in promiſing the act of another, you ſubmit to pay a certain penalty or merely damages, in caſe of the inexecution of the promiſe, it is not to be doubted that in this caſe you did not underſtand to promiſe merely the act of another, *& de alio tantum promittere*, but that you underſtood to promiſe that you would procure him to do or give the thing, *& de te promittere*. Therefore Ulpian ſays: *Si quis velit alienum factum promittere, poenam vel quanti ea res est, potest promittere.* L. 38, §. 2, ff. *d.* t.

§. II.

Cases in which we actually stipulate or promise for ourselves, although another person be mentioned in the agreement.

First Case.

57. It is not to ſtipulate for another to ſay, that the thing or ſum which I ſtipulate ſhall be paid to a third perſon deſignated by the agreement. For example. If by the contract I ſell you an eſtate for the ſum of 1000 livres, *which*

you shall pay to Peter, I do not ſtipulate for another: it is for myſelf and not for Peter that I ſtipulate this ſum of 1000 livres. Peter, in this agreement, is only as a perſon to whom I give power to receive the money for me and in my name. This is what the Romans called *adjectus solutionis gratia*, of which we ſhall treat hereafter, *infra*, *Part* 3, *Chap.* 1, *Art.* 2, §. 4.

It is not in his perſon, but in mine, that the right to this ſum reſides. When he receives it, it is in my behalf and in my name that he receives it, and his receiving it conſtitutes between him and me a contract of mandate, if my intention was that he ſhould account for it; or a gift, if my intention was to beſtow it upon him.

Second Case.

58. I do not ſtipulate for a third perſon, but for myſelf, when I ſtipulate that a thing ſhall be done for a third perſon, if I have a perſonal intereſt, appreciable in money, that it be done. *Puta*, if I be myſelf bound to this third perſon to have it done. For example. If, having bound myſelf to James to rebuild, within a certain time, his houſe which is near falling, and having other work to attend to, I bargain with a maſon for his rebuilding the houſe of James within this time; I am preſumed to ſtipulate rather for myſelf than for James, and the agreement is valid. For being bound to James to rebuild the houſe, and being liable to pay damages if the houſe be not built within the time given, I have an actual perſonal intereſt in its being rebuilt. Therefore in ſtipulating for the rebuilding of the houſe of James, it is only *verbo tenus*, in this caſe, that I ſtipulate for James; *re ipsa* and in reality I ſtipulate for myſelf and for my benefit. *Si stipuler alii cum mea interesset.... ait Marcellus stipulationem valere*; L. 38, §. 20, 21, 22, ff. *de Verb. oblig.*

59. Even if, before the bargain which I made with the maſon, for rebuilding the houſe of James, I ſhould not have been bound to James for the rebuilding of his houſe, and I ſhould conſequently have had no perſonal intereſt in the rebuilding of it; yet, as by this bargain which I have made, I manage the affairs of James, and therefore become liable to James

for the management of them; at the very time of the agreement which I make with the mason for the construction of the house, I begin to have an interest in the rebuilding of the house, for which I am accountable to James: whence it follows that even in this case I am presumed to stipulate for myself rather than for James, and the agreement is valid, since I have a personal interest in the mason's doing what I stipulated he should do.

60. But if I stipulate in my name that a thing be done for a third person, without having had, before the agreement, and without having, at the time of the agreement, any personal interest in its being done; in this case it is really to stipulate for another: and such an agreement is not valid in law. For example. If from a motive of mere affection, I make an agreement with the owner of the house which is opposite the windows of James, that he shall whiten the front of his house, that the rooms of James may be the lighter thereby; this agreement will give no right to James, who was not a party to it, nor to me, who, having no personal interest, appreciable in money, in the execution of this agreement, can claim no damages for its inexecution.

THIRD CASE.

61. It is to stipulate or promise for ourselves and not for others, when we stipulate or promise for our heirs, since they are in a manner a continuation of ourselves. *Hæres personam defuncti sustinet.* Therefore it is not to be doubted that we may stipulate for our heirs: *Hæredi cavere concessum est;* L. 10, ff. *de Pact. dot.* L. 38, §. 14, ff. *de Verb. oblig.*

62. Observe that we validly stipulate, when we stipulate for our heirs, in their capacity of heirs: but if one stipulate for A, although he afterwards should become his heir, the stipulation is not therefore valid. *L.* 17, §. 4, ff. *de Pact.*

Julian has carried the strictness of this principle so far as to say, that when a debtor had agreed with his creditor that he should not require the debt from him, nor from A his daughter, the stipulation is not valid with regard to the daughter, although she since became heir to the debtor; *d.* §. 4. Bruneman is of opinion, and with reason, that this too literal decifion is not to be followed; for if I ftipulate with my creditor that he fhall not require from me, nor from my daughter, the fum which I owe him, it is obvious that I ftipulate for my daughter, in cafe fhe becomes debtor of it, which fhe cannot be unlefs fhe becomes my heir. I then ftipulate this for the cafe in which fhe may become my heir; and confequently I am prefumed to ftipulate for my daughter, in her future capacity of my heir, although this be not expreffed, *ad. d. L.*

It is fafer to recede from the opinion of Julian, for it appears that the Roman lawyers were not unanimous in this queftion: Celfus thought differently in *L.* 33, ff. *de Pact.*

63. We may not only validly ftipulate for our heirs, but we are commonly prefumed to have done fo, although this be not expreffed. *Qui paciscitur, sibi hæredique suo pacisci intelligitur.*

This rule admits of a few exceptions. I. When what is the object of the agreement, is a fact perfonal to him to whom the obligation is contracted; as when I agree with a barber that he fhall come and fhave me twice a week at my villa, during the vacations. II. With regard to the claufe in marriage fettlements, by which the wife ftipulates that fhe fhall refume what fhe brings, in cafe fhe renounces the community. We have amply fpoken of this claufe in our introduction *au titre de la Communaute, de la Coutume d'Orleans, ch.* 2, *art.* 2, §. 5. III. When it is clearly expreffed in the agreement, that the perfon who contracted bound himfelf to the perfon with whom he contracted and not to his heirs. But this muft be clearly expreffed in the agreement. From the naming, in the agreement, the perfon with whom I contract an engagement, it does not follow that the intention of the parties was to reftrain to his perfon the right refulting from it: *Plerumque persona pacto inseritur, non ut personale pactum fiat, sed ut demonstretur cum quo pactum fiat;* L. 7, §. 8. Wiffenbach, ad tit. ff. *de Pact. n.* 7.

64. We may alfo reftrain our ftipulation to one of our heirs: *Non obstat uni tantum ex hæredibus provideri, si hæres*

factus sit, cæteris autem non consuli; L. 33, ff. *de Pact.* For example. If I agreed with my creditor that he ſhould not require his debt from me nor from my daughter, and I ſhould leave my ſon and my daughter my heirs, the agreement will have effect only with regard to the daughter, ſhe alone being mentioned in it; and the creditor will have a right to require the debt from my ſon for the part for which he is my heir; *d.L.* 33. It is improperly that the gloſs ſays the creditor may require the whole from him. Cujas has taken notice of this miſtake.

But from a perſon's having ſtipulated by name for A, his heir, it is not always to be inferred that the intention of the parties was to reſtrain the ſtipulation to this heir. There is room to infer it, if, at the time of the agreement, he who thus ſtipulated knew that he was to have other heirs. For then no reaſon appears which might have induced him to ſtipulate for him by name, but in order to reſtrain the ſtipulation to him. On the contrary, if he who has ſtipulated for a particular perſon his heir, had, at the time of the agreement, room to believe that he would be his only heir, it is to be preſumed that his being named in the agreement is merely enunciative and not with the view to reſtrain the effect of the ſtipulation to his perſon. Papinian ſhews this in the following example.

Having married my daughter, with a portion of which I paid the intereſt, and imagining I ſhould have no iſſue but this daughter, who was already provided for, and intending to inſtitute my brother my ſole heir, I ſtipulated in her marriage ſettlement, that in caſe ſhe ſhould die without iſſue, (on which contingency her portion was, by the Digeſt, acquired by the huſband) my brother, my heir, might retain one half of the portion; afterwards I had other children, and my daughter dying without iſſue before her huſband, the queſtion ariſes whether my children, as my heirs, will be entitled to retain, under the agreement, one half of the portion. The reaſon to doubt reſults from the ſtipulation being made in the name of my brother: whence it may appear to be reſtricted to him and to the caſe in which he might have been my heir. But Papinian holds that my children are well grounded in claiming the one half of the portion: becaufe in ftipulating for the right of retaining it for the benefit of my brother, my heir, I am to be prefumed to have ftipulated it, by ufing the words "my heir" for the benefit of my heirs, whoever they may be, and to have named my brother only as *enunciative*, and to fhew that it was he who I expected was to be my heir. *Ea conventio liberis postea susceptis & hæredibus testamento relictis proderit, cum inter contrahentes id actum sit, ut hæredibus consulatur, & illo tempore quo pater alios filios non habuit, in fratrem suum judicium supremum contulisse videatur;* L. 40, §. fin. ff. *de Pact.* Therefore Cujas, *ad Papinian.* on this law, thinks it would have been fo, whoever might have been my heir, even if they had not been my children.

There remains to be obferved, that when I ftipulate with my creditor that he fhall not require what I owe him, the agreement may be reftrained to one of my heirs, in order that he alone may be difcharged from the debt, for the part for which he would have been liable. But when I ftipulate that a fum of money or any other divifible thing, fhall be given to me, I cannot confine the agreement to one of my heirs, fo as to caufe the whole right which refults from the agreement, to pafs to him alone. *Sciendum est quod dari stipulemur, non posse per nos uni ex hæredibus adquiri, sed necesse est omnibus adquiri;* L. 137, §. fin. ff. *de V. obligat.* What is faid here, *sed necesse omnibus adquiri*, muft be underftood of the cafe in which the reftriction to one of the heirs is only made with the view to transfer to this heir, in exclufion of the others, the whole claim. But I may validly agree that if I have not required the debt before my death, my debtor fhall only be liable for it to the amount of the part to which one of my heirs will fucceed to me, and that he fhall be difcharged as to the reft.

65. This is a confequence of the principle that one can validly ftipulate for another, inafmuch only as he is to be his heir and in the quality of heir, which he is one day to have. Hence it follows that he cannot fucceed for the whole, in the rights which refult from this agreement; but only for the part for which he fhall be heir.

It is otherwife with regard to agreements which have for their object fomething indivifible: fuch are moft of thofe *in faciendo*. For as in thofe each of the heirs fucceed for the whole to the right which refults from them, it being of the nature of that right not to be fufceptible of parts; I can, in ftipulating by name for A, one of my heirs, caufe him to fucceed to the whole right which refults from the agreement. *At cum quid fieri stipulamur, unius personam recte comprehendi*; d. L. 137, §. 8. For example. If in the fale of an eftate to a painter, there be a claufe by which it is ftipulated that he fhall make for me or for A, one of my children and heirs, a painting of the circumcifion of our Saviour, of a certain fize, and I die before it is done; A, who is named in the agreement, will alone fucceed for the whole to the claim againft the painter. But in the provinces, the cuftoms of which do not allow a father to prefer one of his children to the others in the difpofition of his eftate, he would be bound to compenfate his co-heirs for their parts.

66. As we are prefumed to ftipulate for our heirs whatever we ftipulate for ourfelves, fo we are prefumed to promife for our heirs and bind them to every thing we promife: unlefs what is the object of the ftipulation be fomething perfonal; or there be a claufe to the contrary.

Likewife in divifible obligations as one cannot ftipulate for another, but inafmuch as he will be his heir and for the part for which he will be his heir, fo he cannot bind any of his heirs for more than the part for which he fhall be his heir. Therefore a debtor would in vain include, in the agreement, a perfon who is to be his heir; for he will be bound no farther than the other heirs, who are not named. *Te & Titium hæredem tuum decem daturum spondes? Titii persona supervacue comprehensa est: sive enim solus hæres extiterit, in solidum tenebitur; sive pro parte, eodem modo quo cæteri cohæredes ejus*; L. 56, §. 1. ff. *de Verb. oblig.*

Fourth Case.

67. What we ftipulate with regard to a thing which belongs to us, may validly be ftipulated not only for ourfelves and our heirs, but thofe who fhall fucceed to us in the own-

ership of it; who are comprised in the expression *assigns*, commonly used in contracts. It is not in this case to stipulate for another. For example. I may validly stipulate that you shall never exercise against me nor against my heirs or assigns, the claim which you may have one day on a certain estate, by the happening of a contingency: and this stipulation will have effect, in favor of those who may afterwards acquire the estate from me.

This is obvious with regard to those who might acquire it by purchase: for being bound to warrant the title, I have an interest that you should not disturb them: this suffices in order that I should be held to have stipulated for myself what I stipulated for them; *supra*, *n.* 58. But it would be so likewise with regard to those who might acquire it by gift, *L.* 17, §. 5, ff. *de Pact.* although I be not bound to warrant their title: for the interest which I have in preserving the free disposition of the thing is sufficient for me validly to stipulate with you that you shall not disturb those to whom I may see fit to dispose of it, on any terms whatever.

68. In this agreement, and others like it, which we make relatively to the things which belong to us, not only may we validly stipulate for our assigns, but we are presumed to have done so, although this be not expressed, whether the agreement be *in rem*, as when it is said in the contract that you engage *not to exercise the rights which you may have on a certain estate*, without saying against whom; or whether it be *in personam*, as when it is said that you engage *not to exercise against* ME your rights on such an estate. In both cases I am presumed to have stipulated for all those who shall succeed me in the ownership of that estate, even by gift. *Pactum conventum cum venditore, si in rem constituatur, secundum Proculi sententiam, & emptori prodest....Secundum autem Sabini sententiam, etiamsi in personam conceptum est, & in emptorem valet, qui hoc esse existimat, etsi per donationem successio facta sit*; L. 17, §. 5, ff. *de Pact.* The reason is that in stipulating for myself, I am presumed to stipulate for all those who shall represent me: and not only my heirs, but all those who succeed to me, mediately or immediately, in

any manner whatever, in the ownership of the estate which was the object of the agreement, represent me with regard to this estate.

69. If I had stipulated *for my heirs*, by name, I would not be presumed to have extended my stipulations to my assigns. In this case *expressio unius est exclusio alterius.* The expression *my heirs*, excludes my other successors. For example. If in an agreement with the lord of the manor of whom my estate is holden, I have agreed with him, that whenever he should be entitled to relief out of it, he should not demand more from my heirs than a pistole for this his right. This agreement will not avail a third person who may acquire the estate from me or my heirs, by sale, exchange, gift, &c. It would be otherwise if my heirs had not been mentioned in the agreement, and it had been said indefinitely that whenever relief should be due, the lord should not require more than a pistole; or after the word heirs there had been added an *&c.* In either case the clause would extend to the assigns.

§. III.

That what concerns a person not one of the parties, may be the mode or condition of an agreement, although it may not be the object of it.

70. To give to a third person, to do something for a third person, and generally what concerns not the personal interest of the person who stipulates, cannot indeed be the object of a contract, but may be *in conditione aut in modo.*

Thus I cannot indeed validly stipulate in my name that you shall make a present to James of the Thesaurus of Meerman; but I may validly stipulate that if within a given time you do not make a present to James of the Thesaurus of Meerman, you shall pay me ten pistoles above the price for which I sell you an estate. For in this case the present which you are to make to James is only a condition. The object of the stipulation is that you shall pay me the sum of ten pistoles, and this sum is a thing which I stipulate for myself and which I have an interest to have. *Alteri stipulari nemo potest.... Plane si quis velit hoc facere, poenam stipulari conveniet, ut, nisi ita factum sit ut est comprehensum, committatur poenæ stipulatio etiam ei cujus nihil interest.* Juſt. *tit. de inut. stipul.* §. 20.

71. What concerns the intereſt of a third perſon may alſo be *in modo*; i. e. that although I cannot directly ſtipulate what concerns the intereſt of a third perſon, yet I may alien what belongs to me, with a ſtipulation that the perſon to whom I alien it, ſhall do a thing which concerns the intereſt of a third perſon. For example. Although I cannot validly ſtipulate in my name that you ſhall make a preſent of the Theſaurus of Meerman to James, I may validly give you a ſum of money or other thing, ſtipulating that you ſhall make this preſent to James.

According to the principles of the old Roman law, the effect of this condition was, that, on your failing to perform the ſtipulation under which you had received the money or other thing from me, I had a right to claim back what I had given you. For as I gave, and you received it only under this ſtipulation, there has ariſen between us an implied agreement, that you ſhould reſtore the thing to me, if you did not fulfil the ſtipulation under which I gave it. Hence reſults the right of claiming the thing by an action which the law calls *condictio (seu repetitio) ob causam dati, causa non secuta.*

But, according to theſe principles, the third perſon who had not been a party to the contract by which I gave you ſomething, under a charge that you ſhould give him ſomething, had no action to recover it, and this is grounded on the principle that contracts have no effect, except between the contracting parties. Hence it follows that no right can accrue to the third perſon, who was no party to the contract. But according to the conſtitutions of the Emperors, a third perſon in whoſe favor a donor adds a charge to the gift, has an action to compel the donee to fulfil the intention of the donor. *L.* 3, *Cod. de Donat. quæ sub mod.*

72. This engagement, which the donee contracts with this third perſon, according to the charge of the donor, under which the gift was made, and from which this action

results, is an engagement which is not indeed properly formed by the contract of gift, as this contract cannot of itself and *propria virtute* produce an engagement to a third person, and give a right to a third person who was not a party to it. It is natural equity which forms this engagement; because the donee cannot, without acting contrary to equity and without incurring the guilt of perfidy, retain the thing which was given him, if he does not perform what was required by the charge under which the gift was made and to which he submitted, in accepting the gift. Therefore the action which is given to this third person, is called by the law *actio utilis*, ibid. which is the name the Roman lawyers gave to actions which had no other foundation than equity; *quæ contra subtilitatem juris, utilitate ita exigente, ex sola æquitate concedebantur.*

73. Hence arises another question, i. e. whether, having given you a thing, under a charge to restore it to a third person, within a certain time, or to give him something else, I may release you from your obligation without the intervention of this third person, who was no party to the contract and who has not accepted the liberality which I intended to exercise towards him, by imposing this charge on you? Authors have been divided on this question. Grotius, *de Jure belli & pacis*, II, IX, 19, maintains the affirmative, which is also the opinion of Bartolus, Duaren and several other writers, particularly Ricard, *Traite des Substitutions, part.* 1, *ch.* 4. The reason on which they establish it is that this third person not having intervened in the gift, the engagement which the donor contracts to give something to the donee, in accepting the gift under that charge, is contracted by the concurrence of the will of the donor and the donee, and consequently may be dissolved by the contrary will of the same persons, according to the principle, *nihil tam naturale est quæque eodem modo dissolvi quo colligata sunt.* The right which is acquired by this third person is then, according to these writers, a right which is not irrevocable; because being formed by the sole will of the donor and donee, without the intervention of this third person, it is liable to be destroyed by the destruction of their assent, a

destruction which will be operated by the concurrence of the will of the same persons to the contrary. This right becomes irrevocable only when, the death of the donor rendering it impossible that such a concurrence should ever happen, the assent which formed the right ceases to be liable to be destroyed.

The contrary opinion has also its champions. It is that of Fachinæus and the authors quoted by him; *Controv.* VIII. 89. The reason upon which these authors ground themselves is that the clause of the contract of gift, which contains the charge imposed on the donee to give something to a third person, includes a second gift made to this second person. This second gift, without the intervention of the third person to whom it is made, receives its entire perfection by the acceptance which the donee makes of the gift, with the charge annexed to it: since by his acceptance he contracts with this third person, without his being a party to the agreement, the obligation of fulfilling the charge. From this engagement arises the right which this third person acquires of requiring, in due time, the performance of it. This right is an irrevocable right, and it ought not to be in the power of the donor to discharge the donee from his obligation, to the prejudice of the acquired right of the third person. For the clause, which contains this second gift or *fidei-commissa donatio* made to this third person by the donor, being a clause which makes part of an act of donation *inter vivos*, the *fidei-commissa donatio*, contained in this clause, is of the same nature: it is then a donation *inter vivos* and consequently irrevocable. It ought not therefore to be in the power of the donee to revoke it, in discharging the first donee from the charge imposed on him and from the engagement which he has contracted to the second donee. With regard to the principles which are opposed, *Quæque eodem modo dissolvuntur quo colligata sunt; Quæ consensu contrahuntur, consensu dissolvuntur.* These rules apply only to cases between the contracting parties themselves, but cannot destroy a right acquired by a third person. It is upon this ground that the law, ff. *de Pact.* determines that the security who has acquired a plea or exception by the agreement which has intervened between the creditor and principal debtor, cannot be deprived of it by an agreement to the contrary made afterwards by the same parties.

This last sentiment has lately been confined by the new Ordinance of Substitutions, *part.* 1, *art.* 11 & 12. But the dispositions of that ordinance relate only to posterior cases, and the question remains entire with regard to those which are anterior to the ordinance.

We will treat more amply of the gifts *fidei-commissa*, which these clauses contain, in a particular treatise on gifts.

§. IV.

That one may stipulate and promise, by the intervention of a third person, and that this is not to stipulate or promise for another.

74. What has been hitherto said, that we cannot stipulate or promise but for ourselves and not for others, is to be understood of such cases in which we contract in our own names. But we may lend our assistance to another to contract for him, to stipulate or promise for him; and in such case it is not properly we who contract, but it is this other person who contracts by our interposition.

Thus a guardian, when he contracts in that capacity, may stipulate or promise for his ward: for it is the ward who is supposed to contract, stipulate or promise, by the interposition of his guardian. The law giving to the guardian a character which causes the acts of the guardian, with regard to the affairs of the minor, to be presumed to be the acts of the minor.

It is the same with regard to a curator or any other lawful administrator. So it is with regard to an attorney. For the power which the principal has given him, causes the contracts of the attorney to be looked upon as entered into by the principal, by the intervention of the attorney.

75. If I contract in the name of a person who had not given me a power of attorney, his ratification will cause him to be presumed to have contracted by my interposition. For this ratification is equivalent to the power of attorney; *ratihabitio mandato comparatur.*

If he does not ratify, the agreement is void with regard to him. But if I pretended to have authority from him, if I promised to procure him to ratify, this promise is an agreement in my name with the person with whom I contracted, by which I bound myself in my own name, to procure his ratification, and, on failure, to indemnify him for what he loses, or fails to gain, for want of this ratification.

76. That one may be presumed to have contracted by the intervention of his guardian, &c. it is necessary that the contract do not exceed the power of such guardian, &c. For example. If a guardian had, in his quality of guardian, without a decree, sold some real property of his ward, the ward would not be presumed to have contracted by his interposition, and there would result no obligation on the ward. The sale of real property being a thing which exceeds the power of guardians.

Likewise that one may be presumed to have contracted by the intervention of his attorney, it is necessary that the attorney should have confined himself within the bounds of his power. When he exceeds them, he, in whose name he has contracted, is not reputed to have contracted by his interposition, unless he ratifies.

77. It is not to be doubted that an attorney exceeds the limits of his power, when he does some other thing than what is contained in it, even if it be more advantageous. For example. If I have given a power of attorney to a man to buy me a certain estate for a certain sum, and he buys another estate in my name, pretending to have a power of attorney from me, authorising him so to do: even if it were a more advantageous bargain, I should not be bound by it, and I shall not be presumed to have contracted by his interposition, unless I be willing to ratify; L. 5, §. 2, ff. *Mand.*

78. An attorney has also exceeded the limits of his power, when he has made, in my name, the contract which I had given him power to make, but in terms more disadvantageous than those which I had prescribed to him. For example. If I had given him power to buy a certain estate for 28,000 livres, and he buys it, in my name, for £.28200

I ſhall not be reputed to have contracted by his intervention and ſhall not be bound by the contract, becauſe he has exceeded the limits of his power, in buying at a higher price than that which had been preſcribed to him.

Yet, if he offered to place me in the ſame ſituation in which I would have been, had he remained within the limits of his power, as if in the above caſe he offered to indemnify me for the two hundred livres, I ſhould be bound to ratify; L. 3. §. 2, & L. 4, ff. *Mand.*

It is obvious that an attorney cannot be ſaid to have exceeded the limits of his power, when he contracts on terms more advantageous than thoſe which were preſcribed to him; L. 5, §. 5, ff. *d. tit.*

79. That I may be preſumed to have contracted by the interpoſition of an attorney, and that the contract which he made in my name may bind me, it ſuffices that the contract does not exceed what is contained in the power of attorney which he ſhewed to the perſon with whom he contracted; and it would not ſuffice to bring another power containing ſecret inſtructions which he had not followed. This ſecret power indeed gives me a right to an action for damages againſt my attorney, for having acted contrary to the ſecret inſtructions which I had given him, but it cannot impair my obligation to him with whom he has contracted in my name, in conformity to the apparent power which he produced. Otherwiſe there would be no ſecurity in contracting with an abſent perſon.

80. For the ſame reaſon, although a power of attorney be at an end by the revocation of it, yet if my attorney contracts in my name ſince the revocation of his power, but before ſuch a revocation was known to the perſon he contracted with, I ſhall be preſumed to have contracted by his interpoſition and ſhall be bound by the contract.

81. Likewiſe, although the mandate be at an end by the death of the perſon who gives it, and it ſeems to be repugnant that I ſhould be preſumed to have contracted by the interpoſition of him who has contracted in my name ſince my death; nevertheleſs if he has contracted in my name,

since my death, but before it might be known in the place where the contract was made, the contract will bind my estate, as if I had effectually contracted by his intervention.

The last position and that which precedes it, are supported by the principle of law; L. 12, §. 2, & L. 32, ff. *de Solut.* that a payment made to an attorney is valid, although made since the death of the principal or the revocation of the power, if the death or revocation was not known.

82. We contract by the interposition of another, not only when one merely lends us his assistance, in contracting in our name and not in his own, but when we contract by the intervention of guardians, attornies &c. who contract in such their capacities of guardians, attornies &c. and not in their own names. We are also presumed to contract by the interposition of another, although he contracts in his own name, when he contracts in regard to affairs which we have committed to his care. For in committing our affairs to him, we are presumed to have adopted and approved beforehand all the contracts he may make relative to the affairs which we have committed to him, as if we had made them ourselves; and we are presumed to have acceded to all the obligations resulting from them.

It is on this principle that is grounded the action *exercitoria*, which those who have contracted with the master of a vessel in regard to the affairs of the vessel, have against the owner who appointed the master.

It is likewise on the same principles that is grounded,the action *institoria*, which those who have contracted with the manager of a particular branch of trade or a manufacture, in regard to the affairs relative thereto, have against those who employ him: and the action *utilis institoria* respecting contracts made with a person to whom any other kind of business is committed.

We shall treat of these actions hereafter, *Part.* 2, *Chap.* 6, *Sect.* 8.

Note a difference between all these persons and guardians, attornies, trustees, &c. when the former contract, it is they who contract and bind themselves. Their employers are only presumed to accede to their contracts and the obligations that thence result. While the latter are not presumed to contract, themselves, but only to lend their assistance in the contract to those, who are under their guardianship, whose power they have, or the corporations whose officers they are. Therefore they do not bind themselves, but those who contract by their interposition.

83. We are also presumed to contract by the intervention of our partners, when they contract, or are presumed to contract, in regard to the affairs of the partnership. For in entering into partnership with them and allowing them to manage the affairs of the partnership, we are presumed to have adopted and approved, before hand, all the contracts they might make in regard to the affairs of the partnership, as if we had ourselves contracted jointly with them: and we have beforehand acceded to all the obligations resulting therefrom.

Note that a partner is presumed to have contracted for the affairs of the partnership, whenever he adds to his signature the words, *and company*, although the contract did not afterwards turn to the advantage of the partnership. For example. If he has borrowed a sum of money from a person to whom he has given a note with these words, *and company*, at the end of his signature; although he afterwards applied this money to his own private affairs or lost it at play, he shall not be the less presumed to have contracted for the affairs of the partnership, and consequently to have bound his partners, who are reputed to have borrowed the money jointly with him, and to have contracted by his intervention. These partners ought to impute it to themselves to have entered into partnership with a dishonest person; but those who dealt with him ought not to be deceived nor suffer from his infidelity.

The signature *and company* would not nevertheless bind my partners, if it appeared from the nature of the contract, that it does not relate to the affairs of the partnership; as if I put this signature to the lease of an estate which belongs to me individually, and which I had not put into the partnership stock.

When the partner has not subscribed *and company*, he is presumed to have contracted in regard to his private affairs, and he does not bind his partners, unless the creditor proves, by some other means, that he contracted in the name of the partnership, and that the contract actually concerned the affairs of the partnership.

84. A wife, in a community of goods with her husband, is also presumed to have contracted with him and by his interposition, in all the contracts which the husband makes during the community, and to accede to all the obligations which result from them, for the part which she has in the community, with this condition nevertheless, that she is bound only to the amount of the profits she may make during the community.

Article VI.

Of the effect of contracts.

85. Contracts produce obligations. We refer, as to what concerns the effect of these obligations, to what will be said hereafter, *Chap.* 2, in treating generally of the effect of obligations. We shall take notice now of a principle which is peculiar to the effect of contracts and of all agreements.

This principle is, that an agreement has no effect but with regard to things that are the object of the agreement, and only between the parties. *Animadvertendum est ne conventio in alia re facta aut cum alia persona, in alia re, aliave persona noceat;* L. 27, §. 4, ff. *de Pact.*

86. The reason of the first part of this principle is obvious. The agreement being formed by the will of the parties, it can only have effect on what the contracting parties intended and had in view.

We may give as an example of the first part of this principle, the stipulations of proper goods. When bringing a certain sum into the community, I have stipulated in my marriage settlement that the surplus of my property should remain my own private property, this agreement ought not to have the effect of excluding from the community, the private property that may come to me by will or intestacy;

during the marriage. For it has no object but to exclude from the community the overplus of the goods which I had at the time of the marriage. See other examples *in l.* 27, §. 7; *l.* 47, §. 1; *l.* 56, ff. *de Pactis, & passim.*

87. The second part of the principle is not so obvious. The obligations, which arise from agreements and the rights that result from them, being formed by the assent and concurrence of the will of the parties, it cannot bind a third person, nor give a right to a third person whose will has not concurred in forming the agreement.

The following example from the law 25, *Cod. de Pactis,* will illustrate this. If I have agreed with my co-heir that he should take on himself, alone, a certain debt of the estate; this agreement will not prevent the creditor of the debt from requiring of me the part for which I am heir. For this agreement can have no effect with regard to the creditor who was no party to it. *Debitorum pactionibus, creditorum petitio nec tolli, nec minui potest*; d. L. Number of other examples might be adduced. It is not a thing contrary to this principle, that a partner, in contracting, binds his partners, an agent his employer, an husband his wife. For as we have seen in the preceding article, those persons are presumed to have been parties, themselves, through the intervention of the partner, agent or husband.

88. It would seem that what is observed with regard to contracts of compositions, in case of insolvency, might be offered against this principle with more reason. When a debtor, who pretends to be unable to pay his debts, makes an agreement with three-fourths of his creditors (which is reckoned, *non pro numero personarum, sed pro cumulo debiti*); this agreement, which contains a time of payment and a discharge of part of the debt, may be opposed to the other creditors, although they be not parties to the contract: and the debtor may, by citing them, have the agreement declared common with them: so that it prejudices not their rights of hypothecation, if they have any. See the ordinance of 1673, *tit. XI, art.* 5, 6, 7, 8; & L. 7, §. 19; L. 8, L. 9, L. 10, ff. *de Pact.* This is not properly an exception to our princi-

ple. For it is not the agreement made with three fourths of the creditors that binds, *per se*, by itself and by its own virtue, the other creditors to assent to the terms mentioned in it. This agreement serves only to render it evident to the judge, that it is the common interest of the creditors that this agreement be executed by all. The presumption being that this great number of creditors have concurred to grant these terms, because it was the common interest of all to grant it, to secure the rest of what is due to them. And as it is not just that the hardness of a few creditors should prejudice the common interest of all the creditors, the judge condemns them to accede to the agreement, and to allow the terms and discharges mentioned in it. But it is not the agreement to which they were no parties, that binds them to accede to those terms. It is equity alone which produces this obligation, and which binds them to accede to this agreement; it being contrary to equity that, by a rigor subversive of their own interest, they should prevent the common interest of all the creditors.

89. The principle that agreements have no effect, but between the parties, is liable to a sort of exception with regard to securities. For the agreements which intervene between the creditor and the principal debtor, avail the securities, although they were not parties to them, and acquire to them the same rights which the principal debtor acquires. We shall see the reason of this *infra*, *Part*. 2, *Ch*. 6.

90. The same principle is liable to another sort of exception with regard to a remainder created by a contract of gift *inter vivos*. For, on the happening of the contingency on which the remainder vests, the person entitled to the remainder, although he was not a party to the original contract by which it was created, acquires the right of requiring from the donee, or his representative, the thing which is the object of it. See what has been said in the preceding article, §. 3.

ARTICLE VII.

Rules for the interpretation of agreements.

FIRST RULE.

91. We ought, in agreements, to attend to what has been the common intention of the contracting parties, rather than to the grammatical fenfe of their expreffions.

In conventionibus contrahentium voluntatem potius quam verba spectari placuit; L. 219, ff. *de Verbor. signif.*

For example. You rented from me a fmall apartment, in a houfe, the reft of which I occupied. I give you a new leafe in thefe words; "I have let my houfe to B. for three "years, on the terms mentioned in the preceding leafe." Will you have a right to pretend that I leafed the whole houfe to you? No. For although thefe words "my houfe," in their grammatical fenfe, fignify the whole houfe and not a fingle apartment, yet it is plain that our intention was only to renew the leafe of the apartment which you rented from me; and this intention, of which there can be no doubt, ought to prevail over the expreffion in the leafe.

SECOND RULE.

92. When a claufe is fufceptible of two meanings, it ought rather to be underftood in that in which it may have fome effect, than in that in which it cannot have any. *Quoties in stipulationibus, ambigua oratio est, commodissimum est id accipi qua res de qua agitur in tuto sit*; L. 80, *de Verb. Oblig.*

For example. If it be faid at the end of a contract of divifion, "It is agreed between Peter and Paul, that Paul may pafs over his lands:" although the words his lands, in their grammatical fenfe, may extend as well to the lands of Paul as to thofe of Peter, yet it is not to be doubted that they ought to be underftood of the lands of Peter; otherwife the claufe would not have any effect: as Paul had no occafion to ftipulate that he might pafs over his own land.

THIRD RULE.

93. When, in a contract, words are fufceptible of two meanings, they ought to be underftood in the fenfe moft fuitable to the nature of the contract.

For example. If it were ſaid in an inſtrument that I leaſe you, for nine years, a certain eſtate for the ſum of three hundred livres. Theſe words, "the ſum of three hundred livres," ought not to be underſtood of that ſum once paid, but of that ſum annually paid during the nine years of the continuance of the leaſe. It being of the nature of the contract of leaſe, that the price ſhould conſiſt in an annual rent.

It would be otherwiſe, if it were obvious that the ſum of three hundred livres is the value of nine years rent. *Puta*, if in the preceding leaſes the eſtate had been leaſed at an annual rent of thirty or forty livres.

Here is another example of the ſame rule. It is expreſſed in a leaſe that I have rented an eſtate for the annual ſum of three hundred livres and the repairs. Theſe words, *and the repairs*, ought to be underſtood of ſuch repairs only as tenants, according to the nature of the contract of leaſe, are bound to make.

FOURTH RULE.

94. What may appear ambiguous in a contract, is to be interpreted by what is cuſtomary in the place: *Semper in stipulationibus & in cæteris contractibus id sequimur quod actum est; aut si non appareat quod actum est, erit consequens ut id sequamur quod in regione in qua actum est frequentatur*; L. 24, ff. *de Regulis Juris.*

For example. If I have bargained with a vine-tender to cultivate my vineyard for a certain yearly ſum, without expreſſing what number of ploughings he ſhould give it, we are preſumed to have agreed that he ſhould give it the number of ploughings which is uſually given in the neighbourhood.

FIFTH RULE.

95. Cuſtom is of ſo great authority for the interpretation of agreements, that clauſes which are cuſtomary in a contract, are taken as a part of it, by implication, without being expreſſed: *In contractibus tacite veniunt ea quæ sunt moris & consuetudinis.*

For example. In a contract for the hire of a houſe, although it be not expreſſed that the rent ſhall be payable in femi-annual payments, the one at St. John's and the other at Chriftmas, and that the tenant fhall be bound to certain repairs, thefe claufes are implied.

Likewife in a contract of fale, although the claufe that the feller fhall be bound to warrant and defend the buyer's title be not expreffed, it is implied.

Sixth Rule.

96. A claufe is to be interpreted by the other claufes in the fame inftrument, whether they precede or follow.

The Digeft furnifhes an example of this rule, 126, ff. *de Verb. sign.* In this cafe, it was faid, in the firft claufe of a contract of fale, that the eftate was fold *uti optimus maximus.* i. e. free from any charge. In a fecond claufe it was faid that the feller meant only to warrant againft the charges which he himfelf had impofed on the premifes. This fecond claufe ferves for the interpretation of the firft and to reftrain the generality of its expreffion to this meaning, that the feller meant only to promife and affure that he had not impofed any charge on the premifes, that they were free from any he might have impofed; but not that they were free from any that might have been impofed by thofe whofe eftate he had, and of which he had no knowledge.

Seventh Rule.

97. In cafes of doubt, a claufe ought to be interpreted againft him who ftipulated the thing and in favor of him who contracted the obligation.

In stipulationibus cum queritur quid actum sit, verba contra stipulatorem interpretanda sunt; L. 38, §. 18, ff. *de Verb. oblig.*

Fere secundum promissorem interpretamur; L. 99, ff. *d. tit.*

The creditor ought to impute it to his own neglect not to have been more explicit.

For example. If it be faid in a leafe that the leffee fhall pay at certain periods a quantity of corn, as an annual rent, without any place of delivery being expreffed; the claufe in this cafe ought to be underftood that the delivery is to be at the leffee's, to thofe who may come there to take the corn away, in behalf of the leſſor; this ſenſe being moſt favorable to the leſſee, who contracted the obligation. If the leſſor intended to have the corn delivered at his barn, he ought to have expreſſed it.

Eighth Rule.

98. However general may be the words in which an agreement is expreſſed, it comprehends thoſe things only on which it appears the parties intended to contract, and not thoſe which they had not in view. *Iniquum est perimi pacto, id de quo cogitatum non est;* L. 9, §. fin. ff. *de Trans.*

According to this rule, if we have ſettled all our reſpective pretenſions and agreed upon a certain ſum, which you promiſed to pay me, by means of which we hold each other quit from all claims whatever: this ſettlement will not prejudice other claims which I might have upon you and of which I had no knowledge. *His tantum transactio obest de quibus actum probatur: non porrigitur ad ea quorum actiones competere postea compertum est;* d. L. 9, §. fin.

For example. If a legatee has compounded, for a certain ſum, his rights reſulting from the eſtate of the deceaſed, he will not be precluded from demanding a legacy left to him in a codicil, which was not diſcovered till ſome time after; L. 3, §. 1; L. 12, ff. *de Trans.*

Ninth Rule.

99. When the object of the agreement is an univerſality of things, it comprehends all the particular things which compoſe this univerſality, even thoſe of which the parties had no knowledge.

One may give as an example of this caſe, the agreement by which I abandon to you, for a certain ſum, my part in the eſtate of a deceaſed perſon. This agreement comprehends all the things which make part of the eſtate, whether we have any knowledge of them or not; our intention having been to treat of all the things which compoſe it. Wherefore it is held that I cannot be permitted to attack the agreement under pretence that, ſince it took place, a number of things have been diſcovered to belong to the eſtate, of which

I had no knowledge: *Sub prætextu specierum post repertarum, generali transactione finita rescindi prohibent jura;* L. 29, Cod. *de Trans.*

Provided, however, that these things were not concealed by my co-heir, with whom I have treated for my part of the estate, and who had those things in his possession. For otherwise there is on his part a fraud which authorises me to attack the agreement: *Error circa proprietatem rei apud alium* EXTRA PERSONAS TRANSIGENTIUM, *tempore transactionis constitutæ, nihil potest nocere.*

Our principle is grounded on the presumption that the parties who treat of an universality of things, have an intention to treat of all the things which compose it, whether they have knowledge of them or not. It is liable to an exception however, when it appears that they intended to treat of the things contained in this universality, which were known to them, as when they treated on an inventory. *Puta,* if by an instrument between my co-heir and myself, it is said that I cede to him, for a certain sum, my part of the personal property of an estate, *contained in the inventory,* or *according to the inventory.* It is clear that in this case our intention has only been to treat of what is contained in the inventory, and not of what has been omitted and which was not known to us.

TENTH RULE.

When in a contract a case has been mentioned, on account of the doubt there may have been, whether the engagement resulting from the contract, would otherwise extend to it, the parties are not presumed to have intended to restrain the legal extent of the engagement with regard to other cases which are not expressed.

Quæ dubitationis tollendæ causa, contractibus inseruntur, jus commune non lædunt; L. 81, ff. *de Regulis juris;* L. 56, *Mand.*

For example. If in a marriage settlement it is said that there shall be a community of goods between the husband and wife, in which community shall enter the personal property which either party may acquire. This clause will not prevent all other things, which legally fall into the community, from entering into it; because it is only inserted in order to clear the doubt, which the parties, not very conversant in legal matters, might entertain whether such personal property enters into the community of goods.

ELEVENTH RULE.

101. In contracts, as well as in testaments, a clause inserted in the plural number often divides itself into several singular things.

For example. If in a deed of gift to James and Richard, my servants, of a certain estate, it be said, "provided that after *their* death, without issue, it shall revert to the donor or his heir;" this clause in the plural number divides itself into two singular clauses; "provided that after the death of James without issue, his part shall revert to the donor and his heirs, &c."; and likewise "provided that after the death of Richard, without issue, his part shall revert, &c." Arg. L. 78, §. 7, ff. *ad sc. Trebel.*

TWELFTH RULE.

102. What is at the end of a phrase relates commonly to the whole phrase and not to what immediately precedes it. Provided what is thus at the end of a phrase agrees in in gender and number with the whole phrase.

For example. If in a contract of the sale of a farm, it be sold with all the grain, fruit and wines which *were* made on it this year: these words *which were made on it this year*, relate to the whole phrase and not to the wines only, and therefore the old grain is as well excepted from the sale as the old wine. It would have been otherwise, if it had been said, and the *wine which has been made on it this year.* These words *which has been made on it this year*, being in the singular, would relate to the wine only and not to the rest of the phrase. See *Pand. Justin. tit. de Leg. n.* 189 & 190.

ARTICLE VIII.

Of the oath which the contracting parties sometimes add to their contracts.

103. The contracting parties sometimes make use of an oath, the better to insure the future performance of the engagements which they contract.

The oath of which we speak here is a religious act, by which a person declares that he submits to the vengeance of God, or renounces his mercy, if he does not perform what he promises. Such is the result of these formulas: *So help me God. May God punish me, if I fail in my word*, &c.

104. The pretensions of churchmen had heretofore rendered common the use of oaths in all contracts. They pretended that all contestations, on the execution of contracts which were confirmed by an oath, belonged to the ecclesiastical judge. Because an oath was a religious act, and the refusal to perform an obligation, confirmed by an oath, being the violation of an oath, religion was interested in contestations respecting the execution of such engagements, which ought to render them cognizable by the ecclesiastical judge.

Therefore the notaries, who were churchmen, did not fail to insert, in all the contracts which they received, that the parties had made oath not to contravene any clause of the contract and to execute it faithfully, in order to insure to the ecclesiastical judge the cognizance of the execution of the contract. This style is often seen in several ancient manuscripts.

Churchmen have long ago been compelled to abandon these pretensions, to which ignorance had given rise: and the use of oaths has ceased in the contracts of individuals. Nevertheless, as it sometimes happens that persons resort to an oath, in order to insure the future performance of their promises, it will not be improper, summarily, to inquire what may be the effect of such an oath.

105. This oath has little or no effect in courts of justice. For either the obligation is deemed by them valid, of itself, or it is not. When it is deemed valid, of itself, the

oath is superfluous. For without its intervention, the creditor, to whom the obligation is contracted, has an action against the debtor to require the performance of it. The oath adds nothing to this action, and gives to the creditor no right which he had not before it intervened.

When the obligation is, of itself, invalid in those tribunals, and is one of those for which the municipal law has thought proper to deny an action, the oath is likewise of no effect in these tribunals. For the municipal law does not the less, on account of this, deny an action to the creditor.

For example. A tavern keeper is no less inadmissible to claim, by suit, from an inhabitant of the place, payment for what the latter had eaten or drunk in his tavern; a gamester is no less inadmissible to sue for a gaming debt; because, in each case, the debtor had bound himself by an oath to pay. The reason is, that the oath being an accessory to the engagement, the law which deems the engagement void, ought, by a necessary consequence, to deem the oath void: *Quum principalis causa non consistit, ne ea quidem quæ sequuntur locum habent;* L. 129, §. 1, ff. *de Reg. jur.*

Add that it ought not to depend on individuals, by the interposition of an oath, to render any engagement valid which the municipal law has thought proper to reprobate. This would be to elude the law.

106. According to the Roman law, the oath, which one of the parties took, to perform his agreement, was indeed of no effect, when the object of it was something unlawful in itself; L. 7, §. 16, *de Pact.;* or when violence had been used; *Auth. Sacramenta,* Cod. *Si adv. vend.* But when the agreement had no other defect than the minority of one of the contracting parties, the oath which the party who had executed the agreement had taken not to attack it, had the effect to prevent his being admitted to do so. Such was the decision of Alexander Severus, in the case of the sale of an estate by a minor, who had promised to the buyer, by an oath, not to attack it: *nec perfidiæ, nec perjurii, me autorem tibi futurum sperare debuisti.* L. 1, Cod. *Si adv. vend.*

Automne informs us that this decision is not followed in

our jurisprudence. The reafon is that if it were, the laws in favor of minors would be always eluded : it being eafy for thofe who contract with them, to require them to bind themfelves by an oath. The cuftom of Brittany, *art.* 471, formally decides that the contracts of infants are not rendered valid by their oaths.

It is principally in a moral view, that the oath by which one binds himfelf to perform his promife, may have fome effect. It has the effect of ftrengthening the obligation and rendering the breach of the promife more criminal. For he who, having bound himfelf, by an oath, voluntarily fails in his engagement, adds to the infidelity which refults from the voluntary breach of his promife, the guilt of perjury.

107. The oath has this effect, when the engagement is of itfelf valid, at leaft on the confcience. But fuppofing the engagement to be null, is the oath to fulfil it of no effect? We fhall examine this queftion in a fummary review of the defects which may render the engagement void.

When the engagement is void on account of its object, as when one has bound himfelf to give a thing which is not a fubject of commerce, or to do an impoffible thing, it is evident that the oath added to the engagement is not obligatory and has no effect.

All concede alfo that the oath to perform an unlawful engagement is not obligatory ; that it is a crime to take fuch an oath and would be a greater to keep it ; *scelus est fides.*

This pofition is correct, whether the thing be unlawful by the natural or by municipal law. For we are bound in confcience to obey the municipal law and the oath cannot leffen our obligation.

When the agreement is defective on account of error, (of which we have fpoken before) fo as to be void, the oath which accompanies it is alfo void. For the agreement being abfolutely void, there refults from it no obligation to which the oath may attach.

108. There is more difficulty when the defect proceeds from violence. Grotius contends that a promife extorted

by violence does not bind the person who made it; because if it were true that there results from it an obligation vesting a right in the person to whom it was made, he would himself be bound to indemnify the former, for the injury occasioned by such unlawful violence, by releasing him from his obligation. But when the promise, so extorted, has been confirmed by an oath extorted also by violence, Grotius contends that I am still bound in conscience to perform my promise; because if, for the above reason, I be not thus bound towards the person to whom I made the promise, still I am bound towards God, to whom I am presumed to have promised, by the oath which I have taken. Therefore if I do not perform my promise, having it in my power so to do, I am guilty of perjury; *Grotius, lib.* 2, *chap.* 13, *n.* 14.

The same writer observes that the heir of the person who has taken this oath, is not bound by the obligation resulting from it. Because my heir, who succeeds to me in my civil capacity, and represents me as a member of society, succeeds indeed to the obligations which I may have contracted with the persons with whom I have had an intercourse; but he does not succeed to my obligations towards God. *Grotius, lib.* 2, *chap.* 13, *n.* 17.

109. Saint Thomas, 11, 2. *q.* 89. *art.* 7. has also thought that a promise, although accompanied by an oath, is not indeed obligatory towards the person who had extorted it by an unlawful violence, but is obligatory towards God and in *foro conscientiæ;* that this obligation does not result from any vow or promise, but is founded on the reverence due to the holy name of God; which is violated, when we do not perform what we have promised by his name.

He adds nevertheless this modification, that after I have complied with my oath, in paying the thing I was compelled to promise under an oath, I may claim the money back, by law, if I be able to prove the unlawful violence exercised against me.

This modification is liable to an exception. Is it truly to pay a thing and to comply with an oath, to pay it, *dicis causa*, and with an intention of reclaiming what is paid?

Therefore, Grotius refutes this opinion, d. cap. 13, n. 15. *Probare non possum, quod a quibusdam traditum est, cum qui prædoni quicquam promiserit, momentanea solutione posse defungi, ita ut liceat quod solvit recuperare; verba enim juramenti, quod ad Deum, simplissime, & cum effectu sunt accipienda.*

110. The Popes have also decided that although a promise under oath, even when extorted by an unlawful violence is obligatory before God. *Alex. III. ch. 8. extra, de jurejur.* Celestinus III. says that from the Popes' absolution from the violation of this oath, they do not intend to induce those who make similar oaths to violate them, but only to treat such a violation with the indulgence to which venial faults have a claim, and not with the rigor due to a deadly sin. *Non eis dicatur ut juramenta non servent; sed si non ea attenderint, non ob hoc tanquam pro mortali crimine puniendi,* ch. 5, d. t.

111. Puffendorff, *IV.* 2. 8. thinks, on the contrary, that a promise extorted by violence, although confirmed by an oath, is no more obligatory before God than before men. His reasons are, that such an oath when addressed to the person to whom the promise is made, is only a solemn and religious recognition of the promise made to this person, but is not a vow. It does not contain a particular promise to God to perform that made to this person, nor would such promise, if admitted, be obligatory. For as promises, made to men, are only binding when accepted by those to whom they are made; so vows made to God bind only towards him when he may be believed to have acceded to and accepted them. Can it be believed that it is agreeable to God, and that he consents that an honest man should strip himself of his property, in favor of a wretch who has extorted a promise from him by an unjust violence?

As to the reverence due to the holy name of God, on which St. Thomas grounds his opinion, it cannot be denied that it is to fail in that reverence, and a great crime to promise under oath, although through violence, what one does not intend to perform: Since it is to make the name of God subservient to a lie, which Puffendorf admits. But after the oath is taken, (whether the person actually intended at the time to perform his promise, in which case there was no crime, or whether he had not such an intention, in which case there was,) the breach of the oath does not appear to Puffendorf to be sinful or contrary to our duty to God. The repentance which the person, who swore without an intention of performing, ought to have, seems to require him to give what he has promised, or in the other case the fear of scandal on weak minds may also induce a performance. But Puffendorff imagines it would be better to bestow the money in pious uses, rather than to give it to the person who extorted the promise, and who would use it in the further prosecution of his crimes.

112. There remains for us to say a word as to the case of fraud. It is not to be doubted that a promise, although supported by an oath, obtained by the fraud of the person to whom it is made, is no more obligatory towards him, than if he had extorted it by violence. For his fraud does not bind him the less to release it than violence would. But is such an oath obligatory towards God? According to the system of Puffendorf, who thinks that an oath extorted by violence is not binding, this ought not to be any more obligatory. But in adopting the opinion of Grotius and others, who think that an oath extorted by violence is binding, we need not conclude, that an oath, obtained by the fraud of the person who receives the promise, is obligatory. For when it appears that the oath is founded on a false supposition, without which the promise would not have been made, Grotius himself, *ibid*, *n.* 4. admits that the oath has no effect, even before God. The reason of this difference is this. He who promises, though he acts by compulsion, promises absolutely, without making his promise dependent on any condition; whilst the other intends to make his promise in a manner dependent on the truth of the fact he supposes, and which is the foundation of his promise.

SECTION THE SECOND.

Of the other causes of Obligations.

§. I.

Of quasi-contracts.

113. We call a quafi-contract, the act of a perfon, permitted by law, which binds him to another or another to him, without the intervention of any agreement between them.

For example. The acceptance of an inheritance by an heir is a quafi-contract, between him and the legatees: for it is an act permitted by law, which binds him to them to pay the legacies mentioned in the will of the deceafed; without there having intervened any agreement between the heir and legatees.

Another example of a quafi-contract is when one pays, by an error of fact, what he does not owe. The payment of this thing is an act which binds the perfon who has received it to reftore it to him who paid it; though it cannot be faid in this cafe, that there has intervened any agreement for the reftitution of it.

The adminiftration which one undertakes of the affairs of another who is abfent, and who did not requeft it, is alfo a quafi-contract which binds the one to account for his adminiftration, and the other to refund to him his difburfements.

There are a number of other inftances of quafi-contracts which we pafs over in filence.

114. In contracts, it is the affent of the parties which produces the obligation. In quafi-contracts no affent intervenes: it is the law alone or natural equity which produces the obligation in rendering the act, from which it refults, obligatory. For this reafon fuch acts are called quafi-contracts: becaufe, without being contracts and much lefs torts, they produce obligations as contracts do.

115. All perfons, even minors and lunatics, who are incapable of affent, may by the quafi-contract refulting from

the act of another, become bound to him, and bind him to them.

For it is not the assent which forms these obligations: they are contracted by the act of another without any act on our part. The use of reason is indeed required in him who does the act which forms a quasi-contract, but not in those by whom or to whom the obligations resulting from this act are contracted.

For example. If one has administered the affairs of a minor or a lunatic, his administration is a quasi-contract, which binds the minor or lunatic to allow him his useful expences, and reciprocally binds him to the minor or lunatic, to give an account of his administration.

The rule is the same with regard to feme coverts. They may in this manner become bound to others, and bind others to them, without the intervention of their husbands. For the law which prohibits them from binding themselves or doing any thing without their husbands, avoids only what they may do without their husbands' permission, but not the obligations resulting from an act in which they had no agency.

§. II.

Of torts and quasi-torts.

116. Torts are the third cause of obligations, and quasi-torts the fourth.

A tort is an act, by which, through fraud or malice, a person occasions damage or injury to another.

A quasi-tort is an act by which without malice, but through inexcusable imprudence, a person occasions damage or injury to another.

117. Torts and quasi-torts differ from quasi-contracts in this: that the act, from which a quasi-contract results, is an act permitted by the law, while that, which forms the tort or quasi-tort, is prohibited.

118. It results from the definition which we have given of torts and quasi torts, that it is only those persons, who have the use of their reason, who are capable of them. For

those who have it not, as infants and lunatics, are incapable of malice or imprudence.

It is impossible to ascertain the period at which persons begin to have the use of reason, and are consequently capable of malice; that period being earlier in some than in others. This is to be determined by circumstances. But as soon as a person has the use of reason, and malice and reflection are perceived in an act by which he has caused an injury to another, that act is a tort: and the person who is guilty of it, although he has not yet reached the age of puberty, contracts the obligation of repairing the injury which he has occasioned. Hence the maxim, *Neminem in delictis ætas excusat.* Imprudence is more readily excused in young persons.

119. Although ebriety occasions the loss of reason, a person is no less bound to repair the injury which he has done to another, whilst in that situation. For it is his own fault voluntarily to have placed himself in it. In this, a drunken man differs from an infant or lunatic, to whom no fault can be imputed.

120. It is not to be doubted that a person interdicted, on account of prodigality, is bound to the reparation of the injury which he occasions by the torts or quasi-torts which he commits, although he cannot contract any obligation by his agreements. The reason of this difference is obvious. Those with whom he has contracted, ought to impute it to their own folly to have contracted with him. An interdiction is a public thing, and therefore ought to be known to them. But nothing can be imputed to those to whom he has occasioned an injury by his torts or quasi-torts. They ought not to suffer from his interdiction: it ought not to procure him the impunity of his torts. This decision serves also to determine, that a person interdicted may be condemned to pecuniary fines for his torts or quasi-torts, contrary to the opinion in the gloss *ad L. Si quis, 7, Cod. Unde vi;* of Bartolus, and some other doctors, who say *Potest quidem se obligare ad pœnam corporalem, sed non ad pœnam pecuniariam, quia res suas alienare non potest.* For the interdiction is established to prevent him from contracting indis-

creetly, and not to insure to him the impunity of his torts.

All that we have said of persons interdicted, is applicable to minors of the age of puberty, or near that age, who are yet under the power of a tutor: except that the faults of imprudence, which we call quasi-torts, are more readily excused in them, than in persons of age, interdicted on account of prodigality.

121. Not only is the person who has committed the tort or quasi-tort, bound to the reparation of the injury which he has caused: those who have this person under their power, as parents, tutors, preceptors, are liable to this obligation, whenever the tort or quasi-tort has been committed in their presence, and generally whenever, having it in their power to prevent it, they did not. But if they could not prevent it they are not liable, *Nullum crimen patitur is qui non prohibet, quum prohibere non potest*; L. 109, ff. *de Reg. Jur.* even if the tort was committed in their presence: *Culpa caret qui scit, sed prohibere non potest*; L. 50, ff, d. tit.

Masters are also rendered responsible for the injury occasioned by the torts and quasi-torts of their servants or workmen, employed in their service. They are so, even in cases in which it has not been in their power to prevent the tort or quasi-tort, when it has been committed, in the exercise of the duties to which they were employed by their masters; even in the absence of their masters: which has been established in order to render masters cautious, not to employ any but careful servants.

With regard to the torts and quasi-torts which they commit, when not actually employed about the affairs of their masters, the latter are not answerable.

122. Observe that those who are liable for the obligation from a tort committed by another person, in which they did not participate, are liable in a different manner than the trespasser. Although he is liable to be compelled by the imprisonment of his person, to the payment of the damages he may be condemned to, for the reparation of the injury which his tort has occasioned; when the tort is of a nature to authorize his imprisonment: the others who are

liable alſo, are only civilly ſo, and can be compelled to pay the damages, by the ſeizure of their property only, and not by the impriſonment of their perſons.

§. III.

Of the law.

123. Natural law is the cauſe, mediately at leaſt, of all obligations. For if contracts, torts or quaſi-torts produce obligations, it is, primitively, becauſe natural law requires that each ſhould perform what he promiſed, and repair the injury which he occaſioned by his tort.

It is alſo the ſame law that renders obligatory the acts from which an obligation reſults, and which are therefore called quaſi-contracts, as we have before remarked.

There are obligations of which the ſole and immediate cauſe is the law. For example: it is not by virtue of any contract that children are bound to maintain their indigent parents, when they have the ability. Natural law alone produces this obligation.

The obligation which a feme covert contracts to reſtore the money, which ſhe has borrowed without the authority of her huſband, when it has turned to her advantage, is not produced by any contract or quaſi contract: for the contract of loan which has been made with her, without his authority, being void, produces no obligation: *Quod nullum est, nullum producit effectum.* Her obligation is then produced by natural law alone, which does not permit any one to enrich himſelf at the expence of another. *Neminem æquum est cum alterius damno locupletari; L. 206, ff. de Reg. Jur.*

Theſe obligations produce an action which is called *condictio ex lege.*

SECTION THE THIRD.

Of the persons between whom an obligation may exist.

124. There cannot be any obligation without two perſons, the one who contracts the obligation, the other to whom it is contracted.

He, in whoſe favor it is contracted, is called the creditor, and he, by whom it is contracted, the debtor.

125. Although it is of the effence of an obligation, that there be two perfons, one of whom is the creditor, and the other the debtor of it; yet the obligation is not extinguifhed by the death of one or the other. For this perfon is prefumed to have furvived in the perfon of his heir, who fucceeds to all his rights, and all his obligations.

126. Even if the creditor were to leave no heir, ftill he would be prefumed to have furvived in his vacant eftate. For the vacant eftate of a deceafed perfon, reprefents him, holds the place of his perfon, and fucceeds to all his rights and all his obligations. *Hæreditas personæ defuncti vicem sustinet*; and this fictitious perfon either of the creditor or of the debtor, fuffices to preferve the obligation after the death of either.

Not only may an obligation continue to exift in favor or againft the fictitious perfon of a vacant eftate, but there are certain obligations which may be contracted by or to fuch fictitious perfon.

For example. When a perfon who has been appointed curator to a vacant eftate, adminifters the goods of the eftate, he contracts towards the perfon of the vacant eftate, the obligation to render an account of his adminiftration; and the fictitious perfon contracts towards the curator the obligation to allow him his reafonable difburfements, in the execution of the truft.

A number of other examples might be adduced, of obligations contracted by a vacant eftate: as that which it contracts to the perfon who buried the deceafed, for his funeral dues. *Vice versa*, if any one fteals goods, part of a vacant eftate, or injures them, there refults an obligation, which he contracts to the vacant eftate.

127. Corporations are a kind of civil perfons, by whom and to whom obligations may be contracted.

128. It is clear that ideots, lunatics and infants, are incapable of contracting the obligations which refult from torts and quafi-torts, or even thofe which refult from contracts: fince they are incapable of affent, without which there can be no contract, tort or quafi-tort. But they are

capable of those obligations which are contracted without the act of the person by whom they are contracted. For example. If any one has advantageously administered the affairs of an ideot, a lunatic or an infant, this infant, lunatic or ideot, contracts the obligation of allowing this person his useful disbursements, in this administration, as we have already observed, *n.* 115. They contract also all the obligations which their tutors or curators, contract for them and in their names, *n.* 74.

By the Roman law, no obligation could be contracted between a father and the son who was under his power, unless *ex certis causis; puta, ex causa castrensis peculii.* The reason was, that the son, while under the power of his father, *in vinculis paternis,* could not *extra has causas,* have a thing of his own, and acquired for his father all that he did acquire. But as paternal power has no such effect with us, nothing prevents a father from contracting an obligation to his children or his children any to him.

Section the Fourth.

Of what may be the object and subject of obligations.

129. There can be no obligation, unless there be something which is due and which is the object and subject of it.

§. I.

General thesis on what may be the object of obligations.

130. The object of an obligation may be a thing, properly speaking, *res,* which the debtor binds himself to give, or an act, *factum,* which the debtor binds himself to do or not to do. This results from the definition which we have already given of an obligation.

Not only things themselves may be the object of an obligation, but the use of a thing or the possession of a thing may be the object of an obligation. For example. When one hires a thing, it is the use of that thing, rather than the thing itself, which is the object of the contract.

When one binds himself to give me a thing in pledge, it is rather the possession of the thing, than the thing itself, which is the object of his obligation. A number of other examples might be given.

§. II.

What things may be the object of an obligation.

131. Every thing, which is a subject of commerce, may be the object of an obligation.

Not only may a certain and determinate thing, as a certain horse, be the object of an obligation, but also an indeterminate thing may be the object of it, as when one binds himself to give me a horse, without mentioning what horse. It is necessary, however, that the indeterminate thing, which is the object of an obligation, have a certain moral consideration. *Oportet ut genus quod debetur, habeat certam finitionem*; as when one promises a horse, a cow, a hat, generally. But if the thing be so indeterminate, as to be reducible almost to nothing, there will be no obligation for want of a thing, which is the object and subject of it. For, morally speaking, almost nothing is regarded as nothing. For example. Money, corn, wine, without the quantity being determined or determinable, cannot be the object of an obligation; because that may be reduced to almost nothing, as a farthing, a grain of corn or a drop of wine. It is for this reason, that it is decided in L. 94, ff. *de Verb. Oblig.* that the stipulation *triticum dare oportere* produces no obligation: as it cannot be known what quantity the parties had in view.

Yet, it is not necessary that the quantity, which is the object of the obligation, be actually determined at the time the obligation is contracted, provided it be determinable. For example, if one binds himself to indemnify me for the damage which I have sustained or may sustain, on a certain account, the obligation is valid, though the sum to which it may amount is yet undetermined; because it is determinable by the estimation which may be made. Likewise, if one binds himself to supply me with corn for the use of my family, during one year, the obligation is valid, though the quantity be undetermined, because it is determinable, by the estimation which may be made of the quantity that will be necessary.

necessary.

132. Things which do not yet exist, but the existence of which is expected, may be the object of an obligation, provided however the obligation depends on the condition of their existence.

For example, when I bind myself to a wine merchant to deliver him all the wine I shall make this year, the *obligation* is validly contracted, although the wine does not exist. But if my vines are killed by the frost, so that I can make no wine, the obligation vanishes, for want of a thing which is the object of it; as entirely as if it had never been contracted.

This rule, that future things may be the object of an obligation, admits of an exception in the civil law, with regard to future inheritances. This law proscribes, as indecorous and contrary to public honesty, all agreements relative to future inheritances; whether a person contracted for his own estate towards another person to whom he stipulated to leave it, even when this was part of a marriage settlement; L. 15, Cod. *de Pact.*; or whether the agreement related to the inheritance of a third person, which one of the parties expected; L. fin. Cod. *de Pact.*; unless this third person intervened and gave his assent to the agreement. *d. L. fin.*

Our jurisprudence, in favor of marriage, permits the introduction into marriage settlements, of agreements relating to future inheritances. We may by the marriage settlement of another person, bind ourselves to leave him our whole estate or part of it, or to leave it to the issue of this marriage. This is what we term the contractual institution of an heir, which is in use in marriage settlements, and of which we have spoken in the appendix to the title of inheritance, according to the custom of Orleans. It is likewise lawful in marriage settlements to make, for the benefit of either of the contracting parties, such a provision as may be agreed upon for the future disposition of the estate of a third person. The stipulation of *proper* estates in the lineal and collateral lines are agreements of this kind. We have treated of these in our general introduction to the custom of Orleans, *chap.* 3, *art.* 4. §. 3. Except in marriage settlements, agreements relative to future inheritances are as much disallowed by our law as by the civil.

We ought not to mistake for a future inheritance, the substitution or trust estate of any property left to me by will to be restored to a third person at my death. This is no future inheritance, it makes no part of my property. It is a simple debt which I am bound to pay at my death, to those who were the object of the testator's beneficence, and relatively to which they may stipulate during my life with myself or others. L. 1 & 16, Cod. *de Pact.* L. 11, Cod. *de Trans.*

The rule that things which do not yet exist may be the object of an obligation, is liable to another exception by the laws of police; as those forbidding the sale of corn and hay before the harvest, wool before the shearing, and rendering such contracts void. *Traite de Police de Delamare.*

133. Not only may the things which belong to the debtor be the object of his obligation, but even those which do not, when he binds himself to give them: and he is bound to buy them from those to whom they belong, in order to give them to those to whom he has promised them.

If those to whom they belong did not wish to part with them, the debtor could not pretend to be discharged from his obligation, on the pretence that it is not in his power to perform it, and that one is not to be held to what is impossible; for the maxim *ad impossibilia nemo tenetur* is only true when the impossibility is absolute. But when the thing is possible of itself, the obligation does no less exist, although it be not in the power of the debtor to perform it; and he is liable for the damages resulting from its inexecution. It suffices that the thing was possible of itself, to justify the creditor in depending on the promise of the debtor. The debtor was in fault not to have considered, before he bound himself, whether it was in his power to do what he promised.

134. One may bind himself to give a thing which belongs to a third person, but cannot contract the obligation of giving to another what already belongs to him, unless it belonged to him but imperfectly. For in this case the obligation would

be valid so as to bind the debtor to cause the thing to belong perfectly to the other. *Traite du Contrat de Vente, n.* 8 & *seq.*

135. It is evident that things which are not a subject of commerce, cannot be the object of an obligation. For example, one cannot bind himself to give a church, a public square, a canonship, &c.

Neither can one contract the obligation to give to another, what he is incapable of possessing. For example; a right of view, to one who does not possess the neighbouring house or ground. But it is unnecessary that he who contracts to give a thing, should be capable of owning and possessing it, provided he to whom he engages to give it be capable. L. 34, ff. de *Verb. oblig.*

The Edict of 1741, *art.* 14, having disabled persons of mortmain, from owning or possessing real estates, one cannot contract the obligation to give property of this kind to such persons.

Can a venal office be due to a woman? Yes: for though she is incapable of holding the title of the office, she is not incapable of holding the right of finance from it, and it is this right, which is a subject of commerce, that is the object of the obligation.

§. III.

What acts may be the object of an obligation.

136. In order that an act may be the object of an obligation, it must be possible. *Impossibilium nulla obligatio est;* L. 85, ff. *de R. J.*

But it suffices that the act for which a man binds himself to me is possible of itself, though it be impossible to him. For if I knew not that it was not possible to him, I had a right to depend on his promise, and he validly bound himself to me; *in id quanti mea interest non esse deceptum.* He ought to blame himself for not having considered his ability, and having rashly bound himself to what was above it.

137. An act contrary to law or good morals, is like one

absolutely impossible, and can no more be the object of an obligation.

That an act may be the object of an obligation, it is necessary also, that what the debtor engaged to do, be something determinate. Therefore, if one binds himself to another to build him a house, without saying where, he contracts no obligation. *L.* 2, §. 5, ff. *de eo quod certo loco.*

138. The act which one binds himself to do or not to do, must be such an act as the person to whom the obligation is contracted, has an interest to have done or not done; and such interest must be appreciable.

The reason is evident. An obligation being a bond of right, there can be no obligation when he who promised to do or not to do may, with impunity, disregard his promise. It is evident that he may, with impunity, disregard it when I have no appreciable interest in his doing or not doing what he had promised. For damages cannot become due from him on account of the inexecution of his promise: damages being the estimation of the interest which the creditor has in the execution of the promise.

139. An act in which the person who stipulates has no interest, cannot indeed be the object of an obligation; but it may be the condition and charge of it. For example. If you should agree with me that you will come and study law at Orleans, the agreement would be void, and no obligation would result therefrom. For this act, in which I have no interest, cannot be the object of an obligation towards me. But if we had agreed that I should give you ten pistoles if you came to study law at Orléans, or on condition that you should come, the agreement would be valid. For this act, although it interests me in no wise, may be the condition or charge of the obligation resulting from our agreement.

On this principle, the promise made by a nephew to his uncle not to play, under the penalty of paying him 300 livres, if he failed in his promise, was held to be valid, in a case reported by Maynard and by Papon.

140. An act, to be the subject of a civil obligation, must be one in which the creditor to whom the obligation is contracted has an interest appreciable in money, according to the reasons mentioned before. But it is otherwise of the natural obligation: it suffices that the act which is the subject of it, be one in which the person to whom the obligation is contracted has an interest of just affection to render the obligation valid as a natural obligation. He who promised such an act and fails to do it, sins and becomes guilty *in foro conscientiæ*, although he cannot for the breach of his promise, be prosecuted *in foro legis*. See *supra*, *ch.* 1. *art.* 5, §. 1.

CHAPTER II.

ARTICLE THE FIRST.

Of the effect of Obligations on the part of the debtor.

§. I.

Of the obligation to give.

141. HE who has obliged himself to give a thing, is bound to give it, in a convenient time and place, to the creditor or some other person who has power or qualification to receive it in his stead. See *infra*, *Part* III, *chap.* 1.

142. When it is a determinate thing which is the object of the obligation, the obligation has the further effect with regard to the debtor, to bind him to use proper care in the preservation of the thing, until payment is made: and if for want of this care the thing happens to perish, to be lost or impaired, he is liable for the damages which may result. We shall treat of these damages, *infra*, *art.* 3.

The care which he ought to use for this preservation is different, according to the different nature of the contracts or quasi-contracts from which the obligation results:

When the contract is for the sole advantage of him to whom the thing is to be given or restored, the debtor who is obliged to give or reftore it, is bound only to ufe good faith in the prefervation of the thing, and is liable in this refpect only for grofs neglect, which, on account of its enormity, is confidered as fraud. *Tenetur duntaxat de lata culpa & dolo proxima, L. 5, §. 2, ff. commodat.* For example. A depofitary is held only to ufe good faith in the prefervation of the thing depofited with him, and which he has bound himfelf to reftore. Becaufe the contract of depofit is made for the fole advantage of the perfon who depofited the thing, and to whom the depofitary bound himfelf to reftore it. If the contract be for the mutual advantage of the parties, the debtor is held to ufe in the prefervation of the thing, the ordinary care which prudent perfons beftow on their own affairs, and confequently will be liable for flight neglect. For example. The feller is liable for this neglect in regard to the thing fold, which he obliged himfelf to deliver. The creditor is alfo liable in the fame manner in regard to the thing which he received in pledge, and which he obliged himfelf to reftore. Becaufe the contracts of fale and of pledge are for the mutual advantage of the parties. If the contract is for the fole advantage of the debtor, as is the contract of loan to ufe, he is bound to ufe in the prefervation of the thing, not only ordinary care, but every poffible care; he is therefore liable for the flighteft neglect.

This rule however, admits of feveral exceptions, as fhall be fhewn in particular treatifes on the different contracts and quafi-contracts.

As to accidents, and cafes of fuperior force, *vis divina*, the debtor of a determinate thing, while he has not been in arrear in paying it, is not liable for them, unlefs he undertook fpecially to anfwer for them, or the accident was occafioned by fome previous neglect on his part. As if I had lent you my horfe to go to a certain place, and you were attacked by robbers who have taken or killed it. Although this violence which you have fuffered is an accident for which a debtor is not ordinarily liable; yet, if inftead of taking the ufual or fafeft road, you took a bye-path, known to be infefted with robbers, in which you were attacked, you will be liable for this accident, becaufe your own imprudence has occafioned it.

143. It is another effect of the obligation to give, on the part of the debtor, that when he has been in arrear in difcharging his obligation, he be liable to the creditor for the damage refulting from this delay, and that he ought, confequently to indemnify him to the amount of what he would have had, if the thing had been paid on demand.

It is a confequence of this principle that if a thing due has been injured, or has wholly perifhed, fince the arrear of the debtor, by accident or fuperior force, the debtor is liable for the injury or lofs, provided the thing would not equally have perifhed or been impaired, had it been with the creditor.

It is likewife a confequence of this principle that the debtor is liable to the creditor, not only for the profits received, but alfo for thofe which might have been received by the creditor, fince the arrear of the debtor. Of other fpecies of damages, fee *infra, art.* 3.

144. Note that according to our practice, the debtor is not reputed in arrear of paying the thing due, but after a judicial interpellation, validly made, and only from the day of the interpellation.

This is the cafe, although the thing be due to minors or the church. The principle of the civil law, relating to the arrear which is contracted, *re ipsa*, towards thofe perfons, not being in ufe among us.

The rule has, however, an exception with regard to thieves, who are reputed in arrear of fatisfying the obligato reftore the thing ftolen, from the moment they contracted it, by the theft, without there being occafion, in regard to them, for any judicial interpellation; *L. fin. de Cond. furt.*

The debtor ceafes to be in arrear of giving the thing due, by the valid tender of it, whereby he puts the creditor in arrear of receiving.

145. The obligation to give a thing, extends fometimes to the fruits of it, when it produces any, and to intereft, when what is due is a fum of money.

Commonly, the debtor owes only the fruits which were or might have have been received ſince the judicial interpellation which has put him in arrear; and intereſt, likewiſe, runs only from that time. Sometimes, however, the fruits and intereſt are due before the arrear, as in the contract of ſale of a thing which is frugiferous. This depends on the different nature of contracts and other cauſes from which the obligations ariſe. We ſhall ſee this in treating of the different contracts and quaſi-contracts.

§. II.

Of the obligation to do or not to do.

146. The effect of the obligation, which a perſon contracts, to do a thing, is that he ought to do what he engaged to do; and that if he does not do it, after he has been put in arrear, he ought to be liable for the damage of the perſon to whom he contracted the obligation; that is to ſay, *in id quanti creditoris intersit factum fuisse, id quod promissum est*; which ought to be eſtimated in money by proper perſons named by the parties.

Commonly, the debtor cannot be put in arrear, but by the judicial interpellation, made to him by the creditor, to do what he promiſed, in order that on his failure he may be condemned to pay the damages.

The judge, on ſuch a demand, preſcribes a time within which the debtor ſhall be held to do what he has engaged, and on his failing to do it, within that time, condemns him to pay damages and coſts.

If the debtor diſcharges his obligation, within the time given, he avoids the damages and is only to be condemned to pay coſts; unleſs the judge conſiders that damages are due for the delay.

147. Sometimes, the debtor is held to pay damages to the creditor, on his failing to do what he promiſed, though no judicial interpellation was made. This happens when what the debtor bound himſelf to do could be effectually executed within a certain time only, which is paſt. For example. If I have employed an attorney to oppoſe, in my

behalf, the ſale of an eſtate which was mortgaged to me, and he has ſuffered a decree to paſs for the ſale of the eſtate, without oppoſing it; he is liable to pay damages for the injury I ſuſtain, although I made no demand on him for the performance of what he engaged to do: the time within which he ought to know the oppoſition was to be made, ſuffices for a demand.

148. The effect of the obligation which a perſon contracts not to do a thing, is that if he does it, he becomes liable for damages for the injury reſulting from his doing it, to the perſon to whom he bound himſelf not to do it.

149. When he who bound himſelf to do a thing, is prevented from doing it, by ſome accident or ſuperior force; likewiſe, when he who bound himſelf not to do a thing, is compelled to do it by ſome accident or ſuperior force; there is no ground for damages: for *nemo præstat casus fortuitos.*

Obſerve that, in this caſe, I ought to inform you of my being prevented from complying with my engagement; that you may take your meaſur.s accordingly; otherwiſe I could not avoid being condemned to pay damages, unleſs I were prevented by the ſame means from informing you. *L.* 27, §. 2, *ff. Mand.*

Article II.

Of the effect of the obligation in regard to the creditor.

150. The effects of the obligation, in regard to the creditor, are, I. the right which it gives him to proſecute the debtor, judicially, for the payment of that which is contained in the obligation.

II. When the obligation is of a liquidated ſum, it gives to the creditor the right of oppoſing it, as a ſet-off, to the amount of what he may owe to his debtor. We ſhall treat of this ſet-off, *infra, part* 3, *ch.* 4.

III. The obligation ſerves to the creditor as a ground for other obligations which ſecurities may contract with him for the perſon who contracted it. We ſhall ſpeak of theſe ſecurities, *infra, part* 2, *ch.* 6.

IV. It ferves as the fubject for a novation, when one intervenes. We fhall fpeak of novations; *infra, part* 3, *ch.* 2.

We fhall treat, in this place, only of the firft or principal effect of the obligation, which is the right it gives to creditor to demand, by judicial means, the payment of what is due. It is proper, in this refpect, to diftinguifh the cafe in which the obligation is to give, from that in which it is to do or not to do.

§. I.

Of the case in which the obligation is to give.

151. The right which the obligation gives to the creditor to profecute for the payment of the thing which the debtor bound himfelf to give, is not a right which it gives him to the thing, *jus in re;* it is only a right againft the perfon of the debtor to have him condemned to give the thing, *jus ad rem. Obligationum substantia non in eo consistit, ut aliquod corpus nostrum, aut servitutem nostram faciat, sed ut alium nobis obstringat ad dandum vel faciendum;* L. 3, ff. *de Obligat. & act.*

The thing which the debtor bound himfelf to give, continues ftill to belong to him: and the creditor can become owner of it only by the actual or fictitious delivery, which the debtor may make, in difcharge of his obligation. Until this delivery, the creditor has only the right to demand the thing; and he has that right only againft the perfon of him who contracted the debt, his heirs or univerfal fucceffors; becaufe the heir fucceeds to all the rights, and obligations of the anceftor: and becaufe the univerfal fucceffor of the debtor, fucceeding to his property, fucceeds alfo to his debts, which are a charge on his property.

152. Hence it follows, that if my debtor, fince he has contracted the obligation to give me a thing, has transferred it to another, either by fale or gift, I cannot demand it from the buyer or donee, but only from my debtor; who, being unable to give it to me, as he no longer has it, fhall be condemned to pay the damages refulting from the inexecution of his obligation.

G

The reaſon is, that, according to our principles, the obligation not giving to the creditor any right in the thing which is due him, I have in the thing which is due me no right which I may proſecute againſt the perſon in whoſe hands it is. The right which the obligation gives, being a right which the creditor has againſt the debtor and thoſe who ſucceed to his whole property, I cannot have any action againſt the buyer, who, having acquired this thing alone, has not ſucceeded to the obligation of the perſon who was bound to me; *L. Quoties*, 15, *Cod. de Rei vind.*; *Paul, sent. V.* 11, 4.

For the ſame reaſon, if my debtor has bequeathed the thing which he had obliged himſelf to give me, at his death the property of it will be transferred to the legatee, according to the maxim, *Dominium rei legatæ statim a morte testatoris transit a testatore in legatarium.* For having, according to our principles, continued owner, he was able to transfer the property. It will be the legatee, then, who will obtain it; and I ſhall, in this caſe, have only an action for damages againſt the heir of my debtor; L. 32, ff. *locat.*

153. Note, however, that if the debtor, when he transferred to a third perſon the thing which he had obliged himſelf to give me, was not ſolvent, I might proſecute this third perſon to obtain a reſciſſion of the transfer made to him to the prejudice of my claim, provided he had been a partaker in the fraud, *conscius fraudis*, if he had acquired it for a valuable conſideration; if he had acquired it for a gratuitous conſideration, it would not even be neceſſary for this that he ſhould have partaken in the fraud. *Tit.* ff. *his quæ in fraud. cred.*

Note that if the ſale has been made before a notary, and the thing ſold is real property, I have a lien on it for the performance of the obligation which the perſon from whom I bought it contracted towards me; and I may proſecute the right which this lien gives me againſt a ſecond buyer, whom I find in poſſeſſion of the property. It is true, he may turn me back to the diſcuſſion of the property of the ſeller, for the damages which are due me and which re-

sult from the inexecution of the obligation, contracted towards me: but if this discussion is fruitless, on account of the insolvency of the seller, the second buyer will be obliged to abandon the property to my lien, unless he prefers to pay the damages.

154. Although a personal obligation does not, of itself, give any right to the creditor in the thing which is the object of it; yet there are certain obligations, for the execution of which the thing that is the object of them is liable. This gives to the creditor a right in the thing and enables him to prosecute the obligation against third persons who detain the thing. Such is, for example, the obligation which results from the clause of redemption, *by which the buyer* of an estate obliges himself to reconvey to the seller, when he may require it, on being reimbursed, all that he has expended. The estate, which is the object of the obligation of the buyer, is liable for the execution of this obligation, and the seller may prosecute the execution of it against a third person *detaining the estate. But it is not the obligation that* produces this lien; the obligation, of itself, is incapable of giving any right except against the person who contracted it. It results from this, that the seller in the sale of the estate, is reputed to have retained the lien, for the obligation which the buyer has contracted towards him, in regard to the estate.

This lien is stronger than a mortgage. The creditor of a determinate thing, subject to his claim, may procure the possessor of it to be condemned to abandon the very thing, without being liable to be turned back by the possessor to the discussion of the property of the principal debtor, or to be paid, *instead of the thing, the damages resulting from the in*execution of the obligation.

155. As to the means which the creditor has to compel the debtor, his heir or universal successor, to give what is due him, they are two: I. command and execution: II. simple demand.

The first is to make to the debtor, personally or at his

houſe, by an officer, a command to pay, and to ſeize, on his refuſal or neglect, his perſonal and even his real property, and cauſe it to be ſold to raiſe the money.

That the creditor may uſe this method of command and execution, three things muſt concur. I. The debt muſt be of a certain and liquidated ſum of money, or of a certain and liquidated quantity of ſuch things as are regulated by number, weight or meaſure; as corn, wine, &c. Obſerve, however, that although one may ſeize for a debt of the laſt kind, when the quantity is liquidated, it is neceſſary to poſtpone the ſale until an appraiſement is made. *Ord.* 1667, *tit.* 8, *art.* 2.

II. It is, commonly, neceſſary that the creditor have a title of execution; that is to ſay, an inſtrument executed before a Notary, cloathed with all due formalities, by which the debtor ſhould have obliged himſelf to pay; or a judgment, whereby he has been condemned, which ſhould not be ſuſpended by appeal, writ of error, &c. *See Introduction au titre* 20 *de la Coutume d'Orleans, chap.* 2, §. 1. I have ſaid *commonly*, becauſe, in the cuſtom of Orleans, a landlord &c. may proceed by execution for three quarters. *Orleans, art.* 406.

III. It is neceſſary that it be againſt the perſon, who obliged himſelf before the Notary, or againſt whom the judgment was had, that the creditor thus proceeds. For although the heirs of this debtor ſucceed to his obligations, the creditor can only proceed againſt them by the way of ſimple demand, until they give him a new title before a Notary, or the creditor obtains judgment againſt them.

When theſe things concur, the creditor is entitled to execution, and is not permitted to proceed by the way of ſimple demand.

Simple demand is the method which the creditor who is not entitled to execution, is to take; it is to cite the debtor before a competent tribunal, and obtain judgment againſt him.

156. When the thing due is a determinate thing, and

the debtor, against whom there is judgment that it be given, has it in his possession, the Judge, on the petition of the creditor, ought to permit him to have it seized, and thus obtain possession of it; and it does not avail the debtor to offer in this case, to pay the damages resulting from the inexecution of his obligation. *Traite du Contrat de Vente, n. 57.*

§. II.

Of the case in which the obligation is to do, or not to do.

157. When a person has obliged himself to do a thing, the obligation does not give to his creditor the right of compelling him to do, specifically, the thing to which he bound himself, but only to procure him to be condemned to damages, on his failing to perform his obligation.

It is in this obligation of paying damages, that all obligations to do or not to do, resolve themselves. *Nemo potest præcise cogi ad factum.*

158. When one has obliged himself not to do a thing, the right which this obligation vests in the creditor, is that of prosecuting the debtor, judicially, in case he contravenes his obligation, and to have him condemned to the damages resulting therefrom.

If that which he obliged himself not to do, and has done contrary to his obligation, is something which may be undone; the creditor may also demand that it may be so. For example. If my neighbour has obliged himself not to shut up his avenue, but to leave me a free passage, and contrary to his obligation, he has erected a fence, or dug a ditch across it; I may procure a decree that he be held to pull down the fence or fill up the ditch, and that on his failing to do it within a certain time, I may be authorized to procure it to be done at his cost.

ARTICLE III.

Of the damages resulting either from the inexecution of obligations, or from delay in their execution.

159. We call *damages* the loss which a person has sustained, and the profit which he has failed to make. *Quan-*

tum mea interfuit; id est, quantum mihi abest, quantumque lucrari potui; L. 13, ff. *Rat. rem hab.*

When therefore, it is faid that the debtor is bound to pay the damages of the creditor, refulting from his failing to perform his obligation, it is meant that he ought to pay the creditor for the lofs which he has occafioned him, and the gain which he has deprived him of, by failing to perform his obligation.

160. The debtor, however, ought not to be fubjected to indemnify the creditor for all the loffes, indifcriminately, which the inexecution of the obligation may have occafioned him, and much lefs for all the profits he might have made, if the debtor had performed his obligation. It is proper, in this refpect, to take notice of different cafes, and different kinds of damages, and according to circumftances, to ufe moderation, in the affeffment of thofe with which he is chargeable.

When no fraud can be imputed to the debtor, and it is only by fimple fault that he has not performed his obligation, either becaufe he rafhly undertook what he could not accomplifh, or becaufe he has fince, by his own inattention, difabled himfelf from performing it; he ought only to be charged with the damages, which it could have been forefeen at the time of the contract, that the creditor might fuftain from the inexecution of the obligation; for the debtor is prefumed to have fubmitted to thefe only.

161. Commonly, the parties are prefumed to have forefeen only the damages which the creditor might fuftain from the inexecution of the obligation, in regard to the things which was the object of it, and not thofe which the failure of the debtor may occafion him, in regard to the reft of his property. Therefore in this cafe, the debtor is not chargeable with thefe, but only with fuch as are fuffered with regard to the thing itfelf, which was the object of the obligation; *damni & interesse, propter ipsam rem non habitam.*

For example. Suppofe I had fold a horfe, which I obliged myfelf to deliver to the buyer within a certain time, and which I was not able to deliver. If, in the meanwhile, the value of horfes has rifen, and the buyer has been compelled to give a higher price for another horfe of the fame kind, which he was under a neceffity to buy from another perfon; this is a damage for which I fhall be obliged to indemnify him. For it is a damage which he fuffered *propter ipsam rem non habitam*, and which relates only to the thing which was the object of the contract, and which I could have forefeen that he might fuftain. But if the buyer was a canon, who, for want of the horfe which I had engaged to deliver him, and being unable to find another, could not arrive at his church early enough to become entitled to certain extra tithes, I fhall not be chargeable with the lofs of thefe extra tithes, although it was occafioned by the inexecution of my obligation; becaufe it is a damage which is foreign to what was the object of the obligation, which was not forefeen at the time of the contract, and to the reparation of which I cannot be faid to have fubmitted in contracting.

Likewife, if I have leafed to another, for eighteen years, a houfe which I believed, *bona fide*, to belong to me, and at the end of ten or twelve years my leffee was evicted by the true owner, I fhall be chargeable with the damages of the leffee, refulting from his having been obliged, by a rife in the price of houfe-rent, to pay a higher rent for a houfe of the fame kind, during the remainder of the leafe, as well as from the expences of his removal. For thefe damages have a near relation to the enjoyment of the houfe, which was the object of my obligation, and are fuffered by the leffee *propter ipsam rem non habitam*.

But if the leffee had eftablifhed a lucrative branch of trade in the houfe, fince the beginning of the leafe, and his removal has occafioned to him the lofs of many of his cuftomers and injured him much in his trade, I fhall not be obliged to indemnify him for this injury, which was foreign to, and was not forefeen at the time of, the contract.

A fortiori, if in the removal, fome valuable pieces of furniture of the leffee were broken, I fhall not be liable for this lofs; for it is the unfkilfulnefs of the people whom he employed, which is the caufe of it, and not the eviction, which is only the occafion of it.

162. Sometimes the debtor is liable even for the damages of the creditor, although extrinfic; this happens when it appears that they were forefeen at the time of the contract and the debtor exprefsly or impliedly charged himfelf with them, in the cafe of his failure to perform his obligation. For example. I have fold my horfe to a canon, and there was an exprefs claufe in our bargain, by which I obliged myfelf to deliver it to him early enough to arrive at his church in time to fecure his extra tithes. If, in this cafe, I fail by my fault, although without fraud, to perform my obligation, and this canon could not eafily find another horfe, or otherwife procure a conveyance, I fhall be chargeable with the extrinfic damages refulting from the lofs of his extra-tithes. For by the claufe in our bargain, the rifk of this damage was forefeen and expreffed, and I am prefumed to have charged myfelf with it.

Likewife, if I have leafed my houfe to a merchant to keep a ftore, or to an innkeeper to keep an inn, and the leffee is evicted, the damages which he will have a right to claim from me, fhall not be confined to the expences of his removal and the advanced rent he may be obliged to give, as we have faid they fhould in the inftance before adduced; the lofs he may fuftain in his bufinefs, if unable to procure a houfe during the quarter, muft alfo be confidered; for in renting to him my houfe for a ftore or tavern, the rifk of this kind of damage was forefeen, and I am prefumed to have impliedly fubmitted to it.

163. Another example of our diftinction. I have bought feveral pieces of timber, which I made ufe of to ftanchion my building, which fell down from the defect in thefe pieces, which were rotten. If the feller was not a perfon profeffing that kind of trade, and fold me the timber *bona fide*, being himfelf ignorant of its defect, the damages I fhall have a right to, on account of the failure of the ftanchions, will only be a deduction from the price I gave him, in buying for found timber that which was otherwife; they will not

extend to the lofs I fuftain from the fall of the building. For the feller who fold the timber *bona fide*, and who was not bound to be acquainted with its quality any more than myfelf, cannot be prefumed to have undertaken to charge himfelf with for rifk. L. 13, ff. *de act. empt.*

But if the feller profeffed that particular trade, if he was a carpenter who fold to me thofe ftanchions for my building, he will be liable for the damages refulting from the fall of the building, occafioned by the infufficiency of fuch ftanchions. He will not be admitted to alledge that he thought them good and fufficient, and even if this were the cafe, his ignorance in regard to a matter relating to the art or trade which he publicly profeffed, would not excufe him. *Imperitia culpæ annumeratur;* L. 132, ff. *de R. J.* In felling me thefe pieces of timber to ftanchion my building, and felling them as a carpenter, he is prefumed to have engaged that they would prove fufficient, and to have taken on himfelf the rifk of the building, if they did not. *Molin. Tract. de eo quod interest*, n. 51.

Obferve, neverthelefs, that he ought only to be charged with the rifk which he undertook. Therefore if the carpenter fold me thefe ftanchions for a certain houfe, and I ufed them for one much larger, he will not be anfwerable for the fall of the latter, if the ftanchions were fufficient for the former, for which they were intended, becaufe, in this cafe, he was in no fault. But even if he had been in fault, the ftanchions being abfolutely bad and infufficient even for the fmaller houfe, for which they were intended, he will only be liable for the damages refulting from the fall of the large houfe, to the amount of the value of the fmall one. For having fold thefe ftanchions only for the fmall houfe, he intended to make himfelf liable only for the damages which I might fuffer, to the amount of the value of the fmall houfe: confequently he ought not, according to our principle, to be bound farther. Perhaps he would have thought more on the fubject, if he had underftood he was to run a greater rifk and that he was felling the ftanchions for the large houfe. *Molin. ibid.* n. 62.

For a like reafon, Dumoulin is of opinion, that when a

carpenter has fold me ftanchions for a houfe, which, from their infufficiency, has fallen down, the damages with which he is chargeable, are to be confined to the injury which the houfe has received and cannot be extended to the lofs of the furniture that was in it, and which was broken or loft in the fall. For this man, in felling me thefe ftanchions to fupport my houfe, undertook to anfwer for the fafety of the houfe alone. It is againft this rifk only that he undertook to indemnify me, and not againft the lofs of the furniture, which he could not forefee that I would leave in the houfe, it being cuftomary to remove the furniture of a houfe which is to be ftanchioned: therefore the carpenter ought not to be charged with the lofs of the furniture, unlefs he exprefsly took the rifk of it on himfelf. *Molin, ibid. n.* 65 & 64.

It would be otherwife in the cafe of a mafon, who having contracted to build me a houfe, which, foon after it was finifhed, fell down, owing to its not having been built in a workmanlike manner. The damages to which this unfkilful mafon would be holden, for having failed in his contract, would extend not only to the lofs of the houfe, but alfo to that of the furniture which was in it and could not be faved. For this mafon, in contracting to build the houfe, could not be ignorant that furniture would be brought into it, and that it could not be ufed without furniture; confequently he took on himfelf the rifk of the furniture. *Molin, ibid. n.* 64.

164. As to the damages to which a debtor is holden, on account of his failure to perform his obligation, in cafes in which no fraud can be imputed to him, it remains for us to obferve, that when thefe damages are confiderable, they ought not to be affeffed rigoroufly, but with a certain moderation.

It is on this principle that Juftinian, *Cod. de Sentent. quæ pro eo quod interest*, directs that the damages, *in casibus certis*, that s to fay, as Dumoulin explains it, *ibid. n.* 42 & *seq.* when they relate only to the thing which was the object of the obligation, are not to be affeffed above double the value of the thing, this value being included.

This is applicable to the following cafe. I have bought

for 4000 livres an eſtate, with a vineyard, in a diſtant county. At the time of the purchaſe, wine, the only produce made on this eſtate, was very low in that county, there being little demand for it in the neighbourhood and no way of conveying it to a market. Since that time, the king has cauſed a canal to be cut near the eſtate, through which produce may eaſily be conveyed to a good market, and the price of wine has increaſed fourfold: ſo that the eſtate which I bought for 4000 livres, is now really worth more than 16000. It is evident, that if I be evicted, the damages reſulting from the eviction, which are nothing elſe than *id quanti mihi hodie interest hunc fundum habere licere*, amount in reality to more than 16000. Yet according to the law of Juſtinian, for the damages which are due me, as well for the increaſed value of the eſtate as the coſts of the purchaſe, the ſeller, who ſold it to me *bona fide*, can only be charged with 8000 livres, including the purchaſe money. Becauſe the damages, which, in this caſe, are due only *propter rem non habitam & in casu certo*, cannot, according to this law, exceed double the price of the thing which was the object of the obligation.

The reaſon is, that obligations which reſult from contracts can only be produced by the intention and aſſent of the parties. The debtor, in obliging himſelf for the damages which may reſult from the inexecution of his obligation, is preſumed to have meant to bind himſelf no farther than what he could probably foreſee thoſe damages might extend to, and not beyond this: ſo that when theſe damages happen to amount to an exceſſive ſum, far above what the debtor could reaſonably be expected to foreſee, they ought to be moderated and reduced to the ſum to which it might probably have been foreſeen, that they would at moſt amount to; it not being to be preſumed that the debtor intended to bind himſelf farther. *Molin. Tract. de eo quod interest, n.* 60.

This law of Juſtinian, inaſmuch as it confines the reduction of the damages preciſely to double the value of the thing, is an arbitrary law, which has no binding force with us. But the principle whereon it is grounded, which does not allow a debtor, who can be charged with no fraud, to be made liable for the damages resulting from the inexecution of his obligation, above the sum to which he may reasonably have imagined they would amount, being grounded on natural law and equity, we ought to follow it, and consequently to reduce the damages when they happen to be excessive, leaving the quantum of this reduction to the discretion of the judge.

165. It is evident that the principle of reducing the damages to double the value of the thing which was the object of the primitive obligation, is applicable to those only which are due in regard to the thing itself; and that it cannot be extended to those which the creditor has sustained, extrinsically, in regard to the rest of his property, when the debtor has expressly or impliedly submitted to them. For these damages, not being due on account of the thing which is the object of the primitive obligation, cannot be regulated by the value of this thing; they may sometimes amount to tenfold and more. For example. The damages which are due me by a cooper, who has sold me leaky casks, resulting from the loss of the wine which I put in them, may amount to more than tenfold the value of the casks; for in selling me the casks, as a cooper, he made himself responsible for their goodness and tacitly charged himself with the risk of the loss of the wine, which might amount to ten or twenty times more than the price of the casks. This kind of damage, not referring to the casks but to the wine which was put in them, ought not to be regulated by the price of the casks. *Molin. ibid. n.* 49.

Nevertheless, even in the case of extrinsic damages, moderation ought to be used when they are excessive, and the debtor ought not to be charged with more than the highest sum to which he could have foreseen they might amount. For example. If I have put foreign wine or other liquor of immense value, which was lost on account of some defect in the cask, the cooper, who sold it to me, ought not to be obliged to compensate me for the whole loss, but only to the amount of the value of a cask of the best wine of the country: for when he sold me the cask, he could not foresee that I was going to put in it any liquor of greater value, and did not therefore intend to charge himself with any further risk. *Molin. ibid. n.* 60.

On the same principle, the mason who built my house, which fell down on account of some defect in building it, is bound, as we have seen before, to compensate me for the loss of the furniture broken or lost in the fall. But if I had precious stones or valuable manuscripts which were lost, he ought not to be chargeable with the entire loss: his obligation would not extend farther than to the ordinary value of the furniture of a person of my rank.

166. The principle which we have thus far established, is not applicable, when the damages have been occasioned by the fraud of my debtor. In such case he is chargeable with all the damages I have suffered, which were occasioned by his fraud; not only those I have suffered on account of the thing which was the object of the contract, *propter rem ipsam;* but those also, I have suffered in regard to the rest of my goods: without there being any occasion to distinguish or enquire whether the debtor is presumed to have submitted thereto. For he who is guilty of a fraud obliges himself *velit, nolit,* to the reparation of every injury which results from it. *Molin, n.* 155.

For example. If a dealer in cattle, sold to me a cow, which he knew was infested with a contagious distemper, and which he concealed from me; this concealment on his part is a fraud, which makes him responsible for the injury I sustained not only in the cow itself which he sold me, and which is the object of the primitive obligation, but likewise for what I may suffer in my other cattle to which she may have communicated the distemper. *L.* 13, *ff. de act. empt.* For it is the fraud of the seller which has occasioned all this damage.

167. As to other damages which I have sustained, and which are a more distant and indirect consequence of the fraud of the seller, will he be answerable for them? For example. If, extending the same case farther, the distemper which was communicated to my oxen, by the cow he sold

me, prevented me from cultivating my land; the damage I suffer from its remaining uncultivated, seems to be a consequence of his fraud who sold me a distempered cow; but it is a consequence more distant than the loss which I sustained from the communication of the distemper to my cattle. Will this person be answerable for it? *Quid*, if the loss of my cattle and the damage which I have sustained from being unable to make a crop in consequence thereof, disables me from paying my debts, and my creditors prosecute me and sell my goods for a trifling sum; will the seller be chargeable with this loss? The rule which appears to me proper to be followed in this case, is that we ought not to include in the damages with which a debtor is chargeable on account of his fraud, such damages as are only a distant and not a necessary consequence of it, and which may have proceeded from other causes. For example. In the present case the seller will not be chargeable with the loss I sustained from the sale of my goods, which is a very remote and indirect consequence of his fraud, and has no necessary relation to it; for although the loss of my cattle, which was occasioned by his fraud, has had an influence in the derangement of my affairs, this derangement may have had other causes.

This is conformable to the doctrine laid down by Dumoulin, in speaking of the damages with which the lessee of a house, who has maliciously set fire to it, is chargeable. *Et adhuc in doloso intelligitur venire omne detrimentum tunc & proxime secutum, non autem damnum postea succedens ex novo casu, etiam occasione dictæ combustionis, sine qua non contigisset; quia istud est damnum remotum, quod non est in consideratione. Dumoulin, ibid. n.* 179.

The loss which I have sustained from failing to cultivate my land, seems to be a remote consequence of the fraud of the seller. Yet I think he ought not to be chargeable with it, at least not with the whole. This failure is not absolutely a necessary consequence of the loss of my cattle, occasioned by the fraud of the seller. I might, notwithstanding the loss of my cattle, have prevented my land from remaining uncultivated, by buying other cattle; or, if I was not able to buy, by hiring others, or by leafing the land if I had no way to cultivate it myfelf. But as, by recurring to thefe expedients, I fhould not make as much out of the land as if I had cultivated it myfelf with my own cattle, which I loft by the fraud of the feller, this ought to be confidered in affeffing the damages with which he is chargeable.

168. The damages which refult from the fraud of the debtor, differ ftill from the ordinary damages in this, that the moderation which according to the principles of the civil law, *Cod. de sent. quæ pro eo quod interest*, is obferved in regard to ordinary damages, is not obferved in regard to thofe which refult from the fraud of the debtor. The reafon of this difference is evident. The moderation which is obferved in regard to ordinary damages, is grounded on the principle which we have already eftablifhed, that a debtor cannot be prefumed to have meant to oblige himfelf to more than the higheft fum to which he may have imagined the damages that might refult from the inexerution of his obligation would amount. This principle cannot be applied to the damages which are occafioned by fraud. For whoever is guilty of fraud binds himfelf *velit, nolit*, to the reparation of the injury which it may occafion; *ut supra*.

It ought neverthelefs to be left to the prudence of the Judge, even in the cafe of fraud, to ufe fome indulgence in affeffing the damages.

Thefe principles apply whether the fraud be committed *delinquendo* or *contrahendo*; *Molin, ibid. n.* 155.

169. It remains for us to fay a word refpecting the damages refulting from the delay of the debtor in the execution of his obligation.

A debtor is not only chargeable with the damages of the creditor, which refult from the abfolute inexecution of his obligation, when he does not perform it; but likewife with thofe which refult from his delay in the execution of it, when he is put in arrear.

Thefe damages confift in the lofs which the creditor has fuftained and the profit of which he has been deprived, by the delay; provided they be a neceffary confequence of it.

They are assessed with rigor and extended to every kind of loss, when it is by fraud or obstinacy that the debtor has delayed the performance of his obligation.

But when negligence alone can be imputed to him, these damages ought to be assessed with much more moderation, and are to be confined to such as may have been foreseen at the time of the contract, and to which the debtor expressly or impliedly submitted.

170. Such are the general rules. A particular one is followed with regard to the delay in the performance of obligations which consist in giving a certain sum of money. As the different damages which may result from delay in the performance of obligations of this kind, vary infinitely and as it is as difficult to foresee as to prove them, it has been found expedient to reduce them, by a sort of average, to a standard. This has been done by fixing them to the interest due according to the rate established by law.

This interest begins to run against the debtor from the day he has been put in arrear, until payment; because they are the common price or value of the lawful profit which the creditor might have drawn from the sum which was due him, if it had been paid.

In consequence of this sort of average, however great the damages may be which the creditor sustains from the delay of payment of the sum due, whether it proceeds from the negligence, fraud or obstinacy of the debtor, the creditor can have no other compensation than the interest.

But, on the other side, he is not compelled, in order to obtain it, to prove that any damage resulted from the delay of payment.

171. This rule, however, admits of an exception with regard to bills of exchange. When the person on whom a bill of exchange is drawn, refuses to pay it as it becomes due, the bearer of it, on causing it to be duly protested, may, by way of damages for the delay which he suffers, require from the drawer or endorsers the re-exchange, although it would exceed the ordinary rate of interest. We

call re-exchange the profit paid to a banker, to procure money on bills of exchange, in lieu of the money which was to have been received on the ſpot. *Traite des Lettres de change, n.* 64.

172. Such are the rules by which courts decide; but in a moral view, when the creditor has ſuffered no damage from the delay of payment of the ſum which was due him, that is to ſay, when this delay has occaſioned him no loſs, and has deprived him of no gain, he ought not to demand intereſt: for intereſt is only granted as a compenſation, and no compenſation can be due to him who has ſuffered no damage.

Vice verſa, if the damage which the delay has occaſioned to the creditor, be greater than the amount of the intereſt, the debtor is bound in conſcience, when he has delayed payment by fraud or obſtinacy, to compenſate the creditor fully for all the damages he knows him to have ſuſtained in conſequence of the unjuſt delay. It does not ſuffice to pay the intereſt from the time of the arrear.

It is otherwiſe when there has been, on the part of the debtor, no fraud in the delay. The reaſon of this difference is that, except in caſes of fraud, a debtor is only chargeable with the damages to which he is preſumed to have ſubmitted, which, in this caſe, are the intereſt ſince he was in arrear.

Another difference between the principles which are conſidered in *foro legis* and thoſe in *foro conſcientiæ*, is that, according to the former, it is not always neceſſary that there ſhould have been a judicial interpellation to put the debtor in arrear, in order that intereſt may run againſt him. For if my creditor tells me he wants his money, and, at my requeſt, in order to oblige me and to avoid injuring my credit, he refrains from making a judicial interpellation, depending on my honeſty and the promiſe I made him to indemnify him in the ſame manner as if he had proceeded judicially; I am in this caſe, in a moral view, ſufficiently put in arrear by his requeſt, and am obliged to pay him the intereſt that will afterwards accrue. It is without foundation, that the author of the Conferences of Paris, on Usury, vol. 1, page 379, *et seq.* rejects this interest as usurious. There is no usurious interest, but that which is demanded as the reward of a loan which ought to be gratuitous: but this has a just consideration, viz. the compensation of the injury which I occasion to my creditor by the delay in the execution of my obligation. This author grounds his opinion on the following reasoning. We hold, says he, our rights and our property from the law alone. Our law grants to the creditor the right of demanding interest on the sums which are due him, only when they are given by a judgment after a judicial interpellation: therefore, concludes this author, without a judicial interpellation, a creditor has no right to demand interest on the sum due him, and he cannot conscientiously receive it.

The answer is, that if the creditor cannot, in *foro legis*, demand interest, without a judicial interpellation, it is because he cannot, without this, prove that the creditor has been in arrear. A judicial interpellation being the only legal evidence of the arrear. But if the debtor has been really in arrear, the creditor has a right to receive interest as a compensation for the injury which the delay has occasioned him. He holds this right from the most respectable of all laws, the law of nature, which binds every debtor to perform his obligation and to indemnify his creditor for the injury he may sustain from the delay. When the creditor, from a regard for his debtor, forbears to have recourse to a judicial interpellation, which might ruin the credit of his debtor, it is a service which he renders him; the creditor ought not to suffer for having rendered this service to his debtor. *Officium suum nemini debet esse damnosum.* It is an absurdity to say that the creditor, because he has indulged the debtor, ought to be in a worse situation than if he had treated him with rigor.

SECOND PART.

Of the different kinds of obligations.

CHAPTER THE FIRST.

A general exposition of the different kinds of obligations.

§. I.

First division.

173. THE first division of obligations is derived from the nature of the duty, which they create. Obligations considered in this respect are divided into I. natural and civil obligations; II. civil obligations; and III. natural obligations.

We call a *civil obligation* that which is a bond of right, *vinculum juris*, and which gives to the party to whom it is contracted, the right of requiring, by law, the performance of it.

We call a *natural obligation* that which, in honor and conscience, binds him who contracted it to the performance of it.

174. Obligations are commonly both civil and natural. There are, however, some which are merely civil obligations, without being also natural, to the performance of which the debtor may be constrained by law, although they be not binding in conscience. Such is the obligation which results from a judgment erroneous in law or in fact, when the time, within which it might have been reversed, is past; or from an unjust judgment, from which there is no appeal. In either case the defendant is bound by the judgment and may be constrained by legal means to pay, what in conscience he does not owe. It is the authority of the judgment, *rei judicatæ*, which forms this obligation. The decisory oath produces a like obligation. The defendant, who has

deferred it to the plaintiff, is bound by this to pay what is thus ſworn to be due; although in truth and conſcience he does not owe it.

175. There are alſo obligations which are mere natural obligations, without being alſo civil. Theſe obligations in honor and conſcience bind thoſe who contract them to the performance of them; but the municipal law gives no action to thoſe to whom they are contracted for enforcing the performance of them.

Theſe are improperly called obligations; for they are no bond of right, *vinculum juris*: they do not impoſe upon the party an abſolute neceſſity to perform them, ſince he cannot be conſtrained thereto by the perſon with whom he contracted them. It is, however, this *necessity* which conſtitutes the character of the obligation, *vinculum juris quo necessitate adstringimur*; they are merely *pudoris & æquitatis vinculum*.

We ſhall treat particularly of this kind of obligation in the following chapter.

§. II.

Second division.

176. The ſecond diviſion of obligations is derived from the different manner in which they are contracted. In this reſpect we divide them into abſolute or conditional.

Absolute obligations, are thoſe which are not ſuſpended by any condition: whether they were originally contracted without any condition, or under ſuch conditions as have ſince been performed.

Conditional obligations are thoſe which are ſuſpended by ſome condition, under which they were contracted, and which is not yet performed.

177. We call abſolute obligations in a more confined ſenſe, thoſe which are contracted without any of the following modifications: a condition of defeaſance, a time limited for the duration of the obligation, a time and place of payment, the right to pay to ſome other perſon than the creditor,

or to pay another thing than that which is the object of the obligation. The alternative of different things which are the object of the obligation, the joining of feveral creditors or feveral debtors, are alfo modifications.

All thefe different modifications make as many different kinds of obligations of which we fhall treat in the third chapter.

§. III.

Third, fourth and fifth divisions.

178. Thefe divifions are derived from the quality of the different things which are the object of obligation.

There are obligations *to give* and obligations *to do. Stipulationum quædam in dando, quædam in faciendo*; L. 3, ff. *de Verb. obl.*

Obligations to do, comprehend alfo thofe by which a perfon obliges himfelf not to do.

There is this difference between obligations to give, and obligations to do. He who has obliged himfelf to give a thing, may when he has it in poffeffion, be conftrained to give the thing itfelf; the creditor may, againft his oppofition, obtain the poffeffion of it by legal means; whereas he who has obliged himfelf to do a thing cannot be conftrained to do it fpecifically: on his failing to perform his obligation, it refolves itfelf into an obligation to pay the damages which refult from his failure, and thefe damages confift in a fum of money liquidated by proper perfons, appointed by the parties or the court.

179. We divide obligations or debts, farther, into debts liquidated and unliquidated.

Liquidated debts are thofe of a thing certain. *Obligatio rei certæ.* Gaius defines them: *Certum est quod ex ipsa pronuntiatione apparet quid, quale, quantumque sit*; L. 74, §. 1, ff. *de Verb. obl.* Such are the debts of a determinate chattel, a certain quantity of wine, corn, &c. a certain fum of money.

A debt is unliquidated when the thing or fum which is due, is not yet afcertained; *ubi non apparet quid, quale, quan-*

tumque est in stipulatione; L. 75, ff. *dict. tit.* Such are debts of damages, until they are unliquidated, and confequently all obligations to do or not to do; *d. L.* 75, §. 7, fince they refolve themfelves into debts of damages. Debts of a thing indeterminate, or in the alternative, until the debtor has made his election, or until, on failure of the debtor, they are demanded by fuit, are alfo unliquidated debts; *d. L.* 75, §. 1, §. 8. See *Pand. Justin. tit. de Verb. oblig. n.* 78, 79, 80, 81.

There are feveral differences between liquidated and unliquidated debts. The creditor of a liquidated debt, when he has a title of execution, may proceed by command and feizure of the property of the debtor; the creditor of an unliquidated debt cannot. A liquidated debt may be pleaded as a fet off to another liquidated debt; an unliquidated debt cannot.

In regard to debts of grain or other things which confift in quantity, *quæ in quantitate consistunt*, a diftinction is made between liquidation and appreciation. A debt is liquidated when the quantity of a thing which is due is determined, *cum constat quantum debeatur*; it then gives a right to the creditor, who has a title of execution, to feize the property of the debtor, but he cannot fell them until after an appreciation; that is to fay, until the amount of what is due be eftimated in money; *Ord.* 1667, *t.* 33, *art.* 2.

180. We further divide obligations into obligations of a determinate thing, and obligations of an indeterminate thing of a determinate kind of things, which is called *obligatio generis*.

We fhall treat *ex professo* of thefe obligations *infra, chap.* 4, *sect.* 1.

181. Laftly. Obligations are divided into divifible and indivifible obligations, according as the thing due is fufceptible of parts, at leaft in idea, or is not.

We fhall treat of thefe *ex professo infra, chap.* 4, *sect.* 2.

§. IV.

Sixth division.

182. Obligations are divided into principal and acceffory obligations. This divifion is derived from the order in which the things that are the object of them ftand in regard to themfelves.

A *principal* obligation is the obligation of what is the principal object of the engagement contracted between the parties.

We call *accessory* obligations, thofe which are confequences and dependencies of the principal obligation.

For example. In the contract of fale of an eftate, the principal obligation, which the feller contracts, is that of delivering the eftate to the buyer and to warrant and defend his title. *Obligatio præstandi emptori rem habere licere.*

The obligation to give him the title deeds and the neceffary information in regard to the eftate, to act with good faith in the execution of the contract, and to take convenient care in the prefervation of the thing fold; are acceffory obligations.

Note that thefe terms *principal* and *accessory*, are alfo applied in another fenfe, as we fhall fee *infra*, §. 6.

§. V.

Seventh division.

183. We diftinguifh obligations into primitive obligations and fecondary obligations: and this divifion is derived from the order in which they are prefumed to be contracted.

The *primitive* obligation, which may alfo be called *principal* obligation, is that which has been contracted originally, principally and fubftantively.

The *secondary* obligation is that which is contracted, in cafe of the inexecution of a firft obligation.

For example. In the contract of fale, the obligation which the feller contracts to deliver and warrant the thing fold, is the primitive obligation; that to pay damages to the buyer, if he cannot deliver or warrant to him the thing fold, is a fecondary obligation.

184. There are two kinds of fecondary obligations. The firft is that of the fecondary obligations, which are only a natural confequence of the primitive obligation, which, without the intervention of any particular agreement, arife naturally from the inexecution of the primitive obligation, or from delay in the execution of it.

We may adduce, as an example, the obligation of damages, in which is converted naturally and *de jure*, the primitive obligation contracted by a feller to deliver and warrant the thing fold, in cafe the obligation be not performed; likewife, the obligation of intereft, which arifes from delay in the performance of an obligation to pay a certain fum of money.

Secondary obligations of the fecond kind, are thofe which arife from a claufe inferted in the contract, by which the party who undertakes fomething, promifes to give a certain fum of money or any other thing, in cafe he does not comply with his engagement.

Thefe are called *penal claufes*, and the obligations which arife from them, are called *penal obligations*, and are acceffory to the primitive and principal obligation, and are contracted in order to infure the execution of it.

We fhall treat of them *ex professo infra, chap.* 5.

185. Secondary obligations may further be fubdivided into two kinds.

There is a kind of fecondary obligation, into which primitive obligations, that are not executed, are wholly converted. Such is the obligation of damages, of which we have fpoken before. When a feller does not perform his primitive obligation to deliver or warrant the thing fold, the obligation is wholly converted into the fecondary obligation to pay damages to the buyer. This fecondary obligation is fubftituted to the primitive, which no longer remains.

There is another kind of fecondary obligation, which only accedes to the primitive, without deftroying it, when the debtor delays the execution of it. Such is the obligation of intereſt which reſults from the delay of paying the principal ſum.

§. VI.

Eighth diviſion.

186. Obligations, conſidered in regard to the perſons who contract them, are divided into principal and acceſſory obligations.

The *principal* obligation in this ſenſe, is that of him who binds himſelf as principal debtor, and not for any other perſon.

The *acceſſory* obligations are thoſe of perſons who bind themſelves for another, ſuch as the obligations of ſecurities, and of all thoſe who accede to the obligation of another.

We ſhall treat of theſe, *infra, ch.* 6.

§. VII.

Ninth, tenth, eleventh and twelfth diviſions.

187. Obligations, conſidered in regard to the ſecurities and means which the creditor has to procure the payment of them, are divided into obligations privileged and unprivileged, obligations hypothecary and chirographical, obligations with, and without, title of execution, obligations for which the debtor may be perſonally conſtrained, and civil or ordinary obligations.

Privileged obligations are thoſe for which the creditor has a lien, on all or part of the property of the debtor, to be paid in preference to other creditors. See *Introduction au Titre* 20 *de la Coutume d'Orleans, chap.* 2, §. 9, & *Introduction du Titre* 21, §. 16.

Unprivileged obligations are thoſe for which the creditor has no ſuch lien.

188. *Hypothecary* obligations are thoſe which are contracted with an hypothecation or mortgage of the property of the debtor, which is ſuſceptible of hypothecation.

Chirographical obligations are thoſe which are not accompanied by any hypothecation. *Introduction au Titre* 20, *de de la Coutume d'Orleans, chap.* 1.

189. Obligations with *title of execution*, are those for the payment of which the creditor has a right of execution against the debtor; *supra, n.* 45.

190. Lastly. Obligations for which the debtor may be *personally constrained*, are those to enforce the payment of which the debtor may be imprisoned 'till he pays. Other obligations, the payment of which cannot be enforced in this manner, are, by contradistinction, termed *civil* and *ordinary* obligations. *Ord.* 1667, *tit.* 34, *& le Commentaire de M. Jousse.*

CHAPTER II.

Of the first division of obligations, into civil and natural obligations.

191. WE have, thus far, sufficiently seen what is the nature of civil obligations; there remains for us to treat in this chapter of natural obligations.

The principles of our jurisprudence differ, in this respect, from those of the civil law.

The Roman jurists called *natural obligation* that which was destitute of action; that is to say, which did not give the person to whom it was contracted, the right of requiring, in law, the payment of it.

Such were all those which arose from simple agreements, that had neither the quality of a contract, nor the form of a stipulation.

These obligations were much favoured; *Quid enim tam congruum fidei humanæ, quam ea quæ inter eos placuerunt servare?* L. 1, ff. *de Pact.* If they were destitute of action, it was only from a reason derived from the policy of the Patricians, who, for their particular interest, had thought proper to make the right of action dependent on formulas, of which they alone, at first, had the knowledge, in order to oblige the Plebeians to resort to them in their affairs and thereby to keep them in dependence. Therefore, except that they were destitute of action, they had all the other effects which a civil obligation could have. Not only was the payment of what was due by a mere natural obligation valid and not liable to be recalled; but according to the principles of the civil law, I might plead to the action of my creditor, as a set off, what he on his part owed me by a mere natural obligation; L. 6, ff. *de Comp.* According to the same principles, securities could contract a civil obligation, which might accede to an obligation merely natural. L. 16, §. 3, ff. *de Fidej.* And a mere natural obligation might be the subject of a novation to a civil obligation. L. 1, §. 1, *de Novat.*

192. According to the principles of our jurisprudence, which has not admitted the distinction of the civil law between simple pacts and contracts, these natural obligations of the civil law are with us actual civil obligations.

Those which may be called in our law mere natural obligations, are, I. those for which the law denies an action, on account of the disfavor of the cause from which they proceed. Such is the debt due to an innkeeper, for expences incurred in his inn, by an inhabitant of the place. *Coutume de Paris, art.* 128.

II. Those which proceed from the contracts of a person who, having sufficient judgment to contract, is nevertheless, by the municipal law, disabled from contracting. Such is the obligation of a wife who has contracted without being authorised.

193. These obligations which proceed from a cause disapproved by the law, or which have been contracted by a person whom it does not allow to contract, would not have had, by the civil law, even the name of natural obligations; therefore I do not think they ought to have, among us, the effect which the civil law gives to mere natural obligations.

For example. An innkeeper ought not to be permitted to plead to the action of his creditor, what the plaintiff owes him, for expences incurred in his inn; nor the debtor of a wife to plead, as a set off, what she owes him by a contract entered into during her coverture, without her being authorised, unless the contract has turned to her advantage.

194. Likewise, securities do not bind themselves validly

to an innkeeper, for the expences incurred in his inn, by an inhabitant of the place; because the disfavor of the cause of the debt, which causes an action to be denied to the innkeeper, operates equally in regard to the securities as in regard to the principal debtor.

When it is on account only of the quality of the person that the law avoids the obligation, as when a wife binds herself without being authorised, there is more room to doubt whether an action ought to be denied against the securities. For it is from a reason which is personal to the wife, that the law denies an action against her. Nevertheless, it is to be holden, that the obligation of the securities is no more valid than that of the wife. For as the law avoids the obligation of the wife, it cannot exist, except in a moral view. The municipal law disowns and avoids it, and consequently it cannot be a sufficient subject to which other obligations may accede. If, according to the principles of the civil law, securities might accede to a natural obligation, it is because natural obligations were not obligations disapproved of by law and which it avoided. They were only destitute of action. But the civil law decides that securities cannot validly bind themselves for a woman who bound herself contrary to the prohibition of the Velleian Senat. consult. *Quia totam obligationem Senatus improbat*; L. 16, §. 1, ff. *ad sc. Vell.* L. 14, *Cod. dict. tit.* For the same reason, it is to be holden that securities cannot accede to the obligations which a wife contracts, without being authorised, nor to any of the other obligations which are called mere natural obligations on account only of their being forbidden by the municipal law. *Lebrun, Traité de la Communauté, liv.* 2, *ch.* 1. §. 5, *n.* 17.

195. The only effect of the obligation merely natural, is that when the debtor has voluntarily paid, the payment is valid and cannot be recalled; because he had a just cause to pay, that is to say, to discharge his conscience. Therefore it cannot be said that it was done without cause: whence it follows that there is no ground for the actions which are called *condictio sine causa*, and *condictio indebiti*.

Observe, however, that in order that the payment, made

by a woman, of a debt which she has contracted, without the authority of her husband, may be valid, it must be made in her widowhood, or with the authority of her husband, if it be made during the coverture; for then she is no more able to pay without his authority, than to contract.

196. Hitherto, we have spoken of obligations which the disfavor of the cause or the legal inability of the person who contracted them, renders merely natural. A civil obligation, when the debtor has acquired a plea or prescription against the action which results from it, *puta*, by the authority of a judgment or the decisory oath, or by the lapse of the time within which it ought to have been brought, may also be considered as an obligation merely natural, while the plea or prescription remains good and is not removed. See *infra part* 3, *ch.* 8.

197. We ought not to confound the natural obligations of which we have spoken in this chapter, with the imperfect obligations mentioned in the beginning of this treatise. These give to no one a claim against us, even in a moral view. For example. If I have failed to render to my benefactor a service, which gratitude required from me; although he suffers by my neglect of this duty, this does not make him my creditor, even in *foro conscientiæ*. Therefore if he owes me a sum of money, for which I have no action against him, because my claim is barred by the lapse of the time of limitations, he is nevertheless bound, in a moral view, to pay me, without being authorised to oppose to my demand, the loss which he has sustained through my ingratitude, or the advantage which I have reaped from his bounty. On the contrary, the natural obligations of which we have treated in this chapter, give to the person with whom we have contracted them, a claim upon us, not indeed in a legal, but in a moral view. Therefore if I have contracted a debt of one hundred livres for expences in a tavern in the town where I reside, the tavern keeper is really my creditor for this sum, in a moral, although not in a legal view; and if I have a demand against him, which is barred by the limitation, he may conscientiously oppose his tavern bill as a set-off to this demand.

CHAPTER III.

Of the different modifications under which obligations may be contracted.

Article the First.

Of suspending conditions and conditional obligations.

198. A CONDITIONAL obligation is that which is ſuſpended on a condition, under which it has been contracted, that has not yet been performed.

In order to underſtand what a conditional obligation is we ſhall ſee, I. what is a ſuſpending condition, and what are the different kinds of conditions; II. what may make a ſuſpending condition; III. when a condition is preſumed to be performed, or ſo holden. IV. We will treat of the indiviſibility of the performance of conditions; V. of the effect of conditions. VI. We ſhall ſee whether, if the obligation has been contracted under ſeveral conditions, it be neceſſary that they ſhould all be performed in order that the obligation may have its effect.

§. I.

What a condition is, and what are its different kinds.

199. A condition is the contingency of a future and uncertain event, that may or may not happen, on which the the obligation is made to depend.

200. We divide the conditions on which an obligation may be made to depend, into poſitive and negative.

A poſitive condition is that which conſiſts of the contingency of a certain thing which may or may not happen, that it ſhall happen; as *if I marry*.

A negative condition is that which conſiſts in the contingency of a certain thing which may or may not happen, that it ſhall not happen; as *if I do not marry*.

201. We further divide conditions into potential, caſual and mixed.

A potential condition is that which is in the power of him to whom the obligation is contracted; as when I oblige myſelf to my neighbour to give him a ſum of money, if he will cut down a tree in his field, which obſtructs my proſpect.

A caſual condition is that which depends on chance, and is not at all in the power of the creditor; ſuch are theſe, *if I have children; if I have no children; If a certain veſsel arrives safe in the Indies*, &c.

A mixed condition is that which depends on the concurrence of the will of the creditor and that of a third perſon; as is this, *if you marry my cousin.*

§. II.

What may make a condition which suspends an obligation.

202. In order that a condition may have the effect to ſuſpend an obligation, it is neceſſary, I. that it be the condition of a thing future. An obligation contracted under the condition of a thing paſt or preſent, although unknown by the contracting parties, is not properly a conditional obligation. For example. If, after the drawing of a lottery, and before the account arrives, I have promiſed a perſon to give him a certain ſum if the high prize has fallen to my lot; or if I have promiſed a certain ſum in caſe the Pope be now living; theſe obligations are not conditional: they are either complete and abſolute at firſt, if it appears that I have really the high prize, or the Pope is living; or they are no contracts at all, if it appears that I have not the high prize, or the Pope is dead.

This is ſo decided by the law, 100, ff. *de verb. oblig. Conditio in præteritum non tantum in præsens tempus relata, statim aut perimit obligationem, aut omnino non differt. Adde* L. L. 37, 38, 39, ff. *de R. cred.*

Nevertheleſs, although the thing be actually due, the creditor cannot exact it until the fact be rendered certain, and the debtor notified thereof.

203. It is neceſſary, II. that the condition be of a thing which may or may not happen. The condition of a thing which certainly will happen, is not properly a condition, and does not ſuſpend the obligation; but it merely defers the right of demand, and is equivalent to a time of payment.

It is neceſſary, however, to diſtinguiſh in this reſpect, between obligations which are contracted by deed *inter vivos*; by which we contract as well for ourſelves as for our heirs, and thoſe which ariſe from diſpoſitions made for the benefit of a certain perſon and not his heirs, ſuch as legacies and ſubſtitutions by teſtament or by donations *inter vivos*.

With regard to theſe diſpoſitions, although the contingency which is here the ſubject of a condition, muſt certainly happen; yet if the time when is uncertain, and it is during the life of the legatee or perſon ſubſtituted, it may form a true condition. The reaſon is, that as ſuch diſpoſition is made only to the legatee or perſon ſubſtituted, as the right which reſults therefrom can be acquired only by the ſame perſon, and as the condition which is annexed cannot of conſequence be effectually performed but during the life of the legatee, or perſon ſubſtituted, it ſuffices that it be uncertain whether the condition will happen during his life, though it be certain that it will happen on ſome day, for the diſpoſition to be conditional; ſince it is uncertain whether the legacy will become due. Upon theſe principles it is, that the law 1, §. 2, ff. *de Cond. et dem.* decides that if I have charged my heir with a legacy *when he shall die*, this legacy is conditional.—On the contrary, in deeds *inter vivos* by which we contract for ourſelves as well as for our heirs, the contingency of a thing which muſt certainly happen, though it be uncertain when, can never make a condition to ſuſpend an obligation; becauſe the condition of obligations thus contracted, may be as effectually performed after the death of the perſon to whom they were contracted as during his life; as we ſhall ſee, *infra*, *n.* 208, that a debt contracted under the condition of a thing which muſt certainly happen, cannot be uncertain and conſequently not conditional.

204. It is neceſſary, III. in order that a condition be valid and may ſuſpend an obligation, that it be the condition of a thing poſſible, lawful and which may not be contrary to good morals.

The condition of a thing impoſſible, unlawful or contrary to good morals, under which one would promiſe a thing, renders the contract absolutely null, when the condition is *in faciendo*, and no obligation arises from it. *L.* 1, §. 11, ff. *de Obl. & act.*; *L.* 31, *d. tit.*; *L.* 7, ff. *de Verb. obl.*; as if I had promised you a sum of money under this condition, *if you made a triangle without angles*, or under this, *of going naked through the streets.*

It is otherwise in testaments. Legacies given under the like conditions, are not the less valid, and the condition is regarded as null. This is in favor of last wills; L. 3, ff. *de Cond. & dem.* L. 104, §. 1, ff. *de Legat.* 1.

When the impossible condition is in *non faciendo*, as if I had promised you a sum of money *if you did not stop the course of the sun*, it does not render the obligation which is contracted under it null; this condition has no effect, and the obligation is absolute. L. 7, ff. *de verb. oblig.* But the condition not to do a certain thing which is contrary to law or good morals, may render the obligation null, because it is contrary to justice and good faith to stipulate for a sum of money to refrain from doing that which is forbidden.

205. In order that a condition may be valid and suspend the obligation contracted under it, it is necessary, IV. that it should not destroy the nature of the obligation. Such would be the condition that would make the obligation to depend on the mere and sole will of the person bound; as if I had promised to give a thing if it pleased me, *si voluero.* For the obligation, being *juris vinculum quo necessitate adstringimur* and essentially including a necessity of doing or giving something, nothing is more contrary to its nature than to make it depend on the mere will of him who is supposed to have contracted it; and consequently such a condition does not suspend, but destroys the obligation, which is void for want of binding power, as we have said, *supra, n.* 47, & 48. *nulla promissio potest consistere, quæ ex voluntate promittentis statum capit.* L. 108, §. 1, ff. *de verb. oblig.*

It is contrary to the essence of an obligation that it be dependent on the mere and sole will of him who is supposed to have contracted it; but it may depend on the sole will of a third person. Therefore I may validly contract the obligation to do or give something, if a certain third person consent to it; L. 43, L. 44, *de verb.*

§. III.

When conditions are presumed to be performed.

206. Positive conditions are performed when the contingency, which is the subject of the condition, happens.

When the condition consists in giving or doing a thing, it is necessary for the performance of the condition, that he, whose duty it is made, should give or do the thing in the manner in which it is probable the parties understood it. Therefore, if I have contracted an obligation to you under a condition that you give a sum of money to a certain person, who is a minor; the condition is not performed, when instead of paying this sum to his guardian, you have given it to the minor, who has wasted it; L. 68, ff. *de Solut*: for it is evident that my intention, in imposing on you this condition, was that you should pay the sum to the minor in such a manner as that he might be benefited by it, by placing it in the hands of his guardian, and not by abandoning it to his discretion.

The principle that conditions ought to be performed in the manner in which the parties have probably intended, assists in deciding the question whether conditions ought to be literally performed, *in forma specifica?* Generally they ought to be performed *in forma specifica*; they may nevertheless be performed *per equipollens*, when, *pro subjecta materia*, it appears probable that the parties so intended: and this intention is presumed when he in whose favor the condition is, has no interest in having it performed in one manner more than another.

For example. I have contracted an obligation under this condition, if within a certain time you pay me 100 louis d'ors; the condition will be presumed to be performed on your tendering me 2400 livres in silver, it being indifferent to me to receive that sum in gold or silver; the more so, as in money we consider only the value given it by the Prince, and not the pieces which are the sign of it. *Arg.* L. 1, *in fin.* ff. *de cont. empt.*

207. Conditions being to be performed in the manner the parties underſtood them, it is aſked whether, when the condition conſiſts in ſomething to be done by the creditor, the debtor or a third perſon, it muſt neceſſarily be done by that perſon, or whether it may be done by his heirs or ſome perſon appointed by him? The deciſion of this queſtion depends on the nature of the thing to be done and the intention of the parties. If it be ſomething perſonal, ſomething to be done by a *certain perſon*, rather than a thing ſimply and of itſelf, which the parties had in view; in this caſe, the condition muſt be performed by the perſon himſelf. For example. If I have bound myſelf to my ſervant to give him a certain reward, if he remain ten years in my ſervice, it is evident that his ſervices are perſonal, and that ſuch a condition can be performed by him alone. It is the ſame if I have bound myſelf to the pupil of a celebrated painter to pay him a certain ſum if his maſter made me a certain painting; the object of this condition is perſonal, and muſt be performed by the painter himſelf.

But if the thing, in the condition, to be done by the creditor, the debtor or a third perſon, be not perſonal; if it be ſomething which the parties have conſidered abſtractedly and not in relation to the perſon by whom it was to be done, the condition may not only be performed by that perſon, but alſo by his heirs or other ſucceſſors. For example. I have bound myſelf to pay you a certain ſum of money, *if within a year you cut down the trees on your land, which ſhade my vines*. This condition may be performed by your heirs; for there is nothing perſonal in it. It is evident that I have conſidered the thing ſimply and of itſelf, having no other view than to have the trees removed, it being no matter by whom. Likewiſe, if I have bought your land under a condition that your neighbour ſhould give up a right of way which he had over it, and he dies, the condition is performed on his heirs giving up the right.

208. The condition of contracts by acts *inter vivos* by which we contract as well for ourſelves as for our heirs, may as well be performed after the death of the perſon to whom we bind ourſelves as during his life. *Inſtit. tit. de*

Verb. oblig. §. 15. In this, these contracts differ from legacies and the like dispositions, which lapse when he, for whose benefit they were made, dies before the performance of the condition. *L.* 59, ff. *de Cond. & dem.*

The reason of this difference is, that the testator bequeaths only to the person of the legatee; hence it follows that the condition which is not performed till after his death, does not render the legacy due; for it cannot become due to the legatee who is no more, nor to his heirs who were not those to whom the testator intended to bequeath. On the contrary, in acts *inter vivos*, he who stipulates, is presumed to stipulate as well for himself as for his heirs: *Qui paciscitur, sibi hæredique suo paciscitur.* The obligation which results is contracted to him and his heirs; hence the performance of the condition under which the obligation has been contracted, though it happen after his death, must leave the obligation absolute.

Cynus, Bartolus and most of the antient doctors, have maintained that our principle on the performance of conditions in acts *inter vivos*, admits of an exception with regard to potential conditions, that is to say, those which consist of something in the power of him to whom the obligation is contracted. These they pretend cannot be performed after his death. If this decision were confined to potential conditions, consisting of something personal to be done by the creditor, there would be no difficulty in it. It is evident, from what has been already said, that they could not be performed after his death; but it is wrong to say that all potential conditions, indistinctly, may not be performed after the death of the creditor. There is no solid reason on which the opinion of these doctors can be supported. They ground it only on a few texts of law, which are by no means decisive, and which it would require too much time to recite and refute. It will suffice to answer the law 48, ff, *de Verb. Oblig.*, which is the principal foundation of this opinion. It is there said that in a stipulation, these words *cum petiero dabis* are different from the words *si petiero*, and that they include no condition: *admonitionem magis quam conditionem habet hæc stipulatio; et ideo*, adds Ulpian, *Si decessero prius quam petiero, non videtur defecisse conditio.* From these last words, our doctors argue thus; Ul ian says that when the parties have used these words *cum petiero*, the death of the creditor, happening before the demand, does not prevent the effect of the agreement, because the words *cum petiero* include no condition. Therefore, they conclude, if the parties had used words including a condition, as these *si petiero*, it would have been otherwise; and the death of the creditor happening before the demand, the condition would fail and with it the agreement: then the condition *si petierò* cannot be effectually performed but in the lifetime of the creditor: therefore potential conditions cannot be effectually performed in the lifetime of the creditor. I answer that this last consequence is ill drawn. These doctors, against the rules of logic, argue from a particular proposition to a general one. I admit that the condition *si petiero, cannot be performed after the death of the creditor*, because it appears by this condition that it is the personal act of the creditor, the the demand of the creditor himself, which the parties have intended to make a condition; otherwise this condition would have no meaning: but because the condition *si petiero* cannot be performed after the death of the creditor, it does not thence follow that other potential conditions, which include an act that is not personal, cannot be effectually performed after the death of the creditor. This question has been treated of at great length by Covarruvias, *quest. pract.* 39.

209. When the condition includes a time fixed within which it must be performed, as if I oblige myself to give you a certain sum of money *if a certain vessel returns this year to the ports of France*; the thing must happen within the time fixed; and when the time is expired without this event, the condition is presumed to fail, and the obligation contracted under this condition entirely vanishes.

But if the condition does not include any fixed time within which it must be performed, then it may be performed at any time and it is not presumed to fail until it becomes certain that the thing will not happen.

This rule admits of an exception when the condition

consists of a thing to be done by him to whom I have bound myself under this condition, and is a thing which I am interested in having done; as if I have promised my neighbour to give him a sum of money *if he will cut down a tree which incommodes me*: for in this case I may cite him, to whom I bound myself under this condition, to shew cause why a time should not be fixed by the Judge within which he shall perform the condition, so that on his failure, I may be absolutely discharged from my obligation.

210. Negative conditions either have a time fixed or they have not. When they have a fixed time, they are performed or rather accomplished when this time is expired without the happening of the thing. For example. If I have promised something *if a certain vessel does not return this year to our ports*; the condition will be performed when the year shall expire without the vessel's returning. They may be performed before the expiration of this time when it becomes certain that the thing will not happen.

If the negative condition has no fixed time, it is not holden to be performed until it becomes certain that the thing will not happen. For example. If I have obliged myself to give you something, *if a certain vessel does not arrive safe from the Indies*, the condition of my obligation is not performed until it becomes certain that the vessel will not return, *puta*, by certain news of its wreck.

211. If, however, the condition consists of a thing which is in the power of the debtor, and which is for the interest of him for whose benefit the obligation has been contracted; as if one is obliged to me to give me a certain sum of money if he does not cut down a tree on his land which injures my vines: I think that he who is obliged under this condition may be cited to shew cause why, on his failing to do it within a reasonable time to be fixed by the Judge, he should not be condemned to pay what he is bound to give in case he does not do it; and if he does not do it within the time thus fixed, this negative condition is holden to be performed; and he shall be condemned to pay what he has obliged himself to pay under this condition.

This decision however did not appear to the Roman lawyers to be without difficulty. The two schools were divided in opinion upon the question; L. 15, §. 2, ff. *de verb. oblig.* That of the Sabinians, which I have followed, appears to me more conformable to the spirit and simplicity of our jurisprudence.

212. It is a rule common to all the conditions of obligations that they ought to be holden to be performed, when the debtor who has obliged himself under the condition, has prevented its performance. *Quicunque sub conditione obligatus, curaverit ne conditio existeret, nihilominus obligatur*, L. 85, §. 7, ff. *de Verb. obl.* *Pro impleta habetur conditio cum per eum fiat qui, si impleta esset debiturus esset.* L. 81, §. 1, ff. *de Cond. et dem.* This is a consequence of this rule of law. *In omnibus causis pro facto accipitur id in quo per alium mora fit quo minus fiat* L. 39, ff. *de Reg. juris.* We cannot say, however, that it is by the act of the debtor that a condition has not been performed, and that it ought therefore to be holden to be performed, when it was but indirectly and without design of preventing the performance of it, that he opposed an obstacle to it. Therefore Paul says in regard to conditions annexed to legacies, *non omne ab hæredis persona interveniens impedimentum pro expleta conditione cedit.* L. 38, ff. *de statu lib.*

For example. If a testator, to whom I have succeeded, had devised to you a house, *if in a year from his decease you gave to the creditor of Peter a certain sum of money, for which he detained him in prison*; and being myself your creditor to a considerable amount, I have seized your property in order to be paid therefrom; although the seizure which I have made, has disabled you from paying this sum to Peter's creditor and performing the condition annexed to your legacy, I shall not, however, be presumed to have properly prevented, by my own act, the performance of it, and it will not be holden to be performed: for it is but indirectly that I prevented it: the seizure which I made was not made with a design to prevent you from performing the condition; I only intended to exact, by legal means, the sum which you owed me.

Obſerve alſo a difference, in this reſpect, between conditions the performance of which is momentary, and thoſe which can only be performed by lapſe of time: the former are holden to be performed as ſoon as the conditional creditor having offered to perform the condition, has been prevented by the debtor. It is not ſo with the latter. For example. If I had bound myſelf to a labourer under a condition that he do for me ten days work, and I have ſent him back on his offering to work, the condition will be holden to be performed only in part and for a ſingle day; it will not be holden to be entirely performed, until he has offered ten different days. L. 20, §. 5, *dict. tit.*

213. In regard to the rule concerning potential conditions, that they ought to be holden to be performed when he to whom a deceaſed perſon has left ſomething under ſuch a condition, has not had it in his power to perform it; it is a rule which takes place only in the caſe of laſt wills, and which ought not to apply to the conditions of engagements contracted by acts *inter vivos*. For example. If one has bequeathed you a certain ſum, if in a year from his deceaſe you ſet free your negro James, the condition is holden to be performed and the legacy is due, if the death of James, happening ſoon after that of the teſtator, has prevented you from executing and performing the condition; L. 54, §. 2, ff. *de leg.* I. But if one, by an agreement between him and you, has obliged himſelf, under ſuch condition, to give you a certain ſum, I do not think that the ſum would be due you, if the death of the negro ſhould intervene and prevent the performance of the condition. The reaſon of this difference is, that laſt wills are ſuſceptible of a more liberal interpretation. On the contrary, contracts ought only to be extended *quantum ſonant*; and the interpretation in caſes of doubt is always made againſt him to whom the obligation is contracted. *Ambiguitas contra ſtipulatorem eſt.* L. 26, ff. *de R. dub.*; becauſe he ought to impute to himſelf the blame, if the act is not ſufficiently explicit, having had it in his power at the time to render it ſo; L. 39, ff. *de Pact.* L. 99, *de Verb. oblig.* Therefore, according to this principle, when by an act *inter vivos*, one is obliged to me under this condition, that I ſet

my negro free, in the doubt whether the obligation be binding in case I could not set him free, the interpretation should be made against me; and I shall not be able to require what was promised me under this condition, although the death of the negro, happening before I could set him free, prevented me from performing the condition. This decision would take place even when I had made some preparation for this purpose; as if I had sent for the negro from a distant plantation, where he was in order to set him free before the judge, where I reside, and he had died on the way; I could not require what has been promised me under this condition; I can only demand to be indemnified for my expences in sending for him.

214. It is the same as to the rule which applies to mixed *conditions. If one has promised me a certain sum if I would* marry his cousin, I do not think that the sum would be due if I should offer to marry her and she should refuse; altho' if one had left me a legacy under such condition, the condition, would be holden to be performed. L. 31, ff. *de Cond. & dem.*

§. IV.

Of the indivisibility of the performance of conditions.

215. The performance of conditions is indivisible even when that which makes the object of the condition is something divisible. For example. If one has bequeathed to me a certain estate, on condition that I give a certain sum of money to his heir; or if one by a transaction obliges himself to abandon to me an estate in litigation between us, if I would give him, within a certain time, a certain sum: although this condition has for its object a thing divisible, nothing being more so than a sum of money, nevertheless the performance of this condition is indivisible, in this sense, that the legacy which has been given me under this condiand the obligation which has been contracted to me under this condition, will be in suspense till the performance of the whole condition, and the partial performance will not give a partial effect to the legacy or obligation. L. 23. L. 56, ff. *de Cond. & dem.*

Therefore if one left a legacy to Peter, in case he gave to his heir 10,000 livres, and Peter dies after having given only 5,000, the legacy becomes lapsed as to the whole; *d.* L. 56; and the heir of Peter can only recall his 5,000 livres *condictione sine causa*; unless, however, the heir of the testator chooses to pay half of the legacy; for it is in favor of the heir of the testator, debtor of the legacy, that the condition is regarded as indivisible; *Molin. tract. de div. & individ.* 3, *n.* 457.

It would be the same if the legacy had been given to Peter, or, on his decease, to his children, and Peter dying first, one of his children, succeeding to the legacy, had paid to the heir of the testator his part of the 10,000 livres: the condition would not in anywise be holden to be performed; and he could demand nothing until the residue had been paid. *d.* L. 56.

It would be otherwise if the legacy had been at first given to two legatees under this condition. The testator, having at first imposed the condition upon two legatees, is presumed to have divided it between them; *d.* L. 56.

216. Dumoulin decides for the indivisibility of the condition in the following instance. Four heirs of a debtor have been condemned to pay a certain sum, with a stay of two years for the payment, *if they give security in one month* Dumoulin maintains that the three heirs who have given security on their part in the month, cannot avail themselves of the stay, if their co-heir has not done the same on his part. The reason is that the creditor, in this instance, is the party most to be favored, since it is he who suffers inconvenience from the time given to his debtors; whence it follows that the condition under which the time is granted by the judge, ought to be construed favorably to him and with strictness against the debtor. *Molin. tract, de div. & ind. n.* 3, *n.* 534, *& seq.* If the fourth heir, instead of giving security for his part, has paid it, there is no doubt that the three who who have given security, each for his part, ought to have the benefit of the stay granted by the judgment: the creditor in this case, has security for all that is due. *Molin. ibid, n.* 542.

217. The condition annexed to a legacy is divided, when the legacy has not effect but in part. For example. If one has bequeathed to me a thing under a condition to give to some person a certain sum, and this legacy is reduced to a third part because the rest did not belong to the testator, who thought however that he was proprietor of the whole: not only would I not be holden to give more than a third of this sum to perform the condition; but if I had already given the whole, I might recall the surplus. See L. 43, L. 44, §. 9, ff. *de Cond. et dem.*

§. V.

Of the effect of conditions.

218. The effect of a condition is to suspend the obligation until the condition be performed or be so holden; until then, there is nothing due, but there is only an expectation that it will be due. *Pendente conditione nondum debetur, sed spes est debitum iri.* Therefore payment made through error before the condition is performed is subject to be recalled *condictione indebiti.* L. 16, ff. *de Cond. ind.*

219. If the thing which made the object of the conditional obligation, entirely perishes before the performance of the condition, the condition would be ineffectually performed afterwards; for the performance of the condition cannot confirm the obligation of what no longer exists, there being no obligation without a thing which may be the subject of it. If the thing exists at the time of the performance of the condition, the performance of the condition has this effect that the thing is due in the state it may be in: the creditor profits by the augmentation intervening, if the thing is augmented; and he suffers by the loss and diminution which may intervene, provided it does not proceed from the fault of the debtor. L. 8, ff. *de Per. et comm. rei vend.*

220. This performance of the condition has a retrospective effect to the time when the engagement was contracted; and the right that results from the engagement is presumed to have been acquired to him with whom the contract was made, from the making of the contract. L. 18, L. 144, §. 1, ff. *de Reg. Jur.*

Hence if the creditor dies before the performance of the condition, although he had yet no complete right, but a mere possibility, yet if the condition be performed after his death, he will be presumed to have transmitted to his heirs the right resulting from the engagement contracted towards him; because by means of the retrospective effect of the condition, the right will be presumed to have been acquired from the time of the contract, and consequently to have been transmitted to his heirs.

It is otherwise of conditions annexed to legacies. The reason of this distinction is, that the legacy being only made to the person of the legatee, the condition can only be performed for his benefit: while he who contracts being presumed to contract for himself and his heirs, the condition may be performed for the benefit of his heirs, even after the death of the creditor. *Supra, n.* 208. See *Cujas, ad. d.* L. 18.

221. It is also a consequence of the retrospective effect of conditions, that if the conditional engagement has been contracted by an act which produces an hypothecation, the hypothecation will be presumed to be acquired from the day of the contract, although the condition was not performed 'till a long time after.

222. Although the conditional creditor has no right 'till the performance of the condition, yet he is admitted to do all that may be necessary or proper for the preservation of the right which he expects one day to have. For example, He may oppose a decree for the sale of the land, which would be hypothecated to his claim, if the condition, on which it depends, were performed. He will even be considered as a creditor for this conditional claim. But he shall not receive the sum for which he is admitted to be a creditor, 'till after the performance of the condition. The absolute creditor, to whom the funds will fail, in case the admission of the conditional creditor be confirmed, by the performance of the condition, will be paid in his stead, on giving him security to refund, in case the condition be performed.

§. VI.

Whether, when an obligation has been contracted under several conditions, it be necessary that they be all performed.

223. This question is decided by a distinction. When several conditions are put with a disjunctive particle, as when I have bound myself to something towards you, *if a certain vessel arrives safe, or if I am appointed to a certain office*; it suffices that one of the conditions be performed to render the obligation absolute. But if they are put with a conjunctive particle, as when it is said, *if a certain vessel arrives, and if I am appointed to a certain office*, it is necessary that both the conditions be performed; and if either fail, the obligation vanishes. L. 129, ff. *de Verb oblig.*

Note, however, that in testaments, and even in contracts, by acts *inter vivos*, disjunctive particles are taken in a copulative sense, when it is evident that they were so taken by the testator or the contracting parties; as when a father or other relation bequeaths his estate over, after the death of his son or other relation, *if he dies without issue, or without having disposed*, &c. It is evident that in this substitution, by testament or by a donation *inter vivos*, the disjunctive particle *or* was understood by the testator or donor in a copulative sense, and that the substitution is not to take place, but on the performance of both conditions. *Facit*, L. 6, *cod. inst. & subst.*

Article II.

Of resolutive conditions and of obligations dissoluble under a certain condition, and of those the duration of which is limited to a certain period.

224. Resolutive conditions are those which are put, not to suspend the obligation, till the performance of them, but to make it cease when they are performed. An obligation contracted under a resolutive condition is perfect, therefore, at the moment of the contract; the creditor may demand the payment of it. But if, before it be discharged or the debtor has been put in arrear to discharge it, the condition, under which it has been agreed it should be dissolved, happens, the obligation will cease.

This difference between resolutive conditions and suspending conditions of which we have spoken in the preceding article, will be illustrated by an example. You have lent to Peter, by my order, 1000 crowns, and I have bound myself to pay this sum to you, if a certain vessel, in which I have a large interest, arrives safe from the Indies. This condition is a suspending condition, which suspends my obligation: I am not yet your debtor, and will not become such 'till it be performed by the return of the vessel. But if I have bound myself to you *'till the return of the vessel*, that is to say, under a condition that my obligation shall not continue longer than 'till the return of the vessel, the condition of the return of the vessel is only a resolutive condition, which does not prevent my obligation from being perfect from the time of the contract, and consequently, you may demand of me the payment. The whole effect of this condition is, that if the vessel arrives before I discharge the obligation or before I have been put in arrear to discharge it, the performance of the condition will cause the obligation to cease.

225. As the duration of an obligation may be limited to a certain event, so it may be limited to a certain time. For example. If I became security to you for Peter for three years, I shall be discharged from my obligation when this time will be expired.

226. Note, however, that when the debtor, before the expiration of the time, or before the performance of the condition, which was to dissolve the obligation, has been put in arrear by a judicial interpellation, his obligation can no longer be dissolved in this manner. L. 59, §. 5, ff. *mand.* The reason of this is evident; the creditor cannot suffer from the unjust delay of the debtor in the discharge of his obligation whilst it subsisted, and the debtor ought not to avail himself of his own wrong.

See *infra, Part* 3, *ch.* 7, *art.* 2; what is there said of the manner in which obligations are dissolved by a resolutive condition, or by the expiration of the resolutive time.

ARTICLE III.

Of the time of payment.

227. An obligation may be contracted with a time of payment or without. When it is contracted without a time of payment, the creditor may demand the payment of it immediately: when it includes a time of payment, he cannot demand it 'till the expiration of that time.

§. I.

What a time of payment is, and what are its different kinds.

228. The time of payment is a ſpace of time granted to the debtor to diſcharge himſelf from his obligation.

There is an expreſs time of payment which reſults from a poſitive agreement, as when I have bound myſelf to pay you a certain ſum of money within a certain time. There is another which reſults impliedly from the nature of the things which are the object of the engagement, or from the place where it is agreed that the thing ſhall be paid. For example. If a maſon bound himſelf to build me a houſe, I ought to wait the convenient ſeaſon to require from him that he perform his engagement. If one has bound himſelf in Orleans to convey a thing to my correſpondent at Rome, the engagement impliedly includes the time which is neceſſary to ſend it to Rome.

229. The time of payment is either a matter of right or of favor. It is a matter of right when it makes part of the agreement which produced the engagement; being included in it expreſsly, or at leaſt impliedly. It is a matter of favor when it makes no part of the agreement, *puta*, when it is granted ſince, by the Prince or by the Judge, at the prayer of the debtor.

§. II.

Of the effect of the time of payment, and in what it differs from the condition.

230. The time of payment differs from the condition, in this, that the condition ſuſpends the engagement which the agreement is to produce: the time of payment on the con-

trary does not fufpend the engagement, it only delays the execution of it. He who has promifed under a condition is no debtor, 'till the condition be performed; there is only a probability of his becoming fo. Hence it follows, that if thro error he were to pay before the condition was performed, he might reclaim what he has paid as a thing not due, as we have feen in the preceding article.

On the contrary, he who owes and has a time of payment yet to come, is a real debtor, and were he to pay before the time, he could not reclaim, becaufe he would have paid what he really owed; but though he is a debtor, the creditor cannot, till the time of payment arrives, exact from him what he owes.

Sometimes, however, the verb *to owe* is taken more ftrictly for what is actually demandable, and in this fenfe they fay, "*he, who has time, does not owe.*"

231. The time of payment delays the right to demand the debt, till it be entirely elapfed. Thus if I have promifed to pay a fum of money this year, it will not be demandable 'till the laft day of the year. For this laft day makes part of the time of payment; L. 42, ff. *de verb. oblig.*

232. This effect of the time of payment, to prevent the creditor from exacting the debt, 'till it be expired, is common to the time of payment, of right, and to the time of payment, of favor.

The time of payment, of right, has another effect which is peculiar to it, viz. that it prevents the debt from being oppofed as a fet-off, till it be expired.

For example. I lent you on the firft of January, 1755, 1000 crowns, which you bound yourfelf to repay me on the firft of January 1756; fince that time you became heir to my creditor, to whom I owed the fame fum without a time of payment. You demand payment of this fum in July 1755. I cannot oppofe to your claim, as a fet off, the 1000 crowns you owe me, payable the firft of January, 1756. For the fet off being a payment, this would be, on my part, to compel you to pay me before the time of payment, which is contrary to the tenor of the agreement which was made between us.

It is otherwise of the time of payment, of favor: this will prevent the creditor from prosecuting, but it does not include a right to oppose it as a set-off. For example. I lent you on the first of January, 1755, 1000 crowns, payable on demand, and you have obtained from the Prince or Judge, time of payment 'till the first of January, 1756. If, because you have become heir to a person to whom I owe a like sum, you were to demand it of me in July, 1755, the time of payment, of favour, which has been granted to you, would not prevent my opposing, as a set off, the sum of 1000 crowns, which you owe me. This time of payment, of favor, has only the effect to stay the rigorous pursuit of the creditor, and not to prevent or delay a set off. *Aliud est enim diem obligationis non venisse, aliud humanitatis gratia tempus indulgeri solutionis.* L. 16, §. 1, ff. *de Compens.*

233. There remains for us to observe, as to the effect of the time of payment, that as it is presumed to be given in favor of the debtor, L. 17, ff. *de R. J.*, the debtor may well refuse to pay 'till the expiration of the time; but the creditor cannot refuse to receive, if the debtor desires to pay; L. 70, *de soluti;* L. 17, *de Reg. Jur.;* unless it be apparent, from circumstances, that the time of payment was stipulated as well in favor of the creditor as in favor of the debtor.

The time of payment mentioned in a bill of exchange is reputed to have been inserted as well in favor of the creditor, owner of the bill, as in favor of the debtor. *Declaration of the 28th of November*, 1712.

§. III.

Of the cases in which the debt may be demanded before the time of payment.

234. The time granted by the creditor to the debtor is presumed to have for its foundation the creditor's confidence in the debtor's solvency. When, therefore, this foundation fails, the effect of the time of payment ceases.

235. Hence it follows, I. that when the debtor becomes

bankrupt, and his property is divided among his creditors, a creditor may receive his dividend, though the time of payment has not arrived. This is another difference between the time of payment and the condition. For the conditional creditor in ſuch caſe has no right to receive a dividend, but only to require that the other creditors may give ſecurity to refund, in caſe, by the happening of the contingency on which the condition depends, his debt becomes abſolute.

236. Note, that if, of ſeveral debtors *in solidum*, ſome happen to become bankrupts, the creditor may well demand the debt from them before the time of payment; but he cannot demand it from thoſe who remain ſolvent. A ſolvent debtor ought to have the full benefit of his time of payment, neither is he to be required to give any ſecurity on account of the failure of his bankrupt co-debtors. It was thus determined in a caſe, decided the 29th of February, 1592, reported by Anne Robert, IV. 6. The reaſon is, that the debtor who remains ſolvent, cannot, without ſome act of his, be bound to more than he at firſt intended to engage. He therefore cannot be compelled to give a ſecurity which he did not bind himſelf to give. The failure of his creditors being their act, not his, cannot prejudice him, according to the rule, *Nemo ex alterius facto prægravari debet.*

Hence it follows, II. that the hypothecary creditor who has made oppoſition to the ſale of an eſtate that was hypothecated to him, and who finds that there are prior hypothecations under which it muſt be ſold, may demand the payment of what is due him out of the monies ariſing from the ſale, though the time of payment has not yet arrived, becauſe his right of hypothecation, which occaſioned his confidence in the debtor to give him a time of payment, failing, the effect of the time of payment given ought to ceaſe alſo.

§. IV.

Of the time added to the condition.

237. Agreements include ſometimes a condition and a time for its performance. In ſuch caſe, it is neceſſary to examine whether the time is put to the condition alone or to

the payment alſo. In the firſt caſe when the condition is performed, it is not neceſſary to wait for the expiration of the time in order to demand the debt. For example. If it be ſaid, *if I marry within three years, you will pay me* 100 *livres.* On my marrying in ſix months after, I ſhall have a right immediately to demand the 100 livres, without waiting for the expiration of the three years. Likewiſe, if it had been agreed that you ſhould pay me a certain ſum in caſe I did not go to Italy before the month of May, the ſum will bcome due as ſoon as it ſhall be certain, by my death, that I ſhall not go to Italy, L. 10, ff. *de Verb. oblig.*; without there being any neceſſity to wait till the month of May; becauſe the time is put to the condition alone and not to the payment. But if, on the contrary, it has been ſaid, *if I marry between the preſent time and the firſt of January* 1758, *then you will pay me* 100 *livres*; the word *then* ſhews that the time is put to the payment as well as to the condition: therefore, tho' I perform the condition by marrying, I ſhall not be able to demand the ſum promiſed, till the expiration of the time; L. 4, §. 1, ff. *Cond. & dem.* See *Pand. Inſt. tit. de Verb. oblig. n.* 111; *& tit. de Cond. de dem. n.* 10 *&* 11.

ARTICLE IV.

Of the place of payment.

238. When the agreement includes a certain place where the payment is to be made, the place is preſumed to have been agreed upon for the advantage of the creditor as well as of the debtor; therefore the debtor cannot compel the creditor to receive elſewhere. *Is qui certo loco dare promiſit, nullo alio loco quam in quo promiſit, ſolvere invito ſtipulatore poteſt*; L. 9, ff. *de eo quod certo loco.*

But according to the principles of the civil law, the creditor might demand payment from the debtor in another place than the one agreed upon; *puta*, at the place of reſidence of the debtor, or at the place where the contract was made, when he found him there, each allowing to the other a compenſation for the inconvenience ſuffered from the payment not being made at the place agreed upon. This was

239. This action is not in use among us, and the creditor can no more compel the debtor to pay at another place than the one agreed upon, than the debtor can compel the creditor to receive elsewhere. Automne, *d. tit.* says: *Hic titulus non servatur in Gallia.*

Hence it follows that when the creditor does not reside in the place at which the payment is to be made, he ought to appoint where, in that place, the payment may be made; otherwise the debtor cannot be put in arrear. This appointment ought to be notified to the debtor, either by the agreement or by a judicial summons. For want of such appointment by the creditor, the debtor, when he wishes to pay, may summon him judicially to make the appointment; otherwise he will be authorised to consign at the place. See *infra, n.* 536.

240. The debtor cannot, indeed, be compelled to pay elsewhere than at the place designated; but on his failing to do so at this place, his property may be seized, if the obligation be with title of execution, wherever it may be found, and even if it be one for which the debtor may be constrained by his person, he may be imprisoned wherever he may be found; it was so adjudged in a case reported by Mornac, *ad.* L. 1, ff. *de eo quod certo loco.*

241. It remains to be observed that if the agreement includes two different places of payment, put with a conjunctive particle, the payment must be made, one half in one, and the rest in the other. L. 2, §. 4, ff. *de eo quod certo loco....* If they are put with a disjunctive particle, the payment may be made, of the whole, in either place, at the election of the debtor. *Generaliter definit Scævola petitorem habere electionem ubi petat, reum ubi solvat, scilicet ante petitionem*; L. 2, §. 3, ff. *d. t.* See *infra, part* 3, *chap.* 1, *art.* 5.

Article V.

Obligations contracted with a clause giving liberty to pay to a person indicated, or to pay a certain thing instead of the thing due.

242. Regularly the payment of a debt cannot be made to any person other than the creditor, without his consent

It is then an accidental quality of the obligation, when it is contracted with the liberty of paying to another person indicated in the agreement. See *infra, part* 3, *ch.* 1, *art.* 2, §. 4.

243. Nor can one regularly pay to the creditor, without his consent, another thing than that which is due, and which makes the object of the obligation. Nevertheless obligations are sometimes contracted with the liberty of paying another thing instead of that which is due; as when I farm my vineyard for 300 livres a year, which the tenant shall be at liberty to pay me in wine of his vintage, at the price it may be sold at in the neighbourhood. Although it is a sum of 300 livres which is due me by my tenant, yet he may pay me wine instead of it.

Likewise, if one has devised to me his house, if his heir does not choose to pay me three thousand *livres* in its stead; the heir, in accepting the inheritance, contracts towards me *ex quasi contractu*, the obligation to give me the testator's house, but with the liberty of paying me three thousand livres in its stead.

244. We ought not to confound these obligations with obligations under an alternative, of which we shall speak in the following article. In these, all the things promised under an alternative, are due; but in the obligations with liberty to pay another thing than that which makes the object of the obligation, there is but one thing due. That which the debtor has the liberty to pay is not due; it is not *in obligatione*, but only *in facultate solutionis;* as in the example of the devise of a house, with the liberty of paying three thousand livres in the stead of it, there is nothing due but the house.

Hence it follows, I. that the creditor has no right to demand any thing but the house, and not the three thousand livres, although the debtor may, before and after a demand made of the house, pay the three thousand livres.

II. That if the house be destroyed by an earthquake, the debtor will be entirely discharged.

III. That the claim resulting from such a devise is of

the nature of real property, even if the debtor were to make his election to pay me the three thousand livres in order to discharge himself; for the nature of a claim follows that of the thing due, not of that which may be paid in its stead. Therefore if the devise had been made by my grandfather, whilst I was in a community of goods with my wife, I would have, as my separate property, the three thousand livres paid by the heir during the community, this sum being the redemption of the claim of a house and consequently of a claim of real property, which proceeding from the devise made to me by my grandfather, is my separate property.

ARTICLE VI.

Of obligations under an alternative.

245. An obligation under an alternative, is that by which a person binds himself to give or do several things, on condition that the payment of one of them shall discharge him as to all; as if I bind myself to give you a certain horse or twenty crowns, or if I bind myself to build you a house or pay you a hundred pistoles, &c.

When one has bound himself to pay two different sums of money put with a disjunctive particle, the obligation is not therefore in the alternative, and he is debtor only of the smallest; *Si ita stipulatus fuero, decem aut quinque dari spondes, quinque debentur;* L. 12, ff. *de Verb. oblig.*

246. In order that an obligation may be under an alternative, it is necessary that two or more things be promised and put with a disjunctive particle. When several things have been promised with a conjunctive, there are as many obligations as there are things; L. 29, ff. *de Verb. oblig.*; and the debtor is discharged only by the payment of them all: but when they have been promised under an alternative, though they are all due, there is but one obligation. L. 27, ff. *de Leg.* 2, which may be discharged by the payment of either of the things so promised; *Alterius solutio totam obligationem interimit. Adde Gloss. ad* L. 25, ff. *de Pecun. const.*

247. The debtor has the choice of the thing which he would pay; L. 25, ff. *de Contr. empt.*; unless it has been a-

greed that the creditor ſhould have it. This is a conſequence of the rule of interpretation mentioned *ſupra*, *n*. 97.

The debtor may indeed pay which of the things he pleaſes; but he cannot pay part of one and part of another. For example. If he has bound himſelf to give me ſixty livres or twenty buſhels of grain; twenty crowns or a certain acre of land: he cannot give me the half of the money and half of the land or grain; but he muſt give me either all the money, or all the land or grain. So when the creditor has the choice, he cannot require part of the one and part of the other. L. 8, §. 1, ff. *de Leg.* 1.

In rents and annuities which are under an alternative, as a rent of thirty livres or a meaſure of grain yearly, the debtor may chooſe every year which of the two things to pay; although he may have paid the thirty livres for the firſt year, he may elect to pay the meaſure of grain the next, and *vice versa*; L. 21, §. 6, ff. *de Act. empt.*

248. From the principle we have eſtabliſhed, that the things compriſed in an obligation which is under an alternative, are all due, without any one of them, however, being due determinately, it follows, I. that, in order that the demand of the creditor may be regular, he ought to demand all the things, not indeed jointly, but in the alternative under which they are due him. If he demanded only one of the things, his demand would not be regular, becauſe neither of them is determinately due; but all are due in an alternative. If, however, by a ſpecial clauſe, the choice was given to the creditor, he might demand one of them alone.

249. II. That an obligation is not under an alternative when one of the two things that were promiſed was not ſuſceptible of the obligation contracted; but in this caſe the obligation is a determinate one of the thing which was ſuſceptible of it. It is on this ground, that it is decided in the law 72, §. 4, ff. *de ſolut.* that if one has promiſed under an alternative two things, one of which belonged to me already, he is not at liberty to pay this to me inſtead of the other, though it has ſince ceaſed to belong to me; becauſe, as this thing was not, at the time of the contract, ſuſceptible

of the obligation which was contracted towards me, *cum res sua nemini deberi possit*, it is only the other that is due.

250. It follows from our principle, III. that when several things are due under an alternative, the extinction of one of them does not extinguish the obligation; for all being due, the obligation exists in those which remain and they cannot cease to be due but by the payment of one of them.

For the same reason, if the creditor of those things, being so *ex causa lucrativa*, became owner of one of them *ex alia causa lucrativa*, the obligation, which cannot exist with regard to the thing of which he is become owner, exists as to the others. L. 16 *de Verb. obl.*

When one of two things due under an alternative has perished, is the debtor allowed to offer the price of the thing which perished, in order to avoid paying that which remains? No; for the thing which has perished, existing no more, is no longer due; that which remains is the only one due, and consequently the only one which may be paid; L. 2, §. 3, *v. Qui Stichum*, ff. *de eo quod certo loco.* L. 34, §. 6, ff. *de Contr. empt.*; L. 95, §. 1, ff. *de Solut.* The law 47, §. 3, ff. *di Leg.* 1, seems contrary to this position. It is there said, that two slaves being bequeathed under an alternative, and one of them being dead, the heir was holden to give the one which remained; and it was added, "or perhaps the price of "the one who was dead," *fortassis vel mortui pretium*. But this decision, as Dumoulin very properly remarks, *Tract. de Div. & individ. part.* 2, *n.* 150, must be confined to the cases, in which circumstances would shew that such was the testator's intention, which the word *fortassis* indicates.

251. It is immaterial whether one of the things included in the alternative, perished without the act or fault of the debtor and before any delay on his part, or whether it perished by his fault or since his delay. In either case, that which remains is the only thing that is due, and the debtor is not admitted to pay the price of the one which has ceased to exist; *d.* L. 95, §. ff. *de Solut. Nec obstat* that when a thing has perished by the fault of the debtor or since his ar-

rear, it is presumed to continue to be due in the price which the debtor, in this case, owes in the room of it. L. 82, §. 1, *de Verb. obl. & passim.* The answer is, that that which has been established only in favor of the creditor in the case of the obligation of a thing determinately due, cannot be opposed to the creditor in the case of the obligation under an alternative; the fault or delay of the debtor ought not to be prejudicial to the creditor. They would be prejudicial to him and alter his situation, if the debtor who can still perform his obligation, in the one of the two things which remains, were received to offer the price of that which has perished; a price which the creditor would not be bound to receive, were they both remaining.

252. When both the things have perished successively, by the fault of the debtor or since his arrear, the debtor, though he had the choice to give which of the two he pleased, has not in the same manner the choice to give the price of that one of the two which he pleases; for by the extinction of the first he has become debtor of the second: he therefore owes determinately the price of that which perished last.

When the first has perished by his fault, and that which remained has also perished, but not by his fault, and before he has been put in arrear, although, *subtilitate legis*, it would seem that he ought to be absolutely discharged as to both; yet equity requires that he be chargeable in this case with the price of the first which perished by his fault; d. L. 95, §. 1.

253. When, by the agreement, the choice has been given to the creditor, he has the choice of the thing that remains or the price of the one which perished by the fault of the debtor: otherwise this fault would be prejudicial to him, if the first, which perished, was the most valuable. *Molin. Tract. de div. & in div. p. 2, n. 152, 154.*

254. It follows from our principle, IV. that as long as the things due under an alternative exist, the obligation remains indeterminate and uncertain; and it becomes determinate to one of the things comprised in the obligation,

only by the payment of it. Hence it follows that when real property and a perſonal thing are due under an alternative, the nature of this claim is in ſuſpenſe. If the debtor gives the real property, the claim will be reputed to have been a claim of real property; if he gives the perſonal thing it will be reputed to have been a perſonal claim. In this the obligation under an alternative differs from the determinate obligation of a certain thing with liberty to give another in the ſtead of it. See *supra, n.* 244, *in fine.*

255. A teſtator having bequeathed to one a certain picture determinately, has ſince, by a codicil, altered this diſpoſition by bequeathing to the ſame perſon this picture *or a sum of* 500 *livres.* This codicil not being found at the death of the teſtator, the heir delivered to the legatee the picture, which he thought was due determinately. Afterwards the codicil is diſcovered, and the heir, finding that he owed the picture only under the alternative of 500 livres, cites the legatee to reſtore it on being paid the money. Is he well grounded? The two ſchools among the Romans were divided on this queſtion. Celſus, of the ſchool of the Proculeians, decides the queſtion, in law 19, ff. *de Leg.* 2. in the negative. His reaſon is, that the things included in an obligation under an alternative, being all due, the payment which has been made to the legatee of the picture bequeathed, is the payment of a thing due, and conſequently is a valid payment not liable to be reclaimed.

On the contrary, Julian, who was of the Sabinian ſchool, decides in the law 32, §. *fin.* ff. *de Cond. indeb.* that there is room to reclaim, when a debtor has paid a thing which he thought, through miſtake, to be determinately due, though he was debtor only of an indeterminate thing of a certain kind, or was debtor of it only under the alternative of another thing.

The reaſon, on which this deciſion is grounded, is that the innocent error in which the debtor was as to the quality of his obligation, ought not to be prejudicial to him, nor add to his obligation, by depriving him of the choice he had to pay the money inſtead of the picture. As to the reaſon given for the contrary opinion, it is obviated by faying that there is room to reclaim, *condictio indebiti*, not only when one has paid what was in no manner due, but alfo when one had paid more than was due. L. 1, §. 1, *Cod. de cond. ind. & passim;* which is to be eftimated *non solum quantitate debiti, sed & causa. Inst. tit. de act.* §. 34, *vers. Huic autem.* Therefore, in the prefent cafe, he who has paid a thing as due determinately, whilft he owed it only under the alternative of another thing, has paid more than he owed and this payment ought to be liable to be reclaimed by the debtor on his offering to pay the other thing which he had the right to pay inftead of that which he has paid. This laft opinion is much more equitable than the firft; it reftores to each what belongs to him. Therefore Dumoulin decides very properly, *Tract. de div. & ind. p.* 2, *n.* 135, *& seq.*; that it ought to be followed.

256. Dumoulin, *n.* 139. *& seq.*, adds to this decifion a modification which is, that when the creditor has not led the debtor into error, and he has received *bona fide*, the claim of the debtor is only to be admitted, when the creditor will not be injured by it and when he will be placed in the fituation he was in before the payment. The reafon is that the action is grounded only on a principle of equity: *Hæc condictio ex bono & æquo introducta*, L. 66, ff. *de condictione indeb.* It is grounded only on the rule of equity which does not permit any one to benefit himfelf at the expence of another. Therefore it can be allowed only for the amount of the advantage gained by him who has received. L. 65, §. 7 & 8, ff. *d. tit.* According to thefe principles it is to be holden that if, in the above cafe, the legatee had fold *bona fide* the thing which had been delivered to him, the heir cannot claim any thing more than the excefs beyond the fum which he had a right to pay inftead of it.

According to the fame principles, if the debtor has paid to the creditor a fum of money which he thought was due determinately; although he owed it only under the alternative of another thing, he ought not eafily to be admitted to reclaim the money on offering to give the other thing, when the creditor has employed the money, and there is not a great difproportion of value between the fum received and the other thing.

257. There is another queftion on which the fchools were divided. He who owed two things under an alternative, being deceived by the copy of the notary who had written *and* inftead of *or*, as it was in the original, has paid the two at the fame time; he has fince difcovered that he owed but one of the two, at his choice. There is no doubt that he may recall one of them; but may he recall which of them he pleafes? Celfus, cited by Ulpian in law 26, §. 13, *in fin. ff. de Cond. ind.*, thought that the creditor had a right in this cafe to retain which he pleafed. Julian, on the contrary, as related by Juftinian in law *penult. Cod. hoc titulo*, thought the debtor had a right to recall which of the two he might choofe. The opinion of Celfus was probably grounded on this reafoning: the two things which are comprifed under the alternative being both due, the debtor who has paid them both cannot fay that either of thefe two things determinately was not due. He cannot then reclaim either of them determinately as due; he has only a right to reclaim one of the two indeterminately, as having paid more than he owed, in paying both whilft he owed but one of them. The creditor becoming in his turn debtor for the reftitution which is due of one of the things, it is to him, in quality of debtor, that ought to belong the choice of paying back which of them he pleafes. This reafoning, on which the opinion of Celfus is founded, is a mere fubtilty.

The opinion of Julian is founded in equity. The action *condictio indebiti* is a kind of reftitution *in totum* which equity grants againft an erroneous payment. It is of the nature of all reftitutions againft an act, that the parties be reftored to the fame condition in which they were before. Hence it follows that the debtor who has paid the two things, not knowing that he was bound only to pay the one which he pleafed, ought to be reftored by this action to the right he had before the payment, to pay the one only which he chofe, and confequently to reclaim with the fame choice. This laft opinion, as the moft equitable, has been embraced by Papinian and finally confirmed by the conſtitution of Juſtinian; L. *penult. Cod. d. tit.*

Obſerve that the debtor has, in this caſe, the right to claim back one of the two things which he has paid, only whilſt they exiſt. If one of the two had ceaſed to exiſt ſince the payment, there would be no ground for reſtitution as is decided by Julian, in L. 32, ff. *d. tit.* The reaſon of this is evident. The action *condictio indebiti* reſtores the parties to the ſame ſituation as if payment had not been made, and was ſtill to be made. If it were yet to be made, the debtor could not avoid paying that which alone ſhould remain due; it ought therefore in this caſe to remain *in soluto* with the creditor, and the debtor cannot claim it back.

As to the indiviſibility of the payment of obligations under an alternative, ſee *infra, part* 3, *ch.* 1, *art.* 6, §. 3.

ARTICLE VII.

Of obligations in ſolidum *between several creditors.*

258. Regularly when one contracts the obligation of one and the ſame thing towards ſeveral perſons, each of thoſe to whom it is contracted is creditor of this thing only for his part; but it may be contracted towards each of them for the whole, when ſuch is the intention of the parties; ſo that each of thoſe to whom the obligation is contracted may be a creditor for the whole and yet that payment made to any of them may diſcharge the debtor as to all. This is called an obligation *in solidum*, and theſe creditors are called *correi credendi, correi stipulandi.*

259. We may adduce as an example of this kind of obligation, that which ariſes from a teſtamentary diſpoſition in theſe words: *my heir shall give to the Carmelites or Capuchins the sum of* 100 *livres.* The heir, in this caſe, owes but one ſum; but he owes it entire to each of the convents who are creditors *in solidum;* ſo that, however, his paying this ſum to either of them will diſcharge him as to both; L. 16, ff. *de Legat.* 2. This kind of obligation is in little uſe among us; it ought not to be confounded with the indiviſible obligation, of which we ſhall ſpeak *infra.*

260. The effects of the obligation *in solidum* between the creditors are I. that each of the creditors, being a creditor of the whole, may consequently demand the whole, and if the obligation be with title of execution, may constrain the debtor for the whole. II. The acknowledgment of the debt made to one of the creditors, interrupts the prescription for the whole of the debt, and consequently for the benefit of the other creditors. L. fin. *Cod. de duobus reis.* III. The payment to one of the creditors extinguishes the whole debt; for this creditor being a creditor for the whole, the payment of the whole to him is validly made; and this payment discharges the debtor as to all. For although there are several creditors, there is but one debt, which must be extinguished by the entire payment made to one of the creditors.

The debtor has it at his option to pay to which of these creditors he pleases, while the debt remains entire; but if one of them had brought suit, the debtor would no longer be at liberty to pay to any other than him. *Ex duobus reis stipulandi, si semel unus egerit, alteri promissor offerendo pecuniam, nihil agit.* L. 16, ff. *de duobus reis.*

IV. Each of the creditors being creditor for the whole, may, before any one of his co-creditors has brought suit, release the debt to the debtor and discharge him as to all: for as the payment of the whole, made to one of these creditors, discharges the debtor as to all; so the release of the whole, which is equivalent to payment, made by one of the creditors, must discharge the debtor with regard to all. *Acceptilatione unius tollitur obligatio;* L. 2, ff. *de duobus reis.*

ARTICLE VIII.

Of the obligation in solidum *on the part of the debtors.*

§. I.

261. An obligation is *in solidum* on the part of those who have contracted it, when they oblige themselves each for the whole, so, however, that the payment made by one of them may discharge all the others.

Those who bind themselves in this manner are called *correi debendi.*

As an obligation *in solidum* on the part of the creditors confifts in this, that the obligation of the fame thing contracted towards feveral perfons, is contracted towards each of them for the whole, as entirely as if each was the only creditor, faving, neverthelefs, that payment made to one of them difcharges the debt as to all; fo an obligation *in solidum* on the part of the debtors confifts in this, that the obligation of the fame thing is contracted by each for the whole, as entirely as if each was the only debtor, fo, however, that payment made by one of them difcharges all the others.

262. That an obligation may be *in solidum* it does not always fuffice that each of the debtors be debtor of the whole thing; as happens in the cafe of the obligation which is indivifible and not fufceptible of parts, tho' it be not contracted *in solidum*: it is neceffary that each of the debtors *totum & totaliter debeat*; that is to fay, that each be as entirely bound to the payment of the thing, as if he alone had contracted the obligation.

263. It is neceffary, above all, that the debtors be bound to the payment of the fame thing. It would not then be an obligation *in solidum* of two perfons, but there would be two obligations, if two perfons bound themfelves to another for different things.

But provided they are each wholly bound for the payment of the fame thing, though they be differently bound, they are, not the lefs, co-debtors *in solidum*, *correi debendi*; *puta*, if one is bound abfolutely and the other conditionally or with a time of payment; or if they are bound to pay in different places. L. 7, L. 9, §. 2, ff. *de duobus reis*.

It will perhaps be faid that it is inconfiftent that one and the fame obligation fhould have oppofite qualities; that it fhould be abfolute with regard to one of the debtors and conditional with regard to the other. The anfwer is, that the obligation *in solidum* is indeed one and the fame with regard to the thing that is the object, fubject and fubftance of it; but it is compofed of as many ties as there are different perfons who contracted it; and thefe perfons being different between themfelves, the ties by which they are bound are ſo many different ties, which may conſequently have as many different qualities. This is what Papinian intends, when he ſays, *Et si maxima parem causam suscipiunt, nihilominus in cujusque persona, propria singulorum consistit obligatio; d.* L. 9, §. 2. The obligation is one with regard to its object, which is the thing due, but with regard to the perſons who contracted it, it may be ſaid that there are as many obligations as there are perſons bound.

264. When ſeveral perſons contract a debt *in solidum*, it is with regard to the creditor only that each is debtor of the whole. With regard to themſelves, the debt divides itſelf, and each is debtor for himſelf only to the amount of the part he had in the cauſe of the debt. Suppoſe, for example, that two perſons borrow together a ſum of money, which they bind themſelves *in solidum* to repay; or that they buy a thing for the payment of which they bind themſelves *in solidum* to the ſeller. If they have equally divided between them the money borrowed or the thing bought, each of them, though debtor of the whole to the creditor, is, as to his co-debtor, bound only for one half. If they have divided it unequally, *puta*, if one of them has received two thirds of the money borrowed or of the thing bought, and the other has received only one third; the one who has received two thirds will be debtor *for himself* of two thirds and the other only of one third. If one of them alone be benefited by the contract, and the other becomes bound with him *in solidum* in order to ſerve him, the one who has alone been benefited is the only debtor; the other, though a principal debtor with regard to the creditor, is, with regard to his co-debtor with whom he became bound merely to ſerve him, what a ſecurity is with regard to the principal debtor for whom he has become bound.

Likewiſe, if the debt *in solidum* proceeds from a tort committed by four perſons, each of them is a debtor *in solidum* with regard to the perſon againſt whom the tort has been committed; but with regard to themſelves each is a debtor for the part he had in the tort, that is to ſay, each for his fourth part.

§. II.

In what cases the obligation of several debtors is holden to be in solidum.

265. An obligation *in solidum* may be created in all contracts, of whatsoever kind; L. 9, ff. *de duob. reis.* But regularly it ought to be so expressed; otherwise, when several have contracted an obligation towards one, they are presumed to have contracted each only for his part. This is decided by Papinian in law 11, §. 2, ff. *de duobus reis;* and has been confirmed by Justinian in the novel 99. The reason is, that the interpretation of obligations is made, in cases of doubt, in favor of debtors, as we have before observed. According to this principle, in the instance of an estate belonging to four proprietors, three having sold it *in solidum,* and having promised to procure a confirmation of the sale by the fourth, it was adjudged that the fourth, in confirming the sale, was not to be holden to have sold *in solidum;* because, although the three had promised for him that he should accede to the contract of sale, yet it was not expressed that he should accede to it *in solidum.*

266. There are, however, certain cases in which the obligation is *in solidum* between several debtors of the same thing, although it was not expresly stipulated.

The first case is when partners in trade contract an obligation relative to their trade.

This is a decision of our law; *Ordonn. du Commerce de* 1673, *t.* 4, *art.* 7.

Two merchants who purchase together a quantity of merchandise, though there be not otherwise any partnership between them, are holden to be partners as to this purchase, and, as such, are bound *in solidum,* although the obligation be not so expressed. Bornier, upon this article, reports a case in the parliament of Toulouse, in which it was so decided, and this has since been a principle admitted. See *supra, part* 1, *ch.* 1, *art.* 5, *n.* 83.

267. The second case in which several debtors of the same thing are bound *in solidum,* although it be not so ex-

preſſed, is that of the obligation which ſeveral tutors contract who undertake the management of the ſame infant's eſtate; or of that which ſeveral perſons contract who undertake to act as wardens or truſtees of a corporation. Theſe offices create an obligation in the perſons undertaking them, which is *in solidum*, according to the diſpoſition of the laws that are, in this reſpect, obſerved among us, unleſs there be ſome uſage to the contrary.

The civil law granted to tutors who had not acted, the benefit of order and diſcuſſion, which conſiſted in ſending the minor on his coming of age, to proſecute at their coſts the tutor who had acted. It granted alſo to tutors who had acted jointly, the benefit of diviſion when they were all ſolvent. See *infra* 270, *ad med.* But theſe exceptions or pleas granted to tutors, truſtees, &c. are not in uſe among us. Therefore, when Dumoulin, *Tract. de Div. & ind. n.* 3, *n.* 166, ſays that tutors have this benefit of diviſion for the payment of the balance of their accounts, excepting the ſingle caſe in which they are debtors *ex dolo*, he muſt be underſtood to mean that they have this benefit according to the civil law, and in thoſe provinces in which the civil law is in this particular obſerved.

268. The third caſe of an obligation *in solidum* is of that which ariſes when ſeveral perſons have concurred in a tort; they are bound *in solidum* for the damages.

They are not allowed the plea of diſcuſſion or diviſion, being deemed unworthy of it.

269. There may alſo reſult an obligation *in solidum* from a clauſe in a teſtament by which the teſtator expreſsly declares that he charges his heirs or other ſucceſſors *in solidum* with the payment of a legacy.

Even though no charge *in solidum* be expreſſed in the will, thoſe whom the teſtator has charged with the legacy are bound *in solidum* when the teſtator has uſed a disjunctive; as when he has ſaid "my ſon Peter or my ſon James "ſhall give to a certain perſon 10 crowns." This is the deciſion of the law, 8, §. 1, ff. *de leg.* 1. *Si ita scriptum sit. "L. Titius hæres meus, aut Mævius hæres meus decem Scio dato:"*

cum utro velit, Seius aget, at si cum uno actum sit & solutum, alter liberetur, quasi si duo rei promittendi in solidum obligati fuissent. Yet Dumoulin pretends *Tract. de Div. & ind. p.* 3, *n.* 153, 154, 155, that this obligation is not an obligation perfectly *in solidum*; that altho' each of the persons named is bound for the whole of the legacy and they resemble debtors *in solidum*, yet they are not debtors truly *in solidum*, and their obligation has not the other effects of obligations *in solidum*. For example. If two heirs were thus charged with the legacy of a determinate thing which should be destroyed by the act of one of them, he does not think that the other would be bound for the loss as a debtor *in solidum* would be; *infra, n.* 273. In this Dumoulin deviates from the common opinion taught by Bartolus on this law, and by the other doctors, who recognize, in the case put in this law, an obligation truly *in solidum*. Dumoulin grounds his position on these words *quasi si duo rei, &c.* which indicates, he says, that the two heirs are not, in the instance in this law, truly *correi*, the adverb *quasi* being *adverbium improprietatis*. I would rather incline to the opinion of Bartolus. These heirs being, in this case, debtors of the whole, not from the quality of the thing due, but from the intention of the testator, which was that they should be chargeable each for the whole of the legacy, their obligation appears to me to have all the characters of an actual obligation *in solidum*, and I do not perceive any thing wherein it varies. It does not appear to me that the adverb *quasi* ought to be taken *pro adverbio improprietatis*; it ought rather, as it appears to me, to be taken for *quemadmodum* in this sense; these two heirs are bound *in solidum* as much as if they were thus bound by a stipulation. For it is not by stipulation only that one may contract an obligation *in solidum, non tantum verbis stipulationis sed & ceteris contractibus duo rei promittendi fieri possunt*; L. 9, ff. *de duobus reis*; and wills, as well as contracts, ma create such obligations.

§. III.

Of the effects of the obligation in solidum *between several debtors.*

270. These effects are, I. that the creditor may apply

to whom he pleafes of the debtors *in solidum* and exact from him, by demand, if the debt lies only in action, or by conftraint, if it lies in execution, the whole of what is due him. This is a neceffary confequence of the principle that each of the debtors *in solidum* is a debtor for the whole.

I do not even think that the co-debtors, who have bound themfelves *in solidum*, have the benefit of divifion; that is to fay, that the one of them from whom the creditor demands the whole fhould be received, on offering his part, to demand that the creditor be fent back to the other debtors for their refpective parts, when they are folvent. Contracts entered into before a notary, generally contain a claufe renouncing the benefit of divifion; and if they were not to contain fuch claufe, I do not think it fhould be allowed: the law 47, ff. *Locati*, fays it is more juft to deny it to them; *quanquam fortasse sit justius, &c.*

It is true that the novel grants it to debtors *in solidum*, who become fecurities for each other *alterna fidejussione obligatis;* but I do not think this is followed among us. No other advantage is granted to the debtor *in solidum*, who is profecuted for the whole debt, than to allow him to demand the fubrogation or ceffion of the actions of the debtor againft the other debtors *in solidum*. See, on this fubrogation, *infra, part.* 3, *ch.* 1, *art.* 6, §. 2.

271. Note that when the creditor elects one of the debtors againft whom to bring his fuit, this does not difcharge the others, while he remains unpaid; he may withdraw his fuit againft the one he has fued, and fue the others or all at the fame time, if he pleafes; L. 28, *Cod. de Fidejus.*

272. II. The demand made on one of the debtors *in solidum*, interrupts the prefcription with regard to all the others; L. *fin. Cod. de duobus reis.* This is a further confequence of the principle that each of the debtors is a debtor for the whole. For the creditor in making a demand on him, has demanded the whole debt. He has therefore interrupted the prefcription for the whole debt, even with regard to the debtors on whom he made no demand, who could only oppofe the prefcription to the creditor when he had not ex-

ercifed his right in regard to the debt for which they are bound: but this, in the prefent cafe, they cannot pretend, fince the debt for which they are bound is the fame which was demanded in the whole from their co-debtor.

273. III. For the fame reafon, when the thing due has perifhed by the act or fault of one of the debtors *in solidum* or fince he has been put in arrear, the debt is perpetuated not only againft this debtor, but againft all his co-debtors who are all bound *in solidum* to pay the creditor the price of the thing; for the debt of each of them being one and the fame debt, it cannot exift as to one and be extinguifhed as to the others; this is the decifion of the law *penult.* ff. *de duob. reis. Ex duobus reis ejusdem Stichi promittendi factis, alterius factum alteri quoque nocet.* For example. If Peter and Paul have fold me *in solidum* a horfe, and, before a delivery had been made, the horfe died by the fault of Peter, Paul will remain my debtor as well as Peter and I fhall have a right to demand the value of the horfe from him as well as from Peter, faving to him his recourfe againft Peter: whereas if they had fold not *in solidum*, Peter alone would be chargeable for his fault; and Paul by the death of the horfe, altho' it happened thro' the fault of Peter, would be wholly difcharged from his obligation and would, not the lefs, remain my creditor for the half of the price of the horfe, in the fame manner as if the horfe had died by mere accident. *Molin. Tract. de Div. & indiv. part.* 3, *n.* 126.

Obferve that the act, fault or arrear of one of the debtors *in solidum* prejudices, indeed, his co-debtors *ad conservandam et perpetuandam obligationem*, that is to fay, that they be not difcharged from the obligation, by the lofs of the thing, and that they be bound to pay the price of it. It is in this fenfe that the law *penult*, ff. *de duobus reis*, fays, *Alterius factum alteri quoque nocet.* But the fault, act or arrear of one of them does not prejudice the other, *ad augendam ipsorum obligationem;* that is to fay, that it is only he who has committed the fault or who has been put in arrear, who ought to be anfwerable for the damages which may refult from the inexecution of the obligation, befides the price of the thing due. As to the other debtor who has committed no fault and who has not been put in arrear, he is bound to nothing elſe than to pay the price of the thing which has periſhed by the fault or ſince the arrear of his co-debtor. His obligation may be perpetuated, but not increaſed by the fault or delay of his co-debtor. For the ſame reaſon it is only he who has been put in arrear who ought to be anſwerable for the damages reſulting from the delay: it is in this ſenſe that the law 32, §. *penult.* ff. *de Uſuris*, ſays, *Si duo promittendi ſint, alterius mora alteri non nocet.*

Dumoulin confines the deciſion of this law to the damages which have not been expreſsly ſtipulated; if any had been ſtipulated, they would all be liable for them: the act or arrear of one of them cauſing the condition of the inexecution of the obligation, under which they all bound themſelves for theſe damages, to take effect. *Molin. ibid. n.* 127.

274. IV. The payment which is made by one of the debtors, diſcharges all the others; this is a conſequence of the principle that the debt *in ſolidum* is a ſingle debt of the ſame thing of which there are ſeveral debtors.

Not only the actual payment, but every other kind of payment ought to have this effect; therefore, for example, if one of the debtors *in ſolidum*, ſued by the creditor, has oppoſed as a ſet off, to the ſum that was demanded of him, a like ſum which the creditor owed him, his co-debtors will be diſcharged as well by this ſet off as they would have been by the actual payment of the ſum due.

Peter and Paul became my debtors *in ſolidum* of 1000 livres; I afterwards became debtor to Peter of the like ſum. If I have ſued Peter for the payment of the ſum due me by Peter and Paul, and he has oppoſed, as a ſet off, the like ſum which I owe him: according to what has juſt been ſaid, this ſet off is equivalent to payment, the debt which was due me by Peter and Paul *in ſolidum*, is by this ſet off extinguiſhed as to both. But if I have not ſued Peter, and I ſue Paul for the payment of this ſum, may Paul oppoſe, as a ſet off, the debt of 1000 livres which I owe to his co-debtor? Papinian in the law 10, ff. *de duobus reis*, decides the queſtion in the negative: *Si duo rei promittendi socii non sint, non proderit alteri, quod stipulator alteri reo pecuniam debet.*

Yet Domat, in his civil law, *p.* 1, *l.* 3, *t.* 3, §. 4, *art.* 8, decides against this text, that Paul may oppose as a set off the sum which I owe to Peter, for the part of the debt for which Peter with regard to Paul is bound and not for the surplus. His reason is that Peter ceasing to be my debtor of the part, which he owed, of the debt, by the set off of the sum which he had a right to oppose, Paul ought not to be compelled to pay for Peter this part, from which Peter is discharged by the set off. This reason is not absolutely conclusive; for when a debtor *in solidum* pays the whole of the debt it is not with regard to the creditor that he pays the parts of his co-debtors; he pays what he owes himself, and consequently he can only oppose as a set off what is due to him, and not what is due to his co-debtors: on this is founded the decision of Papinian. It may be said in favor of that of Domat that it avoids circuity; for when Paul pays me the whole sum which he owes with Peter *in solidum*, Paul will have recourse against Peter for the part for which he was bound; and for this part he will attach in my hands what I owe to Peter and recover from me, to the amount of this part, what I have received. This last reason should induce us to follow, in our practice, the decision of Domat.

275. A release of the debt *in solidum* made by the creditor to one of the debtors, would also discharge the other, if it appeared that the creditor, by this release, intended to extinguish the whole debt.

If it appeared that his intention was only to extinguish the debt as to the share for which he to whom he made the release was chargeable with regard to his co-debtors, and to discharge from the surplus of the debt the person of this debtor, the debt would, notwithstanding, remain as to the surplus against the other debtors. *Quid*, if the creditor, by the release he made to this debtor, had expressly declared that he intended merely to discharge the person of this debtor, and to preserve his claim entire as to the persons of the other co-debtors? Could he, under this protestation, require the whole from the other debtors, without any deduction for the part of him whom he has difcharged? I think he could not. The reafon is that the debtors *in solidum* would not have bound themfelves *in solidum*, but only for their parts, if they had not counted that on paying the whole debt, they would have recourfe againft their co-debtors, and that they would have, for this purpofe, the ceffion of the actions of the creditor for the other parts. It was only under the implied condition of this ceffion of the creditor's actions that they have bound themfelves *in solidum*; and confequently the creditor has no right to demand from each of them the whole, except under the condition of this ceffion of actions. In this inftance the creditor having difabled himfelf by his own act to cede his actions againft the debtors whom he has difcharged, and confequently put it out of his power to perform the condition under which he has the right to demand the whole debt, it follows that he cannot demand from each the whole debt: *repellitur exceptione cedendarum actionum*. See, of the ceffion of actions, *infra, part.* 3, *ch.* 1, *art.* 6, §. 2. ff

When there are feveral debtors *in solidum* and the creditor has difcharged one of them, does the obligation ceafe entirely to be *in solidum*? Or may he fue each of the other debtors for the whole with the deduction only of the part of him whom he has difcharged and of the part which he whom he has difcharged would have been liable for, in cafe of the infolvency of fome of the other debtors? For example. If I had fix debtors *in solidum*, and I have difcharged one of them; of the five which remained one is infolvent; can I fue each of the others only for their fixth part, or may I fue each of them for the whole with a deduction only of the fixth part for which he whom I have difcharged was liable, and of the part with which he would have been chargeable for the fhare of the infolvent debtor? I think I fhould be well grounded; for this debtor whom I fue, cannot claim to have any other deduction than what he lofes by not having the ceffion of my actions againft him whom I have difcharged: this ceffion would only have given to him the right to demand from him his fhare, and to make him contribute towards that of the infolvent debtors, as we ſhall ſee, *infra*, *n.* 281.

276. When one of the debtors *in solidum* is become the only heir of the creditor, the debt is not extinguiſhed againſt the other debtors: for the confuſion *magis personam debitoris eximit ab obligatione, quam extinguit obligationem.*

But this debtor who has become the heir of the creditor, can exact it from the other debtors only under a deduction of the part for which he was chargeable with regard to the other debtors; and if any of them be inſolvent, he ought, beſides, to bear his part of the ſhare of the inſolvent debtor. It is the ſame in the inverſe caſe, when the creditor has become the ſole heir of one of the debtors *in solidum.*

§. IV.

Of the release of the liability in ſolidum.

277. The right which the creditor has againſt ſeveral debtors of the ſame debt, to demand the whole from each of them, being eſtabliſhed in his favor, it is not to be doubted that according to the maxim, *Cuique licet juri in suum favorem introducto renuntiare*, a creditor of age, having the free diſpoſition of his property, may renounce this right. He may renounce it, either in favor of all the debtors, by conſenting that the debt be divided between them, or in favor of one of the debtors, whom he may diſcharge from his liability *in solidum*, reſerving his right againſt the others, holding each of them liable for the whole; ſo, however, that the diſcharge which he has given to one of them do not prejudice the others, as has been obſerved, *n.* 275.

He may renounce this right expreſsly or impliedly.

He is preſumed to have renounced it impliedly, when he has admitted one of his debtors to pay the debt *for his part*, ſo naming it. This is the deciſion of the law 18, *Cod. de Pact.* *Si creditores vestros,* ex parte *debiti admisisse quemquam vestrum pro sua persona solventem probaveritis, aditus rector provinciæ, pro sua gravitate, ne alter pro altero exigatur providebit.*

The reaſon is, hat when the creditor gives a receipt to

one of the debtors *in solidum* in these words, "I have received of A. B. the sum of ——— for his part," he acknowledges him to be debtor of the debt *for a part;* and consequently he consents that he be no longer liable for the whole, it being two opposite things to be debtor *for a part*, and debtor for the whole.

This decision does not apply when the receipt by which the creditor acknowledges to have received from A. B. ——— *for his part*, expresses a reservation of the debtor's liability for the whole; for the express terms by which the creditor reserves to himself his right to hold the debtor liable for the whole, removes the implication which would be raised from the words *for his part*, used in the receipt, to induce from them a renunciation of the liability *in solidum*. And granting even that these words *for his part*, should be as formal in favor of the renunciation of the liability *in solidum* as the express reservation is formal against this renunciation, it would only follow that these words *for his part*, and these *without prejudice to my claim for the whole*, would destroy each other and the receipt be regarded as if it contained neither; in which case it cannot prejudice the right of the creditor to hold each of the debtors liable for the whole. This is the reasoning of Alciat, *ad d.* L. 18.

It will perhaps be objected that in this receipt the words *without prejudice, &c.* ought to be understood as a reservation, which the creditor makes of his right against the other debtors to hold them liable each for the whole, and not against him to whom he has given the receipt; in this way it may be supposed that these words are reconcileable with the words *for his part*, made use of in the receipt. This explication is a bad one. When in a receipt, as in all other instruments, rights are reserved without its being said against whom, it is natural to understand the rights which the party who reserves them has against the party with whom he treats or to whom he gives the receipt, and not those which he has against others. The words *for his part*, are more properly reconciled with the reservation, by saying that, in this case, the creditor who has reserved his claim for the whole, has intended by these words *for his part*, not the part for which this debtor would be liable to him the creditor, but the part for which this debtor is actually liable with regard to his co-debtors; which part the creditor was willing to receive from him, saving to himself the right to demand from him the surplus in virtue of his liability for the whole, from which he does not discharge him. This is one of the points settled in a case of the 6th of September, 1712, reported in the 6th volume of the *Journal des Audiences*.

When the receipt expresses *without prejudice to my rights*, it is the same as if it had expressed *without prejudice to my claim for the whole*; for the right to claim the whole is included in the general expression *without prejudice to my rights*; and indeed the reservation of this right has the greatest relation to the receipt which I give, and serves as an explanation of the words *for his part* made use of in the receipt. *Alciat, ad dict. leg.*

When the creditor has given to one of the debtors *in solidum* a receipt simply for a certain sum, which makes exactly that for which the debtor is liable for his part of the debt towards his co-debtors, without expressing that he received it *for his part*, ought the creditor to be presumed to have released to the debtor his liability *in solidum*? I think he ought not; the decision of the law *Si creditores*, above cited, ought to be confined to the case there stated, which is that in which one of the co-debtors was admitted to pay expresly his personal part, *ex parte pro persona sua*, and it is this expression in the receipt, that the creditor receives *for the part* of this debtor, from which is derived the presumption in favor of the renunciation of his right to claim the whole. But if the creditor has indeed been willing to receive from one of his debtors a part of his debt, for the whole of which this debtor was liable, it ought not, from this alone, to be concluded that he intended to discharge him from his liability *in solidum*: for this consequence does not necessarily follow; and it ought not to be derived without necessity, as no one is presumed to release his rights: *Nemo facile donare præsumitur.* This is the decision of the law 8, §. 1, ff. *de leg.* I., in the instance of two heirs whom the teſtator had charged *in ſolidum* with the payment of a legacy. Pomponius decides that the legatee who has demanded or even received the part of one of the co-debtors, is not preſumed, for this reaſon, to have diſcharged him from his liability for the whole, and that he may exact from him the ſurplus. *Quid si ab altero partem petierit? Liberum erit ab alterutro reliquum petere: idem erit & si alter partem solvisset.* Bacquet, *Traite des Droits de Justice*, *ch.* 21, *n.* 245; and Baſnage, *Traite des Hypotheq. part.* 2, 4, are of this opinion.

Bartolus pretends that there is in this reſpect a difference between debtors *in ſolidum* by teſtament and thoſe by acts *inter vivos*: but this diſtinction is not founded on any ſolid reaſon.

Obſerve that theſe words of the law, *idem erit & si alter partem solvisset*, muſt be underſtood of the caſe in which the creditor, without having made any demand, voluntarily receives from one of the debtors *in ſolidum* the ſum which amounts to that which the debtor owes for his part, without expreſſing in the receipt that he receives it *for his part* as will be noticed hereafter.

When a creditor has made a judicial interpellation on one of the debtors *in ſolidum* to pay a certain ſum *for his part* of the debt, or when he has cited him to pay *his part* of the debt is he preſumed, for this alone, to have divided the debt and diſcharged this debtor from his liability *in ſolidum*? The authors are divided on this queſtion. Baldus is for the affirmative, and Bartolus for the negative. For the affirmative it will be ſaid that there appears to be the ſame reaſon for the deciſion in this, as in the caſe in the law *Si creditores* above mentioned. In that caſe, the creditor who expreſſed in formal terms in the receipt which he had given to one of the debtors *in ſolidum*, that he had received a certain ſum *for his part*, had, by theſe words, acknowledged and admitted that he was debtor only *for his part*, and conſequently that he was no longer debtor *in ſolidum*, it being two oppoſite things to be debtor *for his part* and debtor for the whole. When a creditor has expreſſed in the judicial interpellation or ſummons to the debtor *in ſolidum* that he demands from him a certain sum *for his part*, has he admitted that this debtor should no longer be liable for the whole? There appears to be the same reason, in this case to decide that the creditor has discharged him from his liability *in solidum*, as in the case of the law *Si creditores*.

On the contrary, they alledge, in behalf of the negative, the law *Reos*, 23, *Cod. de Fid.* and the law 8, §. 1, ff. *de Leg.* 1. above cited. The law *Reos* does not appear to me in any manner to decide the question; but the law 8, §. 1, formally decides that a debtor *in solidum* is not discharged from his liability for the whole, by the demand of the creditor *for his part*; since it decides that the creditor notwithstanding the demand is not precluded from requiring the surplus from either of the debtors and consequently not from him even from whom he had first demanded his part: *Quid, si ab altero partem petierit? Liberum erit ab alterutro reliquum petere.* The reason is, that as debts are contracted by a concurrence of the will of the creditor and the debtor, the release can be made only by the consent to the contrary of the same parties; *part* 3, *ch.* 3, *art.* 1. §. 3. Hence it follows, that supposing the demand on one of the debtors *in solidum* to pay *his part*, should include an intention in the creditor to release his liability for the whole; as long as the will of the debtor has not concurred with that of the creditor, as long as the debtor has not acquiesced in this demand and offered in consequence thereof to pay his part, this demand cannot cause any right to be acquired to the debtor nor cause him to be discharged from his liability *in solidum*, and consequently cannot prevent the creditor from augmenting his demand and claiming from him the whole of the debt. In this the present case differs from the case in the law *Si creditores*, in which the will of the debtor who pays his part of the debt to the creditor who is contented therewith, concurs with that of the creditor in the release of the surplus.

When the debtor who is sued for the payment of his part, before the creditor has augmented his demand, has paid his part or only offered indeed to pay it, it appears to me there would be entirely the same reason to decide, as in the law *Si creditores*, for the discharge of the liability *in soli-*

dum. Therefore I think that these last words of the law 8, §. 1, ff. *de Leg*. 1. *idemque erit & si alter partem solvisset*, which make a separate clause in this paragraph, must be confined to the case of a voluntary payment made without its being expressed in the receipt that the creditor has received *for his part*, and that they ought not to be extended to a payment made in consequence of a suit against the debtor for the payment of *his part*.

Likewise, when, upon the suit of the creditor against one of the debtors *in solidum* for the payment of *his part*, a judgment has intervened, by which he is condemned to pay his part, the creditor can no longer demand from him the surplus; the judgment has supplied, in this respect, the will of the debtor in the acceptance of the release of the surplus: *cum in judiciis quasi contrahamus, & judicatum quandam novationem inducat*. This is the opinion of Bacquet, *ibid. n*. 247.

278. When there are more than two debtors *in solidum*, does the receipt given to one of them, expressing that it is for the payment *of his part*, discharge from the liability *in solidum*, all the debtors, or him only to whom it is given? The authors have again been divided on this question. The ancient doctors maintained the affirmative, grounding themselves on the law *Si creditores*, above cited. Peter de L'Etoile, celebrated professor at the university of Orleans, commonly called Stella, is the first, according to Alciat *ad d. Leg*. who maintained the negative. His opinion seems to be the most accurate, and most conformable to the principles of law. The law *Si creditores* well understood, is not opposed to it. This law is grounded on an agreement, which is presumed to have tacitly intervened for the discharge of the liability *in solidum* between the creditor, and the debtor to whom he has given the receipt. It is one of the most positive principles of law that agreements can create no right to any persons but such as are parties to them *supra, n*. 85, *& seq*. Hence it follows that this could procure a discharge from the liability *in solidum* only to the debtor to whom he gave the receipt, who is the only one with whom he treated, and it cannot give any right to the others whom the creditor had not in view in this agreement.

the favor which the creditor was willing to ſhew to one of his debtors in admitting him to pay the debt for his part only, ought not to prejudice him with regard to the others. *Bonitas creditoris*, ſays Alciat, *ad d. L. non debet esse ei captiosa*; the law *Si creditores* on which the antient doctors ground their opinion, has no reference to this queſtion. It ſeems even that in the caſe in this law, there were but two debtors *in solidum*; if there had been more, the Emperor would have ſaid *Rector providebit, ne unus pro cæteris exigatur*. Theſe words *ne alter pro altero exigatur*, deſignate two debtors only, and are to be underſtood in this ſenſe: *ne alter qui solvit, pro altero qui nondum solvit exigatur*.

This deciſion muſt be followed with this modification, that if among the debtors that remain, there be ſome inſolvent, the others ought to be diſcharged from the part, which the one who was diſcharged from his liability *in solidum*, would have otherwiſe been liable for on account of the inſolvency: for if they ought not to be benefited by this diſcharge they ought not to be prejudiced by it. We muſt, however, admit that Bacquet, *ibid. n.* 245, after having ſaid that the opinion of L'Etoile appeared to him to be equitable, avows that the contrary one, which is that of the ancient authors, is followed in the Chatelet of Paris: but I think this is an error which ought to be reformed, if it has not been already.

When the creditor has obtained judgment againſt one of his debtors *in solidum* for *his part* of the debt, it muſt, according to the ſame principle, be decided that the judgment ought not to diſcharge the other debtors from their liability *in solidum*. *Cum res judicata aliis non prosit*; and that they may only require that, in caſe there be ſome of them inſolvent, the creditor ſhould allow them a deduction of the part which the debtor whom he has diſcharged would have been liable for on account of the inſolvency.

279. There remains for us a queſtion to examine whether, when there are ſeveral debtors *in solidum* of a rent, the receipt which the creditor has given to one of them of a certain ſum for *his part* of the arrearages then due, diſ-

charges him from his liability *in solidum* for the future, or only as to the arrearages then due, for which the receipt was given. It must be decided that it discharges him from his liability *in solidum* only for the arrearages due and for which the receipt was given, and not for the future. This decision is grounded on the principle above cited, *Nemo facile præsumitur donare*. Hence it follows that we ought not to infer from the receipt given by the creditor, that he intended to discharge the debtor from his liability for the whole debt, unless this implication were necessarily to arise and it does not necessarily arise: for from the creditor's having been willing to allow this debtor to pay *his part* of the arrearages that were due, and for which a receipt was given *for his part*, it follows only that the creditor was willing to discharge him from his liability *in solidum* for these arrearages; but it by no means follows that he was willing to discharge him from his liability *in solidum* for the rent that was to accrue. Such is the decision of *Alciat ad d. L. Bacquet, ibid. n.* 246.

Nevertheless, if during the time required for the prescription, (i. e. during the space of 30 years) the debtor had been always admitted to pay the arrearages *for his part*, this debtor would acquire, by the prescription, a discharge from his liability *in solidum*, even for the future. *Alciat, Bacquet, ibid.* But even in this case, as Bacquet observes. *ibid.* the debtor would not have acquired the right of redeeming the rent for his part alone. For from the creditor's having been willing to discharge him from his liability *in solidum*, for the payment of the arrearages, it by no means follows that he likewise consented to the division of the redemption of the rent.

§. V.

Of the cession of the actions of the creditor, which a debtor in solidum, *on paying the whole debt, has a right to demand.*

280. The debtor *in solidum*, who pays the whole debt, may, if he chooses, extinguish the debt only for so much as he is bound, himself, to pay, for his part, and without recourse. See *supra, n.* 264. He has a right to insist on the

ceſſion of the creditor's actions for the ſurplus againſt his co-debtors; and by this ceſſion of actions he is preſumed rather to purchaſe the claim of the creditor for the ſurplus, againſt his co-debtors, than to have diſcharged it. *Creditor non in solutum accepit, sed quodammodo nomen creditoris vendidit* L. 36, ff. *de Fidejus.*

The creditor cannot refuſe this ſubrogation or ceſſion of his actions, to the debtor *in solidum* who pays the whole debt, when he requires it from him; and even if he had diſabled himſelf from making it againſt any of them he would impair his right to claim for the whole as has been ſaid, *supra.*

Further, when the creditor has, by the act of payment, required the ſubrogation; even if the creditor were to refuſe it, the debtors, according to our uſages, would, not the leſs, enjoy the ſubrogation, without ſuing the creditor to make him yield it. The law ſupplies in this caſe what the creditor ought to have done, and ſubrogates the debtor, who has required the ſubrogation, to all the rights and actions of the creditor.

Quid, if the debtor had paid without requiring the ſubrogation? He could not afterwards cauſe himſelf to be ſubrogated to the actions of the creditor. For the abſolute payment having extinguiſhed the claim with all the rights and actions reſulting from it, it is impoſſible to cede to him afterwards what has ceaſed to exiſt. *Si post solutum, sine ullo pacto, omne quod ex causa tutelæ debetur, actiones post aliquod intervallum cessæ sint, nihil ea cessione actum, cum nulla actio superfuit*; L. 76, ff. *de Solut.*

The Doctors, among other texts of law, uſually cite this to ſhew that the ſubrogation does not take place *ipso jure*, if it be not required by the payment which is made by the debtor *in solidum*, or a ſecurity, or ſome other perſon, paying what he owes for or with others: indeed this text ſeems to decide it in words formal enough. Yet Dumoulin in the firſt ſolemn lecture he read at Dole, has pretended, againſt the opinion of all writers, that a debtor *in solidum*, a ſecurity or any other perſon paying what he owes for or with another, was in consequence of the payment, *ipso jure* subrogated, although he may not have required the subrogation. His reason is that they ought always to be presumed to have paid only on condition that they should have this subrogation which they have a right to demand; no one being to be presumed to neglect or renounce his rights. He pretends that the case in this law 76, is not, as they have all thought, the case of a tutor who had paid the balance which he owed *in solidum* with his co-debtors, without requiring the subrogation against them; but that it is the case of the friend of a tutor, who had paid for him without being bound for the debt. Dumoulin pretends that this is the only case in which there is no subrogation, when no mention of it is made in the receipt; because in this case the creditor not being bound to cede his action, a cession of actions in this case is not to be presumed if it be not expressly agreed upon. But whenever he, who has paid, had an interest in paying, and had consequently a right to the subrogation of the creditor's actions against those for or with whom he was debtor for what he has paid, he ought always, according to Dumoulin, to be presumed to have been subrogated; although he did not require the subrogation. He grounds his opinion principally on the law, 1, §. 13, ff. *de Tut. & rat.* which he understands in a sense quite different from that in which this text has always been understood. It is said *si forte quis ex facto alterius tutoris condemnatus præstiterit, vel ex communi gestu, nec ei mandatæ sunt actiones, constitutum est a D. Pio & ab Imperatore nostro & patre ejus, utilem actionem tutori adversus contutorem dandam.* Whereas the text is understood ordinarily of the action *utilis negotiorum gestorum*, which these constitutions grant in this case to the tutor against his co-tutor, in which action there was a difficulty, because this tutor, in paying that to which he was condemned in his own name, *non contutoris, sed magis proprium negotium gessisse videbatur*; Dumoulin, on the contrary, understands this text to be of the action of wardship, which the minor had against the other tutor, called *utilis*, because the law, *utilitate ita suadente* for want of an express cession, subrogates to it the tutor who has paid.

This opinion has not prevailed, and they have continued to teach in the schools and to decide in courts, that a co-debtor *in solidum*, a security and all those who pay what they owe for or with others, are only subrogated to the actions of the creditor, when they have required the subrogation. The reason is, that according to a principle acknowledged by Dumoulin himself, no subrogation is made *ipso jure*, unless the law expresses it. *Non transeunt actiones, nisi in casibus jure expressis.* Dumoulin cannot quote any text of law, establishing in this case the subrogation. The law 1, §. 13, *ff. de Tut. & rat.... distr.* which is the principal ground of his opinion, does not establish it, there being no necessity of construing this text in the sense in which Dumoulin does, of an action *utilis tutelæ*, to which the tutor, who has paid, might be subrogated; and the text may be understood in a sense much more natural, of the action *utilis negotiorum gestorum*. This text, far from establishing that the subrogation is made, in this case, *ipso jure*, on the contrary, supposes that it is not made. This is the natural sense which the law 76, *ff. de Solut.* presents; that which Dumoulin gives to this law is not. The law 39, *ff. de Fidej.* and the law 11, *Cod. de tit.* admit, still less, of objection. These laws decide that the security who has failed, on paying, to cause himself to be subrogated, has no action against his co-securities; which very clearly supposes that he is not subrogated *de jure*, without requiring the subrogation. For if this had been the case, it would have been useless to consult the Emperor Alexander to know whether he had an action. In vain would it be said, in support of the opinion of Dumoulin, that the debtor *in solidum* having a right to cause himself to be subrogated to the action of his creditors against his co-debtors, ought not to be presumed to have renounced this right, because no one is presumed to renounce his rights. The answer is, that this right, consisting of the mere faculty, which he has, of requiring the subrogation, which he may use or forbear to use, it is not enough that he be not to be presumed to have renounced his right, it ought to appear that he used this faculty, which does not appear, if he has not declared it. The debtor who pays, having another motive in paying than to acquire the ſubrogation, viz. that of avoiding the ſuit of his creditor and diſcharging his perſon and his property. The payment, which he makes without requiring the ſubrogation, ſhews only that he wiſhed to diſcharge himſelf, not that he intended to acquire the ſubrogation. Beſides, if it ſhould be ſuppoſed that he had the intention to acquire the ſubrogation, this intention, kept within himſelf, would not be ſufficient; his right conſiſting of the faculty of requiring it, the ſubrogation cannot take place, when he does not require it. It is true the law grants it if the creditor fails to yield it; but in order to ſay that there is a failure in the creditor, he ought to have been put in arrear to yield it, by the demand which the creditor ought to make. It is for this reaſon that modern authors have continued to follow the common opinion.

Renuſſon, *Traite des Subrogations*, *ch.* 7, *n.* 68, *& ch.* 9, *n.* 7, maintains this laſt opinion. It has been followed alſo in a number of adjudged caſes. There is one of them of the 26th of Auguſt, 1706, reported in the fifth volume of the *Journal des Audiences*, in which it was determined that a ſecurity, having paid without requiring the ſubrogation, was not ſubrogated to the actions of the creditor, and that he had conſequently no action againſt the wife of the debtor, who had bound herſelf to the creditor for the return of her huſband to priſon, or to pay for him.

There are, however, certain caſes in which the ſubrogation takes place *ipſo jure*. See *Intr. au tit.* 20. *Cout. d Orleans. ch*, 1, §. 5.

281. The debtor *in ſolidum* who, in paying, has required the ſubrogation, is, for the ſurplus of that for which he was debtor on his own account and without recourſe, ſubrogated to the actions of the creditor, not only againſt his co-debtors, but againſt their ſecurities, if they have given any to the creditor. He is ſubrogated to all the privileges and rights of hypothecation attached to the actions of the creditor, and he may exerciſe them, even againſt third perſons, as well as the creditor, of whom he is *procurator in rem ſuam*, might have done.

When there are several co-debtors, as for example, when an obligation has been contracted *in solidum* y four persons, it is a question much controverted, whether one of the four who has paid the whole debt, with subrogation, may sue each of his co-debtors for the whole debt, deducting only the fourth part, with which he was himself chargeable, and for which he could not be subrogated, or whether he can only sue each of them for his fourth part? The question was anciently decided in favor of the first opinion. Indeed it seems at first, that as the debtor is by the subrogation *procurator in rem suam* of the creditor, he may use the actions of the creditor against each of his co-debtors for the whole as the creditor himself might have done. However, the late decisions have been for the other opinion. One of them is reported in the *Journals du Palais, tom.* 1. *p.* 615, of the 22d of February, 1650, which was followed by another of September 5, 1674. The reason is, that otherwise, there would be a circuity of actions, for the one of my co-debtors from whom I may have exacted the whole debt with a deduction of my part, would have a right, on paying, to be subrogated to the actions of the creditor, deducting the part for which he is himself liable; and in virtue of this subrogation, he would have a right to demand from me, with a deduction of his part, what he may have paid me, since I am, myself, bound for the whole. I could not say, to defend myself against this circuity of actions, that I am no longer a debtor, having paid the creditor; for by means of the subrogation the payment I made has only extinguished the debt, for so much of it as I was myself chargeable with, and not for the surplus: by means of the subrogation, I have rather acquired the creditor's claim for the surplus, than discharged it. But being reimbursed by my co-debtor who would also require the subrogation, this claim for the surplus with the deduction of the part with which he himself is chargeable, would pass to the person of this debtor. It would be no longer I, but he, who would be *procurator in rem suam* of the creditor, and who in this quality would have a right to use against me the actions of the creditor for this surplus and to make me return what he had paid me.

When, after I have paid the whole with ſubrogation, there is among my co-debtors one who is inſolvent, and from whom I cannot recover the part of the debt for which he is liable, this inſolvency ought to be divided between thoſe who are ſolvent and myſelf; equity not permitting that after having paid alone the whole debt, I ſhould alone bear this inſolvency.

§. VI.

Of the actions which the debtor in ſolidum *who has paid without subrogation, may have in his own right against his co-debtors.*

282. Though a debtor *in solidum* has omitted, on paying, to require the ſubrogation, he is not, however, deſtitute of all remedy, and has in his own right, againſt each of his co-debtors, an action to recover the part of the debt with which each of theſe co-debtors is chargeable.

The action is different, according to the different cauſes from which the debt proceeds.

When the debt *in solidum* is contracted by ſeveral perſons, for a joint affair; as when ſeveral perſons have bought together a plantation, for the payment of the price of which they bound themſelves *in solidum*, or when they have borrowed a ſum of money which they have employed in a common ſpeculation, or which they have divided among themſelves, and they bound themſelves *in solidum* to repay it; in this and the like caſes the debtor *in solidum* who has paid the whole, has againſt each of his co-debtors the action *pro socio*.

He has this action againſt each of them, for the part which each has had in the joint affair that has occaſioned the debt, each of them being liable for the debt for this part.

If one of them was inſolvent, he who has paid the whole has, beſides, an action againſt each of thoſe who are ſolvent, to recover ſo much as each ought to bear of the inſolvent's part; and each is to bear *pro rata* his proportion of that part, according to the ſhare he had in the joint concern. For the inſolvency of one of the partners, is a partnerſhip loſs. This loſs, therefore, ought to be born by each partner, in proportion to his ſhare in the partnerſhip.

This will be illuſtrated by an example, *Finge*. Six perſons, Peter, Paul, James, Andrew, John and Thomas purchaſe, together, a quantity of goods, of the value of one thouſand livres, for the payment of the price of which they bind themſelves *in solidum* to the ſeller. They divide them among themſelves. Peter takes half on his own account and is charged with one half of the price. The five others divide the other half among themſelves, in equal ſhares. Thomas pays the whole debt without ſubrogation. Andrew is inſolvent. Thomas, who has paid the whole debt, has recourſe againſt his ſolvent co-debtors firſt, for the part with which each was chargeable of the whole debt; viz. againſt Peter for five hundred livres, and againſt Paul, James and John for one hundred each; and further, he will have recourſe againſt each of the ſaid four co-debtors, for the part which each of them ought to bear, on account of the inſolvent debtor, according to the repartition which ought to be made among them, *pro rata*, in proportion to the ſhare which each had in the debt. Thus the part of the debt with which Peter is chargeable, being the quintuple of that with which each of the other debtors is chargeable, he ought, therefore, to bear, of the hundred livres the part of the inſolvent debtor, the quintuple of that which the other ſolvent debtors ought to bear. Therefore this ſum of one hundred livres is to be divided into nine parts, of eleven livres, two deniers and two-ninths. Peter ought to bear five-ninths or fifty-five livres, one ſous. Thomas, who has paid the whole debt, will have a further claim for fifty livres and one ſous againſt Peter, and for eleven livres and two deniers againſt each of the other ſolvent co-debtors, viz. Paul, James and John: and the reſt will be extinguiſhed by confuſion.

When the affair for which the debt was contracted by ſeveral perſons who bound themſelves *in solidum*, concerns only one of them; though they are all, with regard to the creditor, principal debtors, yet with regard to them, he whom alone the affair concerned, is the only principal debtor and the others are as his ſecurities. For example. If

Peter, James and John, borrow a ſum of money, which they bind themſelves *in solidum* to repay, aud Peter retains the whole ſum, Peter is, with regard to his *co-debtors*, the only principal debtor. If he diſcharges the whole debt, he will have no recourſe againſt his co-debtors, who became debtors with him merely to ſerve him: on the contrary, if James has diſcharged the whole debt, he will have the action *mandati* againſt Peter to claim the whole from him, as a ſecurity has this action againſt the principal, when he, the ſecurity, has paid the whole debt.

But in caſe of Peter's inſolvency, will James who has paid the whole, have an action againſt John to recover the half? This depends on the deciſion of the queſtion, whether the ſecurity has an action againſt his co-ſecurities? See this queſtion, *infra*, *ch.* 6, §. 7, *art.* 4.

When the debt *in solidum* has for cauſe a donation, *puta*, when two or three perſons have, by a contract of marriage, given to one a certain ſum, which they bound themſelves *in solidum* to pay him, and of which one of them has paid the whole, he cannot in this caſe have for it the action *pro socio* againſt the co-debtors: for a partnerſhip may indeed be contracted in purchaſing together and in ſelling together, but not in giving together; partnerſhip being in its nature a contract which is made *lucri in commune quærendi causa*. The action which he who has paid the whole, has in this caſe againſt his co-debtors, is the action *mandati*: for in this inſtance each of the donors is donor and debtor for himſelf, only for his part; and he is in regard to the ſurplus as a ſecurity and mandatary: he has therefore againſt them for the ſurplus, the action *manduti*, ſuch as a ſecurity has.

When the debt *in solidum* proceeds from a tort, *puta*, when ſeveral have been condemned *in solidum* for the payment of a certain ſum, the civil reparation of a tort which they have committed together; he who has paid the whole cannot have againſt his co-debtors either the action *pro socio* or the action *manduti*: *Nec enim ulla societas maleficiorum*; L. 1, §. 14, ff. *Tut. & rat. Nec societas aut mandatum flagitiosæ rei ullas vires habet*; L. 35, §. 2, *contr. empt. Rei turpis nullum mandatum est*; L. 6, §. 3, ff. *mand.* According to the exact principles of the Roman Jurists, the debtor who has paid the whole, has not in this case any recourse against his co-debtors.

According to our practice, which is more indulgent, there is granted in this case to him who has paid the whole, an action against each of the co-debtors, to recover from him his part. See *Papon, liv.* 24, *t.* 12, *n.* 4. This action does not arise from the tort which they have committed together; *nemo enim ex delicto consequi potest actionem*: it arises from the payment which one of the debtors has made of a debt which he owed in common with his co-debtors, and from equity, which does not permit that his co-debtors should profit at his expence by the discharge of a debt for which they were as much bound as he. This is a kind of action *utilis negotiorum gestorum*, founded upon the same principles of equity on which is founded the action that is given in our jurisprudence to the security who has paid, against his co-securities. See *infra, ch.* 6, §. 7, *art.* 4.

CHAPTER IV.

Of some particular kinds of obligations considered with regard to the things which make the object of them.

AMONG the divisions of obligations with regard to the things that are the object of them, which we have noticed *supra, ch.* 1, §. 3, we have said that there were obligations of a certain thing, as to give a certain horse; and obligations of an uncertain and indeterminate thing of a certain kind, *puta*, that to give a horse indeterminately.

We have said also that there were divisible obligations and others indivisible. We shall treat here in a previous section of the obligations of an indeterminate thing of a certain kind; in a subsequent one, of divisible and indivisible obligations.

§. I.

Of the obligation of an indeterminate thing of a certain kind.

283. What is abfolutely indeterminate cannot be the object of an obligation; *supra*, *n.* 138. For example. If I have promifed you to give you *something*, without faying what, there does not refult from this promife any obligation. But one may contract the obligation of an indeterminate thing of a certain kind of things; as when one obliges himfelf to another to give a horfe, a pair of piftols, without determining what horfe, what piftols. The individual thing which makes the object of thefe obligations is indeterminate; but the kind in which this individual thing is to be taken, is certain and determinate: thefe obligations are indeterminate *quoad individuum*, though they are, *quoad genus*, a determinate object.

Thefe obligations are more or lefs indeterminate, according as the kind in which the thing is to be taken is more or lefs general. For example. If one has bound himfelf to give me a horfe of a certain breed, the obligation being confined to a horfe of this breed, is lefs indeterminate than if he had bound himfelf fimply to give me a horfe.

In thefe obligations, each of the things comprifed in the kind in which the thing due is to be taken, is *in facultate solutionis*, provided it be good and merchantable; but not *in obligatione*: for there is not indeed, any individual thing of the kind which the debtor may not pay, yet there is none that may properly be demanded from him.

There is indeed one of the things of this kind which is due; for the obligation muft have an object: but this thing is not any one of the individual things *in concreto*; it is a thing of this kind confidered *in abstracto*, by a tranfcendent idea which makes abftraction of the individuals which compofe the fpecies or of the fpecies comprifed in the genus; it is an uncertain, indeterminate thing which will be determined only by the valid payment which may be made of one of the individual things.

It is true that this thing, thus confidered, is, until it be determined by the payment, a thing which exifts only in idea; but we have feen *supra*, that things which exift only in idea may be the object of obligations, obligations being, themfelves, ideal.

This principle, which we give from Dumoulin, *Tract. de Div. & ind. p.* 2, *quæst.* 5, in regard to the object of an obligation of a thing included in a certain kind, appears more juft and proper than that of thofe who think that thefe obligations have for their object all the individual things comprifed in the fpecies or genus, fo that each of all thefe individuals is due, *non quidem determinate*, but under a fort of alternative or condition, *si alia res ejus generis non solvatur*.

Hence it follows, I. that when a thing of a certain kind is due indeterminately, the creditor is not well grounded in demanding determinately any one of the things comprifed in this kind; but he muft demand generally and indeterminately one of thefe things.

It follows, II. that the lofs of the things of this kind, which happens fince the obligation has been contracted, does not fall upon the creditor: for the things which perifh are not thofe which were due him; and it fuffices that fome one of them remains, for the obligation to continue.

Obferve however, that if the debtor, in order to difcharge himfelf from his obligation, had offered to the creditor one of the things of this kind, good and merchantable, and had, by a judicial fummons, put the creditor in arrear to receive it, the lofs which fhould afterwards happen in regard to this thing, would fall on the creditor, as the debtor ought not to fuffer from the delay of the creditor, and the debt, indeterminate as it was, has been, by the offer, rendered determinate in the thing offered; L. 84, §. 3, ff. *de Leg.* 1.

284. In regard to the things which the debtor of a thing of a certain kind may validly offer in order to difcharge himfelf from his obligation, obferve that it is neceffary they

ſhould be good and merchantable; *L.* 33, *in fine*, ff. *de Solut.*; which is to ſay, that they have no material defect. He who owes a horſe indeterminately, is not admitted to offer a horſe that is blind in an eye, lame, or ſhort-winded, &c. nor one that is very old. Yet, if the thing have no material defect, and the debtor can transfer the irrevocable property in it to the creditor, he may give ſuch a thing of the kind as he pleaſes; *L.* 72, §. 5, ff. *de Solut.*

May he give a thing which could not have been validly promiſed to the creditor towards whom the obligation had been contracted? For example. If I have obliged myſelf to give you a horſe indeterminately, may I diſcharge myſelf from my obligation by giving you a horſe which belonged to you at the time of the contract, and which, having been ſince ſold by you, has become my property? Dumoulin decides for the affirmative; and in this, this obligation differs from that by which I have promiſed a horſe indeterminately under the alternative of another thing; for in this laſt caſe, as my obligation could not exiſt with regard to a thing which belonged to you, there was no other thing due, and conſequently no other thing which I could pay. But in the obligation to give you a horſe indeterminately, no individual horſe being due, and every horſe being *in facultate solutionis*, rather than *in obligatione*, it ſuffices that, at the time of payment, the horſe which I give you, to diſcharge myſelf from my obligation, no longer belongs to you, and that it belongs to me, for the payment of the horſe to be validly made to you. This is plainly decided by Marcellus, in the law 72, §. 4, ff. *de Solut. Ei qui hominem dari stipulatus est, unum etiam ex his qui tunc stipulatori servierunt dando promissor, liberatur.*

It muſt be admitted, however, that the law 66, §. 3, ff. *de Leg.* 2, which is from Papinian, declares the contrary. *Quum duobus testamentis homo generatim legatur; qui solvente altero legatari factus est, quamvis postea sit alienatus, ab altero hærede idem solvi non poterit eademque ratio stipulationis est; hominis enim legatum, orationis compendio singulos homines continet; utque ab initio non consistit in his qui legatarii fuerunt, ita frustra solvitur cujus dominium postea d gatarius adeptus est, tametsi dominus esse desierit.*

Dumoulin, *Tract. de Div. & ind. p.* 2, *n.* 102, according to his custom of making the laws subservient to his decisions, distorts this law. He says that the decision of this law must be confined to the particular instance of two legacies made of a thing of a certain kind by two testators to the same person, or of two gratuitous promises of a thing of a certain kind, clothed in the form of a stipulation, made by two donors to the same person: that it is by a particular reason that in this instance the same thing which has been paid to the legatee or donee in discharge of the first legacy or first gift, can no longer be paid in discharge of the other legacy or gift, *ne scilicet videretur offendi juris regula: Non possunt duæ causæ lucrativæ in eadem re & in eadem persona concurrere:* but that from this law we ought not to make a general decision: that in all the obligations of a thing of a certain kind, the things of this kind which, when the obligation was contracted, belonged to him towards whom it was contracted, or which have belonged to him since, ought to be presumed excepted from this obligation, and cannot therefore be paid to him, although they no longer belong to him. Finally, he says that in this law these words, *hominis legatum, orationis compendio, singulos homines continet,* do not signify that all the slaves in the world are each *in obligatione legati,* under this condition, *si alius non solvitur;* but that they signify only that all the slaves in the world are *in facultate solutionis,* and that the legacy may be performed and discharged *in singulis hominibus.* This interpretation appears to me contrary to the natural sense of the text. I would rather, in recognising a true antinomy between this law and the law 72, as Ant. Faber and Bachovius have done, abandon the decision of Papinian, as founded on the false principle that the obligation of a thing of a certain kind includes, *alternate & orationis compendio,* that of all the individual things which are susceptible of it, and I would rather adopt the decision of Marcellus, in the law 72, §. 4, above cited, for the reasons before alledged. Cujas, upon these laws, has taken an opinion diametrically oppofite to that of Dumoulin: and to reconcile what Marcellus fays, in the law 72, *de Solut.* with what Papinian fays in the law 66, ff. *de Leg.* 1. he makes an alteration in the text of this law, 66; but the end of the paragraph fhews the falfity of this innovation in the text, which is befides without foundation.

283. When the debtor of a thing of a certain kind has paid a certain thing which, through error, he thought was determinately due, he has a right to claim it back, on offering to give another; for having given this thing in payment of his obligation of a thing of a certain kind, only under the falfe perfuafion that he owed this thing determinately, he has paid what he did not owe, and confequently *locus est condictioni indebiti*; L. 32, §. 3, ff. *de Cond. ind.*

On the indivifibility of the payment of obligations of a thing of a certain kind, fee *infra Part* 1, *ch.* 1, *art.* 6, §. 3.

285. Whether the obligation be *generis generalissimi*, as when one has obliged himfelf to give a horfe, generally; or whether the obligation be *generis subalterni*, *aut generis limitati*, as when one has obliged himfelf to give one of his horfes; all we have hitherto faid applies, provided the agreement does not contain any claufe which takes away the choice from the debtor.

But when by a particular claufe in the agreement, the choice is granted to the creditor; as when one has obliged himfelf to give me one of the dogs of his kennel at my choice; in this cafe, although the agreement includes principally the abfolute obligation to give a dog indeterminately, yet it may alfo be faid that in virtue of the claufe which grants me the choice, each of the dogs of the debtor's kennel is due me under a fort of condition, which is the choice I may make; fince in virtue of this claufe there is no one of them which I may not require. Therefore the debtor is in this cafe bound to keep them all for me until I may make my choice; he cannot until this, without contravening his obligation, difpofe of any of them. *Arg.* L. 3, ff. *Qui & a quib. man. Si indistincte homo sit legatus, non potest hæres, quosdam manumittendo, evertere jus electionis; nam quodammodo singuli sub conditione legati videntur.*

It cannot be ſaid in the ſame manner, when the debtor has the choice, that each individual is compriſed in the obligation, in caſe the debtor chooſes to give one rather than another; for it is not in the faculty to pay one thing rather than another, but in the right to require it, that the obligation conſiſts. This is the difference which Dumoulin eſtabliſhes, *Tract de Div. & ind part.* 2, *n.* 112, 113, 114, between the caſe in which the choice is given to the creditor and the caſe in which it is given to the debtor.

SECTION THE SECOND.

Of diviſible and indiviſible obligations.

ARTICLE THE FIRST.

What obligations are diviſible, and what are indiviſible.

§. I.

What is a diviſible obligation and what an indiviſible obligation.

287. A diviſible obligation is that which may be divided: an indiviſible obligation is that which cannot be divided. An obligation is not the leſs diviſible though it be actually undivided; for it ſuffices, to be diviſible, that it *may* be divided. *Molin. Tract. de Div. & ind. part.* 3, *n.* 7, *& seq*

For example. When I have alone contracted the obligation to pay you the ſum of one thouſand crowns, this obligation is undivided; but it is diviſible, becauſe it may be divided, and will in fact divide itſelf between my heirs, if, dying before I have diſcharged it, I leave ſeveral heirs.

Likewiſe, the obligation *in solidum* which ſeveral perſons contract to pay to ſome one ten crowns, is not the leſs, a diviſible obligation. The effect of the liability *in solidum* is that it be not actually divided between the debtors *in solidum*; but their obligation is no leſs a diviſible obligation, becauſe it may be divided, and will in fact be divided among their heirs.

288. It is neceſſary to enquire what obligations may be divided, and what may not be divided.

An obligation may be divided and is diviſible, when the thing due which makes the object and ſubject of it, is ſuſceptible of diviſion, and of parts in which it may be paid; and on the contrary, the obligation is indiviſible and cannot be divided, when the thing due is not ſuſceptible of diviſion and of parts, and can be paid only in the whole.

The diviſion which is here in queſtion is not a phyſical diviſion, which conſiſts *in solutione continuitatis*, as that of a board which is ſawed into two; but it is a *civil* diviſion, and proper to the commerce of things.

There are two kinds of civil diviſions; one which is in actual and divided parts, and another which is in parts ideal and indiviſible. When an acre of land is divided into two parts, by erecting a fence acroſs, it is a diviſion of the firſt kind: the parts of this acre which are ſeparated from each other by the fence, are actual and divided parts.

When the owner of this acre of land, or other thing, dies and leaves two heirs who become owners each of an undivided half, this is a diviſion of the ſecond kind: the parts which reſult from this diviſion and which belong to each of the heirs, are undivided parts which are not actual and which exiſt only *in jure & intellectu.*

The things which are not ſuſceptible of the firſt kind of diviſion are not the leſs ſuſceptible of the ſecond. For example. A horſe, a ſilver plate, are not ſuſceptible of the firſt kind of diviſion; for theſe things are not ſuſceptible, without the deſtruction of their ſubſtance, of actual and divided parts; but they are ſuſceptible of the ſecond kind of diviſion, becauſe theſe things may belong to ſeveral perſons in undivided parts.

It ſuffices that a thing be ſuſceptible of this ſecond diviſion, although it be not of the firſt, for the obligation, to give this thing, to be a diviſible obligation. This reſults from the law 9, §. 1, *de Solut.* where it is ſaid, *Qui Stichum debet, parte Stichi data, in reliquam partem tenetur.* According to this text, the obligation to give the slave Stichus is a divisible obligation, since it may, at least by consent of the creditor, be discharged in part, although the slave is not susceptible of the first kind of division; *Molin. ibid. p.* 1, *n,* 5, *p.* 2, *n.* 200 *&* 201.

Indivisible things are those which are not susceptible either of actual parts or even of ideal parts: such are certain incorporeal hereditaments, *quæ pro parte acquiri non possunt.*

The obligation to give a thing of this nature, is an indivisible obligation; *Molin. p.* 2, *n.* 201.

289. The same rule which we have just given to determine whether obligations *in dando* are divisible or indivisible, must also serve in regard to obligations *in faciendo vel in non faciendo.* Several writers have thought that these obligations were indivisible, without distinction; but Dumoulin, *ibid. p.* 2, *n.* 203, *& seq.* has shewn that they are no less divisible than obligations *in dando,* unless the act which is the object of them be of such a nature as that it cannot be performed in parts, as when I have obliged myself to build a house, &c. But if the act which is the object of the obligation may be performed in parts, as if I have obliged myself to put you in possession of a thing which may be possessed in parts, the obligation will be divisible. This is the fifth key of Dumoulin: *Omnis obligatio etiam facti dividua est, nisi quatenus de contrario apparet. Molin. ibid. & p.* 3, *n.* 112.

Likewise, the obligation *in non faciendo* will be divisible, when what I have obliged myself not to do, may be done in one part and not done in another part: such is the obligation *amplius non agi ad aliquid dividuum;* as when I have bound myself to you not to disturb the possessor of an estate which you have to warrant and defend; this is an obligation *in non faciendo,* which is divisible; for it may be discharged in part. I may contravene it in part, by claiming a part only of this estate, and discharge it in part by forbearing to claim the other part.

290. Observe that is the very thing or act which makes he object of the obligation, that must be considered in order

to decide whether the obligation is divifible or indivifible, and not the benefit which the creditor might derive from the obligation contracted to his advantage, nor the detriment, *onus & diminutio patrimonii*, which would refult therefrom to the debtor; otherwife there would be no obligation which might not be divifible.

Therefore, for example, if two joint proprietors of a houfe have obliged themfelves to the two joint proprietors of an adjoining houfe, to grant a right of view for the benefit of this adjoining houfe, this obligation is indivifible; becaufe the right of view which makes the object of it, is fomething indivifible, although the benefit which refults therefrom to each of thofe to whom the obligation is contracted, and the detriment to be fuftained by each of thofe who contracted it, may be valued in a fum of money which is divifible. This is fhewn by Dumoulin, *ib. p.* 2, *n.* 199: *Cum hic effectus*, he fays, *sit quid remotum & separatum a substantia obligationis & rei debitæ, non dicitur obligatio dividua vel individua penes effectum, sed secundum se & secundum naturam rei immediate in eam deductæ.*

§. II.

Of the different kinds of indivisibility.

291. Dumoulin, *ib. p.* 3, *n.* 57, *& seq. & n.* 75, diftinguifhes very properly three kinds of indivifibility; that which is abfolute, and which he calls *individuum contractu*; that which he calls indivifibility of obligation, *individuum obligatione*; and that which he calls indivifibility of payment, *individuum solutione*.

The abfolute indivifibility, which Dumoulin calls *individuum contractu*, is when a thing is in its nature not fufceptible of parts, fo that it could not be ftipulated or promifed in part: fuch are, as before obferved, certain incorporeal hereditaments, as for example, a right of way. It is impoffible to have an idea of the parts in a right of way; and confequently one could not ftipulate or promife this kind of things in part.

292. The fecond indivifibility is that which Dumoulin

calls *individuum obligatione*. Whatever is *individuum contractu*, is so *obligatione*: but there are certain things, which, although they may be absolutely stipulated or promised in parts, and consequently though they be not *individua contractu*, yet from the manner in which they have been considered by the contracting parties, are something indivisible, and which cannot, consequently, be due in parts.

We may adduce as an example of this indivisibility, the obligation to build a house or ship. This obligation is not indivisible *contractu*; for it is not impossible that it should be contracted in parts. I may agree with a mason that he shall construct a part of the house which I intend to build, *puta*, that he shall carry it up to the first floor. But although the building of a house be not indivisible *contractu*, it is, ordinarily, indivisible *obligatione*: for when one contracts with a builder to build a house, the building of the house, which makes the object of the obligation, is, from the manner in which it is considered by the contracting parties, something indivisible, and *quod nullam recipit partium praestationem*. It is true that this building can only be done by parts and successively; but it is not the building of the house which makes the object of the obligation; it is the work itself completed, it is *domus construenda*. As there cannot then be a house until it be entirely built, as the form and quality of the house can result only from the completion of the work, and as there cannot be parts of what does not yet exist, it follows that the obligation to build a house, can be performed only by the building of the house completed, and consequently that this obligation is not susceptible of parts, and cannot be performed in parts. This is the meaning of the commentator in the law 80, §. 1. ff. *ad leg. Falcid.* in which, in order to prove that the obligation to construct a work, as a theatre, a bath, is indivisible, he alledges the reason: *Neque enim ullum balneum, aut theatrum, aut stadium fecisse intelligitur, qui ei propriam formam quae ex consummatione contingit, non dederit.*

For the same reason it is said in the law 85, §. 2, ff. *de*

Verb. ob'g. that the obligation to conſtruct a work is indiviſible: *Singuli hæredes in solidum tenentur, quia operis effectus in partes scindi non potest. Opus*, ſays Dumoulin, *fit pro parte realiter & naturaliter: sed si illud* OPUS FIERI *referas ad effectum præstationem ejus quod debetur, tunc verum non erit per partes fieri quia parte fabricæ facta, non est debitor liberatus in ea parte: simplex enim fabricatio & operatio transiens non debetur, sed opus effectum, cujus pars non est fabricæ pars, cum nullæ sint partes domus quæ nondum est; nec sum stipulatus fabricam, sed fieri domum, id est tale opus, sub tali forma consummatum, quod ante perfectionem non subsistit, nec ullas actu partes habet. Molid, Tract. de Div. & ind. p.* 3, *d.* 76. We may further adduce here the law 5, ff. *de Verb. signif.*, which ſays *opere locato conducto significari non* OPUS, *id est operationem, sed* EFFECTUS, *id est ex opere facto corpus aliquod factum.*

Certain circumſtances under which the obligation of a thing is contracted, may alſo render the obligation indiviſible, although the thing in itſelf and detached from theſe circumſtances, be indeed diviſible. Such is the obligation which I might contract to furniſh a perſon with a piece of ground for a wine-preſs which he is about to erect: for although the ground which I have promiſed is a thing in itſelf diviſible, yet it being due, not as a piece of ground *simpliciter*, but as a piece of ground deſigned for a wine-preſs, it becomes, in this view, ſomething indiviſible, ſince no part can be taken from it without its ceaſing to be proper for the purpoſe, and without its ceaſing conſequently to be the thing which makes the object of the obligation; *Molin. p.* 2, *n.* 314, 295.

293. The obligation indiviſible *natura & contractu*, is the obligation of a thing which in itſelf, from its nature, and in whatever manner it may be conſidered, is not ſuſceptible of parts: the obligation indiviſible *obligatione*, is the obligation of a thing which, conſidered in the reſpect in which it makes the object of the obligation, is not ſuſceptible of parts.

It is evident that theſe obligations which are indiviſible, whether *contractu* or *obligatione*, are likewiſe ſo *solutione*; for that cannot be paid in parts which is not ſuſceptible of parts.

294. There is a third kind of indiviſibility, which is called *individuum solutione tantum*. It is that which relates only to the payment of the obligation, and not to the obligation itſelf, when the thing due is in itſelf diviſible and ſuſceptible of parts, and may be due in parts, whether to the different heirs of the creditor, or by the different heirs of the debtor, but cannot be paid in parts.

We ſhall adduce ſeveral examples of this kind of indiviſibility in the following article, in which we ſhall treat of the nature and effects of diviſible obligations, to which claſs properly belong the obligations in which is found this kind of indiviſibility, ſince it does not relate to the obligation itſelf, although, however, the law 2, §. 1, ff. *de verb. oblig.*, would make of them a mixed kind, partaking of the nature of obligations diviſible and indiviſible.

§. III.

Some particular kinds of obligations in regard to which it is asked whether they are divisible or indivisible

Of the obligation to deliver a piece of land.

295. The obligation to deliver a piece of land, *fundum tradi*, is a diviſible obligation; for this delivery may be made in parts; a part of this piece of land may be delivered. The act which makes the object of this obligation being then diviſible, it cannot be doubted that, according to the principle we have juſt eſtabliſhed, this obligation is diviſible. Our deciſion is confirmed by texts of law; for although the obligation of a borrower is the obligation to return the thing borrowed, *obligatio rem tradi*, yet the law 3, §. 3, ff. *Commod.*, decides that his heirs are regularly bound for the part only for which they are heirs, which is the character of diviſible obligations: *Hæres ejus qui commodatum accepit, pro ea parte qua hæres est, convenitur.* It is true that this obligation of the borrower, although diviſible *quoad obligationem*, is indiviſible at leaſt *quoad solutionem*: but examples may eaſily be given of obligations *tradi rem*, *fundum tradi*,

which are divisible even *quoad solutionem.* Such is that which Dumoulin gives, *p.* 2, *n.* 305. I compound with a person who has brought suit against me for a certain piece of land, and I bind myself by this composition to abandon it to him without any warranty on my part. This obligation, which is an obligation *fundum tradi*, is divisible even *quoad solutionem;* and if I die before the delivery, and leave four heirs, each of my heirs will discharge himself from this obligation by abandoning the part of the land which has descended to him.

The law 72, ff. *de verb. oblig.*; appears, however, to be diametrically opposite to our decision; for the obligation *fundum tradi* is there adduced in formal terms as an example of an indivisible obligation, with the obligations *fossam fodiri, insulam fabricari, vel si quid simile*, which are indivisible, *tam obligatione quam solutione.* Dumoulin, *p.* 2, *n.* 278, *ad. n.* 359, after having adduced the different opinions of several writers to reconcile this law, adduces his own, to which it is proper to adhere. He thinks with reason that this example of the obligation *fundum tradi* ought not to be understood, without distinction, of every obligation by which one has obliged himself to deliver a piece of land, but only of the obligation to deliver a piece of land, with circumstances which render the obligation indivisible; as, for example, if wishing to build myself a house, and not having any proper place for my materials and conveniences, I agree with my neighbour that he shall give me the use of a piece of ground which he has adjoining my house, to serve me for this purpose: this obligation is an obligation *fundum tradi, non simpliciter, sed ad certum usum finemque principaliter consideratum in contrahendo:* and this purpose renders indivisible this obligation *fundum tradi*; for an obligation is indivisible when that which makes the object of it is not susceptible of a partial performance, *cum id jus quod in obligationem deductum est, non nisi in solidum præstari potest;* which is the case in the present instance: for this piece of ground being to be furnished me for a particular purpose, it can be furnished for this purpose only in the whole, since a part would not be fufficient and could not ferve the purpofe for which it is to be furnifhed me. Dumoulin gives other examples, 312, 313, 314, 315.

Of the obligation of a day's work.

296. The obligation of a day's work is indivifible, in the fame manner as the obligation to build a houfe: for although the labour of a day's work be not in itfelf a thing indivifible, yet the obligation is contracted as of a thing indivifible, and which cannot be difcharged in part. Therefore Ulpian fays: *Nec promitti, nec solvi, nec deberi, nec peti pro parte poterit opera*; L. 15, ff. *de Oper. libert.*

Likewife, Pomponius, in the law 3, §. 1, ff. *de Oper. libert.* decides that the labour of a day's work cannot be difcharged in parts, as for a certain number of hours; and that confequently the debtor of a day's work who had worked until noon and retired, would not in any manner have difcharged his obligation and would ftill remain debtor of the day's work: *Non pars operæ per horas solvi potest, quia id est officii diurni; neque ei liberto, qui sex horis duntaxat meridianis præsto fuisset, liberatio ejus diei contigit.* But after he has performed the day's work of which he remained debtor, he may demand the price of his half-day's work which he did not owe.

Dumoulin, *p.* 2, *n.* 335, *& seq.* remarks very juftly that this indivifibility of the obligation of a day's work is only an indivifibility *obligatione* and not an abfolute indivifibility, or indivifibility *contractu*; for nothing prevents the obligation from being contracted for a part of a day's work, as for half of a day. It is true that the law 15, §. 1, *de Oper. libert.* fays, *Nec promitti pro parte opera potest*: but this is a mere fubtilty. The Jurift takes *opera* for *officium diurnum*, as by the definition in the law 1, ff. *d. tit*, which it regards, according to this idea, as indivifible; fince if you divide it, it is no longer *officium diurnum*: it is *officium horarium*.

Of the obligation to do a piece of work.

297. We underftand here by work, *effectio transiens*

opus specificum permanens, according to the expreffion of Dumoulin, *p.* 2, *n.* 361; and we have already feen *supra*, *n.* 292, that the obligation to do a piece of work taken in this fenfe, fuch as the obilgation to build a houfe, to make a ftatue, a picture, is an indivifible obligation, not of that abfolute indivifiblity which we have called, with Dumoulin, indivifibility *contractu*, but the fimple indivifibility *obligatione*.

Of the obligation to pay a certain sum of money bequeathed for the building of a hospital or for some other purpose.

298. The obligation which refults from fuch a legacy is divifible, fince it is an obligation to give a fum of money: What is added in the teftament to *build a hospital*, expreffes only the motive which the teftator had to make this legacy; it is *ratio legandi*: but this motive, not being united to the difpofition, *ratio legandi non cohæret legato*, L. 72, §. 6, ff. *de Cond. & dem.* cannot confequently have any influence on the nature of the legacy, nor on the obligation which refults therefrom.

If the teftator had charged his heirs to build a hofpital in a certain city, and to employ for this purpofe a certain fum of money; the obligation, which would have for its object the building of the hofpital, would be indivifible. It is to this laft inftance that the law 11, §. 23, ff. *de Leg.* 3, muft be applied. See *Dumoulin*, *p.* 2, *n.* 368 & *seq.*

ARTICLE II.

Of the nature and effect of divisible obligations.

§. I.

General principles.

299. An obligation is called *divisible*, as we have already remarked, not becaufe it is actually divided, but becaufe it may be divided. Therefore, however divifible the thing due may be, the obligation, before the thing has been divided, is indivifible, and cannot be difcharged in parts, as we fhall fee, *infra*, *Part.* 3, *ch.* 1. *art.* 3, §. 2.

It is neceffary then to be careful not to confound what is undivided with what is indivifible. This is the firft key of Dumoulin, *Tract. de Div. & ind. p.* 3, *n*, 7, *& seq. n.* 112.

This division of the obligation takes place on the side of the debtor or on that of the creditor, or sometimes on both together. The obligation is divided on the side of the creditor, when he leaves several heirs. Each of the heirs is creditor only for his part: whence it follows that he can exact the debt only for this part, unless he has authority from his co-heirs to receive their parts. From this it likewise follows that the debtor may pay separately to each of these heirs the parts which are respectively due them.

The obligation is divided likewise on the side of the debtor, when he leaves several heirs: each of the heirs of this debtor is liable for his part only of the debt and, ordinarily, each of the heirs may oblige the creditor to receive the debt for this part.

§. II.

Modifications of the first effect of the division of the obligation on the side of the debtor.

300. The principle which we have established, that in divisible obligations each heir of the debtor is liable only for his part of the debt receives several exceptions and modifications.

The first is in regard to debts with hypothecation. In this case, when the heirs of the debtor are in possession of real estate hypothecated for the debt; although the debt is divided between them, and they are therefore liable to the personal action which results from the obligation of the deceased, only for the part for which they are heirs; yet they may be prosecuted for the whole of this debt, as the possessors of the estate hypothecated to secure it. See what we have said on this subject, in our *Introduction au tit.* 20, *Cout. d'Orleans, ch.* 1, *sect.* 3.

301. The second is in regard to debts of a certain and determinate thing which the deceased has left among other things of his estate. When the deceased has left heirs of different kinds, those who take his acquired property, and those who take that which has descended to him, they are

not all liable for the debt of this determinate thing; the heirs only of the patrimony, of which it makes a part, are liable for it. The reason is that the ancestor would not himself be liable for it, were he still living, unless he continued to possess it, or had ceased by his own act or fault, to possess it. His heirs who succeed to the estate of which the determinate thing does not make part. who have therefore never possessed it, cannot therefore be liable for the debt of this determinate thing, as they could only be liable in the manner in which the deceased whom they represent would have been; the heirs therefore of the patrimony, of which the determinate thing makes part, can alone be liable for it.

But if, by the division between the heirs of this patrimony, this determinate thing due by the deceased, has fallen to the lot of one of them, the others would not therefore be discharged from the debt, even though they have charged the one to whom the determinate thing has fallen, with the payment of the debt when it should become demandable: for having been once liable for this debt, they could not by their own act, in comprising this determinate thing in the mass of property which they have divided, discharge themselves from the obligation to deliver it to the creditor.

302. The third modification is also in regard to debts of a certain and determinate thing. Although the debt of a determinate divisible thing, divides itself between the heirs of the debtor who succeed to the kind of estate of which it makes a part; and although, after the division by which the determinate thing has fallen to the lot of one of them, each of these heirs continues debtor for his part, as we have just seen *supra*; yet he to whom it has fallen, may be prosecuted for the payment of the whole, provided his co-heirs are made parties to the suit, or, if not, provided he had been charged in the division with the payment of the debt.

The reason which Dumoulin renders for this is that, although the action which arises from this debt be divided against each of the heirs of the debtor, yet as the execution muft be made for the whole againft him who has become, by the divifion, the fole poffeffor of the thing, it follows that he may be condemned to the delivery of the thing in the whole; *quia quamvis actio mere sit personalis, tamen executio judicati in rem scripta est, & divisio non debet impedire vim futuri judicii, nec executionem in rem & in ejus possessorem, salvo contra hæredes recursu; Molin, p. 2, n. 84.*

This decifion applies when it is *in his quality of heir*, and by the divifion of the eftate, that this heir of the debtor for a part of the eftate, has come to poffefs the thing due entire. It would be otherwife if it were in his own right t e poffeffed it; he would not in this cafe be the debtor of it, and he could only be condemned to pay the part for which he is heir. An argument in fupport of this may be derived from the law 86, § . 3, ff. *de Leg.* 1, *si fundus ab omnibus hæredibus legatus sit, qui unius hæredis esset; is cujus fundus esset, non amplius quam partem suam præstabit, cæteri in reliquas partes tenebuntur.*

We have juft feen that when the heir for part of the eftate of a debtor of a determinate thing, comes, in this quality of heir, to poffefs the thing entire, he may be condemned to the payment of the whole, provided his co-heirs be parties to the fuit, according to Dumoulin, *ib. n.* 84. This author goes much further, *ib. p.* 3, *n.* 242; for he decides that the heir may be condemned to this, even without making his co-heirs parties to the fuit, when it is evident they could not have any defence. This is decided in the inftance of a feller, who having fold a thing to be delivered in one month, and having received the price, died during the time, leaving feveral heirs: he decides that the fale and the payment of the price being admitted, the heir in whofe poffeffion the thing is, ought, after the expiration of the time, to be condemned to deliver it, without making his co-heirs parties.

303. The fourth modification is when the debt confifts in the fimple reftitution of a thing which belongs to the creditor and is only detained by the debtor. Although the

thing be divisible, and consequently the debt also, yet the heir of the debtor with whom the thing is, is alone liable for the restitution. For example; if one has lent or deposited with you a library, although this debt be divisible, the heir in whose possession it may be, will be liable for the restitution of this library in the whole: *Hæres ejus qui commodatum accepit, pro ea parte qua hæres est, convenitur, nisi forte habuit totius rei facultatem restituendæ, nec faciat; tunc enim condemnatur in solidum, quia hoc boni judicis arbitrio conveniat;* L. 5, §. 3, ff. *Commod.*

The reason is, that as this heir who has the possession of the thing entire, has it in his power to restore it, and has no need for this purpose to wait for the consent of his co-heirs, who have no right in the thing, and to whom the restitution which he may make, cannot be otherwise than advantageous, by discharging them from the obligation in which they are also to restore it; good faith does not permit him to refuse this restitution.

This is intended by the words, *quia hoc boni judicis arbitrio conveniat.* If this heir is liable only for the part for which he is heir, *ex prima and primitiva obligatione depositi aut commodati, quæ dividua est,* he is liable for the whole of this restitution which is in his power, *ex obligatione accessoria præstandi bonam fidem,* the obligation of good faith being an indivisible obligation; *neque enim bona fides potest præstari pro parte.* This is also one of the keys of Dumoulin: *Lex 12 tabularum,* he says, *non dividit obligationes, etiam dividuas, quatenus respiciunt bonam fidem; unde obligatio etiam dividua, ad officium bonæ fidei obligat in solidum, concurrente facultate præstandi, & quatenus concurrit, & quemdocumque hoc contigerit. Molin, p. 3, n.* 112.

304. A fifth modification is that the heir by whose act or fault the thing has perished, is liable for the whole of the debt. The reason is derived from the principle of Dumoulin, that the principal obligation *rem dividuam dandi,* is indeed divisible; but that the accessory obligation *præstandi bonam fidem & diligentiam,* which accompanies it, i indivisi-

ble. Each of the heirs is in this respect bound *in solidum : nec enim pro parte diligentia præstari potest :* whence it follows that the heir who has failed in this, and by whose act or fault the thing has perished, ought to be liable for the whole. According to these principles, if a person has bound himself to suffer me to enjoy an estate, either by a lease or a sale of the use of it, and he has left four heirs ; if one of the heirs, without having any title to this estate in his own right, unjustly disturbs me in the enjoyment of the whole of this estate, he will be liable for the whole damages, and not for part only in the proportion in which he is heir : for although the principal obligation, to suffer me to enjoy, be divisible, the accessory obligation *præstandi bonam fidem*, which is not to oppose any disturbance, is indivisible, and passes consequently to each of the heirs in the whole : thus the heir who contravenes it ought to be liable for the whole damages.

From this principle, that an heir cannot indeed be sued for a divisible debt, for more than the part for which he is heir, when he is sued in his sole capacity of heir and for the act of the ancestor, but that he may be sued for the whole when he is sued for his own act : *multum refert unum hæredum debitoris teneri secundaria obligatione ut hæredem tantum, id est ex facto, vel non facto defuncti tantum ; an vero ut ipsum, id est ex suo facto proprio vel non facto ; Molin, p. 3, n. 5.*

305. In regard to the other heirs who have not concurred by any act or fault of theirs, in the loss of the thing due, they are discharged; for this heir is liable for the debt, in the same manner as the ancestor was The ancestor would have been discharged by the loss of the thing due which had happened without his fault; the heir therefore ought likewise to be discharged by the loss of the thing which has happened without the fault of the ancestor or his own. The heir is indeed liable for the acts of the ancestor, since he succeeds to his obligations; but he is not liable for the act of his co-heirs. This is decided by the law 9 & 10, ff, *Depos. In depositi actione, si de facto defuncti agatur, adversus unum ex pluribus hæredibus pro parte hæreditaria*

agere debeo; si vero ex suo delicto, pro parte non ago; merito, quia estimatio refertur ad dolum quem in solidum ipse admisit, nec adversus cohæredes qui dolo carent, actio competit. Paul decides the ſame thing in the loan to uſe; L. 17, §. 2, *Commod. Molin. p.* 3, *n.* 439 & 440.

If a penalty had been ſtipulated in caſe the thing ſhould not be reſtored; in this caſe, although it had periſhed by the fault of one of them, and without the act or fault of the others, they would, not the leſs, be liable for the penalty, for their reſpective parts. For the obligation to pay the ſum ſtipulated in the penalty, is a ſecond obligation which the anceſtor contracted, and which is conditional; it has for condition the inexecution of the firſt.

The heirs of the deceaſed have each, to the amount of the part for which they are heirs, ſucceeded to this ſecond obligation under the ſame condition: they are therefore liable, each for their part in the eſtate, to pay this ſum on the accompliſhment of the condition, which is to ſay, in caſe the firſt obligation be not performed, whether by the act or fault of the anceſtor, or by that of one of his heirs; ſaving their recourſe againſt the heir by whoſe act or fault the thing has periſhed. This is taught by Dumoulin, who ſays that the co-heirs of him by whoſe act the thing has periſhed, are liable in this caſe for the penalty, *non immediate ex facto & culpa dolosi, sed ejus occasione & tanquam ex eventu conditionis, ex obligatione defuncti quæ in eos sub ea conditione descendit;* Molin. *d. n.* 443.

This is the caſe which Paul intends to ſpeak of in the law 44, §. 5, ff. *Fam. ercisc.*, when he ſays, *Si reliqui propter factum unius teneri cæperint, tanquam conditio stipulationis hæreditariæ extiterit habebunt familiæ erciscundæ judicium cum eo propter quem commissa sit stipulatio.*

Obſerve that in order that the contravention by one of the heirs may prejudice the others, it is neceſſary that there ſhould have been a ſecond expreſs agreement; by which the anceſtor bound himſelf for the payment of a certain penalty in caſe of the inexecution of the principal obligation, or by which he bound himſelf for the damages in caſe of a contravention by himſelf *or his heirs*. But it does not ſuffice that it be ſaid at the end of the inſtrument that the parties have all bound themſelves for its contents under the penalty of all coſts and damages; for this clauſe does not include a ſecond obligation: *Hæc clausula nihil novi addit, cum sit ex stylo communi ad confirmandam tantum, secundum materiam subjectam, & ejus limites; ib.* 442.

It will perhaps be ſaid againſt the diſtinction of Dumoulin, that in all agreements which contain a principal obligation, a ſecond obligation muſt always be implied as acceſſory to the firſt, by which the debtor binds himſelf for the damages in caſe of a contravention, by himſelf or by his heirs, of the principal obligation; that this ſecond implied agreement muſt have the ſame effect as if it had been expreſſed. The anſwer is that it is not true that this ſecond agreement ought to be implied when it is not expreſſed. If the debtor who contravenes his principal obligation, is liable for the damages reſulting from his contravention, it is not from any ſecond implied agreement by which he ſubmitted to theſe damages; it is ſolely becauſe this obligation of damages is included in the principal obligation, and this principal obligation, *ex propria natura*, is converted, againſt the debtor, into an obligation of damages. But in this caſe, when it is one of the heirs of the debtor, who has contravened the obligation, the other heirs who have not contravened it, are not liable for any damages; theſe heirs being liable indeed for the acts of their anceſtor and for their own but not for thoſe of their co-heir, as we have before obſerved.

306. When the thing has periſhed by the act or fraud of ſeveral of the heirs, each of them is liable *in solidum*: *Nec enim*, ſays Dumoulin, *qui peccavit, ex eo relevari debet, quod peccati habet consortem*.

If, however, theſe heirs had, each by a particular act, deſtroyed or diverted different parts of the thing due, each would be liable only for the particular loſs which he occaſioned; for in this caſe, *unusquisque non in solidum, sed in parte duntaxat dolum admisit*; this is what Marcellus decides in the law 22, §. *Deposit. Si duo hæredes rem apud defunctum depositam dolo intervenerint, quodam casu in partes duntaxat tenebuntur; nam si diviserunt decem millia, quæ apud defunctum fuerant, & quina millia singuli abstulerint, & uterque solvendo est, in partes adstricti erunt: quod si quæ species dolo eorum interversa fuerit, in solidum conveniri poterunt; nam certe verum est in solidum quemque dolo fecisse.*

Obſerve in regard to the firſt inſtance in the law 22, that it is ſaid, *si uterque solvendo est*; for if one of the two heirs had been inſolvent, the one who was ſolvent, would have been in fault, not only with regard to his half, but even with regard to the other half, as he ought not to have divided the ſum given to the anceſtor in depoſit, with his inſolvent co-heir. If the obligation to reſtore the ſum was a diviſible obligation, the acceſſory obligation to keep and preſerve it with good faith, was an indiviſible obligation, for the whole of which each was liable, and which the ſolvent heir has contravened, not only with regard to the half which he ought to have paid, but alſo with regard to the other half which he abandoned to his inſolvent co-heir.

307. A ſixth exception is that, although an obligation be diviſible, one of the heirs of the debtor may be chargeable with the whole, either by an agreement, or by the teſtament of the deceaſed who may have ſo charged him, or by the act of the Judge who makes the diviſion of the eſtate. In all theſe caſes, one of the heirs is liable for the whole of the debt, without the other heirs ceaſing to be liable each for their part.

308. There reſults from all theſe modifications, *ut aliud est unum ex pluribus sive principalibus sive hæredibus teneri in solidum, aliud obligationem esse individuam.* This is the third key of Dumoulin, *part.* 3, *n.* 112.

309. Excepting theſe caſes, each heir of the debtor is liable for diviſible debts only in the proportion in which he is heir; and he is not liable even ſubſidiarily for the ſurplus, in caſe of the inſolvency of his co-heirs. The law 2, *Cod. de*

Hered. act., which decides that each heir is liable only for his part of the debts of the anceſtor, does not diſtinguiſh whether all the heirs are ſolvent or not. It is derived from the very idea of an heir, who is one that ſucceeds to the rights active and paſſive, which is to ſay, the debts and obligations of the anceſtor. He who is heir for a part only, ſucceeds only for this part; he is therefore chargeable only with this part. The inſolvency of his co-heirs which happens, does not render him ſucceſſor to all the rights of the anceſtor; he continues heir for his part only and conſequently ought to be liable only for his part of the debts.

It is ſaid that as the debts are a charge upon the eſtate, they ought to be diſcharged in the whole, from the eſtate which this heir for part retains. The anſwer is, that the whole of the eſtate is charged with the whole of the debts; but the parts of this whole of the eſtate are charged only with the like parts of the debts. It is inſiſted, that if the debtor had diſſipated the half of his eſtate, the other half which ſhould remain, would be chargeable with the whole of the debts: therefore when one of the heirs of the debtor has diſſipated his half, the other half, which belongs to the other heir, ought likewiſe to be charged with the whole of the debts. I deny the conſequence. When the debtor has diſſipated the half of his eſtate, that which remains is the whole eſtate of the perſon bound for the whole of the debts, and conſequently the whole of the debts is a proper charge on what remains of the eſtate; but when my co-heir has diſſipated the half which has fallen to him, that which I have is only the portion of an heir for half, who is perſonally liable for the debts to the amount of this half: this portion ought not therefore to be charged with more than the half of the debts. It is further inſiſted that the creditor ought not to ſuffer from the number of heirs the debtor leaves: therefore the diſſipation of half of the eſtate, by one of the heirs, ought not to ſubject him to loſe the half of his debt; ſince if the debtor or his ſole heir had deſtroyed this half of the eſtate, the creditor would loſe nothing of his debt. The anſwer to this is, that it is only *ex accidenti* that the creditor suffers in this case from the number of heirs which the debtor leaves: he might have avoided any loss, by attaching the estate before the division, or otherwise using more diligence in causing himself to be paid.

This decision, that the heir for part is not liable for the debts for the parts of his co-heirs who have become insolvent, although his part should be more than sufficient to pay the whole, being derived from principles of natural reason and from the nature of the very quality of an heir, it ought to apply in *foro conscientiæ* as well as in *foro legis*; *Molin. part.* 2, *n.* 82.

310. This principle, that an heir is not liable for the insolvency of his co-heirs, admits of several exceptions. The first, which is attended with no difficulty, is when it is by the act and fraud of one heir that the creditor has not been able to cause himself to be paid by the other heirs who have become insolvent; *puta*, when this heir has pretended to be the sole heir. *Molin. ib. n.* 85, *in fine.*

Dumoulin adduces a second exception, which is, when a father should leave two sons his heirs, one of whom had wasted beforehand what he received of the estate in advancement, and to whom, by reason of the account he would have to render, there would come, of the active property of the estate of the father, much less than the part of the debts of this estate for which he would be liable in acceding to the succession. The other son ought to answer in this case to the creditors of the estate for the part of the debts for which his insolvent brother is liable, although the creditors have not had the precaution to attach the property of the estate before the division. The reason is, that as this son has received almost all the active property of the estate of the deceased, by means of the account which his brother had to render for what he received in the life-time of the father, it is just that he should not profit, at the expence of the creditors of the estate, by the improper accession of his brother to the inheritance: there is room in this case to presume a collusion between the two brothers, and that it was with a view to discharge himself from a part of the debts and thereby to defraud the creditors, that the solvent heir has induced his insolvent brother to accede to the succession: *Hoc est injustum*, says Dumoulin, *nec suspicione collusionis vacat. ib. n.* 93, *in fine.*

This author, *n.* 92, adduces a third exception, which is when the creditor had made a loan to the ancestor which was the cause of his fortune: in this case the solvent heir being in a manner indebted to the creditor for his part in the inheritance of a valuable estate, ought not to suffer the creditor to lose the part of this debt for which his insolvent co-heir is liable. This decision admits of much objection; Gratitude indeed requires this; but gratitude produces only imperfect obligations, which are not binding *in foro legis*.

§. III.

Of the second effect of the division of the debt which is that it may be paid in parts.

311. We have seen that one of the effects of the division of the debt, whether it be on the side of the creditor or on that of the debtor, is that the payment of the debt may be made in parts; viz. in the parts which are due to each of the heirs of the creditor, and in those due by each of the heirs of the debtor. This principle has also its exceptions and modifications, *non propter individuitatem obligationis, sed propter incongruitatem solutionis*, says Dumoulin; which is to say, not because the partial payment of a divisible obligation is not always, absolutely speaking, possible; for since the thing due has parts, it is a necessary consequence that it may be paid in parts; but if the payment of these obligations sometimes ought not to be made in parts, it it is because a partial payment is not always equitable: *Aliud quippe individuitas obligationis, aliud incongruitas solutionis.* This is a fourth key of Dumoulin, *part.* 3, *n.* 112.

312. The first case in which the partial payment of a debt, although divisible, is not valid, is the case of debts in an alternative, or of things indeterminate. For example; if he who is debtor of a certain house *or the sum of* 10,000

livres, leaves two heirs, one of the heirs will not be admitted to pay the half of one of these two things until the other heir pays also the other half of the same thing: for if one of the heirs had paid the half, for example, of the house, and the other wished to pay the half of the money, there would result a prejudice to the creditor, who is entitled to receive one of the two things entire, and not two halves of two different things. For the same reason, although indeed the creditor had voluntarily received the half of one of the two things, *puta*, the half of the money, this payment would not receive its perfection even for this half, until the other half should be paid him; and if afterwards, the house should be given in payment, there would be room to claim back what had been paid in money. *Infra, Part.* 3. *n.* 525.

It is the same of debts of things indeterminate; as if the ancestor owed indeterminately an acre of land, one of his heirs is not admitted to offer to the creditor the half of a certain acre of land, until the other heir gives also in payment the other half of the same acre: otherwise there would result a prejudice to the creditor, to whom there is due an entire acre, and who has an interest in receiving an entire acre rather than the half of two different acres. This results from the law 85, §. 4, & L. 2, §. 2, ff. *pe Verb. oblig. Molin. part.* 2, *n.* 125.

This indivision of payment must apply, not only when the debt has been divided on the side of the debtor, but also when it has been divided on that of the creditor, who has left several heirs; for it is the interest of these heirs of the creditor to receive a single thing that is their due, which would be in common only with themselves, rather than the parts of different things which they would each have in common with strangers. *Molin. ib. part.* 2, *n.* 130.

When one of the heirs of the debtor has been discharged for his part of the debt, whether by the release which the creditor has given him, or otherwise, nothing prevents the other heir from paying the half which he owes in either of the things he pleases; *d. L.* 2, §. 3. The reason which prevents the partial payment, ceafes; for there is no room to apprehend that the payment would be made in parts of different things.

Obferve that in the text cited, after the words, *si tamen hominem stipulatus, cum uno ex hæredibus egero*, it is neceffary to add, *& victus fuero per injuriam judicis.* See *Cuj. ad. l. Molin. ib. ch.* 2, *n.* 188.

Obferve alfo that the indivifion of the payment of a debt in an alternative ceafes to apply, when this debt, by the extinction of one of the two things, ceafes to be in an alternative, and becomes determinate in the thing which remains: nothing here prevents this thing from being payable in parts, whether by the different heirs of the debtor, or to the different heirs of the creditor.

313. The fecond cafe in which the payment of an obligation, although divifible and divided among feveral heirs of the creditor, cannot be made in parts, is when it is fo agreed in contracting the obligation, or fince. It might, however, be doubted whether this agreement is valid; for the law 56, ff. 1, *de Verb. oblig.*, decides that a perfon cannot, in contracting, caufe one of his heirs to be bound for more of his debt than in the proportion in which he fhall be heir. *Te & Titium hæredem tuum decem daturum spondes: Titii persona supervacue comprehensa est; sive enim solus hæres extiterit, in solidum tenebitur; sive pro parte, eodem modo quo cæteri cohæredes ejus.* That is to fay that he fhall be bound, notwithftanding this ftipulation, for the part only for which he may be heir: and the reafon is that being heir of the contracting party only for this part, and confequently a ftranger in regard to the other parts, he cannot be bound for the other parts by the promife of the contracting party, according to the rule of law, *Nemo nisi de se promittere potest, non de extraneo.*

Notwithftanding this, Dumoulin properly decides that one may validly agree that a debt may be difcharged in parts by the different heirs of the debtor; and he very juftly remarks that this agreement differs widely from that in the

the inſtance in the law above quoted, which relates to the ſubſtance of the obligation, while this agreement relates only to the manner in which the payment is to be made: *Non concernit substantiam obligationis sed modum; unde quemadmodum potest in prajudicium haredum determinari locus & tempus solutionis, ita & modus; Molin. ib. part.* 2, *n.* 30 & 31. This agreement does not prevent one of the heirs of the debtor from being bound only for his part of the debt; but the effect is that he may make the payment only in the entire thing, jointly with his co-heirs; ſo that the offer which he ſhould make, to give his part, would be inſufficient to diſcharge, even for his part, the obligation for which he is liable, if his co-heirs do not equally offer their part. See *infra, n.* 316.

314. This agreement that the debt ſhall not be paid in parts, prevents indeed the heirs of the debtor from paying it in parts; but it does not prevent it from being payable in parts to the different heirs of the creditor.

The debtor cannot indeed validly pay to either of them but for his part; and if he ſhould pay the whole to one of them, he would not be diſcharged from the claim of the others.

Yet it may alſo be agreed that one of the heirs of the creditor ſhall have power to exact the whole, and that the payment of the whole may be made to him; in which caſe the payment made to him diſcharges the debtor towards all the heirs of the creditor, in regard to whom he who received the payment is as an agent for their parts, or as *adjectus solutionis gratia; Molin. ib. n.* 33.

315. The third caſe in which the debt, although divided between the heirs of the debtor, ought not to be diſcharged in parts, is when, without there having been any agreement, it reſults from the nature of the engagement, or from the thing which is the object of it, or from the end propoſed in the making of the contract, that the intention of the parties was really that the debt ſhould not be diſcharged in parts. This is eaſily preſumed when the thing which makes

the object of the agreement, is susceptible, indeed, of ideal parts and is therefore divisible, but cannot be divided into actual parts. *Molin. part.* 3, *n.* 223.

This is presumed even in regard to the things which may be divided into actual parts, when they cannot be divided without a prejudice resulting to the creditor.

For example. If I have purchased or leased a certain plantation; although this plantation be susceptible of parts, yet one of the heirs of him who sold or leased it to me, would not be admitted to offer me his undivided or divided part of this estate, in order to discharge himself from his obligation to me, unless his co-heirs were likewise, on their side, ready to deliver me theirs; because the division of this plantation would occasion me a prejudice, I purchased or leased it only with a view to have and use it in the whole, and I would not have purchased or leased it in part.

The end which the contracting parties had in view may also prevent the payment from being made in part, even of a debt of a sum of money. For example; if by a composition you have obliged yourself to pay me the sum of one thousand crowns, it being declared that it was to procure my liberation from prison, in which I was detained for the said sum by a creditor, and afterwards you should die, leaving four heirs; one of these heirs would not be admitted to offer me separately the fourth part of this sum, which could not procure the liberation of my person and which I could not safely keep in the prison while waiting for the surplus, *Molin. part.* 2, *n.* 40.

316. In all the cases above adduced, in which an obligation, although divisible in itself, cannot however be discharged in parts, the creditor cannot, indeed, put the heirs of his debtor in arrear without making his demand against all; the demand which he might make against one of them to pay him the whole, would not be valid and would not put him in arrear, since, as the obligation is divisible, he does not owe it in the whole; but although one of the heirs is debtor only for the part for which he is heir, and cannot be sued for the whole, yet the indivision of the payment

prevents him from validly tendering the part for which he is debtor, unlefs the furplus is tendered at the fame time by his co-heirs; therefore fuch partial offers not only do not put the creditor in arrear of receiving and do not ftop the intereft, if the debt is of a nature to produce any, but if the heir who has made thefe offers, had been before put in arrear by a demand made on all the heirs, thefe imperfect effers would not cure his arrear, nor prevent him from being fubject, with regard to the creditor, to all the confequences of his arrear; faving his recourfe againft his co-heirs. *Molin. p.* 2, *n.* 243.

Obferve that an annuity which is not accompanied with hypothecation, divides itfelf among the heirs of the debtor as do other debts: each of the heirs is bound to continue it and pay the arrearages only in the proportion in which he is heir: but the right to redeem it under which it was contracted, is not divided. We have treated of this fubject in our *Traite du Cont. de Const. de Rente. ch.* 7, *art.* 3. 'See *Dumoulin, Tract. de Div. & ind. p.* 2, *n.* 207, 209; *& p.* 3, *n.* 23, *& seq.*

§. IV.

Of the case in which the division of the debt takes place, as well on the side of the creditor as on that of the debtor.

317. When the debt has become divided as well on the fide of the creditor as on that of the debtor, *puta*, if the creditor has left four heirs, and the debtor has likewife left four; each of the heirs of the debtor, who, by the divifion on the fide of the debtor, is bound only for the fourth of the debt, may pay feparately, and for the fourth only of which he is debtor, the fourth part that is due to each of the heirs of the creditor; which is to fay, he may pay to each of them the fourth of a fourth, or fixteenth of the whole.

§. V.

Whether the reunion of the parts either of the heirs of the creditor, or of the heirs of the debtor, in a single person, destroys the right to pay in parts.

318. The decifion of this queftion depends on fol-

lowing principle. The divifion of the debt, which takes place by the death of the creditor or debtor who leaves feveral heirs, does not make feveral debts of one; but it only affigns to each of the heirs, whether of the creditor or of the debtor, parts of this debt, which before had no parts, but was only fufceptible of them. In this alone it is that this divifion confifts: there ftill is but a fingle debt, *unum debitum:* the law 9, ff. *de Pact.* fays this in formal terms. In fact, the different heirs of the creditor are creditors only of the debt which was contracted to their anceftor; the different heirs of the debtor are debtors only of that which was contracted by their anceftor. There is ftill, therefore, but one debt: but this debt which was undivided and had no parts, while there was only one perfon who was debtor, and one only who was creditor, now comes to have parts and to be due in parts, whether to each of the heirs of the creditor or by each of the heirs of the debtor. It is in this that the divifion confifts.

From this principle is derived the decifion of the queftion: the parts of the debt, in which this divifion confifts, being produced by the number of perfons to whom the debt is due when the creditor has left feveral heirs, or by the number of perfons by whom the debt is due, when the debtor has left feveral, it follows that when this number of perfons ceafes, there ceafes to be parts in the debt; *cessante causa, cessat effectus;* and confequently the divifion of the debt ceafes, and it can no longer be paid in parts.

If, then, a debtor or a creditor has left feveral heirs, and one of them has himfelf become the fole heir of all the others, the debt will ceafe to be payable in parts; becaufe there being now but one creditor and one debtor of the debt, there are no longer parts in the debt.

In vain is it faid that the debtor, having once acquired the right to pay in parts, when the creditor has left feveral heirs, cannot afterwards lofe it; that the obligation in which each of the heirs of the creditor was to receive his part feparately, muft pafs to the furviving heir, who has fucceeded to all the obligations of the preceding heirs. This would be true, if this right to pay in parts were intrinfically inherent in the obligation, and did not on the contrary depend folely on the extrinfic circumftance of the number of perfons to whom or by whom the debt is due: this circumftance ceafing, its effect muft therefore ceafe. See *Dumoulin, p. 2, n. 18, & seq.*

This decifion does not apply when the furvivor of feveral heirs of a debtor has fucceeded indeed to the inheritance of his predeceffors, but with the benefit of inventory; for this manner of inheriting, prev enting the confufion of the beneficiary inheritance with the proper eftate of the heir, prevents alfo a reunion of the parts of the debt. The furvivor owes feparately and in different *rights the part of the* debt for which he is liable on his own account, and that for which he is liable as beneficiary heir of his former coheirs, fince he is liable for the firft in his proper eftate and for the laft only in the beneficiary eftate of his former coheirs. Being therefore liable for thefe different parts of the debt feparately and in different rights, it is a natural confequence that he may pay them feparately. This is the opinion of Dumoulin, *p.* 2, *n.* 22.

319. The reunion of the parts of the heirs of the creditor in a fingle perfon, deftroys the right to pay in parts, in whatever manner this reunion may take place, not only when one of the heirs has become the heir of all the others, but alfo when he has acquired by ceffion the rights of all the others.

Quid, if there was no ceffion, could one of the heirs who had only a power of attorney from all the other co-heirs to demand the debt, or a third perfon who had this power from all, refufe to receive the payment in parts? It feems he could not; for there is not in this cafe a reunion. There are in *reality feveral perfons* to each *of whom the debt is* due in part, and confequently it feems that the debt may be paid in parts: notwithftanding this, Dumoulin, *p.* 2, *n.* 25, decides that this attorney of all the heirs may refufe to receive the payment of the debt in parts. This is his reason. As, when the debt is divided between the heirs of the debtor, this divifion is made for the benefit of thefe heirs, in order that they may be liable for the debt only in the proportion in which they are heirs, and may be difcharged on paying their parts; fo, when the debt is divided between the heirs of the creditor, the divifion in this cafe is made only for the benefit of the heirs of the creditor, in order that each may demand and receive his part without being obliged to wait for his co-heirs to demand or receive theirs. Thefe co-heirs of the creditor may therefore forbear to ufe this right that is derived from the divifion of the debt, which is only in their favor, according to this rule of law, *Unicuique liberum est juri in favorem suum introducto renuntiare;* and confequently he who has from all the heirs a power to receive the debt, may refufe to receive it in parts.

320. All we have hitherto faid applies when the parts of feveral heirs of a creditor or debtor unite in the fame perfon. It is different when a debt has been contracted at firft to two creditors or by two debtors, not *in solidum*, but for their feveral parts. In this cafe there are two debts truly diftinct and feparate; and they do not ceafe to be fo, although one of the two creditors or one of the two debtors may have fucceeded to the other: therefore the right to pay them feparately muft continue. *Molin. ib. n.* 29.

§. VI.

The difference between the debt of several determinate things, and that of several indeterminate things, with regard to the manner in which they are divided.

321. When the debt of feveral determinate things, *puta*, of one determinate acre of land, and of another determinate acre, and the debt comes to be divided, *puta*, by the death of the creditor, who has left two heirs, the divifion takes place *in partes singularum rerum*. The debtor does not owe one of the two acres to one of the heirs, and the other acre to the other heir; but he owes to each of the heirs the half of each acre; faving to thefe heirs the divifion.

It is otherwise when the debt is of two indeterminate things; *puta*, if, in the instance proposed, the debtor owed, not a determinate acre, but two acres indeterminately. In this case he would owe to each of the heirs of the creditor one acre, and not the half of two. The division does not take place *in partes singularum rerum*, but numerally: *numero dividit obligatio*. This is the decision of the law 54, ff. *de Verb. oblig.*; & 29, ff. *de Solut.*

ARTICLE III.

Of the nature and effect of indivisible obligations.

§. I.

General principles respecting the nature of indivisible obligations.

322. An indivisible obligation being the obligation of a thing or act which is not susceptible of actual or of ideal parts, it is a necessary consequence that when two or more persons have contracted a debt of this kind, although they have not contracted it *in solidum & tanquam correi debendi*, yet each of them is debtor for the whole thing or act which is the object of the obligation; for he cannot be debtor of it for a part only, since it is premised that this thing or act is not susceptible of parts.

For the same reason when the person who has contracted a like debt, has left several heirs, each of the heirs is debtor for the whole of the thing, as he cannot be debtor for a part of what is not susceptible of parts. *Ea quæ in partes dividi non possunt, solida a singulis heredibus debentur*; L. 192, ff. *de Reg. jur.*

Likewise, when the creditor of a like debt has left several heirs, the thing is due in the whole to each of the heirs; as it cannot be due in parts, since it is not susceptible of parts.

323. In this the indivisibility of obligation differs from the quality of the obligation *in solidum*: but it differs principally in this that in the indivisibility of obligation, that which makes each of the debtors debtor for the whole pro-

ceeding from the nature of the thing due, which is not susceptible of parts, this indivisibility is an actual property of the obligation, which passes with this property to the heirs and which makes each of the heirs of the debtor debtor for the whole. On the contrary, the quality of the obligation *in solidum*, proceeding from the act of the persons who have bound themselves each for the whole, is a personal quality which does not prevent this obligation *in solidum* from dividing itself between the heirs of each of the debtors *in solidum* who have contracted it, and between the heirs of the creditor to whom it has been contracted. This is perfectly explained by Dumoulin with his usual clearness: *In correis credendi vel debendi qualitas distributiva seu multiplicativa solidi, personalis est, & non transit in hærede nec ad hæredes, inter quos active nec passive dividitur; sed qualitas solidi in individuis realis est, quia non personis, ut illa correorum; sed obligationi ipsi & rei debitæ adhæret, & transit ad hæredes, & in singulorum hæredum hæredes singulos in solidum*, p. 2, n. 222.

324. Hence arises another difference between the indivisibility of the obligation and its quality *in solidum*. As the latter does not proceed from the nature of the thing due, but from the personal act of the creditors who have each contracted the whole obligation, these co-debtors are not only debtors of the thing for the whole, but they are debtors of it *totaliter*. Although the primitive obligation which they have contracted *in solidum*, becomes converted, by its inexecution, into a secondary obligation, they are bound *in solidum* for this secondary obligation as they were for the primitive. For example, if two masons had obliged themselves *in solidum* to build me a house within a certain time; in case of the inexecution of this primitive obligation they will each be bound *in solidum* for the obligation of damages into which the primitive obligation is converted.

On the contrary, when the obligation is not *in solidum*, but indivisible, as when several persons have obliged themselves, not *in solidum*, for something indivisible; in this case, the indivisibility proceeding only from the nature of the thing due, which is not susceptible of parts, the debtors of such an obligation are, indeed, each debtors for the whole, as they cannot be debtors of a thing in parts which is not susceptible of parts; *singuli solidum debent;* but not having obliged themselves *in solidum, non debent totaliter. Aliud est,* says Dumoulin, *p.* 3, *n.* 112, *quem teneri ad totum, aliud totaliter.* Being debtors for the whole only from the nature of the thing due, which is not susceptible of parts; when the primitive obligation becomes converted into the secondary obligation of a thing divisible, these debtors will be liable each for their part only. For example. If two masons have bound themselves, not *in solidum,* to build me a house; although they are each liable for the whole of the primitive obligation, because it has for its object an act which is not susceptible of parts; yet in case of the inexecution of this obligation, they would be liable each only for their part of the secondary obligation of damages into which the primitive obligation is converted; because these damages consist in a sum of money which is divisible. It results from this, *ut longe aliud est plures teneri ad idem in solidum, & aliud obligationem esse individuam.* This is another key of Dumoulin, *ibid.*

The same must be said in regard to several creditors, or several heirs of a creditor of a thing indivisible. They are creditors of the whole, *singulis solidum debetur;* but they are not so *totaliter,* as are creditors *in solidum,* who are called *correi debendi; & aliud est pluribus deberi idem in solidum, aliud obligationem esse individuam.* This will be explained *in decursu* in the following paragraphs.

325. From this principle, *aliud est debere totum, aliud est debere totaliter,* it follows that an indivisible obligation is, not the less, susceptible of deduction. For example, if my relation to whom I have succeeded, has charged me with a right of way to Peter over my land, and there remains of the estate, after the debts are paid, only the sum of 200 livres, and this right of way is worth 300 livres; although this charge and the obligation resulting therefrom are indivisible, and the right of way which is the object thereof are

alfo indivifible, yet, as I am not bound by this obligation *totaliter*, but only to the amount of the 200 livres which remain of the eftate, this charge and this obligation, although indivifible, are fufceptible of deduction, not indeed with regard to the thing itfelf which is not fufceptible of parts, but with regard to its value; therefore I would owe to Peter a right of way entire, but with this modification that he could not require it without allowing me the fum which it is worth beyond the 200 livres, to which amount alone I am liable for the difpofition of the teftator; *Arg. l.* 76, ff. *de Leg.* 2.

§. II.

Of the effect of the indivisibility of the obligation in dando aut in faciendo, *with regard to the heirs of the creditor.*

326. When the obligation is indivifible, each heir of the creditor being creditor of the whole thing, it refults that each of the heirs may demand the whole thing from the debtor.

For example; if one has bound himfelf to give me, for the benefit of my land, a right of way over his, or procure it through fome other adjoining; this right being indivifible, each of my heirs may demand from the debtor the whole; L. 2, §. 2, ff. *de Verb. oblig.*

Likewife, if one has obliged himfelf to me to make a picture, or build a houfe, each of my heirs may demand from him that he make the picture or build the houfe entire.

But as each of my heirs, although creditor of the whole thing, is not however creditor *totaliter*; if, on the demand of the whole thing, by one of my heirs, the debtor, failing to perform his obligation, be condemned to the damages, he will not be liable to this heir for more than the part for which he is heir; for, although creditor of the whole thing, he is neverthelefs creditor as my heir only for part. If he has a right to demand the whole thing, it is becaufe the thing cannot be demanded in part, not being fufceptible of parts: but the obligation of this indivifible thing converting itfelf, by the failure of the debtor, into an obligation of damages, which is divisible, my heir for part cannot claim, of these damages, more than for his part; L. 25, §. 9, ff. *Fam. ercisc.*

In this the heirs of the creditor of an indivisible debt are different from creditors *in solidum* who are called *correi credendi.* Each of these being creditor not only of the whole thing due, but being so *totaliter;* if, on the demand of the creditor, the debtor does not perform his obligation, he may be condemned towards him for the damages in the whole.

327. From this, that the heir for part of an indivisible debt, although creditor of the whole thing, is not so however *totaliter*, it follows also that he cannot release the debt for the whole as a creditor *in solidum* could. L. 10, §. 12, ff. *de Accept.*

Therefore if the creditor of an indivisible debt left two heirs, and one of them has released to the debtor his interest in the debt, the debtor will not be discharged from the other. Yet the release will have its effect. The other heir may, indeed, demand from the debtor the thing entire; but he can only demand it on offering to allow one half of the value of this thing; for the thing due, although indivisible in itself, has however a value, which is divisible, and which may, in this case, be resorted to: this is a modification which the indivisibility of the debt in this case admits of.

It would not be sufficient for the debtor to offer to him who has not released his right, the half of the price of the thing due: for this heir is creditor of the thing itself, and his co-heir, in releasing his own right, could not prejudice that of this heir. This is taught by Dumoulin, *Tract. de Div. & ind. p. 3, n. 189. Stipulator servitutis reliquit duos hæredes, quorum unus accepto fecit promissori ..... debet alteri hæredum totam servitutem, sed non totaliter, utpote deducenda æstimatione dimidiæ partis ..... sed cujus est electio? Breviter dico creditoris, videlicet alterius hæredis, quia cohæres etiam vendendo & pretium recipiendo, nocere non potuit, nisi in refusio-*

ne pretii, si hic hæres noluit jus suum vendere; igitur gratis remittendo non potest in plus nocere.

328. The fame principle muft apply when the debtor has become the heir of the creditor for half; the other may demand from him the thing entire, on offering to allow him the half of the value.

329. All that we have faid of the feveral heirs of the creditor of an indivifible debt, applies in regard to the feveral creditors not *in solidum*, to whom a like debt may have been contracted.

§. III.

Of the effect of indivisible obligations in dando aut faciendo, *with regard to the heirs of the debtor.*

330. When the debt is indivifible, each of the heirs of the debtor being debtor for the whole thing, it refults that a demand may be made on each of the heirs for the whole thing: but as he is not debtor of it *totaliter*, but only as heir in part of the debtor and conjointly with his co-heirs, it follows that, on being fued, he may demand a time to call in his co-heirs, and that he cannot be condemned alone except on his failing to call them in to be made parties with him. Dumoulin grounds this decifion upon the law 11, §. 23, ff. *de Leg.* 3, *Si in opere civitatis faciendo relictum sit, unumquemque hæredem in solidum teneri D. Marcus & Verus Proculæ rescripserunt: tempus tamen cohæredi Proculæ, quem Proculà vocari desideravit, ut secum curaret opus fieri, præstiterunt, intra quod mittat ad opus faciendum, postquam solam Proculam voluerunt facere, imputaturum sumptum cohæredi.* Dumoulin, *p.* 3, *n.* 90 & 104; & *p.* 2, *n.* 469, & *seq.*

331. Further, when the heir who is fued by the creditor of an indivifible debt, is heir only for a fmall part, and there is another heir for a much greater part; *puta*, if, in fome cuftomary provinces, a creditor has fued a younger brother who is heir only for a fmall part, the eldeft being principal heir; in this cafe the heir who is fued may not only afk a time to bring in his co-heir, but may require that the creditor fhall proceed againft the principal heir,

the younger brother offering to pay his part. *Molin. ib. n.* 105.

352. Further, as to the effect of the indivifible obligation *in dando vel in faciendo*, with regard to the heirs of the debtor, three cafes are to be diftinguifhed, according to Dumoulin. This debt is either of a nature that it may be difcharged only by the heir of the debtor who is fued; or it is of a nature that it may be difcharged feparately, either by him who is fued or by each of his co-heirs; or it is of a nature that it may be difcharged only by them all jointly.

We may adduce, as an example of the firft cafe, the debt of a right of way, which the anceftor promifed to grant over a piece of land, that has fallen by the divifion to one of his heirs. It is this heir alone, to whom the land has fallen in the divifion, who can difcharge this debt; becaufe fuch a right can be granted only by the owner of the land. In this cafe he will alone be condemned to grant it, by a judgment, which, on his failure to do fo, will be equivalent to the deed by which he ought to grant it: *Molin. p.* 3, *n.* 100. faving to him his recourfe or indemnity againft his co-heirs if he was not charged, by the divifion, with the grant of this right.

353. We may adduce, as a firft example of the fecond cafe, the debt of a fimilar right, which the anceftor bound himfelf to procure to another over the land of a third perfon. The thing, which is the object of this obligation, is an indivifible thing, and which in its nature may be difcharged feparately by each of the heirs of the debtor. For it is in the power of each of them, at leaft *natura*, to treat with the owner of the land over which this anceftor engaged to procure this right. The creditor will then be entitled to demand this right of way for the whole from each of the heirs of the debtor. For this right, being indivifible, each is liable for the whole debt. But as this heir, though debtor of this right for the whole, is not however bound for it *totaliter*, and as he is bound jointly with his co-heirs,

he may ask a delay to bring them into court, that they may jointly with him procure to the creditor the right which is due him; otherwise, that they be all condemned to the damages of the creditor, and being all condemned thereto, they will be liable, each for his part only; because this obligation of damages is divisible.

If he neglects to call in his co-heirs and have them made parties, he will be condemned alone to procure to the plaintiff the right which was promised him by the ancestor; and on failure will alone be condemned to the damages: saving his recourse against his co-heirs. *Molin. p.* 2, *n.* 175. For having neglected to bring them in, he ought alone to suffer the condemnation. He is bound in this case, *quasi ex facto proprio*; having alone submitted to the suit, & *non tantum quasi hæres.*

Observe that this judgment for damages ought to be given, although the heirs of him who promised this right, should be ready to purchase it from the owner of the land on which it was to be given, and this owner would not grant it on any terms. For as we have seen before, it suffices that what was promised be possible in itself, although it was not in the power of the ancestor who promised it or of his heirs, for the obligation to be valid, and to give a claim, in case of its inexecution, for damages. He who contracted the obligation ought to impute it to his own folly that he unadvisedly promised to procure it to be done by this third person.

A second example is the obligation I have contracted to another to build him a house on his land. This obligation is indivisible: the creditor may sue each of my heirs and demand that they be condemned to build the house entire. But as each heir, although bound for the building of the whole house, is not however debtor *in solidum*, he may require that his co-heirs be brought in, and this being done, on their failure to perform the obligation, they will be condemned to damages, each in the proportion of his part in the inheritance.

Thofe who were ready to concur will be condemned as well as thofe who refuſed; faving their recourſe againſt the latter: becauſe each is bound to build the whole houſe, and it is ſomething which each may do ſeparately.

If one of the heirs, who was ſued for the building of the whole houſe, did not cauſe his co-heirs to be brought in, he would alone be condemned to damages for the whole, in caſe of the *inexecution of the obligation*. *It is* his own fault that he did not bring in the other heirs.

334. It remains for us to ſpeak of the third caſe, in which the indiviſible debt cannot be diſcharged but by all the debtors jointly. We may adduce, as an example, the caſe of one who, by a compoſition, had bound himſelf to grant you a right of way over his land, in ſuch part of it as he ſhould indicate. If he died without performing this obligation, leaving ſeveral heirs, who ſucceed in common to his eſtate, the obligation to grant the right of way, to which they ſucceed, is an indiviſible obligation, which cannot be diſcharged but by all the heirs jointly, as a right of way, and the like, can only be granted by thoſe who are owners of the land. L. 2, ff. *de Serv.* L. 18, ff. *Comm. Præd.*

In the caſe of this kind of obligation, if one of the heirs declares that he is ready, as far as it in him lies, to perform the obligation, and it depends on the other heirs alone to complete the performance of it, it is only he who refuſes who muſt be condemned to the damages: for he who tenders is not in arrear. *Molin. ib. p.* 3, *n.* 95.

If a penalty had been ſtipulated in caſe of the inexecution of the obligation, the co-debtor or co-heir who had not been in arrear, would, not the leſs, be liable for his part of the penalty incurred by the delay of the other, *non immediate, sed ejus occasione, & tanquam ex conditionis eventu;* as in diviſible obligations.

335. Obſerve that the law 25, §. 10, ff. *Fam. erciſc.* contains nothing contrary to the diſtinctions we have hitherto made: for, as Dumoulin remarks, *p.* 8, *n.* 99, this text does not ſuppoſe that the heir, for part, of the debtor of an

indivisible thing, would always and without distinction be liable to pay the value of the whole in case of the inexecution of the obligation; but it decides only that in the case in which he should be liable, *puta*, when he has suffered himself to be condemned without bringing in his co-heirs, who were bound as well as he, he would have against them the action *familiæ erciscundæ*, to obtain an allowance for it in the division.

§. IV.

Of the effect of indivisible obligations in non faciendo.

336. When one has bound himself to another not to do a certain thing; if what he bound himself not to do is something indivisible, *puta*, if he bound himself to his neighbour not to prevent him from passing over his land, the contravention by one of his heirs will give room to the action of the creditor against all the heirs, that they may be prohibited from contravening the obligation, and condemned to damages; with this difference, that he who has contravened it, ought to be condemned for the whole, *quia non tenetur tantum tanquam hæres, sed tanquam ipse & ex facto proprio*; and the other heirs ought to be condemned only in the part for which they are heirs and saving their recourse against him who contravened the obligation, that he be holden to pay in their discharge, or indemnify them if they have been compelled to pay. They are not bound, *in solidum*, as is he who contravened the obligation, but only for their part in the inheritance, *quia tenentur tantum ut hæredes*. It is in this sense that Dumoulin says we ought to understand the law 2, §. 5, ff. *de verb, oblig*. *Si stipulatus fuero per te non fieri, neque per hæredem tuum quominus mihi ire, agere liceat, & unus ex pluribus hæredibus prohibuerit, tenentur & cohæredes ejus; sed familiæ erciscundæ repetent ab eo quod præstiterint. Dumoulin, part, 3, n. 168, & seq.*

With regard to the creditor, those who have not contravened are bound for the contravention of this co-heir; and in this the obligations *in non faciendo* differ from obligations *in faciendo*. For when the obligation consists in doing ſomething indiviſible, which can only be done by both jointly and one of them offers to do it, while the other refuſes to concur. We have ſeen *supra, n.* 334, that, according to the opinion of Dumouiin, the creditor has no action againſt him who was not in arrear, but only againſt him who refuſed.

The reaſon of this diſtinction is, that it is the arrear of the debtor that gives room for the action, in obligations *in faciendo*. Hence it follows that it cannot ariſe, againſt him who is ready and willing *quantum in se est* to perform the obligation, and who conſequently is not in arrear. On the contrary in obligations *in non faciendo* it is the act itſelf, from which the debtor promiſed that he and his heirs would abſtain, which gives room to the action of the creditor. Therefore it ſuffices that one of the heirs do it, to give room to the action againſt all. It muſt be ſuppoſed that ſuch was the intention of the contracting parties. For otherwiſe he, to whom another has bound himſelf not to do a thing, would not be ſafe, and it would often happen that when what was ſtipulated not to be done ſhould be done, he could not ſue any one, for want of knowing who did it: it not often being eaſy, when a thing has been done, to know who it was done by. Whereas in obligations that conſiſt in doing a thing, it cannot be difficult to know who is in arrear or refuſes, by making a demand.

Dumoulin, *part.* 1, *n.* 27, gives to the heirs who have not contravened, the plea of diſcuſſion by which they may compel the creditor previouſly to aſcertain, at their coſts, the inſolvency of the one who has contravened.

CHAPTER V.

Of penal obligations.

337. A PENAL obligation is, as we have already ſeen, that which reſults from the clauſe of an agreement, by which a perſon, in order to aſſure the execution of a pre-

vious engagement, binds himſelf, in the form of a penalty, to ſomething, in caſe of the inexecution of this engagement. For example. If you lent me a horſe to perform a journey, which I bound myſelf to return to you ſound and in good order, and to pay you fifty piſtoles, if I did not return him ſo; this obligation which I contracted to pay fifty piſtoles, if I did not return him ſound and in good order, is a penal obligation.

To treat this ſubject in order, after having ſhewn in the firſt article the general principles reſpecting the nature of penal obligations, we ſhall ſee in the ſecond, when the penalty is incurred; we ſhall examine in the third, whether the debtor may, in diſcharging his obligation in part, avoid a part of the penalty: we ſhall diſcuſs in the fourth, whether the penalty is incurred for the whole and by all the heirs of the debtor, on the contravention by one of them; and in the fifth, whether the contravention made towards one of the heirs of the creditor, cauſes the penalty to be incurred for the whole and towards all the heirs of the creditor.

ARTICLE THE FIRST.

Of the nature of penal obligations.

First Principle.

338. A penal obligation being from its nature acceſſory to the principal and primitive obligation, the nullity of this carries with it the nullity of the penal obligation. The reaſon of this is that it is of the nature of acceſſory things, that they cannot exiſt without the principal thing. *Quum causa principalis non consistit, ne ea quidem quæ sequuntur locum obtinent.* L. 129, §. 1, ff. *de Reg. Jur.* Beſides the penal obligation, being the obligation of a penalty ſtipulated in caſe of the inexecution of the primitive obligation, if the primitive obligation is not valid, the penal obligation cannot take place; for there cannot be a penalty for the inexecution of an obligation, which, not being valid, could not and ought not to be performed.

The law 69, ff. *de Verb. oblig.*, contains an example of

this division. You had promised to me to give me a certain slave, of the death of whom you were ignorant, and to pay me a sum of money, as a penalty, if you failed to give him to me. Ulpian decides that the penal obligation is no more valid than the principal one, which, being that of an impossibility, cannot be valid. *Si homo mortuus sisti non potest, nec pæna rei impossibilis committetur, quemadmodum si quis Stichum mortuum dare stipulatus, si datus non esset, pænam stipuletur.*

339. This principle that the nullity of the primitive obligation carries with it that of the penal obligation, admits of an exception, in the case of an obligation, in the performance of which, he, to whom it has been contracted, had no appreciable interest; *puta, cum quis alteri stipulatus est.* We have seen *supra, n.* 54, that such an obligation is not valid. Yet, the penal obligation that is annexed to it is valid. *Alteri stipulari nemo potest . . . . Plane si quis velit hoc facere, pænam stipulari conveniet, ut nisi ita factum sicut est comprehensum, committatur pæna, stipulatio etiam ei cujus nihil interest, &c. Instit. tit. de inut. Stip.* §. 18. The reason is that the principal obligation is void in this case, only because the debtor may contravene it with impunity; he to whom it has been contracted having in such case, no damage to claim on account of its inexecution; the penal obligation that is added cures this defect, in preventing the debtor from contravening the obligation with impunity.

Likewise, although one could not validly promise the act of another, the penal obligation added to an agreement, by which one has promised the act of another, is valid. For the penal clause shews that he who promised had not simply an intention to promise the act of another, but that he had authority from this person, and consequently he has promised *non de alio, sed de se.* Supra, *n.* 56.

Frain, in his reports of cases, determined in the Parliament of Brittany, relates one, of the 12th of January 1621, which was decided on this principle. The relation of a canon, who had offended the bishop of St. Malo, had promised to the bishop that the canon should not appear in the city during four months, and bound himself to pay the sum of three hundred livres in case of a contravention. The canon coming into the city within that time, the agreement was holden to be valid and the penalty incurred.

Second Principle.

340. The nullity of the penal obligation does not carry with it the nullity of the principal obligation. The reason is that the accessory cannot indeed exist without the principal; but the principal does not depend on the accessory and may exist without it. This is the decision of the law 27, ff. *de Verb. oblig. Si stipulatus sum te sisti, nisi stiteris, hippocentaurum dari, perinde erit atque si te sisti solummodo stipulatus essem:* and as Paul says in L. 126, §. 3, *d. tit. Detracta prima stipulatione, prior manet utilis.*

Third Principle.

341. The penal obligation has for its object to assure the performance of the principal obligation.

Hence it must be concluded that the intention of the contracting parties was not, by the penal obligation, to extinguish or dissolve the principal obligation, nor to merge the latter in the former. L. 21, §. 2, ff. *de Verb. oblig.*

Therefore, although the penal obligation be incurred by the arrear of the debtor to perform the principal obligation, the creditor may, instead of demanding the penalty, sue for the performance of the principal obligation. L. 28, ff. *de Act. empt.* L. 122, §. 2, ff. *de Verb. oblig. & passim.*

Therefore, when stipulating a penalty in case of the inexecution of a principal obligation, the intention of the parties was that in such case, as soon as the debtor should have been put in arrear to perform the principal obligation, nothing more should remain due than the sum stipulated. Such stipulation is not a penal stipulation; the obligation which results from it is not a penal obligation, but as much a principal obligation as the first, of which the party intended to make a novation. It is this that is ſpoken of in the law 4, §. *fin.* ff. *de oblig. & act.*

On the queſtion when it is to be preſumed that the parties intended to make a novation, ſee what is ſaid *infra, part.* 3, *chap.* 2, *art.* 4, §. 2.

Fourth Principle.

342. The penalty is ſtipulated with an intention to indemnify the creditor from the inexecution of the principal obligation. It is conſequently in compenſation of the damages, which he ſuffers from the inexecution of the principal obligation.

It follows from thence that he ought, in ſuch caſe, to chuſe either to proſecute for the performance of the principal obligation, or for the penalty; that he ought to be ſatisfied with the one or the other, and that he cannot exact both.

Yet as the penal obligation cannot impair the principal one; if the penalty which the creditor had received for the inexecution of the principal obligation did not ſufficiently indemnify him, he would not be prevented, although he received the penalty, from demanding the damages reſulting from the inexecution of the principal obligation, deducting from ſuch damages the penalty which he had received. This is the deciſion of the law 28, ff. *de Act. empt.* 41 & 42, ff. *pro socio.*

However the judge ought not eaſily to liſten to a creditor who pretends that the penalty which he has received does not ſufficiently indemnify him for the inexecution of the agreement; for the parties having, in fixing the penalty, valued and ſettled, themſelves, the damages that would reſult from the inexecution of the agreement, the creditor, by aſking larger damages, appears to depart from a valuation, which he, himſelf, has made, which it ſeems he ought not be allowed to do, unleſs he has proof that the damages which he has ſuſtained exceed the penalty; as in the following caſe. If a merchant who lent me his chair, on condition that I returned it on a certain day, when he would want it to go to the fair; and I bound myself to pay him thirty livres if I failed to return it on the appointed day: the merchant may refuse to be satisfied with the thirty livres, if he has proof that he was compelled to pay fifty livres for a chair, and that the common price of chairs to go to the fair was fifty livres, at the time I was to return him his.

343. As the penal clause does not take away from him, who stipulated, the action that results from the principal obligation; so it does not take away the pleas and prescriptions that might result from it.

For example. If I agreed with a person coming of age, that he should not disagree to the sale of an estate which he made to me during his minority, and I stipulated, with a penalty, that he should pay a certain sum in case he contravened this agreement; if he should afterwards sue for a rescission of the sale, the penal clause inserted in our contract would not prevent my opposing to his suit the plea which results from the principal engagement stipulated, that he should not disagree to the sale. But as he who stipulates a penalty cannot receive the penalty and what is contained in the principal engagement, if I avail myself of the plea resulting from this engagement and cause the suit to be dismissed, I shall not be admitted to claim the penalty; and *vice versa*, if I have exacted the penalty from him, I shall not be allowed the plea. This results from the law 10, §. 1, ff. *de pact.*

The decision of this law has nothing contrary to that of the law 122, §. 6, ff *de Verb. oblig.*, related *infra*, in the article following, *n.* 348. When I have, under a certain penalty, stipulated with you on your coming of age, that you should not disagree to the sale of an estate you made me in your minority, the object of this agreement is to procure me the release of a rescissory action which you might truly have against me: therefore when, in pleading this agreement, I have caused your suit to fail, and thereby procured the effect of this release, I cannot demand the penalty: for otherwise I should have, at the same time, the thing and the penalty, which ought not to be. Such is the instance in the law 10, §. 1, ff. *de Pact.* which we have just quoted. That in the law 122, which is opposed to us, is very different. After a division which is in itself valid and not subject to any rescissory action, we had, in order to avoid a suit, however groundless, agreed under a certain penalty not to litigate it. The object of this agreement was not, as in the preceding case, to procure to me the release of an action which you might have against me to set aside the division, because you could have none; the only object of this agreement was to avoid a suit; therefore if you have brought one, although it has been dismissed by a judgment in my favor, the penalty will be incurred: for the only thing which was the object of the agreement being to avoid a suit, however groundless, as you have obliged me to defend a suit, it is true to say that you have contravened the agreement in regard to that which was the object of it; whence it follows that the penalty is incurred.

344. Our rule that the creditor cannot have both the principal and the penalty, admits of an exception, not only when it is said expressly in the penal clause that on failure of the debtor to perform his obligation within a certain time, the penalty shall then be incurred and shall become due, without prejudice to the principal obligation, which would be expressed by these words *rato manente pacto;* L. 16, ff. *de trans.;* but also whenever it appears that the penalty was stipulated as an indemnification of what the creditor may suffer, not from the absolute inexecution of the obligation, but from the mere delay in the performance of it: for in this case the creditor who has suffered from the delay, may receive the principal and the penalty.

Fifth Principle.

345. The penalty stipulated in case the obligation be not performed, may, when it is excessive, be reduced and moderated by the judge.

This principle is derived from a decision of Dumoulin, in his treatise *de eo quod interest, n.* 156, *& seq.* He grounds it on this, that it is of the nature of the penalty that it be in lieu of the damages which might be claimed by the creditor in case the obligation be not performed. Therefore, says he, as, when the creditor claims an excessive sum for the damages which he pretends to have sustained from the inexecution of the obligation, the judge ought to reduce it; and as the law, *Cod. de sent. quæ pro eo quod interest prof.*, does not allow that the damages should exceed double the value of the thing which made the object of the primitive obligation; so, when the penalty stipulated in lieu of damages is excessive, it ought to be reduced: for this penalty may well, indeed, exceed the amount of the damages, and even be due when the creditor might not have sustained any, because it has been stipulated to avoid the discussion of the question whether the creditor has actually sustained any damages and to what amount; but being in lieu of the damages of the creditor, it is contrary to its nature that it should be carried beyond the limits which the law prescribes to damages. If the law above cited restrains them, and does not permit that they should be claimed *ultra duplum*, even when the inexecution of the contract may have really occasioned a greater loss to the creditor, who finds himself, on this account, *versari in damno; a fortiori* the excessive penalty, to which the debtor unadvisedly submitted, ought to be moderated and reduced when the creditor has not suffered any loss, or has suffered one much below the amount of the penalty stipulated, and consequently in the case in which *certat de lucro captando*. In fine, Dumoulin grounds his opinion on the text of the law before cited, *Cod. de sent. pro eo quod interest, &c.* which from its general terms seems to include *interesse conventionale*, as well as other kinds of damages.

Azon is of an opinion contrary to that of Dumoulin. He decides that a penalty stipulated in the form of damages, is not subject to be moderated. It may be said in favor of his opinion, that there is a difference between the damages stipulated, and those which are regulated by the contract. With regard to the latter, it is true, indeed, that the debtor, in contracting the primitive obligation, is presumed to have contracted the secondary obligation of damages which might result from the inexecution of the primitive obligation; but there is room to presume that he did not intend to bind himself *in immensum* for the damages, but only *intra justum modum*, and to the extent of the sum to which it was probable they could amount. But the same cannot be said of the damages which are stipulated; for *ubi est evidens voluntas, non relinquitur præsumptioni locus.* However excessive the sum may be which is stipulated in the form of damages in case of the inexecution of the agreement, the debtor cannot deny that he intended to bind himself for it, when the clause of the contract has so expressed it. Notwithstanding these reasons, the decision of Dumoulin appears more equitable. When a debtor binds himself for an excessive penalty in case of the inexecution of a primitive obligation which he contracts, there is cause to presume that it was the confidence of the debtor that he should not fail in the performance of the primitive obligation which induced him to subject himself to so excessive a sum; that he did not think to engage any thing in subjecting himself to it, and that he would not have bound himself in such penalty if he had thought the case would happen in which the penalty was to be incurred: thus the consent which he gave to the obligation of a penalty so excessive, being a consent founded on error, is not a valid consent: therefore these excessive penalties ought to be reduced to the sum to which the damages of the creditor, resulting from the inexecution of the primitive obligation, may amount at the highest. This decision ought to apply in commutative contracts, because as equity, which ought to reign in these contracts, does not permit that one of the parties should profit and enrich himself at the expence of another, it would be contrary to this equity that the creditor should enrich himself at the expence of the debtor in exacting from him a penalty too excessive and manifestly too much above what he has suffered from the inexecution of the primitive obligation. The decision ought likewise to apply in donations, *cum nemini sua liberalitas debeat esse captiosa.*

The text of the Inſtitutes, *tit. de inut. Stip.* §. 20, does not more than the law 38, §. 17, ff. *de Verb. oblig.*, decide any thing againſt the deciſion of Dumoulin: for from what is there ſaid, *Pœnam cum quis stipulatur, non inspicitur quod intersit ejus, sed quæ sit quantitas in conditione stipulationis*, it follows that the penalty may be due, although he in whoſe favor it has been ſtipulated has not ſuffered any thing from the inexecution of the primitive obligation or has ſuffered leſs than the penalty; but it does not in any manner follow that this penalty may be immenſe and in no proportion to the object of the primitive obligation.

With regard to the law 56, *de Evict.*, which ſuppoſes that one may ſtipulate in a contract of ſale, the reſtitution of the triple or quadruple of the price in caſe of eviction, it is anſwered in different ways. Noodt pretends that the words *triplum aut quadruplum* are a bad gloſs, which is not in the text, and ought to be retrenched. Dumoulin, *ibid. n.* 167, *& seq.* anſwers better in ſaying that the queſtion in this law is not what may be validly ſtipulated in caſe of eviction, and therefore that it is not to be concluded that one may always and without diſtinction, in all contracts of ſale, ſtipulate validly the reſtitution of the triple or quadruple, in caſe of eviction; that it is only to be concluded that ſuch a ſtipulation may be ſometimes inſerted in contracts of ſale, and theſe caſes are when a thing has been ſold not ſimply, but in circumſtances in which the purchaſer might ſuffer a great loſs in the reſt of his property, in caſe of eviction from the thing ſold, which riſk was known and foreſeen by the contracting parties, as in the following caſe. I ſell to a merchant, a little before the fair, a booth, and it is expreſsly mentioned in the contract, that it is for the purpoſe of putting his goods in. The riſk which the purchaſer runs in caſe of eviction, during the time of the fair, not to find a booth to be hired or ſold, and conſequently to loſe the ſale of his goods, is the riſk of a damage foreſeen by the contracting parties at the time of the contract, which damage may conſiderably exceed the price of the booth, and to which the ſeller ſubjects himſelf. Therefore, in this caſe, the damages which were not fixed by the contract would be valued above the double, triple or quadruple of the price of the thing sold. Likewise one may, in the same case, stipulate a penalty above the double of the price of this thing; and the penalty is not in this case judged excessive, for not being in any proportion to the price of the thing sold; provided it be in some proportion to the damage, which the purchaser has sustained by the loss of the sale of the goods. Since it was in lieu of this damage that it was stipulated.

346. It remains to be observed that if the penalty which is in lieu of the ordinary damages, is subject to be reduced when it is excessive, *a fortiori*, the penalty stipulated in case of the failure to pay a sum of money or other thing which is consumed in the use, ought to be reduced to the lawful rate of interest of which it is in lieu, or even entirely rejected, when interest may not lawfully be stipulated.

Article II.

When the penalty of the obligation is incurred.

§. II.

Of the case in which a penal clause has been added to an obligagation to do something.

347. It is evident in this case that the penalty is incurred, as soon as he who bound himself under the penalty not to do a thing, has done the thing which he bound himself not to do.

348. Is it necessary that the act on which the penalty is to be incurred, should have its effect? This depends on what was the intention of the parties. Suppose that in making a division or a composition we have reciprocally promised not to litigate the same, under the penalty of a certain sum, payable by the party contravening his promise to the other. Afterwards you have brought suit against me to procure this division or composition to be annulled. This suit, although it has had no effect and has been dismissed by a judgment in my favor, causes the penalty to be incurred; *Arg.* L. 1, 122, §. 6, ff. *de Verb. obl.* The

reason is, that in stipulating with you, under a certain penalty that you should not litigate what we had done, I did not precisely understand that you should not set aside the division or composition, which being valid of themselves, would have remained so notwithstanding the stipulation. What I intended to stipulate with you was, that you should not oblige me to contest a suit. It suffices then that you have brought suit, though you have failed in it, for the penalty to be incurred. It cannot be said, in this case, that I am paid for both the principal obligation and the penalty, which is contrary to the fourth principle we have established in the preceding article: for the principal obligation which you contracted to me, not to litigate the division or composition, and to which the penal obligation was attached, had for its object that you should not bring a suit against me: and you failed to perform this principal obligation, because you have made me sustain one; I may therefore exact the penalty.

On the contrary, if I have stipulated with you, under a certain penalty that you should not let your house, adjoining the one I occupy, to a blacksmith, or other person of the like trade; the lease you made of it to such a person, if he did not come into the house, will not cause the penalty to be incurred. For what I had in view in stipulating this with you, was only to avoid the inconvenience of the noise which such workmen make. As the house was not used for a purpose creating this inconvenience, the penalty ought not to be incurred.

For the same reason Papinian decides in the law 6. ff. *de Serv. export.* that when a slave has been sold under a condition that the purchaser should not emancipate him, and under a certain penalty, if he did, a void deed of emancipation does not cause the penalty to be incurred.

§. II.

Of the case in which a penal clause has been added to the obligation to giv or do some thing.

349. In this case the penalty is incurred when the

debtor has been put in arrear to give or do what he has promifed. The civil law makes a diftinction, when the agreement contains a fixed time in which the debtor is to give or do what has been agreed, and when it does not contain fuch a time. In the firft cafe, they decide that the penalty is due, *de pleno jure*, as foon as the time is expired, without there being any neceffity for an interpellation on the debtor, and that he could not be difcharged from it, by offering, after the expiration of the time, to perform the principal obligation: L. 23, ff. *de obl. & act.*

The expiration of the time appeared to the Roman jurifts fo fully fufficient to operate a forfeiture of the penalty, without the neceffity of otherwife putting the debtor in arrear, that they held the penalty to be forfeited, even when the debtor had died before, without leaving any heirs, and there was confequently no one who could be put in arrear. This is the decifion ot the law 77, ff. *de Verb. oblig.*

Further, the law 112, ff. *de Verb. oblig.* decides that when the obligation to which a penal claufe has been added, is to do within a certain time a certain piece of work, the execution of which requires a particular time, the penalty is due, even before the expiration of the time ftipulated, as foon as it becomes certain that the work cannot be done in this time; fo that the enlargement of the time which might afterwards be granted to the debtor, would not difcharge him from the penalty incurred before this enlargement.

In the fecond cafe, when the obligation to give or to do a thing includes no fixed time, the law 122, §. 2, decides that the penalty is incurred only on the demand of the creditor *litis contestatione*,

With us, whether the primitive obligation includes a time within which it is to be performed, or not, it is commonly neceffary that there be a judicial demand in order to put the debtor in arrear, and thereby caufe the penalty to be incurred. I have faid *commonly;* for there are cafes in which the penalty as well as damages may be incurred, without any demand, *supra*, *n.* 147.

It is to be obferved that the penalty cannot be incurred, when it is by the act of the creditor that the debtor is prevented from performing his obligation. L. 122, §. 3, *de Verb. oblig.*

Article III.

Whether the debtor may, in performing his obligation in part, avoid part of the penalty.

350. A debtor cannot pay to the creditor, againft his confent, part of what he owes, as long as his obligation, although divifible, is ftill undivided, as we fhall fee *infra, part 3, chap. 1, art. 3, §. 2.* Therefore the tender he fhould make to the craditor of part of what is due, would not difcharge him from the penalty ftipulated in cafe of the inexecution of the obligation, if the creditor refufed the partial payment.

But if the creditor has willingly received part of the payment of his debt, is the penalty incurred for the whole, in cafe of failure to pay the part that remains due? Ulpian, in the law 9, §. 1, ff. *Si quis caution. in jud.*, decides that although, *subtilitate juris*, it may appear that in this cafe the penalty ought to be incurred for the whole, yet it is equitable it fhould be fo only in proportion to the part of the principal obligation that remains to be performed. The true reafon of this decifion is that given by Dumoulin, and which we have mentioned above: namely, that the penalty being prefumed to be promifed as an indemnification for the inexecution of the obligation, the creditor cannot receive both. When therefore he has been paid for part of the principal obligation, he cannot receive the penalty for that part, otherwife he would receive both, which ought not to be. This is the tenth key of Dumoulin, in his treatife *de div. & ind. p. 3, n.* 112. *In omnibus sive individuis, sive dividuis, pœna non committitur, nisi pro parte contraventionis efficacis, nec potest exigi cum principali; sed creditor non tenetur partem principalis & partem pœnæ accipere.*

This will be illuftrated by an example. In felling me a farm not ftocked with cattle for its neceffary ufe, you have bound yourself to supply me with two yoke of oxen, under the penalty of five hundred livres, for the damages, in case you failed to deliver them. You will not be allowed in this case to compel me to receive one yoke of oxen, as I am not compellable to receive a part of what is due me; and consequently the tender you should make of one yoke, if I do not chuse to receive it, would not prevent your being liable to me for the whole penalty of five hundred livres. But if I willingly received the yoke of oxen which you tendered me, on your failing to deliver me the other yoke, I shall be entitled only to one half of the penalty. For having received a part of what was the object of the agreement, I cannot have the entire penalty, as I cannot have both.

351. Our principle that the penalty is due only in the proportion, and as to the parts in which the principal obligation is not performed, applies equally, whether you bound yourself, under a penalty, in case you did a certain thing, or in case a third person did it. If you bound yourself under a penalty of three hundred livres, that Peter should not claim a piece of land in my possession, the penalty will be incurred only for one half, if Peter claims only one half of it, unless the contrary appeared to have been the intention of the parties. *Molin. ibid. p. 3, n. 531.*

352. These decisions apply especially in regard to obligations of things divisible. It would seem that they could not apply to obligations of indivisible things, yet they do sometimes apply to such.

I. Although the use of a right of way, or the like, is something indivisible, and consequently the obligation which the owner of the land over which it is granted contracts to allow it, is an indivisible obligation; yet, when the right of way is limited to a particular purpose for which it was instituted, which purpose terminates in something divisible, if this purpose has been accomplished in part, the penalty will be divided and will be due only for the part for which it has not been accomplished. This will be illustrated by an example.

I own a piece of land to which is attached a right of way over yours, by which the possessors of yours are bound, during the time of vintage, to suffer me to convey my wine over your land, under a penalty of three hundred livres in case I be disturbed in this right. In this case, if, after suffering one half of my wine to be carried over your land, you have prevented the rest from being carried, you will only incur one half of the penalty of three hundred livres. For although the right of way is indivisible and the obligation to allow the exercise of the right is the obligation of something indivisible, yet as the right is limited to a purpose which is the transporting of my wine, and my wine is something divisible, it cannot be denied that I have partially obtained the purpose for which the right of way was established, and that you have permitted me partially to exercise it, by suffering me to transport one half of my wine over your land. I can demand, therefore, only one half of the penalty; for I cannot receive the penalty for the whole, and enjoy a part of the benefit of the right of way. I cannot have both. This Dumoulin teaches in the case which we have quoted. *Quia*, says he, *hæc servitus de se individua, dividuatur ex accidenti, & ex fine dividuo .... & debet judicari secundum regulam dividuorum*; *p.* 3, *n.* 363.

355. II. These principles also apply even in the case of indivisible obligations, in the following instances and others similar to it. You have bound yourself by a contract under a certain penalty to procure me a right of way over a piece of land of which you are tenant for life, imagining you could cause the grant of this right to be confirmed by the reversioners. Three of these confirm it, but the fourth refuses. The penalty, it is true, is due me for the whole; for the refusal of one of the reversioners to confirm it, prevents the validity of the grants, notwithstanding its confirmation by the three others; as a right of way cannot be granted for part, but must be granted by all the owners of the land. But as the confirmation of three of the reversioners, though it is of no use in passing the right, has nevertheless some effect, which is to bind personally those who have confirmed,

to suffer me to pass, I cannot demand the whole penalty, without surrendering the right which results from this obligation: otherwise I shall only have a right to part of the penalty. For I cannot receive the whole penalty and at the same time receive advantage from the principal obligation. *Molin. part.* 3. *n.* 4&2, 473.

354. The principle that the penalty is due only in proportion to the part for which the principal obligation was not performed, takes place even when the penalty consists in something indivisible. *Finge.* I sold you an estate, the price of which you paid me except fifty pistoles, which you bound yourself to pay me in twelve months, and we have agreed that on your failure to pay that sum within the time you should grant me a right of view over your house adjoining mine: I received of you twenty-five pistoles. On your failing to pay the overplus, I cannot exact the penalty for the whole, but only for the half for which the principal obligation was not performed, and as the penalty consists in a right of view, which is indivisible and not susceptible of parts, in demanding that you grant me the right of view, it will be necessary that I tender you payment of half of its value; the penalty being due me only for one half. *Molin. part* 3, *n.* 323, *& seq.* See *infra.*

Article IV.

Whether the penalty is incurred for the whole, and by all the heirs of the debtor, on the contravention of one of them.

It is necessary in deciding this question, to distinguish between divisible obligations and obligations indivisible.

§. I.

Decision of the question with regard to obligations indivisible.

355. When the primitive obligation which has been contracted under a penal clause is the obligation of an indivisible thing, the contravention of this obligation by one only of the heirs of the debtors causes the penalty to be incurred not only by the one who has contravened it, but also by his coheirs, who are liable for the penalty, in the proportion in which they are heirs, saving their recourse

against him, who by his contravention has occasioned the forfeiture of the penalty, in order that they may be reimbursed by him.

For example; one has bound himself to permit me to pass over his land adjoining the house which I occupy, as long as I should occupy it, under the penalty of ten livres, in case of disturbance. If one of the heirs of my debtor stop my way, although without the participation and against the will of his coheirs, the whole penalty of ten livres will be incurred, and it will be incurred by each of the heirs of my debtor, who will be respectively liable for it to the amount of their part in the inheritance. For that which is the object of the primitive obligation being indivisible and not susceptible of parts, the contravention of this obligation, which is made by one of the heirs of the debtor is a contravention of the whole obligation. It ought consequently to occasion the forfeiture of the whole penalty by all who are liable for it as heirs of the debtor who bound himself to the penalty in case of contravention.

This is the decision of Cato, in the law 4, §. 1, ff. *de Verb. oblig. Cato scribit: Poena certæ pecuniæ promissa, si quid aliter sit factum, mortuo promissore, si ex pluribus hæredibus unus contra quam cautum sit, fecerit, aut ab omnibus hæredibus poenam committi pro portione hæreditaria, aut ab uno pro portione sua: ab omnibus, si id factum de quo cautum est, individuum sit, veluti iter fieri; quia quod in partes dividi non potest, ab omnibus quodam modo factum videtur.* Et seq. *Omnes commisisse videntur, quod nisi in solidum peccari poterit, illam stipulationem per te non fieri quominus mihi e, agere liceat.*

Paul decides the same question in the law 85, §. 3, ff. *d. tit. Quoniam licet ab uno prohibeor, non tamen in parte prohibeor;* and he adds *sed cæteri familiæ erciscundæ judicio sarcient damnum.*

The heirs being bound for the penalty, each only for the part for which he is heir, are in this case different from debtors *in solidum*, who are debtors of the penalty for the whole, when it is incurred by one of them, as they are with regard to the principal obligation.

356. May the creditor demand the whole penalty from the heir who has made the contravention? The reafon to doubt is that the law does not fay it, and that it fays on the contrary that the penalty is due by all the heirs, for their hereditary part alone. It is added that the contravention by the heir caufes the penalty to be incurred, inafmuch as this contravention is as the condition under which the obligation of the penalty was contracted by the anceftor. This debt of the penalty which was contracted by the anceftor, being a debt of the anceftor and a divifible one, the heir can be liable for it only in the proportion for which he is heir, and in which he fucceeds in this quality to the debts of the anceftor.

It muft be decided, however, that the heir who contravenes the indivifible obligation contracted by the anceftor, becomes debtor of the penalty for the whole. It cannot be doubted that he is liable for it, at leaft obliquely or indirectly: for being bound to indemnify his co-heirs for the part for which they are liable, the creditor ought to be admitted, in order to avoid a circuity of actions, to require the penalty from him not only for his fhare, but alfo for that of his co-heirs, whom he is bound to indemnify, and confequently he is liable for the whole.

Dumoulin, *part 3, n. 173 & 174, & passim alibi*, goes much farther and maintains that the heir owes the penalty for the whole not obliquely, but indeed directly. For the primitive obligation being fuppofed indivifible, he is debtor of it for the whole, and debtor under the penalty ftipulated. His contravening an obligation to which he is liable for the whole, ought to make him incur the whole penalty. This is proved by an argument from the law 9, ff. *depos.* which we have before quoted. It is there decided that the heir in part, of a depofitary, who by his own act has occafioned the lofs of the thing depofited with his anceftor, is liable for the whole damage to him who made the depofit. In fact, although the principal obligation to reftore the thing depofited, is a divifible obligation, the acceffory obligation to ufe good faith in the prefervation of the thing depofited, is an indivisible obligation, for which each heir is liable for the whole, and which renders him debtor of the whole of the damages of the creditor, if he contravenes it. If an heir for part who contravenes by his own act an indivisible obligation of the ancestor, is debtor for the whole damages, he ought to be so for the whole penalty, since the penalty is in lieu of the damages, and is only a liquidation of them agreed upon by the parties themselves. Such is the reasoning of Dumoulin.

With regard to the first objection drawn from the paragraph *Cato*, this is the objection to it. When Cato decides that in the case of indivisible obligations, the contravention by one of the heirs causes the penalty to be incurred by each of them for their hereditary parts, he means to speak only of the heirs who have not participated in the contravention. As to the second objection, which is that as the obligation of the penalty, is an indivisible obligation contracted by the ancestor, each heir can be bound only for the part for which he is heir: the answer of Dumoulin is, that this is true when the heir is liable as heir, *tamquam hæres*, but when he is liable *ut ipse, & ex proprio facto*, he is liable for the whole, and this is one of his keys to determine questions on this subject. *Aliud est teneri hæredem ut hæredem, aliud teneri ut ipsum.* Tract. de Div. & ind. *part* 3, *n.* 5, & 112.

357. When an indivisible obligation is contravened by one of the heirs of the debtor, the heir who has contravened it being liable for the whole penalty, it follows that if the contravention has been made by one of several heirs, each heir is bound *in solidum* for the whole penalty; for the contravention of his co-heir does not diminish his own: *Nec qui peccavit, ex eo relevari debet, quod peccati consortem habuit; multitudo peccantium non exonerat, sed potius aggravat.* Molin. *ibid. part* 3, *n.* 148.

358. All we have said in this paragraph, with regard to the heirs of the debtor of an indivisible obligation, applies to several principal debtors, who have contracted to-

gether, not *in solidum*, under a penalty, an indivisible obligation. The contravention by one of them, binds the others to the payment of the penalty, each for his part, saving their recourse; and it binds, for the whole, him who has contravened. When the contravention has been made by several, it binds *in solidum*.

§. II.

Decision of the question with regard to divisible obligations.

359. When the primitive obligation contracted under a penal clause is that of a divisible act, Cato, in the paragraph above cited, seems to decide that the one of the heirs who contravenes the obligation, alone incurs the penalty, for the part for which he is heir. *Si de eo cautum sit quod divisionem recipiat, veluti amplius non agi, eum hæredem qui adversus ea facit, pro portione sua solum pœnam committere.*

The case in this law may be thus stated. A person bound himself to me, under a penalty of three hundred livres, to abide by the award of arbitrators, who have discharged me from a claim he pretended to have against me, for two hundred bushels of wheat. One of his heirs, who inherits a fifth of his estate, has, contrary to the faith of this agreement, sued me for his fifth of the two hundred bushels of wheat, which by the award it was adjudged I did not owe. He alone incurs the penalty stipulated, and he incurs it only for his fifth, which is his hereditary part. The reason is that the obligation is divisible, and as this heir can contravene it only for the part for which he is heir, he can consequently be liable only for part of the penalty. His coheirs, who, far from contravening this obligation, have performed it in part, in submitting for their part to the award, cannot be liable for this penalty. The creditor, who is satisfied as to their part of the award, cannot demand the penalty for their part, for he cannot be paid both the principal obligation and the penalty, as we have seen *supra*, *n.* 342, *& seq.*

The paragraph 4. *Si sortem*, of the law 5, *de tit.* seems contrary to this decision of Cato. It is there decided that when one of the heirs of the debtor has discharged the obligation for the part for which he was liable, he, not the less, incurs the penalty, if his co-heir does not likewise perform the obligation, saving his recourse against his co-heir, who occasions the forfeiture of the penalty, by failing in the performance of his part of the obligation: *Si sortem promiseris, & si ea soluta non esset, pœnam; etiam si unus ex hæredibus tuis portionem suam ex sorte solverit, nihilominus pœnam committet, donec portio cohæredis solvatur .... sed a cohærede ei satisfieri debet; nec enim aliud, in his stipulationibus sine injuria stipulatoris constitui potest.*

The interpreters, as well ancient as modern, have endeavoured to reconcile these two texts. Dumoulin relates several concordances of ancient interpreters, and refutes them all.

It is best to coincide with those of Cujas and Dumoulin, *Tract. de div. & ind. p.* 1, *n.* 62, *& seq.* which are alike. When the obligation is indivisible *tam solutione quam conditione*, when the intention of the parties, in adding the penal clause, has been simply to assure the performance of the obligation and not to prevent the payment of it from being made in parcels, by the several heirs of the debtor, especially when the act which is the object of the primitive obligation is such that it cannot be performed by the several heirs of the debtor, otherwise than by each for the part for which he is heir; in this case the decision of Cato ought to apply, the one of the heirs who contravened the obligation ought alone to incur the penalty, and for the part only for which he is heir. The act mentioned in the case in the paragraph *Cato, amplius non agi*, is the case of an act divisible *tam solutione quam obligatione*, and which, from the nature of the thing, cannot be performed by the several heirs of him who has contracted the engagement, otherwise than by each for the part for which he is heir. For each of these heirs succeeding only for his share to the right or pretension which the ancestor bound himself not to exercise, each of these heirs can only for his part contravene this engagement, or execute it, in renewing or not renewing his pretensions for the part he has.

On the contrary, when the obligation is divisible, indeed, *quoad obligationem*, but indivisible *quoad solutionem* and the intention of the parties was in adding the penal clause that the payment might not be made but for the whole, in this case each of the heirs, in discharging for his part the principal obligation, will not avoid the forfeiture of the penalty; and to this case ought to be confined the paragraph *Si sortem*, which is reconciled with the paragraph *Cato*.

Dumoulin, *p.* 1, *n.* 72, gives as an example of the decision of the paragraph *Si sortem*, the case of a merchant, who had stipulated with his debtor a certain sum as a penalty, in case the principal sum due him should not be paid in a certain place during a particular fair. The tender which one of the heirs should make him to pay his part ought not to prevent the penalty from being due for the whole, on failure of the payment of the whole sum. Because this merchant not being able to transact his business at the fair, without the whole of the sum due him, the intention of the parties was, in stipulating the penalty, that it should be incurred for the whole, on failure of the payment for the whole, and notwithstanding the partial payment that might be made. For this partial payment cannot indemnify the creditor even for part of the injury which he sustains from the delay of payment of the whole; and it is for the indemnification of the injury that the penalty is stipulated. Note, also that in the case of the paragraph *Si sortem*, the penalty is stipulated for the delay, and not for the inexecution. Therefore the creditor ought to receive both the principal and the penalty.

The law 85, §. 6, *d. tit.* is also the case of an obligation divisible, it is true, *quoad obligationem*, but indivisible *quoad solutionem*; it is said in the case of this stipulation *Si fundus Titianus datus non erit, centum dari; nisi totus detur, pœna committitur centum; nec prodest partes fundi dare cessante uno, quemadmodum nec prodest ad liberandum pignus, partes creditori solvere*. Although the obligation *dare fundum Titianum* be an obligation divisible *quoad obligationem*, yet this obligation, whether it arises from a contract of sale, a contract of exchange or a composition, or in any other manner, is indivisible *quoad solutionem*, as the creditor has an interest in not taking a part of the land, having intended to purchase the whole. Therefore if one of the heirs of the debtor is in arrear to give his part of the land, the tender of the other heirs to give their parts, the transfer which they should even make of them to the creditor, who only accepted them provisionally and expecting the transfer of the rest, would not prevent the creditor from demanding the whole penalty, on offering nevertheless the parts which he had received. For he cannot have them both.

360. In the case of the paragraph *Si sortem*, when one of the heirs, for part, of the debtor, in neglecting to discharge the principal obligation for the part for which he is liable, has occasioned the forfeiture of the penalty, against the others who were ready to discharge the obligation for their parts, does he incur the penalty for the whole? He incurs it directly for the part only for which he is heir: for being liable for the principal obligation for his part; he can only contravene it for this part; then he can for this part only incur the penalty: for the penalty ought to be proportioned to the contravention. In this, divisible obligations differ from those which are indivisible. But although he be liable directly for this part only of the penalty, he is indirectly bound for the whole. For his co-heirs, who were ready to perform the obligation for their part, having incurred the penalty for their part, by his delay in perform ing his part of the obligation, he is bound to them, *judicio familiæ erciscundæ*, to indemnify them; *d.* §. *Si sortem*, to avoid an useless circuity of actions and the creditor may be received to demand from this heir the penalty not only for the part for which he is directly liable, but also for that of his co-heirs, for which he is bound to indemnify them, and consequently for the whole.

361. We have spoken thus far of the case in which the heir for part has failed to perform a divisible obligation of the ancestor, for the part for which he was liable. The instance in the paragraph *Cato*; and that in the paragraph *Si sortem*, although different from each other, as we have observed, are both put in this case. We may suppose another, for which there is no express authority; it is the one in which the heir, for part, of him who had contracted, under a penal clause, a divisible obligation should contravene it for the whole and not for the part only for which he is heir.

For example. A person has let his land to farm, and leaves four heirs, one of whom evicts the tenant for the whole. On this case two questions arise, I. whether the penalty is incurred for the whole by this heir? II. whether it be incurred not only by him, but also by his co-heirs? The reason to doubt on these questions is, that this heir being liable as heir, only for the part for which he is heir, to continue the lease, he ought to be looked upon as a stranger for the rest. The disturbance he occasions to the tenant, is only as heir for his part; for the rest he disturbs him as a stranger. Hence they conclude, that as the disturbance which a stranger, without right, should oppose to the enjoyment of the lease, would not occasion the forfeiture of the penalty against this stranger, who would only have been liable for damages; nor against the heirs of the lessor, who would have been holden to remit the rent to the tenant only in proportion to the eviction, in case of the insolvency of the person who disturbed him; so, in this case, the penalty ought not to be incurred by this heir in part, except for the part for which he is heir: he ought to be chargeable only with damages for the remainder and the penalty ought not to be incurred by his co-heirs. Yet, Dumoulin, who discusses this question, *part* 3, *n.* 412, *& seq.* decides that in this case the penalty is incurred for the whole, by this heir in part, and that it is also incurred by his co-heirs, for the part for which each is heir. To establish this decision and to refute at the same time the reasoning which we have noticed, he distinguishes in this obligation to continue the leafe, and in all other kinds of divifible obligations, two kinds of obligations, the principal obligation, as in this cafe that to continue the leafe, which is divifible, and the acceffory obligation or that of good faith, which is indivifible, and for which each heir is confequently bound for the whole. The heir in part of the leffor, who evicted the tenant, was, indeed, liable, as to the principal obligation for his part; but he was liable for the whole and indivifibly, to ufe good faith. Good faith obliged him to oppofe no difturbance to the enjoyment of the leafe, not only for his part, but alfo for the other parts. In evicting the tenant for the whole, he ought not to be confidered as having trefpaffed fimply as a ftranger with regard to the other parts, but as having contravened the obligation to ufe good faith, which he was under in his capacity of heir, even with regard to the other parts. This contravention being then, even with regard to the other parts and confequently for the whole, the contravention of an obligation contracted by the anceftor, under the penalty included in the agreement, it ought to occafion the forfeiture of the penalty for the whole, againft the heir who has contravened it. Such is the opinion of Dumoulin on the firft queftion. Dumoulin confirms his opinion by the following reafoning. Were it true, fays he, that in evicting the tenant from the whole, this heir ought to be confidered to have contravened for his part only, and to be confidered to have trefpaffed as a ftranger for the other parts, it would follow that the tenant would not, on account of his contravention for thefe parts, have the hypothecation refulting from his leafe on the property of the anceftor. It would follow that although the leafe was made under a feal giving jurifdiction, as that of the Chatelet of Orleans, the tenant could not profecute the heir, who had evicted him, before the Bailli of Orleans, except for the part for which he is heir. This is what no one will pretend to fay. Then this heir in part, in evicting the tenant, ought to be holden to have contravened the obligation, not only for his part, but for the others and for the whole, and confequently he ought to incur the whole penalty ftipulated in the cafe of contravention.

With regard to the ſecond queſtion, Dumoulin for the ſame reaſon holds that the penalty is incurred, not only by this heir, but alſo by each of his coheirs for the part for which they are heirs: for by the penal clauſe the anceſtor bound himſelf and all his heirs to the payment of the penalty, in caſe of a contravention of the primitive obligation. It ſuffices then that there has been a contravention, for it to be ſaid that the condition, under which the obligation of the penalty was contracted, has become accompliſhed, and conſequently that all the heirs of the anceſtor are liable.

If the anceſtor had given ſecurities *in omnem causam*, which ſecuritiſhip extended as well to the primitive as to the penal obligation, the act of the heir who evicted the tenant would have bound the ſecurities to the payment of the penalty; *a fortiori*, ought it to bind his co-heirs, who ſucceed to this obligation as principal debtors.

362. This deciſion on the ſecond queſtion applies even when the heir who has evicted the tenant would alone be bound by the primitive obligation to continue the leaſe, as in this caſe: I have leaſed a paternal eſtate to a tenant, under a penalty of two hundred livres, in caſe I fail in permitting him to enjoy the leaſe; I leave an heir to this paternal eſtate and ſeveral heirs of another line. This paternal heir prevents by his own act the leſſee from enjoying the leaſe, *puta*, by ſelling the eſtate, without binding the purchaſer to continue the leaſe. Although this heir is alone liable for the primitive obligation to continue the leaſe, according to the principle ſtated *supra*, *n.* 301, this obligation being the obligation of a certain determinate thing, to which he has alone ſucceeded, yet his contravention will occaſion the forfeiture of the penalty, with regard to my other heirs, for the parts for which they are heirs. For the debt of the penalty is the debt of a ſum of money, contracted by the anceſtor, on the condition of this contravention, to which debt conſequently, all the heirs of the anceſtor ſucceed. They have recourſe, however, againſt the one who contravened the obligation. *Molin. part* 3, *n.* 430.

363. Another example may be given. A tenant for life has made a lease of the land, concealing the nature of the estate he had in it and pretending to be tenant in fee. There is a penalty of two hundred livres, stipulated for the benefit of the lessee, if he be not suffered to enjoy. The tenant for life dies, leaving four heirs, one of whom is the proprietor of the land, and who as such evicts the lessee. The penalty is incurred by the four heirs; but he who evicted the lessee is liable only for his part, and is not bound, as in the former case, to indemnify his co-heirs. For, having, as proprietor, the right of enjoying his own estate, he has not acted contrary to good faith. *Dolo non facit qui jure suo utitur.* He is liable for the violation of the lease and the penalty, in his capacity of heir only and therefore only for his hereditary part. *Molin. ib. n.* 432.

Article V.

Whether the penalty is incurred for the whole, and towards all the heirs of the creditor, by a contravention affecting one of them.

364. Paul, in the law 2, §. *fin. de verb. oblig.*, determines this question, in the instance of a penal stipulation added to an indivisible primitive obligation. For example. You bound yourself by a composition to suffer me and my heirs to pass through your park, a foot or on horseback, and with beasts of burden, under a penalty of twelve livres, in case of a contravention of this obligation: I have left four heirs; you prevented one of them from passing through the park and you suffered the other three to pass. Paul determines that in this case the contravention being of an obligation indivisible and not susceptible of parts, cannot be a partial contravention, therefore the forfeiture of the penalty which it occasions, it would seem *subtilitate juris*, ought to be incurred for the whole and to the benefit of all the heirs. Yet according to equity which in this case ought to prevail over the subtilty of the law, the penalty can be incurred towards him only to whom a passage was denied and only for his hereditary part: *Si stipulator decesserit qui stipulatus erit sibi hæredique suo agere licere; & unus ex hæredibus ejus prohibeatur; si pæna sit adjecta, in solidum committetur; sed qui non*

sunt prohibiti, doli exceptione submovebuntur, d. §. The reason is that equity does not allow that the three heirs to whom a passage through the park was allowed, should, at the same time, reap the benefit of the performance of the obligation and receive the penalty stipulated in case of a contravention: nor that they should complain of the contravention of the debtor towards their co-heir, in which contravention they had no interest: *Non debet aliquis habere simul implementum obligationis & pœnam contraventionis; & pœna quæ subrogatur loco ejus quod interest, non debet committi his qui non sunt prohibiti, & quorum nulla interest cohæredem ipsorum esse prohibitum; Molin. p.* 1, *n.* 32 & 35. The law 3, §. 1. *d. tit.* seems contrary to this. The reason is that Ulpian speaks only *subtilitate juris.*

As the contravention of the obligation, made by the debtor towards one of the heirs of the creditor, occasions the forfeiture of the penalty only with regard to this heir, and with regard to his hereditary part only, although the primitive obligation might have been indivisible; a *fortiori* ought it to be so holden when the primitive obligation is a divisible one.

CHAPTER VI.

Of the accessory obligation of securities and others, who accede to that of a principal debtor.

THIS chapter is divided into eight sections, the seven first of which relate to securitiship. We shall treat in the first of the nature of securitiship. We shall see in the second what are the different kinds of securities. In the third we shall speak of the qualifications which securities ought to have. We shall see in the fourth, for whom, to whom, for what kind of obligations, and in what manner securitiship is contracted. In the fifth, to what it extends. In the sixth we shall speak of the manner in which securitiship is extinguished, and the different exceptions or pleas, which the law allows to fecurities: In the feventh, of the action which the fecurity has in his own right, againft the principal debtor and againft his co-fecurities. In the eighth and laft fection, we fhall treat of the other kinds of acceffory obligations.

SECTION THE FIRST.

Of the nature of securitiship. Definition of securities, and the corollaries resulting therefrom.

365. Securitifhip is a contract by which one binds himfelf for a debtor to the creditor, to pay, in the whole or a part, what the debtor owes him, by acceding to his obligation.

We call a fecurity him who contracts fuch an obligation.

Securitifhip, befides the contract that takes place between the fecurity and the creditor, includes alfo, in moft cafes, another contract, which is prefumed to take place between the fecurity and the debtor for whom the fecurity binds himfelf; and this contract is the contract of mandate, which is always implied, when it is with the knowledge and approbation of the principal debtor that the fecurity binds himfelf for him, according to the rule of law: *Semper qui non prohibet pro se intervenire, mandare creditur;* L. 60, ff. *de Reg. jur.* When the fecuritifhip has been entered into without the knowledge of the debtor for whom the fecurity binds himfelf, it cannot be prefumed to include a contract between the fecurity and this debtor; but there is prefumed in this cafe a kind of *quasi* contract between them, which is called *negotiorum gestorum*. We fhall treat of the obligations which arife from the contract of mandate, or from the contract *negotiorum gestorum*, in the feventh fection of this chapter.

The contract which takes place between the fecurity and the creditor to whom he binds himfelf, is not of the clafs of contracts of beneficence; for the creditor receives nothing, by this contract, above what is due him: he only procures to himfelf a fecurity for what is due him, without which he would not have contracted with the principal debtor, or would not have granted him the terms he has granted: but the securitiship includes a benefit to the debtor for whom it is entered into.

From the definition we have just given of securitiship and securities, several corollaries result.

First corollary.

366. The obligation of securities being, according to our definition, an obligation accessory to that of the principal debtor, it results therefrom that it is of the essence of the obligation of securities that there be an obligation of a principal debtor which is valid: consequently, if he for whom the security has bound himself to you, was not your debtor, the security would not be liable, as the accessory obligation cannot exist without a principal obligation, according to this rule of law; *Cum causa principalis non consistit ea quidem quæ sequuntur locum habet;* L. 178, ff. *de Reg. jur.*

Second corollary.

367. A second consequence of our definition is, that the security, in binding himself for the principal debtor, does not discharge him from his obligation, but contracts another, which accedes to his. In this the security differs from him who is called in law *expromissor*, who binds himself to the creditor, in such a manner that the creditor accepts him as the debtor in the room of the principal debtor, whom he discharges.

Third corollary.

368. It results from our definition, that the security can validly bind himself only to the payment of the same thing for which the debtor is bound, or of part of the same thing. Therefore if one has become security to me for one hundred bushels of wheat, in favor of a person who owed me two thousand livres, the securitiship would be null. L. 42, ff. *de Fidej.* 232.

Contra, vice versa, one may validly become security to me for two thousand livres, in favor of one who owes me one hundred bushels of wheat. For money being the common thing by which all things are valued; he who owes me one hundred bushels of wheat of the value of two thousand livres, owes me in fact and validly two thousand livres, and consequently he who binds himself for him to pay me two thousand livres, does not bind himself to any thing different from what is due me by the principal debtor.

369. If one had bound himself to give me a certain piece of land, in fee, and another became his security that he should give me a life estate in it, would this securitiship be valid? Yes: for this part of the fee, being a right in the land which is due me, is in a manner part of the thing that is due me, and consequently it cannot be said that the security bound himself for a thing different from that due by the principal debtor. This is the decision of Caius in the law 70, §. 2, ff. *de Fidej. In eo,* says he, *videtur dubitatio esse, ususfructus pars rei sit an proprium quiddam? Sed cum ususfructus, fundi jus est, incivile est fidejussorem ex sua promissione non teneri.*

Fourth corollary.

370. It results from this definition, that the security cannot validly bind himself to more than that to which the principal debtor is bound: and as more is estimated not only *quantitate*, but also *die, loco, conditione, modo,* it results that the creditor cannot bind himself to harder conditions than the principal debtor; for the accessory obligation cannot surpass the principal; but he may bind himself to conditions more easy. Such is the decision of the law 8, §. 7, ff. *de Fidej. Illud commune est in universis qui pro aliis obligantur, quod si fuerint in duriorem causam adhibiti, placuit eos omnino non obligari; in leviorem plane causam accipi possunt.*

It results from this principle, that if one has bound himself for a determinate sum, *puta,* for three hundred livres, for a debtor, whose debt was unliquidated, the securitiship ought to be presumed to have been fixed to three hundred livres in favor only of the security, and only for the purpose that if by the liquidation that should afterwards be made, the debt amounted to a larger sum, the security ſhould be bound only for three hundred livres. But if, by the liquidation, the debt was fixed at a leſs ſum, *puta*, two hundred and fifty livres, the ſecurity, who cannot owe more than the principal debtor, would be debtor only of two hundred and eighty livres, and if he had paid the three hundred livres mentioned in the contract of ſecuritiſhip, he would have a right to reclaim the overplus.

May the creditor in ſuch caſe, before the liquidation of the debt, compel the ſecurity to pay the three hundred livres proviſionally, notwithſtanding the latter ſhould require that the debt be liquidated, and ſhould contend that it does not amount to ſo much? The cuſtom of Brittany, *art.* 189, decides for the affirmative; but this deciſion ought not to be followed, out of that province. For according to the principle which we have eſtabliſhed, as the ſecurity cannot be bound for more than the principal debtor, he ought not to be compellable to the payment of the debt ſooner than the principal debtor: as the latter cannot be compellable till after the liquidation of the debt, *Ord.* 1661, *tit.* 33, *art.* 2, the ſecurity ought not to be compellable to pay before this. D'Argentre, in his note on this article of the cuſtoms above cited, admits that it is contrary to law, *contra Jus Romanum*, and in his commentary on the *art.* 206 of the old cuſtoms from which this is drawn, he ſays, *Hic ſe Authores Conſuetudinis produnt non Juriſconſultos.*

371. According to this principle, when the principal debtor is bound abſolutely, the ſecurity may validly bind himſelf to pay within a certain time or on a certain condition; but on the contrary, if the principal debtor is bound only under a certain condition, ſtill depending, or within a certain time yet unexpired, the ſecurity cannot bind himſelf to pay preſently and on demand; *dicta lege*, 8, §. 7.

Note that if nothing be expreſſed in the contract of ſecuritiſhip, the time and condition expreſſed in the principal obligation are implied; ſo it is determined in the law 61, ff. *d. tit.* that the place of payment mentioned in the principal obligation is implied in the ſecuritiſhip.

372. If the principal debtor is bound to pay within a

certain period, the security may bind himself to pay within the same or a longer period; but he cannot bind himself to pay within a shorter one.

Hence it follows that when the principal debtor is bound to pay within a certain time, and the security binds himself to pay, under a certain condition, *as soon as* the condition is accomplished; this securitiship will not be valid if the condition is accomplished before the time of payment, within which the principal debtor is bound to pay, is expired. L. 16, §. 5, ff. *de tit.* For if the securitiship should be valid, the security would be bound to pay before the debt might be demanded from the principal debtor, and consequently *in duriorem causam*, which cannot be.

When the principal debtor is bound under a condition, the security may validly bind himself under this condition and another likewise; for in this case the situation of the security is better than that of the debtor, since he cannot be bound but on the accomplishment of both conditions. If the security binds himself under the alternative of the condition under which the principal debtor is bound and of another condition, or simply under a different condition, the securitiship will be valid, if the condition under which the principal debtor bound himself is first accomplished: but if the other is accomplished first, the securitiship will not be valid, as the security cannot be bound before the principal debtor becomes so; L. 70, *pp.*º & §. 1, ff. *de Fidejuss.*

373. The place of payment may also render the obligation more difficult to be performed: therefore if the security had promised to pay in a more distant place than that in which the principal debtor is to pay, the securitiship would not be valid, being made under a harder condition than the principal obligation; *d.* L. 15. §. 1 & 2.

374. If a person had bound himself to another to give him one or the other of two certain negroes, *puta*, James or John, which were nearly of the same price, would the contract, by which the security should bind himself for the debtor to give John determinately, be valid? The law 54.

ff. *de Fidej.* decides that it is valid and that the situation of the security is, in this case, better than that of the principal debtor, since the security may be discharged by the death of John alone, whereas the principal debtor cannot be discharged but by the death of both.

Contra, if the principal debtor had bound himself to give John determinately, the contract by which the security should bind himself to give John or James, would not be valid, not only for the reason we have given that this alternative condition is harder than the determinate one of James; but also for another reason, which is that if the security chuse to give James, he would find himself to owe another thing than what was to be given by the principal debtor, who is debtor only of John; which cannot be, *supra n.* 368. This is the decision of the law 8, §. 1, ff. *d. tit.*

This is not to be apprehended in the last case in which the principal debtor promised John or James, and the security promised James determinately. For, in this case, if the principal debtor tenders James to the creditor, and puts him in arrear to receive it, in determining by this choice his obligation to deliver James, he discharges himself from the obligation to give John; and consequently discharges his security from it. *Nam reo liberato, liberantur fidejussores.* The security who has acceded only to the obligation to give John, owes nothing more. If, on the contrary, the principal debtor had offered John, he would owe the same thing as his security: therefore it cannot happen, in this case, that the principal debtor and his security should owe different things.

If the principal debtor had bound himself to give the negroes John and James, *at the choice of the creditor*, the security might validly bind himself to give the one of the two *which he pleased*, *d. L.* 8, §. 10. For the creditor preserving his choice against the principal debtor, till the payment, the principal debtor would always be debtor of both negroes, and consequently of that whom the security should chuse to pay.

375. A question is made whether the securitiship is entirely void, when the security has bound himself for more than the principal debtor; or whether it be void only for so much as exceeds the principal obligation? It appears that the Roman lawyers thought it was entirely void; though Dumoulin, *ad* L. 51, *Si stipulanti*, §. *Sed si mihi*, *n.* 30, *&* *seq.* wishes to make them say the contrary. This evidently results from the words of the law 8, §. 7, above cited, *placuit eos omnino non obligari.* It is true that Halcander, in his edition, reads *non omnino;* but he has, on his own private authority, altered the text, against the faith of the copies, and against the authority of the Greek interpreters, who consider these words *omnino non* to have the same meaning as *nullo modo.* This likewise results from the other texts above quoted. The reason which Connanus gives, *Comment. Jur.* 68, for this opinion of the Roman lawyers, is that securitiship being necessarily an obligation accessory to the principal obligation, and it being of the essence of an accessory obligation, that it contain nothing more than the principal, a contract of securitiship by which the security binds himself to something more, is defective in the essential form of securitiship, and must therefore be absolutely null. This reasoning, on which there is room to believe the Roman lawyers grounded their opinion, is more subtle than solid. From a securitiship being an accessory of the principal obligation, it follows only that when the security has bound himself to more, he is not validly bound to this addition: nothing ought to prevent him from being bound to the amount for which the principal debtor is liable. For by agreeing to be bound to a greater sum, he has agreed to be bound to the sum for which the principal debtor is liable. Therefore, as the Roman laws are followed in our provinces only when they are conformable to natural equity, I think they ought not to be followed in this instance, and that it is to be holden that a security who bound himself to a greater sum than the one mentioned in the principal obligation, or who bound himself to pay immediately what the principal debtor owed only at a future period, or under a certain

condition, is validly bound to pay the sum mentioned in the principal obligation, on the terms and conditions there expressed. The custom of Brittany, *art.* 118, has adopted this opinion, and Wissembach, *ad. Tr. de Fid. n.* 10, admits that, although it is contrary to some texts of law, it is followed in practice.

376. The principle which we have established that the security cannot bind himself to harder terms than the principal debtor, *in duriorem causam*, ought to be understood with regard to what is due and what is the object of the obligation. The security cannot indeed owe more than is due by the debtor, *quantitate, die, loco, conditione, modo*, but as to the nature of the obligation, he may be harder and more strictly bound.

For example, I. According to the principles of the civil law, the security who accedes to a mere natural obligation is more strictly bound than the principal debtor; since he may be compelled to pay while the principal debtor cannot: the creditor having no action against him.

II. According to the same principles, when one has been security for a person who has what is called *exceptionem competentiæ*; as if one has been security for the father to the son, a creditor of his father; the security is more strictly bound than the principal debtor. Since the security may be constrained, with all rigor, to pay the whole debt, while the principal debtor is compellable only to the amount of what remains of his estate, after deducting what is necessary for his subsistence, L. 173, ff. *de Reg. jur.*

III. The security of a minor is often more strictly bound than the principal debtor, who may, if he has been overreached, be relieved against his obligation; whereas the security is bound without any hope of remedy. L. 13, *de minor*, L. 1, *Cod. de Fidejuss. minor.*

IV. According to our practice, a judicial security may be constrained by his person, although the principal debtor be not so; *puta*, if a priest, a minor, a woman, a septuagenarian: he is therefore more strictly bound, and as to the nature of the obligation, is bound *in duriorem causam*.

Fifth corollary.

377. It results from our definition that, as the securitiship is an accessory obligation to that of the principal debtor, the extinction of the principal obligation carries with it the extinction of the securitiship also, since it is of the nature of accessory things that they cannot exist without the principal thing. Whenever, then, the principal debtor is discharged, in what manner soever, not only by the actual payment he may have made, by a set-off or by a release given him by the creditor, the security is also discharged. For it being of the essence of the securitiship, that the security be bound for a principal debtor, he can no longer be bound, when there is no longer a principal debtor, for whom he may be bound.

378. Likewise, the security is discharged by the novation that is made of the debt: for the security can no longer be bound for the first debt for which he became security of the debtor, since it no longer exists, having been extinguished by the novation. Neither can he be bound for the new debt into which the former is converted, since this new debt is not the one to which he acceded. *Novatione legitimè perfecta debiti in aliam speciem translati, prioris contractus fidejussores, vel mandatores liberatos esse non ambigitur, si modo in sequenti se non obligaverint; L. 4, Cod. de Fidejus.*

379. Likewise when the principal debtor becomes sole and absolute heir of the creditor, *aut vice versa*, when the creditor becomes sole and absolute heir of the principal debtor, or when the same person becomes successively heir of both, the security is discharged, for there remains no longer a principal debtor, from the confusion that takes place of the qualities of creditor and debtor, which, happening to unite in the same person, mutually destroy each other; as no one can be his own creditor or his own debtor.

It would be otherwise, if the debtor had become heir of the creditor, with the benefit of inventory, *aut vice versa*. For one of the effects of the benefit of inventory being to prevent the confusion of qualities, and to distinguish the proper estate of the heir from the beneficiary estate, the debtor, beneficiary heir of the creditor, remaining always debtor to the beneficiary estate, his securities are not discharged: for there is still a principal debtor.

When the creditor succeeds to his debtor, not as heir, but as universal donee, or universal legatee, by escheat or by confiscation; as in all these cases he is not indiscriminately liable for his debts, but only to the value of the estate to which he succeeds, the confusion takes place only to that amount. Hence it follows that the securities are discharged no further; and if there be not, of the estate which the debtor has left, enough to pay the debt, the securities remain liable for the rest; but the creditor cannot prosecute them, until he has given them an account of the estate of the debtor to which he succeeds.

When the debtor becomes absolute heir indeed of the creditor, but only for part, *aut vice versa*, the confusion taking place only for the share for which he is heir, his security is discharged only in that proportion.

330. When the principal debtor is not discharged *de pleno jure*, but by some plea or bar, which he may oppose to the demand of the creditor, may the security oppose the same plea or bar, which the principal debtor might. It is necessary, in this case, to distinguish between the pleas or bars which are called *exceptiones in personam* and those that are called *exceptiones in rem*. The pleas *in personam* are those which are grounded on some reasons that are personal to the principal debtor. The pleas *in rem* are those which are thus called because they are not grounded on any thing that is personal to the debtor, but on the thing itself, which is to say, on the debt itself.

These pleas *in rem* may be pleaded by the security as well as the principal debtor: *Rei cohærentes exceptiones etiam fidejussoribus competunt*; L. 7, §. 1, ff. *de except*; and it is with regard to these pleas that we are to understand what is said in the law 19, ff. *de tit. Omnes exceptiones quæ reo competunt, fidejussori quoque, etiam invito reo competunt.*

Such is the plea of fraud or violence; such is also the

plea of the thing judged, *rei judicatæ*, or the decisory oath, *d.* L. 7, §. 1; for these pleas being founded on what has been settled by the judgment or decisory oath, are pleas that affect the thing, and are not founded on any thing that is personal to the debtor, and consequently are pleas not *in personam* but *in rem*; and these last pleas may be pleaded as well by the security as by the principal debtor in whose favor the judgment was, or to whom the oath was deferred. *Nec obstat regula juris*, that the judgment or decisory oath can procure no right to third persons not parties to the suit. L. 2. *Cod. Quib. res jud. non noc.*; L. 3, §. 3, ff. *de jurejur.* for this rule ought not to be understood of those whose right is essentially connected with that of the person who was a party, as the security is with the principal debtor.

When a principal debtor, by a composition made with the creditor respecting the legality of the debt, has agreed to pay it, on condition that three years should be given him; the plea which this agreement gives against the creditor, if he sues before that time, is also a plea *in rem*; for it is founded on the thing itself; it is founded on the doubt there was about the legality of the debt, which doubt was the object of the composition. This plea, therefore, may be pleaded by the security as well as the principal debtor, although he was not a party to the composition. Hence arises another question, whether the debtor, by a new agreement with the creditor, may, to the prejudice of the security, permit the creditor to exact the debt before the time mentioned in the first agreement? Paul, in the law 27, §. 2, ff. *de Pact.*, decides formally that he may, although several interpreters, in order to reconcile this text with the law *fin.* ff. *d. t.* which decides differently, have distorted the text, in order to make it say the contrary. The reason of the decision of Paul is, that as the right which results from the first agreement has been formed by a concurrence of the will of the creditor and debtor alone, without the intervention of that of the security, it may be destroyed by a contrary consent; *cum quæque eodem modo dissolvantur quo colligata sunt.* On the contrary, Furius-Anthianus decides that the new agreement cannot deprive the security of the plea he had acquired by the first. L. *fin.* ff. *de Pact.* and I think we ought to adhere to this decision. The reason alledged for that of Paul can apply only when there is no right acquired by a third person. Several interpreters whose opinion I have heretofore followed, in order to reconcile Furius-Anthianus with Paul, say that the decision of Furius applies only to the case in which the security has accepted and ratified the first agreement: but this concordance is conjectural. It is not said in this law that the security had accepted the first agreement; this cannot even be supposed. For in supposing it, Furius would have stated as doubtful, a case on which no doubt could arise.

Let us pass now to the pleas *in personam.*

These pleas, which are grounded on the insolvency or partial solvency of the principal debtor, and the personal privilege which he has, not to be compellable to pay out of his necessary subsistence, cannot be offered by the security. This is what we learn from the law 7, ff. *de except.* which teaches that the plea granted to a debtor, who should be the parent, husband, patron or partner of the creditor, to avoid being compelled to pay the debt, out of what is necessary to his subsistence, cannot be offered by the security. The reason is evident. The indigence of the principal debtor does not discharge him from his obligation, and were he afterwards to be in a better situation, he might be compelled to pay. In the mean time his obligation exists for the whole and is a sufficient foundation to support that of the security. His indigence does not extinguish it: it only suspends the execution, on the ground that he cannot be compelled to pay out of what is necessary to his subsistence. But this plea being grounded on the relation in which he stands to the creditor, as parent, husband, &c. which is personal to him, cannot be offered by his security.

It is the same with regard to the plea which results from the cession of property. When the principal debtor has made a cession of his property, which is not sufficient to pay what he owes, he is not discharged from the balance, L. 1. *Cod. qui bon. ced.*; and his obligation that remains for the balance, is a sufficient foundation to support the obligation of his security for the balance. Yet as long as he has not acquired other property, beyond what is necessary for his subsistence, he cannot plead to the suit of the creditor against him, the plea resulting from the cession of his property. L. 3, ff. *Cod. de bon. author. jud. de possid.*; L. 4, ff. *de cess. bonor.* It is evident that this bar is grounded on a reason of favor that is personal to the debtor; and it is *exceptio in personam*, which his securities cannot plead.

I think it is the same with the plea that arises from a contract of composition to which the creditor should have been compelled to accede, by which part of the debt is remitted to the debtor and time stipulated for the payment of the rest. I think that the pleas which this contract affords to the principal debtor, against the suit that might be brought before the expiration of the time allowed him by the contract, or to recover the part remitted, cannot be used by the security, who may be sued immediately for the payment of the whole debt. For it is evident that this is a plea *in personam*, allowed to the debtor on account of his state of indigence, which is personal to him. The remittance and delay granted by the contract of composition, not being granted *animo donandi*, but by necessity, the plea which results from this contract, like that in the preceding case, affects only the civil obligation. The natural obligation for what remains to be paid, continues in its totality and is a sufficient foundation for that of the securities. This reason is an answer to what has been alledged in the first place for the contrary opinion, which is in saying that it is of the essence of the contract of securitiship that the security be bound to no more than the principal debtor. As to the second position in favor of the contrary opinion, which is in saying that if the security had not the benefit of the contract of composition and might be bound to pay the whole debt, it would happen indirectly, that it could not avail the principal debtor himself on account of the recourse which the security, who had paid the whole debt would have againſt him. The anſwer is, that this will not happen, becauſe the ſecurity who has paid the whole is, as a creditor of the ſum for his indemnity, bound like the other creditors, to accede to the contract of compoſition, and to allow to the principal debtor, on this indemnity, the ſame deductions as are ſtipulated in the contract. It is however neceſſary to admit that the contrary opinion is authoriſed by two caſes cited by Baſnage, one determined in the Parliament of Paris, the other in that of Normandy; the laſt is the 114th caſe reported by Montholon. But I do not think that the deciſion in theſe two caſes ought to be followed, for the reaſons above ſtated. This deciſion ſeems alſo to be contrary to the nature of the contract of ſecuritiſhip; which is a contract to which the creditor reſorts for his ſafety, againſt the riſk of the inſolvency of the principal debtor. What then would become of this ſafety if the creditor had not the right of exacting from the ſecurity what the inſolvency of the principal debtor ſhould bind him to remit to the principal debtor? Our opinion is conformable to the 13th article of the *Arretes de M. de Lamoignon*, under this title.

When there was an agreement between a creditor and the principal debtor, by which the creditor, in order to accommodate the principal debtor, had agreed not to demand from him the payment of the debt; if the creditor afterwards demanded the payment of the debt from the ſecurities, the ſecurities might indeed oppoſe to him, the plea reſulting from the agreement he had made with the principal debtor: but according to the ancient Roman law, the ſecurities had the plea only becauſe the ſuit, brought againſt the ſecurities, affected the principal debtor, who was bound to indemnify them, *actione contraria mandati aut negotiorum geſtorum*. Therefore, when the ſuit, brought againſt the ſecurities, could not affect the principal debtor, *puta*, becauſe the ſecurities had bound themſelves *animo donandi*, with proteſtation not to claim any thing from the principal debtor if they were obliged to pay for him, the ſecurities could not in this caſe, according to the principles of the ancient Roman law, oppofe the plea refulting from the agreement that had taken place between the creditor and the principal debtor, becaufe as this agreement and the plea refulting from it, were grounded on the perfonal confideration which the creditor had for the principal debtor, whom he was willing to accommodate, it is a plea *in personam*, which does not belong to the fecurities. This we learn from the law 32, ff. *de Pact.* where it is faid: *Quod dictum est, si cum reo pactum sit ut non petatur, fidejussori quoque competere exceptionem, propter rei personam placuit, ne mandati judicio conveniatur: igitur si mandati actio nulla sit, forte si donandi animo fidejusserit, dicendum est non prodesse exceptionem fidejussori.*

Even if the fecurity were an ordinary fecurity, who might have his recourfe againft the principal debtor for what he fhould be compelled to pay, he could not, according to the principles of the Roman law, oppofe the plea refulting from the agreement which had taken place between the creditor and the principal debtor, if by this agreement, the creditor, in promifing not to demand the payment from the principal debtor, had exprefsly referved the power of demanding it from the fecurity: *Debitoris conventio fidejussoribus proficiet, nisi hoc actum est, ut duntaxat a reo non petatur, a fidejussore petatur: tunc enim fidejussor exceptione non utetur;* L. 21, §. 5, *in fin.* 22, ff. *d. tit.*

Cujas, in his commentary on the paragraph 5, before cited, obferves very properly, that in this fecurities differed from thofe who were called in law *mandatores pecuniæ credendæ;* for if, at your requeft, I had lent another a fum of money, I could not afterwards, by agreeing with the debtor that I would not demand from him the payment of the debt, validly referve to myfelf the right to demand it from you. He gives this reafon for the diftinction. When, at your requeft, I have lent a fum of money to another, I am, from the nature of the contract of mandate that has taken place between us, bound to cede to you the action that refults from the loan I made in the execution of your mandate;

every mandatary being bound, *actione mandati directa*, to account to the mandator for all he has received in the execution of the mandate. Therefore, when by my own act I have disabled myself from performing my obligation to you, and to cede to you the action that results from the loan I made to the debtor, either by agreeing with the debtor not to demand any thing from him, or by suffering, through my own fault, a judgment to be rendered against me in a suit I had brought, or in any other manner, I ought not to be allowed to claim from you, *actione mandati contraria*, the sum which I lent by your order to this debtor. L. 95, §. *pen.* ff. *de Solut.*: for it is a principle common to all synallagmatic contracts, that the party who fails in his obligation, is not to be received to demand from the other party the performance of his.

It is not the same with securities. A creditor according to the principles of the antient Roman law, as Cujas observes, *ad. d.* §., does not contract any obligation to the securities to keep for them his actions against the principal debtor, against whom they have one in their own right. It is from a reason of equity merely, that he cannot refuse the cession of them to the security when he pays; but he is bound only to cede them such as they are; therefore the agreement he made with the debtor, by which his action has been rendered ineffectual, does not preclude him from demanding from the security the payment of the debt.

Such was the antient law, which, as Cujas observes, *ad d.* §. 5, can hardly apply since the novel of Justinian: *Jure novo*, says Cujas, *haud facile procedere potest*: for Justinian having, by his novel, granted to securities the benefit of discussion, *beneficium ordinis*, which consists in the right it gives them, when they are prosecuted by the creditor, to send him back to prosecute, first, the principal debtor, and to discuss, for this purpose, his property, it is evident that the creditor cannot now, by agreeing with the debtor not to demand from him the payment of the debt, reserve to himself the right to demand it from the securities; for he cannot, by his own act, deprive them of the right and the plea which the law gives them.

According to the principles of our jurisprudence, besides this reason derived from the novel, that a creditor may not, in agreeing with his debtor not to demand the debt from him, reserve to himself the right to demand it from the securities, there is another reason which is no less decisive; it is derived from the difference in the civil law and ours, on simple pacts.

According to the principles of the civil law, they were only the obligations which had been formed by the sole assent of the parties, that might be dissolved by a contrary assent. With regard to all others, when the creditor wished to release any of them to the debtor, he could do it only by the acceptilation, either simple or Aquilian: without this the agreement he had made with the debtor, not to demand the debt from him, was a simple pact which could not dissolve the obligation of the debtor; for as a simple pact cannot produce a civil obligation, it cannot dissolve one. It is true that this gave to the debtor a plea to preclude the creditor from the suit he might have brought against him, contrary to the faith of the agreement; but the debtor had a right to this plea only from the equity of the Prætor against the rigor of law: the obligation he had contracted still continued, *ipso jure*, in his person, and was a sufficient foundation to support that of the securities who had acceded to it.

It was so likewise when the creditor had agreed, through liberality, to grant a certain time to the debtor who had first contracted an absolute obligation, without any time of payment. This agreement was but a simple pact which only afforded to the creditor a plea against the suit which the creditor, contrary to the faith of the agreement, might have brought before the time. But if by the agreement the creditor had declared that he intended to grant the time to the debtor alone and not to the securities, this agreement, according to the principles of the antient law, did not prevent him from suing the securities, before the end of the time: and they could not oppose to him the principle, that it is of the nature and essence of securitiship that the security be not bound to more than the principal debtor, and should have the same time of payment: for the agreement by which a time has been granted to the debtor, being only a simple pact, could not impair his obligation or diminish it; it continues *ipso jure*, as it was contracted, an obligation without a time of payment, and it leaves that of the securities likewise to continue. If the debtor may have the advantage of the delay that has been granted him by the agreement, it is an advantage which he holds only from the equity of the Prætor against the rigor of the law, and which, being grounded on a consideration personal to the debtor, does not pass to his securities.

These principles of the civil law, on the effect of simple pacts, are not derived from natural law, and are grounded only on subtilties very much opposed to the spirit and simplicity of our jurisprudence. We are not acquainted with the solemnity of acceptilation. Every agreement may create a civil obligation, dissolve or modify it. When a creditor has agreed with the debtor not to demand the debt from him, this agreement, according to the simplicity of our law, discharges the debtor *de jure*. Therefore the creditor cannot validly reserve to himself the right of demanding payment from the securities: the discharge of the debtor, necessarily carries with it that of the securities.

Likewise, in our jurisprudence, when, since the contract, a creditor grants, through liberality, a day of payment to his debtor, he cannot validly exclude the securities from this delay; for this new agreement having the effect to modify, *de jure*, the obligation of the debtor and to make of an absolute obligation an obligation with a day of payment, the obligation of the securities receives the same modification, and has the same time of payment as the obligation of the principal debtor, because it is of the essence of a securitiship, that the security be not bound to any more than the principal debtor.

If, in the cafe of a contract of compofition made between the creditor and the debtor, the fecurities do not enjoy the allowance and delay granted to the debtor, as we have feen before, it is becaufe thofe allowances and delays that are granted to the debtor by this contract, affect only the civil obligation. The natural obligation remains entire, in confequence of which, the debtor himfelf, were he to have the opportunity of paying, could not confcientioufly avail himfelf of the allowances and delays that were granted him. This natural obligation fuffices, as we have faid, to ferve as a foundation for that of the fecurities. But when the creditor, of his own accord and through liberality, difcharges the debtor or gives him a time of payment, the debtor being no longer bound, naturally or civilly, to pay the fum which has been remitted; being no longer bound, *naturally or civilly*, to pay before the time is expired; it follows, confequently, that the fecurities fhould be no longer bound.

381. When the principal debtor obtains a reftitution againft his obligation by letters of refciffion, does this refciffion carry with it the refciffion of the obligation of the fecurities? The fame diftinction is to be made as before. If the refciffion is grounded on fome actual defect in the obligation, as fraud, violence, error, enormous lefion, the re*fciffion of the principal obligation carries with it that of the* fecurities. If, on the contrary, the refciffion is grounded on reafons that are perfonal to the principal debtor, as, for example, his non-age, in this cafe the refciffion which he obtains of this obligation does not carry with it that of the fecurities. The principal debtor, by the refciffion of his obligation, obtains only a plea which is perfonal to him againft his creditor, and his obligation, notwithftanding the refciffion of it, exifts in a manner *naturaliter*, and is a fubject to be acceded to by the fecurities. This is the decifion of the law 13, ff. *de minorib.* and, very explicitly, of the law 1, *Cod. de fidejus. min.*

There is however a cafe in which the refciffion of the principal obligation, although for the mere reafon of nonage, carries with it that of the obligation of the securities. It is when the principal debtor bound himself in a capacity which the judgment of rescission has destroyed, as if he bound himself in the capacity of heir, and he obtains the rescission of his acceptance of the inheritance. For the principal debtor not being bound in his own right, but in the capacity of heir, which he no longer has, and which he lost by the rescission, he is no longer debtor, not even *naturaliter*; his obligation, attached to a capacity that is destroyed, has ceased. This is the decision of the law 89, ff. *de acquir. hæred.*

382. The rule we have established, that the extinction of the principal obligation carries that of the security, suffers a kind of exception in the case in which the thing should have perished by the fault of the security, or since he has been put in arrear. In this case though the obligation of the principal debtor, who was not put in arrear, be extinguished by the destruction of the thing that was the object of it, the security remains bound. This is the decision of the law 32, §. 5, *de Usur. Si fidejussor solus moram fecerit, reus non tenetur; sicuti si Stichum promissum acciderit; sed UTILIS ACTIO in hunc (fidejussorem) dabitur.* This was established against the maxim which does not permit the obligation of the security to continue after the extinction of that of the principal debtor; which the Jurist teaches us by saying that in this case the action given against the security is *actio utilis*, that is to say, which is given *contra tenorem juris, ita suadente utilitate & æquitate*, by way of damages and as a punishment of the fault the security.

Sixth corollary.

383. From the security's being, according to our definition, he who binds himself for another and who accedes to the obligation of another, the Roman lawyers had drawn this consequence, that whenever the two capacities of principal debtor and of security of this debtor met in the same person, which happens when the security becomes heir of the principal debtor, *aut vice versa*, when the principal debt-

or becomes heir of the debtor, or when a third perſon becomes heir of both, in all theſe caſes the capacity of principal debtor deſtroyed that of ſecurity; as a ſecurity is, eſſentially, one who is bound for another, and as no one can be the ſecurity of himſelf. Hence they concluded that the obligation of the ſecurity was extinguiſhed, and that nothing remained but the principal obligation. L. 93, §. 2, & *fin.* ff. *de Solut.* L. 5, ff. *de Fid.* L. 24, *Cod. de Fidej.*

Hence they concluded that if the ſecurity had himſelf given a ſecurity, who acceded to his obligation, in all theſe caſes the obligation of this ſecurity of the firſt ſecurity was extinguiſhed by the extinction of the obligation of the firſt ſecurity, which was like a principal obligation in regard to that of this ſecurity of the ſecurity. L. 38, §. *fin.* ff. *de Solut.*

In our juriſprudence, this nicety is not obſerved, and a ſecurity of a ſecurity, *fidejussor fidejussoris*, is not diſcharged becauſe the ſecurity for whom he has been ſecurity has become heir to the principal debtor, *aut vice versa.* There is room to think the Roman Juriſts were divided on this queſtion, *d.* L. 83, §. *fin.* and although it ſhould be holden, according to the civil law, that there is a confuſion of the obligation of the ſecurity, the hypothecation given by this ſecurity would ſtill continue, for hypothecations are extinguiſhed only by payment, and the confuſion which, according to the ſubtilty of the law, diſcharges the ſecurity, in his capacity of ſecurity, is not equivalent to a payment; this is the deciſion of the law, *d.* L. 38, §. *fin.*

When the ſecurity becomes heir of his co-ſecurity it is not to be doubted that there is then no confuſion, and that both the capacities remain, though united in the ſame perſon; L. 21, §. 1, ff. *de fidejuss*; as the two obligations continue when the principal debtor ſucceeds to his principal co-debtor, L. 5, ff. *d. tit.*

384. From its being of the eſſence of the obligation of the ſecurity to accede to the obligation of the principal debtor, it is not therefore to be concluded that it is extin-

guished when the principal debtor dies without leaving any heirs. The reason to doubt is that there remains no principal debtor to whose obligation the security may accede. The reason to decide, which may also seem an answer to this objection, is that the estate of the principal debtor, though vacant, represents him and takes the place of his person, according to the maxim *hæreditas jacens personæ defuncti vicem sustinet*; consequently there remains, at least *fictione juris*, a principal debtor to whose obligation that of the security accedes; *vice versa*, when the creditor to whom the security became bound, dies without leaving any heirs, his estate represents him and is a fictitious person in whose favor the securitiship continues to exist.

385. When the securitiship was entered into in favor of a creditor, in a certain capacity which this creditor had, the securitiship continues in favor of the person to whom that capacity passes. For example. If I have been security for the debtor of an estate, to the heir, in his capacity of heir; this heir having since relinquished the estate to a person for whom it was holden in trust, and to whom the capacity of heir and all the hereditary rights have passed, the securitiship continues in favor of the *cestui que trust*; L. 21, ff. *de Fidej.*

§. II.

Division of securities.

386. We have in our jurisprudence three kinds of securities: conventional securities, legal, and judicial securities.

Conventional securities are those who intervene by the agreement of the parties in different contracts, as in the contracts of sale, hire, loan, &c. For example. One borrows money and gives a security, who binds himself to the lender for the return of the money; one buys a thing or hires it, and gives a security who binds himself with him for the payment of the price: such securities are *conventional securities*; they are not by law, nor are they ordered by the judge: it is the sole agreement of the parties which caufes them to intervene, becaufe the borrower, buyer or bailee to hire, has agreed with the lender, vendor or bailor, to give fecurity.

Legal fecurities are thofe which the law requires to be given, fuch as a mutual donee or legatee is bound to give before he receives what is given or bequeathed to him, &c.

Judicial fecurities are thofe which the judge requires to be given. As when the judge decrees that a perfon may receive provifionally a fum of money, on giving fecurity to reftore it, if it be fo decreed afterwards.

SECTION III.

Of the qualifications which a security ought to have.

§. I.

Of the qualifications a person ought to have, in order to contract validly a securitiship.

387. It is neceffary, the firft of all, that the fecurity be able to contract and bind himfelf as a fecurity.

All thofe who are incapable of contracting, as idiots, perfons interdicted, minors, feme coverts not authorifed by their hufbands, monks profeffed, cannot be fecurities.

388. According to the civil law women could not bind themfelves as fecurities for others; the Velleian fenatus-confultus invalidated their obligation.

Juftinian by his novel, 134, *cap.* 8, permitted women, in binding themfelves, to renounce the plea given them by the fenatus-confultus.

This principle was heretofore obferved with us: but as the claufe renouncing the Velleian fenatus-confultus, which had become a matter of courfe in all notarial inftruments, rendered it ineffectual, and was only a fource of lawfuits, King Henry IV entirely abrogated, by his edict of 1606, the Velleian fenatus-confultus; confequently it has ceafed to be law in the jurifdiction of the Parliament of Paris, who regiftered this edict.

In Normandy, where the edict was not regiftered, the

Velleian senatus-consultus is observed in all its rigor, and the novel permitting women to renounce it, is not followed.

In this diversity of jurisprudence, the law of the place where the woman dwelt when she contracted the securitiship, is to be followed. For the laws that regulate the obligation of persons, such as the Velleian senatus-consultus, which disables women from binding themselves for others, are statutes *in personam* extending their power over all persons subject to them by dwelling within the district in which they are in force, wherever may be their property and wherever they may contract. Therefore if a woman dwelling in Normandy becomes security for another, though the contract of securitiship may have been entered into in Paris, where the Velleian senatus-consultus is abrogated, the securitiship would be null.

But although a woman was married in Normandy, if her husband removes his residence to Paris, this wife having ceased by the change of her place of residence to be bound by the laws of Normandy, any securitiship she may enter into since her arrival, will be valid.

The personal obligation which a woman of Normandy has contracted in becoming security for another, being null, it follows as a consequence that the hypothecation of her property under which she has bound herself, is likewise null. Even when it is situated within the jurisdiction of the Parliament of Paris. The hypothecation cannot exist without the personal obligation to which it is an accessory.

Vice versa. If a Parisian woman becomes security before a notary-public, her property though situated in Normandy, will be hypothecated, this hypothecation being a consequence of the obligation which she contracted by a notarial instrument.

This objection will be made; it is admitted that the Velleian senatus-consultus is a statute *in personam* with regard to the first part of it, which disables women from binding their perſons for others. But it has a ſecond part which diſables them from binding their property for the debts of others. This ſenatus-conſultus having for the object of its ſecond part, things, it is, as to this ſecond part, a ſtatute, *in rem*, and, according to the nature of ſuch ſtatutes, its power extends to every thing ſituated in the diſtrict within which it is in force, whoever may be the perſon who is the owner of it: therefore it avoids the hypothecation which a woman, tho' perſonally ſubject to its power, makes of her property ſituated in Normandy, for the debt of another.

My anſwer is, that this argument proves only that if a Pariſian woman, without becoming ſecurity for another, and without binding herſelf perſonally, bound her property ſituated in Normandy for the debts of another, her obligation would be void, becauſe the Velleian ſenatus-conſultus obſerved in Normandy, and binding the property ſituated within that province, avoids ſuch an obligation for the debt of another. But when the obligation of her property is only a conſequence of a perſonal obligation which the Pariſian woman has contracted before a notary-public, the law of Normandy cannot invalidate it; for this law, having no effect on the perſonal obligation of a Pariſian woman, can have none on what is only an acceſſory to it.

The Velleian ſenatus-conſultus being a ſtatute *in perſonam* only with regard to its firſt part, and being a ſtatute *in rem* with regard to the ſecond, it follows that a woman of Normandy may, in not becoming ſecurity and contracting no perſonal obligation, bind, for the debt of another, her lands ſituated out of Normandy, in ſome province in which the Velleian ſenatus-conſultus is abrogated; for ſtatutes *in rem* extend their power only over things ſituated within the diſtrict in which they are in force.

389. Minors, though emancipated, may not validly bind themſelves for others; for emancipation gives them the power only of adminiſtering their eſtates, and it is evident that becoming ſecurity for the affairs of another, does not make part of this adminiſtration.

This applies even with regard to a merchant minor who should be security for another merchant, in a mercantile affair, in which he should have no interest; for his quality of merchant gives him no power to contract without hope of restitution except for affairs relating to his trade; the affairs of another merchant, in which he has no interest, are not affairs of his trade. *Basnage, Traite des Hypot. part 2, chap. 2, Despeisses, Traite des Cautions,* §. 1.

For the same reason, a minor who, by a dispensation from the Prince, exercises a public office, is not the less to be relieved from a securitiship he may have entered into. For the dispensation of the Prince makes him to be presumed of age only in regard to what relates to the public office which he permits him to exercise. Hence it is only with regard to engagements relative to the discharge of his office, that he may contract without hope of restitution; these principles are certain, notwithstanding the case reported by *Despeisses, ib.*

There are cases extremely favorable, in which the securitiship of a minor may be valid. For example; a minor has been determined not to be relievable against his securitiship, entered into to release his father from prison.

The securitiship of a minor for this cause ought, above all, to be confirmed, if the father could not share the benefit of a cession of goods to procure his release, and when the securitiship did not occasion an excessive detriment to the affairs of the son. But if the father might have made the cession of his goods, the minor ought to be relieved, who submitted to a considerable securitiship that was not necessary. The age of the minor may also be regarded. He who was near being of age ought with less facility to be relieved against his securitiship than he who was of an age not so much advanced. Basnage pretends that the securitiship of a minor would not in this case be liable to be revoked; it is necessary that the minor be at least of the age of eighteen; which is the age of puberty complete, and that at which children were bound by the novel 115, *chap.*

3, §. 15, under pain of difinherifon, to redeem their captive father. He cites a cafe in which the fecuritifhip of a minor of the age of fixteen, for this caufe, was annulled. In all thefe cafes great regard is to be paid to circumftances. Hence the difference in the cafes reported by Brodeau on Louet, L. A. *chap.* 9.

§. II.

Of the qualifications requisite for one to be received to be a security.

390. When a debtor is bound either by the law, the judge, or his own agreement, to give fecurity to his creditor; in order that the fecurity may be received, it is not fufficient that he have the above qualification which is required, the firft of all, and which confifts in being able to bind himfelf as a fecurity; it is neceffary, befides, I. that the fecurity be folvent and have property fufficient to fatisfy the debt he accedes to.

When the creditor to whom the fecurity is offered, contefts his folvency, the fecurity ought to juftify it by producing his titles to the real property he poffeffes; otherwife he ought to be rejected.

In judging of the folvency of a fecurity, and whether his property be fufficient to anfwer the debt, no regard, commonly, is paid to his perfonal property, becaufe that kind of property is eafily difpofed of and cannot be hypothecated: yet when the debt is fmall and the time of payment not far off, merchants well eftablifhed in trade are received, though their fortune confifts entirely of perfonal property. *Basnage*, *ibid.*

Neither is any regard paid to real property the title to which is difputed; nor fuch as is fituated at a great diftance; as it would be difficult to difcufs it. *ibid.*

II. The fecurity muft be a refident in the place, which is to fay, within the jurifdiction of the court, that it may not be too difficult to difcufs the property. *Fidejussor locuples videtur non tantum ex facultatibus, sed ex conveniendi facilitate.)* L. 2, ff. *Qui satisd.* In this cafe more indulgence is shewn to those who are required by law or by the judge to give securities, than to those who submitted to do so by their own agreement. The latter ought not to be allowed to say they cannot find any on the spot, having of their own accord submitted to give securities, *sibi imputare debent:* the former ought to be easily permitted to give persons of their neighbourhood, when they cannot find any in the place in which the securities are required. *Basnage, Despeisses.*

III. For the same reason, if a person of power was offered, the creditor might refuse him: so he might reject a person who having the privilege of a particular court, might take the creditor out of the jurisdiction of the place, or a military man who might obtain letters of state. *Basnage, Traite des Hypot. p. 2, ch. 2.*

Another qualification required in those who are offered as securities, is that they be subject to an imprisonment: therefore they may reject, for judicial securities, women, clergymen in sacred orders, and septuagenarians; because these persons are not liable to be so constrained.

As to the form of receiving securities, see *Ord. of* 1667, *t.* 28.

§. III.

Of the cases in which the debtor is bound to give another security in place of the one who has been received.

391. If the security had the necessary qualifications when he was received, and has since ceased to have them, *puta,* if from being solvent, he has now become insolvent, will the debtor be obliged to give another? A distinction is to be made. He will be obliged to do so in the case of a legal or judicial security. *Si calamitas insignis fidejussoribus vel magna inopia accidit, ex integro satisdandum erit.* L. 10, §. 1, *Qui satisd. cog.* L. 4. ff. *stipul. prœt.*

If it be a conventional security, a sub-distinction is to be made. If I bound myself to give a security indeterminately, and in performance of this obligation I gave one who has since become insolvent, I shall be bound to give another.

But if I contracted at first, with A. B. my ſecurity, or bound myſelf to give A. B. for a ſecurity, and A. B. afterwards becomes inſolvent, I ſhall not be compelled to give another, becauſe I promiſed only to give for a ſecurity the perſon whom I have given.

392. It remains to inquire whether he who is bound to give a ſecurity, may be received to give in lieu of it pledges ſufficient to anſwer the debt. For the negative this maxim is alledged, *aliud pro alio invito creditori solvi non potest*; which chiefly applies when the thing offered ſhould be better: hence it ſeems to follow that a creditor to whom a ſecurity is to be given, cannot be compelled to receive pledges inſtead of it. Nevertheleſs he who is to give a ſecurity ought eaſily to be permitted to give pledges inſtead of it, when he cannot obtain a ſecurity. Becauſe he to whom the ſecurity is to be given, having no intereſt but his ſafety, which pledges will as well and better provide for, *cum plus cautionis sit in re quam in persona, & tutius sit pignori incumbere quam in personam agere*, it would be, on his part, mere ill nature to refuſe the pledges, in lieu of a ſecurity, if what is offered in pledge can be kept without any trouble or riſk. *Basnage, ibid.*

SECTION IV.

For whom, to whom, for what obligation and how securitiship may be entered into.

§. I.

For whom and to whom.

393. One may become a ſecurity for any debtor whatever, even for a vacant eſtate, *cum personæ vicem sustineat*, L. 22, ff. *de Fidej.*; and likewiſe to any creditor of the perſon for whom one binds himſelf. One may likewiſe become a ſecurity for minors, idiots, interdicted prodigals, in all caſes in which thoſe perſons may, without any act of their own, become bound. For example. If I have uſefully managed the affairs of a minor or an interdicted prodigal, this minor or interdicted prodigal, being in this caſe bound to

me, *ex quasi contractu*, to reftore the fums I have difburfed in the management of his affairs, and which have turned to his profit, one may, as to thefe fums, become fecurity for him. It is in this fenfe, Cujas teaches us that we ought to underftand the law 25, ff. *de Fidejuss.*, which fays: *Si quis pro pupillo sine tutoris autoritate obligato, prodigove, vel furioso fidejusserit, magis esse ut ei non subveniatur.* This explanation removes the contrariety, which Bafnage finds between this law and the law 6, ff. *de Verb. oblig.* which fays: *Is cui bonis interdictum est .... non potest promittendo obligari, & ideo nec fidejussor pro eo intervenire potest.* For as in the preceding cafe, the interdicted prodigal ought to be validly bound, on the contrary, in this he is not bound, being incapable of contracting. Hence it follows that his fecurity is not bound; as there cannot be a fecuritifhip without a principal obligation. *Supra, n.* 366. Gaius proves clearly our diftinction, in the law 70, §. 4, ff. *de Fidejuss. Si a furioso*, fays he, *stipulatus fueris, non posse te fidejussorem accipere certum est. Quod si pro furioso jure obligato fidejussorem acceperis, tenetur fidejussor.*

It is evident that one cannot be a fecurity for one's felf. L. 21, §. 2, ff. *d. tit.* nor to one's felf.

394. One can be a fecurity only to the creditor of him for whom he becomes fecurity: the fecuritifhip which one might contract to a perfon not his creditor, but who has power only to receive the debt, would not be valid; L. 23, ff. *d. tit.*

§. II.

For what obligation.

395. One may become a fecurity for the performance of any obligation whatever: *Fidejussor accipi potest, quoties est aliqua obligatio civilis vel naturalis, cui applicetur*; L. 16, §. 3, ff, *d. tit.*

Obferve that the natural obligations for which it is faid, under this head, that fecurities may intervene, are thofe for which the municipal law does not grant an action; fuch are thofe formed by a fimple pact, thofe contracted by flaves, and which were not besides forbidden by law: but securities cannot validly intervene for obligations forbidden by law, although they may be binding in *foro conscientiæ*, and may in this sense be called natural obligations.

It is upon this principle the laws decide that a security cannot validly accede to the obligation of a woman who has bound herself contrary to the prohibition of the Velleian senatus-consultus; L. 16, §. 1, ff. *ad sen. vell.*; L. 14, *Cod. d. tit.* For although in *foro conscientiæ*, this woman may be bound to perform her obligation, yet as the obligation has been contracted against the prohibition of the law, it is in *foro legis*, regarded as null, and it cannot consequently serve as a foundation to the obligation of a security. The law in annulling the obligation of the woman, annuls every thing dependent on it, and consequently the contracts of securitiship which are accessory. This is the meaning of these words of the law 16, §. 1, *quia totum obligationem senatus improbat.*

It appears to me that the same decision should be made in regard to a securitiship entered into for a feme covert who had contracted an obligation without being authorised, Indeed it should be so decided *a fortiori*: for it was only *per exceptionem* that the law annulled the obligation of a woman who bound herself contrary to the Velleian senatus-consultus; but it may be said that, according to our customary law, the obligation of a woman who has contracted without being authorised, although it may be valid in *foro conscientiæ*, is null, even *ipso jure*, in *foro legis*, since our customs declare her absolutely incapable of contracting and binding herself. *A married woman* CANNOT BIND HERSELF, &c. Paris, *art.* 234; CAN IN NO MANNER CONTRACT; Orleans, *art.* 194. Domat, *tit. caut.* §. 1, *n.* 4, is of an opinion contrary to ours; and Basnage cites a case in the Parliament of Burgundy, reported by Bouvet, in which it was determined that a securitiship entered into for a woman who had contracted without being authorised was valid: but I do not think that the decision of this case ought to be followed. The distinction upon which Basnage wishes to ground this decision, whether the principal obligation is null *ratione rei in obligationem deductæ*, or is so *ratione personæ*, does not appear to me to be solid. An obligation, in whatever manner it may be null, *ratione rei*, or *ratione personæ*, is not truly an obligation, and it is of the nature of contracts of securitiship, that they cannot take place without a true principal obligation; *supra*, *n*. 365. A feme covert ought not to be compared to a minor: the obligation of a minor is not null; the relief which the law grants him against his obligation, supposes an obligation: there is one then to which the securities may accede. But the obligation of a feme covert who contracts without being authorised, is absolutely null; there is no obligation to which a security may accede.

But if one has bound himself jointly with a feme covert, who contracted without being authorised, not as the security of this woman, but as a principal debtor, the nullity of the obligation of the feme covert will not carry with it the nullity of his. For example; if a feme covert, without being authorised, and I have borrowed of you a certain sum of money which was received by her, and we bound ourselves *in solidum* to return it to you; the feme covert would not be bound to you, if she wasted the sum; but I would, not the less, be bound to repay it to you, being myself a principal debtor and having borrowed it from you: for, in order that I may be the borrower, it is not necessary that I should have received the sum myself; it suffices that you have really paid it to this woman with my concurrence

The obligations which are against morality, *contra bones mores*, being null, do not admit of securitiship. For example, if a person, in charging me to commit a crime, has bound himself to indemnify me for all the consequences which might follow, and to give me a certain reward, one could not validly become a security for the performance of such an obligation, which, being *contra bones mores*, is null and consequently cannot be the object of a securitiship. It is in this sense that it is said *maleficiorum fidejussorem accipi non posse:* but one may validly become a security for a person who has committed a tort, for the reparation of the injury he has done; *L.* 70, §. *fin.* ff. *de fidejussor.*

396. One may become a security even for the obligation of a personal act which can be performed only by the principal debtor; L. 8, §. 1, ff. *de op. lib.*; for this obligation, by its inexecution, is converted into an obligation of damages, which the security may pay; and this suffices for the securitiship to be validly contracted.

397. The civil law did not permit a wife to receive from her husband a security for the restitution of her portion; this distrust of him to whom she had submitted her person, did not appear to the Emperors to be becoming; L. 1 & 2, *Cod. de fid. vel mand. dot.* These laws are not observed with us.

398. One may become a security not only for a principal obligation, but even for a securitiship: *Pro fidejussore fidejussorem accibi posse nequaquam dubium est;* L. 8, §. 12.

399. Finally, a person may become a security not only for an obligation already contracted, but for one which is to be contracted, though it be not yet contracted; *Adhiberi fidejussor tam futuræ quam præsenti obligationi potest;* L. 6, §. *fin. d. tit.*; so, however, that the obligation resulting from this securitiship, will commence only from the time the principal obligation shall be contracted: for it is of its essence that it cannot take place without a principal obligation. According to these principles I may validly become a security to you for the sum of a thousand crowns, which you propose to lend to Peter: but the obligation from this securitiship, will not begin to have effect until the day when you shall actually make this loan to Peter; while you have not yet made it, and the thing is entire, I may withdraw my assent, by notifying to you not to make the loan to Peter, and declaring that I do not intend any longer to be a security for him; *Basnage, Traite des Hypoth. n.* 2, *ch.* 6.

§. III.

How securitiship is contracted.

400. In the civil law, securitiship was contracted only

by stipulation; stipulation is not in use among us. Securitiship may be entered into by a simple agreement, either by a notarial instrument, or under a private signature, or even orally; except that if the object be above the value of one hundred livres, the proof, by witnesses, of an oral agreement is not admitted.

401. Although securitiship may be entered into by letter or even orally, care must be had however, not to take for a promise to become security, what one says or writes, unless there be a well marked intention to do so. Therefore if I wrote or said to you that a man who asked you to lend him money was solvent, this could not be taken for a securitiship, for I might well have no other intention than to inform you what I believed to be the case, and not to bind myself. On this principle it was adjudged in a case reported by Papon X. 1, 12, that these words in a letter to the keeper of a boarding house, *A. B. intends to send his son to board with you. He is an honest man and will pay you well,* did not include any obligation. On the same principle, if I accompany a person to a woollen draper's, where he buys cloth, the draper cannot conclude that I am a security for him.

Although a person makes a partial payment for another, even for his son, it cannot hence be concluded that he meant to be security for him; for the remainder of the debt; L. 4. *Cod. ne uxor, pro marito, &c.*

If it were mentioned in an obligation that it was made in my presence, and that I had subscribed it, it could not be concluded that I became a security; I ought to be holden in such case to have subscribed it only as a witness. L. 6, *Cod. de Fidej.*

402. When the debtor is bound to give a security, either by his own agreement or by the law, the creditor may require that the security should bind himself by a notarial instrument.

Judicial securities bind themselves in the office of the clerk of the court, by an instrument which he receives.

403. It is immaterial whether the securitiship is entered into at the same time with the principal obligation, or at a different time, before or since.

It is not necessary that he for whom a security is given, should consent; L. 30, ff. *d. tit.*

SECTION V.

Of the extent of securitiship.

404. To judge of the extent of the obligation of a security, much attention is to be paid to the manner in which it is expressed.

When the security has expressed the sum and cause for which he became a security, his obligation does not extend beyond the sum and cause expressed: For example; if one had become a security for my lessee for the payment of his rent, he will not be answerable for the other obligations of the lease, such as might result from waste, or from the advances that I might have made to the lessee, &c.

If one had become a security for the principal sum due by the debtor, he will not therefore be liable for the interest that may accrue. L. 68, §. 1, ff. *d. tit.*

On the contrary, when the words *of the securitiship* are general and indeterminate, the security is presumed to have bound himself for all the obligations of the principal debtor resulting from the contract to which he acceded. He is presumed to have become a security for him *in omnem causam.*

For example; if the contract of securitiship, by which one bound himself to me for my lessee, expresses in general terms that he becomes a security for the lease, he will not only be answerable for the rents, but generally for all the obligations of the lease; as for example, for waste, to refund advances or restore the furniture or utensils that may have been left for the use of the lessee, *dotes prædiorum*; L. 52, §. 2, ff. *d. tit.*; for interest accruing on the rent in arrear, &c.

He who becomes a security in general terms, is bound

not only for the principal sum due by the debtor, but also for all the interest that may be due. L. 2, §. 11 & 12, ff. *de adm. rer. ad civit. pertin.* L. 54, ff. *locat.*

He is liable not only for those that are due *ex rei natura*, but even for those which are occasioned by the delay of the principal debtor: *Paulus respondit, si in omnem causam conductionis se obligavit, eum quoque exemplo coloni, tardius illatarum per moram coloni pensionum præstare debere usuras*; *d.* L. 54.

He ought also to be liable for the costs of suit against the principal debtor; for these costs are an accessory of the debt; but he ought to be liable only from the day the suit was notified to him; which has been established to prevent a security from being ruined by costs incurred without his knowledge, and which he could avoid by paying, if he had notice; therefore till the suit be notified to him, he ought to be chargeable only for the costs of the original process.

405. However extended or general the securitiship may be, it reaches only the obligations that result from the contract for which the security bound himself, and not those that would result from a foreign clause.

For example. A creditor in our West-India Islands lent a sum of money to a person who, for the safety of the creditor, has given him a negro in pledge, whom he knew to be a thief, without giving notice to the creditor. The negro robbed the creditor to whom he was given in pledge. The creditor may sue the debtor who did not give him notice, for the damages, *contraria pignoratitia actione*. But the securitiship will not extend to those damages which arise from a cause foreign to the loan for which the debtor's security bound himself: *Ea actio fidejussorem onerare non poterit, cum non pro pignore, sed pro pecunia mutua fidem suam obliget*; L. 54, ff. *de fidejuss.*

For the same reason, he who became a security for an administrator of public monies, is bound only for the payment of public monies, and not for the fines which the administrator may have incurred by his mal-administration.

Such is the decision of the Emperor Severus: *Fidejussores magistratuum in pœnam vel mulctam non conveniri debere decrevit;* L. 68, ff. *d. tit.* And in general, however unlimited the securitiship may be, it does not extend to the penalties to which the debtor may be condemned, *officio judicis, propter suam contumaciam;* for this is a cause foreign to the contract: *Non debet imputari fidejussoribus, quod ille reus propter suam pœnam præstitit;* L. 73, *d. tit.*

SECTION VI.

Of the manner in which securitiship is extinguished, and of the different pleas which the law grants to securities.

ARTICLE THE FIRST.

In what manner securitiship is extinguished.

405. The obligation that results from a securitiship is extinguished, I. in the different ways in which all obligations are extinguished: we shall relate them *infra, part* 3.

II. It is of the nature of securitiship, as it is of all accessory obligations, that the extinction of the principal obligation carries with it the extinction of the securitiship, and the discharge of the securities. *Supra, n.* 377, *& seq.*

III. The security is discharged, when the creditor has by his own act disabled himself from ceding his actions against any of the principal debtors, to which the security has an interest to be subrogated; *infra, part* 3, *ch.* 1, *art.* 6, §. 4.

IV. When the creditor has voluntarily received from the debtor a piece of land in payment of a sum of money due, is the security discharged, although, a long time after, the creditor be evicted from the land? The reason to doubt is, that in this case the payment is invalid, not having transferred to him to whom it is made the property of the thing; *infra, part* 3, *chap.* 1, *art.* 3, §. 3. Consequently the principal obligation continues: whence it seems to follow that the obligation of the securities must likewise remain. Basset IV. 22, 5, reports a case in which it was thus determined. Notwithstanding these reasons and although it cannot be denied that the payment, in this case, is not valid and that the principal obligation remains, it has been adjudged in several cases cited by Basnage, *Trait. Hypoth. p.* 3, *ch. fin.*, that the creditor in such cases cannot be allowed to proceed against the securities, if, in the mean while, the principal debtor becomes insolvent. The decision in these cases is grounded on this maxim of equity, *Nemo ex alterius facto prægravari debet.* The security ought not to suffer from the arrangement that has taken place between the creditor and principal debtor. Therefore if, in this case, the creditor might proceed against the security, the security would suffer from the arrangement by which the creditor received the land in payment; the creditor having, by this arrangement, deprived the security of the opportunity of paying the creditor, and recovering from the debtor, whilst he remained solvent, the sum to which he had been bound for him.

Quid, if the creditor had simply granted to the debtor a delay for the payment, and in the mean while the debtor became insolvent, could the security refuse to pay? *Vinnius, Q. illustr.* 11, 42, holds the negative. This case is widely different from the preceding. In the preceding case the delivery of the land given in payment having, till the eviction, made the debt appear to be discharged, such an arrangement deprived the security of every way to provide for his own safety, even if he had discovered that the affairs of the debtor began to be deranged; for he could not demand from this debtor to be freed from his securitiship, which seemed to be discharged as well as the principal debt: whereas the simple delay, not making the debt to appear discharged, deprives the security of none of the means of providing for his safety, and of proceeding against the principal debtor, if he perceives his affairs are falling into disorder, *si bona dilapidare cœperit.* L. 10, *Cod. mand.* The security cannot then pretend that this delay granted to the principal debtor prejudices him, since he himself derives an advantage from it.

The obligation of the contract of securitiship was also extinguished, according to the principles of the civil law, by confufion, of which we have fpoken, *supra*, n. 383, but this does not apply with us.

The bringing of a fuit by the creditor againft the principal debtor, does not difcharge the fecurity, who always remains bound till payment. L. 28, *Cod. de Fidej.* Therefore the creditor may abandon his fuit againft the principal debtor, to profecute the fecurity. But ordinarily the fecurity may oppofe to him the plea of difcuffion, of which we are going to treat in the next article.

Article II.

Of the plea of discussion.

§. I.

The origin of this right.

407. According to the principles of law which were in ufe before the novel 4, of Juftinian, the creditor could not demand from the fecurities the payment of what was due him, without reforting firft to the principal debtor: *Jure nostro*, fays Antonine Caracalla, in L. 5, *Cod. de Fidej.*, *est potestas creditori, relicto reo, eligendi fidejussores, nisi inter contrahentes aliud placitum doceatur.* The Emperors Diocletian and Maximilian decide the fame in the law 19, *Cod. d. tit.* Juftinian, *de Nov. cap.* 1, granted to fecurities a plea of *discussion* or *plea of order*, which is to fay, a plea by which they may fend the creditor, who demands from them the payment of the debt, to the previous difcuffion of the principal debtor. This law of the novel is followed by us, but not with regard to all kinds of fecurities, nor in all cafes.

§. II.

What securities may plead the plea of discussion.

408. Judicial fecurities may not avail themfelves of this plea. *Louet, letter F*, 23.

Securities for the king's rents are not at the prefent day allowed to avail themfelves of this plea, though the Ordinance of Louis XII, 1513, had granted it to them. This alteration in our jurifprudence was introduced in the time of M. Lebret, who gives this reafon for it, that thefe fecurities are presumed to be secret partners of the principal debtor. *Le Bret, Plaid.* 42, *in fine.*

Lastly, securities who have by their contract renounced this plea, are not allowed to avail themselves of it: *Unicuique enim licet juri in favorem suum introducto renuntiare.*

Is the security presumed to have renounced this plea, when it is expressed in the contract of securitiship, that he binds himself as principal debtor? The authors are divided on this question. Several old cases determined in the Parliament of Paris are cited, in which it has been holden that this is not sufficient, and that the renunciation must be express. Basnage, in his treatise on Hypothecations, says that in the Parliament of Normandy they hold that these words are sufficient to establish the renunciation of the plea of discussion, and that it ought not to be presumed that they were inserted with an intention that they should mean nothing. This is conformable to the rules for the interpretation of agreements, *supra, n.* 92.

The renunciation of the pleas of discussion and division, is not to be inferred from these words, which might be at the end of a contract of securitiship, *promising, engaging*, and *renouncing, &c.* The word *renouncing* is vague and indeterminate, unless what the parties renounce be expressed, and can be looked upon only as mere style, signifying nothing: *Ea quæ sunt styli, non operantur.* This decision is admitted, even if the notary, in his copy, had extended this clause *renouncing, &c.* and had expressed a renunciation of the plea of division and discussion. Dumoulin, *Tract. Usur. quæst.* 7, *in fine*, mentions that it has been so decided. The reason is that the notary cannot, by what he adds in the copy, add to the obligation of the parties; *infra, part* 4, *chap.* 1, *art.* 3, *in princ.*

§. III.

In what case the creditor is bound to a discussion, and when the plea of discussion is to be pleaded.

409. The creditor is not bound to a discussion in all cases, and it may in this respect, be established as a princi-

ple, that the creditor is not bound to a difcuffion that would be too difficult.

It is for this reafon that the novel, in granting to the fecurity the benefit of difcuffion, excepts the cafe in which the principal debtor fhould be abfent, unlefs the fecurity offered to produce him, in a fhort time to be fixed by the judge.

This exception which the novel puts to the plea of difcuffion, is not admitted with us. The reafons on which it is grounded are drawn from the difficulty there was in the proceedings among the Romans againft an abfent perfon. They do not exift here; the fummons and notice at the place of abode being as effectual, in our practice, as if perfonally given, render the difcuffion of the property of the principal debtor as eafy when he is abfent as when prefent.

410. The creditor is not bound to difcufs the property of the principal debtor before he proceeds againft the fecurity, except when the fecurity requires it and pleads his privilege; therefore though the creditor has not difcuffed the property of the principal debtor, his demand and his fuit againft the fecurity are proper until the fecurity avails himfelf of this plea.

It is in confequence of this principle that it has been determined in a cafe of the firft of September 1705, cited by Bretonnier on Henrys, that the judge cannot *ex officio* order the difcuffion.

The plea of difcuffion is ranked among dilatory pleas; fince it tends only to delay the fuit of the creditor againft the fecurity, till after the time of the difcuffion, and not to bar it. Therefore according to the rule common to all dilatory pleas, L. 12, *Cod. de except.*, it ought to be pleaded before a plea in chief. If the fecurity were to plead in chief, without pleading the difcuffion, he would not be allowed to avail himfelf of it; being prefumed, by pleading in chief, to have waved his right; *Gui Pape, and the authors by him cited, q.* 59. He might however be permitted to avail himself of it, if the property of which he demands the discussion, had only come to the principal debtor since the plea in chief, *puta*, if an estate had been left to him. For the rule that dilatory pleas must be pleaded before pleas in chief; can only apply when the plea existed at the time, and not when it has arisen since: as the defendant cannot be presumed by his plea in chief to have waved a right, that has accrued since. *Guthieres, and the authors cited by him, Tract. de Contr. Jurati* xxij. 18.

§. IV.

What property the creditor is bound to discuss.

411. When the discussion is pleaded, the creditor, if he has not a title on which execution may be issued against the principal debtor, ought to sue him and obtain a judgment against him. In consequence of this judgment, or, without suit, in consequence of his title of execution, he ought to proceed by summons against the principal debtor, and to seize and attach the moveable property which may be in his house.

If there can be found no property on which the execution may be levied, the officer ought so to certify, and his return will be equivalent to the discussion of the personal property.

As to any other real or personal property, which the principal debtor may have, the creditor, not being bound to know it, is not obliged to discuss it unless it be indicated by the security. This indication ought to be made at one time, and ought to contain all the property of the debtor which it is intended that the creditor should discuss. One would not be allowed, after the discussion of the property that has been indicated, to indicate other property. *Arretes de Lamoignon, tit. des discussions, art.* 9; a case of the 20th January 1701, cited by Bretonnier on Henrys, *vol.* 4, 34.

412. As the discussion ought not to be too difficult, the creditor cannot be bound to discuss property of the debtor which is out of the kingdom. M. de Lamoignon thought they ought not to be compelled to discuss property in the

jurifdiction of a other parliament; *Arretes de Lamoignon, ibid.*

Nor is the creditor bound to difcufs the property of the debtor which is in difpute; for he is not to be compelled to maintain fuits, nor to wait the event of them in order to be paid: this is a further confequence of the fame principle, that the difcuffion ought not to be too long or too difficult.

For the fame reafon, he is not bound to difcufs the property hypothecated by the principal debtor, when the principal debtor has aliened it, and it has paffed into the poffeffion of third perfons; thefe perfons in poffeffion have, on the contrary, the right to fend back the creditors, who fhould claim this property, to difcufs the other property of the principal debtor or that of the fecurities; *d. Nov. cap.* 2.

It is not fo with regard to thofe who have fucceeded to the whole eftate of the principal debtor, fuch as univerfal donees or legatees, and even the treafury, when it has fucceeded to the principal debtor by efcheat or confifcation. Thefe univerfal fucceffors are *loco heradis*: they reprefent the principal debtor, taking the place of his heirs; they ought therefore to be liable to the difcuffion, in the fame manner as the principal debtor would have been, to the amount of the debts of the principal debtor, for which they are liable.

When feveral principal debtors have contracted an obligation *in solidum*, and one of them has given a third perfon for a fecurity, it is afked whether this fecurity can oblige the creditor to difcufs, not only the property of the debtor for whom he is a fecurity, but likewife that of all the other principal debtors? I think he can. It fuffices, to be convinced of this, to examine the reafon on which the plea of difcuffion is founded. It is not becaufe it is prefumed that the fecurity intended to bind himfelf only in cafe of the failure and infolvency of him for whom he became a fecurity: this intention ought to be expreffed; when it is not expreffed it is not to be prefumed, and the obligation is abfolute. If this prefumption applied in ordinary fecuritiſhip, the right which the ſecurity would have to ſend the creditor to a diſcuſſion againſt the principal debtor, would be a right which he would have in ſtrictneſs of law; the creditor would not have an action againſt the ſecurity before the inſolvency of the principal debtor had been proved by the diſcuſſion. All agree that the plea of diſcuſſion which the law grants to the ſecurity, is granted merely through favor, and that the action of the creditor againſt the ſecurity is by ſtrictneſs of law and is well grounded, although the principal debtor is ſolvent and his property has not been diſcuſſed; it is neceſſary then to ſeek another reaſon for this plea of diſcuſſion, and there is no other than this, which is that it is equitable a debt ſhould be paid, as far as it may be, by thoſe who are the true debtors and who have been benefited by the contract, rather than by thoſe who are debtors only for another; that it is always a hardſhip to be obliged to pay for another: therefore equity requires that the creditor, when it muſt be of little or no difference to him, ſhould ſave the ſecurity from this hardſhip, and ſhould cauſe himſelf to be paid rather by the true debtors than by the ſecurity. This is the reaſon which Quintilian, *declam.* 273, gives for the benefit of diſcuſſion. After having ſaid that it is a hardſhip for a ſecurity to be obliged to pay for another, *miserabile est,* he concludes that a creditor cannot with a good grace bring this hardſhip upon a ſecurity, while he may cauſe himſelf to be paid by the true debtor: *Non aliter salvo pudore, ad sponsorem venit creditor, quam si recipere a debitore non possit.* It is evident that theſe reaſons operate to oblige the creditor to diſcuſs the property, not only of the debtor *in solidum* for whom he became a ſecurity, but alſo that of all the other principal debtors: therefore the ſecurity is well grounded in demanding the diſcuſſion of the property, not only of the debtor for whom he became a ſecurity, but alſo of the other principal debtors. It may even be ſaid that he who has become a ſecurity for one of ſeveral debtors *in solidum*, is alſo in a manner a ſecurity for the others; for the obligation of all theſe debtors being the ſame obligation, in acceding to the obligation of the one for whom he became a fecurity, he has acceded to that of them all.

§. V.

At whose cost the discussion is to be made.

413. The difcuffion is to be made at the coft and peril of the fecurity who demanded to have it made: and as the difcuffion of real property cannot be made without great expence, the creditor may require that the fecurity fhould defray it. This is a general rule in all cafes in which the plea of difcuffion is pleaded. *Journal des audiences, Vol.* 1, l. 5, *ch.* 25; and it is a confequence of our principle.

§. VI.

Is the creditor who has failed to make the discussion, liable for the insolvency of the debtor.

414. May the creditor to whom the plea of difcuffion is oppofed and who has fuffered feveral years to elapfe without making a difcuffion, during which time the debtor has become infolvent, proceed, on the difcuffion of his property fince he became infolvent, againft the fecurity? I think he may; and that the fecurity cannot plead that he did not make in due time the difcuffion of the property of the principal debtor which was required of him. The reafon is that the right which the fecurities have to the plea of difcuffion granted them by the novel is limited to the ftopping of the fuit of the creditor againft them, 'till he has profecuted the principal debtor, and has made a difcuffion of his property. The advantage this novel gives them is confined, as has been faid, to this, that the creditor may not firft proceed againft the fecurity; *creditor non primum ad fidejussorem aut sponsorem accedat.* It fuffices then that the creditor fhould not profecute his fuit againft the fecurities before he has fued the principal debtor and made a difcuffion of his property. The creditor may make this difcuffion whenever he pleafes, and nothing binds him to do it at the pleafure of the fecurity. The law having fixed the time within which the creditor may bring his fuit, the fecurity cannot fix

400. In the civil law, fecuritifhip was contracted only

shorter time than is granted by the law: *Nemo invitus agere compellitur*; *toto tit. Cod. Ut nemo invitus, &c. Creditor ad petitionem debiti urgeri minime potest*; L. 20, *Cod. de pign.* Therefore, if the principal debtor, to the discussion of whose property the creditor has been sent back, is since become insolvent, the security cannot complain of the creditor who did not prosecute him whilst he was solvent; the creditor was not bound to do so, and the security, if he had been apprehensive of the insolvency which has happened, might have guarded against it by prosecuting, himself, the principal debtor, as he had a right to do, as soon as he himself was sued; *infra, n.* 440, Henrys, *vol.* 2, L. 4, *art.* 34, is of this opinion. He supports it by a decision in a similar case and informs us that in his time such was the received opinion in the Parliament of Paris. The custom of Brittany, *art.* 192, has a contrary disposition. I imagine it ought to be confined to that province. D'Argentré on this article, says that this disposition derived from the ancient custom, was preserved, at the reformation, against his opinion.

We have considered this question with regard to ordinary securities: but if the security had bound himself only to pay what the creditor could not obtain from the principal debtor, *in id quod servari non poterit*, the creditor who should have had it in his power for a considerable time to procure the payment from the principal debtor, would not be easily admitted to bring his action against the security, after the debtor, at the end of a considerable time, should have become insolvent; L. 41, ff. *d. tit.*; because this security who bound himself only to pay what the creditor *could not obtain*, would plead that he might easily have obtained from the principal debtor what was due him, and therefore, that he, the security, owes nothing. L. 41, ff, *tit.*

ARTICLE III.

Of the plea of division.

§. I.

The origin of this right.

415. When several persons become the securities of a principal debtor for the same debt, they are holden to have bound themselves each for the whole debt: *Si plures sint fidejussores, quotquot erunt numero, singuli in solidum tenentur. Instit. tit. de fidej.* §. 4.

In this, several securities differ from several principal debtors who are not holden to bind themselves otherwise than each for his part of what they jointly promise, if it be not expressed that they bind themselves *in solidum*. The reason of this distinction is that it is of the nature of the contract of securitiship to bind to all that which the principal debtor owes: and consequently each of those who are securities for him are presumed to contract such an engagement, unless he expressly declares that he binds himself only for a part; this is the reason given by Vinnius, *select. quæst. lib.* 2, *cap.* 40.

The Emperor Adrian modified this liability for the whole by the plea of division which he granted to securities: the security from whom the creditor demands the whole debt, by this plea obliges the creditor to divide the debt between him and his co-securities, when they are solvent, and is consequently allowed to pay his part to the creditor; saving to the creditor his right for the surplus against the others. This modification has been adopted in our jurisprudence.

§. II.

Of those who may, or may not, avail themselves of the plea of division.

416. There are some securities who cannot avail themselves of this plea; such are securities for public monies. See *Lebret, plaid.* 42, *in fin.*

Judicial fecurities alfo are excluded from the benefit of this plea: fuch is the opinion of Bafnage. The fecurities who by their contract of fecuritifhip have renounced it, are alfo excluded.

When the contract of fecuritifhip expreffes that the fecurities have bound themfelves *in solidum and as principal debtors*, does this claufe include an implied renunciation of the plea of divifion? Thofe who think that this claufe does not include a renunciation of the plea of difcuffion, ought alfo to think that it does not include a renunciation of the plea of divifion; but the reafons that induced us to think it includes a renunciation of the plea of difcuffion, and which we have ftated *supra, n.* 408, induce us alfo to think that it does include a renunciation of the plea of divifion.

Finally, the laws refufe the plea of divifion to the fecurities who have at firft, *malâ fide*, denied the fecuritifhip. *Inficiantibus auxilium divisionis non est indulgendum*; L. 10, §. 1, ff. *de fidej.*

417. Not only fecurities themfelves but alfo their heirs may have the benefit of this plea.

The fecurity of a fecurity may alfo avail himfelf of the fame pleas that might have been pleaded by the fecurity whofe fecurity he himfelf is, and demand the divifion of the debt between him and the co-fecurities of the fecurity for whom he is bound.

§. III.

Who are those between whom the debt ought to be divided.

418. The fecurity may demand the divifion of the action between himfelf and the other fecurities who are alfo principal fecurities. He could not demand that it fhould be divided between himfelf and his own fecurity, for he is himfelf a principal debtor with regard to his fecurity; L. 57, §. 4, ff. *de fidej.*

419. It is neceffary alfo that thofe with whom the fecurity demands the divifion of the action be fecurities of the fame debtor. If two debtors *in solidum*, of the fame debt, had each given a fecurity, the fecurity of one of thofe debtors

could not require that the action should be divided between him and the security of the other debtor *in solidum*; for although they are securities for the same debt, yet as they are not securities of the same debtor, they are not properly co-securities. This is the decision of the law 43, 51, §. 2, ff. *d. tit.*

420. Finally, it is necessary that the co-securities, with whom the security requires the division of the action, be solvent; and they are presumed to be solvent, when not being so themselves, they are solvent by their own securities: it is thus decided by the law 27, §. 2, *Si quæratur an solvendo sit principalis fidejussor, etiam vires sequentis fidejussoris ei aggreganda sunt.*

But if my co-security was solvent, in the beginning of the suit, and the action was therefore divided between him and me, although afterwards, and since the suit, he became insolvent, the creditor will not be allowed to resort to me for his part: this is the decision of Papinian, L. 51, §. 4, & L. 52, §. 1.

In this, the plea of division differs from the plea of discussion. The reason of this distinction is drawn from the different nature of these pleas. The plea of discussion is only a dilatory plea. It only delays the action of the creditor against the security, 'till the creditor shall have discussed the property of the principal debtor: whereas the plea of division is a peremptory plea or a plea in bar; when it is admitted, it entirely destroys the action of the security who pleads it, for the part of his co-securities with whom the division is allowed. This is the reason why the creditor can no longer resort to him, even when the co-securities should afterwards become insolvent.

Further; although indeed, when the creditor brings his action, my co-security was already insolvent, if the creditor has willingly divided his action, by demanding from each only his part, he will not be allowed afterwards to demand from me the part of my insolvent co-security. This is the decision of Gordian, in the law 16, *Cod. d. tit.*

421. Provided my co-security be solvent, although the time annexed to the obligation is not arrived, or the condition under which he bound himself is not yet performed, yet I may demand the division of the action provisionally between him and me: saving to the creditor his recourse against me, for the part of this security, if, when the time is arrived or the condition is performed, he was not solvent. L. 37, ff. *de fid.*; and *a fortiori*, if the condition under which he bound himself is not performed.

422. As the action of the creditor is to be divided only when the securities are all solvent, if there is a contest between the creditor and the security, upon the fact of the solvency of the co-securities, the security is allowed, on tendering his part, to require that, before any decision take place as to the surplus, the creditor be bound to discuss the property of the co-securities; L. 10, ff. *d. tit.* But this is to be done at the risk of the security.

423. I cannot avail myself of the plea of division, if my co-security resides out of the kingdom; for this plea is a favor which the law grants only when the creditor does not, by the allowance of it, suffer too great an inconvenience. 10 *Papon*, 4, 25.

§. IV.

Whether the securitiship may be divided with a security who did not validly contract, or with a minor security.

424. When I have bound myself as a security for another, together with a person who was incapable of contracting such an obligation, as were women at Rome, I cannot avoid paying the whole of the debt to the creditor, in the same manner as if I were a sole security. The person who was incapable ought not to be regarded. No distinction is to be made in such case, whether I have entered into the securitiship before the person who was incapable, or whether I entered into it at the time or since.

It is otherwise, according to the civil law, when I have bound myself with a minor, who afterwards procures himself to be relieved from his obligation. I am liable for the whole debt only in cafe I bound myfelf at firft as a fecurity, without depending on the minor, who afterwards became a fecurity for the fame perfon; but if we became fecurity together, the relief which he may obtain from his obligation, ought not, according to the civil law, to charge me alone with the whole debt, which I expected he would pay jointly with me. L. 48, *pp.* & §. 1, ff. *de fidej.*

Papinian adduces this reafon for the difference between a woman and a minor. He who has become a fecurity jointly with a woman, ought not to have depended on her dividing the obligation, fince he ought to have known that fhe was incapable of it, *cum ignorare non debuerit mulierem frustra intercedere*. But it is not fo with regard to him who became a fecurity with a minor; *propter*, fays Papinian, *incertum ætatis & restitutionis*, becaufe he might be ignorant that he was a minor, or hope that he would not avoid his obligation. It is the creditor, rather than he, who ought to have inquired into this, when he received him for a fecurity; and it is the creditor, rather than he, who ought to fuffer from the relief which the minor has procured againft his obligation: *d. L.* 48, *pp.* & *L.* 1.

Whatever refpect I may have for the decifions of Papinian, this one appears to me very queftionable. The feveral fecurities being, as we have faid, debtors of the whole debt, the divifion of it, which is granted by the conftitution of Adrian when they are all folvent, is only a favor which ought not to prejudice the creditor. This reafon which forbids the divifion of the debt with my co-fecurity when he has become infolvent, ought to prevent its being allowed with my co-fecurity who has procured himfelf to be relieved againft his fecuritifhip. There is no greater reafon to grant it in one cafe than in the other. If I could have forefeen the infolvency, I could with more facility have forefeen that he might obtain the relief. It cannot be faid that the creditor was willing to take the rifk on himfelf in accepting the fecuritifhip of a minor; for as he has not been fatisfied with the fecuritifhip of the minor and has required that another security should be added, it is rather a proof that he thought to seek his safety against the relief which the minor might obtain, and that he was not willing to take that risk on himself.

These reasons appear to me sufficient to decide, without distinction, against the authority of the civil law, that the relief obtained by my co-security on account of his minority, ought, like his insolvency, to charge me with the whole debt.

Further; if before the minor security seeks relief against his securitiship, I was sued by the creditor and availed myself of the plea of division, I think it would be equitable that he should not be compelled to divide his action between the minor security and me, unless with the reservation of his recourse against me in case the minor procured himself to be relieved from his securitiship.

But if the creditor had consented to the division of his action without reservation, there is room to think that he took on himself the risk of the minor's procuring relief, and that he would not have any recourse against me.

§. V.

When the plea of division is to be pleaded.

425. It is asked whether the plea of division can be pleaded only before a plea in chief? Several ancient authors as Pierre de Belleperche, Cynus, and others, were of this opinion: but the contrary opinion, which is adopted by Vinnius, *sel. quæst.* 11, 40, is the most just. It is grounded on the formal text of the law 10, §. 1; *Cod. h. tit. Ut..... dividatur actio inter eos qui solvendo sunt, ante condemnationem ex ordine solet postulari.* It suffices, according to the words of this law, to demand the division of the action before judgment, and consequently it may be demanded after a plea in chief. Indeed this is rather a *plea in bar, than a dilatory plea*; since it tends to destroy entirely the action of the creditor against him who pleads it, for the parts of his co-securities. The text of the Institutes, *tit. de fidej*, §. 4, on which the other opinion is grounded proves nothing. It says indeed, that all the co-securities ought to be solvent,

at the beginning of the suit, in order that there may be room for this division, but it does not say that it cannot be demanded after.

The law 10, §. 1, ff. *de fid.*, in which it is said that the security who has denied his securitiship, is not admitted to demand a division, is not contrary to our principle. For it is this denial *mala fide*, that renders him unworthy of this favor and prevents him from availing himself of this plea and not his pleading in chief. The plea in chief that has intervened between the creditor and the security, does not suppose that the security has denied his securitiship. It may have intervened on other grounds, *puta*, that the debt is paid or that there is some other cause that prevents the creditor's action. Some authors have fallen into the opposite extreme, deciding that the division may be demanded even after judgment, like the plea *cedendarum actionum*, and the pleas *SC. Macedoniani & SC. Velleiani*. This opinion is contradicted by the law 10, §. 1, *Cod. de fidej.*, where it is said that the securities may require the division before judgment, *ante condemnationem*, therefore they cannot afterwards. With regard to the examples of pleas that may be offered after judgment, the answer is, that there is a great difference between the plea of division and the plea *cedendarum actionum*. The latter does not attack the judgment nor the right acquired to the creditor by the judgment; and when the security against whom he has obtained a judgment, has satisfied it, he has no interest in refusing to him the cession of his actions; whereas the plea of division if offered after the judgment obtained by the creditor, would attack this judgment and the right acquired by it to the creditor, since it restricts, to a part, the right which the creditor has acquired by the judgment to exact the whole from the security against whom he has obtained the judgment. As to what is decided in regard to the pleas *SC. Macedoniani & SC. Velleiani*, it is a particular right grounded on the favor afforded to these pleas and on a kind of public interest, *ad coercendos fæneratores & ad subveniendum sexui muliebri.* This particular right cannot be made a precedent, nor be extended to the plea of division or to peremptory pleas.

When the judgment in favor of the creditor is suspended by an appeal, it may be said that there is no judgment, 'till there be a final judgment in the court of appeals; hence it follows that the security may be admitted in the appeal to plead his plea of division. This is the opinion of the authors cited by Bruneman, *ad* L. 10, *Cod. de fidej.* It is also that of *Vinnius*.

§. VI.

Of the effect of the plea of division.

426. The effect of the plea of division is to obtain by the order of the judge the division of the debt between securities who are solvent, and by this method to restrict the action to the part of the security who pleads the division.

Before the division of the debt is ordered by the judge on the plea of division, or before it is voluntarily made by the creditor by his suing each of the securities for his part, L. 16, *Cod. de fidej.*, each of the securities is a debtor of the whole debt. Therefore if either has paid the whole, he cannot have against the creditor any claim for the parts of his co-securities. L. 49, §. 1, ff. *de fidej.:* for he really owed the whole of what he has paid. In not availing himself of the plea of division which he might have done, *plenius fidem exsolvit.* But after the division of the debt has been ordered, the debt is so far divided that even if one of the securities between whom the debt has been divided, should become insolvent, the creditor would have no recourse against the others for the part of the insolvent security. L. 51, §. 4, ff. *de fidej.*

There remains a question. If the security, who demands the division of the action of the creditor between himself and his co-securities, has paid part of the debt, ought he to pay the half of what remains due, without deducting what he has paid? Papinian decided it thus, *eam enim quantitatem inter eos convenit dividi, quam litis tempore debent.* This decision, though conformable to the strictness of the the principle, has not been followed; it has been found more equitable to allow the security to deduct from the part of the debt for which he is liable, what he has already paid, to compel him to pay only the surplus of his part of the whole debt, and to charge his co-security with the whole of the rest: *Sed humanius est*, says the annotator, *si & alter solvendo sit, per exceptionem ei qui solvit succurri; d.* L. 51, §. 1.

Article IV.

Of the cession of actions, or subrogation, which the creditor is bound to grant to the security who pays.

427. A third advantage which the law grants to the security, is that when he pays, he may require the creditor to subrogate him to all his rights and hypothecations, as well against the principal debtor for whom he was a security as against all other persons who are liable for the debt. This is the result of the law 17, ff. *de fid.*; L. 21, *Cod. d. tit.*; and a number of other texts. See, on this cession of actions, and on the plea which the security has, who has disabled himself, by his own act, to cede them, *infra, Part* 3, *ch.* 1, *Art.* 6, §. 2.

Section VII.

Of the right which the security has against the principal debtor and against his debtors.

428. The security, after he has paid, has recourse against the principal debtor. We shall treat of this recourse in the first succeeding article. There are indeed some cases in which the security has an action against the principal debtor even before he has paid; we shall treat of these in the second article. We shall treat in the third of the particular question, whether the security for an annuity may, after a certain time, oblige the debtor to redeem it. We shall treat in the fourth of the right which the security has against his co-securities.

ARTICLE THE FIRST.

Of the recourse of the security, after he has paid, against the principal debtor.

§ I.

What are the actions which the security, after he has paid, has against the principal debtor.

429. After the ſecurity has paid, if he has cauſed himſelf to be ſubrogated to the rights and actions of the creditor, he may proſecute them againſt the debtor, as the creditor himſelf could have done. If he has neglected to acquire this ſubrogation, he may notwithſtanding, have in his own right an action againſt the principal debtor, in order to be reimburſed for what he has paid for him.

This action is the action *mandati contraria*, if it was with the knowledge and conſent of the principal debtor that he became a ſecurity for him: for this conſent of the principal debtor includes a tacit contract of mandate, according to this rule of law: *Semper qui non prohibet pro se intervenire, mandare creditur*; L. 60, ff.; *de R. J.* If the ſecurity bound himſelf for the principal debtor without his knowledge, he cannot have againſt him the action *mandati*; but he has againſt him the action *contraria negotiorum gestorum*, which has the ſame effect.

§. II.

What payment gives rise to these actions.

430. It is not material whether the ſecurity has paid in conſequence of a judgment, or voluntarily and without judgment; for in either caſe, *utiliter debitoris negotium gessit.* He has procured to the debtor the diſcharge of his debt, and conſequently he ought to be reimburſed for what he has paid to procure it.

It is not material whether the payment was an actual payment, or a ſet-off or a novation. In all theſe caſes the ſecurity has the right to demand that the principal debtor reimburſe him, either for the ſum which he has paid, or that which he has admitted in the ſet-off, or that which he has bound himſelf to pay in order to extinguiſh the obligation of the principal debtor.

431. If the creditor, from favor to the ſecurity, had releaſed the debt by a mere gift, the ſecurity cannot demand any thing from the principal debtor who has profited by this releaſe, becauſe the ſecurity has paid nothing. If the releaſe was made as the recompence of ſervices which the ſecurity had rendered to the creditor, the ſecurity might demand to be reimburſed for this ſum by the principal debtor; for in this caſe the ſecurity has paid the recompence he was entitled to for his ſervices, which he admitted in the ſet-off for the debt of this principal debtor, that he acceded to as a ſecurity. This is the deciſion of the law 12, ff. *mandat.*: and it is conformable to the principle, *sciendum est non plus fidejussorem consequi debere mandati judicio, quam quod solverit.* L. 26, §. 4, ff. *d. tit.*

§. III.

The three conditions under which the payment made by the security may give rise to the action against the principal debtor.

432. In order that the payment made by the ſecurity may give riſe to theſe actions, it is neceſſary, I. that the ſecurity ſhould not have neglected by his fault any plea which he might have oppoſed to the creditor: II. that the payment ſhould have been valid and ſhould have diſcharged the principal debtor. III. that the principal debtor ſhould not have paid a ſecond time by the fault of the ſecurity.

First condition.

433. In order that the ſecurity who has paid may have his recourſe againſt the principal debtor, it is neceſſary that he ſhould not have omitted by his own fault to plead the proper pleas to the ſuit of the creditor. For example, If one was my ſecurity for the price of a piece of land which I bought, and knowing that I was evicted from it, he nevertheleſs pays the price to the ſeller to whom he bound himſelf as a ſecurity for me, he will not have any recourſe againſt me; becauſe he might have ſaved himſelf from

paying by opposing to the seller the plea resulting from the eviction which I suffered. If the security was ignorant of the eviction and consequently of the plea which resulted from it to the action brought against him by the seller, for the price, I shall be obliged to restore to him what he has paid, saving my recourse against the seller: for he was not in fault in not opposing a plea of which he had not any knowledge, and it is I, on the contrary, who was in fault for not having informed him of it. The law 29, ff. *mand.*, establishes these principles in a similar case. However, it is only an ignorance of the fact which can in this case defend the security; it would be otherwise in regard to an ignorance of law. *Finge.* I purchased, under your securitiship, a house which had been entirely destroyed before the contract, being, at the time, ignorant of its destruction; although you were afterwards informed of it, you have paid the price which, through an ignorance of law, you believed to be due: you ought not to have any recourse against me; *d.* L. 29, §. 1.

434. If the security had a plea to oppose to the creditor's suit, but such as he could not honorably plead, in this case the security is not indeed bound to plead it; but he ought not to deprive the principal debtor from pleading it. Therefore he ought to suffer himself to be sued, and bring in the debtor as a party, to plead it if he see fit. On failure to do this, the security will have no recourse against the principal debtor, for what he has paid. This is the result of the law 41, ff. *mand.* & L. 10, §. 12, *d. tit.*

We may adduce as an example of these pleas which cannot be honorably pleaded, that which may be pleaded to the creditor of an annuity who has suffered more than five year's arrearages to accumulate.

435. The rule which we have given that the security, in order to have his recourse against the principal debtor, ought not to have omitted through his own fault to plead any of the pleas he may have had, admits of an exception when the pleas were personal to him and could not have

been pleaded by the principal debtor. For example: If the security who had bound himself for me till a certain time pays for me after the time has elapsed; although he may have avoided paying, yet he may have his recompence against me, because he has paid for me that which I could not have avoided paying. This is the decision of the law 29, §. 6, ff. *mand. Quamquam enim jam liberatus solverit, fidem implevit & debitorem liberavit.* It suffices that he has procured me the discharge at his expence, in order that I may be bound to indemnify him; otherwise I should enrich myself at his expence, which equity does not allow: *Neminem æquum est cum alterius detrimento locupletari.*

Second condition.

436. That the security may have his recourse against the principal debtor, it is necessary that the payment he has made should be valid. Therefore if he who owed me a horse indeterminately, gave me a security and this security should afterwards give me one that happened not to belong to him, the security will have no recourse against the principal debtor, because the payment he made is not valid and has not procured to the debtor his discharge.

437. This rule admits of an exception in the case in which the security when sued by the creditor should pay, being ignorant that the principal debtor had already paid. For though this payment made by the security, being the payment of a sum which had ceased to be due, is not a valid payment, yet the security will, not the less, have his recourse, *actione mandati contraria*, against the principal debtor, to be reimbursed for the sum he has paid; on condition only of subrogating the principal debtor to his remedy over against the creditor who may be insolvent, in order that the principal debtor may procure payment if he can. This is the decision of the law 29, §. 2, ff. *mand.* The principal debtor is in fault for not having informed the security that he had paid.

This decision ought not to be admitted when the security bound himself for the debtor without his knowledge;

for in this cafe the principal debtor is not in fault for having failed to give this fecurity, whom he did not know, notice of the payment.

Third condition.

438. A third cafe, in which the fecurity who has paid has no recourfe againft the principal debtor for the fum which he has paid, is when, on account of his failing to give notice of it to the principal debtor, the latter has paid the creditor a fecond time. But he may require the debtor to cede to him his action againft the creditor who has received what was not due him, to claim it back. This is the decifion of the law 29, §. 3, ff. *mand.*

In our jurifprudence, thefe ceffions are prefumed; and the fecurity in fuch cafe would be allowed to claim back from the creditor *recta via*, what he received a fecond time.

§. IV.

When may the security who has paid have his recourse.

439. Regularly the fecurity who has paid, may have his recourfe againft the principal debtor, as foon as he has paid for him: but if he had paid before the time of payment had arrived, he could not have his recourfe till the arrival of the time. For he ought not by his own act to deprive him of the delay to which he was entitled; L. 22, §. 1, L. 41, ff. *mand.*

§. V.

Whether, when there are several principal debtors, the security has an action against each of them and for how much.

440. The fecurity may by the action *contraria mandati*, or by the action *contraria negotiorum gestorum* proceed againft each of the principal debtors for whom he was a fecurity to recover the whole of what he has paid. For each of thefe principal debtors being debtor of the whole debt towards the creditor, the fecurity by binding himfelf for them, and by paying, has difcharged each of them from the whole and confequently he has the right of claiming from each of

them the reimburfement of the whole of what he has paid, with intereft from the day of his demand.

If what the fecurity has paid was for arrearages and intereft, thefe arrearages and intereft, form a principal with regard to the fecurity who has paid them, againft the debtor for whom he has paid them, and intereft on it is due to the fecurity from the day of his demand. See a cafe reported by Papon, 4, 20; obferve however, that for the fum which he has paid for thefe arrearages and intereft, the fecurity who caufed himfelf to be fubrogated to the rights of the creditor, will ftand in regard to the property of the debtor againft whom he ufed his recourfe, in the fame condition, as the creditor would if he had not been paid: but as to the intereft of that fum which we fay is due him from the day of the demand, as it is in his own right that he may require it, he will have a claim on the debtor's property only from the day of the contract of indemnity made before a notary-public, if fuch an inftrument was made, or if there were none from the day of the judgment obtained againft him.

The fecurity, who requires from one of the principal debtors for whom he was bound, the whole debt which he has paid, ought to cede to this debtor not only the actions which he has, in his own right againft the other debtors, but alfo the actions of the creditor to which he ought to have procured himfelf to be fubrogated on paying him. If the fecurity in paying the creditor, has neglected to require the fubrogation, and thus difabled himfelf from procuring the fubrogation to the one of the principal debtors from whom he requires the whole debt which he has paid, this debtor will be allowed, on tendering to reimburfe him for his part, to claim, *per oppositam exceptionem cedendarum actionum*, to be difcharged from the demand of the fecurity for the part of the other principal debtors.

It is fo when the debtor has really an intereft to have the fubrogation of the actions of the creditor. But if he had no intereft in this fubrogation, if the fubrogation to the actions which the security has in his own right, gives him the same claim upon the property of his co-debtors, as the subrogation to the actions of the creditor, in this case he is not to be allowed to complain that the security did not, on paying, require the subrogation to the actions of the creditor and cannot procure it. He is therefore not to be allowed the plea *cedendarum actionum*.

This will be illustrated by the following example. *Finge.* Several debtors have borrowed *in solidum* a sum of money from a creditor under my securitiship, and they have given me a deed of indemnification, before a notary-public, of the same date with the obligation contracted towards the creditor. I have paid the debt without requiring the subrogation to the actions of the creditor; I demand the reimbursement of the whole from one of the debtors. It is evident that he cannot complain that I am unable to procure him the subrogation to the actions of the creditor; for the action which I have in my own right against the co-debtors and to which I am ready to subrogate him, having an hypothecation resulting from the deed of indemnification bearing the same date with the hypothecation of the actions of the creditor, the subrogation to the actions which I offer him, procures him the same claim upon the property of his co-debtors, as the subrogation to the actions of the creditor would have procured him, and consequently renders him without interest and prevents his being received to complain that I cannot procure it.

When the security bound himself only for one of the debtors *in solidum* and not for the others, he has, after he has paid the debt, a direct action only against him for whom he was a security. He can only, as using the rights and actions of his debtor, use those which this debtor, on paying the debt, might have used against them, and in the same manner; of which see *supra, n.* 281.

Article II.

Of the cases in which the security has an action against the principal debtor, even before he has paid.

441. The law 10, *Cod. mand*, recognizes only three

cases in which the security may, before he has paid the debt, proceed against the debtor for whom he was bound, in order to procure himself to be indemnified by him. *Si pro ea contra quam supplicas fidejussor, seu mandator intercessisti, & neque condemnatus es, neque bona sua eam dilapidare postea cæpisse comprobare possis, ut tibi justam metuendi causam præbeat; neque ab initio ita te obligationem suscepisse, ut eam possis & ante solutionem convenire; nulla ratione, antequam satis creditori pro ea feceris, eam ad solutionem urgeri certum est;* d. L. 10.

The first case mentioned in this law, is when a judgment has been had against the security, *si neque condemnatus es.*

According to our jurisprudence, the security is not obliged to wait till there is a judgment against him. As soon as he is sued by the creditor, he may cite the principal debtor to defend and exonerate him. He is even bound to do so. On his failing, the debtor is not bound to reimburse him for the costs that may accrue before he is brought in as a party to the suit, excepting the costs of the first process and the costs that may accrue since he is made a party to the suit.

The debtor whom the security has not called in, may sometimes indeed defend himself from paying the debt for which judgment has been had against the security, when the debtor had a good plea against the creditor's demand, which he might have availed himself of had he been called in; *supra, n.* 432.

The second case is, when the affairs of the debtor are deranged, *neque postea bona sua dilapidare comprobare possis.* In this case the security, though he may not yet have paid, may attach the property of the principal debtor that it may be holden to answer the debt for which he is bound.

The third case mentioned in the law is when the debtor bound himself to procure to the security the discharge of his securitiship within a certain time. In such case, when the time is expired, the security may sue the principal debtor to make him procure the discharge or to pay the debt.

The law says, *neque ab initio*, because according to the principles of the civil law, this agreement ought to have intervened at the time of the mandate; the agreements which do no not intervene till after the contract being only simple pacts, which according to the subtilty of the civil law produced no action. See in *Pand. Justin. tit. de pactis, n.* 34. These subtilties have not been received in our jurisprudence; it is immaterial whether the agreement intervened at the time of the contract or since.

The law 38, §. 1, *mand.* mentions a fourth case, *si diu reus in solutione cessavit.* According to this law, although there had been no clause, by which the principal debtor bound himself to procure the discharge of his security within a certain time, yet the security whose obligation has continued a considerable time after, may sue the principal debtor to compel him to procure his discharge. The law, by this word *diu*, designates a considerable time, but does not determine it precisely. Bartolus judges it to be two or three years; several other authors hold it ten years from the date of the securitiship. Nothing can be determined in regard to it. It ought to depend on circumstances and should be left to the arbitration of the Judge *gl. ad. d. L.* 38.

442. When the obligation to which the security has acceded is from its nature to continue a certain time, however long it may be, the security cannot during this time require the principal debtor to procure his discharge, for he knew or might have known the nature of the obligation to which he acceded, and ought to have considered that he would remain bound during the whole of that time. Therefore he who became the security of a guardian for the management of the affairs of his ward, cannot require from the guardian, while the guardianship continues, that he should procure the discharge of his securitiship; because the obligation that results from the administration of the guardianship, cannot have an end before the guardianship. For the same

reason, he who has become the security of a husband to his wife, for the restitution of her portion, cannot require from the husband, while the marriage continues, to be discharged from his suretiship; because the obligation is of a nature that it cannot be discharged till after the dissolution of the marriage.

ARTICLE III.

Whether the security for an annuity may compel the debtor to redeem it.

443. There is either an agreement between the principal debtor and the security, that the debtor shall be bound to discharge him from his suretiship at the end of a certain time agreed upon by the parties, or there is no agreement to this purpose. The first case has less difficulty, yet it is not without some apparent difficulty. It may be said that such an agreement is not valid, being contrary to the nature of annuities, of the essence of which it is that the debtor can never be compellable to redeem. It is added that such agreements, were they permitted, would give room for the frauds of creditors, who in order to provide the means of compelling their debtors to the redemption of the annuities, would not purchase without a secret condition that a confidential person should intervene as a security, with whom the debtor would agree to redeem the annuity at the end of a certain time, and in this way these creditors would procure to themselves usurious annuities, without passing the principal. Notwithstanding these reasons, Dumoulin, *Tract de Usur.* 9, 30, decides that this agreement is valid; that the security may, at the end of the appointed time, require from the principal debtor that he procure his discharge from the suretiship, and that for this purpose he should be holden to reimburse the principal. If it be opposed to this agreement that it is of the essence of annuities that the debtor cannot be compelled to redeem, the answer is that it is indeed of the essence of these annuities that the debtor cannot be compelled by the creditor to redeem, but nothing prevents his being compellable thereto by a third person. It is the perfect alienation of the

principal, which the creditor has paid for the purchafe of the annuity, that conftitutes the effence of the annuity; but it fuffices, for this alienation, that the creditor of the annuity fhould not have retained the right to recall the principal, and that he can never compel the debtor to pay it. It is indifferent that the debtor may be compelled thereto by a third perfon. As to the fecond objection drawn from the fraud, the anfwer is that fraud is not to be prefumed. It is true that the allowance of fuch an agreement may fometimes give room for the kind of fraud mentioned above, and this is an inconvenience: but if, under the pretence of this inconvenience, this agreement, which in itfelf has nothing unlawful, fhould be prohibited, a greater evil would refult, that men could feldom procure money to anfwer their exigencies, not being able to find fecurities who would be willing to contract an obligation the duration of which fhould be unlimited.

The fecond cafe, which is that in which there has been no agreement between the principal debtor and the fecurity, has more difficulty. Dumoulin, *ibid*, decides that in this cafe the fecurity can at no period whatever compel the debtor to redeem the annuity in order to difcharge him from his fecuritifhip; becaufe the nature of the annuity being that it continues for ever till the debtor is pleafed to repay the principal, the fecurity who knew its nature, and was willing to be a fecurity for it, has fubmitted to contract an obligation which is perpetual as is the annuity: *Non obstat*, fays he, *quod diu vel perpetuo remanebit in obligatione, quia hoc est de natura obligationis, & sic prævisum fuit, & tamen fidejussit, & se perpetuo obligavit: simplex autem promissio indemnitatis intelligitur secundum naturam obligationis principalis.* Thus, he adds, he who becomes a fecurity for one who takes a leafe of eighty years, contracts a fecuritifhip of this duration: thus the fecurities for a guardianfhip, the fecurities of a hufband for the reftitution of the marriage portion, contract a fecuritifhip which is to continue as long as the guardianfhip or marriage, and from which they cannot fooner be difcharged. Such have been the decifions in the

Parliament of Toulouſe, as Catelan ſhews, in v. 2, L. 5. *ch.* 21. Notwithſtanding theſe reaſons, we hold in our courts that even in the caſe in which there has been no agreement between the principal debtor and the ſecurity, when the ſecurity bound himſelf at the ſolicitation of the debtor and his ſecuritiſhip has continued a very conſiderable time, as, at the leaſt, ten years, the ſecurity is well grounded in requiring the principal debtor to diſcharge him, on paying the principal within a reaſonable time to be fixed by the judge. The reaſon is, that if an annuity is of a nature to continue 'till it be redeemed, it is alſo of a nature to be always redeemable. If the ſecurity for the leſſee of a long leaſe, the ſecurity of a guardian, or of a huſband for the reſtitution of the marriage portion, cannot be diſcharged till after the expiration of the leaſe, guardianſhip, or marriage; it is becauſe it is of the nature of theſe obligations not to be determinable before. Therefore he who becomes a ſecurity for ſuch obligations, ought to have conſidered that his ſecuritiſhip would not ſooner have an end. But annuities being always redeemable, and being frequently redeemed, he who became a ſecurity for the debtor, depended on the debtor's redeeming the annuity and that his ſecuritiſhip would not endure for ever. Therefore when it continues too long he ought to be admitted to demand that the debtor ſhould diſcharge him by redeeming the annuity. This is the opinion of Baſnage, *p.* 2, *ch.* 5. Lacombe has reported a caſe in which it was thus adjudged.

The right which reſults from this agreement, that the creditor ſhall be bound to redeem the annuity within a certain time agreed upon, in order to diſcharge his ſecurity, is not to be exerciſed with rigor; therefore if the ſecurity at the end of the time, proſecutes the debtor to compel him to redeem, the judge ought readily to grant the debtor a further time to perform this obligation, when he cannot conveniently do it immediately. *Molin, ibid.*

444. When the ſecurity who has required an agreement that the debtor ſhould redeem the annuity within a certain time, has become the ſole heir of the creditor of

the annuity, or when, on his becoming heir, for part, of his estate, the whole of the annuity has fallen to his share; it is evident that he can no longer require from the principal debtor the redemption of the annuity: for his securitiship is in this case extinguished, as he cannot be a security to himself. He can no longer be admitted therefore to demand that the debtor discharge him from a securitiship which no longer remains and from which he is already freed.

Quid, if the annuity for which he became a security to the ancestor, has fallen to the share of his co-heir, or the division has not yet been made? Dumoulin, *ibid.*, decides that if the security has become the heir of the creditor only for a small part, he may in both cases, in his own right, compel the debtor to procure him the discharg of his securitiship, by redeeming the annuity; but that if he has become the heir of the creditor for a considerable part, as for a half or a third, he cannot, in either case, require from the debtor this discharge. The reason he alledges is that the security in becoming heir for a considerable part of the annuity, has become a creditor of this annuity for a considerable part; and that this quality of creditor of a considerable part of the annuity, which he has, or had before the division, opposes his right to require from the debtor the redemption, in order to be discharged from his securitiship; the more so, as it is or has been easy for him to procure this discharge in another manner, by taking the annuity to himself in the division.

I should find much difficulty in yielding to this decision of Dumoulin, especially in the case in which the whole annuity has fallen to the co-heir of the security; for, according to the principles of our jurisprudence, with regard to the declarative and retroactive effect of the division, which was not so well established in the time of Dumoulin as at this day, an heir is holden to have succeeded to the ancestor only for the estate which has fallen to his share by the division. The security, therefore, is never holden to have succeeded to the annuity for which he became a security to the ancester, the whole of which annuity has fallen in the division, to the ſhare of his co-heir: he therefore has not, and is holden never to have had, as to any part, the quality of creditor of this annuity; nothing then can prevent him from requiring in his own right that the debtor redeem the annuity and thereby diſcharge him from his ſecuritiſhip. As to what Dumoulin adds, that it was eaſy for the ſecurity to procure to himſelf in another manner a diſcharge from his ſecuritiſhip, by taking the annuity to himſelf in the diviſion, I anſwer, I. that this did not depend entirely upon the ſecurity; his co-heir, who might have preferred the annuity to the other parts of the eſtate could have required that chance ſhould decide it. II. Although this had depended on the ſecurity, I do not ſee that he could have been obliged, for the ſake of the debtor, to take the annuity rather than other parts of the eſtate, which he might think more advantageous to him.

The caſe in which the diviſion has not been made, has more difficulty. I would think that in this caſe, the action being brought by the ſecurity againſt the debtor for the redemption of the annuity, the proceedings ſhould be ſtayed till after the diviſion; for it is not equitable that the ſecurity ſhould proſecute the debtor for the redemption, while he has the expectation of acquiring the diſcharge of his ſecuritiſhip by the diviſion in which this annuity may fall to his ſhare.

Quid, if the diviſion was made, and the annuity remained in common to the ſecurity and his co-heir? I grant that in this caſe the capacity of creditor for a part of the annuity which the ſecurity has, prevents him from requiring the debtor to redeem the whole annuity. But why could he not, in declaring that he conſents that it may be continued for the part that fell to his ſhare, require him to redeem it for the part that fell to the ſhare of his co-heirs, ſo that he may be releaſed from his ſecuritiſhip? I ſee nothing that ought to prevent it.

The ſecurity ceaſes to have the right of requiring that the principal debtor redeem the annuity, not only when it is as heir that he became owner and creditor of the annuity, but also when he becomes so in any other manner, either by title to the whole or a part, *puta*, if he becomes universal donee or legatee of the creditor of the annuity, or particular donee or legatee: for he has only a right to require the redemption of it, to be discharged from his securitiship, and he has no longer any need to be discharged, when he has become owner of the annuity in any manner; for then his securitiship is extinguished, since no one can be a security to himself.

If the property in the annuity which the security has acquired, be a defeasible right, *puta*, if he were donee or legatee of the annuity under the charge of a substitution; the obligation of his securitiship would be suspended rather than extinguished. It would revive if his right should be defeated, *puta*, by the happening of the contingency on which the substitution was to take place. Therefore the security could not indeed require the redemption of the annuity whilst he was owner of it; but his right to the property happening to be determined and consequently the obligation of his securitiship being revived towards him to whom the property of the annuity had passed, the right of requiring the debtor to redeem the annuity in order to discharge him from the securitiship, ought likewise to be revived; and the time during which the debtor had agreed to redeem, which had ceased to run while the security was owner of the annuity, will begin again to run.

But if the security who became owner of the annuity, ceases to be owner of it, by a voluntary alienation which he makes, and not by the determination of his right, the obligation of his securitiship is not revived, nor, consequently, his right of requiring from the debtor the redemption of the annuity. *Molin. ibid. quæst.* 29, *n.* 246.

If the security himself had redeemed the annuity, though he had procured himself to be subrogated to the actions of the creditor, and by means of this subrogation he might revive it against the debtor, yet he may, by not availing himself of the subrogation, claim back from the debtor the principal ſum which he has paid for this redemption. The reaſon is, that a mandatary may reclaim, *actione mandati contraria*, all that he has been obliged to diſburſe, *quidquid ex causa mandati ipsi inculpabiliter abest.* (*V. Pand. Justin. tit. mand. n.* 53, *& seq.*) It is the ſecuritiſhip which the ſecurity has entered into at the ſolicitation of the debtor that compelled him to redeem, in order to put an end to his obligation: therefore this ſum *ipsi abest ex causa mandati, & quidem inculpabiliter.* For the principal debtor cannot diſapprove of this diſburſement, ſince he had bound himſelf to redeem in order to put an end to the obligation of his mandatary, if the ſecurity had not. Therefore this principal debtor cannot defend himſelf from reimburſing this ſum. *Molin. ibid. quæst.* 30.

Whether the ſecurity has paid money for the redemption of the annuity, or whether, with the conſent of the creditor, he has paid any thing elſe as an equivalent for the ſum by which the annuity was redeemable, he has a right to claim back the money from the principal debtor: for in either caſe, *ipsi ex causa mandati abest.*

Obſerve that if the ſecurity had redeemed the annuity before the expiration of the time within which the debtor had bound himſelf to redeem, he could not claim this money back till after that time. Indeed after this time, the claim ought not to be rigorouſly urged, and when it is made the judge ought eaſily to grant ſome delay to the debtor to procure the money.

We have ſaid that the ſecurity who has redeemed the annuity can only claim the reimburſement of the monies paid for the redemption of the annuity from the principal debtor, inaſmuch as he has not uſed the ſubrogation allowed him in order to revive the annuity. Why? It would ſeem on the contrary, that the ſecurity having two capacities, *duarum personarum vices sustinens*, might exerciſe at once the different rights that reſult from theſe two capacities, viz. that of requiring the continuation of the annuity as being ſubrogated to the rights of the creditor, and that which he has in his own right of requiring that the principal debtor ſhould redeem the annuity. It ſeems that he may the more ſo, as the principal debtor does not appear to ſuffer by this any inconvenience; ſince if the ſecurity had not made the redemption, the ſecurity might require that he ſhould make it; and notwithſtanding this demand of the ſecurity, he would not ceaſe to be liable to pay the arrearages to the creditor, until he had made the redemption: it is indifferent to him whether he pays to the ſecurity who is ſubrogated to the rights of the creditor, or to the creditc Notwithſtanding theſe reaſons, Dumoulin, *quæst.* 29. decides that the ſecurity who wiſhes to avail himſelf of the right of ſubrogation and to take the annuity, cannot afterwards exerciſe the right which he had to require the redemption; becauſe theſe are rights abſolutely incompatible. The creditor of an annuity, or he who wiſhes to exerciſe his rights, is, in this capacity, bound to procure to the debtor the free enjoyment of the principal of the annuity, as long as he pleaſes; which is inconſiſtent with the right to require the reimburſement of the principal.

Dumoulin, *quæst.* 30, *n.* 249, adds this modification to his deciſion, that if the ſecurity, being ignorant of the law that he could not have at the ſame time the right to revive the annuity for his benefit, and that to require the redemption of it, had received one or two years arrearages, he would notwithſtanding be allowed to require the redemption, on offering to renounce his ſubrogation to the rights of the creditor, and conſequently to apply the arrearages he has received to the principal.

ARTICLE IV.

Of the actions of the security against his co-securities.

445. A ſecurity may indeed bring againſt his co-ſecurities the actions of the creditor, when he has had the precaution to cauſe himſelf to be ſubrogated; but, according to the civil law, he had not in his own right any action a-

gainst them, even in the case in which he had paid the debt: this is the decision of the law 39, ff. *de fid.;* L. 11, *Cod. d. tit.*

The Roman jurists ground their decision on the following principle. When several persons become securities for the same debtor, they do not contract towards each other any obligation: neither of them has any other intention than to serve the principal debtor; each proposes to himself the accommodation of the principal debtor and not that of his co-securities: *Solius rei principalis negotium gerit, non alter alterius negotium gerit.*

This principle is true and it may indeed be said, evident: but the consequence which the Roman jurists have derived from it, that a security can never, without the subrogation of actions, have any recourse against his co-securities, even when he has paid the whole debt for which they were all liable, is a consequence too hard and which we have not admitted in our jurisprudence. On the contrary, our jurists have thought that the security who has paid the whole debt, may, without a subrogation, claim back a part of it from each of his co-securities. This was the opinion of d'Argentré, on *art.* 213 of the antient custom of Brittany; and it was incorporated into the present system at the reformation. *art.* 194.

This action does not arise from the securitiship which this security has entered into with his co-securities, since by this securitiship they have not contracted any obligation towards each other, according to the principle above established: it arises only from the payment which this security has made of the whole debt, and from equity, which does not permit that his co-securities, who were liable equally with him for the debt, should profit at his expence by the payment which he has made of it. This action is not the true action *negotiorum gestorum.* This security who has paid the whole debt, having paid what he really owed, has discharged his own obligation, *proprium negotium gessit, magis quam cofidejussorum:* but it is an action *utilis negotiorum ges-*

tarum, quæ non ex subtili juris ratione, sed ex sola utilitatis & æquitatis ratione proficiscitur; becaufe, although this fecurity, *ipsius inspecto proposito,* in paying the whole debt, has done an affair of his own rather than that of his co-fecurities; yet, *effectu inspecto,* having, as to the effect, done an affair which concerned his co-fecurities equally with himfelf, having by the payment which he had made difcharged them from a debt which they owed equally with him, equity requires that they fhould bear their part of this payment, by which they have profited as much as he.

There are fome authors who have gone much farther and have maintained that in the cafe of the infolvency of the principal debtor, a fecurity had an action in his own right againft his co-fecurities, not only after he had paid the creditor, to recover from them their parts of what they were bound equally with him to pay to the creditor; but even before he had paid, to make them contribute with him towards the payment of the fum which they all owed to the creditor. They have gone fo far even as to fay that in the cafe of the infolvency of a debtor of an annuity, a fecurity who had been for a confiderable time a fecurity for the annuity, had an action againft his co-fecurities to compel them to contribute with him towards the redemption of the annuity. See Bafnage, *Trait. des Hypoth. part.* 2, *ch.* 6, who cites fome cafes in the Parliament of Normandy which have been fo adjudged; and Brodeau *on Louet, letter F. ch.* 27, who cites alfo a cafe determined in the Parliament of Paris. But I think that thefe authors have proceeded too far. I grant that when one of the fecurities is fued by the creditor, this fecurity who is fued has an action againft his co-fecurities to compel them to furnifh each his part of the fum demanded, the payment of which would difcharge the action; and that on their failure to pay their proportion, they would be liable each for his part of the cofts incurred fince the fuit has been notified to them. This action arifes from the fuit brought againft the fecurity, and from equity, which does not permit that among feveral perfons who are equally liable for the fame debt, one of them fhould be fued rather than the others. It is on this reafon of equity that the benefit of divifion among the co-fecurities has been eftablifhed. This fame reafon of equity which allows one fecurity who is fued for the payment, to require the creditor to divide his action and fue all the fecurities, ought likewife to allow him to require his co-fecurities to contribute, each his part, towards the payment of the debt, and on failure, towards the payment of the cofts incurred fince the fuit was notified to them. He ought to be allowed to require this, even when he has renounced the benefit of divifion, or when he is excluded from it by the nature of the debt for which the fecuritifhip was contracted; this renunciation and this exclufion applying only in favor of the creditor.

But while the fecurity is not fued for the payment, he has no action againft his co-fecurities to oblige them to contribute with him towards the payment of the debt: for the co-fecurities, according to the principle above eftablifhed, not having intended to contract between themfelves any obligation, that from which arifes the action which the fecurity has againft his co-fecurities, when he is fued, is founded only on a reafon of equity which proceeds from the fuit that is brought againft him; whence it follows that he cannot have any action until he is fued. *A fortiori*, the fecurity of an annuity cannot, in cafe of the infolvency of the principal debtor, have an action againft his co-fecurities to compel them to contribute with him towards the redemption of the annuity; for from what obligation could this action arife? When the fecurity has redeemed the annuity, he can demand nothing more from his co-fecurities than the continuation of the annuity, each for his part: for the action which he has againft them can only arife from the rule of equity which does not permit his co-fecurities to profit at his expence by this redemption; thefe co-fecurities deriving from this redemption no other benefit than the difcharge from the payment of the annuity, they cannot be liable for any thing elfe than to continue each for his part an annuity equal to that from which the redemption had discharged them in regard to the creditor.

A security who has paid a debt that is demandable, or redeemed an annuity, has an action against the other principal securities, and in case of the insolvency of one of them, against the securities of this insolvent security, who represent him; but he has no action against his own security who bound himself for him: for he is simply the security of him for whom is bound, *fidejussor fidejussoris*; the security in regard to his own securities holds the place of a principal debtor, *instar rei principalis*.

By the same reason, when the security of a security has paid, he has a recourse for the whole against the security for whom he bound himself.

SECTION VIII.

Of several other kinds of accessory obligations.

ARTICLE THE FIRST.

Of the obligation of those who are called in law MANDATORES.

446. He by whose order I have lent money to another, is called in law *mandator pecuniæ credendæ; toto tit. ff. de Fidej. & mand.*

When you give me an order to lend a certain sum of money to Peter, this order which I undertake to execute, includes a contract of mandate which takes place between us.

According to the principles of the contract of mandate, the mandatary being bound towards the mandator, *actione mandati directa*, to account with him for all he has *ex causa mandati*, I am by this contract, in my capacity of mandatary, bound *actione mandati directa*, towards you who are the mandator, to cede to you the action which arises from the loan of the sum of money which I have made in the execution of your mandate, and which is consequently *ex causa mandati*.

On your side you are bound towards me *actione mandati*

contraria to reimburſe and indemniſy me for the ſum which I have diſburſed in the execution of your mandate, by lending the ſum of money through your order to Peter. By this obligation you become bound towards me to anſwer for the debt of Peter which he had contracted to me by the loan which I have made to him.

In this *mandatores pecuniæ credendæ* agree with ſecurities.

We need not however confound them; there is an eſſential difference between the one and the other.

The obligation of a ſecurity is no other than a ſimple acceſſory to the obligation of the principal debtor, which has for its conſideration that of the obligation of the principal debtor. *For example. When you become a ſecurity* towards me for a ſum of money which I have lent to Peter, or for a ſum of money which Peter owes me for the price of a thing which I have ſold him, the ſecuritiſhip which you contract is only a ſimple acceſſion to the obligation of Peter; the cauſe of your obligation, as well as that of Peter's to which you have acceded, is the ſale or the loan which I have made to Peter.

It is not the ſame of the obligation which you contract with me by the order you give me to lend a certain ſum to Peter. It is true that it has the ſame object with that which Peter contracts with me by the loan which I have made to him through your order: the ſum of money, for which you are bound, *actione mandati contraria*, to reimburſe me, is not a like ſum, but it is *preciſely the ſame ſum which is* due me by Peter, and I am not allowed to receive it from you and from him, according to the rule, *bona fides non patitur ut idem bis exigatur*; L. 57, ff. *de. R. J.* But although your obligation has the ſame object with that of Peter's, although the ſum which is due me by you and by him, is one and the ſame thing, of which Peter is the principal debtor, ſince he is debtor of it for himſelf abſolutely, and you are debtor of it rather for him than for yourſelf; yet our obligation is not a mere acceſſion to that of Peter; it has a different confideration from that of the obligation of Peter, which is the contract of mandate that took place between us. This contract is not merely a fimple acceffory contract, fuch as is a fecuritiſhip; it is a principal contract: your obligation which arifes from this contract, which is an obligation *ex causa mandati*, has therefore a confideration different from that of the obligation of Peter, who is my debtor *ex causa mutui.*

From thefe principles on the difference of the obligation of a *mandator pecuniæ credendæ*, and of that of a fimple fecurity, follows this difference between the one and the other, that when a fimple fecurity has paid the debt for, which he became a fecurity, without requiring, in making the payment, the ceffion of the actions of the creditor againſt the principal debtor, he extinguiſhes by this payment the debt of the principal debtor, and he cannot afterwards caufe the actions of the creditor to be ceded to him, when thefe actions have been extinguiſhed by this payment; for his debt being not only a debt of the fame thing, but precifely the fame debt as that of the principal debtor, to which he has only acceded, the payment which he has made has extinguiſhed the debt of the principal debtor.

On the contrary when a *mandator pecuniæ credendæ*, by the order of whom I have lent a certain fum to a third perfon, *puta*, to Peter, reimburfes me for this fum; although he has not required the ceffion of my actions againſt Peter, the payment which he makes me extinguiſhes *only his* own obligation, and that of Peter is not extinguiſhed: I remain, notwithſtanding this payment, creditor of Peter *ex causa mutui*, not to the effect that I may exact for my benefit the fum which is due me by Peter *ex causa mutui*, having already been paid *ex causa mandati;* but I remain his creditor to the effect that I may cede the rights of this debt to my mandator when he ſhall require me to do fo, as I am bound *obligatione mandati directa* to cede them to him. This we learn from the law 28, ff. *mand. Papinianus ait mandatorem debitoris solventem ipso jure reum non liberare, propter enim mandatum suum solvit & suo nomine; ideoque mandatori actiones putat adversus reum cedi debere;* although he did not require this ceſſion at the time of the payment.

Theſe differences being excepted, the *mandatores pecuniæ credendæ* agree with ſecurities: altho' the obligation *contraria mandati*, which they contract towards him who has lent to another a ſum of money thro' their order, is not entirely, as is a ſecuritiſhip, a mere acceſſion to the obligation of the debtor to whom the ſum has been lent thro' their order and it has its own conſideration, *propriam causam*, it is however, as is that of ſecurities, acceſſory to the obligation of this debtor, and depends upon it: it is valid only in the ſame manner as the obligation of this debtor is valid; mandators may plead all pleas *in rem*, which could be pleaded by the debtor to whom the thing has been lent thro' their order; L. 32, ff. *de fidej.* The extinction of the obligation of this debtor, in whatever manner it may take place, whether by actual payment of the ſum lent, or by ſet-off, novation, releaſe, or confuſion, extinguiſhes the obligation of theſe mandators, in the ſame manner as it extinguiſhes that of ſecurities. The novel 4, §. 1, has given them, as it has to ſecurities, the plea of diſcuſſion. All we have ſaid of this plea, *supra, sect.* 6, *art.* 2, applies to mandators in the ſame manner as it does to ſecurities.

In order that one may be reputed *mandator pecuniæ credendæ*, and conſequently anſwerable to me for the ſum of money which I have lent to a third perſon through his order, it is neceſſary that what he ſaid or wrote to me ſhould include an actual mandate, by which he has required me to lend this ſum to this perſon, with the intention of indemnifying me for it. But if in a converſation, I told you that I had a thouſand crowns to place at intereſt, and you informed me that Peter was ſeeking to take money at intereſt and that you thought the money would be ſafe in his hands, theſe expreſſions include no mandate, but mere advice by which you contract no obligation towards me, according to this rule of law: *Consilii non fraudulenti nulla est obligatio, nisi dolus intervenerit*; L. 47, ff. *de Reg. Jur.*

Obferve, however, that in order that advice may not bind the perfon who gave it, it is neceffary that it be given *bona fide*; therefore the law adds, *nisi dolus intervenerit*: for if you knew that the affairs of Peter were deranged when you advifed me to lend him money, this would be a fraud on your part which would bind you, at leaft in a moral view, to indemnify me for the lofs I fhould fuftain by the infolvency of Peter.

You might even be holden to be bound thereto *in foro legis*, if I had evident proof that you were well acquainted with his circumftances. Likewife, we ought not to take for a *mandatum credendæ pecuniæ* what is only a recommendation. Thus, if you told me, "Peter, our common friend, wants "to borrow ten piftoles from you, I recommend him to you;" thefe words contain no mandate, but only a recommendation, which is not obligatory; L. 12, §. 12, ff. *mand.*

It would be otherwife if you had faid to me: "Peter "wants ten piftoles, I cannot now conveniently lend them "to him, I pray you to lend him that fum for me." This is an actual mandate.

In order that a *mandator pecuniæ credendæ* may be obliged to indemnify you for the money which you lent to a third perfon, through his order, it is neceffary that you fhould have confined yourfelf ftrictly to the terms of the mandate; *diligenter enim fines mandati custodiendi sunt*; L. 5, ff. *mand.* If then you have done another thing than that which is contained in my mandate; *puta*, if I had directed you to lend a fum of money to Peter, and you have given it to him on a contract of annuity; *aut vice versa*, if I had directed you to give it to him on a contract of annuity, and you have lent it to him, I fhall not be bound to you; for a contract of annuity and a contract of loan being different things, it cannot be faid that you have done what was contained in my mandate.

If I had given you an order to lend a certain fum of

money to Peter, *puta*, five hundred livres, and you lent him fix hundred livres, the fum of five hundred livres mentioned in my mandate being included in that of fix hundred livres, which you lent him, according to this rule of law, *in eo quod plus sit, semper inest & minus*; L. 110. ff. *de Reg. Jur.*; it is proper to fay that you have done what was contained in my mandate, and confequently I am bound to you, *obligatione mandati contraria*, for Peter, to the amount of five hundred livres. With regard to the remaining one hundred livres, as you have in this refpect exceeded the limits of my mandate I am not bound to you for this overplus.

Vice versa, if you have lent to Peter, a lefs fum than the one mentioned in my mandate, I am bound to you for Peter; for you have executed my mandate in part.

If you have done indeed what was mentioned in my mandate, but not in the manner which I prefcribed, I fhall not be bound towards you. For example. If in the order which I gave you to lend a fum of money to Peter, it was mentioned that you fhould require pledges from him, which you did not require; or if it was mentioned that you fhould procure him to bind himfelf before a notary, in order that I might have a lien on his lands; and you only took his note. In thefe and like cafes, I fhall not be bound to you, becaufe you have not done what was mentioned in the order which I gave you; L. 7, *Cod. de fidej.*

Contra, vice versa, if I had given you an order to lend Peter a certain fum of money, and to take only his note, without requiring any pledge or a fecurity, and you caufed him to bind himfelf before a notary, or required from him a pledge or a fecurity, I cannot in this cafe complain that you did not confine yourfelf to the limits of my mandate; for you have done what was mentioned in it, in lending to Peter, the fum of money which I had requefted you to lend him; and as what you have done befides cannot be otherwife than advantageous to me, I cannot complain of it.

If I gave you an order to lend a fum of money to Peter absolutely, and in lending it to him you have granted him a certain time to pay it in, or the liberty of paying something else instead of it, I shall not be bound to you; for in granting him this you have exceeded the limits of my mandate. I only bound myself, *actione mandati contraria*, to reimburse you for the sum which I had given you an order to lend him, provided you placed yourself in a situation, to cede to me, after I should have reimbursed you for that sum, such actions as would have enabled me to require the sum from Peter, as soon as I pleased, without his being able to give me any thing else in lieu of it: thus as, by the terms which you have granted to Peter, you have disabled yourself from ceding such actions to me, I am not bound to you for the loan which you made to Peter.

On the contrary, if I had given you an order to lend to Peter, a certain sum, and to give him a certain time to pay it in, and you lent it to him without giving him any time to pay it in, I shall be bound to you for this sum, but you will not have a right to demand it from me till after the time mentioned in my mandate. I cannot complain that you did not grant to Peter the time mentioned in my mandate; for, provided you have no right to require it from me before the expirat on of that time, it is indifferent to me whether you may demand it sooner from the principal debtor or not.

Article II.

Of the obligation of principals.

We shall see under this head, I. in what sense principals accede to the obligations resulting from the contracts of their agents, and in what they differ from other accessory debtors. II. In what cases the obligation of these principals takes place. III. We shall speak of the effects of this obligation. IV. Of the obligation of principals, accessory to the obligations which result from the torts of their agents.

§. I.

In what sense principals accede to the obligations resulting from the contracts of their agents.

447. When a merchant has committed to a person the management of a trading house or the command of a vessel; and likewise, when the king's farmers have committed to a person the direction of a branch of the revenue, in all the engagements, which this agent contracts, even in his own name, relative to the affairs he is entrusted with, he binds himself as principal debtor, and he binds at the same time his principal as an accessory debtor: for this principal is presumed, by the authority which he has given to his agent, to have agreed beforehand to all the engagements he should contract relative to the affairs he intrusted him with, and to have made himself answerable therefor.

These principals are accessory debtors of a different kind from securities and *mandatores pecuniæ credendæ*. These, ordinarily, in acceding to the obligation of the principal debtor, bind themselves for the business of the principal debtor, and not for their own. On the contrary a principal, in acceding to the contracts of his agent, transacts his own business rather than that of his agent. If in the contract, of the agent, the agent is looked upon as principal debtor and the principal as an accessory debtor, it is only because the contract is made with the agent: the principal, who often has not even a knowledge of the contract, accedes to it only by the general adherence which he is holden to have given beforehand to the contracts his agent was to make, when he committed his business to him. But these contracts of the agent are rather the business of the principal than his own: while securities and *mandatores pecuniæ credendæ* ought to be indemnified by the principal debtors for the obligations which they contract, it is on the contrary the principal who ought to indemnify the agent.

§. II.

In what cases the accessory obligation of principals takes place.

448. In order that this accessory obligation of the

principal may take place, it is requisite that the agent should have contracted in his own name, although for the affairs of the principal: but when he contracts in his capacity of factor or attorney of his principal, it is not he who contracts, it is the principal who contracts through his intervention; *supra, n.* 74: the agent in this case does not bind himself. It is the principal alone who, through the intervention of his agent, contracts a principal obligation.

When the agent contracts in his own name, in order that he may bind his principal, it is requisite the contract should relate to the business which is committed to him, and that the agent do not exceed the limits of his commission. L. 1, §. 7, *tit.* 12, *de exerc. act.*

Such are the contracts of sale, or purchase of goods made by an agent, in a trading house, the purchase made by the master of a vessel of the things necessary to the repairs or fitting out of his vessel, &c.

Money borrowed by an agent is also presumed to have been borrowed for the business which is committed to him, when the contract contains a declaration of the cause for which the money is borrowed, and this cause actually relates to the business committed to the care of the borrower.

For example. If the master or supercargo of a vessel, after a storm or fight, during which the vessel has suffered much injury, puts into port, and borrows money, declaring that he wants it to repair the vessel, the owner or principal who employed him, will be bound by this loan.

It would even be holden that the owner or principal is bound, in such case, even if his agent had wasted the money, and failed to employ it on the vessel, if the want he was in was probable, and the sum borrowed was not much above the sum necessary for the purpose for which it was declared to be borrowed; L. 1, §. 8 & 9; L. 7, *princip.* & §. 1, ff. *de exerc. act.*

Agents bind their principals as long as their commission continues; and it is always holden to continue until it be revoked, and until the revocation be publicly known.

Although regularly every mandate terminates with the death of the mandator; yet it has been eftablifhed for the convenience of commerce, that the commiffion of fuch perfons fhould continue even after the death of the merchant who employed them, until it be revoked by the heir or other fucceffor: and in contracting in regard to the bufinefs which was committed to their management, they bind the heir of the merchant who employed them, or his vacant eftate if he left no heir; L. 17, §. 2 & 3, 11, ff. *instit. act.*

For the fame reafon, the director of an office of finance, binds the fucceffors of the financier who employed him, as long as his commiffion is not revoked.

§. III.

Of the effect of the accessory obligation of the principal.

449. This obligation extends to all that is contained in the obligation of the agent: it depends upon it, as all acceffory obligations depend on the principal obligation to which they accede: therefore this obligation of the principal is extinguifhed, when that of the agent is extinguifhed by payment or novation, L. 13, §. 1, ff. *de inst. act.* or in any other manner whatever. The principal may avail himfelf of all the pleas *in rem* or to the action, which the agent might have pleaded. He cannot take advantage of any defect in the obligation of his agent, arifing from any incapacity of that agent: for the principal who employed him cannot argue againft his own act and the choice which he made. Therefore, although a minor, in contracting, does not bind himfelf validly, *ne quidem naturaliter*, unlefs *quatenus locupletior factus est*, and confequently fecurities cannot intervene for him; yet when a merchant has entrufted his affairs to a minor, he is liable *institoria actione* for all the obligations which refult from the contracts of the minor, without being allowed to plead the nonage of the contractor. *Pupillus institor obligat eum qui eum præposuit, institoria actione; quoniam sibi imputare debet qui eum præposuit;* L. 7. §. *fin.* ff. *de inst. act.*

The law ff. *de obl. & act.* says formally that a minor cannot bind himself, *ne quidem naturaliter.* I know, however, that there are contrary opinions. We have followed that of Cujas. See *in Pand. Just.* a scholium, after *n.* 17 of the title *de obl. & act.* in which we related at length the reasons on which this opinion is established and the objections against it. By natural obligation we mean that which, *in foro legis*, is recognized as a natural obligation and has *juris effectus:* for we do not deny that a minor *pubertati proximus*, if he knows what he is doing may bind himself *in foro conscientiæ.*

Cujas says that the law 127, *de Verb. obl.* which holds that securities may intervene for an infant, must be understood of the case in which he has been benefited by the contract.

450. With regard to the extent of the action *institoria*, which results from the accessory obligation of principals, some difference is to be observed between them and securities.

When several merchants, or several of the king's farmers-general, have entrusted a person with their commerce, the command of a vessel, or the direction of an office of revenue, they are liable *in solidum* for the obligations of their agent; L. 1, §. *fin.* & L. 2, ff. *de exerc. act.*; and they are not entitled to the plea of division, which is granted to securities. There is the more reason for its being so with us, as in our jurisprudence, partners are liable *in solidum*, for all the engagements relative to the partnership.

451. Securities, and even *mandatores pecuniæ credendæ*, have the plea of division, which was granted them by the novel of Justinian, of which we have spoken *supra, sect.* 6, *art.* 2, because they have contracted their obligation rather for the business of the principal debtor than for their own: but the obligation which a principal contracts *ex contractu institoris*, being an obligation which the principal contracts for his own business, he has not the benefit of the plea of

division: even if he had beforehand indemnified his agent, and given him money to pay; but in this case the creditor ought, if it be required at the time of payment, to make him a cession of his actions.

The ordinance of Marine, *tit.* 8. *art.* 2. grants a peculiar advantage to the owners of vessels. It is that of discharging themselves from the engagement contracted by the master, to whom they gave the command of their vessel, by abandoning to the creditors, the vessel and freight.

(What was in the first edition, under n. 452, has been inserted in the beginning of this paragraph; therefore we have suppressed that number.)

§. IV.

Of the accessory obligation of principals resulting from the torts of their agents.

453. It is not only, by contracting, that agents bind their principals. Whoever has committed to a person any function, is answerable for the torts and quasi torts which his agent is guilty of in the exercise of the function which is committed to him; L. 5, §. 8, ff. *de inst. act.* and if there be several principals they are all bound *in solidum* without being entitled to any plea of discussion or division. For example. If an officer of the revenue, in making his visit in an alehouse, were to injure the keeper of it in his person or property, the King's farmers-general who employed him are bound by his tort, and are liable for the damages to which their agent will be condemned, saving their recourse against him; because their agent committed the tort in the exercise of his functions. If he had ill-treated or robbed the alehouse-keeper, out of the exercise of his functions, they would not be liable for it.

This obligation of the principal is an accessory obligation to the principal obligation of the agent who committed the tort.

It extends to all that is contained in the principal obligation for the damages due to the perfon againft whom the tort has been committed; but the principal is bound only *civiliter*, although the perfon who committed the tort, be conftrainable by the imprifonment of his perfon. The principals cannot oppofe to the action refulting from the tort, the plea of divifion, nor that of difcuffion; they may only, when they pay, require the ceffion of the creditors actions.

§. V.

Of heads of families and masters.

454. Another kind of acceffory obligation is that of heads of families who are refponfible for the torts of their minor children and wives, not preventing them when they had it in their power to do fo.

They are holden to have it in their power to prevent the tort when it was committed in their prefence. If it was committed in their abfence, we are to judge from circumftances, whether they had it in their power to prevent it. For example. If a boy had a quarrel with his comrade and wounded him with his fword, even in the abfence of his father, the laft may be liable for the tort, as having had it in his power to prevent it; which he might have done, by not permitting his fon to wear a fword, efpecially if he was of a quarrelfome temper.

455 What is faid here of a father extends to a mother, when after the death of her hufband, fhe had the management of her children. It may likewife be extended to fchoolmafters, preceptors and all thofe who have the care of children.

456. Mafters are alfo liable *for the torts of their* fervants, not preventing them when they had it in their power fo to do.

They are even liable for the torts which they could not prevent, when their fervants committed them in the fervice in which they were employed. For example. If your coachman, in driving your carriage brutally, carelefsly or through want of skill, has caused any injury, you are personally liable for it; saving your recourse against him who is the principal debtor.

Heads of families and masters are not liable for the engagements contracted by their children or servants, unless it be proved that they committed and entrusted such children or servants with some business to which these engagements relate.

For example. If it were proved that I am in the habit of paying shop-keepers for the provisions delivered to my daughter or servant, a shop-keeper will be authorised to demand payment from me for the provisions which my daughter or servant bought from him, in my name; unless I could prove I had given him notice not to furnish any, or what had been taken exceeded by a great deal what was necessary for the use of my family. If the shop-keeper fails in proving this, I ought to be discharged from his demand, on my swearing that when I sent my daughter or servant for provisions I gave them money to pay for them. *Arret du Journal des Audiences, vol. 5.*

SECTION IX. *and last.*
(Added in this new Edition*.)
Of the pact CONSTITUTÆ PECUNIÆ.

We omitted, in the first edition of this work, to treat of the pact *constitutæ pecuniæ*, and of the obligation resulting from it, which is in a manner an accessory obligation, since it is added to a prior obligation and is contracted, only to strengthen it. We shall speak of it here.

1. The pact *constitutæ pecuniæ*, among the Romans, was an agreement by which one assigned to a creditor, a certain day or time, within which he promised to pay him; *diem solvendæ pecuniæ constituebat*. This is the result of the terms of the edict *de constituta pecunia.*

---

* *This section is numbered separately, in order that the numbers of the second volume may be conformable to those of the first edition.*

The word *pecunia*, in this edict, as in the law of the twelve tables, and in the other edicts of the Prætor, was used for all things corporeal as well as incorporeal, which constitute property, and which may be the object of obligations; *Pecuniæ nomine non solum numerata pecunia, sed omnes res, tam soli quam mobiles, & tam corpora quam jura continentur*; L. 222. ff. *de verb. sign. Pecuniæ appellatione* REM *significari Proculus ait*; L. 4. ff. *d. tit.*

According to our jurisprudence, the pact *constitutæ pecuniæ* may simply be defined an agreement by which one promises to a creditor to pay him.

2. This promise may be made to one's own creditor or to that of another.

When one, by this pact, promises to his own creditor to pay him, there arises a new obligation which does not destroy the first, by which he was bound, but accedes to it; and by this multiplication of obligations the right of the creditor is strengthened.

In this the right resulting from a personal claim differs from that of dominion and property. When I have, by virtue of any title, dominion or property over a certain thing, I can no more acquire this dominion or property by virtue of any other title. *Dominium non potest nisi ex una causa contingere*; L. 3. §. 4, ff. *de acq. poss.*

On the contrary, although I be already creditor of a certain thing, by virtue of a title, I may still afterwards become creditor of the same thing, either from the same debtor, who may bind himself anew to give it to me, or from other debtors.

Paul, in L. 159, ff. *de Reg. Jur.* observes this difference between the right of dominion and the right of personal claim: *non, ut ex pluribus causis idem nobis deberi potest, ita ex pluribus causis idem potest nostrum esse.*

3. Of what use, will it be asked, may be to the creditor this new obligation contracted by the principal debtor towards him by the pact *constitutæ pecuniæ?* It is useful to him both in *foro conscientiæ* and in *foro legis*. In *foro conscientiæ*,

the more the obligations of the debtor are multiplied, the greater is the infidelity on his part if he fails in difcharging them; and confequently the ftronger is the right of the creditor to expect the performance of them. In *foro legis*, when the obligation of the debtor, who by this pact had promifed to his creditor to pay him, was a mere natural obligation, fuch as were at Rome all thofe which were formed of fimple pacts, unclothed with the formalities of a ftipulation: it is evident, in this cafe, that the obligation which the debtor contracted by the pact *constitutæ pecuniæ*, was very ufeful, fince it gave him an action which the firft did not. The degree of infidelity which there is in violating repeated obligations, induced the Prætor to give an action againft the debtor to compel him to perform the obligation arifing from this pact: *quoniam grave est fidem fallere*; L. 1, ff. *de pec. const.*

When the obligation of the debtor, who by this pact had promifed to his creditor to pay him, was a civil obligation, which gave him an action, the obligation and action which refulted from this pact were not indeed neceffary; the pact however was not ufelefs, and it feems it intervened as well with regard to civil obligations as with regard to natural obligations: *Debitum ex quocumque causa constitui potest, ex quocumque contractu, &c.* L. 1, §. 6, *& seq. de const. pec.* This pact was ufeful in determining the time within which payment was to be made, when none was expreffed by the contract: and this determination ferved, according to the principles of the civil law, to put the debtor in arrear, *de jure*, by the lapfe of time alone, when he did not perform his obligation: while, when no time was determined, the debtor could be put in arrear only by a judicial demand.

4. Even in the cafe in which the creditor would have no occafion for the pact *constitutæ pecuniæ* to fix the time of payment, which was already fixed and determined by the contract, Ulpian decides that the pact might be of fome utility: *Si is qui & jure civili & Pretorio debebat, in diem sit*

obligatus, an constituendo teneatur ..... habet utilitatem, ut ex die obligatus constituendo se eadem die soluturum teneatur; L. 3, §. 2, ff. *d. tit.*

To understand in what this utility might consist, we ought to reflect that according to the principles of the ancient Roman law, actions depended on embarrassing formulas, the least neglect of which caused the action to fail. It was consequently useful to have several actions for a debt of the same thing, so that if by any fault one of them failed, the creditor might resort to another. Hence altho the obligation was a civil obligation which gave an action to the creditor, the pact *constitutæ pecuniæ*, which gave a new action, was not altogether useless.

5. The pacts *constitutæ pecuniæ* which had for object to determine a certain day, or a certain time within which one bound himself to a creditor to pay what was due him, are not much in use among us: for this determination of the time within which payment ought to be made, which, according to the principles of the civil law, was useful to the creditor, that the debtor might more easily be put in arrear, is ordinarily, according to the principles of our jurisprudence, of no use to the creditor; since in our practice, whether there be a time of payment or not, the debtor cannot ordinarily be put in arrear without process.

There are however, among us, certain agreements, which may be called pacts *constitutæ pecuniæ*, by which one promises to pay to a creditor what is due him. Such are those by which the heirs of a debtor give a new title to the creditor and bind themselves to pay what they owe him in their capacity of heirs. The new obligation which results from such an agreement is useful to the creditor, since it gives him the right of proceeding directly against those heirs, which he had not before.

We shall see on this pact, I. what is necessary to its validity; II. whether it necessarily includes a time within which the payment is to be made; III. whether, by this pact, one may bind himself to more, to another thing, or in a different manner than by the first obligation; IV. what is the nature of the obligation which results from this pact. We shall speak, in a fifth paragraph, of the pact by which one promises to a creditor to give him certain sureties.

§ I.

Of what is necessary to the validity of the pact constitutæ pecuniæ.

6. It results from the definition which we have given of the pact *constitutæ pecuniæ*, that it supposes the pre-existence of a debt which is promised to be paid to him who is the creditor of it. Therefore if, through error, I have agreed to pay you a certain sum which I thought was due you by myself or another; the error being since discovered, you cannot require the payment; because the pact is void, for want of a debt which may be the foundation of it: *Hactenus constitutum valebit, si quod constituitur debitum sit*; L. 11, ff. *de const. pec.*

Quid, if I promised to pay you a sum which I declared I owed you, although I then knew that I did not owe it? This agreement cannot be valid as a pact *constitutæ pecuniæ*, for want of a debt, which ought to be the foundation of it: it contains in this case a donation which I wished to make to you; and cannot be valid, if it be not clothed with all the formalities which the municipal law requires for the validity of donations.

7. When the debt of which payment has been promised by the pact *constitutæ pecuniæ*, was suspended by a condition under which it was contracted, and which was not yet performed; although there was then as yet no debt, yet if afterwards the condition be performed, the pact will be valid: for conditions, when they are performed, have a retrospective effect to the time of the contract: the debt will be presumed to have existed from the time it was contracted, and consequently at the time of the pact *constitutæ pecuniæ*, which intervened some time after. L. 19. ff. *d. tit.*

But if the condition is not performed, the pact will not be valid: it necessarily depends on the condition under which the debt was due: although this was not expressed by the parties.

Quid, if I had expressly promised to pay, even if the condition should happen to fail? The promise to pay cannot in this case be valid as a pact *constitutæ pecuniæ*, for want of a debt which is the foundation of it; it contains, in case of the failure of the condition, a donation, which cannot be valid, unless clothed with the formalities required for the validity of donations *inter vivos*.

8. It is immaterial in what manner, what is promised to be paid by the pact *constitutæ pecuniæ* be due: for in whatever manner what I promise to pay you may be due, were it only a mere natural obligation, it is not a donation that I make; it is a payment which I promise to make, and consequently this is a true case of the pact *pecuniæ constitutæ*.

Quid, if the debt was one of those which the municipal law disallows, would the pact *constitutæ pecuniæ*, by which one should promise to pay it, be valid? I think that if the debt was disallowed by the municipal law, not on account of some defective cause from which it proceeded, but on account of some incapacity of the person who contracted it, and this incapacity did not exist at the time of the pact, the pact would be valid.

For example. If a feme-covert has borrowed a sum, which did not turn to her advantage, I think that, on her becoming a widow, she may validly bind herself to pay it. For although such a debt be disallowed by the municipal law, which declares it void, it suffices that it is due *in foro conscientiæ*, that the payment made by this woman may be an actual payment and not a donation. Hence it follows that the agreement, by which she has promised to pay it, does not contain a donation, but a promise to pay and consequently it is a true pact *constitutæ pecuniæ*, which the woman might validly make, since she was then free and able to bind herself. It will be replied that we have said *supra, n.* 395, that this obligation cannot be the foundation of a securitiship; consequently it cannot be the foundation of a pact *constitutae pecuniae.*

I answer that there is much difference between the two cases. A securitiship is a mere accession to the obligation of a principal debtor: the obligation of a security cannot exist alone; there must necessarily be a principal obligation, to which it is an accessory. An obligation which the municipal law disallows, and which it declares absolutely null, is not susceptible of accessories, and cannot consequently be the subject of a contract of securitiship. The right which I acquire against you, when you become a security to me for another, is only an extension of the right which I had against the person for whom you become a security. If I have none against him, the law declaring his obligation absolutely null, I cannot have any against you. It is not so with regard to the pact *constitutae pecuniae.* If it be said that the obligation which results from it is *accessory* to the principal obligation, which one promises by this pact to discharge, this is only said in this sense, that it is added to this principal obligation, but it is not said in the same sense as it is said in the case of a securitiship. This is not an obligation, like a securitiship, which is a simple accession to the principal obligation: it is an obligation which exists by itself, *propriis viribus,* and even in some cases, after the principal obligation has ceased to exist, as shall be shewn *infra,* by the law 18, §. 1, ff. *d. tit.*

If it is of the essence of the pact *constitutae pecuniae* that there be a pre-existing debt, it is only because it ought to have for its object a payment; otherwise it would include a donation. In order that this pact may not contain a donation, and that it may have for its object a payment, *it* suffices that the debt which one promises to pay by this pact be due, at least in *foro conscientiae,* and that there be consequently a just cause to pay it; although in *foro legis,* it be declared null by the municipal law.

9. Obferve, neverthelefs, that for the validity of the pact *constitutæ pecuniæ*, by which one promifes to pay one of thofe debts which are difallowed and annulled by the municipal law, it is neceffary that the debt be not difallowed on account of fome defect in the caufe from which it refults, but only on account of fome civil incapacity of the perfon who contracted it, and it is requifite that this perfon be under no incapacity at the time of the pact by which he promifes to pay; fuch as in the cafe of which we have given an example. But if the debt, which one promifed to pay by the pact *constitutæ pecuniæ*, be a debt which the municipal law difallows on account of fome defect in the caufe from which it refults; *puta*, if it be due for the expences incurred in a tavern by an inhabitant of the place; although fuch a debt be due in *foro conscientiae*, and the payment of it would be valid, yet the pact, by which one fhould promife to the tavern-keeper to pay it, would not be valid, and he would not be admitted to fue for it. The reafon is that the defect in the caufe of the debt ftill exifts, whether the tavern-keeper claims the payment of it by virtue of the firft obligation contracted by him who originally incurred the debt in the tavern, or by virtue of the pact *constitutæ pecuniæ*; it is always a tavern-debt, which the judge cannot admit.

10. When the debt is due only *subtilitate juris*, as that which would refult from a promife extorted by fraud or violence, for which I am neither bound in *foro legis*, where I may oppofe the plea refulting from the fraud or violence, nor in *foro conscientiæ*, it cannot be the foundation of a pact *constitutæ pecuniæ*. *Si quis constituerit quod jure civili debebat, jure prætorio non debebat, id est, per exceptionem, an constituendo teneatur? Et est verum non teneri, quia debita juribus non est pecunia quæ constituta est*; L. 3, §. 1, ff. *pec. const. Juribus; id est, nec jure naturali, nec quoad effectum jure civili, propter exceptionem.*

The reafon is that as it is of the effence of the pact *constitutæ pecuniæ*, that it have for its object the payment of a debt, such a debt as that a valid payment of it cannot be made, cannot serve as a foundation to this pact, for either the payment has been made by mistake, and it is not valid since there is ground to reclaim what is paid, L. 26, §. 3, ff. *de Cond. ind.*; or the payment is made, with knowledge of the defect in the debt, and in this case it is rather a donation than a payment; according to the rule, *Cujus per errorem dati conditio est, ejus per errorem dati donatio est*, L. 53, ff. *de R. J.* A donation cannot be the object of a pact *constitutae pecuniae*; nothing can be, but the payment of a debt.

11. It is indeed necessary, as we have seen thus far, in order that the pact *constitutae pecuniae* be valid, that at the time of this pact, there exist a debt which one promises by this pact to pay. But the existence of the thing which is promised, by the pact, to be paid, is not in the same manner always necessary. For if this thing had perished by the act or fault of him who was debtor of it, or since he was put in arrear, the thing will continue in this case to be due, although it had ceased to exist, as we shall see *infra, part* 3, *chap.* 6, *art.* 3, which suffices that the pact *constitutae pecuniae*, by which this thing is promised to be paid, though it has ceased to exist, may be valid, and bind him who made the promise to pay the price of this thing. This is the decision of Julian: *Promissor hominis, homine mortuo quum per eum staret quominus traderetur, si hominem daturum se constituerit, de constituta pecunia tenebitur ut pretium ejus solvat*; L. 23, ff. *d. tit.*

12. Provided that at the time of the pact there exist a debt, the payment of which may be the object of it, it is immaterial to the validity of the pact, whether it be the debtor who promises to pay it, or whether it be another person who promises to pay it for him; *& quod ego debeo, tu constituendo teneberis.* L. 5, §. 2, *d. tit.*

It is not necessary that the assent of the debtor should intervene, when another binds himself by this pact to pay for him what he owes; one may even make this pact against his will; for as one may pay for another without his consent and even against his will, L. 52, ff. *de solut.*, so one may bind himself to pay for another without his consent, and even against his will. This is taught by Ulpian: *Utrum praesente debitore an absente constituat quis, parvi refert: Hoc amplius etiam invito.... unde falsam putat opinionem Labeonis existimantis, si postquam quis constituit pro alio, dominus ei denuntiet ne solvat, exceptionem dandam: Nec immerito; nam cum semel sit obligatus qui constituit, factum debitoris non debet eum excusare*; L. 27, ff. *d. tit.*

I may indeed, by the pact *constitutæ pecuniæ*, promise to pay what is due by another; but it is necessary, in order that the pact may be valid, that I should promise to pay it as a thing due by him who is really the debtor of it: if I promised to pay it as under a supposition that I was myself the debtor of it, the pact would not be valid, if I were not the debtor; L. 11, ff. *d. tit.*

13. As a payment is valid, not only when it is made to the creditor, but when it is made to another by his order or by his consent; so this pact is valid, whether it be to the creditor himself that one promises to pay or whether it be to another, provided it be with his consent. It is thus we ought to understand what Ulpian says: *Quod constituitur, in rem exactum est, non utique ut is cui constituitur creditor sit; nam quod tibi debetur, si mihi constituatur, debetur*; L. 5, §. 2; provided, as we have said, that this be with the consent of the creditor. But if one promised to pay to another than the creditor without his consent, the pact would not be valid, although this should be to him to whom one could validly pay. *Titio stipuler; Titio constitui suo nomine.* This is taught by Ulpian. *Si mihi aut non posse Julianus ait; quia non habet petitionem, tametsi ei solvi possit*; L. 7, §. 1, ff. *d. tit.*

§. II.

Whether the pact constitutæ pecuniæ *necessarily includes a time in which one promises to pay.*

14. Among the Romans, as we have already observed, the pact *constitutæ pecuniæ* ordinarily contained a certain day or

time within which payment was promifed. The word *constitutum* appeared fo much to include the idea of a time, that it had been doubted whether the pact *constitutæ pecuniæ* might be valid, when there was no time expreffed. This we learn from Ulpian, who thinks neverthelefs that the pact in this cafe is no lefs valid, but that a delay of eight days at leaft ought to be implied. L. 21, §. 1, ff. *d. tit.*

This decifion ought not, I think, to be admitted, except when the parties had not been more explicit as to the time of payment in the contract by which the debt was created, than in the pact *constitutæ pecuniæ* by which one has bound himfelf to pay it. But if the contract mentioned the time within which it is to be paid, I think that the parties, who mentioned nothing as to this in the pact *constitutae pecuniæ*, ought to be prefumed to have refted fatisfied with the time mentioned in the contract.

This principle of the Roman law, that the pact *constitutæ pecuniæ* muft always include a time expreffed or implied, within which ought to be made the payment which by this pact is promifed to be made, is not received among us, according to what we have obferved in the beginning of this fection.

§. III.

Whether one may by the pact conftitutæ pecuniæ *bind one's self for more than is due, or to another thing than what is due, or bind one's self thereto in a different manner.*

15. It is not neceffary to the validity of the pact *constitutæ pecuniæ*, that one fhould promife by this pact to pay precifely the fame fum as that which is due; it may be a lefs fum: *Si quis viginti debens, decem constituit se soluturum, tenebitur*, L. 15, ff. *de. pec. const.* Note that in this cafe, although the debtor be not liable *ex pacto constitutæ pecuniæ* but in *decem*, he ftill remains debtor of the whole fum *ex pristina obligatione*, as the pact *constitutæ pecuniæ* does not deftroy the firft obligation, but only accedes to it.

16. One may validly promife by the pact *constitutæ pecuniæ* to pay a lefs fum than the one that is due; but one

cannot validly promise to pay a greater sum; and if this be promised the pact will be valid only to the amount of the sum due. *V. G. Si quis centum aureos debens, ducentos constituat, in centum tantummodo tenetur*; L. 11. ff. *d. tit.*

The reason is that what should be given above the sum due, would not be a payment, but a donation, and, as we have already said several times, the pact *constitutæ pecuniæ* can be valid only as a promise to pay, and not as a donation.

For the same reason, if one had promised by this pact to pay something else besides the thing which he owes, the pact would be valid only for that sum; *Si decem debeantur, & decem & Stichum constituat, potest dici decem tantummodo nomine teneri*; L. 12.

It is not however necessary to the validity of the pact *constitutae pecuniae* that one should bind himself precisely to pay the same thing which is due. One may validly promise to pay another thing, not besides that which is due, but in its stead. For the payment which is made of another thing, in the room of that which is due being valid, when the creditor consents to it, as we shall see *infra*, *part* 3, *n.* 495, the agreement to paying another thing than that which is due, ought likewise to be valid. This is taught by Ulpian: *An potest constitui aliud quam quod debetur quaesitum est? Sed cum jam placet rem pro re solvi posse, nihil prohibet & aliud pro debito constitui*; L. 1, §. 5, ff. *d. tit.*

17. The pact to pay another thing than that which is due may be made validly, not only by the debtor but by a third person who promises to pay this other thing for the debtor. For as a third person may validly pay for a debtor another thing in lieu of that which is due, when the creditor consents to it, he may also validly promise by this pact to make this payment.

In this the pact differs from the securitiship, for as we have seen *supra*, *n.* 368, a security cannot validly bind himself for another thing than that which is due by the principal debtor. *In aliam rem quam quæ credita est, fidejussor obligari non potest*; L. 42, ff. *de fidej.* The reason of this difference is that a securitiship is only a simple adherence of the security to the obligation of the principal debtor: it cannot then have a different object. On the contrary, the pact *constitutæ pecuniæ* supposes indeed the pre-existence of a debt, having for its object the payment of that debt; but it is not on this account a simple adherence to the principal obligation; it may have a different object from that of the principal obligation. For, as the payment of this principal debt, which is the object of the pact, may be made, with the consent of the creditor, in any other thing than that which is due, one may promise by this pact to pay another thing than that which is due; in which case, the pact has another object than the principal obligation. Another proof that the pact *constitutæ pecuniæ* is not a simple adherence to the principal obligation, is that the obligation, which results from this pact, exists sometimes after the principal obligation is extinguished, as we shall see in the next paragraph.

18. One may bind himself, by this pact, in a different manner from the principal obligation. For example. One may bind himself, by this pact, to pay in another place than that expressed in the principal obligation: *Eum qui Ephesi promisit se soluturum, si constituit alio loco, teneri constat*; L. 5, ff. *de pec. cons.*

One may even bind himself by this pact to pay in a shorter time than that mentioned in the principal obligation: *sed & si citeriore die constituat se soluturum, similiter tenetur*; L. 4, ff. *d. tit.*

The pact by which one promises to pay within a shorter time, is valid whether it be interposed by the debtor or whether it be interposed by a third person who promises to pay for him, as Accursius has well remarked in his gloss on this law.

This is not contrary to the principle which we have cited *supra*, n. 370: *Illud commune est in universis qui pro aliis obligantur, quod si fuerint in duriorem causam adhibiti, placuit eos omnino non obligari*; L. 8, §. 7, ff. *de fidej.* For this principle applies to those only whose obligation is but a mere adherence to that of the principal debtor, such as securities. But the obligation which is contracted by the pact *constitutæ pecuniæ*, although it ought to have for object the payment of a pre-existing obligation, is not, as we have already remarked a mere adherence to this obligation; since as we have already seen one may bind himself by this pact to give another thing than that which is due, provided it be in payment and in lieu of that which is due, that one promises to give it. Likewise provided the pact have no other object than the payment of the debt, one may, by this pact bind himself on harder terms to make the payment than the creditor was bound to by the principal obligation and consequently to do it within a shorter time. Accursus observes very well on this law that he who binds himself by this pact and whom he calls *reus constitutae pecuniae*, differs in this from the security.

I cannot approve of the opinion of Cujas who in his commentary on Paulus *ad. Ed.* on this law, blames Accursus for distinguishing the *reus pecuniae constitutae* from the security and who contends that the security may, like the *reus consitutae pecuniae*, bind himself to pay within a shorter time than the principal debtor is bound to pay in, and that it will not be found in any law that he cannot. I answer, that it suffices that the law should say generally that securities may not bind themselves *in duriorem causam*, for it to be concluded that they may not bind themselves to pay within a shorter time than that in which the principal debtor is bound to pay; for it is clear that the condition of him who is bound to pay *hic & nunc* and without delay, is harder than that of him who has a day of payment, and it is true to say that he is bound to more, since more is to be considered *non solum quantitate sed DIE, conditione, loco, &c.* Further, the law 16, s. 5, ff. *de fidej.* decides expressly that if one has become a security under a certain condition for a principal debtor, who was bound to pay at the end of a certain time, and the condition is accomplished before the time, the security will not be bound. Is not this saying very exprefsly that a fecurity cannot be bound to pay immediately, when the principal debtor has a day of payment?

19. The law 8, ff. *de pec. const.* furnifhes another example of the principle that one may bind himfelf differently and on harder terms by the pact *constitutae pecuniae*, than by the principal obligation. It decides that I may validly agree by this pact that that which by the principal obligation might have been paid either to me or into the hands of another perfon, fhall be paid to me alone. The condition of the fecurity who fhould be deprived of the convenience which the debtor has of paying into the hands of a third perfon, would be harder than that of the principal debtor. L. 34, ff. *de fidej*,

Cujas, in the fame work, *ad. leg.* 10 & 13, fays that this law ought to be reftricted to its particular cafe which is when it is the debtor himfelf who promifes to pay to me, alone, what was payable to me, or into the hands of a third perfon; and that a third perfon could not make fuch a pact, for he cannot any more than a fecurity bind himfelf *in duriorem causam*. I think on the contrary that as this pact is not a mere adherence to the principal obligation, a third perfon may by it bind himfelf *in duriorem causam*, as we have feen above.

20. It remains for us to obferve that in new titles, which heirs give and by which they bind themfelves to the payment of what was due by the anceftor, they may indeed, according to the principles which we have given, bind themfelves to pay under different claufes than thofe mentioned in the primitive title. But, for this purpofe they ought to declare that they mean to alter the primitive title: otherwife all that is found in the new title, different from the primitive title, is prefumed to have crept in through error, and is not valid; the prefumption being that thofe who give fuch titles, intend to acknowledge and confirm, what is mentioned in the primitive title and not to change any thing therein.

§. IV.

Of the effect of the pact constitutæ pecuniæ, *and of the obligation which results from it.*

First principle.

21. The pact *constitutæ pecuniæ* which has for its object the payment of a pre-existing obligation contains no novation. It produces a new obligation which does not extinguish the first but accedes to it.

Second principle.

Although the pact *constitutæ pecuniæ* does not extinguish the first obligation; it sometimes occasions changes and modifications in it, which, however, according to the subtilty of the principles of the civil law, was not done *ipso jure*, but *per exceptionem*.

Third principle.

Although the obligation, which results from the pact *constitutæ pecuniæ*, accedes to the first, it is not however a mere adherence to the first obligation, it exists of itself, and it sometimes indeed continues to exist after the extinction of the first.

Fourth principle.

The payment of either of these obligations extinguishes and discharges both.

22. The first of these principles requires no illustration.

The second will be illustrated by examples.

First example.

We have seen in the preceding article that one might, by the pact *constitutæ pecuniæ*, promise to pay in lieu of the sum or thing which is due another thing or sum. Let us suppose that my debtor of thirty pistoles promises to pay me at All-Saints, six barrels of wine from his vintage, in payment of the sum of thirty pistoles which he owes me. This pact does not destroy the first obligation. I may by virtue of the first obligation demand from my debtor the thirty pistoles, and my suit proceeds *ipso jure*; but as by the pact have agreed that he might pay me instead of this sum six barrels of wine, he may, by pleading the pact and tendering the six barrels of wine, require to be discharged from my demand of thirty pistoles. By means of this plea, of which he may avail himself, his first obligation, which was an absolute obligation to pay me precisely thirty pistoles, receives a modification from the pact, and becomes an obligation of thirty pistoles, which may be discharged by the delivery of six barrels of wine in lieu of it.

The creditor, being creditor of the thirty pistoles, by virtue of the first obligation and creditor of the six barrels of wine, by virtue of that which results from the pact *constitutae pecuniae*, may, if he sees fit, bring the action which results from the pact and demand the six barrels of wine; but if the debtor choose to pay the thirty pistoles, he might in tendering them, procure himself to be discharged from the demand for the six barrels of wine, because according to our fourth principle, the payment of the thirty pistoles, which discharges the first obligation, discharges them both.

Second example.

23. If being debtor to you of a sum which was payable to you alone, at your house, I promised to you, by the pact *constitutae pecuniae*, to pay into your hands, or into those of your correspondent, at a less distant place; this pact brings in my favor a modification to my obligation, in this, that whereas before the pact, I was bound to pay into your hands and at your house, I acquire by this pact the convenience of paying it into the hands of your correspondent and in a place which is more convenient to me; this is done however, according to the subtilty of the civil law, only *per exceptionem. Si quis pecuniam constituerit* TIBI AUT TITIO; *etsi stricto jure*, PRIORI *actione, pecuniae constitutae manet obligatus, etiamsi Titio solverit, tamen per exceptionem adjuvatur;* L. 30, ff. *de pec. const. Priori;* Cujas has substituted this word to the word *propria*, which has no meaning. By this correction, the sense of this text is clear. Although the debtor who has paid into the hands of Titius, remains al-

ways, *stricto jure*, debtor of the first obligation, which is payable only into the hands of the creditor, yet this payment discharges him *per exceptionem doli aut pacti*; because he may plead to the demand of the creditor that this payment was made in consequence of the permission which was granted by the pact.

Third example.

24. When by the pact *constitutae pecuniae* my debtor has promised to pay me in a certain time the sum which he owed without a time, or with a shorter time, this pact brings a modification to his first obligation, and renders it payable at the time expressed in this pact: for I am presumed to have granted him by this pact the time in which he has promised to pay me; which must prevent my being received to demand it sooner, even by the action which arises from the first obligation.

It would be otherwise, if it were a third person who had promised me to pay for you in a certain time, what you owed me without a time or with a shorter time. This pact would make no change in your obligation and would not prevent my demanding from you, before the time expressed in this pact, what you owe me: for it is not to you that I have granted the time expressed in this pact, to which you were not a party.

25. There are however some cases in which you may profit indirectly by the pact by which a third person has promised to pay for you: such is the case in which a third person may have promised to pay for you a certain sum instead of the thing which you owed. You acquire indirectly by this pact the convenience of discharging yourself from your obligation by the payment of this sum. For as all persons have power to make, in the name of the debtor, payment of what is due by another, when they have an interest to make this payment, it suffices that you have an interest in the payment of the sum which the third person bound himself by the pact *constitutae pecuniae*, to pay in-

ſtead of the thing which you owe, in order that you may be admitted to make, in the name of this third perſon, the payment of this ſum, and on paying it for this third perſon and diſcharging him from his obligation, you likewiſe diſcharge yourſelf from yours: for according to the fourth of our principles, the payment of one of the obligations extinguiſhes both.

For the ſame reaſon, if a third perſon has promiſed by this pact to pay in another place than that in which the debtor was bound to pay or if he has promiſed to pay to the creditor or into the hands of a third perſon what the debtor could only pay into the hands of the creditor: the debtor may indirectly avail himſelf of this pact, by making, in the name of this third perſon, the payment in the place in which he is permitted by the pact *conſtitutæ pecuniæ* to do it, and into the hands of the perſon to whom he is permitted to pay, and on making this payment for this third perſon you diſcharge yourſelf from your obligation by which you were bound to pay preciſely into the hands of the creditor, or in another place: for, according to the fourth of our principles, the payment of the obligation which reſults from the pact *conſtitutæ pecuniæ* extinguiſhes the firſt, and *vice verſa.*

26. We have related ſeveral examples of changes and modifications which the firſt obligation might receive from the pact *conſtitutæ pecuniæ* in favor of the debtor: it may receive others in favor of the creditor.

Here is an example. When he who was my debtor of a ſum payable to me, or into the hands of another perſon, promiſes me by the pact *conſtitutæ pecuniæ* to pay it to me alone; the firſt obligation receives by this pact a change in favor of the creditor. For whereas it was before an obligation with the liberty of paying into the hands of a third perſon, it becomes by this pact an obligation payable only to myſelf. *Si (mihi aut Titio dare obligatus) poſtea quam ſoli mihi te ſoluturum conſtituiſti, ſolveris Titio, nihilominus mihi teneberis.* L. 8, ff. *de conſt. pec.* For by this pact you are presumed to have renounced the liberty which you had reserved by the first obligation to pay to Titius; therefore the payment you made to him is not valid.

It would be otherwise if it were a third person who had promised to make this payment for you. For this pact to which you were not a party, cannot deprive you of the liberty you had to pay into the hands of Titius.

27. Here is a case in which the pact *constitutæ pecuniæ* makes a change in the first obligation as well on the part of the creditor as on that of the debtor. It is when he who was debtor to me of two things under an alternative, promises to pay me one of them determinately. This pact makes in regard to the creditor a change in the first obligation, in this, that from being alternative as it was, this pact, which determines it to the thing which the debtor has promised to pay, gives the creditor the right to exact this thing determinately, without the debtor's having afterwards the choice to pay the other. This is taught by Papinian: *Illud aut illud debuit, & constituit alterum; an vel alterum quod non constituit, solvere possit quæsitum est? Dixi, non esse audiendum, si velit hodie fidem constitutæ rei frangere*; L. 25, ff. *d. tit.*

The first obligation receives also a change in regard to the debtor; for being by this pact determined to the single thing which the debtor has promised to pay, the debtor may acquire the discharge of his obligation by the extinction of this thing, happening without his fault before his arrear; whereas before this pact, his obligation could not have been extinguished but by the extinction of the two things.

28. Our third principle, that the obligation which arises from the pact *constitutæ pecuniæ*, is not a mere adherence to the first, results sufficiently from what we have said in the preceding articles; and it might have a different object, as when one promises by this pact to pay another thing in the place of that which is due by the first obligation.

This results also from this that it may be contracted under harder conditions; as when one promises to pay in a shorter time than that expressed in the first obligation; *supra, n.* 18.

What proves more fully that the obligation which arises from the pact, is not a simple adherence to the first obligation which one has bound himself by this pact to discharge, and that it exists by itself, is that it may continue to exist after the extinction of this first obligation.

This is taught by Ulpian: *Si quid debitum tunc fuit quum constitueretur, nunc non sit, nihilominus tenet constitutum; quia retrorsum se actio refert: proinde temporali actione obligatum, constituendo Celsus & Julianus teneri debere, licet post constitutum dies temporalis actionis exierit. Quare etsi post tempus obligationis se soluturum constituit, adhuc idem Julianus petat, quoniam eo tempore constituit quo erat obligatio, licet in id tempus quo non tenebatur;* L. 18, §. 1, ff. *de pec. const.*

The commentary adduces as an example of this decision, the case in which a vendor, by a pact *constitutæ pecuniæ*, should have promised the purchaser to pay him a certain sum as an indemnification for a defect in the thing sold for which he was liable to him *actione æstimatoria.* According to the decision in this law, the obligation which results from this pact to pay this sum, continues even after the lapse of the six months to which the action *æstimatoria* was limited; and one might by the pact even have given for the payment of the sum a day beyond the six months or duration of the action *æstimatoria.*

In the example adduced in the commentary, it may be said that although the action *æstimatoria* be extinguished by the expiration of the six months, there remains nevertheless after this time a natural obligation to indemnify the buyer, which may be the subject of the payment, which the latter promised to make by the pact *constitutæ pecuniæ.*

Quid, if the debt for the payment of which the pact *constitutæ pecuniæ* has intervened and which existed at the time of this pact, has since been extinguished otherwise than by an actual or fictitious payment, so that there remains no obligation natural or civil? Will the obligation contracted by the pact *constitutæ pecuniæ* for the payment of this debt continue to exist? Yes. Such is the decision of Paul in the law 19, §. 2, ff. *de pec. const.* where he says that if a father debtor towards the creditor of his son, of the sum which was then in the *peculium* of his son, has promised by this pact to the creditor to pay him this sum, he continues to owe it by virtue of this pact, although the obligation *de peculio* for which he was liable, and in payment of which he promised to pay this sum, be extinguished, if there be nothing remaining of the *peculium* of his son. *Licet interierit peculium, non tamen liberatur.*

We will add further examples more conformable to our usages. *Finge.* I became a security to you for Peter, for the sum of one thousand livres which he owed you, on condition that my securitiship should continue only two years, at the end of which I should be exonerated. Before the expiration of the two years and consequently whilst my securitiship continued, James promised you to pay you this sum for me, and he assigned to you a time of payment which does not happen till after the two years. Will James, after the end of the two years, be bound by the pact *constitutæ pecuniæ* to pay you? The reason to doubt is that having bound myself only on condition that my securitiship should continue but two years, and that I should be discharged from it after that time, there exists no debt due from me naturally or civilly that may be the subject of the payment which he promised to make for me. The reason to decide that the obligation of James still continues to exist, notwithstanding the extinction of my debt, in payment of which he promised to give you the sum of one thousand livres, is that one ought to judge of the existence of the debt, for the payment of which the pact *constitutæ pecuniæ* has intervened, by the time when this pact intervened. If at the time it intervened I really owed you the sum of one thousand livres, the pact has validly intervened; James has validly contracted the obligation to pay you that ſum. It is not material that my debt has ſince been extinguiſhed; that which he contracted continues: *Si quid debitum tunc fuit quum constitueretur, nunc non sit, tenet constitutum; QUIA RETRORSUM SE ACTIO REFERT.* It will be objected that he bound himſelf to pay my debt; that he cannot pay it when it is extinguiſhed: that his obligation cannot then any longer exiſt, that it is reduced to ſomething impoſſible. I anſwer that it is indeed in payment of my debt that he bound himſelf to pay you one thouſand livres, and it was neceſſary for this that I ſhould then have owed them to you: but after he has contracted the obligation, the payment he ought to make and which he does make of this ſum, is the payment of his own debt; it is only indirectly that it might be alſo the payment of mine, if it yet exiſted.

Here is another example. A third perſon bound himſelf to pay you three hundred livres for me, in lieu of a horſe which I owed you: although ſince that time, my obligation has been extinguiſhed by the death of the horſe, that of the third perſon muſt continue.

This caſe is very different from that of a perſon who ſhould be debtor of a certain horſe, or of three hundred livres at his choice; in this caſe the death of the horſe diſcharges him entirely from his obligation, becauſe in ſuch caſe nothing is due but the horſe; the three hundred livres are *in facultate solutionis.* But in the above caſe the third perſon was actually debtor of the three hundred livres, he was not alſo of the horſe; it was only of the ſum that he was debtor; therefore the death of the horſe which extinguiſhes my obligation, does not extinguiſh his.

29. The obligation that reſults from the pact *constitutæ pecuniæ* may well continue after the extinction of the principal obligation for the payment of which the pact has intervened. But it is neceſſary for this, as we have already obſerved, that it ſhould have been extinguiſhed in ſome other manner than by an actual or fictitious payment: for according to the fourth of our principles, the payment of

Rr

one of the two obligations, either of the principal obligation, or of that of the pact, extinguishes them both.

30. The reason of the fourth principle is evident. What is promised by the pact *constitutæ pecuniæ* being promised in payment of the principal obligation, this promise, when it is carried into effect by the payment that is made, includes a payment of the principal obligation; the payment then of what is promised by the pact, is a payment of the two obligations, and consequently extinguishes them both.

Vice versa, the payment of the principal obligation extinguishes that of the pact, in barring the creditor from demanding the payment of it; for what was promised him by the pact having been promised to him, and being due to him, only to pay him the principal obligation, if after having been in another manner paid the principal obligation, he required payment of what has been promised him by the pact *constitutæ pecuniæ*, he would be paid the principal obligation twice, which good faith does not permit. *Bona-fides non patitur ut idem bis exigatur*; L. 57, ff. *de R. J.* one cannot twice require payment of the same debt.

31. This principle that the payment of one of the two obligations extinguishes them both, is true, not only with regard to actual payments, but also with regard to fictitious payments; as a novation, set-off, and even a release. The creditor requiring by the set-off of a like sum which he owed, the discharge of that sum, finds himself, by this discharge, paid that which was due him. The creditor in the case of a novation finds himself paid the debt of which he has made a novation, by the new debt that is contracted to him. He cannot then in such case require to be paid what has been promised to him by the pact *constitutae pecuniae*, since it would be to require to be paid twice.

It is the same in case of a release; for though in such case he may not have received any thing, it suffices that by this release he should consider himself paid the principal obligation, that he may no longer be allowed to require to be paid a second time.

32. Our principle that the payment of one of the two obligations extinguishes both, applies when what has been promised by the pact *constitutae pecuniae* has been promised for the payment of all that was due by the principal obligation. When one promised to pay but a part, the payment of what was promised by the pact extinguishes the principal obligation only for that part. For example. If being your debtor for twenty pistoles, I promised or another promised to pay fifteen of them within a certain time, the payment of the fifteen pistoles promised by the pact, will extinguish the principal obligation only to the amount of the fifteen pistoles.

33. It remains for us to observe, with regard to the obligation *constitutae pecuniae*, that according to the law 16, ff. *de pec. const.* When two persons have promised to pay what is due by a third, they are liable each for the whole. In which they resemble securities, *supra, n.* 415: but they have, like securities, the pleas of division, when they are solvent. L. *fin. cod. de pec. const.*

Haloander has thought that those who have promised by the pact *constitutæ pecuniæ* what is due by a third person, have also the plea of discussion when they are sued for having failed to pay on the day appointed; and that they are included in the disposition of the novel 4, *chap.* 1, under the words *constitutæ pecuniæ reus.*

§. V.

Of the kind of pact, by which one promises to the creditor to give him certain sureties.

34. There is a kind of pact *constitutæ pecuniæ* when one promises to the creditor, not to pay him; but to give him within a certain time certain sureties, as pledges, hypothecation, securities: *si quis constituerit se pignus daturum, debet hoc constitutum admitti;* L. 14, §. 1, ff. *de pec. const.*

The effect of this pact is that he who promised by this pact to give certain sureties may, on his failing to give them be compelled to pay the debt, even before the time when it is payable, and if it be an annuity he may be compelled to reimburse the principal.

35. He who has promised by this pact to give for a security a certain person, is discharged from his obligation, if, before he has performed it, or has been put in arrear to perform it, the person whom he promised to give for a security happens to die; *d.* L. 14, §. 2. The reason is that his obligation becomes impossible by the death of this person who cannot now become a security.

It would be otherwise, if the person whom he promised to give for a security, refused to be bound as his security: *si nolit fidejubere, puto teneri eum qui constituit, nisi aliud actum est*; *d.* §. The reason is that in order that my obligation may be valid, it suffices that the securitiship of the person whom I promised to give for a security, be something possible in itself, though it be not possible to me on account of the refusal of this person to enter into the securitiship. It is my own fault to have promised what I could not perform. This is conformable to the principles established *supra*, n. 136.

END OF THE FIRST VOLUME.

A TREATISE ON OBLIGATIONS,

CONSIDERED IN A

MORAL AND *LEGAL* VIEW.

Translated from the French of POTHIER.

IN TWO VOLUMES.

VOLUME THE SECOND.

NEWBERN, N. C.

MARTIN & OGDEN.

1802.

TABLE.

PART III.

CHAPTER II.

CHAPTER III.

A

TREATISE

ON

OBLIGATIONS.

THIRD PART.

Of the manner in which obligations are extinguished and of the different pleas and prescriptions against them.

457. OBLIGATIONS may be extinguished in different ways; by actual payment, by consignation, by set-off, by confusion, by novation, by release, by extinction of the thing due.

Those which have been contracted under some resolutive condition, are extinguished by the happening of this condition; others by the death of the debtor or that of the creditor.

We shall treat of these different ways separately in seven chapters. We shall add an eighth, in which we shall treat of pleas and prescriptions.

CHAPTER THE FIRST.

Of actual payment, and of consignation.

458. ACTUAL payment is the actual performance of what one has obliged himself to give or to do.

When the obligation is to do something, the actual payment of this obligation consists in doing the thing which one has bound himself to do.

When the obligation is to give something, payment is the donation and translation of the property of this thing.

It is evident that he who has performed his obligation is acquitted and discharged: hence it follows that actual payment, which is nothing else but the performance of the obligation, is the most natural way in which obligations may be extinguished.

We shall see in the two first articles of this chapter by whom and to whom payment ought to be made; in the third what ought to be paid, how, and in what condition; in the fourth and fifth, when payment ought to be made, where and at whose expence. We shall treat in the sixth of the effect of payments. The seventh will contain the rules of their application. Lastly, in the eighth we shall treat of consignation and tender.

ARTICLE THE FIRST.

By whom payment ought to be made.

459. When the obligation is to give something, the payment consisting as we have said in the giving or transferring of the property of the thing, it follows thence that, in order that the payment may be valid, it should be by a person capable of transferring the property of the thing paid.

From this it follows that the payment is not valid if it be not made by the owner of the thing or by his consent; for otherwise he who pays cannot transfer to the creditor to whom he makes the payment, the property of the thing.

Nemo plus juris in alium transferre potest quam ipse habet; L. 54, ff. *de reg. juris.*

According to this principle, although the debt of a deceased person were of a thing determinately due, one of the heirs of the deceased who pays this thing to the creditor without the consent of his co-heirs, does not validly pay it except for his own part, in strictness of law, not being owner of the other parts, which belong to his co-heirs; but as to the effect, this payment is valid, unless the thing were due under the alternative of another thing, or with liberty to pay another thing in its stead; otherwise the co-heirs are bound to ratify this payment, which they would be obliged to make themselves if it were not made. *Quod utiliter gestum est, necesse est apud judicem pro rato haberi.* L. 9, ff. *de neg. gest.* *Molin. Tract. de Div. & ind. part* 2, *n.* 166 & 169. If the debt did not consist in *dando*, but in the simple restitution of a thing of which the deceased had only a naked possession, *puta*, if it had been lent or deposited; the restitution which one of the heirs, having the thing, should make of it, would be a valid payment even *ipso jure*, without the consent of the other heirs: for these co-heirs having no right in the thing, nor any interest in preventing the restitution, their consent is not requisite. *Molin, ibid.*

460. As the payment is not valid when he who has paid the thing was not the owner of it, so it is not valid if, although the owner of it, he were, on account of some personal defect, incapable of aliening it.

For this reason, payment is not valid when it is made by a feme covert unauthorised, a minor, or a person interdicted. L. 14, §. *fin.* ff. *de solut.*

461. When the payment made by a person who was not the owner, or who was incapable of aliening, is of a sum of money or other thing which is consumed in the use, the consumption which is made of it, *bona fide*, by the creditor, renders the payment of it valid; *d.* §. The reason is, that the use which he makes *bona fide* of the sum of money or other like thing which has been paid to him, is equiva-

lent to the translation of the property of it. Indeed the translation of the property would not have given any thing more to the creditor; he has used and consumed the thing as if the property had been transferred. He is no longer liable to have the sum of money or other thing which he has consumed *bona fide*, recalled, any more than if he had been the actual owner of it; since the thing which is out of his possession, without any fault on his part, can no longer be demanded from him, as the demand can only be made against the possessor of the thing, or him who has wrongfully parted with the possession.

462. Although the payment of a thing, the property of which has not been transferred to the creditor, be not valid, yet while he has it in his hands, he is not to be admitted to demand from the debtor what is due him; it is necessary that the thing should have been recovered from him, or that he should offer to restore it to the debtor. L. 94, ff. *de solut.*

463. In order that the payment may be valid, it is not necessary that it should be made by the debtor, or some one who has power from him. Any person whatever may make the payment, even without any power from the debtor and even against his will, provided it be done in the name and in discharge of the debtor, and the person who pays be capable of transferring the property of the thing paid, the payment is valid; it operates the extinction of the obligation, and discharges the debtor even against his will. *Solvere pro invito & ignorante cuique licet, cum sit jure civili constitutum licere etiam ignorantis invitique meliorem conditionem facere.* *Gaius ad.* L. 53, ff. *de solut.* L. 23, L. 40, ff. *d. tit.* and L. 39, ff. *de neg. gest.*

If the payment were not made in the name of the true debtor, it would not be valid; as if one pays me in his own name a sum of money, believing himself to be the debtor of it, when it is not due from him but from another; this payment extinguishes not the obligation of the true debtor, and I am bound to return the sum to him who has paid it to me through error.

This decision applies in strictness of law even in the case in which you have paid me in your name a sum of money not due from you, out of the monies and by the order of him who indeed owed it. But if I sued him for it, he might defend himself by bringing you in as a party and praying with you that this sum which you had improperly paid to me in your own name out of his monies, should remain in my hands as the payment of the debt and that he be consequently discharged therefrom. If you were to sue me to recover back this sum which you have paid without owing it, I might avoid your demand by causing my debtor to be made a party, who would pray that this sum, having been furnished by him to be paid in his name, should remain with me in discharge of his debt.

Although the payment of a sum or thing due me be not valid when paid by him who did not owe it in his own name, yet if he afterwards becomes debtor of it, the payment is thereby rendered valid, if not *ipso jure*, at least *per exceptionem doli*. L. 25, ff. *de solut.*

481. The principle which we have established that payment is valid by whomsoever made, if made in the name of the debtor, admits of no difficulty when it is effectually made and is received by the creditor. Whether a stranger without power or authority to manage the affairs of the debtor, having no interest in the discharge of the debt, can compel the creditor to receive the payment which he tenders in the name of the debtor, is a question of more difficulty. The laws which we have quoted do not decide it. They say, it is true, that payment made by any person whatever in the name of the debtor, discharges the debtor; but they leave it undecided whether the creditor may be compelled to receive it. We are to seek the solution of this question from the law 72, §. 2, ff. *de solut.* It decides that the tender of payment made by any person whatever in the name and without the knowledge of the debtor, puts the creditor in arrear. The ordinance of 1673 *tit.* 5, *art.* 3, also permits bills of exchange in case of protest to be dis-

charged by any perfon whatever. From thefe texts this rule is to be drawn, that the tender made to the creditor by any perfon whatever in the name of the debtor is valid and puts the creditor in arrear when the debtor has an intereft in the payment; as when the tender is made to ftop a fuit already commenced, to fave intereft or difcharge a mortgage. But if the payment procures no advantage to the debtor and has no other effect than to change the creditor, the tender ought not to be regarded. *Molin. Tract. de Usur.* 2, 45. The principle that the payment may be made by any perfon whatever for the debtor, is true with regard to obligations to give. The reafon is that it is never material to the creditor by whom the thing due is given, provided it be effectually given.

As to obligations to do, the rule has not the fame latitude. It applies when the act which is the object of the obligation is of fuch a nature that it is immaterial to the creditor by whom it be done. For example. If I have bargained with a vine-dreffer that he fhould drefs an acre of my vines, any other may difcharge him by doing it for him.

It is not the fame when, in the obligation to do, the perfonal fkill and ability of the workman who contracted the obligation is confidered. The obligation in this cafe cannot be difcharged by another; L. 31, ff. *de solut.* For example. If I have contracted with a painter to make me a painting, he cannot difcharge his obligation by caufing it without my confent to be done by another.

ARTICLE II.

To whom payment ought to be made.

455. Payment, to be valid, ought to be made to the creditor or to fome perfon who has power from him, or capacity, to receive it.

§. I.

Of payment made to the creditor.

466. We underftand by a creditor not only the perfon

with whom the contract was made, but also his heirs and general or special assigns.

When the creditor has left several heirs, each becoming creditor only for the part for which he is heir, payment cannot validly be made to any one of them, of more than this part, unless he has power from his co-heirs to receive the whole. He to whom the creditor has transferred his claim, either by sale, gift or legacy, becomes creditor of it by notifying his title to the debtor or by the voluntary admission of the debtor, and consequently the payment which is made to him is valid. On the contrary, the former creditor ceases to be such, after notice to the debtor or his admission, and the payment afterwards made to him would not be valid.

Likewise when by a judgment, the garnishee has been condemned to pay to the plaintiff what he owes the defendant, and final judgment has been had, the plaintiff succeeds by this judgment to the right of the defendant, and payment made to him is valid.

467. A person who may justly be taken for the creditor, is sometimes presumed to be such although another is the real creditor, and payment made to this presumptive creditor is as valid as if made to the real one. For example. You are in possession of a manor which does not belong to you, to the true proprietor of which rent and feudal duties are due. Payment made to you while you are in possession, for the arrearages of such rents and duties, is valid, though, not being the proprietor, you are not properly the creditor: and when the true proprietor shall appear and the manor be restored to him, although he was the true creditor of those rights of the manor which have been paid to you, he will not be admitted to demand them from those who have so paid them; the payment which they have made to you has discharged them. The reason is, that every possessor being of right reputed and presumed the proprietor of the thing which he possesses, while the true proprietor does not appear, the debtors have had just

cause to believe, seeing you in possession of the manor, that you were the proprietor of it, and consequently the creditor of what they have paid you. Their good faith ought to render valid the payment which they have made. It is the fault of the true proprietor who did not sooner make himself known.

For the same reason payments made to him who is in good and lawful possession of an inheritance, by the debtors of this estate, are valid, although the inheritance does not of right belong to him; saving to the true heir, when he shall appear, a right to require an account to be rendered by the possessor of the inheritance of what he has received.

A fortiori, payments made by the debtors of an estate to the beneficiary heir are valid, although afterwards this heir be excluded from the inheritance by a relation who becomes the absolute heir; for if by means of this exclusion he was not the heir, he was at least an administrator of the inheritance, which gave him a capacity to receive.

Further, a payment made to an heir who has afterwards procured himself to be relieved against his acceptance is, not the less, valid.

468. In order that the payment made either to the creditor himself or those who represent him, may be valid, it is necessary that the person be capable of administering his own estate. Therefore, if the creditor was for example, a minor, under interdict, or a feme covert, the payment which should be made to him would not be valid, and would not procure to the debtor a discharge.

Nevertheless, if this creditor or his tutor or curator for him, pretending the nullity of the payment, should demand to be paid a second time, and the debtor could prove that this creditor has been benefited by the sum paid to him and that this benefit still continues at the time of the demand; as if his debts have been thereby discharged or his buildings repaired, the creditor ought to be barred from his demand, as contrary to good faith, which does not permit one to benefit and enrich himself at the expence of another. *Neminem æquum est cum alterius damno locupletari.*

Observe that if the sum has been laid out in the purchase of a thing necessary, although this thing has since perished by chance, before the demand, he is not the less to be presumed at the time of his demand to be benefited thereby; for in the supposition that the thing was necessary, if he had not laid out the sum which was paid him, in the purchase of it, he would have been obliged to lay out another sum which he has in this way preserved. *Hoc ipso quo non est pauperior factus, locupletior est;* L. 47, §. 1. ff. *de solut.*

If the sum has been employed in the purchase of things which were not necessary to the creditor, he will be admitted to his demand, if they do not continue to exist; if they do, he will still be admitted to his demand by tendering them to the debtor; *d.* L. 47, *princ.* L. 4, ff. *de except.*

469. The payment which the debtor makes to his creditor to the prejudice of an attachment in his hands by the creditors of his creditor, is a good payment against his creditor, but not against the attaching creditors, who may oblige this debtor to pay a second time if it be adjudged that the attachment is valid, saving to him his recourse against *his own creditor to whom he has* paid in prejudice of the attachment.

Lastly, altho' a man be under an arrest of his body, his debtors may validly pay him, while there are no attachments in their hands; L. 46, §. 6, ff. *de jur. fisc.* L. 41. ff. *de solut.*

§. II.

Of those who have power from the creditor to receive.

470. Payment made to those who have power from the creditor to receive for him, is presumed to be to the creditor himself, and consequently is as valid as if made to him. L. 180, ff. *de reg. jur. Quod jussu alterius solvitur, pro eo est quasi ipsi solutum esset.*

471. It follows from this rule, I. that it is not material to what person the creditor has given power; whether it be to a minor or to a monk professed, the payment is good. The reason is, that the payment being presumed to be made to him who has given the power, he, and not the person to whom it was given, ought to be considered; it was the fault of the creditor to choose him. L. 4, *Cod. de solut.*

472. It follows, II. from this rule, that one may validly pay, not only to him who has power from the creditor himself to receive, but also to him who has such power from one having capacity to receive for the creditor. For example. If the creditor is a minor or a feme covert, payment made to one who has power from the tutor or husband is valid. L. 96, ff. *de solut.*

473. It follows, III. from this rule, that payment made to him who has power from the creditor, is no further valid than as if made to the creditor himself. Therefore if the creditor is a minor or under interdict, payment made to one who has power from him, is no more valid than if made to the minor or person interdicted.

474. Payment made to him who has a power to receive, is valid only when the power continues at the time of payment.

Therefore if a creditor has given power to one to receive what is due to him, during a certain time or during his absence, payment made to this person after the expiration of the time or after the return of the creditor, would not be valid, because the power no longer continued.

Likewise, if the creditor has revoked the power which he had given, payment made after the revocation is not valid; but it is necessary, for this, that the debtor who has paid since the revocation should have had knowledge of the revocation, or that it should have been so notified to him, as that he might have had knowledge of it; otherwise the payment made, altho' after the revocation, will be valid. L. 12, §. 2; L. 24, §. 3; L. 51, ff. *de solut.*

The reason is, that the error of the debtor who pays after the revocation of the power proceeds rather from the fault of the creditor, who ought to notify the debtor of this revocation, than from that of the debtor, who, seeing a power to receive and not imagining any revocation, has had just cause to pay the person who had the power. Therefore it is not just that the debtor should suffer from this error, and be obliged to pay twice; the creditor who is in fault ought alone to suffer.

This case is very different from that in which the debtor should pay upon a forged power from the creditor; for in this case there would be no fault of the creditor: it is that of the debtor in not having sufficiently informed himself of the validity of the power; therefore such payment is void and does not discharge the debtor. L. 34, §. 4, ff. *de solut.*

475. The power expires also by the death of the creditor who gave it, and sometimes by a change of condition, as by the marriage of the creditor, being a woman; consequently payment to him who has this power, is not valid, if made since the death or change of condition of the creditor who gave it. L. 108, ff. *de solut. arg.* L. 38, §. 1.

But if the death or change of condition of the creditor was not known at the time of the payment, the good faith of the debtor would render the payment valid. L. 32, ff. *d. tit.*

476. The power given by one who has capacity to receive for the creditor, expires when this capacity ceases. For example. If the tutor of a minor has given power to one to receive the debts of the minor, payment may not be made after the tutorship expires, to the person who had the power; because the capacity of him who gave it has ceased and payment could no longer be made to him. L. 180, ff. *de Reg. juris.*

477. It remains to be observed that it is not material whether the power from the creditor be a special power, or a general one, *omnium negotiorum.* l. 12. *de solut.*

An execution in favor of the *creditor in the hands* of the officer, is equivalent to a power to receive the debt contained therein, and the discharge which he gives to the debtor is as valid as if given by the creditor.

It is otherwise of an attorney at law to whom I have given power to bring suit against my debtor; this does not include a power to receive the debt. L. 86, ff. *de solut.*

It is a celebrated question whether the power which we give to one to contract for us, as to sell or let a thing, includes that of receiving for us the price. Bartolus maintains the affirmative and is followed by Fachin, II. *contr.* 94. I think the most plausible opinion is that of Willembach, *ad. tit.* ff. *de solut. n.* 14, who holds that the power to sell does not include that to receive the price, unless there are circumstances which give room to presume it.

The Digest, L. 1, §. 12, *de exerc. act.*, appears to me decisive for this opinion. It is there said that he whose only charge on board of a vessel, is to agree with the passengers for the price of their passage, has no power to receive the money. One could not say more formally that the power to sell or to let, does not include that to receive the price.

But there may be circumstances in which he who has a power to sell, is presumed to have a power to receive the price. For example. If there are in a city certain persons whose trade it is to carry about what they are employed to dispose of, and receive the price from the purchasers; in delivering to one of these persons a thing to be sold, I am presumed to give him also a power to receive the price.

§. III.

Of those to whom the law gives capacity to receive.

478. Payment made to those to whom the law gives capacity to receive in the stead of the creditor, is valid.

The law gives this capacity to tutors to receive what is due to their minors, to the curator of persons under interdict to receive what is due to these persons, to husbands to receive what is due to their wives who are not separated from them, to trustees of hospitals, parish officers, &c. to receive what is due to the said hospitals, parishes, &c.

Such persons have capacity to receive not only the revenues of those whom they thus represent, but also the principal of annuities when the debtors think proper to redeem them, without the intervention of any decree to this effect from the judge, and the debtors who have paid into their hands are fully discharged, and no recourse can be had against them, even if these persons to whom they have paid should become insolvent. The law 25, *Cod. de adm. tut.*, which requires the decree of the judge to protect the debtor, in case of the insolvency of the tutor to whom he has paid, is not received in our jurisprudence.

479. The single reason of relationship to the creditor, however near, is not a sufficient capacity to receive what is due to him.

Therefore neither the father has capacity to receive what is due to the son who is no longer under his power, nor the son to receive what is due to his father, nor the husband to receive what is due to his wife who is separated from him, much less the wife to receive what is due to her husband. L. 22, ff. *hoc. tit.* L. 11, *Cod. hoc tit.*

§. IV.

Of those to whom the agreement gives capacity to receive.

480. Sometimes in a contract by which a person obliges himself to pay something to another, a third person is indicated, into whose hands it is agreed that payment may be made as well as to the creditor; such person has by the agreement itself a capacity to receive for the creditor; and consequently the payment which is made to him is as valid as if made to the creditor himself. These third persons to whom it is agreed that the debtor may pay are called by the civilians *adjecti solutionis gratia.*

These third persons are most frequently creditors of the creditor who indicates them. For example. You sell me an eftate for the fum of ten thoufand livres, and it is agreed in the contract that I may pay this fum in your discharge, to a third perfon who is your creditor for the like fum.

Sometimes alfo, the perfon whom I have indicated to you is a third perfon who is not my creditor, but who is to receive this fum for me as my mandatary, or indeed as my donee if I intended to give it to him. Such are properly *adjecti solutionis gratia*, fpoken of in the civil law.

481. A perfon may be indicated to receive not only the thing itfelf which the debtor owes to his creditor, but fometimes even a different thing; as if I let you a right of pafture in my woods for your hogs, on condition that you pay me the fum of thirty livres at my houfe, or deliver a hog of one hundred pounds weight to my overfeer at D—. In this cafe the delivery of the hog made to my overfeer, difcharges you from the thirty livres which you owe me. L. 34, §. 2, ff. *de solut.* L. 141, §. 5, ff. *de Verb. oblig.*

482. The fum which is mentioned in the contract to be paid to a third perfon, may be lefs than that which the debtor obliges himfelf by his contract to pay to the creditor.

Hence arifes the queftion, L. 98, §. 5, ff. *de solut.*, whether in this cafe the payment of the lefs fum to this third perfon difcharges the debtor from the creditor entirely, or only to the amount of this fum. We ought on this queftion to feek from the circumftances what was the intention of the parties; but unlefs the contrary is evident, the prefumption is, that it was the intention of the parties that the payment of the lefs fum made to the perfon indicated, fhould difcharge the debtor to the amount only of this fum.

483. The indication of a third perfon to whom payment is to be made, may be for a place or time different from that in which the thing is payable to the creditor himfelf. For example. I may agree that you pay a fum of money to me at my houfe in Orleans, or to my banker

in Paris. Likewise, I may agree that you pay a sum of money either to me at the time of a certain fair or to a certain person after the time of the said fair. L. 98, §. 4, 6, ff. *de solut. Vice versa*, I may agree that you pay such sum either to me at the time of the fair or to a certain person before the fair. L. 141, §. 6, *de Verb. oblig.*

484. The indication may also be made to depend on a condition, although the obligation be absolute; but if the obligation itself depends on a condition, the indication, although made absolute or under another condition, would necessarily depend on the condition upon which the obligation depends; for one cannot make a valid payment to the person indicated except of a thing due, and it cannot be due if the condition of the obligation has not happened. L. 141, §. 7, 8, ff. *de Verb. oblig.*

It is not the same in regard to the time of payment. As the payment may be validly made before the time, the indication to pay to a third person is not necessarily confined to the time I have granted to my debtor to pay me; therefore I may, in contracting, permit my debtor to pay a third person provided he do it in a month, although I have granted him two months to pay to me *d.* L. 98, §. 4.

485. Payment made to the person indicated is valid, not only when it is made by the debtor himself to whom the indication is made, but when by any other person. L. 59, *vers. & si a filio*, ff. *de solut.*

486. This right which the debtor has to pay the sum to the person indicated as validly as if to the creditor himself, is a right which passes to the heirs of the debtor. They have this right, although it was omitted to be mentioned in the new title which has been given; for an intention to alter a primitive title by a new one is never presumed.

487. Regularly it can only be the person indicated by the contract to whom payment may be made, not his heirs or other persons who may represent him. L. 55, ff. *de Verb. oblig.* L. 81, ff. *de solut.*

Neverthelefs when a feller indicates to the buyer in the contract of fale to pay the price to one of his creditors, the payment may be validly made not only to this creditor, but to his heirs or other perfons who may fucceed to his right. The reafon is, that in this indication it is not fo much the perfon indicated, as the quality of creditor which has been confidered, on account of the intereft which the feller had to be difcharged from his debt and that which the buyer had to pay to the creditor in order to be fubftituted to the rights and fecurities of this creditor.

488. One can no longer validly pay to the perfon indicated when he has changed his condition. Therefore if the perfon indicated in the contract, has fince loft his civil capacity, payment to him cannot validly be made. L. 38, *de solut.* Although the creditor might have indicated a perfon who at the time of the contract had loft his civil capacity. L. 95, §. 6, *dict. tit. Cujac. in Comment. ad Papin. ad h. L.*

The reafon of this difference is, that one may prefume that the creditor would not have wifhed that payment fhould be made into the hands of this perfon, if he had forefeen this change. But when at the time of the contract this perfon was civilly dead and the creditor knew it, the intention of the creditor that payment fhould be made into his hands, although he had loft his civil capacity, cannot be ambiguous.

The fame may be faid of a perfon indicated who fhould afterwards be interdicted, take a hufband or become a bankrupt. In all thefe cafes the debtor can no longer validly pay to fuch perfon; the prefumption being that fuch perfon would not have been indicated if thefe circumftances had been forefeen.

489. He whom the creditor by the agreement itfelf has indicated, is very different from him who has only a power of attorney from the creditor to receive. The right of paying to an attorney ceafes with the revocation of the power, notified to the debtor, which the creditor may

make when he fees fit. The reafon is, that the right of paying to the attorney is founded on the power, which is as revocable as any other; from which it follows that as the power comes to an end by the revocation, the right to pay to the attorney alfo ceafes.

On the contrary, the right to pay to the perfon indicated by the agreement, having its foundation in the agreement itfelf, of which it makes a part, and from which one of the parties cannot detract without the confent of the other, the creditor cannot deprive the debtor of the benefit of it, who may, againft the will of the creditor, pay into the hands of the perfon indicated, according to the agreement. L. 12, §. 3, & L. 106, ff. *de solut.*

Neverthelefs if the creditor alledges that he has reafons why the payment fhould not be made into the hands of this perfon indicated by the contract, and that the debtor can have no intereft in paying into his hands rather than to the creditor himfelf, or to fome other perfon who might be indicated in the place of the one already indicated, it would be on the part of the debtor an ill temper and an unreafonable obftinacy to infift on paying into the hands of the perfon indicated; an obftinacy which a court ought not to favor.

490. By the civil law, the right to pay to the perfon indicated by the contract, ceafed when in a fuit which had intervened, the defendant pleaded to the merits; L. 57, §. 1, ff. *de solut.*; a ftrictnefs which ought not to be admitted in our law.

491. There is no doubt that payment made of a part to the creditor himfelf does not take away the right to pay the remainder to the perfon indicated. L. 71, ff. *de solut.*

§. V.

In what manner payment made to a perfon who had neither power nor capacity to receive, may be rendered valid.

492. Payment made to a perfon who had neither power nor capacity, becomes valid, firft, by the ratification

and approbation which the creditor makes afterwards of this payment. L. 12, §. 4, *de solut.* L. 12, *Cod. dict. tit.* L. 24, ff. *de neg. gest.*

Ratifications having a retroactive effect, according to the rule *Ratihabitio mandato comparatur, d.* L. 12, §. 4, the payment will be presumed to have been good from the time it was made. Therefore if one becomes a security to me for my debtor with a clause that his securitiship shall continue only to the first of January one thousand seven hundred and fifty, at the end of which time he shall rest acquitted and discharged *pleno jure;* the payment which he made in the course of the year one thousand seven hundred and forty nine to a person who had not power from me, would be valid and he could not recall this sum of money, although I had not ratified the payment till the year one thousand seven hundred and fifty, when he would have ceased to be my debtor, if he had not paid: for by means of the retroactive effect of my ratification the payment is valid from the day it was made, which was while his obligation continued. L. 71, §. 1, ff. *de solut.*

According to the same principle if I owe a thousand livres to Peter and Paul, creditors *in solidum,* and I have paid this sum in the first place to a person who received it for Peter without any power from him, and have paid it a second time to Paul, the validity of the payment made to Paul would depend on the ratification by Peter. The first payment would be valid if Peter ratified it, and that made to Paul would be void as being the payment of a debt discharged. If Peter does not ratify, the first payment would not be valid and that made to Paul would be. L. 58, §. 2, ff. *d. tit.*

493. The second case in which the payment would become valid when made to a person who had not a capacity to receive, is when the sum paid has afterwards come to the benefit of the creditor. L. 28, L. 34, §. 9, ff. *de solut.*, as if it has discharged him from what he owed. L. 66, verbo *sed exceptione,* ff. *d. tit.*

The third cafe is, when the perfon, to whom payment has been made, has become the heir of the creditor, or has fucceeded to his right by fome other title. L. 96, §. 4, ff. *de tit.*.

ARTICLE III.

What thing ought to be paid, how and in what condition.

§. I.

May one thing be paid for another.

494. Regularly it is the thing due which ought to be paid, and a debtor cannot oblige his creditor to receive in payment another thing than what he owes him. L. 16, *Cod. de solut.*

We do not follow the novel 4, *cap.* 3, which permits the debtor of a fum of money, who has neither money nor goods from which it may be made, to oblige his creditor to receive in payment lands, according to eftimation made thereof, unlefs the creditor would rather find him a purchafer.

495. Not only the debtor cannot oblige the creditor to receive in payment another thing than what is due to him, but if through error the creditor, thinking he was receiving what was due, had received another thing, the payment would not be valid, and the creditor could, on offering to return what he has received, exact the thing which is due him. Paul, L. 50, ff. *de solut. Si quum aurum tibi promisissem, tibi ignoranti quasi aurum æs solverim, non liberabor.*

If the creditor was willing however to receive another thing inftead of what was due, there is no doubt that the payment is valid; L. 17, *Cod. de solut*; unlefs there was room for relief againft the payment in the cafe of lefion, on account of the minority of the creditor who had imprudently given his confent, or on account of fraud, &c. L. 26, ff. *de lib. leg.*

496. The debtor may fometimes oblige the creditor to receive fome other thing in payment, in the room of that which is due, that is to fay, when this right has been

granted to him either by the contract, or by some subsequent agreement with the creditor, intervening. L. 57, L. 96, §. 2, ff. *de solut.*

By the civil law this right ceased when in a suit by the creditor the debtor had pleaded to the merits; *d.* L. 57, which I do not think ought to be followed in our law.

497. These agreements to pay something in lieu of what is due, are always presumed to be made in favor of the debtor: thus it is always lawful for the debtor to pay the sum itself which is due, and the creditor cannot exact any other thing.

Therefore if by a marriage-settlement, a husband receives a certain sum as a portion, to secure which he subjects certain lands, and it is agreed *that after the dissolution* of the marriage, the wife shall receive them in payment of her portion, this does not prevent the husband or his heirs from retaining the said lands, on tendering the portion received, of which the restitution is due. L. 45, ff. *de solut.*

By the same reason if I have leased a vineyard for the sum of five hundred livres a year, payable in wine to be made from it, the right to pay in wine is presumed to be given in favor of the lessee, and I cannot oblige him to give me wine, if he offers to pay me in money the five hundred livres, which is the price of his lease.

But if the payment had been made of a thing in the stead of what was due, the thing being consumed, the debtor would not be admitted to recall it on offering to pay the sum which is due; L. 10, L. 24, *Cod. de solut.*

§. II.

Is the creditor bound to receive in parts what is due to him.

498. Although a debt be divisible, while it is yet undivided, the creditor is not obliged to receive in parts what is due to him.

It is upon this principle that Modestin, L. 41, §. 1, ff. *de usur.*, holds that if there is no clause in the contract that the debtor may pay in parts, the consignation made by him of a part does not stop the interest even for this part. This supposes the principle well established that a creditor is not obliged to receive in parts what is due to him. If he were so obliged, and the consignation of the part tendered were valid, the interest would cease to run; for when a debt is discharged in part, interest runs only upon what remains due. *Cod. de comp.*

What interest, it will be asked, has the creditor to refuse to his debtor the convenience of paying in parts? The answer is that he has an advantage in receiving all at once a gross sum from which he may derive a profit, rather than several small sums at different times which are imperceptibly expended as they are received. Besides it is an *inconvenience to the creditor to credit several small* sums and to have calculations to make. *Molin. Tract. de div. & ind. part* 2, *n.* 14.

It is not even sufficient for the debtor to tender the whole sum of the principal which he owes when it bears interest; the creditor is not obliged to receive it, if all the interest which is due is not paid at the same time.

499. Where several persons become securities for a debtor, although they have between them the benefit of a division, yet until they are prosecuted by the creditor for the payment, neither can oblige him to receive payment in part.

The reason is, that the debt for which several persons have become securities, is not *pleno jure* divided between them; these securities have *only* a plea to demand a division when they are sued: but while they are all solvent this plea cannot be received; the debt until this time not being divided, it follows that the creditor cannot be holden to receive a part.

The interpellation made by the security who is not sued, upon the creditor to receive his part unless he will discharge him, is not well founded, however long may be the time for which the security is bound; for it is only against the principal debtor for whom he is a security, and not against the creditor, that the security has the action *mandati* to procure himself to be discharged from the securitiship.

This interpellation is not well founded, even when the security alledges that the principal debtor and his co-security, although yet solvent, begin to waste their property, and that he ought not to suffer from the negligence of the creditor to pursue them; this security would have no other resource than to pay the whole debt and procure himself to be substituted to the rights and actions of the creditor. *Molin. Tract. de div. et ind. part.* 2, *n.* 54, 55, 56.

Dumoulin, *n.* 57, goes much further. Even when the obligation of the securities would of right be divided between them, as if three persons had become securities for a debtor, each for a third; he thinks even in this case that the security who is not prosecuted for payment, cannot oblige the creditor to receive the payment of his third; because, says he, the obligation of securities ought not indirectly to impair the principal obligation, and make it payable in parts before it be divided.

I think that Dumoulin goes too far. In fact, the security being bound only for a third, ought to have the right to discharge himself by paying this third, which is all he owes; for every debtor may discharge himself by tendering all that he owes. I think even that the principal debtor who could in his own name pay in part, could pay for one of the securities the third part which this security owed. The debtor having an interest to pay for the security, in order to discharge himself from the indemnity which he owes him, the creditor cannot refuse this payment. Dumoulin, *ibid. n.* 50, admits that this is the common opinion of authors, though contrary to his.

500. The rule that the creditor cannot be obliged to receive in parts that which is due, while the debt remains undivided, receives an exception, first, when there is a clause in the contract that the sum shall be divided into a certain number of instalments, *puta*, into two or three, or

when in confideration of the poverty of the debtor it is fo ordered by the judge. The creditor is holden in all thefe cafes to conform himfelf to what is prefcribed by the agreement or by the judgment.

When it is not expreffed what fum each payment fhall be, the payments ought to be underftood to be of equal parts. For example. If I am obliged to pay you ten thoufand crowns in four payments, each payment fhould be of a fourth of this fum, neither more nor lefs, excepting that I may make feveral payments at once of the half or three parts of the fum.

When the agreement is that the payment fhall be made in two different places, which are united by a conjunctive, as if it be faid that I fhall pay at Orleans at my houfe, and at Paris at the houfe of my banker; by this claufe it is intended that the payment be by moiety in each of the faid places. *Secus*, if the particle is disjunctive; as *if it be faid that I fhall pay at Paris or at Orleans*; the creditor is holden to receive the payment in either of the faid places which the debtor may choofe.

501. Secondly, when there is a conteft refpecting the quantity of what is due. As if by an account ftated, I acknowledge myfelf debtor of a certain balance and my creditor pretends that it fhould be a greater fum than is ftated, by the Digeft, *l.* 31, *de reb. cred.*, the creditor may be obliged to receive the fum which I acknowledge to be due, faving his right to more, if due, on the decifion of the fuit. This being very equitable, it is prudent in the judge to order this provifional payment when the debtor fo requires.

502. Thirdly, in the cafe of a fet-off; for a creditor is obliged to credit to the amount of the fum which is due him, that which he owes to his debtor, although it may be lefs than what is due him.

503. He who is creditor of a perfon for different debts is obliged to receive the payment, which his debtor tenders, of one of thefe debts; although he does not tender at the fame time payment of the others.

For the same reason the debtor of several years arrearages may oblige the creditor to receive the payment of one year's, though he does not tender at the same time payment of the others; for these terms of arrears are as many different debts. The creditor cannot however be obliged to receive those of the last year before the preceding; *ne rationes ejus conturbentur. Molin. ibid. n.* 44.

According to this principle, Dumoulin, *ibid.*, holds that one who has a long lease, viz. from nine to one hundred years, subject by a clause of the lease to the loss of his right on failure of payment of three years rent, may avoid this penalty by tendering the payment of one year's, before the expiration of the third.

§. III.

How may the thing which is due be paid.

504. The payment of a thing is made only by transfering to the creditor by delivery, he irrevocable property of the thing. *Non videntur data quæ eo tempore quo dantur, accipientis non fiunt;* L. 167, ff. *de R. juris.*

Hence it follows, as has been already said in *art.* I, that the payment of a thing is not valid, when it does not belong to him who gives it in payment without the consent of the owner.

Nevertheless this payment may afterwards become valid, if the creditor who has received it in payment becomes owner of it by the length of time required for a title by prescription, or at least when he has no longer room to fear a recovery back; as when he who has given it to him in payment has become the sole heir of the owner of the thing, or when the thing has ceased to exist, or has been consumed *bona fide* by the creditor who received it in payment. L. 60, L. 78, L. 94, §. 2, ff. *de solut.*

The reason is that in these cases what has happened since, has supplied the defect in the payment by acquiring to the creditor either the property of the thing which he has received in payment, or something equivalent to the right of property.

505. But when a creditor receives in payment, through error, a thing of his own, the payment which is made to him of it, is null in ſuch manner as that it can never become valid; for he never can be preſumed to have acquired either really or by equivalent, what belonged to him already. *Quod meum est, amplius meum esse non potest.*

506. When the payment is made to a third perſon by order of the creditor, it is likewiſe neceſſary that the property of the thing which is paid be transferred, either to the creditor when this third perſon receives it in the name of the creditor and in order to acquire it for him, or to this third perſon when the intention of the creditor was that it ſhould be acquired by this third perſon.

Hence it follows that when I have given an order to him who has ſold me a tract of land, to make livery of it to my wife to whom I intended to give it, as the payment or delivery which he makes by my order to my wife of this land could not transfer the property to my wife, becauſe gifts between huſband and wife are forbidden by the law, nor to me as it was not received for me, the ſeller remains owner of the land which he has delivered to my wife. This payment then in ſtrictneſs of law is invalid, and has not diſcharged the ſeller; but if it has not diſcharged him *ipso jure* and in ſtrictneſs of law, he is diſcharged *per exceptionem doli*; good faith not permitting me to demand from him a thing which, by my own act, he has been diſabled from delivering to me, in delivering it according to my order to my wife. Therefore he no longer remains in this caſe bound towards me for any thing elſe but the ceſſion of his right of reclaiming, which I may exerciſe at my riſque. This reſults from the law 26, ff. *de donat. inter vir. & uxor.*, and from the law 38, §. 1, ff. *de solut.* According to our practice, it would not be neceſſary even that my debtor ſhould ſubſtitute me to his right to claim back; I ſhould be ſubſtituted to it *de pleno jure:* L. 54, §. 7, ff. *de solut.*, and notes on this law in *Pand. Justin. tit. de solut. n.* 27.

507. That the payment may be valid, it ſuffices not

that the property be transferred to the creditor. It ought, as we have said, to be transferred irrevocably; for it is not to transfer it truly, to transfer it in a manner that he may not always retain it. *Quod evincitur, in bonis non est*; L. 190, ff. *de R. Jur.*

For example. If the thing given in payment was hypothecated, whether it be the very thing due, or whether it be given in payment of a sum of money, the debtor would not by such payment be discharged from his debt, unless he should free the thing from the hypothecation. L. 20, L. 69, L. 98, ff. *de solut.* For such payment not having transferred to the creditor to whom it is made the property of a thing which he may always retain, is not a valid payment and consequently has not extinguished the debt.

If by a clause in the contract the debtor who bound himself to give a certain thing, had charged the creditor with the risk of certain evictions, or the thing was declared by the contract to be of a nature liable to a certain species of evictions, its subjection to these evictions, provided there be none to be feared but those with which the creditor was charged, would not invalidate the payment which has been made to him of this thing.

§. IV.

In what condition the thing ought to be paid.

503. When the debt is of a thing certain and determinate, it may validly be paid in whatever condition it may be, provided that any losses or decays which have happened since the contract, did not proceed either from the act or neglect of the debtor, nor from that of those for whom he is answerable, as his workmen or domestics.

If it is by chance or the act of a stranger that the thing has become injured, the debtor may validly pay it in the condition in which it may be; he is not bound further than to cede to his creditor the actions which he may have against him who has caused the injury; and when he will not cede them to him, the judge will substitute the creditor who happens to be the person who suffers the loss.

509. It is otherwise when the debt is of a thing indeterminate; as if a dealer in horses has promised to his son in law, by a contract of marriage, to give him a horse as part of the portion of his daughter, without specifying what horse. If one of his horses becomes blind or disordered, he cannot give this horse to discharge himself from the debt. He ought to give one which has no material defect. L. 33, *in fin.* ff. *de solut.* Otherwise if he had obliged himself determinately to give to his son in law a certain horse, he would acquit himself of his obligation in giving him the horse such as it may be.

ARTICLE IV.

When payment ought to be made.

510. It is evident that one cannot make payment of a thing before it is due; for while there is yet no debt, there can be no payment. Hence it follows that when a debt is suspended, because the condition under which it was contracted is not yet accomplished, payment cannot be made. Not only cannot the debtor be obliged to pay nor the creditor to receive, before the accomplishment of the condition, but if the debtor, ignorant of the condition, has paid thro' error, he may recall it *per condictionem indebiti*: for in this case it is true that he has paid what he did not owe. But the payment which was not valid, is confirmed and becomes valid by the accomplishment of the condition; for this accomplishment has an effect retroactive to the time of the contract, which in causing the debt to be presumed to be due from the time of the contract, *supra, n.* 220, causes, by necessary consequence, the payment which has been made before the condition, to be presumed to be valid. L. 16, ff. *de cond. indebit.*

511. It is otherwise of the time of payment; the time not having the effect to suspend the debt but only to delay the right to demand it, *supra, n.* 230. Payment made before the time of payment, is valid. L. 1, §. 1, ff. *de cond. & dem.*

This rule however is liable to some exceptions. For

example. If a testator has bequeathed a certain sum to a minor, and in order to prevent the tutor from dissipating it, he had ordered that it should not be paid till the coming of age of the legatee, the heir by whom the legacy is to be paid, who should pay it before, would not be discharged in the case of the tutor's insolvency. L. 15, ff. *de ann. leg. tom.* 2. See, on the time of payment, what we have said *supra, part* 2, *chap.* 3, *art.* 3.

ARTICLE V.

Where the payment ought to be made and at whose cost.

§. I.

Where payment ought to be made.

512. When by the agreement there is a place agreed upon where the payment must be made, it ought to be made at this place. If there is no place designated and the debt is of a thing certain, the payment must be made at the place where the thing is. For example. If I have sold a merchant the wine of my vintage, it is at the place where my wine is stored that he ought to receive the payment of it; he ought to send there for it at his own expence, I delivering it to him where it is. I am not obliged to remove it, but only to give him the key of my store-house and to suffer him to take it away. L. 47, §. 1, ff. *de leg.* 1. *Si quidem certum corpus legatum est, . . ibi præstabitur ubi relictum est.*

If the debtor, since the bargain, has transported the thing from the place where it was to another place, from which the removal by the creditor becomes more expensive, the creditor might claim, by way of damages, what the removal should cost more than it would have cost if the thing had remained where it was at the time of the bargain; as the debtor ought not by his own act to make the conditon of the creditor worse.

513. If the debt is not of a thing certain but of a thing indeterminate, as if one were to give me a pair of gloves indeterminately, a certain sum of money, a certain quantity of corn, wine, &c. the place of payment cannot in this

case be the place where the thing is, since the uncertainty prevents the assigning of any place where it might be. Where then shall it be? According to the law before cited, in this case the thing ought to be paid in the place where it is demanded, *ubi petitur*; which is to say, at the place of residence of the debtor. *Molin. Tr. de Usur.* 9, 9.

The reason is, that as agreements respecting things in regard to which the parties have not explained themselves ought to be interpreted rather in favor of the debtor than of the creditor, *in cujus potestate fuit legem apertius dicere*, *supra n.* 97, it follows from these principles, that when they have not explained themselves respecting the place where payment ought to be made, the agreement, should in this respect be interpreted in a manner the least burdensome and expensive to the debtor.

Our principle, that things indeterminate are payable at the residence of the debtor, when there is no place of payment marked out by the agreement, is liable to an exception when two things concur, that is to say when the residence of the creditor and that of the debtor, are not at much distance from each other, as when they reside in the same city, and when the thing due consists in a sum of money, or in some other thing which may be carried or sent, without expence, to the creditor. When these two things concur, the payment ought to be made at the house of the creditor; *Molin. ibid.* The debtor owes in this case this deference, which costs him nothing. For want of payment at the house of the creditor, the creditor may make a demand on his debtor at the residence of the debtor who ought to pay the charges thereof; and the debtor, may pay to the officer who makes the demand.

Although it be expressly agreed that the sum be payable at the house of the creditor, which was at the time of the agreement in the same city with that of the debtor, and for a stonger reason, when there is no explanation respecting the place of payment; if since the contract the creditor has changed his dwelling to another city at a diftance from that of the debtor, the debtor will be well grounded in demanding that the creditor elect where, in the place in which the contract was entered into, the payment shall be made; this change of the place of payment to a place where the debtor is not accustomed to resort, ought not to be burdensome to the debtor, and to render his condition worse than it was before, according to this rule, *nemo alterius facto prægravari debet.* See, on the place of payment, what has been said *supra part.* 2, *ch.* 3, *art.* 4.

§. II.

At whose expence the payment is to be made.

514. The payment is to be made at the expence of the debtor; therefore if he should require a discharge before a notary, it is at his expence that it should be given.

It is also for this reason that he who has sold wine, should pay at the custom-house for the necessary permit to deliver it.

ARTICLE VI.

Of the effect of payments.

515. The effect of payment is to extinguish the obligation and all that is accessory to it, and to discharge all those who are debtors of it; L. 43, ff. *de solut.*

§. I.

Whether a single payment may extinguish several obligations.

516. Sometimes a single payment may extinguish several obligations: this happens when the thing which is given in payment of the obligation, is the same thing which was the object of another obligation.

For example. If I have agreed with you to sell you, in payment of the sum which you have lent me, the thing which I have given you in pledge; the payment which I make you of this thing extinguishes at the same time the obligation resulting from the loan which you have made me, and that resulting from the sale which I have made you of the thing; L. 44, ff. *de solut*: for this thing which I pay you in performance of the obligation resulting from the loan of money which you have made to me, is the fame thing which makes the object of my obligation refulting from the fale which I have made to you.

517. This rule applies even in regard to different creditors. For example. If, owing you ten thoufand livres, I have paid them by your order to your creditor to whom you owed the like fum, this payment extinguifhes at the fame time two obligations, mine and yours; L. 64, ff. *d. tit*; it difcharges me towards you, and it difcharges you towards your creditor. This payment contains two, *juris effectu*; for it is as if I had paid you the fum, and you had paid it afterwards to your creditor: *Celeritate conjungendarum inter se actionum, unam actionem occultari*; L. 3, §. 12, ff. *don. inter vir. & uxor.*

518. This rule that the payment made in performance of one obligation, extinguifhes the other obligations which have the fame object, applies alfo in regard to different debtors.

For example. If by your order I have lent a fum of money to Peter, the payment which Peter makes me of the fum which I have lent him, extinguifhes at the fame time the obligation of Peter and your obligation refulting from the mandate which you gave me.

What we have juft faid, that when there are obligations which, although they proceed from different caufes, have however one and the fame object, the payment which is made of one of thefe obligations extinguifhes both, applies only in the cafe in which the debtor who has paid had not the right to require the ceffion of the actions of the creditor againft the debtor of the other obligation. But in the contrary cafe, when he who has paid had the right to require the ceffion of the rights and actions of the creditor againft the debtor of the other obligation, he extinguifhes, in paying, only his own obligation; the other continues, not to the effect that the creditor may caufe himfelf to be paid a fecond time, but to the effect that he may cede the action which arises from it, to him to whom he ought to cede it.

For example. If, in the instance above mentioned, I have by your order lent a sum of money to Peter, we have seen that the payment made by Peter extinguishes his obligation and yours: but if before Peter had paid me, you had yourself paid me this sum, in order to be discharged from the obligation resulting from the mandate which you gave me, this payment extinguishes only your obligation, and not that of Peter; because in paying me, you have the right to require from me the cession of my rights and actions against Peter, who therefore remains bound, no longer indeed towards me, who cannot twice exact the same thing, but towards you, in consequence of the cession of my actions which I ought to make to you; L. 95, §. 10. ff. *de solut.* L. 28, ff. *mand.*

This cession of actions against the debtor of a different obligation, may even be made *ex intervallo*, after the payment; in which it differs from that which is made against the co-debtors of the same obligation, of which we are going to speak in the following paragraph.

§. II.

Whether the payment made by one of the debtors extinguishes the obligation of all the other debtors of the same obligation; and of the cession of actions.

519. If the payment of one obligation may discharge the debtor of another obligation, different from it but having the same object, as we have seen in the preceding paragraph, *a fortiori* the payment made by one of the debtors of the same obligation, ought to discharge all the other debtors of this obligation, whether they be principal debtors, or whether accessory debtors, such as are securities.

This rule admits of a limitation in the case of the cession of actions; for if one of the co-debtors or securities, in paying the debt, has caused the rights and actions of the creditor to be ceded to him, the debt is not holden to be extinguished in regard to those against whom the actions of the creditor have been ceded to him.

Several questions arise in regard to this cession of actions; I. who are those who, on paying a debt, have a right to require the cession of the actions of the creditor against the other debtors who are liable for it? II. Is the creditor bound in such a manner to make this cession of actions, that he cannot demand his debt in the whole or in part, from those to whom he is bound to make it, when he has disabled himself by his own act from making it? III. Is this cession of actions made *de jure* or ought it to be required and when may it be required? IV. What are the effects of this cession of actions?

On the first question it is to be holden as a principle that all who are bound for a debt for others or with others, by whom they ought to be discharged, either for the whole, or a part, have a right, in paying such debt, to require the cession of the actions of the creditor against the other debtors who are liable for it.

It is on this principle that Julian decides that the security ought, in paying, to obtain the cession of the actions of the creditor as well against the principal debtor as against all the others who are liable for it: *Fidejussoribus succurri solet, ut stipulator compellatur ei qui solidum solvere paratus est vendere cæterorum nomina*; L. 17, ff. *fidej.*

For the same reason, the creditor cannot refuse to a debtor *in solidum* from whom he exacts the whole debt, the cession of his actions against the other debtors; L. 47, ff. *locat.*

This obligation of the debtor to cede his actions, is grounded on this rule of equity that, being commanded to love all men, we are bound to grant them every thing which they have an interest in having, when we may do so without injuring ourselves.

A debtor *in solidum* having, then, a just interest in having the actions of the creditor against his co-debtors, to make them pay their part of a debt which they owe as well as he, the creditor cannot refuſe it. For the ſame reaſon he cannot refuſe it to a ſecurity, and generally to all thoſe who, being bound for the debt, have an intereſt in being diſcharged, in the whole or in part, by thoſe for or with whom they are debtors.

But when a ſtranger pays a debt for which he was not bound, and in the diſcharge of which he had no intereſt, the creditor is not bound, unleſs he pleaſes, to cede to him his actions. L. 5, *Cod. de solut.*; for he was not in need of them, ſince nothing compelled him to pay the debt.

This is liable to an exception in the caſe of bills of exchange. When a ſtranger for the honor of the drawer, one of the indorſers or the acceptor, pays a bill of exchange, of which he is not debtor, not only cannot the ceſſion of the actions of the creditor of the bill of exchange be refuſed him, but he is ſubrogated to them *de jure* by the ordinance of 1673, as we have ſeen in our treatiſe on bills of exchange; this has been eſtabliſhed in favor of commerce.

520. As to the ſecond queſtion, whether the creditor ought to be excluded from his demand *per exceptionem cedendarum actionum*, againſt one of his debtors, when by his own act he is diſabled from ceding to him his actions againſt the other debtors; this is liable to no difficulty in regard to *mandatores pecuniæ credendæ*. Papinian decides it in formal terms in the law 95, §. 11, ff. *de solut. Si creditor a debitore culpa sua causa ceciderit, prope est ut actione mandati nihil a mandatore consequi debeat; cum ipsius vitio acciderit ne mandatori possit actionibus cedere.*

The reaſon of this is evident. It is a common principle in all ſynallagmatic contracts, that when we have contracted reciprocal obligations, I am not to be admitted to demand from you the performance of yours, when by my own fault I fail in the performance of mine. According to this principle when by my order you have lent a certain ſum of money to Peter, and by your own fault you have loſt the action, which you had acquired by this loan, and you cannot consequently cede it to me, you ought not to be admitted to demand from me this sum, for the reimbursement of which I am bound by the contract of mandate which took place between us; since on your part you have, by your own fault, disabled yourself from performing the obligation which you have, by this contract, contracted towards me, to cede to me the action which you have acquired by the loan you made to Peter in the execution of my mandate. See *supra*, n. 445.

Ought the same decision to be applied to the case of securities? May a security from whom the creditor demands the payment of a debt for which he has become a security, prevent the demand from being received, because the creditor has by his own act disabled himself from making the cession of his actions to the security, which he, by the payment, might require? The reason to doubt is that I do not see any text of law which formally decides thus in regard to securities. The law 15, §. 11, above cited, which gives this plea to *mandatores pecuniæ credendæ*, does not appear to me decisive for securities; as there is not the same reason for it. He who has lent a sum of money to Peter by the order of another, has, by the contract of mandate included in the order which he has executed, contracted a formal obligation towards the *mandator pecuniæ credendæ*, to secure and cede to him the action which he acquired by the loan made to Peter in execution of the mandate. The same cannot be said in regard to a security, that the creditor has contracted towards him the obligation to secure and cede to him his actions: the securityship is an unilateral contract by which the security alone is bound. If the creditor is obliged to cede his actions to the security at the time of the payment which he makes him, it is equity alone which obliges him, because he has no interest to refuse to cede them; but he ought only to be obliged to cede them as far and such as he has them, and he ought not to be blamed for not having kept them and for having disabled himself from ceding them. Another difference may be added which is observed by Cujas, *ad l. 21, ff. de pact.* He by whose order I have sent a sum of money to Peter, having no action against Peter, has need absolutely that I should cede to him my actions against Peter; but a security, having in his own right an action against the principal debtor for whom he has become a security, has not an absolute need of the cession of the action of the creditor against the principal debtor, although the cession of the hypothecations might be useful to him; *Nec usquam legitur*, says *Cujas*, *cogi creditorem fidejussori cedere actionibus sortis.*

Not only is there no text of law which decides that the security may exclude the creditor from his demand for the whole or a part, when he has by his own act disabled himself from ceding his actions, whether against the principal debtor, or against the other securities; there is also room to suppose the contrary. The law 22, ff. *de pactis*, decides that a creditor may agree with the principal debtor not to demand from him the payment of the debt, and yet reserve to himself the right to demand it from the security. In this instance, the creditor may demand from the security the payment of the debt, although he has disabled himself from ceding to him his action against the principal debtor, which has become ineffectual by the agreement which the creditor has made with this debtor, who has thereby acquired the plea *pacti*. The law 15, §. 1, ff. *de fidej.*, appears also to decide that the creditor who by his own act has disabled himself from ceding to one of the securities his actions against the other, was not thereby in any manner excluded from his demand: *Si ex duobus qui apud te fidejusserant in viginti, alter, NE AB EO PETERES, quinque tibi dederit vel promiserit; nec alter liberabitur; & si ab altero quindecim petere institueris, nulla exceptione summoveris.* Yet the creditor had disabled himself from making to him from whom he demanded the fifteen crowns which remain due to him, the cession of his actions against the other, by which he would have had recourse against him for the five crowns. Notwithstanding these reasons, it must he decided that when the creditor has disabled himself from ceding to the security his actions, whether against the principal debtor or against the other securities, whether because he has discharged them or whether he has by his own fault suffered them to become discharged from his demand against them, the security may, *per exceptionem cedendarum actionum*, prevent the demand of the creditor from being received, because the creditor has disabled himself from making the cession of his actions which the security has a right to require.

There is no difficulty in this with regard to the action against the principal debtor: for as we have observed *supra*, *n.* 370, it being of the essence of securitiship that the security should not be bound to more than the principal debtor, the discharge which the creditor grants to the principal debtor, discharges likewise the security, and all the pleas *in rem* and prescriptions which the principal debtor acquires, are acquired by the security. We have replied *supra*, *n.* 380, to the law 22, *de pactis*.

When the creditor has disabled himself from ceding to the other securities the action which he has against one of them, in discharging this security or in suffering him to become discharged, we must likewise decide that the creditor ought, *per exceptionem cedendarum actionum*, to be excluded from his demand against the other securities, not for the whole, but for the part for which they would have had recourse against the security who has been discharged, if the creditor had not disabled himself from ceding his action against him. For example. If there were four securities all solvent, the creditor cannot demand his debt from three of them, except with a deduction of a fourth for which they would have recourse against him who has been discharged; and if among the three there was one insolvent, the creditor ought to make to the two that are solvent a deduction, not only of the fourth for which he who has been discharged was liable in his own right, but also of the third part which this security ought to bear of the share of the insolvent.

The reafon of this decifion is, that when feveral perfons together become fecurities for a principal debtor, they count upon the recourfe which they may have againft one another; it is in this confidence that they contract an engagement which they would not have contracted without it; it is not juft then that the creditor fhould deprive them of it by his own act.

Obferve that if the fecurity, difcharged by the creditor, had only become a fecurity fince the fecuritifhip of the others, thefe would not have the plea *cedendarum actionum* againft the creditor; for in contracting their fecuritifhip they had no right to count on a recourfe againft him who has been difcharged, fince he was not then a fecurity. It is to this cafe that the decifion of the law 15, §. 1, above cited, muft be reftricted.

It is neceffary to fay in regard to debtors *in solidum* what we have faid in regard to fecurities. When feveral perfons contract an obligation *in solidum*, they oblige themfelves each for the whole, only in the confidence that they may have recourfe againft one another on paying the whole. Therefore when the creditor by his own act has deprived them of this recourfe, in difabling himfelf by his own act from ceding his actions againft one of them whom he has difcharged, he ought no longer to be allowed to proceed againft the others *in solidum*, except with a deduction of the part for which they would have had recourfe againft him whom he has difcharged. See *supra n.* 275.

When the creditor has loft fome hypothecary claim upon the property of one of his debtors, whether by failing to oppofe the decrees which may have been made refpecting it, or by failing to interrupt third purchafers, who have acquired it without the charge of hypothecation or have obtained a difcharge therefrom by the poffeffion of ten or twenty years, may the co-debtors *in solidum* and the fecurities oppofe to this creditor the plea *cedendarum actionum*, on the ground that he has difabled himfelf from ceding to them the hypothecary action which refults from the hypo thecation he has suffered to be lost and upon which action they counted for the safety of the recourse which they would have had, in paying the whole against the debtor to whom the property, of which the creditor has lost the hypothecation, belonged? I do not think they would be well grounded in this. The plea *cedendarum actionum* ought not, it appears, to me, to be opposed to him when it is either by a positive act on his part that he is disabled from ceding his actions against one of the debtors, in discharging his person or property, or when, by suffering his demand against the debtor to come to be without remedy, he is suspected of collusion. But a simple negligence on his part, in not having interrupted the purchasers, or in not having opposed the decrees, ought not to be imputed to him as a fault; I. because, as he is not bound to make the cession of his actions but by a mere reason of equity, and as he has not contracted in this respect towards the other debtors and securities, any precise obligation to secure his actions to them, it suffices that he act in this respect with good faith, that is to say, that he do nothing contrary to this obligation; and he ought not in this respect to be liable for a mere negligence. II. The other debtors and securities have power also to watch the preservation of the hypothecary right which is lost; they may summon him to interrupt at their risk the third purchasers, or to oppose the decrees. It is only in this case in which they may have put the creditor in default, that they may complain that he has lost his hypothecation; but when they have been no more vigilant than he, they shall not be allowed to oppose to him a negligence which is theirs in common with him.

521. The third question, whether the cession of the actions of the creditor is made *de pleno jure*, has already been discussed, *supra*, *n.* 280, in regard to joint debtors *in solidum*. We have established, contrary to the opinion of Dumoulin, that it does not take place *de pleno jure*, and that it should be required; but that when it has been required, it is not necessary in our practice to prosecute the creditor who had refused; that the law would apply itself to the re-

fusal of the creditor, and transfer his actions to him who had required the cession of them. All which we said in regard to debtors *in solidum*, takes place likewise in regard to securities.

This cession should be made or required at the time of payment; otherwise, as the payment has extinguished the debt and the actions of the creditor, one can no longer make a cession of actions which no longer exist.

Mandatores pecuniæ credendæ are the only persons who, for a particular reason, can, *ex intervallo*, cause themselves to be subrogated to the actions of the creditor. See this reason *supra*, *n.* 445.

Observe that there are cases in which the law transfers the rights and actions of the creditor, to the person who has paid the debt, although he has not required this cession. These cases are, I. when one, in order to prevent the protest and for the honor of the drawer, has of his own accord paid a bill of exchange, he is then subrogated *de jure ipso* to all the rights and actions of the creditor of the bill of exchange, as we have seen *supra*, *n.* 520, *in fine*.

II. When, during the community of property between husband and wife an annuity due only from the wife, has been redeemed out of the monies of the community, the husband or his heirs are for his part in the community subrogated *de jure* to all the actions of the creditor against the wife, who was the debtor of the annuity, or against her heirs; *& sic vice versa*. Paris, 244, 245.

See what we have said on this subject in our introduction to title 10 of the custom of Orleans, *chap.* 6, L. 4.

III. When a creditor with hypothecation, to fortify his hypothecation, pays to another creditor with hypothecation, what is due him by the common debtor, this creditor has no need to require the subrogation; he is subrogated *de jure* to the claim which he has discharged, and to the hypothecations and rights which are attached to it. L. 4, *Cod. de his qui in prior.* It is evident that he paid only to have this subrogation. See our introduction to title 20 of the custom of Orleans, n. 71.

In regard to a third person detaining the possession of an estate; who, in order to avoid the delay, has paid the debt for which his estate was hypothecated; if, in paying, he has failed to require a subrogation to the rights of the creditor, he will not indeed be subrogated to all the rights of the creditor; but he may at least, according to our usages, exercise them upon the estate of which he detains the possession, against all the other creditors posterior to the one he has paid: for in exonerating the estate from this hypothecation, *meliorem fecit in eo fundo caeterorum creditorum pignoris causam*; which gives him a plea against them, *exceptionem doli*, to retain what he has paid to discharge this hypothecation. Good faith does not permit that they should profit at his expence by this discharge. *Dolo faciunt, si velint cum ejus damno locupletari.* This case is like that of a person detaining an estate subject to hypothecation, who has made improvements upon it. See our introduction, *ibid.* n. 72.

The cession of actions, or at least the requiring of this cession, is necessary for the subrogation to the claims of the hypothecation, except in the cases which we have just reported. But in regard to claims which have a personal privilege attached to them, such as those for funeral expences, expences of last sickness, house-rents, ground-rents, duties, &c., it is not necessary to require the subrogation to them: the privilege attached to these claims passes *de jure* to those who have acquired them, and they exercise them in the manner in which the privileged creditor whom they have paid out of their money might have exercised them. *Eorum ratio prior est creditorum quorum pecunia ad creditores privilegiarios pervenit.* L. 24, §. 3, ff. *de reb. auth. Jud. poss. alias.* L. 9, §. 3, ff. *de privil. cred.*

527. On the fourth question, what is the effect of the cession of actions, it is necessary to consult the law 36, ff.

de fidej. It informs us that the payment which is made by any one to a creditor, with fubrogation to his rights and actions, is confidered to be a payment, only as being a fale which this creditor is confidered to make of his claim and of all the rights which are attached to it, to him from whom he received the money. *Non in solutum accepit, sed quodammodo nomen debitoris vendidit. d. L.* Therefore the claim which is thus difcharged, is, in favor of him who is fubrogated, reputed to continue with all the rights which are attached to it; he may exercife them as the creditor might have done, for whom he is confidered to be an attorney *in rem suam.*

This fubrogation is not for the whole, except when he who pays ought to have recourfe for the whole; as when he who pays is a fecurity who has recourfe for the whole againft the principal debtor.

But when he who pays ought not to have recourfe but for part, and is debtor without recourfe and for himfelf of the furplus, the fubrogation will not take place but for the part for which he may have recourfe; and the payment would be, for the part of which he is debtor without recourfe and for himfelf, an abfolute payment, which will entirely extinguifh the debt for this part.

For example. Suppofe there were four debtors *in solidum*, of a debt; if one of them, who is debtor for the whole towards the creditor and for a fourth part with regard to his co-debtors, pays this debt in the whole, with fubrogation, the fubrogation cannot take place but for the three fourths for which he ought to have recourfe againft his co-debtors; but for the fourth of which he is debtor without recourfe, the payment made by this debtor, is an abfolute payment, which extinguifhes the debt for this part.

523. It is a great queftion, whether the debtor may have *in solidum* againft each of his co-debtors the actions of the creditor to which he is fubrogated for the three fourths we have treated of this at large *supra, n.* 281. One may make the fame queftion in regard to a fecurity, fubrogated

to the actions of a creditor against his co-securities, and the same decision ought to be made; the same reasons obtain.

It remains for us to observe that it is only by a fiction of law, established in favor of him who has paid with subrogation, that the claim is considered to continue. In truth it is paid and extinguished; for the true intention of the parties was to make a payment and not a transfer. Therefore when one, in redeeming an annuity of which he was a debtor *in solidum* or a security, is subrogated to the rights of the creditor of this annuity, he is not liable for the hypothecations which the creditors of the creditor who was proprietor of this annuity had upon it, as he would be a person to whom it was truly ceded, to whom the creditor has made a transfer of it: the redemption which he has made of it, although *with subrogation, being a true payment*, has extinguished the annuity and consequently the hypothecations, which are extinguished *rei obligatæ interitu.* The subrogation to the actions of the creditor, being established in favor of him who has paid, cannot be opposed to him, according to this maxim: *Quod in favorem alicujus introductum est, non debet contra ipsum retorqueri.*

§. III.

Of the effect of partial payments.

524. Regularly the payment of a part of what is due, extinguishes the debt for this part. For example. If you owed me ten crowns, and you have paid me five of them, the debt is extinguished as to half. L. 9, §. 1, ff. *de so'ut.*

525. This rule admits of three exceptions. The first is in regard to obligations in an alternative, which are not discharged in part by the payment which is made of a part of one of the two things which are due in the alternative, until the other part of the same thing is paid. For example. If a peasant has promised to give his daughter in marriage a certain cow or twenty crowns, and he pays his son in law ten crowns; he does not discharge by this payment any part of his obligation, while the cow is living,

until he has paid the remaining ten crowns. The payment which he has made is until this time in fufpence; it is that of the ten crowns remaining which will make it valid, and wholly difcharge the debt. If he fhould think proper to pay the cow, the payment of the ten crowns which he had before made would be null, and he might recall this fum as paid and not due; L. 26, §. 13, ff. *de cond. ind.*

If after having paid the firft ten crowns, the cow dies, in this cafe the cow can no longer be paid; and the obligation becoming determinate for the fum of twenty crowns promifed, the payment of the firft ten crowns will become valid, and the debt will be extinguifhed as to half.

526. The fecond exception is in regard to obligations of a thing indeterminate, *obligationes generis*. It is neceffary to fay in this refpect the fame that we have faid in regard to obligations in an alternative. For example. If a peafant has promifed to his daughter in marriage, a horfe indeterminately, and in difcharge of this obligation he gives the part which he has in a certain horfe in common with his neighbour; he is not difcharged from any part of his obligation, until he has redeemed the part which his neighbour has in this horfe, and has ceded it to his fon in law. Until then, notwithftanding the payment which he has made of the part which he had in this horfe, his fon in law may demand of him an entire horfe, on offering however to render to him what he has given for part. L. 9, §. 1, ff. *de solut.* Thefe decifions apply whether the obligation in an alternative, or of a thing indeterminate, has been contracted by one or by feveral debtors, whether towards one or feveral creditors. L. 34, §. 1, ff. *de solut. d.* L. 26, §. ff. 14, *de cond. indeb.*

527. The third exception is, when a debtor has given one or feveral determinate things in payment of a fum which he owed. If this payment is found not to be valid for a part, by the eviction which the creditor fhould fuffer as to a part of the things which he received in payment, it would not extinguifh the debt for any part; and the cred-

itor might, on offering to render him what remained of the things which were given him in payment, exact the entire debt; because he would not have received the thing in payment, if he had not believed he could retain the whole; L. 46, *pr.* L. §. 1, ff. *de solut.*

Article VII.

Rules respecting the application of payments.

First rule.

528. The debtor, when he pays, has the right to declare to what debt he intends to apply the sum which he pays: *Quoties quis debitor ex pluribus causis, unum solvit debitum, est in arbitrio solventis, dicere quod potius debitum voluerit solutum;* L. 1, ff. *de solut.*

The reason Ulpian adduces for this, is an evident one; *possumus enim certam legem dicere ei quod solvimus; d.* L.

According to our rule, although regularly the interest ought to be paid before the principal, yet if the debtor who owed principal and interest, in paying a sum of money, declared that he paid it upon the principal, the creditor who was willing to receive, cannot afterwards contest this application. *Respondi si qui dabat, in sortem se dare dixisset, usuris non debere proficere.* L. 102, §. 1, ff. *de solut.*

Second rule.

529. When the debtor, in paying, makes no application, the creditor to whom it is due for different causes, may apply it to the discharge of which he pleases. *Quoties non dicimus in id quod solutum sit, in arbitrio est accipientis, cui potius debito acceptum ferat. d.* L.

It is necessary, first, that this application should have been made at the time. *Dummodo in re præsenti fiat, in re agenda, ut vel creditori liberum sit non accipere, vel debitori non dare, si alio nomine solutum quis eorum velit; postea non permittitur.* L. 2, §. 3, ff. *hoc. tit.*

It is necessary, II. that the application which the creditor makes should be equitable: *In arbitrio est accipientis qui potius debito acceptum ferat; dummodo,* adds the law, *in* *id constituat solutum, in quod ipse si deberet, esset soluturus, id est,* non in id debitum quod est in controversia, aut in illud quod pro alio quis fidejusserat, aut cujus dies nondum venerat*; d. L. 1, ff. *de solut.*

Bachovius, *ad Treut. t.* 2, *disp.* 29, *th.* 3, *l.* 6, says that this limitation ought to be understood in this sense, that while the thing is yet entire, while the debtor has not yet received from the creditor an acquittance which includes the application, he may prevent the creditor from applying the payment he has made to those debts which the debtor has less interest to discharge, and consequently may demand that the creditor should make an equitable application by his acquittance, or return him his money. But when the debtor has consented to the application in receiving an acquittance which includes it, he cannot, according to Bachovius, contradict this application, although it be made to a debt which he has the least interest to discharge; because *volenti non fit injuria*, and because otherwise it would not be true to say that, when the application has not been made by the debtor, the choice of the application is referred to the creditor: for if we suppose that the creditor may only make the application to the debt which the debtor has the most interest to discharge, and consequently to the debt upon which the right of application applies, in the case in which the creditor has not made any, it follows that that which the creditor does make is useless and that he has not the choice. Such is the reasoning of Bachovius.

We may answer to this reasoning, that in order that the rule which refers to the creditor the choice of the application, when the debtor does not make it, may be true, it is not necessary that the creditor in all these cases, should make his choice; it suffices that he may make it in certain cases: and he may when the different debts for which the debtor is bound, are such as that it is not material to the debtor

* *It is here the negation ought to be placed, which is misplaced in the Florentine text: this correction is necessary for the sense of the text.*

that one should be discharged rather than the other. In these cases the creditor has the choice of application, when the debtor does not make it; and as, if he had not in fact made any application, it would be made to the oldest debt, or to all by contribution, in case of a concurrence of debts, as we shall see hereafter, the application would be to that to which the creditor would choose to make it.

Suppose, for example, that I am your creditor of the sum of one thousand livres for the price of an estate which I sold you in the year one thousand seven hundred and fifty, by a deed before a notary; and further, of another sum of one thousand livres for the price of another estate which I sold you in one thousand seven hundred and sixty. After having paid me the interest on these two sums, you pay me the sum of one thousand livres without appointing to which of the two debts you intend to pay it; it is indifferent to you to which of the two I make the application, since both are with hypothecation, are demandable and produce interest; but it is of much consequence to me to make this application to the debt of one thousand seven hundred and sixty in order to preserve my hypothecation for that of one thousand seven hundred and fifty; for if I do not so make the application, it will be the debt of one thousand seven hundred and fifty which, as the oldest, would be presumed to be paid.

The other plea of Bachovius appears more plausible, which is, that the debtor, who, in accepting the acquittance which includes the application, has consented to this application, is not to be received to contradict it, whatever interest he may have that it should be made to another debt. However I do not think we ought to decide, without distinction, that he should not be received: for if the debtor is a person who does not know how to read, or is a simple and untaught person, this application which has slipped into the acquittance, ought not to prejudice him, when the sum paid equals or surpasses that of the debt which the debtor had the most interest to discharge, so that the creditor could not have had any reason to dispense with making the application which the debtor had an interest in having made. For example. Suppose that a peasant owed an attorney on one account the sum of three hundred livres, demandable, for the price of a piece of land which he had sold him and about a year's interest; and that he owed him on another account, five or six hundred livres for fees. If this peasant brings to the attorney the sum of four hundred livres, and the attorney gives him an acquittance for this sum, mentioning that it is on account of fees due him; it is evident that this application which he makes of the payment, to his fees, is a surprise upon the debtor, and that the debtor has a right to demand that, notwithstanding what is made to appear by the acquittance, the payment should be applied to the three hundred livres which he owed for the price of the land, and that the interest should be declared in consequence thereof to have ceased from the day of the acquittance. On the contrary, when the creditor can have sufficient reason to dispense with making the application to the debt which it most concerns the debtor to discharge, *puta*, because the sum paid was less than that due for this cause, and the creditor was not obliged to receive in part the payment of this debt, the application made to another debt cannot in this case be contradicted; because in this case the creditor who had a right to refuse the payment which was made to him, has not accepted it but on the condition of the application which he has made of it, and which was agreed between him and the debtor.

Observe that when it is expressed in the acquittance that the sum is received to be credited on all the different demands of the creditor, *ex universo credito*, this general application is presumed to comprehend only the demands for which the creditor has an action, and not claims merely natural; L. 94, §. *fin de solut.*

This expression, it also appears to me, ought only to comprehend those debts of which the time of payment has arrived.

Third rule.

530. When the application has not been made either by the debtor or the creditor, the application ought to be made to that of the different debts which the debtor had, at the time, the moſt intereſt to diſcharge.

First corollary.

The application ought to be made rather to the deb not conteſted, than to that which was conteſted; rather to that of which the payment had fallen due when the debtor paid, than to that of which the time had not yet arrived. L. 3, §. 1, L. 103, ff. *de solut.*

Second corollary.

Among ſeveral debts of which the time of payment is come, the application ought to be made rather to that for which the debtor was conſtrainable by his perſon, than to debts merely civil.

Third corollary.

Among civil debts the application ought rather to be made to thoſe which produce intereſt, than to thoſe which do not.

Fourth corollary.

The application ought to be made rather to an hypothecary debt than to a debt which is chirographical; L. 97, ff. *de solut.*

Fifth corollary.

The application is made rather to the debt for which the debtor has given a ſecurity, than to thoſe which he owes alone; *d.* L. 4, *in fine;* L. 5, ff. *d. tit.* The reaſon is, that in paying the former, he diſcharges himſelf towards two creditors, towards his principal creditor, and towards his ſecurity, whom he is bound to indemnify. One has more intereſt to diſcharge himſelf towards two than towards one alone.

Sixth corollary.

The application ought to be made rather to a debt of

which he who has paid was principal debtor, than to those which he owed as a security for other persons; *d.* L. 97; L. 4, ff. *d. tit.*

All these corollaries may, from the circumstances, admit of exceptions, which are left to the discretion of the judge.

For example. Although the debt, of which the time of payment has arrived, has a preference, in regard to the application, to that of which the time has not arrived, yet if that, whereof the time has not arrived, would become due in a few days, and would make his person liable, I think that it ought to be preferred, in regard to the application, to another debt whereof the time had arrived; for it was the interest of the debtor to discharge rather a debt for which he would in a few days be constrainable by his person, although the time of payment had not yet arrived, than to discharge other ordinary debts of which the time had arrived.

Likewise, although the debt which brings this constraint, be preferable, in the application, to other debts merely civil, yet if the debtor was a person who, from his dignity and wealth, had room to expect that his creditor would not use towards him the rigor of this constraint by his person, this debt, if it did not bear interest, ought to yield in the application, to another debt, merely civil which would have carried interest.

Fourth rule.

531. When the debts were of equal nature and such as that the debtor had no interest to discharge one sooner than the other, the application ought to be made to the oldest. *Si nulla causa prægravet, in antiquiorem;* L. 5, ff. *d. tit.*

Observe that of two debts contracted the same day, but with different times of payment that, whereof the time is the shortest, and which is consequently soonest due, is presumed to be the oldest. L. 89, §. 2, ff. *hoc. tit.*

Fifth rule.

532. If the different debts were of the same date, and

all other things equal, the application will be made proportionably to each. *Si par et dierum et contractuum causa sit, ex summis omnibus proportione solutum*; L. 8, ff. *de solut.*

Sixth rule.

533. In debts which are of a nature to produce interest, the application is made to the interest, before the principal: *Primo in usuras, id quod solvitur, deinde in sortem, accepto feretur*; L. 1, *Cod. hoc. tit.*

This applies even when the acquittance should express that the sum was paid on account of principal and interest, *IN SORTEM et usuras.* The clause is understood in this sense, that the sum is received on account of the principal after the interest is discharged. L. 5, §. *fin.* ff. *de solut.*

Observe that if the sum paid exceeds what is due for interest, the application is made to the principal, even when it was expressed to be made to the interest, without mention of the principal; L. 102, §. *fin.* ff. *de solut.*

This decision ought to be understood of such principal as is demandable. But if the debtor of an annuity has, through error, paid more than he owed for the arrearages of this annuity, he may recall the overplus and it cannot be demanded that the application should be made to the principal of this annuity; for, properly speaking, the principal of an annuity is not due; it is only *in facultate luitionis*, and the creditor is not presumed to have consented to the redemption of his annuity in part.

534. The rule which we have established that the application ought to be made to the interest before it is made to the principal, does not apply in regard to such interest and damages as are due by a debtor as the penalty of his arrear, from the day of a judicial demand. These are adjudged as damages and form a debt distinct from the principal; and what the debtor pays, when there is in fact no application, is applied rather to the principal than to these damages, according to the third corollary, *supra.* Such is our law. Decree, 8th July, 1649, 1st vol. *Journal des Au-*

diences. Another, 15th July, 1706, *Journal des Audiences.*

535. When the creditor himself pays the price of a thing which was hypothecated to him, and which he has sold, there are other rules, than those which have been above established, for the application of the payment.

First rule.

The first rule is, that the application ought in this case to be made to the debt for which the thing was hypothecated, rather than to those for which it was not. Whatever interest the debtor may have to discharge them rather than this; L. 101, §. 1, ff. *de solut.*

Nota. When the debt for which the thing was hypothecated carries interest, the creditor may make the application to the interest before he does to the principal; L. 48, *d. tit.*

Second rule.

When the thing was liable for different debts, the application is made to that whereof the hypothecation was the strongest. For example. If one of the debts has a privileged hypothecation and the others only a simple hypothecation, the application will be made first to the debt of which the hypothecation was privileged. In the case of simple hypothecations, the application is to be made to the debt, the hypothecation of which is the oldest. If the hypothecations are equal, the application ought to be made to all by contribution, *pro modo debiti;* L. 96, §. 3, ff. *d. tit.*

ARTICLE VIII.

Of consignation, and tender of payment.

536. Consignation is a deposit which the debtor makes by authority of the court, of the thing or sum which he owes, in the hands of a third person.

537. Consignation is not properly a payment; for payment essentially includes the transferring of the property of the thing which is paid, to the creditor; *supra, n,* 504. And it is evident that the consignation does not transfer the property of the thing consigned, to the creditor; as the

creditor can only acquire it by receiving voluntarily the thing which is tendered to him. *Dominium non acquiritur nisi corpore & animo.* But though the consignation which is made on the refusal of the creditor to receive the thing or sum due him, which is tendered to him, be not an actual payment; yet when it is made validly, it is equivalent to a payment, and extinguishes the debt, as well as actual payment made to the creditor. *Obsignatione totius debitæ pecuniæ solemniter facta, liberationem contingere manifestum est;* L. 9, *Cod. de solut.*

538. In order that the consignation may be valid and may be equivalent to payment, it is necessary that it should not have been in the power of the debtor to pay the creditor, and that the creditor should have been put in arrear to receive, by a valid tender made to him.

In order that the tender may be valid it is necessary, I. that it be made to the creditor, if he be capable of receiving, otherwise to him who is qualified to receive in his stead, as his tutor, his curator, &c.

If there was a person indicated in the contract to whom the payment might be made, the tender might be made to that person: for the debtor having a right by the law of the agreement, to pay to this person, it is a consequence of this right, that he should not be obliged to seek the creditor.

539. It is necessary II. that the tender should be made by a person capable of paying; for he who is incapable of paying is incapable of tendering.

540. It is necessary, III. that the tender should be of the entire sum, unless the agreement gives to the debtor the right to pay in parts; otherwise the tender does not put the creditor in arrear, who was not bound to receive his debt in parts.

541. It is necessary, IV. that, when the debt has been contracted under a condition, this condition should have happened; and if there has been a time of payment

ſtipulated in favor of the creditor, that this time ſhould have arrived: for as long as the creditor cannot be compelled to receive, the tender which is made to him, does not put him in arrear.

542. It is neceſſary, V. that the tender ſhould be made at the place where the payment ought to be made: *Ita demum oblatio debiti liberationem parit, si eo loco quo debetur, solutio fuerit celebrata;* L. 9, *Cod. solut.*

Therefore if the ſum due be payable to the creditor at his houſe, the tender cannot be validly made but at his houſe. If the ſum be payable at another place, the tender may be made to him where, in this place, he elected to receive it; and if he has not elected where, the debtor ſhould cite him, perſonally or at his houſe, to appear before the judge, to ſhew cauſe why he ſhould not be compelled by order of the judge to appoint where, in that place, the debtor may make payment; otherwiſe, why the debtor ſhould not have leave to conſign.

If the thing due be a thing determinate which ought to be delivered at the place where it is, the creditor is to be cited, perſonally or at his houſe, to take it away; and on this citation, which is equal to a tender, the debtor may be authoriſed by the judge to depoſit the thing ſomewhere elſe, if he has occaſion for the room which it occupies.

543. Finally, an inſtrument ought to be drawn out ſtating the tender and the ſummons made in conſequence of it to the creditor to receive. This ought to be done by an officer and clothed with the ordinary formalities: it is cuſtomary to have it atteſted by witneſſes who may prove the tender.

The creditor ſhould be ſummoned to appear before the judge, without delay, that the conſignation may be ordered. The judgment by which the conſignation is ordered, ought to be notified to the creditor with a ſummons to be preſent at the conſignation, at a certain place, day and hour.

It is not however neceſſary to the validity of the conſignation, that it be preceded by the order of the judge. Although the debtor has not cited the creditor before the judge, yet if he has ſimply declared to the creditor that on his refuſal he would conſign at a certain place, day and hour, the conſignation purſuantly made and duly notified to the creditor, will be valid, and the judgment which may be afterwards obtained, confirming it, will have a retroactive effect to the time when it was made. Decree, 11th Auguſt, 1773, *Journal des Audiences.*

544. This conſignation ought to be made at the day and hour appointed: in order to be valid, it ought to be of the whole ſum due, unleſs the debtor has, by the agreement, a right to pay in parts. An inſtrument, ſtating the conſignation and containing an account of the money in which the ſum has been paid, is drawn up and notified to the creditor.

545. The effect of the conſignation is, that if it be judged valid, the debtor is holden to have been diſcharged by it: and although, *subtilitate juris*, he remains proprietor of the coins conſigned, till they be taken by the creditor, they ceaſe to be at his riſque and lie at the creditor's, who from being a creditor of a ſum of money, as he was before, is now become creditor of thoſe coins, *tanquam certorum corporum;* and he is a creditor no longer of his debtor, who has been fully diſcharged by the conſignation, but he is a creditor of the conſignee, who by the conſignation, obliges himſelf, *tanquam ex quasi contractu*, to reſtore the coins to the creditor, if the conſignation be judged valid, or to the debtor who conſigned them, if it be declared null.

Hence it follows that the appreciation or depreciation of the money ought to be to the profit or loſs of the creditor, if the conſignation be judged valid; for when the thing due is a thing certain, it is at the riſque of the creditor. If the conſignation be not judged valid, the debtor will take back the money as it may be.

In caſe of an appreciation of the money happening ſince

the consignation, the creditor will not be received, in order to avail himself of this appreciation, to ask to withdraw the money consigned, and hold the consignation to be null; for no one is to be received to argue against his own act. The formalities which the debtor might have neglected having been established in favor of the creditor, he only has a right to complain, if they have not been observed.

There remains a question, which is, whether, the consignation having been regularly made and the debtor having voluntarily withdrawn the money consigned by him, this consignation ought to be regarded as of no effect with regard to the securities and the co-obligors of the debtor; and whether therefore the securities and co-obligors remain bound. For the negative it may be said, that the consignation, having been regularly made, has extinguished the debt, and discharged all those who were liable for it; that, the securities and co-obligors having been once discharged, it cannot be in the power of the debtor, by withdrawing the money consigned, to revive their obligation which has been extinguished. An argument is drawn from the law *fin. ff. de pact.*, which decides that when the debtor has acquired to himself and his securities, by the pact *de non petendò*, which has taken place between the creditor and him, a plea to the action of the creditor, he can no longer, in renouncing the pact by a contrary agreement, deprive his securities of the plea they have acquired: *a fortiori*, say they, it ought not to be in his power to revive the obligation of his securities, after they have been discharged *de jure* by the consignation. It is added that as, after an actual payment which has extinguished the debt, the voluntary restitution which the creditor might make to the debtor of the money he had paid, would not revive the debt; so, after the consignation which is in lieu of the payment and has the same effect in extinguishing the debt, the restitution made to the debtor, of the money consigned, cannot revive the debt. Notwithstanding these reasons, it has been adjudged in a case, 1624, reported by Basset, IV, 21, that the consignation should be holden as null, and that the securities should remain bound. Basset gives for the reason of this decision, that the consignation which extinguishes the debt is not a momentary consignation, but a consignation *quæ in suo statu permanserit*, and which has not been withdrawn by the debtor who made it. But may it not be replied that this is begging the question? For it is precisely a question whether the debtor who has made a consignation according to law, may withdraw it to the prejudice of his securities. I should think we ought to distinguish whether the consignation has been withdrawn by the debtor before it was ordered or declared valid, or whether it has been withdrawn since. In the first case, I think that the consignation ought to be regarded as of no effect, and that the securities are not discharged: for the consignation not being in itself a payment, it is from the authority of the judge that it holds the effect which is equivalent to a payment and extinguishes the debt. The sentence of the judge which declares the consignation valid, has, I confess, a retroactive effect, and the consignation, confirmed by this sentence, is presumed to have extinguished the debt from the instant it was made; but a consignation, which has neither been ordered nor confirmed by the judge, and which the debtor has withdrawn, could not have the effect to extinguish the debt, nor to discharge, in consequence thereof, the securities, and it ought to be regarded as null. In the second case when the debtor has not withdrawn the monies by him consigned, until after the consignation has been declared valid, I do not think that this should prejudice the securities and co-debtors who have been discharged by this consignation.

CHAPTER II.

Of novation.

THIS chapter will be divided into six articles. We shall see in the first, what a novation is, and what are its different kinds. In the second we will treat of the debts which ought to make a ground for novation: in the third, of the perfons who may make a novation. In the fourth, how novation is made. In the fifth, of the effect of a novation. We will treat in the fixth of the effect of delegation, which is a particular kind of novation.

ARTICLE THE FIRST.

What a novation is and what are its different kinds.

546. Novation is the fubftitution of a new debt in the place of an old one.

The old debt is extinguifhed by the new one which is contracted in its place: therefore novation is reckoned among the ways in which obligations are extinguifhed.

547. Novation may be made in three different ways, which form three different forts of novation.

The firft is that which is made without the intervention of any new perfon, when a debtor contracts a new engagement with his creditor, on condition that he fhall be difcharged from a preceding one. This fort of novation is called fimple novation.

548. The fecond fort of novation is that which is made by the intervention of a new debtor, when one becomes debtor in my place to my creditor, who accepts him for his debtor and difcharges me in confequence thereof.

He who thus becomes debtor for another who is confequently difcharged, is called in law *expromissor*; and this fort of novation is called *expromissio*. This *expromissor* is very different from the fecurity whom they call in law *adpromissor*: for he who becomes a fecurity for one, does not difcharge him from his obligation; but he accedes to it and becomes debtor jointly with him.

549. The third fort of novation is that which is made by the intervention of a new creditor, when a debtor, in order to be difcharged from an old creditor, by the order of this creditor, contracts fome engagement with a new creditor.

There is a particular kind of novation which we call

delegation, which very often includes a double novation. We will treat of it in article VI.

We shall say nothing of that which results *ex litis contestatione*, the principles of the Roman law in this respect being no longer in use among us.

ARTICLE II.

Of the debts which make the necessary ground for novation.

550. It results from the definition which we have just given of novation, that there cannot be a novation unless there have been two debts contracted, of which one is extinguished by the other which is substituted to it.

Hence it follows that the debt of which one intends to make a novation by another engagement, is a conditional debt; the novation cannot take place till the condition happens. L. 8, §. 1, ff. *de novat.*

Therefore if the condition fails, there will be no novation; because there has not been a first debt to which the new one could be substituted.

Likewise, if the conditional debt of which one has intended to make a novation by another engagement, was of a thing certain, and before the accomplishment of the condition the thing should perish, there would be no novation, even when the condition should be accomplished: for the condition not confirming the debt of a thing which does not exist; there has not yet been a first debt to which the new one could be substituted.

551. *Vice versa*, if the first debt did not depend on any condition, but the second engagement by which one has intended to make a novation of this first debt, depends on a condition, the novation cannot be accomplished but by the accomplishment of the condition of the new engagement before the extinction of the first debt.

Therefore there will be no novation, not only in the case in which the condition should fail, but even in the case in which, before the accomplishment of this condition, the first debt should have been extinguished; *puta*, by the extinction of the thing which made the object of it: for the accomplishment of the condition cannot effect the novation of a debt which is no more. L. 14, ff. *de novat.*

552. The simple time of payment is very different from the condition: the debt exists, although the time of payment may not yet have arrived. Therefore one may make a novation of a debt whereof the time of payment has not yet arrived, by another absolute engagement; or of an absolute debt, by another which contains a time of payment; and in both cases the novation is accomplished at first, without waiting the arrival of the time. L. 5, L. 8, §. 1, ff. *de novat.*

553. It is indeed of the essence of a novation that there should have been two debts contracted; a first, and a second which has been substituted to it: but it suffices that the first has preceded the second for an imaginary moment. The novation of the first debt may be made by the second, in the same instant that the first is contracted.

For example. If you sell me an estate for the price of ten thousand livres, and by the same contract a third person engages in my place to pay you this sum, and you accept him for your only debtor, we must suppose for a moment, a debt which I contract for the price of the estate that I purchase, and of which novation is made by the engagement contracted by this third person to pay the price in my place. Although this debt which I contract has not existed a moment in reality, a novation of it is made in the same instant that I contracted it. See another example in the law 8, §. 2, ff. *de novat.*

554. The novation is valid, whatever may be the first debt to which a new one is substituted, and whatever that may be which is substituted. *Non interest qualis præcessit obligatio, seu civilis, seu naturalis; qualiscumque sit novari potest; dummodo sequens obligatio, aut civiliter teneat, aut naturaliter;* L. 1, §. 1, ff. *de novat.*

It is necessary however that these obligations be not such as the law formally condemns and declares null; for what is null cannot be fusceptible of any effect. See *supra*, *part*. 2, *ch*. 2.

Article III.

What persons may make a novation.

555. The confent which the creditor gives to the novation of the debt, being fomething equivalent, as to the extinction of the debt, to a payment which might be made of it, it follows that thofe only to whom one may validly pay, may make a novation of the debt.

Therefore, by the fame reafon that one cannot validly pay to a minor, to a feme covert not authorifed by her hufband, to one interdicted, we muft decide that thefe perfons cannot make a novation of what is due to them. L. 3. L. 20, §. 1, *de tit.*

556. *Vice versa*, he to whom one may pay a debt, may commonly alfo make a novation. *Cui recté solvitur, is etiam novare potest*; L. 10, ff. *de novat.*

It follows thence that a creditor *in solidum* may make a novation. So decides Venulius, L. 31, §. 1, ff. *de novat. & de leg.*, whofe decifion, it appears to me, ought to be followed, though Paul is of a different opinion. L. 27, ff. *de pactis*. The commentators have endeavoured in vain to reconcile them. See Wiffembach, *ad tit. de novat*. 10.

557. Likewife, a tutor, a curator, a hufband may make a novation; L. 20, §. 1, L. *fin*. §. 1, ff. *de tit.* He who has a general power of attorney may alfo. He who has only a particular power to receive from the debtors may not, becaufe, as his power is limited to receive, *non debet egredi fines mandati.*

It is the fame with thofe who are called *adjecti solutionis gratia*, of whom we have fpoken in a preceding chapter, *art*. 2, §. 4: they cannot make a novation, L. 10, ff. *de solut.*, although one may validly pay to them.

ARTICLE IV.

How novation is made.

§. I.

Of the form of a novation.

558. By the civil law novation could only be made by ftipulation. The form of ftipulation is not in ufe in our law. Simple agreements here have the fame effect which ftipulation had in the civil law; therefore novation is made by fimple agreement.

§. II.

Of the intention to make a novation.

559. It is neceffary for the novation that there fhould have been an intention to make it in the creditor, or in the perfon who has power from him or capacity to make the novation in his place.

By the antient Roman law, this intention was eafily prefumed; but according to the conftitution of Juftinian in the laft law *Cod. de novat.*, this intention to make a novation fhould have been exprefsly declared, without which there could not have been a novation; and the new engagement which is contracted, is prefumed to have been made rather to confirm the firft and to accede to it, than to extinguifh it.

The reafon of this law is, that no one fhould flightly be prefumed to give up the rights which belong to him. Therefore, as a novation includes an abdication which the creditor makes of the firft debt, to which the fecond is fubftituted, this novation ought not to be flightly prefumed, and the parties ought to explain themfelves.

We do not however adhere, in our *jurifprudence*, fo literally to this law, that it fhould always be neceffary that the creditor declare in precife and formal terms that he intends to make a novation; it fuffices, that his intention to make a novation fhould, in fome manner or other, appear fo evident that it could never be called into doubt. This is what d'Argentre eſtabliſhes, on the article 273 of the antient cuſtom of Brittany.

For example. I am the creditor of Peter for the ſum of one thouſand livres; an inſtrument is paſſed between James, the debtor of Peter, and me, by which it is ſaid that James obliges himſelf towards me to pay me the ſum of one thouſand livres which is due me by Peter, and it is added that I intend, *in order to accommodate Peter*, to content myſelf with the preſent obligation which is made to me by James. We ought to decide in this inſtance that there was a novation and that Peter is diſcharged towards me, although it be not ſaid in formal and preciſe terms that I diſcharge Peter, and that I accept the obligation of James, in making a novation of that of Peter: for the terms which I have made uſe of, that I would *content* myſelf with the obligation of James *in order to accommodate Peter* declare ſufficiently that I intended to diſcharge Peter, and rely on James for my debtor in his place.

But unleſs it ſhould appear evident that the creditor had an intention to make a novation, the novation is not preſumed. Therefore if, in the ſame inſtance, having made a ſeizure and attachment upon James for the act of Peter, my debtor, James has bound himſelf to me abſolutely by an inſtrument of writing, to pay me the ſum of one thouſand livres which is due me by Peter and for which I have made ſeizure, without there being added, as in the above caſe, *that I intended, in order to accommodate Peter, to content myſelf with the obligation of James*, or ſuch other words from which it would be evident that I had intended to diſcharge Peter, I ſhall not be preſumed to have made a novation, and James will be holden to have acceded to the obligation of Peter who ſtill remains bound to me. It was ſo adjudged by the parliament of Toulouſe in a caſe reported by Catelan, *vol.* 2, *l.* 5, *ch.* 38.

Likewiſe, if ſince the debt was contracted, a new agreement has taken place between the creditor and the debtor, by which a longer time of payment may have been given or a new place for the payment appointed, or the debtor allowed the liberty of paying to another person than the creditor, or to pay another thing in the room of that which was due, or even by which the debtor should have bound himself to pay a larger sum, or a less one to which the creditor was willing to confine his demand; in all these cases and the like, according to our principle that the novation is not to be presumed, it must be decided that there has been no novation and that the parties intended only to modify, diminish or augment the debt, rather than extinguish it in order to substitute a new one to it, if they did not explain themselves.

§. III.

Whether an annuity to the amount of a sum due by him who contracts it, essentially includes a novation.

When by an agreement between the creditor and debtor of a sum of money, the debtor has contracted an annuity to his creditor, is there necessarily in this case a novation? Many hold that in this case there is no novation, when the parties have not mentioned it, and especially when they have expressly declared in the contract that they did not intend to make a novation. They hold that by the contract the creditor gives no discharge of the sum that is due him; that he only consents not to exact the sum that is due as long as the interest of that sum is paid to him; consequently that it is always the old debt which exists, although under a new modification; that is to say, that from being demandable as it was, it has now become a debt whereof the principal is aliened and cannot be exacted as long as the debtor pays the arrearages. This opinion appears to me to be liable to many objections. It is of the essence of the contract of annuity, which is a contract real or *in rem*, that he who contracts the annuity receive the price of the annuity. When my debtor of a certain sum, as of a thousand livres, contracts for that sum an annuity of fifty livres, it is then necessary that he receive the sum of a thousand livres as the price of the annuity which he contracts, and he can only be holden to have received it by the discharge which I give in payment of the annuity he contracts. This contract of annuity includes then a discharge which I give him of that sum: it includes a compensation of the debt for the sum which he owed me, with a like sum which I was obliged to give him as the price of the annuity he contracts. Hence it is evident that this discharge and this compensation extinguish the debt and form a novation.

It cannot be said that the principal of the annuity which is contracted, is the old debt of a thousand livres due by Peter, which continues to exist under a new modification of the principal of the annuity, instead of the debt demandable as it was: for besides that it is extinguished by the contract of annuity as we have just now shewn, the debt of an annuity is properly the debt of the arrearages, which will run forever till the redemption, rather than of the principal, which, as it cannot be exacted, is not properly due, and is *in facultate luitionis, magis quam in obligatione.*

These reasons appear conclusive in determining that the contract by which the debtor of a certain sum contracts an annuity to his creditor for that sum, essentially includes a novation, even though it should be expressly mentioned that the parties intend not to make a novation; for a protestation cannot prevent the natural and essential effect of a contract. Therefore it appears to me that this clause cannot have any other effect than to prevent the extinction of the hypothecations for the former debt, and transfer them to the new, as may be done according to the law 12, § 6, ff. *Qui potior.*

Although these reasons appear to me very strong to determine that the contract by which a demandable debt is converted into a contract of annuity, essentially includes a novation, yet the contrary opinion seems to be advocated by most authors. They ground it on two cases decided, which they say have settled the question. The first, which is of the 13th April, 1783, is reported in *Journal des Palais*, *vol.* 2, *ed. fol.*

In this case Ligondez, a debtor *in solidum* with Sablon of the sum of six thousand livres, afterwards contracted an annuity as well in his own name as in acting for Sablon. The creditor brought a suit against Sablon to compel him to enter into a contract of annuity or pay the said sum of six thousand livres, and judgment was given for the plaintiff. The reporter infers from this case that it was adjudged, that a debtor of a sum of money might contract an annuity for that sum without a novation of the debt taking place. But I think the consequence is badly drawn, and that the respective pleas of the parties which are reported in the journal did not bring this question before the court. The reason for which judgment was given against the debtor to pay or contract the annuity, appears to me to have been this, that as Ligondez contracted the annuity as well in his own name as in acting for Sablon, and as the plaintiff therefore consented to the conversion of his claim of six thousand livres, into an annuity under the condition that it should be contracted by both the debtors; the conversion of the debt of six thousand livres into an annuity, the novation and the extinction of the claim which was to result from it, depended on this condition: therefore on the refusal of Sablon to contract the annuity, the condition failed and there was no novation; the debt continued and judgemnt was rightly given for the plaintiff. The other case is of the 6th September 1712, and is reported in *vol.* 6, *Journal des Audiences*. In this case several persons were bound *in solidum* to pay a certain sum: two had actually paid each a third part, and the creditor, in receiving it, had reserved his right against each for the whole. Lebegue and de Villemenard had, by a note, promised to contract an annuity for the remaining third and it was expressed in the note that this should not impair the creditor's right against the others as to their liability for the whole. A long time after, the creditors brought a suit against Montpensier, one of those who had paid his third under the above reservation, to compel him to pay the remainder or to accede to the contract of annuity, and judgment was rendered to this effect. Therefore it is said to have been adjudged that a contract of annuity, made by a debtor for the sum which he owed, did not necessarily include a novation and an extinction of the debt of this sum: otherwise, in the present case, Montpensier, debtor *in solidum* of the sum which remained due and for which the annuity was contracted, would have been discharged from this debt by the annuity, and would not have been condemned by the judgment to pay it.

I do not know what were the reasons upon which this judgment was grounded; but in order to support our principles, it might be said that the judgment has not determined what is inferred but that it has determined that, by the reservation, the creditor was reputed to have made the conversion of his claim into an annuity dependent on the condition, that all the debtors *in solidum* would accede to the contract of annuity, and that consequently on the refusal of Montpensier to accede to it, the condition failed and the debt continued in force.

§. IV.

Of the necessity that there should be some difference between the new and the old debt.

560. When there is a new agreement between the same creditor and the same debtor without the intervention of any new person, although it be expressly declared by the instrument which contains the new engagement that the parties intend to make a novation, it is necessary, in order that the novation may be valid, that this instrument contain something different from the first obligation which was contracted, whether in the quality of the obligation, if the first was determinate, and the second in an alternaternative, or *vice versa;* or whether in regard to the accidental accessories of the obligation, as the time or place of payment. It is also a sufficient difference if the first obliga-

tion was contracted under the securitiship of another person, or under the hypothecation of my goods, and by the new one I have bound myself without a security and without hypothecation or *vice versa*.

If the new engagement made without the intervention of a new person, does not contain any thing different from the first, it is evident that this new engagement is ineffectively contracted. *Instit. tit. quib. mod. toll. ob.* §. 4.

561. When the novation is made with the intervention of a new debtor or of a new creditor, the difference of creditor or debtor is a sufficient difference to render the novation effective, without the necessity of any other intervening.

§. V.

Whether the consent of the old debtor is necessary for the novation.

562. The novation which is made by the intervention of a new debtor, may be made between the creditor and this new debtor, without the first, whose debt is to be extinguished by the novation having any part in it, and without his consenting thereto. *Liberat me is qui quod debeo promittit, etiamsi nolim;* L. 8, §. 5, *de novat.* The reason is, that the novation, in regard to the first debtor, includes nothing else than the discharge of his debt, by the novation which this third person contracts in his place: one may discharge the debt of another without his consent thereto, as we have seen in a preceding chapter: *Ignorantis enim et inviti conditio melior fieri potest.* L. 53, *de solut.*

ARTICLE V.

Of the effect of novation.

563. The effect of a novation is that the first debt is extinguished in the same manner that it would be by an actual payment.

When one of several debtors *in solidum* contracts alone a new engagement with the creditor in order to make a novation of the first, the first debt being extinguished by the novation as it would be by an actual payment, all his co-debtors are discharged as well as himself. Likewise as the extinction of the principal obligation carries with it that of all the accessory obligations, the novation which is made of the principal debt extinguishes all the accessory obligations, such as that of securities.

If the creditor wished to preserve the obligation of the other debtors and securities, it is necessary that he should annex a condition to the novation, that the co-debtors and securities should accede to the new debt; in which case, if they were not willing to accede to it, there would be no novation, and the creditor would preserve his old debt.

From the principle that a novation extinguishes the old debt, it follows also that it extinguishes the hypothecations which were accessory to it. *Novatione legitime facta liberantur hypothecæ*; L. 18, ff. *de novat.*

But the creditor may by the same act which contains the novation, transfer to the second debt the hypothecations which were attached to the first. L. 12, §. 5, ff. *qui potior.*

For example. If by a writing between us of one thousand seven hundred and fifty you have borrowed from me the sum of a thousand livres under the hypothecation of your property, and by another of one thousand seven hundred and sixty you have contracted towards me a new obligation, and it is expressed in this last that by the means of this new obligation you should rest discharged from that of one thousand seven hundred and fifty, *of which the parties have intended to make a novation under the reserve of the hypothecations*, I shall, by this clause, be continued in my order of hypothecation for my new debt, from the day of the date of the old one. L. 3. L. 21. ff. *dicto titulo.*

Observe that if the new debt was greater than the old, I should not be continued in my order of hypothecation, except to the amount of the sum which was due me by the instrument of one thousand seven hundred and fifty; this transferring of the hypothecations from the old debt to the new one, not being allowed to prejudice intermediate creditors.

Observe also that this transferring of the hypothecations from the old debt to the new, cannot be made but with the consent of the person to whom the things hypothecated belong. In the instance above mentioned, it is clear that you have consented to this transferring of the hypothecation, since you were party to the instrument in which the reservation of the hypothecation is stipulated. But if a third person by a deed of one thousand seven hundred and sixty is obliged towards me to pay me the sum which you owed me by a deed of one thousand seven hundred and fifty, and it is said that by means of the premises, the debt of one thousand seven hundred and fifty remains discharged, *under the reserve of the hypothecations,* although the novation may be made without your intervention in the deed, the transferring of the hypothecation of your property attached to your debt of one thousand seven hundred and fifty cannot be made to the new debts of one thousand seven hundred and sixty, if you are not a party to the deed to consent to it; the new debtor to whom the things hypothecated do not belong, cannot without you, to whom they do belong, hypothecate them for the new debt. This is what Paul decides in the law 30, ff. *de novat.* *Paulus respondit, si creditor a Sempronio, animo novandi stipulatus esset, ita ut a prima obligatione in universum discederetur, rursum easdem res a posteriore debitore, sine consensu debitoris prioris, obligari non posse.*

According to the same principles, if one of several debtors *in solidum* contracts towards the creditor a new obligation, and it be expressed in the deed, that the parties have intended to make a novation of the first debt, *under the reserve of the hypothecations;* the reserve can only have effect as to the hypothecations of the property of this debtor who contracts the new debt, and not the hypothecation of the property of his co-debtors; as their property cannot be hypothecated for this new debt without their consent.

Whatever reſerve the creditor ſhould make by the deed which contains the novation, the ſecurities of the old debt cannot be obliged to the new one, if they do not conſent to it.

ARTICLE VI.

Of delegation.

§. I.

What delegation is, and how it is made.

564. Delegation is a kind of novation by which the old debtor, in order to diſcharge himſelf from his creditor, gives him a third perſon who obliges himſelf in his place towards this creditor, or towards the perſon whom he indicates to him. *Delegare est vice sua alium reum dare creditori, vel cui jusserit.* L. 11, ff. *de novat.*

It reſults from this definition, that a delegation is made by the concurrence of three perſons, and that there intervenes ſometimes a fourth.

It is neceſſary that there ſhould be the concurrence, I. of the perſon delegating, that is to ſay, of the old debtor who gives to his creditor another debtor in his place.

II. Of the perſon delegated, who obliges himſelf towards the creditor in the place of the old debtor, or towards the perſon indicated by the creditor.

III. Of the creditor, who in conſequence of the obligation which the perſon delegated contracts towards him or towards the perſon whom he indicates to him, diſcharges the perſon delegating.

Sometimes there intervenes in the delegation a fourth perſon, viz. the one whom the creditor indicates, and towards whom, upon the indication of the creditor, and by the order of the perſon delegating, the perſon delegated binds himſelf.

In order that there may be a delegation, it is neceſſary that the will of the creditor to diſcharge the firſt debtor, and to content himſelf with the obligation of this new debtor, who obliges himſelf towards him in the place of the firſt, ſhould well appear. Therefore if Peter, one of the heirs of my debtor, in order to diſcharge himſelf from an annuity towards me, has, by a diviſion, charged James, his coheir, to pay it to me in his diſcharge, there will be no delegation; and Peter will not be diſcharged towards me, if I have not, by ſome deed, declared formally that I diſcharged Peter: without this, although I have received from James alone the arrearages during a conſiderable time, it cannot thereby be concluded that I have accepted him for my only debtor in the place of Peter, and that I have diſcharged Peter; *arg.* L. 40, §. 2, ff. *de pact.*

§. II.

Of the effect of delegation.

565. The delegation includes a novation, which is the extinction of the debt of the perſon delegating; and the obligation which the perſon delegated contracts in his place. Commonly indeed the delegation contains a double novation; for commonly the perſon delegated is a debtor of the perſon delegating, who, in order to diſcharge himſelf, towards the perſon delegating, of his obligation, contracts, by the order of the perſon delegating, a new obligation towards the creditor of the perſon delegating. There is in this caſe a novation, both of the obligation of the perſon delegating towards his creditor to whom the perſon delegating gives another debtor in his place, and alſo of the obligation of the perſon delegated towards the perſon delegating, in conſequence of that which he contracts by his order towards his creditor.

566. If the perſon delegated was not the debtor of the perſon delegating, although he bound himſelf to his creditor only on the falſe ſuppoſition that he was debtor of the perſon delegating, the obligation he ſhould contract with this creditor would, not the leſs, be valid, and he could not avoid paying it; ſaving his recourſe againſt the perſon delegating, that he might be compelled to reimburſe him. The creditor who, by the obligation which the perſon dele-

gated contracts towards him, receives only what was due him by his former creditor whom he has discharged, ought not to suffer by this error. *Si per ignorantiam promiserit, nulla quidem exceptione uti poterit adversus creditorem, quia ille suum recepit; sed is qui delegavit, tenetur conditione;* L. 12, ff. *de novat.*

It would be otherwise if he towards whom the person delegated bound himself, was not creditor of the person delegating, either if the person delegating was himself in the error and thought himself debtor, or if he wished to make him a donation. In either case, the person delegated who bound himself to him through error, in the false supposition that he was debtor of the person delegating, will not be validly bound, and will be able to defend himself from paying, on discovering the error; L. 7, ff. *de dol. excep.*; L. 2, §. 4, ff. *de novat.*

The reason of this difference is, that in this case, he towards whom the person delegated bound himself, *certat de lucro captando;* whilst the person delegated, who through error bound himself to him, *certat de damno vitando.* He is more entitled to favor *qui certat de damno*, than he *qui certat de lucro.* Therefore he ought not only to be discharged from his obligation contracted through error, but also to recover back what he may have paid in consequence thereof, according to this rule of law, *Melius est favere repetitioni, quam adventitio lucro.* On the contrary, in the preceding case, the creditor to whom the person delegated bound himself, *versaretur in damno*, would sustain a loss, if the person delegated was discharged from his obligation.

567. If the person delegated binds himself only under a condition, all the effect of the delegation will be suspended until the condition be performed, and as in this case it depends on the performance of the condition, that the person delegated should be bound, so it depends on the performance of the same condition that the person delegating be discharged from his obligation, which can only be extinguish-

ed by the new obligation of the person delegated, which is to be substituted to it. The obligation of the person delegated to the person delegating, depends likewise on this condition; for the person delegated can only be discharged from his obligation to the person delegating, by becoming bound to the creditor in his stead.

Although the person delegated be not discharged from his obligation towards the person delegating, until the performance of the condition, yet the person delegating, by whose order he conditionally bound himself, cannot prosecute him till there be a failure in the performance of the condition; for as long as it may be performed, it is uncertain whether he will remain bound to him, or whether he will become bound to the new creditor; this is the decision of the law 36, ff. *de reb. cred.*

§. III.

Whether the person delegating is liable for the insolvency of the person delegated.

568. Regularly, when the person delegated is validly bound to the creditor to whom he has been delegated, the person delegating is fully discharged from his obligation to this creditor, who can have no recourse against him in case the new debtor delegated to him should become insolvent; this creditor, in accepting the delegation, has relied on the solvency of the debtor who was delegated to him; *nomen ejus secutus est.*

This principle is liable to an exception in the case in which it should be agreed that the person delegating should give *at his own risk* a new debtor in his stead. Paul decides that in this case the creditor may prosecute, *actione mandati contraria*, the person delegating, in order to be indemnified for the sum for which he could not procure payment, on account of the insolvency of the new debtor delegated to him. For when at the request of my old debtor, I accept at his risk another debtor in his stead, it is a contract of *mandate* which intervenes between us. I am his mandatary in accepting the delegation, and consequently ought to be indemnified by him for what this acceptance may cost me. It costs me the sum which I could not obtain from the person delegated; for this therefore he ought to indemnify me.

Observe that it is necessary that I should not be subject to be reproached for having neglected to use the diligence which might have procured my payment, whilst the debtor delegated was solvent; for in that case it is my own fault if I have not been paid. According to the rules of the contract of mandate, the mandatary has only an action to be indemnified for what it has cost him without his fault. *Venit in actione mandati quod mandatario ex causa mandati abest inculpabiliter.*

As it is not the delegation of itself, but the contract of mandate which is supposed to have taken place between the person delegating and the creditor, which renders the former responsible for the insolvency of the debtor delegated, it is for the creditor who claims to avail himself of this contract of mandate, to prove by some writing that it has intervened and that he has only accepted the delegation at the risk of the person delegating. Such an agreement is not presumed: it was thus determined in a case reported by Bouvot.

Cujas *ad* L. 26, §. 2, ff. *mand. ad libr.* 33, *Paul. ad edic.* adduces a second exception to this principle, that although the delegation was not made on the condition that it should be at the risk of the person delegating, yet if, at the time of the delegation, the debtor delegated was insolvent, and his insolvency was unknown to the creditor, the person delegating ought to be answerable for it. This opinion of Cujas is grounded on equity. The delegation includes, between the person delegating and the creditor, a contract of the kind of those which are contracts of interest on both sides, in which each intends to receive as much as he gives. The equity of these agreements consists in their equality; they are iniquitous when one of the parties gives much and receives little in its place. According to these principles the delegation which you make to me of the sum of one thousand livres due you by Peter an insolvent person, in the room of a like sum which you owe me, is manifestly iniquitous; for by this delegation you receive the discharge of your debt of one thousand livres, which discharge is of the real and actual value of a thousand livres, and for this value of one thousand livres, which you receive of me, you give me a claim on an insolvent debtor, which is of no value or almost of none: it is therefore necessary, in order to repair the iniquity of the agreement, that you should be answerable to me for the insolvency of this debtor, whom I accepted through error for my debtor in your stead.

It would be otherwise if at the time of the delegation which you made me of this debtor in your stead, I had knowledge of his insolvency. The delegation in this case does not include a contract of the kind of those which are of interest on both sides; but it includes a beneficence which I have been willing to exercise towards you by accepting this debtor however insolvent, in your stead. You have done me no injury, since knowing this, I was willing to accept him: *volenti non fit injuria*.

Despeisses rejects the opinion of Cujas, and contends that unless it be expressly agreed that the person delegating delegates at his risk, *suo periculo*, the creditor can never complain of the insolvency of the debtor who was delegated to him, and whom he was willing to accept, notwithstanding any ignorance he may plead. His reason is, that otherwise the delegation would never have the effect of discharging the person delegating, which is the effect which it ought from its nature to have, since the creditor would always pretend that he was ignorant of the insolvency of of the debtor who was delegated to him.

These reasons may cause the opinion of Cujas to be rejected *in foro legis*; but it appears to me unquestionable *in foro conscientiæ*.

§. IV.

Difference between delegation, transfer, and simple indication.

569. It remains for us to obſerve that delegation differs from a transfer, as well as from ſimple indication.

The transfer which a creditor makes to another of his claim, includes no novation. It is the ſame claim that paſſes from the transferor to the transferee, who indeed is, properly ſpeaking, only a procurator *in rem suam* of the creditor who cedes it to him. Beſides this transfer paſſes only between two perſons, the transferor and transferee, without there being any occaſion for the intervention of the conſent of the debtor.

We have treated of the transfer in our treatiſe on the contract of ſale, *part* 6, *ch.* 3.

The novation differs alſo from ſimple indication.

When I indicate to my creditor a perſon from whom he ſhall receive the payment of the ſum which I owe him, and on whom I give him an order to this effect, this includes only a ſimple mandate. It includes neither a transfer nor a novation; I ſtill remain the debtor of my creditor; the perſon whom I indicate to him and on whom I give him an order, does not become his debtor in my ſtead.

Likewiſe, when a creditor indicates to his debtor a perſon to whom he may pay, this indication includes no novation; the debtor does not become a debtor of the perſon indicated to him, but remains always a debtor of the ſame creditor. See, on this kind of indication, *supra*, *ch.* 1, *art.* 2, §. 4.

CHAPTER III.

Of the release of a debt.

570. The releaſe which the creditor makes of the debt, is alſo one of the ways in which obligations are extinguiſhed; for it diſcharges the debtor *de jure*,

Article the First.

How the release of a debt is made.

§. I.

Whether the release of a debt may be made by a simple agreement.

571. According to the principles of the civil law there was a difference between civil obligations which resulted from contracts *ex consensu* or *consential*, which were contracted by the mere consent of the parties, and other civil obligations which resulted from contracts real, *in rem*, or from stipulation. With regard to those which were contracted by the mere consent of the parties, the release might have been made by a simple agreement, by which the creditor agreed with the debtor to hold him discharged; and this agreement extinguished the obligation *de pleno jure*. L. 35, ff. *de R. juris*. With regard to other civil obligations, in order that the release which the creditor made of it to the debtor might extinguish the obligation *de jure*, it was necessary to have recourse to the formality of the acceptilation, either *simple*, if the obligation resulted from a stipulation, or *Aquilian*, if it resulted from a contract real. See *tit. acceptil. in Instit. et Pandect.* The simple agreement by which the creditor agreed with the debtor to hold him discharged, did not extinguish these obligations *de jure*; but it only gave to the debtor an exception or plea to the action of the creditor who should have demanded the payment of the debt against the faith of the agreement.

This distinction and these subtilties are not received in our law: we do not recognise the form of acceptilation; and all the debts, whatever they may be, and in whatever manner they have been contracted, are extinguished *de jure* by the simple agreement of release between the creditor and the debtor, provided that the creditor be capable of disposing of his property, and the debtor was not a person to whom it was unlawful for the creditor to give.

Therefore what is said under the title in the Digest *de*

accept.; of the form of acceptilation, does not receive any application in our law, and particularly the acceptilation cannot be made under a condition; L. 4, ff. *de acceptilat.*

Among us nothing prevents the creditor from making the release which he makes of the debt depend on a condition; and the effect of such release is to render the debt conditional, as if it had been contracted under a contrary condition.

§. II.

In what case one may presume a tacit release.

572. The release of a debt may be made not only by an express agreement but also by a tacit agreement, which results from certain facts which give room to presume it. For example. If the creditor has given the debtor his note of hand or obligation before a notary, he is presumed to have released the debt. *Si debitori meo reddiderim cautionem, videtur inter nos convenisse ne peterem;* L. 2, §. 1, ff. *de pact.*

If the note was subscribed by several debtors *in solidum*, and the creditor had delivered it to one of them, some authors cited by Bruneman *ad* L. 2, ff. *de pact.*, have thought that the return of the note ought to be presumed in this case only a personal discharge of the debt, which the creditor intended to grant to him to whom he has released the note. It appears to me on the contrary that one ought to presume that he intended to release and extinguish entirely the debt; for if he had intended to discharge only one of his debtors, he would have retained the note which would have been necessary to him in order to procure payment from the others.

573. Does the possession of the note which the debtor is found to have, make it presumable that the creditor has returned it to him? Boiceau, after some antient authors, makes a distinction; he says that if the debtor alledges that he has paid, his possession of the note makes the payment presumable and gives room to believe that the note has been rendered up to him as paid, unless the creditor proves

the contrary; but if he alledges that the creditor has released to him the debt, his possession of the note is not of itself sufficient, and he ought to prove that the creditor has intentionally released to him and rendered up his note; because the release is a donation which is not to be presumed, according to this rule, *Nemo donare facile præsumitur*; and besides that it is an agreement which ought, according to the ordinance, to be established by writing. I do not think this distinction solid. I think we ought to decide without distinction that the possession of the note by the debtor should make it presumable that it has been rendered to him by the creditor, either as discharged or as released; unless the creditor proves the contrary, *putà*, that the note has been stolen from him. In vain may it be said that the donation is not to be presumed; for this signifies that it is not slightly to be presumed, and without a sufficient ground for such presumption. According to the law cited, there is a sufficient ground to presume the donation and the release of the debt, when the creditor has released the note to the debtor; and the possession of the note by the debtor ought also to make it presumable that the creditor has returned it to him, since this is the natural way by which the possession of it has passed from the creditor with whom it was, to the debtor. The agreement drawn from the ordinance which directs that agreements, the object of which exceeds one hundred livres, should be proved by writing, is not better. The ordinance intended only to exclude proof by witnesses, and not presumptions resulting from facts avowed by the parties.

The distinction of Boiceau upon the quality of the debtor is more plausible. If the debtor was the factor of the creditor, or other domestic who had it in his power to take the note, the possession which he should have of the note would not be a sufficient presumption, either of the release or of the payment of the debt. *Idem*, if it was a neighbour to whose house the creditor had carried his effects, in the case of fire.

What is decided in regard to a note or obligation before a notary, ought not to extend to an engrossed copy of a contract of annuity, or of an obligation of which there is a minute. Although this engrossed instrument is found in the hands of the debtor, there does not result therefrom a sufficient presumption of the payment or the release of the debt, unless other circumstances concur: for the copy which remains with the notary and which is not discharged, reclaims the debt in favor of the creditor, from whom the engrossed instrument has been stolen, or who, trusting to the copy, has parted with it and confided it to the debtor.

574. The restitution which the creditor has made to the debtor of the things which he has given him in pledge for his debt, causes neither the release nor the payment of the debt to be presumed. L. 3, ff. *de pact.*: for he has only intended by this to release to him the pledge, and not to release to him the debt.

575. A creditor is presumed to have released the liability *in solidum* of the debtors *in solidum*, when he has admitted them to pay only their part. See *supra*, *n.* 277, *& seq.*

576. When after a synallagmatic contract made between us, before it has been performed on either part, a new agreement takes place between us, by which it is said that I discharge you from this contract, you are presumed tacitly to have discharged me from the reciprocal obligation which I have contracted towards you. For example. If after you have sold me a thing, we agree that I discharge you from the sale which you have made to me, you are presumed likewise to have discharged me from my purchase. L. 23, ff. *de accept.*

577. The omission to reserve a debt, in the acquittance which the creditor gives of another debt, forms no presumption of the release of the debt of which there has not been a reservation. L. 29, ff. *de oblig. & act.*

Likewife, if in an account between two parties who had dealings together in trade, one of them has not comprifed an article of debt which he had againft the other, there refults no prefumption of the releafe of this debt: it will be prefumed on the contrary that it was an omiffion made by forgetfulnefs, which fhould not prevent the creditor from exacting his debt, notwithftanding the account in which it has not been comprifed.

Yet there may refult a prefumption of the releafe of a debt not comprifed in the account, when three circumftances concur. I. When the creditor and the debtor were united by the ties of blood or ftrict friendfhip; II. when it is not made for a fingle account between the parties, but feveral, in neither of which the debt has been comprifed; III. when the creditor is dead without having demanded it. From the concurrence of thefe three circumftances, Papinian derives a prefumption fufficient to releafe the debt. This is the decifion of the celebrated law *Procula*, 26, ff. *de probat.*

§. III.

Whether the release may be made by the single will of the creditor without an agreement.

578. We have feen that the releafe of a debt may be validly made by an agreement expreffed or tacit, between the creditor and the debtor. Some authors think that it may be made by the fingle will of the creditor who fhould declare that he makes the releafe, provided he fhould be capable of difpofing of his property. This is the opinion of Barbeyrac in his notes on Puffendorf. His reafon is that every one who has the difpofal of his property may by his fingle will renounce the rights which belong to him, and that he lofes them in renouncing them. Paul, in law 2, §. 1, ff. *pro derel.*, decides expreffly that one may by his fingle will renounce and lofe the right of property in a thing corporate which belongs to him. For the fame reafon we may by our fingle will renounce the right of a claim which we have againft a debtor; and as there cannot be any debt

without a claim by him towards whom it has been contracted, the renunciation and abandonment which the creditor makes of his claim, necessarily draws after it the extinction of the debt. According to these principles, if a creditor at Orleans has written to his debtor at Marseilles a letter, in which he mentions to him that he has released to him his debt, although the debtor be dead since the writing of the letter, but before it had reached him, so that one could not say that any engagement took place between the creditor and him, yet according to the principles of Barbeyrac, it must be decided that the debt is extinguished, and that the creditor who has by this letter declared his intention to renounce his debt, is not to be received to demand it from the heirs of the debtor.

I do not think that the opinion of Barbeyrac can be followed in practice. I would willingly agree with him that, in supposing an abstract case, a creditor who should have an absolute intent to abdicate his claim, might by his single will extinguish it; but when a creditor declares that he makes a release to his debtor of his debt, it is not this absolute will to renounce his claim which we ought to suppose in him, but rather the intention to make of it a donation to his debtor. Therefore, as every donation requires the acceptance of the donee, we ought to think that this creditor only intended to abdicate his right when the release and the donation which he was willing to make to his debtor, should receive their perfection by the acceptance of this debtor. Therefore, in the instance proposed, I think we ought to decide, contrary to the principle of Barbeyrac, that the release of a debt expressed by a letter ought not to have any effect, if the debtor to whom the release may have been made, is dead before the letter reached him. Admitting even that the principle of Barbeyrac ought to be followed, this could only be when the release is absolute: when it is made under certain conditions, it is evident that it cannot have effect before the debtor has accepted the conditions.

§. IV.

Whether the release may be made for a part.

579. The releafe of a debt may be made for the whole or for a part. The civil law excepted, in regard to the acceptilation, the cafe in which the thing was not fufceptible of parts. For example. If I had obliged myfelf towards you to impofe upon my eftate a certain right of way for the benefit of yours, the acceptilation of this debt could not be made by parts; L. 13, §. 1, ff. *de acceptil.* But among us nothing prevents a like debt from being releafed for a part, as for the half, third, &c. and the effect of this releafe will be that you can not exact from me this right of way without making me fatisfaction for the moiety of the price or for the third.

ARTICLE II.

Of the different kinds of release.

We may diftinguifh two different kinds of releafe, which a creditor may make of his debt; one which we call a releafe *rei*, the other which we call a difcharge *personæ*.

§.

Of the release rei.

580. The releafe *rei* is when the creditor declares that he holds the debt to be difcharged, or when he gives an acquittance of it, as if he had received payment; although he had not received it.

This releafe is equivalent to payment, and makes the thing no longer due; and confequently it difcharges all thofe who were debtors of it; as there can be no longer debtors when there is nothing due.

§. II.

Of the discharge perfonæ.

581. The releafe or difcharge *personæ* is that by which the creditor fimply difcharges the debtor of his obligation. This difcharge *magis eximit personam debitoris ab obligatione, quam extinguit obligationem:* it only extinguifhes the debt

indirectly, in the case in which the debtor to whom it should be granted, should be the only principal debtor; because there cannot be a debt without a debtor.

But if there are two or several debtors *in solidum*, the discharge granted to one does not extinguish the debt; it discharges him only to whom it is granted and not his co-debtor. The debt is extinguished however for the part of him to whom the discharge is granted, and the other remains bound only for the surplus. The reason is, that if each owed the whole, this was only on condition that the creditor should grant to him his rights and actions against the other. The creditor having put it, by his own act, out of his power to cede them against him whom he has discharged, the other ought not to suffer therefor, as we have seen *supra, n.* 520, *page* 67. The discharge granted to the principal debtor carries with it that of his securities; for he would be ineffectually discharged if his securities were not: since his securities, being obliged to pay, would have recourse against this debtor; besides there cannot be a security without a principal debtor. This rule receives however a sort of exception in regard to contracts of composition, *supra, n.* 380.

Contra, vice versa, the discharge granted to the security, does not discharge the principal debtor: for the obligation of the security depends entirely upon that of the principal debtor, but that of the principal debtor does not depend upon that of the security. There cannot be a security without a principal debtor, but there may be a principal debtor without a security.

The discharge *personæ* granted to a security, does not any more discharge his co-securities. L. 23, ff. *de pact.* L. 15, §. 1, ff. *de fidejuss.* Yet if the securities could have counted upon the recourse which they would have in paying, against this security whom the creditor has discharged, having contracted their securityship with him, or after, it is equitable that the discharge granted to this security should discharge them, as to the part for which, in paying, they would have had recourse against this security if he had not been discharged. The creditor not having power, in discharging this security and depriving them of this recourse, to prejudice them, they may in this case oppose, for this part, to the creditor, the plea *cedendarum actionum*, as we have seen, *supra, n.* 520.

This decision, that the discharge granted to a security, neither discharges the principal debtor nor the co-securities, applies even when the creditor had received a sum of money from the security for his discharge from the securitiship. This principal debtor will not therefore be discharged from any thing; for this sum is not given in payment and to come in deduction of the debt, but it is given for the price of the discharge from the securitiship.

§. III.

Whether the creditor may lawfully receive any thing from a security for his discharge, without applying it to the debt; and several questions which depend hereon.

582. What we have just said brings us to the celebrated question, whether, when a person has become a security towards me, for a debtor to whom I have lent a sum of money, I may not only in *foro legis*, but also in *foro conscientiæ*, receive something from the security for his discharge from the securitiship, and exact afterwards from the principal debtor the entire sum which I have lent him, without allowing him what I have received from the security. Dumoulin in his treatise on Usury, 9, 34, decides that I may lawfully do so, provided that when I discharged the security there was room to apprehend the insolvency of the principal debtor. I do not commit in so doing any usury; for usury consists in receiving something beyond the sum loaned, as the price and reward of the loan; it consists in making a gain for a service which ought to be gratuitous; but in this case the sum which I have received from the security, and which I retain besides the sum that I loaned, which has since been paid to me in full, is not a sum which I receive as the price and reward of the loan I made; I have received it for quite a different cause. The

risque of the insolvency of the debtor which was to be feared, was a risque that was to fall on the security and not on me. I am willing to take this risque on myself, and discharge the security from it. I am not obliged to do it for nothing. This risque is appreciable and I may lawfully receive a sum of money as the price of this risque. *Finge.* I was creditor of Peter for the sum of twelve thousand livres; you were his security. The affairs of Peter were on a decline; there was room to fear that he would not be able to pay ten shillings in the pound. This risque was yours. You offer me three thousand livres to take that risque on myself, in discharging you from your securitiship. I accept your offer. It happens afterwards that the affairs of Peter take a better turn, and he pays me in full. I gain the three thousand livres which I received from you. This gain is quite lawful; it is the price of the risque which I have been willing to run, in your place, of losing six thousand livres and perhaps more. The principal debtor has no room to complain, nor have you. The principal debtor cannot; for he has paid only what he owed and no more: nor can you complain, for if you have given me three thousand livres above the sum that was due me, I have given you an equivalent for it, by taking on myself, in your stead, the risque of losing six thousand livres or more. It is an aleatory contract that has intervened, which is as lawful as a contract of insurance. It will be said, perhaps, that it is a principle in matters of loan, that the risque of the insolvency of the debtor cannot give a right to the creditor to receive any thing beyond the principal sum that is due him. I answer that this principle is true only with regard to the debtor. The risque that the creditor runs of losing the money he lends him, by his insolvency, cannot give him the right to exact from him any thing beyond this sum; because to the debtor this overplus would be an absolute loss; he receives nothing for it: his poverty ought to be a reason that he should be favored rather than charged. But the risque of the insolvency of the debtor may give a right to the creditor to receive something from a third perſon who has undertaken this riſque, when the creditor takes it on himſelf, in his ſtead; for this third perſon receives ſomething for what he gives, viz. a diſcharge from the riſque.

When there is no room to apprehend the inſolvency of the debtor, Dumoulin in this caſe, decides, *ibidem*, that the creditor cannot lawfully receive any thing from the ſecurity to diſcharge him from the ſecuritiſhip. It may be objected to this opinion, that the right which I had againſt the ſecurity was a right that was in *bonis*, which made part of my property. I give him this right when I diſcharge him; why may I not be permitted to receive ſomething from him in the place of what I give him? I anſwer that according to the rules of commutative juſtice, I cannot exact in the place of the thing which I have given, more than the equivalent of this thing, that is to ſay, more than the amount to which it is appreciable. If it be appreciable to nothing, I cannot exact any thing for it. Such is, in this caſe, the right which I had againſt the ſecurity and of which I have made him a gift and releaſe. *Finge*. I have a good claim againſt Peter for one thouſand piſtoles; there is no room to fear his inſolvency: he has real property to the amount of ten times that ſum, which is hypothecated for my claim. You were his ſecurity. I diſcharge you from your ſecuritiſhip: to how much can the right which reſulted from this ſecuritiſhip be appreciated? My claim, with all the rights that reſulted from it, was worth one thouſand piſtoles and no more; without the ſecuritiſhip from which I have diſcharged you, my claim is ſtill worth the full ſum of one thouſand piſtoles; ſince it is well ſecured: conſequently the right which I have given up to you is not appreciable to any thing; in giving it I ſuffer no diminution in my property, and conſequently I cannot lawfully receive any thing for it.

Obſerve that when a ſecurity has given ſomething to the creditor to be diſcharged from his ſecuritiſhip, it ought to be preſumed *in foro legis* that there was room to fear the infolvency of the debtor; for one is not prefumed to give without caufe; *Nemo res suas jactare facile præsumitur.*

Although it fhould be fully proved that there was no room to fear that the debtor would become infolvent, when the fecurity gave money to be difcharged from his fecuritihip, the fecurity, in the cafe in which the debt was not yet difcharged, would not have the right to recall what he has given, except under offers to become and continue bound as he was before the difcharge which has been given to him. *Molin. ibidem.*

The fecurity may alfo in this cafe offer to pay the debt, in applying and deducting what he has given, without caufe to be difcharged from his fecuritifhip; and if it was an annuity for which the fecurity was given, this application fhould be made firft upon the arrearages which are due, and afterwards upon the principal. He may, in making the payment, exact the fubrogation to the rights of the creditor; for although he has been difcharged, he ought not to be regarded as an entire ftranger, fince he makes the payment in order to procure for himfelf a fatisfaction for what he has already given to be difcharged. *Molin. ibidem.*

In regard to the principal debtor, he may never reclaim from the creditor what the creditor has unduly received in order to difcharge the fecurity, nor retain for it any part of the fum which he owes, when he pays: for the fecurity having no recourfe againft the principal debtor for the fum which he has unduly given for the difcharge of his fecuritifhip, the principal debtor is without intereft.

But if the fecurity had a recourfe againft the principal debtor for the fum which he has given for the difcharge of his fecuritifhip, as if the principal debtor was obliged towards him to pay the debt in a certain time, and they had agreed that after the debtor had made default of fo doing, he fhould permit the fecurity to purchafe from the creditor the difcharge of his fecuritifhip on the beft terms he could, for which he ſhould be indemnified by the principal debtor; in this caſe it is not to be doubted that the principal debtor may retain this ſum and deduct it from the debt when he ſhall pay it to the creditor; for by means of the recourſe which the ſecurity has againſt him it is the ſame as if he had paid it to the creditor. *Molin. ibidem.*

ARTICLE III.

What persons may make a release and to whom.

§. I.

What persons may make a release.

583. It is only ſuch a creditor as has the power to diſpoſe of his property who may releaſe a debt, or one deriving a ſpecial power from him to make this releaſe.

An attorney with general power, for all one's affairs, a tutor, a curator, an adminiſtrator, have not this right. L. 37, ff. *de pact.* L. 22, ff. *de adm. tut. & passim;* for all thoſe perſons have only a power and capacity to adminiſter and not to give: the releaſe is a donation.

We muſt except the releaſe which is made of part of the debt to a debtor in caſe of his bankruptcy. As it is not made ſo much *animo donandi*, as with the intention of ſecuring in this way the payment of the ſurplus of the debt, and preventing a loſs of the whole, this releaſe may paſs for an act of adminiſtration, of which theſe perſons are capable. The releaſes which are made of a part of feudal rent to a perſon who comes to compound for ſuch rents, before he concludes the bargain for the eſtate which he propoſes to purchaſe, are alſo acts of adminiſtration which tutors and other adminiſtrators may make; for theſe releaſes are as compoſitions rather than donations: they are not made as much *animo donandi*, as to avoid the loſs of a profit; the refuſal of the releaſe may cauſe the bargain for the eſtate to fail.

Tutors and other adminiſtrators may make a releaſe of part of the rents, even after the bargain is concluded, and in the caſe of neceſſary commutations, provided they be not excessive and are conformable to those which are usually made: for although one cannot deny that such releases are true donations, *liberalitas nullo jure cogente facta*, yet custom has made these releases, not indeed an obligation, but a sort of duty of prudence; and donations which are of this description are not forbidden to tutors and other administrators. *Arg.* L. 12, §. 3, ff. *de adm. tut.*

It is upon this foundation that the receivers of the king's rents are authorised to make a release of a fourth, which is passed to them in the chamber of accounts, provided that the purchasers declare their purchase and pay in three months. *Letters patent*, 1556, cited by Livoniere, *Traite des Fiefs.*

When there are several creditors *in solidum, correi credendi*, one of them may without the others make a release of the debt; and this release discharges the debtor towards all the creditors, as if the payment had beeu really made to all. L. 13, §. 12, ff. *de accept.*

§. II.

To whom the release may be made.

584. It is evident that the release of a debt can only be made to the debtor. For it is presumed to be made to the debtor, whether the agreement which includes this release intervene with the debtor himself or with his tutor, curator, attorney or other administrators of his goods.

Relations in the ascending line having by the ordinance of one thousand seven hundred and thirty one, *art.* 7, capacity to accept of donations made to their minors, although they be not under their tutorship; it is a consequence that they may validly accept the release which the creditor of their minors would make to them.

585. When there are several debtors *in solidum*, the creditor may by the release of the debt which he makes to one of them, extinguish the debt and discharge all the others: L. 16, ff. *d. tit.*; but it is necessary that it should appear that the creditor had an intention to discharge the debt: for if he had only an intention to discharge the person

of the debtor, his co-debtors are not discharged, except for the part of him who has been discharged, as it has been said in a preceding paragraph.

586. The release being a donation, it is necessary, in order that it may be valid, that the debtor to whom it is given should not be a person to whom the laws forbid it to be given: the release which a woman should make to her husband of what he owed her, or that which a sick man should make to his physician, would not be valid.

This ought not to extend to releases which are made rather by composition than by donation, such as those made in case of bankruptcy and compositions for feudal rents.

Although the release of a part of a feudal rent, made to a person to whom the laws do not permit it to be given, has not been made in the form of a composition, but as an absolute gift, as in the case of a necessary commutation, it ought to be valid, and ought not to pass for a prohibited donation, when it does not exceed those which the lord is accustomed to make to strangers, as when it is only the release of a fourth.

CHAPTER IV.

Of set-off.

587. SET-OFF is the extinction which is made of debts of which two persons are reciprocally the debtors, one to the other, by the credits of which they are reciprocally creditors, one to the other: *Compensatio debiti & crediti inter se contributio.* L. 1, ff. *de compens.* For example. If I owe you the sum of five hundred livres, as for a loan which you have made me of this sum, and on the other side I am your creditor of the like sum of five hundred livres, as for the lease of my house, which has since run out; the debt for which I am bound towards you will be extinguished by the right to oppose as a set-off the claim of the like

ſum which I have againſt you; and *vice versa*, the debt for which you are bound towards me will be extinguiſhed by the claim which you have againſt me.

The equity of a ſet-off is evident. It is eſtabliſhed upon the common intereſt of the parties between whom the ſet-off is made. It is evident that they have each an intereſt to make the ſet-off, rather than to be obliged to draw from the pocket to pay what they owe and bring ſuit for the payment of what is due to them. This is the reaſon which Pomponius adduces in the law 3, ff. *de compens. Ideo compensatio necessaria est, quia interest nostra potius non solvere, quam solutum repetere.* Add that the ſet-off avoids an uſeleſs circuity. *Quod potest brevius per unum actum expediri compensando, incassum protraheretur per plures solutiones & repetitiones.* This is the reaſon which Baldus gives of the right of ſet-off.

We ſhall ſee on this ſubject, I. againſt what debts a ſet-off may be oppoſed; II. what debts may be oppoſed as a ſet-off; III. how a ſet-off is made, and what are its effects.

§. I.

Against what debts a set-off may be opposed.

588. One may regularly oppoſe a ſet-off againſt debts of all things which are ſuſceptible of it.

Debts of things ſuſceptible of a ſet-off are the debts of a certain ſum of money, of a certain quantity of corn, wine and of other things determinable by number, weight or meaſure. The debt of a thing indeterminate of a certain kind, although it be not of the number of things ſo determinable, is alſo ſuſceptible of a ſet-off. For example. If by a bargain made between us, you have obliged yourſelf to give me a horſe *indeterminately*, without ſaying what horſe; this debt of a horſe, of which I am creditor by our bargain, is ſuſceptible of a ſet-off, and if afterwards, before I have been paid it, I become the only heir of a perſon who has bequeathed to you a horſe *indeterminately*, and in this quality your debtor of a horſe, it is evident that you could oppose to me as a set-off this debt of a horse of which I am debtor towards you by the testament of him to whom I have succeeded, against the debt of a horse of which you are debtor towards me by our bargain.

On the contrary, when a thing, although in its nature a thing determinable by number, weight or measure, is due as a thing certain and determinate, the debt is not susceptible of a set-off. For example, If I have purchased of you the six hogsheads of wine which you have made this year in your vineyard of St. Denis, and on the other side before you have delivered them to me, I have become the only heir of a person who has bequeathed to you six hogsheads of wine by his will, and in this quality your debtor of this quantity of six hogsheads of wine; you cannot oppose to me, against the debt of six hogsheads of wine of your vintage, which I have purchased of you, that of six hogsheads of wine of which I am the debtor towards you: and I shall be right in demanding that, without having regard to this set-off, you should be holden to deliver to me the six hogsheads of your vintage which I have purchased of you, on offering to give you six other hogsheads of wine good and merchantable, such as I might choose. The reason is, that as a set-off is a reciprocal payment which the two parties make to each other, a creditor cannot be obliged to receive as a set-off any other thing than what he would be obliged to receive in payment: according to the rule, *Aliud prò alio invito creditori solvi non potest, supra, n.* 494. The creditor of a thing certain and determinate cannot be obliged to receive in payment another thing than the thing certain and determinate which is due him; and one will not be received to offer him in payment another thing, although of the same kind with the thing certain and determinate which is due him. For the same reason, one cannot oblige him to accept as a set-off against the debt of a thing certain and determinate which is due him, the debt of things of the same kind of which he is debtor. The debt of a thing certain and determinate, although of the number, of things determinable by number, weight or measure, does not therefore admit of a set-off.

There is one case however in which the debt of a thing certain and determinate may be susceptible of a set-off; for if I were your creditor of an undivided part of a thing certain, as if you had sold me the undivided part which you had in a certain estate, and before you delivered it to me, I should become the heir of a person who was your debtor of another undivided part in the same estate; you might oppose, against the debt of the part of this estate for which you were bound towards me, the set-off of the debt of the part in the same estate for which I was bound towards you. *Sebast. de Medicis, Tract. de compens. p.* 1, §. 3.

589. When the thing due is susceptible of a set-off, one may oppose a set-off against the debt of this thing, from whatever cause this debt may proceed.

One may oppose it even against the debt of a sum due in virtue of a judgment. L. 2. *Cod. de compens.*

There are however some debts against which the debtor is not listened to in proposing a set-off.

I. In the case of spoliation, one may not oppose any set-off against the demand for the restitution of the things of which one has been despoiled, according to this maxim so well known: *Spoliatus ante omnia restituendus.* See *Sebast. de Medicis, Tract. de Compens. p.* 2, §. 28.

II. A depositary is not admitted to oppose any set-off against the demand which is made on him for the restitution of the deposit that has been confided to him. *In causa depositi compensationi locus non est.* *Paul, sent.* 11, 12, 13.

This text of Paul ought to be understood principally of an irregular deposit, such as that which is spoken of in the laws 24, 25, §. 1, & 26, §. 1, ff. *depos.*, by which one gives in trust to another a sum of money, to put it with other sums which are deposited by other persons and return, not the same pieces of money, but the same sum. If the deposit was an ordinary deposit, such as that of a bag of money sealed and marked, there would be no room for a set-off, not only because it is a deposit, but from the general rule that debts of a thing certain are not susceptible of it.

The depositary cannot indeed oppose, against the restitution of the deposit which is demanded from him, a set-off of claims which he might have against him who has confided it to him, when these claims have a cause not connected with the deposit; but when the cause for which the depositary is a creditor of him who has confided to him the deposit, proceeds from the deposit itself, as when he is a creditor for the expences which were necessary for the preservation of the deposit; not only has he in this case the right to a set-off, when the deposit is an irregular deposit; but even when it is a thing certain which is the object of the deposit, he has the right to retain it, *quasi quodam jure pignoris*, until he shall be paid his claim. This is the common decision of the authors cited by *Sebast. Med. Tract. de Compens. p.* 1, §. 19.

It is according to this principle that the receivers of consignations retain upon the sums consigned, the fees of consignation attributed to their offices.

III. The debt of a sum which has been given or bequeathed to me to serve for my maintenance, and with the clause that it shall not be liable to my creditors, is a debt against which one cannot oppose to me any set-off: for as this clause prevents it from being seised by third persons and employed in the payment of what I might owe to third persons, it prevents it, for the same reason, from being employed as a set-off in the payment of what I might owe to him who is the debtor of it. Sebastian de Medicis, *Tract. de comp. p.* 1, §. 11, adduces another reason for this decision, viz. that as maintenance is a thing necessary for life, this would be a sort of homicide, which he would commit who is charged to furnish them, if he should refuse them under any pretext whatever, even that of a set-off. *Necare videtur qui alimonia denegat*; L. 4, *de agnosc. liber.*

IV. A tenant cannot oppose as a set-off a sum which should be due him from the lord, in order to discharge himself from his obligation to go or send, at the day and place accustomed, to pay him the rent which he owes him.

The reaſon is that the debt of feudal rent includes not only a debt of a ſum of money, but that of an acknowlegment of tenure, which is ſomething valuable and therefore is not ſuſceptible of a ſet-off.

Feudal rent is not ſuſceptible of a ſet-off even againſt a debt of the like nature. *Finge.* I owe you for an eſtate ſituated within your ſeigniory three farthings rent, payable at your manor-houſe on St. Martin's day, on pain of five ſous for default. You owe me for an eſtate ſituated within my ſeigniory the like ſum of three farthings rent, payable the ſame day under the penalty of three other farthings only for default; a ſet-off cannot take place in this inſtance and we cannot thus diſcharge one another from going to pay the feudal rents. The reaſon is that a ſet-off, in order that it may take place, ſhould give to each of the parties what belongs to him. For example. If I owe you five hundred livres, and you ſhould owe me as much, a ſet-off, by the diſcharge which it procures me from the five hundred livres, I owe you, gives me truly the five hundred livres which were due me by you; for the diſcharge from your claim of five hundred livres, is worth truly five hundred livres. But in our inſtance, the diſcharge from the acknowlegment of tenure for the eſtate which I hold of you, cannot cauſe the like acknowlegment to me for that which you hold of me: there cannot therefore in this caſe be room for a ſet-off, ſince it cannot give to each of us what belongs to us: beſides *monumenta cenſuum interturbarentur; Molin. in Conſ. Par. ad art.* 85, *gl.* 1, *n.* 38.

Obſerve that feudal rent is not ſuſceptible of a ſet-off, in this ſenſe, that the tenant cannot be diſcharged from going or ſending to pay the rent; but it may be ſuſceptible of it in this ſenſe, that the tenant who is a creditor of his lord for a ſum of money, may go at the day and place at which the rent is payable and offer to his lord in the place of the ſum of money which he owes for rent, a diſcharge of the like ſum for that which is due him by his lord; for he ſatisfies, in going to the place and making these offers, the obligation of attornment. This set-off ought not however to be permitted, except when the rent consists of a considerable sum, and it ought not to take place for small rents; *Molin. ibid.*

A question has heretofore been put, whether the debtor who has obliged himself by oath to the payment of the debt, may in *foro conscientiæ*, as in *foro legis*, oppose as a set-off what is due him by his creditor. Several authors, especially canonists, have maintained the negative, for a frivolous reason that the oath ought to be accomplished *in forma specifica*. The opinion of those who hold the affirmative is the best. The oath, added to an obligation, serves only to render the debtor more culpable when he contravenes it, and to induce him, by the fear of rendering himself guilty of perjury, not to contravene it; but the obligation, although confirmed by an oath, remains the same, and the oath cannot prevent its being discharged in any way in which obligations may be discharged, and consequently by set-off. *Seb. Medicis, Tract. de Comp. p.* 2, §. 25.

One may oppose a set-off not only against debts which are due from particular persons, but also against those which are due from cities, bodies corporate or communities. The law 3, *Cod. de compens.*, excepts however certain kinds of debts due to cities, against which it does not permit a debter to oppose any set-off of what the city should owe him.

The law 1, *Cod. d. tit.*, admits of a set-off even against the treasury, provided however that the debt from which I defend myself by the set-off as well as that which is opposed as a set-off, are depending each in the same office. *Rescriptum est compensationi in causa fiscali locum esse, si eadem statio quid debeat quæ petit; d. L.* 1. For example. I cannot oppose a set-off against my capitation tax which I owe at Orleans, the arrearages which are due me from another branch of the revenue at Paris.

§. II.

What debts may be opposed as a set-off.

590. In order that a debt may be opposed as a set-off, it is necessary, 1. that the thing due be of the same kind with that which makes the object of the debt against which the set-off is opposed. *Compensatio debiti ex pari specie, licet ex causa dispari, admittitur. Paul. sent.* 11, v. 3. For example, I would oppose as a set-off against a sum of money which I owe you, the debt of a like sum of money which you owe me: these debts are of the same kind, *ex pari specie*. But I cannot oppose as a set-off against a sum of money which I owe you, the debt of a certain quantity of corn which you owe me.

The reason is, that as a set-off is a payment, and as I cannot pay my creditor against his will another thing than what I owe him, *supra, n.* 494, I cannot, for the same reason, oblige him to receive as a set-off against the sum of money which I owe him, the corn which he owes me: for this would oblige him to receive corn for the money which is due to him; consequently to receive in payment another thing than what is due him.

Although one cannot oppose, against the debt of a thing certain and determinate, the debt of a quantity, although of things of the same kind, as we have seen in the preceding article, *n.* 588; *contra, vice versa*, one may against the debt of a quantity oppose the set-off of a thing certain and determinate of the same kind. For example. I am your creditor of six hogsheads of wine of your vintage, which you have sold me, and at the same time your debtor of six hogsheads of wine *in genere*, which a person to whom I have succeeded has bequeathed to you; you cannot oppose to me, against the debt of six hogsheads of wine which you have sold me, that of the six hogsheads *in genere* which I owe you: because you are not permitted to pay me any other thing than the same six hogsheads of wine. On the contrary, if you demand of me the payment of six hogsheads of wine *in genere* which I owe you, I may oppose to you as a set-off, the debt of the six hogsheads of wine which you have sold me; because if you had delivered them to me, I might give them to you in payment of the six hogsheads of wine which I owe you.

Observe however that as this set-off *speciei mihi debitæ ad quantitatem*, depends on my choice, it does not take place but from the day on which I declare my choice and oppose the set-off; whereas a set-off which is made *quantitatis ad quantitatem*, takes place from the moment the creditor becomes debtor, as we shall see, *infra*.

591. It is necessary, II. that the debt which is opposed as a set-off should be a debt whereof the payment has fallen due. *Quod in diem debetur, non compensabitur antequam dies veniat.* L. 7, ff. *de compens.* The reason is evident. A set-off is a reciprocal payment which the parties make to each other; the debtor of a debt whereof the payment has not yet fallen due, not being yet bound to pay, is not yet bound to admit the set-off of it against his demand.

The time of payment, the arrival of which is necessary for the set-off, is the time which the debtor has of right in virtue of the agreement. It is otherwise of a time of grace which may have been granted to him. For example. If I have a judgment against my debtor for the sum of one thousand livres, which I lent him, and by the judgment he has granted him the time of three months to pay it, and in one month after the judgment this debtor, becoming heir of my creditor to whom I owe the like sum of one thousand livres, demands of me this sum, I may oppose to him as a set-off the debt of one thousand livres which he owes me, although the time of three months which was granted him is not expired: for this time is but a time of grace granted only for the purpose of arresting the rigor of constraint, but which cannot arrest the set-off: *Aliud est diem obligationis non venisse, aliud humanitatis gratia tempus indulgeri solutionis*; L. 16, §. 1, ff. *de compens.*

592. It is necessary, III. that the debt which is opposed as a set-off should be liquidated; L. *fin.* §. 1, *Cod. de compens.*

A debt is liquidated when it is known what is due, and how much; *cum certum est an et quantum debeatur.*

A contested debt therefore is not liquidated and cannot be opposed as a set-off, unless he who opposes it has the proof of it at hand and is able to prove it readily and summarily.

Although it should even be known that something is due, yet while it is not known how much is due, and the liquidation depends on an acount which would require a long discussion, the debt is not liquidated and cannot be opposed as a set-off.

593. It is necessary, IV. that the debt should be determinate. Therefore if one has charged his heir to give me one hundred pistoles, or his two carriage horses, and I owe the like sum of one hundred pistoles to this heir, I cannot oppose to him as a set-off the hundred pistoles which have been bequeathed to me, while he has a choice of the hundred pistoles or the horses: because this sum is not due *determinately.* But if the testator had given me the choice of them, I might oppose the set-off, which however would take place only from the day on which I made my choice: *Si debeas decem millia aut hominem, utrum volet adversarius; ita compensatio admittitur, si adversarius palam dixisset utrum voluisset;* L. 22.

594. It is necessary, V. that the debt be due to the same person who opposes it as a set-off. *Ejus quod non ei debetur qui convenitur, sed alii, compensatio fieri non potest.* L. 9, *cod. d. tit.*

Therefore I cannot oppose, against what I owe, a set-off of what my creditor owes to my father, my children, to those of whom I am tutor, curator or administrator, or to my wife who has a separation of estate. If there is a community of estate between us, what is due to her, is actually due to me; consequently I may oppose it as a set-off.

Papinian, in the law 18. §. 1, ff. *de compens.*, carries this principle so far as to decide that my creditor is not obliged to accept the set-off of what he owes to another as well as to me, although this third person, his creditor should intervene and offer to make a set-off for me of what is due him. *Creditor compensare non cogitur quod alii quam debitori suo debet, quamvis creditor ejus, pro eo qui convehitur, proprium debitum velit compensare. Finge.* You bring a suit against me for the sum of one hundred livres, which I owe you; you owe the like sum to Peter, and I signify to you an instrument of writing by which Peter consents that the sum of one hundred livres which you owe him should be opposed as a set-off against that which you demand of me; and I consequently plead the set-off to be discharged from your suit, of which I offer to pay the costs. Papinian pretends that you are not obliged to admit this set-off; but Barbeyrac in his notes on Puffendorf thinks, with reason, that Papinian has carried too far the subtilty, and that the set-off ought to be admitted, for it being indifferent to you to receive of me or Peter the hundred livres which I owe you, it is unjust that your suit should be maintained against me for the payment of this sum, when Peter is willing that you should receive this sum of him for me as a set-off of that which you owe him.

We may reconcile Barbeyrac with Papinian by a distinction. If the sum which I owe Peter is equal to that which you owe me, I cannot prevent its being opposed as a set-off against that which you owe me, when you make Peter intervene, who consents that it should be so opposed: this is the case in which the decision of Barbeyrac ought to be followed. But if the sum which I owe to Peter is less than that which you owe me, any offer which Peter should make to suffer the sum which you owe him to be opposed as a set-off against that which I owe you, would not oblige you, according to the decision of Papinian, to admit this set-off, unless I offer at the same time to pay you the surplus: for otherwise it would oblige you to receive your debt in parts, a thing to which you cannot be holden. It is only in the case in which I am myself your creditor of a part of the sum which I owe you, that the set-off takes place, and to the effect to extinguish, against your will, my debt for part, to the amount of the sum which I owe you.

It is the concurrence of the qualities of creditor and debtor in the same persons which effects this set-off *de jure*, to the amount due and concurring; no person being indeed my creditor but under the deduction of what he owes me, nor indeed my debtor but under the deduction of what I owe him.

He to whom are ceded the rights of a creditor is not truly, according to the subtilty of the law, a creditor, but only an attorney *in rem suam* of the creditor. Yet as he is in effect a creditor when he has signified the cession to the debtor, he may oppose this claim as a set-off to the debtor towards whom he is himself a debtor, as well as every other of which he should be creditor in his own right. *In rem suam procurator datus, si vice mutua conveniatur, æquitate compensationis utetur*; L. 18, ff. *de compens.*

595. The rule which we have just established that one can oppose as a set-off only what is due to himself, receives an exception in regard to securities. He from whom is demanded the payment of a sum which he is obliged to pay as a security of another person, may oppose to the plaintiff the set-off, not only of what is due him himself by the plaintiff, but also of what is due by the plaintiff to the principal debtor: *Si quid a fidejussore petitur, æquissimum est fidejussorem eligere quod ipsi an quod reo debetur, compensare malit*; L. 5, ff. *d. tit.*

The reason is, that it is of the substance of suretiship that the security be not obliged to more than the principal, and that he may therefore use the same pleas which the principal debtor could use; *supra*, n. 380: the principal debtor could oppose to the creditor a set-off of what his creditor owed him; the security therefore may also oppose the set-off of the same debt.

It is not the same *vice versa*; the principal debtor cannot oppose to his creditor a set-off of what his creditor owes to the securities.

May a debtor *in solidum* oppose as a set-off what is due to his co-debtor? See *supra, n.* 274.

596. It is necessary, VI. that the debt which is opposed as a set-off should be due by the same person to whom it is opposed. For example. If one demands of me the payment of what I owe him, I cannot oppose to him as a set-off what is due me by the minors of whom he is tutor; and *vice versa*, if, in quality of tutor, he demands of me the payment of what I owe to his minors, I may not oppose to him the set-off of what he owes me himself. *Is quod pupillorum nomine debetur si tutor petat, non posse compensationem objici ejus pecuniæ quam ipse tutor suo nomine debet;* L. 23, *d. tit.*

For the same reason, I cannot oppose to my creditor the set-off of what his wife owes me, when she has a separation of property; but I may oppose it if she is in a community of property with him; because he is himself bound for the debts of his wife; he has himself become the debtor of it by the community of property which he has contracted with her. This takes place even when there was a clause for the separation of debts; unless he could prove by the detail of an inventory that there does not remain to him in his hands any monies of the property of his wife; for without this he is debtor himself of what is due by his wife. We may, in support of our decision, derive an argument from the law 15, which decides that one may oppose to the master, to the amount of the wages of his servant, the set-off of what is due by his servant; this debt of the servant being the debt of the master, to the amount of his wages that are due.

When my creditor has made to some one a transfer of the claim he had against me, I may oppose to the assignee a set-off, not only of what is due me by him, but also of what is due me by his assignor; provided I commenced to be creditor of his affignor before the fignification or acceptance of the transfer: for this claim not having paffed fooner to the perfon of the affignee according to the maxim of our law, that a transfer does not take effect until it be made known; and having therefore until this time refided in the perfon of the affignor, all the rights which I might until this time have acquired againft the affignor, have by virtue of the fet-off extinguifhed and diminifhed *de jure*, to the amount due and concurring, that which he had againft me and of which he made a transfer.

If I do become a creditor of the affignor only from the time of the fignification of the transfer, there will be no room for the fet-off; for he has ceafed to be my creditor by this fignification: or if he were my creditor, it would be only *juris subtilitate & non juris effectu.*

Although I fhould become a creditor of the affignor before the transfer, yet if having a knowledge of my claim, I neverthelefs accepted the transfer abfolutely, I am prefumed by my abfolute acceptance to have renounced the fet-off, and I cannot oppofe it to the affignee, who has counted upon my acceptance; faving to myfelf my claim againft the affignor. This is what has been adjudged in the cafes cited by Defpeiffes.

597. According to the principles of the civil law, I may oppofe to you as a fet-off of what you owe me at this place, a fum which you you owe me and which is payable in another place, making you at the fame time fatisfaction for the coft of the remittance from the place where it was payable to this other. L. 15, ff. *de compens.* The creditor, according to the principles of the civil law, having the action *de eo quod certo loco*, to oblige his debtor to pay wherever he finds him, the fum which was payable elfewhere, allowing him the coft of remitting it, it was a confequence that he might likewife oblige him to admit a fet-off. But this action *de eo quod certo loco* not being in ufe among us, and the creditor not having power to exact the payment of a fum, payable in a certain place, in any other than the

place where it is payable, *supra, n.* 239. it would seem that we ought to conclude from this, that he cannot oppose the set-off of what he owes in another place. Yet Domat, *p.* 1, *l.* 4, *t.* 2, §. 2, *n.* 8, thinks that this set-off ought to be admitted, satisfaction being made for the cost of remittance. This would appear equitable enough, as the set-off is much to be favored.

598. It is evident that I cannot oppose to you as a set-off against what I owe you, the principal of an annuity which you owe me, but only the arrearages of it which have fallen due; for the principal of an annuity is not properly due, it is only *in facultate luitionis.*

§. III.

How a set-off takes place, and of its effects.

599. A set-off takes place *de pleno jure: Placuit id quod invicem debetur,* IPSO JURE *compensari;* L. 21, ff. *de compens.* There was however a difference with regard to this in the antient Roman law, between debts which proceeded from contracts *bonæ fidei,* and those which proceeded from contracts *stricti juris.* This difference was abrogated by the constitution of Justinian, in the law *fin. cod. d. tit. Compensationes ex omnibus actionibus* IPSO JURE *fieri sancimus; d. L.*

When it is said that a set-off takes place *de pleno jure, ipso jure,* this signifies that it takes place by the mere operation of law, without being pronounced by the judge or even being proposed by either of the parties.

As soon as he who was creditor of a person, becomes his debtor of a sum of money or other *quantity* susceptible of a set-off against that of which he was creditor; & *vice versa,* as soon as he who was debtor of a person becomes his creditor of a sum susceptible of a set-off against that of which he was debtor; the set-off takes place, and the respective debts are from that time extinguished to the amount due and concurring, by the mere operation of law.

This interpretation is conformable to the explanation which all lexicographers give of these words *ipso jure.*

Ipso jure fieri dicitur, says Brisson, *quod ipsa legis potestate & autoritate, absque magistratus auxilio & sine exceptionis ope fit..... Verba* IPSO JURE, says Spigelius, *intelliguntur, sine facto hominis.* IPSO JURE *consistere dicitur*, says Pratejus, *quod ex sola legum potestate & autoritate, sine magistratus opera consistit.*

Our principle that the set-off extinguishes reciprocal debts *ipsa juris potestate*, without its being pleaded or pronounced, is established not only by the words *ipso jure* which the laws make use of, words to which no other signification can be given, but also by the effects which the texts of law give to the set-off. For example. Paul, *sent.* 11, 5, 3, says that if my creditor demands the whole sum which he is my creditor, without offering to deduct that of which he has become my debtor, he incurs by his demand the penalty of the surplus demand: *Si totum petat, plus petendo causa cadit:* which evidently supposes our principle, to wit, that before I opposed the set-off to my creditor, the debt for which he has become my debtor had already diminished and extinguished his claim for so much; otherwise it would not be the case of a surplus demand.

The other effects of the set-off which will be presently adduced, likewise establish our principle.

With regard to the texts of law commonly brought against our principle which relate to the set-off opposed to the demand of the creditor, and of set-offs admitted or rejected by the judge, they decide nothing against our principle, and it cannot be concluded from them, that the set-off ought to be pleaded or declared in order to take place. It is true that if he who was my creditor of a given sum and who has since become my debtor to the same amount, brings suit against me for the payment of that sum, I shall be obliged, in order to defend myself from his demand, to plead against him a set-off of the sum of which he has become my debtor; without this, the judge who would see this right and who could not imagine the claim which I on my part have against him, could not fail to sustain his suit. It is for this that mention is made in those texts, of set-offs pleaded by one party, admitted or rejected by the judge; but it cannot thence be concluded that the debt was not discharged by the set-off before it was pleaded. I am obliged to plead the set-off only in order to inform the judge that the debt has been extinguished by the set-off; in the same manner as when one has demanded from me a debt which I have paid, I am obliged, in order to instruct the judge, to plead the payment and bring forward my receipts.

It is usual also to oppose to our principle the law 6, *Cod. de compens.*, in which the set-off is called *mutua petitio*, which would seem to suppose that the respective actions of the parties exist before the judge pronounces the set-off. The answer is that it is only in a very improper sense that the set-off opposed by the defendant is called *mutua petitio* in this law; which signifies nothing else but the simple allegation of the claim which the defendant had against the plaintiff and by which that of the plaintiff has been extinguished. Our answer is founded on the law 21, ff. *de comp.*, where it is expressly said that he who alledges the set-off does not make a demand, but only defends himself from that which is made against him, by making it appear that it does not amount to the sum opposed as a set-off. *Postquam placuit inter omnes*, says this law, *id quod invicem debetur ipso jure compensari, si procurator absentis conveniatur, non debebit de rato cavere*, (to be admitted to alledge the set-off, as he would be obliged if he were to make a demand); *quia nihil compensat, sed ab initio minus ab eo petitur:* that is to say, *non ipse compensat, non ipse aliquid mutuo petit, sed allegat compensationem ipso jure factam, quæ ab initio jus petitoris ipso jure minuit.*

600. The effects of the set-off are consequences from the principle which I have established.

These effects are, I. that if my creditor to whom I have given goods in pledge, has become my debtor, I may claim those goods, on offering him only what I owe him above what he owes me; the set-off which is made of our reciprocal debts to the amount due and concurring, being equivalent to the payment of the furplus. This is the decifion of the law 12, *Cod. de compens.*

II. If you had againft me a claim of a certain fum of money, from its nature producing intereft, and you have fince become my debtor of a fum of money; although my claim fhould not be of a nature, like yours, to produce intereft, yet my claim will be holden by virtue of the fet-off to have difcharged yours to the amount due and concurring, from the day that you become my debtor of it, and from that day the intereft to the amount due will ceafe to run. For example. If you were my creditor for the fum of one thoufand livres for the price of a piece of land which you had fold and delivered to me and you have fince become fole heir of Peter who owed me the fum of eight hundred livres on a loan; from the day that you became heir of Peter and in this capacity my debtor of that fum of eight hundred livres, that is to fay, from the day of the death of Peter, your claim of one thoufand livres is confidered to have been difcharged to the amount of the faid fum of eight hundred livres, and to exift only for the two hundred livres remaining: and from that day the intereft will ceafe to run, except upon the remaining fum of two hundred livres. This is the decifion of the conftitution of Septimius Severus, reported by Ulpian: *Quum alter alteri pecuniam sine usuris, alter usurariam debet, constitutum est a divo Severo concurrentis apud utrumque quantitatis usuras non esse præstandas*; L. 11, ff. *de compens.*

The fame decifion is found in the conftitution of Alexander; *Si constat pecuniam invicem deberi, ipso jure pro soluto compensationem haberi oportet ex eo tempore, ex quo ab utraque parte debetur utique quoad concurrentes quantitates, ejusque solius quoad amplius apud alterum est usuræ debentur*; L. 4, *Cod. d. tit.*

This effect of the fet-off takes place only in ordinary fet-offs, *quantitatis certæ ac determinatæ ad certam ac determinatem quantitatem*, which are *de pleno jure*: but in fet-offs which do not take place but from the day when they are pleaded, the intereſt ought not to ceaſe to run but from this day. For example. If you were my creditor for the ſum of one thouſand livres, for the price of an eſtate which you have ſold me, and which conſequently bears intereſt, and you have ſince become the only heir of Peter who has bequeathed to me two carriage horſes or the ſum of one thouſand livres, at my choice; the intereſt of the ſum of one thouſand livres which I owe you, does not ceaſe to run from the day of the death of Peter, which is the day when you become debtor of the legacy which he bequeathed to me; they would ceaſe only from the day when I ſhould declare that I would chooſe the ſum of one thouſand livres for my legacy; it is only from this day that the ſet-off is made of this ſum againſt that which I owe you, as we have already obſerved *supra*, *n.* 593.

601. III. Although my creditor cannot be obliged to receive in part the actual payment which I would make him, *supra*, *n.* 478; yet if he has become my debtor of a ſum leſs than that which I owe him, he is obliged to ſuffer the partial diſcharge of his demand, which is made in this caſe by virtue of the ſet-off, as it reſults from the laws above adduced.

602. IV. If I were your debtor for three different cauſes, and have ſince become your creditor of the ſum of one thouſand livres, the ſet-off of the claim of one thouſand livres which I have acquired againſt you, ought to be made againſt that one of the three debts from which I have the greateſt intereſt to be diſcharged. The reaſon is, that as the ſet-off is in the place of payment, for the ſame reaſon that in payments the application is made upon that one of the debts which the debtor has the greateſt intereſt to diſcharge, *supra*, *n.* 550, the ſet-off ought likewiſe to be made upon that one of the debts which he has the moſt intereſt to diſcharge.

This deciſion obtains only when the different debts of which I was your debtor have all preceded the claim which I have ſince acquired againſt you. But if being your debtor of the ſum of one thouſand livres, I have ſince become your creditor of the like ſum, and have ſince contracted a new debt towards you, although this ſhould be a debt from which I might have more intereſt to be diſcharged than from the firſt, yet you may demand of me payment of it, without my being able to oppoſe as a ſet-off of the claim I have acquired; this claim having been extinguiſhed as ſoon as I had acquired it, by the ſet-off which is made *de jure*, of this claim againſt the firſt which you had againſt me. *Tindar. Tract. de compens. art. 7, in fin. Sebast. Medicis, p. 2, §. 12.*

603. If he who was my creditor of a certain ſum of money, has ſince become my debtor of as much, and notwithſtanding the ſet-off which has extinguiſhed, *de pleno jure*, our reſpective claims, I have paid it to him, I may reclaim the ſum which I have paid him, as not due, by the action which is called *condictio indebiti*. This is what Ulpian decides in the law 10, §. 1, ff. *de compens. Si quis compensare potens solverit, condicere poterit quasi indebito soluto.*

This text proves very clearly the principle which we have eſtabliſhed, that the ſet-off is made of full right, and extinguiſhes by mere virtue of the law, the reſpective debts of the parties, without its being pleaded by either of the parties or pronounced by the judge; otherwiſe in this inſtance, in which, when I have paid, the ſet-off has neither been pleaded nor pronounced by the judge, one could not ſay that I have paid what I no longer owed.

Hence ariſes a queſtion which may be put in the following hypotheſis. I was your debtor of the ſum of one thouſand livres; I have ſince become the only heir of Peter, who was your creditor of the like ſum, for the return of a diviſion. Notwithſtanding the ſet-off of which I could have availed myſelf, I have paid you this ſum of one thouſand livres. Afterwards your goods have been actually ſeized by your creditors and particularly thoſe to whom you have fallen in debt by the diviſion you made with Peter. I oppoſe this decree and demand to be placed in the order of a privilege upon the price of these goods; for the return of the division which you owed Peter to whom I have succeeded. Are the other creditors well grounded in opposing it? It seems that they are well grounded; for the demand of Peter for the return of the division, has been extinguished at the same time that I succeeded to it, by virtue of the set-off which is made of this claim which I have acquired against you, against that of the like sum of one thousand livres which you have against me. The payment which I have since made you has not power to revive our respective claims which the set-off has extinguished; it can only give me a simple action to reclaim the sum which I have paid you, as having been paid without being due, and this action has no hypothecation, or it has at the most a simple hypothecation from the day of the discharge, if it was before a notary. It was not in my power, in paying you voluntarily a debt which was extinguished by the set-off of this debt against the claim which I have acquired against you, to revive my claim with the hypothecations that were attached to it, to the prejudice of creditors who have followed me, and of the right of priority in the hypothecations which has been acquired to them by the set-off which has extinguished our reciprocal claims.

Notwithstanding these reasons I think it is necessary to use a distinction on this question. If, since I have succeeded to Peter, but before I had knowledge that there was in this estate a claim of one thousand livres against you, I have paid you the one thousand livres which I owed you myself, I think that in this case I ought to be put in the order of privilege, for the claim of one thousand livres for which I have succeeded to Peter, and that we ought to judge in this case that there is not made of it any set-off. The reason is, that as the set-off is a fiction of law which supposes that the parties have respectively paid themselves, as far as they were creditors and debtors at the same time of one another, this fiction which is established in favor of the parties between whom the set-off is made, ought not to be extended so far as to be prejudicial to them and to lead them into error; a benefit of the law ought never to become prejudicial to those to whom the law grants it. *Beneficium legis non debet esse captiosum.* We ought not then to suppose in this case that there has been a set-off; for it would be prejudicial to me, it would lead me into error. It would make me, without my fault, lose the sum of one thousand livres for which I had a privileged hypothecation. We must decide otherwise in the case in which I had not paid you the one thousand livres which I owed you myself, till after the inventory of the estate of Peter, which has given me knowledge of the claim which the succession to this estate has given against you. Nothing hinders the supposition in this case that the set-off has extinguished our respective claims. It is not in this case the law of the set-off which has caused me a prejudice or led me into error. If I lose the thousand livres which I have unadvisedly paid you, I ought not to impute it to the law of set-off, but to myself, who have been willing to pay you a debt which I knew to be discharged by the set-off. It was not in our power to revive my claim by this payment, in fraud of the right acquired by the creditors who followed me.

604. How ought we to decide in the following instance? I was your debtor of the sum of one thousand livres. I have since become your creditor of as much, *puta*, in becoming the only heir of Peter, to whom you owed the like sum. Upon the suit which you have brought against me for the payment of this sum of one thousand livres, which I owed you, having neglected to oppose the set-off of that which you owed me, I have been condemned to pay you this sum and have paid it to you in execution of the judgment. Have I in this case any recourse? I cannot have, as in the preceding case, the action *condictio indebiti.* The law 2, *Cod. de compens.*, decides that although I might yet oppose the set-off of my claim against your proceedings in execution of the judgment, there will be no ground for the action

condictio indebiti; because what is paid in execution of a judgment cannot be regarded as paid without cause. This action *condictio indebiti* does not take place but when the payment has been made without any cause, and consequently without a judgment. *Pecuniæ indebitæ per errorem, NON EX CAUSA JUDICATI solutæ, esse repetitionem jure condictionis non ambigitur.* L. 1, *Cod. de cond. indeb.* Shall I then in this case be deprived of all remedy? It must be said that in this case, although, according to the subtilty of the law, the set-off has extinguished our respective claims in the same instant I succeeded to that which Peter had against you, yet this set-off ought, in this instance, to be regarded as not having taken place: this claim to which I have succeeded, and the action which grows from it, ought to be restored to me, and I ought to be admitted to bring suit upon it.

The reason is, that as this set-off has not had its effect with regard to you, and relatively to the claim which you had against me, by the judgment which has been rendered against me for the payment of this claim, equity does not permit it to exist with regard to me, and relatively to the claim which I had on my side against you. This is what Tindarus decides very properly in his treatise *de compens.*, and it is in this sense that he explains the law 7, §. 1, ff. *de compens.*, which says, *Si rationem compensationis Judex non habuerit, salva manet petitio*; which is to say, when the judge has condemned one of the parties towards the other, notwithstanding the set-off which had extinguished their reciprocal claims, either because it was not pleaded, or because being pleaded, the judge has omitted to pronounce upon it, the claim which the party condemned had against the other is preserved to him, *salva manet petitio. Lex enim*, says Tindarus, *hoc casu restituit actionem peremptam, ex maxima necessitate, sicut facit in multis casibus, æquitate suggerente.* See L. 1, *in fin.* ff. *ad Velleian.*

Is my claim restored to me with the hypothecations that were attached to it, or without them? I imagine that it is neceſſary in this caſe to make a diſtinction. If there is no room to ſuſpect that it was by colluſion with you and to make you receive money to the prejudice of your creditors, that I have not pleaded the ſet-off of the claim which I had inherited from Peter againſt you; *puta*, becauſe I had no knowlege of it at the time of the judgment; the death of Peter being ſcarcely known in public, or at leaſt no inventory having been made of his papers, from which alone I could have knowlege of this claim; in this caſe I think my claim ought to be reſtored with its hypothecations. But if, having already a knowlege of the claim I had againſt you, I have ſuffered myſelf to be condemned without oppoſing to you the ſet-off, or if I have only oppoſed it *perfunctorie*, without eſtabliſhing it, ſo that the judge has n t pronounced upon it, in this caſe my claim againſt you will be preſerved to me; but I ſhall not be permitted to exerciſe the hypothecations that were attached to this claim, to the prejudice of the creditors who followed me in the order of hypothecation, and by whom the right of priority of hypothecation was acquired, as ſoon as I ſucceeded to the claim of Peter, by the ſet-off and extinction of our reciprocal claims which then took place: equity does not permit that by a colluſion with you I ſhould deprive thoſe creditors of this right which was acquired by them.

CHAPTER V.

Of the extinction of the debt by confusion.

605. WE call *confusion* the concurrence in the ſame ſubject, of two qualities, which mutually deſtroy each other. That of which we mean to ſpeak here is the concurrence of the qualities of creditor and debtor, of the ſame debt, in the ſame perſon. We ſhall ſee, I. in what caſes this confuſion takes place; II. what are its effects.

The Roman Juriſts admitted another kind of confuſion, in the caſe in which a ſecurity became heir to the principal debtor, *aut vice versa.* We ſhall ſay nothing of it here; having already treated of it *supra, part.* 2 *ch.* 6, §. 1, *coroll.* 6.

§. I.

In what cases confusion takes place.

606. Confuſion takes place when the creditor becomes heir to his debtor, *aut vice versa,* when the debtor becomes heir to his creditor. For as the heir ſucceeds to all the rights, as well active as paſſive, of the deceaſed, when the creditor becomes heir of his debtor; he becomes, in this capacity of heir, debtor of the debt of which he is in his own right the creditor: and *vice versa,* when the debtor becomes heir of his creditor, he becomes, in this capacity of heir, creditor of the ſame debt of which he is in his own right the debtor. In both caſes the qualities of the creditor and debtor of the ſame debt happen to concur in the ſame perſon.

The ſame thing happens when the creditor ſucceeds to the debtor in ſome other manner which renders him liable for his debts, as when he becomes his univerſal donee; or when the debtor ſucceeds in any manner to the claim of the creditor. In all theſe caſes the qualities of creditor and debtor of the ſame debt happen to concur in the ſame perſon.

The ſame thing happens alſo when the ſame perſon becomes heir of the creditor and of the debtor, or ſucceeds to both by ſome other univerſal title.

The acceptance of a ſucceſſion with the benefit of inventory, does not operate any confuſion: for it is one of the effects of the benefit of inventory, that the beneficiary heir and the eſtate ſhould be regarded as two different perſons, and that their reſpective rights be not confounded.

§. II.

Of the effect of confusion.

607. It is evident that by the concurrence of theſe two contrary qualities of creditor and debtor in the ſame perſon,

they mutually deſtroy themſelves: for one cannot be creditor and debtor at the ſame time; one cannot be creditor of one's ſelf or debtor towards one's ſelf. From this reſults indirectly the extinction of the debt, when there is no other debtor; for as there cannot be a debt without a debtor, the confuſion extinguiſhing, in the perſon who was the only debtor, the quality of debtor, and there remaining conſequently no longer a debtor, there can no longer be a debt. *Non potest esse obligatio, sine persona obligata.*

608. The extinction of the principal obligation which is made by the confuſion, when the creditor becomes heir of the principal debtor, *aut vice versa*, draws after it alſo the extinction of that of the ſecurities; L. 38, §. 1, ff. *de fidej.* L. 34, §. 8, L. 71, ff. *de solut.* The reaſon is, that the obligations of the ſecurities are only acceſſory to the obligation of the principal debtor. *Fidejussor accedit obligationi rei principalis.* Whence it follows that they cannot exiſt when the principal obligation no longer exiſts, according to this rule of law, *Quum principalis causa non subsistit, ne ea quidem quæ sequuntur locum habent*; L. 129, §. 1, ff. *de reg. jur.*; and this other, *Quæ accessionum locum obtinent, extinguuntur, cum principales res peremptæ fuerint.* L. 2, ff. *de pecul. leg.*

Add that a ſecurity ſuppoſes a principal debtor for whom the ſecurity is obliged: whence it follows that when by means of the confuſion there is no longer a principal debtor for whom the ſecurity is obliged, there can no longer be a ſecurity. This is the reaſon which the law 38, §. 1, ff. *de fid.*, adduces; *Quia nec reus est pro quo debeat.*

Add alſo that it is repugnant that I ſhould be a ſecurity for one towards myſelf: it is then neceſſary that the obligation of the ſecurity ſhould extinguiſh itſelf, when the perſon for whom he is obliged becomes, by the acceptance of the ſucceſſion to the creditor, the ſame perſon with the one towards whom the ſecurity is obliged: *Fidejussores ideo liberari, quia pro eodem apud eumdem debere non possunt.* This is the reaſon of the law 34, §. 8, *de solut.*

609. *Contra vice versa,* the extinction which is made

of the obligation of the security by the confusion, when the creditor becomes the heir of the security, or the security becomes the heir of the creditor, does not draw after it the extinction of the principal obligation. *Si creditor fidejussori hæres fuerit, vel fidejussor creditori, puto convenire confusione obligationis non liberari reum;* L. 71, ff. *de fidejussor.* The reason of this difference is, that the accessory obligation cannot in truth exist without the principal obligation, but the principal obligation has no need of the accessory obligation in order to exist.

Confusion differs in this from payment. The reason of this difference is, that payment makes the thing no longer due; for the thing ceases to be due when it has been paid by any one. There can no longer remain a debtor, either principal or accessory, when there is no longer any thing due; the payment made by the security having therefore made the thing due by the security, which is the same with that due by the creditor, no longer due, and it no longer remaining a thing due, it is necessary that the obligation of the principal debtor should be extinguished, as well as that of the principal debtor who has paid.

The same thing may be said of an actual release, of set-off, of novation and of the other kinds of discharges which are equivalent to payment.

On the contrary, the confusion makes only the debtor in whom is found to concur the qualities of creditor, cease to be bound, because he cannot be so towards himself. *Personam eximit ab obligatione;* but nothing prevents the obligation of the principal debtor from existing, although the security has ceased to be bound.

For the same reason when the creditor of two debtors *in solidum* becomes heir of one of them, the other co-debtor remains bound.

Is he for the whole? The law 71, ff. *de fidej.*, decides that if the two debtors *in solidum* were partners, this debtor, who was not in this case debtor of the whole, except with a remedy over against the person with whom confusion is made, would not remain bound but under a deduction of the part for which he would have had this recourse against him: it not being just that the confusion should deprive him of this recourse.

In our jurisprudence, each of the debtors *in solidum*, although they be not partners, having, on payment, a recourse against the others for their part, as we have seen *supra n.* 281., it is necessary to decide without distinction, that when there is made a confusion of the debt in the person of one of the debtors *in solidum*, the other remains bound only under a deduction of the part for which he would have had recourse against him with whom the confusion is made. We have already seen, *supra, n.* 275, that when the creditor has discharged one of the debtors *in solidum*, the other would not remain bound but under a deduction of the part for which he would have had recourse against his co-debtor who has been discharged; for the same reason, the co-debtor of him who has been discharged by the confusion, ought to remain debtor only under a deduction of the part for which he would have had recourse against him.

610. If he who was creditor of Peter of a certain sum, has transferred to me his claim, and before Peter has accepted the transfer or I have signified it to him, he becomes heir of Peter who is the debtor, there will indeed be a confusion and an extinction of the debt of Peter which he has transferred to me; but as he was, by the transfer which he made to me, debtor towards me of this claim which he has transferred to me, and it is by the acceptance which he has made of the succession of the debtor, and consequently by his own act, that this claim which he had transferred to me has been extinguished, he is bound to render me the value of it: for every debtor is bound to pay the price or the value of the thing which he owed, when it is by his own act that it has ceased to exist, as we shall see, *infra, n.* 625.

If the transfer had already been accepted or signified when the person transferring to me became the heir of the debtor, confusion would not take place: because he was no longer actually the creditor, and I had become so in his place.

611. When the creditor becomes heir, not of the debtor, but of him who was obliged to discharge the debtor, there is not indeed a confusion of the debt, but it is extinguished at least indirectly and as to the effect. He can no longer demand it from the debtor, having succeeded to the obligation to guaranty and indemnify him from it.

612. In order that a total confusion may be made of the debt, it is necessary that the same person unite not only the quality of creditor, but that of the creditor of the whole; he ought also to unite not only the quality of the debtor, but that of the debtor of the whole.

If he who is only creditor for a part, had become the only heir of the debtor, it is evident that there would not be a confusion and an extinction but of the part of the debt of which he is creditor; *& vice versa*, if the creditor of the whole had become heir of him who was only debtor for a part, there would not be a confusion but of this part of the debt.

It is not less evident that, when the creditor of the whole becomes one of the heirs of the debtor of the whole, there is a confusion and an extinction of the debt, only as to the part for which he is heir, and for which he is bound for the other debts of the estate; but the claim exists against the co-heirs for the part for which each of them is bound for the debts. L. 50, ff. *de fidejuss.* L. 1, *Cod. de hæred. act.*

CHAPTER VI.

Of the extinction of the obligation by the extinction of the thing due, or when it has ceased to be susceptible of obligation, or when it is so lost as that one is ignorant where it is.

ARTICLE THE FIRST.

A general exposition of the principles upon this manner in which debts are extinguished.

613. THERE cannot be a debt without there be fomething due, which may be the fubject and object of the obligation; whence it follows that when the thing which was due comes to perifh, as there no longer remains any thing which may be the fubject and object of the obligation, there can no longer be an obligation. The extinction of the thing due neceffarily carries therefore the extinction of the obligation; L. 33, 37, ff. *de verb. oblig.*

614. For the fame reafon, if the thing due has afterwards become not fufceptible of being the fubject and object of an obligation, there can no longer remain an obligation. This happens when the thing which was due becomes not a fubject of commerce. Therefore Ulpian fays, *Is qui alienum servum promisit, perducto eo ad libertatem, non tenetur*; L. 51, ff. *de verb. oblig.*

According to this principle, if you have obliged yourfelf to deliver me a certain piece of ground, and fince, by public authority they have taken it to make a high way, the claim which I have to this piece of ground is extinguifhed; becaufe this piece of ground, becoming not a fubject of commerce, is no longer fufceptible of being the fubject and object of a claim and of an obligation: as there remains therefore nothing that may be the object of the claim which I had, it cannot exift.

615. Not only when the thing which made the object of the obligation ceafes to be abfolutely fufceptible of an obligation, is the obligation extinguifhed; it is extinguifhed alfo when the thing which was due me can no longer be

due to me, although it be fufceptible of an obligation with regard to another.

There is a firft example of this in the law 136, §. 1, ff. *de verb. oblig.* You bound yourfelf to give me for my plantation a right of way over the adjoining one: before this right of way is given, I have fold my land, without ceding to the purchafer my claim for this right of way. This claim is extinguifhed; becaufe the right of way, which was the object of it, can no longer be due to me, as the right of way can only belong to the owner of the land.

616. A fecond example is, when he who is creditor of a determinate thing, *lucrativo titulo*, becomes owner of it *alio lucrativo titulo*. The claim for this thing is extinguifhed in this cafe. *Omnes debitores qui speciem ex causa lucrativa debent, liberantur, quum ea species ex causa lucrativa ad creditores pervenisset;* L. 17, ff. *de oblig. & act.*

The reafon is drawn from our principle. When I become owner of the thing that was due me, it can no longer be due me; for one cannot owe me that which is already mine: it is repugnant that one fhould be bound to give me that which is already mine; *nam quod meum est, amplius meum fieri non potest.* As there remains nothing that may be the object of the obligation, it cannot exift.

Hence this rule, *Duæ causæ lucrativæ in eamdem rem et personam, concurrere non possunt.*

617. In order that the debt may be extinguifhed when the creditor has become owner of the thing that was due him, it is neceffary that he fhould have acquired a full and perfect property in that thing; otherwife the debt exifts and the debtor of this thing is bound to fupply to the creditor what is wanting for the perfection of the right of property which he has in the thing.

For example. If one has bequeathed to me a plantation which he knew did not belong to him, and, fince his death and before the difcharge of the legacy, the owner made a gift of it to me, referving to himfelf a life eftate, the claim for that plantation, which I have againft the heir of the teſtator, is not extinguiſhed, although I have become owner of the thing that was due to me; becauſe ſomething is wanting to the perfection of my right, viz. the uſe of it during the life of the donor. The heir of the teſtator remains therefore debtor of this plantation, in this ſenſe that he is bound to purchaſe for me the life eſtate of the donor, or to pay me the value of it.

If the full property has been given to me, but the donation is liable to be revoked, *puta*, by the birth of children, the donor having none when he made it, there wants in this caſe ſomething for the perfection of my title, according to this rule: *Non videtur perfecte cujusque id esse, quod ei ex causa auferri potest*; L. 139, §. 1, ff. *de regul. jur.* Therefore the debtor remains bound to procure the land for me in caſe the donation which was made to me ſhould happen afterwards to be revoked by the birth of children.

618. It is neceſſary alſo that I ſhould become owner of the thing of which I was creditor, *lucrativo titulo*, that my claim may be extinguiſhed. If it were only *oneroso titulo* that I required it, *puta*, if it were ſold to me, he who was my debtor would not be diſcharged; for I ſhall not be holden to have perfectly acquired this thing, when I have paid any thing for the acquiſition of it: *Hactenus mihi abesse res videtur, quatenus sum præstaturus*; L. 34, §. 8, ff. *de leg.* I. The claim which I had for this thing does not therefore ceaſe to exiſt, ſo that I may demand to be reimburſed for what I have paid.

619. Finally that my claim may be extinguiſhed when I become owner, although *lucrativo titulo*, of the thing which was due me, it is neceſſary that my claim ſhould have proceeded likewiſe *a lucrativo titulo*; for if I were crèditor *ab oneroso titulo, puta*, by purchaſe, my claim would not be extinguiſhed: *Quum creditor, ex causa onerosa, vel emptor, ex lucrativa causa rem habere cœperit, nihilominus integras actiones retinent*; L. 19, ff. *oblig. & act.* *Adde* L. 13, §. 15, ff. *de act. empt.*

For example. If I have purchaſed of you an eſtate

which did not belong to you, and I have since become proprietor of it by the donation or legacy which has been made to me of it by the true proprietor; my claim resulting from the sale which you have made to me of it, is not extinguished. The reason is, that every debtor *oneroso titulo*, such as is a seller, is obliged to guaranty the thing which he owes, and that this consists in the obligation which the seller contracts, that the buyer should have the thing in virtue of the sale which has been made to him of it, *præstare emptori rem habere licere ex causa venditionis ipsi factæ*. It suffices that it should not be in virtue of the sale which you have made to me, that I hold the thing, although I be proprietor of it otherwise, in order that there may be room for the warranty.

620. A thing which is so lost as that one is ignorant where it is, is little different from that which has ceased to exist; therefore when this loss happens without the fault of the debtor, as when, by a violence which he could not resist, the thing which he owed him has been carried away by thieves, one knows not where, the debtor is discharged from his obligation in the same manner as if the thing had ceased to exist; with this difference, however, that as a thing which has ceased to exist is not to be revived, the debtor is discharged from his obligation absolutely, when the thing has ceased to exist; whereas when a thing is so lost as that it may be found again, the debtor is not discharged in this case from his obligation, but while it is lost and cannot be found.

There remains one question on this subject. When the debtor of a thing certain, who is not chargeable for accidents, and who is liable only for losses which should happen by his fault, alledges that the thing by him due has perished or has been lost without his fault or by accident must the creditor prove that the loss has happened by the fault of the debtor, or on the contrary must the debtor prove the accident by which he pretends it was lost? I think we ought to decide that the debtor must prove the accident.

If a plaintiff is obliged to furnish the roof of what makes the foundation of his demand, the defendant is obliged likewise to furnish the proof of what makes the foundation of his defence. The creditor who demands from his debtor the payment of the thing which his debtor is bound to give him, ought to prove the claim which makes the foundation of his demand; and he proves it by producing the evidence of his claim. The debtor who pleads for his defence against this demand, that he is discharged from the debt of this thing by the accident which has caused the loss of it, ought to prove the accident which makes the foundation of his defence.

This is conformable to what Ulpian illustrates in the law 19, ff. *de prob. In exceptionibus dicendum est reum partibus actoris fingi oportere, ipsumque exceptionem velut intentionem implere, id est probare debere.*

ARTICLE II.

What kinds of obligations are subject to be extinguished by the extinction of the thing due, or when it can no longer be due.

621. It is evident that the obligations of a thing certain and determinate are extinguished by the extinction of the thing certain and determinate.

In regard to obligations under an alternative, they are not extinguished by the extinction of one of the two things which are due under an alternative; but this obligation, in an alternative as it was, becomes determinate as to the other which remains. The reason is, that in the obligation under an alternative of two things, the two things are due, *supra, n.* 246: it suffices that there should remain one of them that there may be a thing due, and consequently a sufficient subject of the obligation.

For example. If having two horses, you have obliged yourself to give me one of the two; the death of one of them does not extinguish the obligation, and you would owe me that which remains, *non jam alternate, sed determinate.*

It is the ſame, if one of the things which are due me under an alternative, can no longer be due to me, *puta*, if I become proprietor of it *lucrativo titulo:* the obligation would continue for the other thing which remains. *Si Stichum aut Pamphilum mihi debeas, & alter ex eis meus sit factus ex alia causa, reliquus debetur mihi a te;* L. 16, ff. *de verb. oblig.*

The principle which we have eſtabliſhed, that the obligation under an alternative is not extinguiſhed by the extinction of one of the things which were due under an alternative, nor when it can no longer be due to me, takes place only when this happens while the obligation is yet in the alternative; but if this obligation has been determined to one of the things, *puta*, by the offer which the debtor had made, and the arrear in which he had put the creditor of receiving, in this caſe it is not to be doubted that the obligation would be extinguiſhed by the extinction which ſhould happen of this thing. L. 105, ff. *de verb. oblig.*

623. The extinction of obligations by the extinction of the thing due, cannot happen to obligations of a ſum of money, or of a quantity, as of a meaſure of grain, &c; nor to that of a thing indeterminate, as of a cow, of a horſe, without determining what cow, what horſe: there cannot be in this caſe an extinction of the thing due, as there cannot be an extinction of what is indeterminate; *genus non perit.* Therefore the law 11, *Cod. Si certum pet.*, decides that the debtor of a ſum of money is not diſcharged by the burning of his effects. *Incendium ære alieno non exuit debitorem:* for the money and his other effects which have periſhed by the fire, are not the thing which he owed; it is a ſum of money, which being indeterminate cannot periſh. But if the indeterminate obligation was determined to an obligation of a thing certain, by the offer which the debtor had made of it, and the arrear in which he had put the creditor of receiving, it is not to be doubted that this obligation would become from that time ſubject to be extinguiſhed, by the extinction of the thing which has been offered.

623. When the obligation is not absolutely indeterminate, and is of a thing indeterminate indeed, but which makes part of an indeterminate number of certain things, it may be extinguished by the extinction of all these things.

For example. If one owes me a tun of the *wine which he has in a certain house*, and he has a hundred in this house; while there remains one of them, his obligation will continue: but if none of them remains, *puta*, if an inundation has carried them all away, the obligation will be extinguished.

This decision takes place when the terms of the obligation are restrictive, and limit the obligation to this number of things; it would be otherwise if the terms were only demonstrative. For example. If one had obliged himself to furnish me a tun of wine, *to be taken from those of his cellar*; although every tun which were in the cellar of the debtor, may have perished by accident, the obligation would not be extinguished: because it is not limited to those tuns only which were in the cellar of the debtor. These terms *to be taken*, are not restrictive, they are only demonstrative; they only designate *unde solvetur*: they do not relate to the disposition, they do not restrain it; they concern only its execution. See *in Pandect. Justinian. tit. de cond. & dem. n.* 235.

Article III.

What extinctions of the thing due extinguish the debt; when and against whom it is perpetuated notwithstanding this extinction.

624. The extinction of the thing due extinguishes the debt, when the thing is totally destroyed; if there remains any part of it, the debt continues at least for what remains. For example. If I were creditor of a herd of cattle which has been sold or bequeathed to me, and one only of them remains, the others having perished by mortality; or if I were creditor of a house which has since been burnt; the debt of the herd would continue as to the one of them which should remain, and likewise the debt of the house would con-

tinue as to the ground on which it ftood, and the materials which fhould remain.

625. In order that the extinction of the thing due may extinguifh the debt, it is neceffary alfo that it happen without the act or fault of the debtor, and before he has been put in arrear.

If the lofs of the thing due happens by the act of the debtor, it is evident that the obligation ought not to be extinguifhed, and that it muft be converted into an obligation of the price of this thing; for the debtor cannot by his own act difcharge himfelf from his obligation and make his creditor lofe his claim.

This decifion takes place even when the debtor had deftroyed the thing before he knew that he was debtor of it: L. 2, ff. *de verb. oblig.*

626. If the lofs of the thing due has happened not precifely by the act of the debtor, but by his fault, becaufe he has not taken the care which he ought to have taken, the debt is not extinguifhed, and it is converted likewife into an obligation of the price of the thing.

We confider in this refpect the fault of the debtor differently according to the different nature of the contracts from whichthe obligation arifes, *supra*, *n.* 142.

627. In fine the lofs of the thing due does not extinguifh the obligation, when it has happened fince the debtor has been put in arrear to give it. L. 82, ff. *de verb. oblig.*

According to our law a debtor is put in arrear, either by the command which is ferved upon him, when the title of the claim is with execution, or by the fimple demand made when the title is not with execution.

In order that the lofs of the thing due, happening fince the debtor was in arrear, may extinguifh the obligation, it is neceffary, I. that it fhould happen whilft he ftill continues in arrear: for if he had ceafed to be in arrear by actual offers made to the creditor, whereby he would have put the creditor himfelf in arrear to receive, or by fome agreement betwixt the creditor and debtor, the loſs of the thing due, happening ſince the debtor had ceaſed to be in arrear, would extinguiſh the obligation. The arrear of the debtor, ceaſing to exiſt, can no longer have the effect to perpetuate the obligation, notwithſtanding the extinction of the thing due. L. 91, §. 3, ff. *de verb. oblig.*

628. That the loſs of the thing due, happening ſince the arrear of the debtor, may not extinguiſh the debt, it is neceſſary, II. that the thing might not equally have periſhed with the creditor, if it had been delivered to him at the time of the demand. L. 47, §. *fin. de leg.* 1. L. 14, §. 1. ff. *depos.*; L. 12, §. 4, ff. *ad exhib.*; L. 15, §. 5, ff. *de rei vind.* For the arrear of the debtor perpetuates the debt, notwithſtanding the extinction of the thing due, only by way of damages. If the creditor has not ſuffered from the delay of the debtor, damages are not due him: it is evident that he has not ſuffered, if the thing would equally have periſhed with him.

It is eaſily preſumed that the thing would not equally have periſhed with the creditor, if the creditor was a merchant who bought it to ſell again.

If the thing periſhed by fire in the houſe of the debtor, it is evident that it would not have periſhed if it had been delivered to the creditor.

No enquiry is made whether the thing would equally have periſhed with the creditor, in regard to the reſtitution of things due from thoſe who ſtole or took them by violence; they are bound without diſtinction for the price of the thing, when it has periſhed in their hands. L. *fin.* ff. *de cond. furt.* L. 19, ff. *de vi & vi arm. quod ita receptum odio furti & violentiæ.* Note alſo, in regard to thoſe perſons, that they are conſidered in arrear from the day of the theft or taking, without the neceſſity of any previous demand.

629. When the thing due has periſhed by the act or fault of the principal debtor or ſince his arrear, the debt of the price of this thing exiſts not only againſt him and

his heirs, but even againſt his ſecurities, and in general againſt all thoſe who have acceded to his obligation. L. 91, §. 4, 5, ff. *de verb. oblig.* L. 58, §. 1, ff. *de fidejus.* L. 24, §. 1, ff. *de usur.* Paul gives this reaſon for it: *Quia in totam causam spoponderunt.* The ſecurities, in becoming for the principal debtor ſecurities for the principal obligation to give the thing, are conſidered to have likewiſe become ſecurities for the ſecondary obligation which reſults from the principal obligation, ſuch as that of keeping the thing with proper care until the delivery, and generally to uſe good faith and due fidelity in the performance of the principal obligation; they cannot be diſcharged from their obligation by the loſs of the thing, when this loſs happened by the fault of the principal debtor, or ſince he was in arrear; while being, as we have ſaid, ſecurities for the care which he was to take in the keeping of the thing, and of the fidelity with which he was to perform his obligation, they are anſwerable for the fault through which this debtor has ſuffered the thing to periſh, and for the unjuſt delay by which he has contravened the fidelity which he ought to have uſed in the performance of his obligation.

Theſe principles appear contrary to the rule of law, *unicuique sua mora nocet.* L. 173, §. 2, ff. *de reg. jur*; for it ſeems to follow from this rule that the delay of the principal debtor can only prejudice him and not the ſecurities. Cujas and the other commentators reconcile this rule with our principles by this diſtinction: the delay of the principal debtor cannot it is true prejudice his ſecurities ſo as to add to their obligation; *non nocet ad augendam obligationem.* For example. In debts of a ſum of money, the arrear of the debtor cannot prejudice the ſecurities who are only bound for a certain determinate ſum, ſo as to render them liable for the damages which become due by this debtor from the day he becomes in arrear; for the delay of the debtor does not prejudice the ſecurities *ad augendam eorum obligationem:* it cannot then bind for the damages theſe ſecurities, who are bound only for the principal ſum. This is the caſe of the law 173. But in debts of a thing certain, the arrear of the debtor may prejudice the securities whose securityship is unlimited, so as to perpetuate their obligation, and to prevent them from being discharged by the loss of the thing, happening since the arrear; *non nocet ad augendam obligationem, sed nocet ad perpetuandam obligationem.*

630. *Contra, vice versa,* if the thing has perished by the act or fault of the security, or since he has been put in arrear, the security alone will remain bound for the price of the thing: the principal debtor will be discharged by the extinction of the thing; L. 32, §. *fin.* ff. *de usur.*; L. 49, *de verb. oblig.* The reason of this difference is, that the security is indeed bound for the principal debtor; but the principal debtor is not bound for the security; and consequently he cannot be holden to the obligation which the security has contracted by his own act, by his fault or arrear.

631. If the thing due has perished by the act or fault of one of the co-debtors *in solidum*, or since his arrear, the other co-debtors will be bound therefor; L. 18, ff. *de duobus reis.* See what we have said in treating of obligations *in solidum, supra n.* 273.

If the thing had perished by the act or by the fault of one of the heirs of the debtor, or since his arrear, his co-debtors will not be bound therefor; L. 48. §. 1, ff. *de leg.* 1: for although, as holding the estate, they are bound with hypothecation for the whole debt, they are personally bound each only for their parts; they are not between themselves debtors *in solidum*, they are not bound one for the other.

632. The principle which we have established, that the debtor of a thing certain is discharged from his obligation when the thing has perished without his act or fault, and before he has been put in arrear, receives an exception in the case in which the debtor makes himself by a particular clause of the contract liable for the risque of accidents. For example. If I have given a stone to a lapidary to cut, and it be broken without any fault of the workman, but by the defect of the thing itself; although regularly this loss, which has happened without his fault and by

a ſort of accident, ought to diſcharge him from the obligation which he has contracted to reſtore to me this ſtone, yet if by a particular clauſe in our bargain, he has charged himſelf with this riſque, he will not be diſcharged; he will be bound to pay me the price of this ſtone. It is the ſame of the law 13, §. 5, ff. *locat*. Theſe agreements, by which a debtor charges himſelf with accidents, have nothing contrary to the equity which ought to reign in contracts, eſpecially when the debtor who charges himſelf with this riſque, receives from the other party ſomething equivalent to the eſtimation of the riſque with which he charges himſelf; for theſe riſques are ſomething appreciable. For example. In the inſtance juſt propoſed, the lapidary who has taken on himſelf the riſque of the thing is preſumed to be compenſated for it by a price for his work, greater than it would have been if he had not charged himſelf with this riſque.

Likewiſe in the contract of loan to uſe, when the borrower takes upon himſelf the riſque of accidents in regard to the thing which is lent him, as in the inſtance of the law 1, *Cod. commod.*, he is compenſated for this riſque which he takes upon himſelf, by the enjoyment of the thing which the lender was not obliged to lend him gratuitouſly, and which he might have hired to him.

In the contract of pledge, the creditor who takes on himſelf the riſque of the things given him in pledge, as in the inſtance of the law 6, *Cod. de pign. act.*, is compenſated for the riſque by the aſſurance which he procures himſelf; the perſon giving the pledge being only his debtor, who was not obliged to give him pledges, was not obliged to procure it for him.

Even when the debtor who has charged himſelf with the riſque of accidents, ſhould not receive any thing for this riſque with which he is charged; if, in taking it on himſelf, he intended to exerciſe a liberality towards the other party, the clauſe does not contain in this caſe any injuſtice. If on the contrary the debtor, not intending to exerciſe any liberality, but to receive as much he gave, has taken on himself the risque of accidents, the clause, in *foro conscientiæ*, is unjust, when he does not derive any advantage from the bargain, which might be equivalent to this risque with which he is charged: in *foro legis* he is presumed to be compensated.

A debtor may take on himself not only the risque of a certain kind of accidents, as in the instance of the law 13, §. 5, ff. *locat.*, just mentioned; he may also charge himself generally with every accident by which the thing may perish, as in the instance of the law 6, *Cod. de pign. act.* However general the clause may be, it comprehends those only which may be prevented by the parties, and not those which they could not prevent, and which they could not guard against; *arg.* L. 9, §. 1, ff. *de transact.* Guthier, *Tr. de Con. jur.* §. 24, thinks that this decision ought to take place even when the clause should be expressed in these terms, *to be liable for all accidents, foreseen and unforeseen.* See our treatise on the contract of hire, *part* 3, *ch.* 1, *art.* §. 5, where we have treated at large of all these clauses.

Article IV.

Whether the obligation which is extinguished by the extinction of the thing due, is so extinguished as that it does not continue for the part which remains of this thing, nor for the rights and actions which the debtor has in regard to this thing.

633. When the extinction of the thing due is not a total extinction, and there remains some part of this thing, it cannot be doubted in this case that the obligation continues for the part which remains of the thing due. For example. If you were debtor to me of a herd of cattle which has perished by a mortality and of which there remains but one; or if you were debtor to me of a house which has been consumed by lightning; it is not to be doubted that you would continue towards me debtor of the one which remains of the herd, or of the ground and materials which remain of the house: for the one which remains of the

herd, although it could not itself compose a herd, is nevertheless, in a very proper sense, a part of this herd; the ground and materials escaped from the flames are, in a very proper sense, a part of this house. It may then be said in these two cases, that the herd of cattle which was due me yet remains, not totally but in part, in the one which remains of it; and likewise that the house which was due me yet remains in part, in what remains of this house; and these parts which remain may yet be the subject of the obligation.

There is more difficulty in the case in which the extinction of the thing due is a total extinction, so that what remains cannot be regarded as a part of this thing. This happens when the thing due is an individual thing, as an animal. It is a question whether in this case the obligation continues in what remains of the thing due. For example. If you were debtor to me of a certain ox, it is a question whether, if the ox be dead without your fault, I would be well grounded in demanding the hide. The reason to doubt is, that the death of the ox is a total extinction of the thing which was due me. One cannot say that this ox which was due me still continues for a part, after the death of the ox. The hide of the ox is indeed something which remains of the ox, but one cannot say that it would properly be a part of the living ox which was due me. There being in this case a total extinction of the thing due, the obligation, it is said, ought to be totally extinguished; I can demand nothing, not even the hide: for it is only the ox which you were obliged to give me. There was no question between us respecting the hide which should remain after the death of the ox: you have not obliged yourself to give me this hide; it is not the hide which is due me, and consequently I can have no right to demand it from you. In fine they pretend that the law 49, ff. *de leg.* 2, decides this question against the creditor: *Mortuo bove qui legatus est, neque corium neque caro debetur.* Notwithstanding these reasons, I think we ought to decide that the creditor is well grounded even in this caſe, to demand what remains of the thing due. I. Equity calls for this deciſion. In fact, when the ox which I have purchaſed of you and paid for, is dead without your fault, before the delivery which you ought to have made me, would it not be a manifeſt injuſtice that you ſhould profit by the misfortune which I have to bear from the loſs of this ox in retaining to your benefit and my prejudice, the hide of this ox of which you were my debtor? II. The principles of law alſo eſtabliſh our deciſion: it is not to be queſtioned that, is whatever manner a thing which belongs to me ſhould periſh, what remains of this thing belongs to me likewiſe: *meum est quod ex re mea superest.* L. 49, §. 1, ff. *de rei vind.* If the *jus in re*, if the right which one has in a thing, ſuch as the *dominium* or the right of property, continues to exiſt, after the extinction of the thing, in what remains of it; why ſhould not the *jus ad rem*, the right which one has to a thing, the right of demanding the thing, continue likewiſe to exiſt after the extinction of the thing, in what remains of it? As it is a principle *ut meum est quod ex re mea superest*, ſo is it *ut mihi debetur quod ex re mihi debita superest.* This is what Brunus very properly decides in his treatiſe *de Interitu.* After having eſtabliſhed *ut forma dat esse rei*, and *ut destructa forma substantiali, res interiisse videtur*, he ſays, *perempta forma, si quid ex re superest, potest durare circa illud quod remanet, jus, actio & obligatio.*

In regard to the reaſons to doubt propoſed above, it is eaſy to anſwer them. It is ſaid that the total extinction of the thing due ſhould totally extinguiſh the debt, and that conſequently there can no longer continue to the creditor a right to demand what remains of it. I anſwer. When the extinction of the thing is ſo entire as that nothing remains of it. I willingly grant that in this caſe the obligation is totally extinguiſhed; but when the thing due is not ſo entirely extinguiſhed as that nothing of it remains, although what remains of it be not properly a part of the thing. I deny that ſuch an extinction is an extinction of the thing fully and perfectly entire, and that it ought to extinguish totally the obligation; I maintain that it ought to continue in what remains of this thing. It is ill reasoning, and a begging of the question, in those who urge the reasons to doubt, to have advanced the contrary as a principle; since it is precisely what is in question. In fine, it is said that the debtor was obliged to give the ox which was living at the time of the contract, and that he is not obliged to give the hide which might remain after the death of the ox. I answer, that he is not obliged *formaliter* to give this hide; but he is obliged to do so *implicite & eminenter*; the obligation to give a thing containing *eminenter* whatever this thing includes and contains, and consequently whatever may remain of it, after the extinction of the thing. In regard to the law 49, ff. *de leg.* 2, which they plead, by which it is said that when the ox which has been bequeathed to me is dead, the legatee may not demand of it either the hide or the flesh, the answer is, that we must necessarily suppose, in the instance of this law, the ox to be dead before the legacy took effect and became due, that is to say in the life-time of the testator, if absolute, or before the accomplishment of the condition, if conditional. For if the ox was not dead till after the legacy took effect and became due, the property having been transferred to the legatee, it cannot be doubted that all which should remain of the ox would belong to him. According to the rule of law, *meum est quod ex re mea superest; ideoque vindicari potest.* L. 49, §. 1, ff. *de rei vind.* In supposing, as it ought necessarily to be supposed, that the ox died before the legacy became due, nothing can be inferred from this law against our decision; for if it be decided by this law that the legatee cannot demand what remains of the ox, it is not because the death of the ox has totally extinguished the debt: since as the ox was dead before the legacy became due, this debt never could be contracted; but it is because the legacy could have no effect, the death of the testator not being able to confirm the legacy of that which did not exist.

The obligation exists also after the extinction of the thing due, in that which was its accessory. For example. If you were debtor to me of a horse and furniture, and the horse died since the contract, without your fault, I am well grounded in demanding the harness of this horse which has remained with you. The law 2, ff. *de pecul. leg.*, is not contrary to this decision. It is there said, *Quæ accessionum locum obtinent extinguuntur, qùum principales res peremptæ fuerint.* The answer is, that this rule takes place when there has been as yet no obligation contracted. This law is in the instance of a slave who having been bequeathed with his *peculium*, died before the legacy became due. The *peculium* not being bequeathed *per se*, but as an accessory to the legacy of the slave, and the legacy of the slave having no effect, the whole lapsed. In this case there was yet no obligation contracted; but when once the obligation of a thing with its accessories has been contracted, the creditor having acquired a right, *jus ad rem*, to the accessories as well as to the principal thing, he ought to retain it even after the extinction of the principal thing.

634. When, without the fault of the debtor, the thing which he owed has perished or become not a subject of commerce, or is lost so that one does not know what has become of it; if the debtor has any rights or actions relative to this thing, his obligation continues so as to bind him to subrogate his creditor to the said rights or actions. For example. If you were my debtor of a horse which without your fault has been killed by a third person, or has been taken away by violence, without its being known what has become of the horse, you will indeed be discharged from the obligation to deliver the horse; but you will be bound to subrogate me to the actions which you have against those who killed or carried the horse away. Likewise, if you were debtor to me of a piece of ground which has since been taken for a public square, you will be discharged towards me with regard to the ground; but you will be bound

to subrogate me to the indemnity which you have a right to claim: it will remain with me to prosecute it at my costs and for my benefit.

CHAPTER VII.

Of several other ways in which obligations are extinguished.

ARTICLE THE FIRST.

Of time.

635. REGULARLY time does not extinguish obligations; those who bind themselves, bind forever themselves and their heirs, until the perfect performance of their obligation.

It may however be validly agreed that one shall be bound only until a certain time. For example. I may be a security for one with a clause that I shall not be holden to my securitiship longer than for three years.

By the civil law, the agreement by which the debtor stipulated that he should be bound only for a certain time, or until the event of a certain condition, although valid, did not however procure at the end of this time, or on the happening of the condition, the extinction of the debt *de jure*; but it gave to the debtor a plea against the demand of the creditor, *exceptionem pacti*. L. 44. §. 1, & 2, ff. *de oblig. & act.*; L. 56, ff. *de verb. oblig.* §. 4. The reason which the jurists give for it is, that obligations once contracted, cannot be extinguished but in the natural or lawful ways in which obligations are extinguished; and that the lapse of time or the happening of a condition are not such ways of extinguishing them. Our law does not admit of these subtilties and we consider the debt extinguished *de jure* by the expiration of the time to which the debtor intended to limit his obligation.

If he who is obliged only for a certain time had been put in arrear of paying, by a suit before the expiration of the time, he would remain obliged for ever, and could not be discharged but by payment; for the unjust default which he has made, ought not to be profitable to him and injurious to the creditor; L. 59, L. 5, *mandat*. This is conformable to this rule of law: *Omnes actiones quæ morte aut tempore pereunt, semel inclusæ judicio, salvæ permanent.*; L. 39, ff. *de reg. jur.*

Observe that in instruments of writing which express that one of the contracting parties has bound himself for a certain time, it is necessary to pay good attention to what has been intended by the parties. For example. If Peter has borrowed of you the sum of one hundred livres, which he binds himself to return you on your demand, and it is expressed that I become a security for him for this sum during the period of three years only, it is evident that the meaning of this clause is, that if during the said time I have not been put in arrear to discharge this debt, I shall, at the end of the said time of three years, be discharged *de jure* from my securitiship; as the clause in this case can have no other meaning. But if in a lease which you have made for the term of six years, it is expressed that I become a security for the lessee for the term of *six years only*, this would not signify that at the end of six years I should be discharged and acquitted from my securitiship, although the obligations of the lease should not be discharged; but these terms should be understood in this sense, that by the precaution and although it might not be necessary to be so explicit, I meant thereby to declare that I intended to become a security only for the obligations of this lease which would endure for six years, and not for the leases which you might, after the expiration of this time, renew to this lessee, either expresly or impliedly.

Article II.

Of resolutive conditions.

636. In the same manner as one may contract an obligation with a clause that it shall endure only for a certain time, one may also contract an obligation with a clause

that it ſhall endure only till the event of a certain condition; as when, in becoming a ſecurity for Peter, I have ſtipulated that I would bind myſelf for him until the return of a certain veſſel in which he has a large intereſt; my obligation endures only until the return of the veſſel: the return of the veſſel extinguiſhes it.

We call this kind of condition a reſolutive condition. See what we have ſaid *supra, part* 2, *ch.* 3, *art.* 2.

In ſynallagmatic contracts, which contain the reciprocal engagements between each of the contracting parties, they often put for a reſolutive condition of the obligation which one of the parties contracts, the inexecution of ſome one of the engagements of the other.

For example. If I ſell you my wine with a clauſe that if you do not come to take it away and pay me in eight days, I ſhall be diſcharged from my obligation; this is a reſolutive condition.

According to the ſimplicity of theſe principles, the ſingle lapſe of the time limited by the contract, in which you ought to ſatisfy the condition, when it has paſſed without your having ſatisfied it, ought to extinguiſh and diſſolve my engagement in all theſe and ſimilar caſes. Yet in our practice, it is uſual to cite the creditor by an officer, to ſatisfy the condition, or appear before the judge and ſhew cauſe why the engagement ſhould not be declared null for his default of ſatisfying it.

Even when we have not expreſſed in the agreement the inexecution of your engagement, as a reſolutive condition of that which I have contracted towards you, yet this inexecution may often operate the diſſolution of the bargain, and conſequently the extinction of my obligation. But it is neceſſary that I ſhould procure this diſſolution to be pronounced by the judge, upon notice which I ought to give you to this effect. Suppoſe for example, that I have ſold you my library abſolutely: if you delay to pay me the price of it, the inexecution of the engagement which you have contracted to pay me the price agreed, will give room for the extinction of that which I have contracted to deliver you my library. But this extinction of my engagement will not be made *ipso jure*; it will be made by the sentence which will intervene upon the notice which I shall give you, to shew cause why, on your default in taking away my library and paying me the price of it, the bargain should not be annulled. It is in this case at the discretion of the judge to allow you such delay as he may think proper to satisfy your obligation, after which I may obtain a judgement by which the dissolution of the bargain will be pronounced and I be discharged from my engagement.

ARTICLE III.

Of the death of the creditor and of the debtor.

§. I.

General rules.

637. Regularly claims are not extinguished by the death of the creditor; for he stipulates or is presumed to stipulate as well for his heirs and other universal successors as for himself.

Therefore the claim by the death of the creditor passes to his heirs who succeed to all his rights; and if he has no heirs, the claim is supposed to reside in the vacant succession, which in this respect *personæ vicem sustinet defuncti.*

Likewise, the obligation is not extinguished by the death of the debtor; for we are presumed to bind ourselves as well for our heirs and all other successors as for ourselves. Therefore when the debtor dies, the obligation passes to his heirs, who succeed to all his rights, active and passive; and if he leave no heirs, it resides in the vacant succession which represents him.

The principle that obligations pass to the heirs of the debtor, and the rights which result therefrom to the heirs of the creditor, applies not only in regard to obligations which are to give something, but also to those which are to do something, according to the constitution of Justinian in the law 13, *Cod, de cont. & comm. stipul.*

§. II.

Of claims which are extinguished by the death of the creditor.

638. There are however certain claims which are extinguifhed by the death of the creditor; fuch are thofe which have for their object fomething which is perfonal to the creditor; as if one binds himfelf to grant me the ufe of a certain book as often as I fhould require it, or to accompany me in the travels which I fhould perform; thefe things which make the object of my claim being perfonal to me, my claim would be extinguifhed by my death.

But if on the default of the debtor to perform his obligation, I had obtained a judgment againft him for the damages, this right to damages, into which my claim is converted, would pafs to my heirs.

A claim for the reparation of an injury is extinguifhed alfo by the death of the perfon injured, when he has not, during his life, brought any fuit therefor: he is prefumed in this cafe to have remitted and pardoned the injury; L. 13, ff. *de injur.*

Annuities are alfo debts which are extinguifhed for the future by the death of the creditor, when they have been conftituted on his life; but the debt of arrearages which have run till the day of his death, paffes to his heirs.

§. III.

Of debts which are extinguished by the death of the debtor.

639. There are alfo fome debts which are extinguifhed by the death of the debtor; fuch are thofe which have for their object fomething perfonal to the debtor, as when one is bound to ferve another in the quality of fhepherd, coachman, or in any other quality.

If the debtor, on default of performing this kind of obligation, has fuffered a judgment for the damages, this obligation, which fucceeds to his principal and original obligation, paffes to his heirs.

Excepting the cafe of perfonal acts, he who has promifed to do fomething, and is dead without having done it. although he has not been put in arrear of doing it, transmits his obligation to his heirs, who are obliged to do what the deceased was obliged to do.

By the civil law, obligations which arose *ex delicto*, were extinguished, for the most part, by the death of the debtor, when the demand had not been brought to a judgment against him in his life-time, and they did not pass to his heirs; except to the amount of what they had profited by them in their succession to the deceased. They had only the action which was called *condictio furtiva*, to demand the thing stolen, which was given against the heir of the thief, even when the heir had not profited by it. L. 19, ff. *de cond. furt.*

The principles of the canon law are different. It is only the penalty due for the trespass, which is extinguished by the death of him who has committed it; but the obligation to repair the injury which one has committed *ex delicto*, passes to his heirs. This is the decision of *cap. fin. de sepult.* and of *cap.* 5, 10, *de rapt.* We have on this point preferred, as most equitable, the principles of the canon law, to those of the civil law; and in our practice although the heirs of him who has committed a tort have not profited by it, they are liable for the damages due to him towards whom it has been committed; even when he had not brought his action against the deceased. This is attested by *J. Fab.* upon the *Instit. tit. de act.* §. *pœnales*; and by d'Argentre, *art.* 189, of the custom of Brittany.

CHAPTER VIII.

Of pleas in bar and prescriptions against claims.

Article the First.

General principles on pleas in bar and prescriptions.

640. PLEAS in bar against claims, are pleas shewing certain causes which prevent the creditor from being heard in court to make his demand.

The first kind of pleas in bar is the authority of the thing judged, *rei judicatæ*. When a debtor has had a judgment against the complaint of the creditor, there results from this judgment a plea in bar against the creditor, which disables him from suing for the debt; unless he causes the judgment to be set aside by a writ of error or appeal, when the judgment has not yet had the force of the thing judged: or, when it has acquired the force of the thing judged, by having it revoked in the tribunal of errors, if the case be such as that it could be brought there. With regard to cases in which a judgment is presumed to have obtained the force of the thing judged, and as to cases in which judgments which have obtained the force of the thing judged, may be set aside by the tribunal of errors, see the ordinance of 1667, *t.* 27, *art.* 5, & *t.* 35. This plea in bar is called in the civil law *exceptio rei judicatæ*, on which see the the Digest, *tit. de excep. rei jud.*

A second plea in bar is that which results from the decisory oath of the debtor who has sworn that he owed nothing, when this oath was deferred to him by the creditor. There results from this oath a plea in bar called *exceptio jurisjurandi*, which prevents the creditor from being received to prosecute his demand, notwithstanding any proof he may have obtained since. We will treat of this oath *infra*, *part.* 4, *ch.* 3, §. 3, *art.* 1.

641. A third plea in bar is that which results from the lapse of the time within which the law has confined the duration of the action which results from the claim. We call this kind of plea properly *prescription*; although the term prescription be a general expression which may also suit all other pleas in bar.

It is of this kind of pleas in bar which we shall treat of in the sequel of this chapter.

642. Pleas in bar do not extinguish the claim but they render it ineffectual, in rendering the creditor not receivable to bring the action which results from it.

Besides this, although pleas in bar do not extinguish

the claim *in rei veritate*, yet they cause it to be presumed to be extinguished and discharged, while the plea in bar exists.

Therefore when the debtor has acquired a plea in bar against my claim, not only am I, unable to bring an action against him, I cannot even oppose to him this claim as a set off against the claim which he may on his part have acquired against me since the plea in bar acquired against mine; for the plea in bar which exists against my claim, induces a presumption of the extinction of my claim.

But if my debtor of a sum of money, before the time of the prescription against my claim was accomplished, and consequently before the plea in bar was acquired, had become my creditor of a like sum of money, and afterwards, since the time of the prescription against my claim was accomplished, should demand the payment of his; although I should not be receiveable to bring an action against him for mine, I would be receivable to oppose it to him as a set-off against his. This is according to this maxim: *Quae temporalia sunt ad agendum, perpetua sunt ad excipiendum.* The reason is, that as the set-off is made *ipso jure, supra, n.* 599, from the time that you became my creditor, your claim and mine which was not yet prescribed, were mutually destroyed by the set-off and extinguished.

From the principle that the plea in bar while it exists, causes the claim to be presumed to be extinguished, it follows also that one would ineffectually become a security for a claim which is already barred. Add that the same pleas *in rem* which may be opposed against the principal obligation by the debtor, may be opposed by the security.

Pleas in bar ought to be pleaded by the debtor: the judge cannot supply them.

They may be waved by the renunciation which the debtor makes of them whether expresly, or tacitly.

These pleas in bar, being thus waved, cannot afterwards arrest either the execution or the demand. A plea in bar cannot be more effectually waved than by the payment which the debtor makes of the debt. As the plea in bar had not extinguifhed the debt, it cannot be doubted that the payment would be valid. Yet if the debtor who had paid the debt was a minor, he might procure a reftitution againft this payment, as alfo againft all other renunciations which he fhould make of pleas in bar that had been acquired by him.

Article II.

Of the prescription of thirty years.

643. Regularly the actions which arife on claims ought to be brought within the period of thirty years. When the creditor has fuffered this time to elapfe without bringing his action, thd debtor acquires againft him a prefcription which renders the creditors not receivable to make his demand.

§. I.

On what reason it is founded.

644. This prefcription is founded, I. on a prefumption of the payment or releafe of the debt, which refults from this lapfe of time; as it is not common that a creditor fhould delay for fo confiderable a time to caufe himfelf to be paid what is due him: and as prefumptions are derived, *ex eo quod plerumque fit*; Cujas, *in parat. ad tit. de prob.*; the laws have hence derived a prefumption that the debt has been difcharged or releafed,

Befides, the care which a debtor muft take to preferve the acquittances which are the proof of the payment he has made, ought not to be neceffary for ever: and a time fhould be fixed after which he fhould not be required to fhew them.

II. This plea in bar is alfo eftablifhed as a penalty for the negligence of the creditor. The law having given him a certain time in which he might bring the action which is given him to caufe himfelf to be paid, he is not entitled to be heard when he has fuffered this time to pafs.

§. II.

When, and against whom it runs.

645. It results from what has just been said, that, the time of the prescription cannot begin to run, but from the day when the creditor has had power to bring his action; for it cannot be said that he has delayed to sue while he was unable to bring suit. Hence this general maxim on the subject: *Contra non valentem agere, nulla currit prescriptio.*

Hence it follows that the time of the prescription cannot run while the action is not yet open and the claim is yet suspended by a condition, the event of which it waits.

Although the right of the creditor be already complete and the action has arisen, if there was a time of payment, the time of the prescription cannot begin to run but from the day of the completion of this time; because the creditor could not sooner effectually demand it.

When a debt is payable at several times, I see no difficulty in saying that the time of the prescription begins to run from the day of the expiration of the first time, for the part of the debt which was payable at this time; and that it does not run for the other parts till the day of the expiration of each of the other times in which they are payable. For example: If you owed me the sum of three thousand livres, payable in three times, from year to year, of which the first payment should be to be made on the first of January, 1735, the time of the prescription would begin to run for the first third part of the debt from the said first of January, 1735; for the second third part from the first of January, 1736; for the last third part from the first of January, 1737: and the debt would be barred for one third part in 1765, for another third part in 1766, and for the remainder in 1767.

646. From our principle that the time of the prescription cannot run while the creditor has not power to bring suit for his demand, it follows further that the time of the prescription cannot run, while the marriage continues, against the claims which a feme covert, although with a se-

paration of property, has againſt her huſband ; for being under his power, ſhe is during this time prevented from bringing a ſuit againſt him.

It is the ſame of claims and actions which ſhe ſhould have againſt third perſons, if theſe third perſons had a recourſe againſt the huſband to be diſcharged from them ; for in this caſe the wiſe is preſumed to have been prevented by her huſband from ſuing on account of the recourſe which the debtor had againſt him. Excepting this caſe, the time of the preſcription runs during the time of the marriage, againſt the claims which the wiſe has againſt third perſons.

The time of the preſcription cannot run againſt the beneficiary heir for the claims which he has againſt the beneficiary eſtate ; for he cannot bring a ſuit againſt himſelf.

647. The preſcription does not run againſt minors, although they have a tutor. This is not by the rule, *contra non volentem agere, non currit preſcriptio*, ſince they have tutors who may bring their actions for them. A particular favor, which this age requires, excepts minors from the law of preſcription. The cuſtom of Paris and of Orleans have regulations reſpecting it : they except minors from the law of preſcription, in ſaying that it runs againſt *perſons of age*.

When the creditor leaves heirs of whom ſome are of age and others minors, if the claim has for its object ſomething diviſible *natura aut ſaltem intellectu*, as if it is a claim for a certain eſtate ; the time of the preſcription which does not run againſt the minors for their part of the claim, does not ceaſe to run againſt thoſe of age for their parts.

But if the claim is indiviſible, as if I have promiſed ſome one to give for the benefit of his houſe a right of way ; while one of the heirs ſhould be a minor, the time of the preſcription would not run at all even againſt thoſe of age ; becauſe, as the debt is indiviſible, not ſuſceptible of parts, it cannot be barred for part. It is in this caſe that it is ſaid that the minor relieves the major *in individuis*.

648. Another queſtion is aſked. Does the time of the preſcription run againſt idiots or perſons inſane ?

These persons are either provided with curators or they are not. When they are not, they are within the rule, *contra non valentem, &c.* and it is not to be doubted in this case that the prescription could not run against them. The question falls then upon idiots who are provided with curators. We may say in their favor, in order to except them from the law of prescription, that the law has excepted minors from it, although provided with tutors: these persons are commonly compared to minors; they are still more incapable than minors of watching the preservation of their property: their condition is worthy of compassion and of the protection of the laws. Therefore it seems that the exception from the law of prescription, which has been granted to minors, ought to be extended to these persons. *Catelan, t.* 11, *l.* 7, 13, reports a case in his parliament, in which it was so adjudged.

The reasons which may be brought for the contrary opinion are that the laws in excepting minors from the law of prescription, have in this granted them a privilege: it is of the nature of privileges granted to a certain class of persons, not to be extended to others even under the pretext of a parity of reason. It may even be said that there is not here entirely a parity of reason. The law could very easily except from the prescription the time of minority, because this time has certain limits; whereas, as the insanity of a person continues commonly all his life, which may go to eighty or a hundred years, the prescription so necessary for the tranquillity of citizens, would often be arrested during too long a time, if idiots were excepted from the law of prescription. Add that minors being the hope of the state, there is a reason to aid them which does not operate in regard to other persons. This opinion may be supported by the authority of the commentary upon the *chap.* 15, *extra, de præscript.*, which in reporting all the cases against which the prescription does not run, does not comprehend in it idiots or persons insane. Bretonnier on *Henrys, t.* 2, 4, 21, appears to incline to this opinion.

649. When a person is absent in a distant country, for example in the East-Indies; although the person who had his power of attorney in his own country was dead, and there was no person who could take care of his affairs, the time of the prescription does nevertheless run against him: he is not for this reason within the rule, *contra non valentem, &c.* for however distant he might be it is not impossible for for him to inform himself of the news of his country, and to send a power of attorney to another person in the stead of him who is dead. See *Catelan*, as above cited.

Circumstances may however happen in which a person absent has been under an actual disability, and when this is evidently proved, we may aid him by applying the rule *contra non valentem, &c.*

650. The time of prescription runs against an estate, although vacant, abandoned and destitute of a curator: for the creditors of this estate, who are those who have an interest in preserving the rights of this estate, had it in their power to name a curator te this estate; theref ore they cannot avail themselves of the rule *contra non valen tem, &c.*

Henrys has thought that the prescription ought not to run against the rights of an estate while the heir has used the delay which the ordinance gives him to deliberate. This opinion has not had followers. The heir during this time had the power, without being bound thereby, to assume the quality of heir, to make use of all the conservatory actions and to interrupt the prescription: he is not therefore within the rule *contra non valentem, &c.*

651. The prescription takes place even against the king's farmers, for the claims depending on the rights which are farmed to them. *Nec obstat* that there is no prescription against the king: for this maxim relates only to the funds of the king's domain which are imprescriptible; but the claims of the farmers of the king, which concern the rights that are farmed to them, are not the funds of the king's domain: they are only the fruits, and the fruits are the property of the farmers.

The king indeed is not himself subject to any human law, consequently not to that of prescription: but his farmers are subject to the laws, and consequently to that of prescription, as well as to all others, and they ought to bring suit for their demands within the time prescribed by the laws.

652. The prescription of thirty years does not take place against the church, but only that of forty years, of which we shall speak *infra.*

Observe that it is the church rather than the beneficiary, which is exempted from the prescription of thirty years. Therefore this prescription is not rejected but when it operates against the ground itself of the claim. But the arrearages of annuities due to the church, the rents, profits, and other like claims, which concern rather the personal advantage of the beneficiary than the church itself, are subject to the prescription of thirty years. When the church succeeds to the claim of an individual, it ought to make use of the same right as this individual had, for the time the claim belonged to him, according to the rule: *Qui alterius jure utitur, eodem jure uti debet.*

The time of the prescription therefore ought only to be augmented in proportion to the time which remained to run when the church has succeeded to an individual. Therefore as ten years are added to the time of the ordinary prescription of thirty years, which is the third part on from the time of the prescription when it began to run against the church; so, when it has begun to run against an individual to whom the church has succeeded, one ought to add to the time of the prescription the third part on from the time which remained to run when the church succeeded to this individual. For example. If fifteen years had already run against an individual since the time of the prescription began to run, it would not be necessary to add ten years to the fifteen which remained to run, but only five years, the third of fifteen which remained, and the prescription would be accomplished at the end of thirty-five years.

Vice versa, when an individual has acquired a claim of the church, the individual ought to enjoy, for the paſt, the privilege of the church as to the preſcription of forty years, and the time of the preſcription ought not to be reduced to the preſcripton of thirty years, except for the future. For example. If twenty years had run againſt the church when the individual acquired the claim of the church, the time of twenty years being but half of that which is neceſſary againſt the church, there would be wanting for the accompliſhment of the preſcription, the other half of the time, not of that which is neceſſary againſt the church, but of that which is neceſſary againſt individuals; that is to ſay, there would be wanting fifteen years more. The time of the preſcription againſt individuals being leſs by a fourth than that of the preſcription againſt the church, when an individual ſucceeds to the church, we muſt ſubtract the fourth of the time which would remain to run againſt the church, if the claim had always continued to belong to it. Therefore in the inſtance propoſed, we have ſubſtracted five years from the time of twenty which remained to run againſt the church when the individual ſucceeded to the church.

Secular corporations have the ſame privilege as the church and are barred only by the preſcription of forty years; *Troncon on Paris*; *Lemaitre*, &c.

§. III.

Of the effect of the prescription of thirty years.

653. The effect of this preſcription is, that when it is accompliſhed, the debtor againſt whom the creditor ſhould bring a ſuit after the accompliſhment of the preſcription, may in oppoſing to the creditor to this preſcription, cauſe him to be declared not receivable in his demand.

654. May the creditor however in this caſe defer to the debtor the oath upon the payment? No: for this preſcription is not only eſtabliſhed upon the preſumption of payment which reſults from the long time which has paſſed; it is alſo eſtabliſhed as a penalty for the negligence of the creditor. The law having limited the time of the duration of

the action which it gives, after the expiration of this time, the creditor has indeed preserved his claim, if it has not been discharged, but he has no longer an action: he has no longer *jus persequendi in judicio quod sibi debetur*, and consequently he has no longer the right to exact from his debtor the oath which makes part of this right of action.

655. The prescription, whether begun or accomplished against the creditor, takes effect against his heirs and other successors, whether by a general or particular title, so that it would no longer remain to them to demand the payment of the claim but for the time which remained when they succeeded to him; and if it has been accomplished against the creditor, the same plea in bar which took place against him, ought to take place against them. This is evident: for being in the rights of the creditor, holding from him all the rights which they can have, they cannot have more than he could have had himself. *Nemo plus juris in alium potest transferre, &c.*

656. There is more difficulty in regard to the substitute. May the time of the prescription which has run before the vesting of the substitution against the heir, for a claim of the succession which makes part of the property comprised in the substitution, after the vesting of the substitution, be imputed to this substitute? The reason to doubt is, that this substitute does not hold his right to the property substituted, from him who was charged with the substitution for his benefit, and against whom the time of the prescription has run. Nevertheless it must be decided that the prescription, whether commenced or accomplished against the person charged, likewise takes effect against him: for although the substitute does not hold his right from the person charged, but from the testator who has made the substitution, yet this claim passes from the person charged to that of the substitute; and it cannot pass but such as it is, and consequently barred by the prescription in part or entirely, if it was so in the life of the person charged. The

person charged having been the true creditor until the vesting of the substitution, it is against him that the time of the prescription ought to run and in fact has run. The person charged would not have power *faciendo*, in disposing of this claim, transferring, hypothecating it, to prejudice the substitute: because he cannot transfer it but as he has it, and consequently *cum causa fideicommissi*, with the charge of the substitution: but he may, *non faciendo, non utendo*, suffer the action which resulted from this claim to perish. This is the precise disposition of the law 70, §. *fin.* ff. *ad Trebell. Si temporalis actio in hæreditate relicta fuerit, tempus quo hæres experiri ante restitutam hæreditatem potuit, imputabitur ei cui restituta fuerit.*

It is true that the law does not speak of actions limited to a number of years, because in the time of the jurists from whom we have this law, common actions were not subject to the prescription of any lapse of time: but since they have been subjected to the prescription of thirty years, there is the same reason so to decide. This is also the opinion of Ricard, *Tr. Subst. p.* 2, *ch.* 13, *n.* 93, 94.

657. The prescription has not only effect *in foro legis*, it may sometimes have effect *in foro conscientiæ*. The debtor who cannot be ignorant that he has not paid, may not indeed *in foro conscientiæ* have recourse to the prescription, and it is for this that it is called *improborum præsidium*: but as the prescription forms a presumption that the debt has been discharged, the heirs of the debtor may even *in foro conscientiæ* presume that the debt has been discharged and consequently avail themselves of the prescription, when they have no knowledge or just cause to believe that the debt has not been discharged.

§. IV.

How prescriptions not yet accomplished, are interrupted.

658. The time of the prescription is interrupted either by the acknowledgment which the debtor makes of the debt, or by a judicial demand.

By whatever instrument the debtor acknowledges the

debt, it interrupts the time of the prescription, whether it be passed with the creditor or without him. For example. If in the inventory of the property of the debtor the debt is comprised among the passive, this inventory, although it be not made with the creditor, is an act acknowledging the debt, which interrupts the time of the prescription.

659. As to the debtor it is immaterial whether the instrument acknowledging the debt be before a notary or under private signature: but as to third persons who have an interest that the claim should be barred, the instrument acknowledging the debt, when it is under private signature, will not be of any use to the creditor, if he has not acquired a date anterior to the accomplishment of the time of the prescription, which date must appear either by the register or by the decease of one of those who have subscribed it: for without this, deeds under private signature have no effect against third persons, but from the day when they are shewn: which has been introduced to prevent the frauds to which the facility of ante-dating might give room.

660. The verbal acknowledgment which the debtor should make of the debt, when it exceeds one hundred livres, can hardly be of any effect to the creditor, because according to the ordinance of 1667, he is not admitted to prove by witnesses things whereof the object exceeds one hundred livres, and of which he had power to procure for himself proof by writing. I think however that he would be receivable to defer to the debtor the oath, whether he has not in fact acknowledged the debt in the time and in the manner in which it is contended that he has. *Nec obstat* that the creditor after the time of the prescription is accomplished, may not defer the oath to the debtor upon the payment, as we have decided above; the difference is, that as it is avowed by the parties that the time of the prescription is accomplished, it remains established that the creditor has no longer an action, and that consequently he has no right to defer the oath. But in this instance it is not avowed by the parties that the time of the prescription is accomplished and that the creditor has no longer an action; the credi

tor maintains to the contrary, that there has been an interruption of the time. It is true that it is for him to prove it; *nam incumbit onus probandi, ei qui dicit*: but, *inopia probationis*, he may upon this fact defer the oath. If the debt did not exceed one hundred livres, I think that the creditor might be admitted to prove by witnesses, that the debtor has within such time acknowledged the debt and promised to pay.

661. The payment of the arrearages which the debtor makes of an annuity, is an acknowledgment of this annuity; but as the acquittances are with the debtor, this acknowledgment is commonly of no effect to the creditor, who cannot prove it unless he requires from the debtor counter acquittances, or unless the acquittances are before a notary, and a minute of them remains.

The journal of the creditor in which he has entered the payments which may have been made to him, cannot serve to prove for him that he has received such payments; because one cannot make himself a witness for himself. L. 5, *Cod. de probat.*

If the annuity was due to a corporation, as to the corporation of a city, or to a company of artificers, I think that the accounts solemnly rendered, in which the receiver charges himself with the payments, ought to give faith to the payment, and consequently to the interruption of the prescription: for it is not likely that a receiver, if he had not actually received these arrearages, would have been foolish enough to charge himself with the receipt of them, and thereby oblige himself to pay them in the stead of the debtor. Besides, whether the debtor has actually paid the arrearages of this annuity, or whether, without their having been paid, the receiver has charged himself with the receipt of them, as if he had received them, and had accounted for them: in both cases the corporation to whom the annuity is due, has received the said arrearages and has availed itself of the annuity. There can be no room then for the prescription: it takes place only when the creditor has not availed himself of his right and has used no diligence to do so. This is the jurisprudence of the *Chatelet d'Orleans*.

662. The second manner in which the time of the prescription is interrupted, is by judicial demand made upon the debtor. This judicial demand, when the title of the claim is with execution, is made by a command to pay served upon the debtor, or when the title is not with execution, by a writ of summons which is brought against him.

As both these acts are done by the assistance of an officer, who is an officer of justice, both contain a judicial demand.

Both acts interrupt the time of the prescription, provided they are clothed with all the formalities with which these acts ought to be clothed, in order to be valid.

If one of these acts should be null, by the omission of of some formality, it would not interrupt the prescription according to the rule, *Quod nullum est, nullum producit effectum*.

An adjournment given before an incompetent judge, in the strictness of principles, does not interrupt the prescription: however when the competency might have been doubtful, the court, in pronouncing the incompetency of the judge before whom the suit was brought, sometimes sends back the parties before the judge who has cognizance of the subject, with this clause, *that they proceed before him in the same condition they were in at the time of the adjournment*; *Imbert*, 1, 22, 7 & 8. *Dumoulin, in styl. Parlam. p.* 7, *art.* 102, cites a decree of the 27th July, 1515, which with this clause remanded before the judge of Angers a suit which had been erroneously brought before the judge of Saumur.

There is a difference between a command and a writ of summons, that this is liable to abatement by the discontinuance of the proceedings upon the summons during the time of three years; and when the abatement has been declared to be acquired, this writ of summons is regarded as nothing, and cannot have the effect to have interrupted the time of the prescription. On the contrary the simple command, not forming a suit, is not liable to the abatement of suits; and even when it should not be followed by any other proceedings, it preserves its effect to interrupt the time of the prescription, and establish the action of the creditor during thirty years from the day of its date.

663. When there are several debtors *in solidum*, the acknowledgement of one of them or the judicial demand made upon one of them, interrupts the prescription in regard to all the others. This is what Justinian decides in the law *fin. Cod. de duobus reis*, as we have already seen *supra, n.* 272.

It is not the same in regard to several heirs of the same debtor. The acknowlegement which one of them makes of the debt, or the judicial demand made upon one of them, does not interrupt the time of the prescription but for the part of which he is personally the debtor, and does not prevent the prescription for the part due by the other heir, who has neither acknowleged the debt, nor has had a judicial demand made upon him: for as a debt may be extinguished in part, it may also be prescribed in part.

This takes place even when the debt should be a debt with hypothecation, for which each of the heirs should be bound with hypothecation for the whole: for as each of the heirs is personally bound for the debt only as to his part, although he should be bound with hypothecation for the whole, the creditor by the judicial demand which has been made upon one of the heirs, has made use of his personal right of action only for the part of the debt for which the said heir against whom a judicial demand has been made was liable, and he has made use of his right of hypothecation only for the part of the property fallen to this heir against whom a judicial demand has been made; but he has not made use of his right of action for the parts for which the other heirs upon whom the judicial demand has not been made were liable, tor of his right of hypothecation upon the part of the property fallen to these heirs; consequently the prescription is acquired by these heirs against whom a judicial demand has not been made as well against the action which the creditor had against them personally for the parts of the debt for which they were liable, as against the hypothecation which he had upon the property which had fallen to them.

An objection may perhaps be made. Why, it will be asked, does not the demand upon one of the holders of property hypothecated to my claim, interrupt the time of the prescription against other holders of property hypothecated to the same claim, in the same manner as the demand made upon one of the debtors *in solidum* interrupts the time of the prescription of my claim against the other debtors *in solidum?* The answer is, that the personal claim which I have against several debtors *in solidum* is a single claim *in personam*, a claim that resides in my person: therefore in making a judicial demand upon one of my debtors, I exercise my right for the whole and interrupt the time of the prescription not only against the debtor upon whom I made the demand, but against all others; for as the right which I have against them is not a different right but precisely the same which I have against him on whom I made the demand, in exercising for the whole the right which I have against him, I have exercised that which I have against them. On the contrary the rights of hypothecation which I have in the different estates hypothecated to my claim are rights *in rem*, rights which consequently reside in the different things in which I have the rights of hypothecation, and which are consequently as distinct one from another as the things in which these rights reside are distinguished one from another. For example. When black acre and white acre are hypothecated to me for a certain claim, the right of hypothecation which I have in black acre is as different from the one that I have in white acre as black acre is different from white acre. When therefore by an hypothecary action which I bring against the person in possession of white acre, I exercise the right of hypothecation which I have in it, I do not thereby exercise the right of hypothecation which I have in black acre, and consequently this action cannot interrupt the prescription against the hypothecation which I have in black acre. According to these principles the hypothecary action which I bring against one of the heirs of my debtors, interrupts the prescription against my rights of hypothecation in the part only of the estate which this heir inherits from my debtor; but it does not interrupt the prescription against the rights of hypothecation which I have in the parts of the other heirs. When the debt is of a thing indivisible, such as a right of way, every one of the heirs being in this case a personal debtor of the whole, the interruption of the prescription with regard to one ought to interrupt it with regard to the other; *secus* when the thing due is susceptible of parts, at least of intellectual parts.

The judicial demand made upon one of the debtors *in solidum* interrupts the prescription not only against the other debtors *in solidum*, but likewise against the heirs of the other debtors *in solidum*; the reason for it is the same.

Likewise a judicial demand made upon all the heirs of one of the debtors *in solidum*, interrupts the prescription against all the other debtors *in solidum*. But the judicial demand made upon one of the heirs of one of the debtors *in solidum*, of a divisible debt, interrupts the prescription against the other debtors *in solidum* only for the part for which this heir was liable. *Puta*, if I had two debtors *in solidum*, one of whom left four heirs, the judicial demand made upon one of those heirs would interrupt the prescription against the other debtors *in solidum* only for the fourth of the debt for which the heir on whom the demand was made was liable; for in making a demand upon this heir, who was bound only for one fourth of the debt, I have exercised my right only for a fourth of it, consequently the prescription is acquired for the surplus to the other debtor *in solidum*, and it is acquired entirely to the co-heirs of him on whom the demand was made, as I have not exercised my right and my action for the parts for which each of them was bound.

664. It is a question much controverted among writers, whether the judicial demand made upon the principal debtor, or the acknowlegement of the debt made by him, interrupts the prescription against his securities. Bruneman *ad L. fin. Cod. de duob. reis*, with the authors by him cited, and, among the moderns, Catelan, hold the affirmative. They pretend that the same reason which has led Justinian to decide thus in regard to co-debtors *in solidum* is found to operate in regard to securities. This reason is, that as the claim of a creditor against several debtors *in solidum* is a single and personal claim, when a judicial demand has been made upon one of them, those on whom the demand has not been made, cannot say to this creditor that he has not exercised the claim which he had against them; since that which he had against them is the same as that which he has exercised in making the demand upon one of them. And, say these authors, the same reason operates in regard to securities: the claim which the creditor has against them is the same as that which he has against the principal debtor, to whose obligation the securities have only acceded: whence it follows that the creditor, in exercising the claim which he has against the principal debtor by the judicial demand which I have made upon him, has exercised the claim which he has against the securities, since it is the same. They add that if Justinian has not spoken of securities, it is because they are as to this point, comprised under the word *correi*, since they are *rei ejusdem obligationis:* they are co-debtors of the principal debtor; not indeed principal co-debtors, but codebtors accessory to the same obligation.

Duperrier and the authors by him cited, hold the negative. They say there is a great difference between securities and co-debtors *in solidum*. When I have sold a thing to several purchasers who have bound themselves to me *in solidum* for the payment of the price, the claim which I have against each of the co-debtors *in solidum* is a single and personal claim, which has the same cause, and from which arises but one and the same action, which is the action *ex vendito*, which I have againſt each of them; whence it follows that in exerciſing my claim by the judicial demand which I have made upon one of them, I exercife the claim which I have againſt all the other co-debtors upon whom I have not made the demand; becauſe it is the ſame claim which I have againſt all. It is not the ſame, ſay they, as to the principal debtor and his ſecurities. The claim which I have againſt the principal debtor, and that which I have againſt the ſecurities, are indeed claims of one and the ſame thing; therefore the payment actual or fictitious by the one, diſcharges the others. But although the claims be claims of one and the ſame thing, they are nevertheleſs claims diſtinct from one another, which ariſe from different contracts and which produce different actions. For example. When I have ſold a thing to ſome perſon for a certain ſum, for which he has given me a ſecurity, the claim which I have againſt the purchaſer and that which I have againſt the ſecurity are indeed claims of a ſingle and the ſame thing, but they are nevertheleſs claims diſtinct from one another. That which I have againſt the principal debtor, is a claim which reſults from a contract of ſale, and from which ariſes the action, *ex vendito*; that which I have againſt the ſecurity, is a claim which ariſes from the ſecuritiſhip to which he has ſubjected himſelf to me. The ſecuritiſhip is a different agreement from the contract of ſale, from which ariſes a different action, which is the action *ex stipulatu*. Theſe claims being diſtinct claims, when the creditor has exerciſed his claim againſt the purchaſer and principal debtor, by the judicial demand which he has made upon him, it cannot be ſaid that he has exerciſed the claim which he has againſt the ſecurity, and conſequently this demand does not interrupt the preſcription of the debt of the ſecurity. Theſe authors derive an argument from the law *fin. Cod. de duob. reis*. This law deciding that the acknowlegement of one of the debtors, or the judicial demand which has been made upon him, interrupts the preſcription againſt all the others, alledges this reaſon for it; *quum ex una stirpe unoque fonte unus effluxit contractus, vel debiti causa ex eadem actione apparuit.* The fecurities, fay they, are not within the terms of the law; for fecurities although debtors of the fame thing with the principal debtor, are debtors in virtue of another contract, and the action which the creditor has againft them is different from that which he has againft the principal debtor.

It may be replied, that the fecuritifhip is a contract merely acceffory. The fecurities do nothing elfe than accede by this contract to the debt of the principal debtor. This contract does not form properly a new claim; it only gives the creditor new debtors who accede to the debt of the principal debtor: the claim which the creditor has againft them is the fame claim which he has againft the principal debtor. As to the objection, that by the Roman law the creditor has againft the fecurities an action *ex stipulatu*, which is an action different from that which he had againft the principal debtor, I anfwer that we need not conclude that the claim againft the fecurities muft be a claim different from that againft the principal debtor. The ftipulation from which arofe the action *ex stipulatu*, was not of itfelf a ground of the claim, it was rather a corroboration of it; it was only an act corroborative of the different agreements in which they had made it intervene; the ftipulation by which the fecuritifhip was contracted, did not therefore form a new claim, it only corroborated the claim which the creditor had already, and caufed the fecurities to accede to it.

§. V.

How prescriptions accomplished are avoided.

665. The prefcription, although accomplifhed, is avoided, when the debtor has acknowledged the debt, notwithftanding this be fince the accomplifhment of the prefcription. This acknowledgment prevents him from being able to plead againft the creditor the bar which refulted from the accomplifhment of the time of the prefcription, and confequently avoids and annuls it.

There is a great difference between the acknowledgment which is made after the time of the prescription is accomplished, to the effect of avoiding the prescription, and that which is made before, to the effect only of interrupting it. This may be made not only by the debtor himself, but also by a tutor, a curator, a person having a general power from the debtor: it may be made by the debtor himself, although a minor, without the possibility of relief against it.

On the contrary, the acknowledgment which should be made of the debt after the time of the prescription is accomplished, to the effect of reviving the debt, cannot be made but by the debtor himself, and it is necessary that he be of age, without which he would be relievable against this acknowledgment. It cannot be made by a tutor, a curator, nor by a person having a power which was not special *ad hoc*, but only general. The reason is, that this acknowledgment, which is made after the time of the prescription is accomplished, to the effect of avoiding it, includes a gratuitous alienation of a right to the plea in bar which the debtor has acquired by the accomplishment of the time of the prescription. A gratuitous alienation of a right acquired exceeds the power of a tutor, a curator, or other person having a general power.

There results from the same principle a second difference between the acknowledgment made after the time of the prescription is accomplished, and that made before. This interrupts the time of the prescription towards and against all; whereas the acknowledgment of a debt made after the time of the prescription accomplished, does not avoid the prescription but against the debtor who has made the acknowledgment, and against his heirs. It does not avoid it against the co-debtors *in solidum* of him who has made the acknowledgment, nor against his securities nor against third persons who detain the possession of what they may have acquired, before this acknowledgment, of the estates hypothecated for the debt, nor against intermediate creditors. For as the right which results from the prescription against the debt has been once acquired by the accomplishment of the time, the debtor who has ſince acknowledged the debt, may indeed by this acknowledgment renounce the preſcription for himſelf and his heirs, but cannot renounce it to the prejudice of a right acquired by third perſons.

666. If the ſimple acknowledgment of the debt avoids and aboliſhes the preſcription, *a fortiori* ought the payment which ſhould be made of the debt after the time of the preſcription accompliſhed.

He who pays, although after the time of the preſcription accompliſhed, is therefore preſumed to pay what he owed and he cannot recall it.

Further; he who pays a part of a debt againſt which a preſcription has been acquired, is preſumed entirely to renounce this preſcription even for the ſurplus which remains to be paid. *arg.* L. 7. §. *pen. & fin.* ff. *de senatusc. Maced.*; unleſs he had proteſted in paying, that he did not intend to acknowlege the debt but for the ſum which he paid.

According to theſe principles, it is not to be doubted that the payment which the debtor of an annuity makes of ſome arrearages ſince the time of the preſcription accompliſhed, avoids the preſcription.

667. A judgment intervening againſt the debtor alſo aboliſhes the preſcription, when it has become effectual as a thing judged, that is to ſay, when there is no farther room for appeal: the debtor after this judgment, is no longer receivable to plead the preſcription, even when he had omitted to plead it in the ſuit in which the judgment intervened; for this judgment gives the creditor a new title.

Article III.

Of the prescription of forty years.

668. According to the diſpoſitions of ſeveral cuſtoms, of the number of which is our cuſtom of Orleans, the hypothecary debtor, that is to ſay, he who has bound himſelf by an inſtrument before a notary, and his heirs, may not plead the preſcription of thirty years, but only that of forty.

Theſe diſpoſitions are conformable to the principles of

the civil law, and to the constitution of the emperor Justinian, in the law *Quum notissimi, Cod de præscr. trig. vel. quadr.* which establishes this prescription of forty years and it seems that they ought to be followed when the custom is in this respect silent. This is the opinion of the commentators on the custom of Paris, cited by Lemaitre.

In order to understand well this law, and why the hypothecary debtor has not the prescription of thirty years as other debtors, it is necessary to examine the nature of the prescription of thirty years.

This prescription includes two kinds; the prescription against personal claims and the prescription against rights of property and other rights *in rem.* These two kinds of prescriptions ought not to be confounded: they have no resemblance but in the time, and are very different in the manner, in which they are acquired.

The prescription against personal claims is acquired by the debtor without any act on his part, and results solely from this that the creditor, during the time defined by the law, has not brought the action which his claim gave him, and has had no acknowlegement of it. It does not extinguish properly the claim, which cannot be extinguished but by a payment real or fictitious; it extinguishes only the action which the creditor had to procure to himself the payment: which action before this law had no limits in its duration, and is by this law limited to thirty years. This action is extinguished by this law, not *ipso jure*, but by a plea in bar which the law grants to the debtor against this action.

The second kind of the prescription of thirty years is that by which he who has possessed during thirty years an estate as belonging to him, and as free from the claims to which it was subject, although he does not adduce any title for his possession, acquires the property of this estate, and a discharge from all the claims to which it was liable. While the first kind of prescription is acquired by the sole neglect of the creditor against whom it is made, without any act of the debtor who makes it, this on the contrary is acquired by the fact of the possession of the possessor who prescribes.

The debtor who had himself hypothecated his estate, could not acquire a discharge from the hypothecation by this kind of prescription, because he could not be presumed to have possessed this estate as free from an hypothecation which he had himself made. Nor could the heir of the debtor any more, according to this rule: *Hæres succedit in virtutes & vitia possessionis defuncti*; L. 11, *Cod. de acq. possess.*, the possession of the heir being presumed to be the same with that of the deceased. Therefore although the debtor or his heirs had acquired by the first kind of prescription of thirty years a plea in bar against the personal action of the creditor, they remained always subject to the hypothecary action of the same creditor; the estate remaining always hypothecated for the debt, which, although prescribed and deprived of action, remained always as a natural debt, and served as a sufficient foundation for the hypothecation; L. 5, ff. *de pign. & hypoth.*

Although Anastase, by the law 4, *Cod. de prescript. trigint.*, had introduced the prescription of forty years against all the actions which were not subject to this of thirty, yet it was not thought that this could extend to the hypothecary action of the creditor against the debtor, for the reasons which we have above deduced.

In fine, Justinian, as we have said, extended the prescription of forty years to the hypothecary action of the creditor against the debtor and the heir of the debtor; this is the disposition of the law *Quum notissimi.*

669. If the debtor, bound personally and with hypothecation, had sold the estate to a third person, this third person who, in the prescription of thirty years which he would oppose, should wish to comprehend the time of his predecessor who was personally bound, ought to add to the thirty years a third of the number of years yet to come of the time of the prescription of his predecessor; for as his predecessor could not prescribe but by a time longer by a third

yet to come than that of thirty years, he cannot, in the place of his predecessor prescribe by a less time, according to this rule, *Qui alterius jure utitur, eodem jure uti debet.*

670. The disposition of the law *Quum notissimi*, has not been adopted but in regard to hypothecations which result from obligations contained in instruments before a notary. Debtors against whom judgment has passed, prescribe by the common time of thirty years, although the ordinance of Moulins has given the effect of hypothecations to judgments: for the law grants this hypothecation rather to the personal action *ex judicato*, than to the claim upon which the judgment has intervened; therefore it is extinguished by the prescription of thirty years, which extinguishes the personal action *ex judicato.*

It is the same with all other legal hypothecations: they are extinguished when the personal action is extinguished.

671. It is the same with the personal action *in rem* for the arrearages of feudal rents and profits, the right of redemption and other like causes; this action is subject to the common prescription of thirty years. See the commentators on the custom of Paris.

Article IV.

Of the prescriptions of six months and of one year against the actions of shop-keepers, artisans and other persons.

§. I V.

In what cases the prescription of six months takes place.

672. According to the ordinance of Lewis XII, in the year 1510, *art.* 6, 8, "All drapers, apothecaries, bakers "and other kinds of tradesmen and shop-keepers selling in "retail, are not receivable, after six months from the first "delivery, to demand the price thereof, unless there has "been a judicial demand, or a settlement of the account."

This ordinance has not been exactly observed.

The custom of Paris has made a distinction: it gives, according to the ordinance of Lewis XII. the time only of six months to shop-keepers and artisans who deal in small sums and small commodities, to demand the payment of their claims; after which time, counting from the day of the first delivery, it declares them not receivable. Such is the article 126 of this custom, "shop-keepers, tradesmen and "other persons selling provisions and commodities in retail, "as bakers, pastry-cooks, taylors, sadlers, butchers, har-"ness-makers, lace-makers, farriers, keepers of cook-shops, "cooks and other like persons, cannot bring their ac-"tion after six months passed from the day of the first de-"livery of the said provisions or commodities, summons or "judicial demand made, note or obligation."

In regard to shop-keepers and artisans who sell wares more considerable, and deal more largely, such as drapers, mercers, grocers, goldsmiths, and other dealers in the gross, masons, carpenters, tilers; it grants them a year to bring suit for what is due to them, *art.* 127.

Apothecaries have also a year, *art.* 125.

673. The ordinance of 1673, which at the present day is in this respect the general law of the kingdom, appears to have followed the distinction of the custom of Paris. It expresses in the first title, *art.* 7, "that shop-keepers by "wholesale and retail, masons, carpenters, tilers, lock-"smiths, glaziers, plumbers, pavers, and others of the like "quality, shall be holden to demand their payment within "a year after the delivery."

And in article 8, it expresses: "The action shall be "brought within six months for provisions and commodi-"ties in retail, sold by bakers, pastry-cooks, butchers, cooks "and keepers of cook-shops, taylors, lace-makers, sadlers, "harness-makers, and other like persons." Under these words, "and other like persons," are comprised shoe-makers, coblers, cooks and sellers of swine flesh, &c.

674. Our custom of Orleans has not admited the prescription of six months except against the demands of letters of horses and other beasts; *art.* 266.

It gives expressly, in the article 265, one year for

demands for fmall commodities; and notwithftanding the ordinance of 1673, the cuftom is always preferved, in this bailiwick, of granting a year without diftinction to all fhop-keepers and artifans, to demand payment for their wares and manufactures.

§. II.

In what cases the prescription of a year takes place.

675. The prefcription of a year takes place, I. againft the demands of fhop-keepers and artifans comprifed in the article 126 of the cuftom of Paris, and of thofe comprifed in the article 7 of the firft title of the ordinance of 1673. In the cuftom of Orleans, this prefcription takes place againft the demands of all fhop-keepers and artifans, without any diftinction of large and fmall quantities.

II. Againft demands for bills of doctors and furgeons, according to the article 125 of the cuftom of Paris, which is obferved where the cuftom is not explicit on that fubject.

III. Againft the demands of fchool-mafters, preceptors ufhers, regents and others for the inftruction of children. Our cuftom of Orleans *art.* 265. has a difpofition to this effect, and it is a common law.

IV. Againft demands for board and neceffaries; *Orleans*, 265. this is alfo a common law.

V. Againft demands for wages of fervants labourers and others; *Orleans*, 265. This is alfo a general law.

This term *servants*, comprehends not only thofe who ferve about the perfon of the head of a family, but alfo thofe who labour in hufbandry fuch as labourers, reapers, gatherers, vineyardsmen, herdsmen, &c., thofe who work at manufactures, fuch as fervants to refiners, and thofe who ferve as journeymen with artifans. Under this term *servants* are not comprifed thofe who work by the day, who have only forty days to make their demand as we fhall *infra.*

§. III.

In what cases prescriptions do not take place.

676. These prefcriptions of fix months and of one year do not take place, I. when the claim is eftablifhed by fome inftrument in writing, whether before a notary, or under private fignature, or finally by an account fettled which contains the articles, or the journal of a fhop-keeper containing the account fettled and figned by the debtor: this is the fenfe of the terms of the article 9, firft title of the ordinance of 1673: "It is our will that the contents take "place, unlefs before the year and the fix months there "may have been *an account settled*, a note or obligation." In this cafe the claim is fubject only to the prefcription of thirty years.

677. II. Thefe prefcriptions do not take place, if they have been interrupted by a fuit brought before the time of the prefcription had expired, and which had not fince failed by *nonpross*: this is common to all prefcriptions.

678. III. Thefe prefcriptions of a year and of fix months are not obferved in the confular jurifdictions, when the articles or workmanfhip of a fhop-keeper or artifan have been delivered to another fhop-keeper or artifan for his trade or art, and the parties have upon their journals accounts current with each other for the faid articles. There is on this fubject a celebrated cafe decided, of the 12 July 1672, *Journal du Palais*. The cuftom of Troyes, *art.* 201, has a difpofition to this effect.

For example. A fhoemaker to whom a currier has furnifhed leather, a joiner to whom a lumber dealer has furnifhed timber, cannot plead this prefcription againft the currier or the lumber dealer, who fhew a journal by which it appears that they have an account current with the fhoemaker or joiner.

679. IV. Thefe prefcriptions do not take place againft common perfons who fell fmall commodities and provifions, the produce of their land, as their corn, their wine.

their wood: for the ordinance as well as the custom has subjected to the prescription only shop-keepers and tradesmen.

One should in this respect, consider as a common person and not a shop-keeper, a person who, although a shop-keeper by profession, sells provisions from his land, and of which he does not make a trade; as if a grocer had sold the wine from his vineyard.

Although a common person be not subject to the prescription of a year, however if he had brought suit after a very considerable time, although less than thirty years, against a shop-keeper, to whom he had sold provisions of his own raising, and the shop-keeper should maintain that he had paid for them, although he had no discharge therefrom, it would be in the discretion of the judge, according to the circumstances, to discharge the defendant from the demand.

§. IV.

From what time prescriptions run and against whom.

680. The prescription against the demands of shop-keepers and artisans, for the price of the articles and manufactures which they have furnished, runs from the date of each article, and the continuation of the articles makes no interruption. This was expressed by the ordinance of Lewis XII. which says from the the first article; by the custom of Paris, which expresses from the day of the first delivery: and finally the ordinance of 1679, *art*, 9, expresses that the prescription shall take place, though there should be a further continuation of the articles.

The reason is, that the claim of the shop-keeper or artisan who has furnished several articles at different times, is composed as well of particular claims which he has for the article that produce as many particular actions, beginning each to run from the day when the articles were furnished.

681. In regard to doctors and surgeons, I think we ought not to consider the claim of a doctor or surgeon who has attended a sick person during his sickness, as composed

of as many separate claims as the doctor or surgeon has rendered attentions, but as a single and the same claim, which has not been completed till the attentions of the doctor or surgeon have been finished, either by the recovery or by the death of the patient, which has put an end to his sickness, or when the doctor or surgeon has been dismissed. Therefore I think that the prescription ought only to run from the day of the death of the patient, when the patient died in the sickness, or from the day of the last visit or last attentions when the patient has been restored, or when the doctor or surgeon has been dismissed before the end of the sickness.

But if the doctor or surgeon has attended one in different maladies, there are as many different claims and actions as there were maladies, which actions ought to be separately prescribed from the day of the termination of each malady.

682. Where the custom is not explicit in regard to servants, there is room to think that we ought to follow the ordinance of Lewis XII., which expresses that they are not receiveable to demand their wages after a year from leaving the house of their masters, and that during the said year they may only demand the wages for the three last years. This is the opinion of Henry, and of Bretonnier.

The custom of Paris and of Orleans having subjected the action of servants for their wages to the prescription of a year, without distinguishing whether these are yet, or not, in the service of their masters, we may maintain that the prescription against the action which the servant has for each period of his service, ought to run from the day of the expiration of each period. For example, according to this opinion, if a servant is hired by the year, he can only demand his wages for the year before the last period and the price of his services since the last period; and if he is hired by the month, he can only demand the wages of the last twelve months, and what has run since the last month.

We must decide the same in regard to the boarding of children for the purpose of their instruction.

683. Duplessis and Lemaitre have thought that these prescriptions ought not to run against minors. For myself, I think that they run as well against minors as against persons of age; I. because the contracts from which arise the action of shop-keepers and artisans against whom this prescription is established, are contracts which they make in their quality of shop-keepers and artisans. It is a principle that they contract as of age when they contract in this quality, and for something relative to their trade or business; whence it follows that they are not relievable against these contracts. They ought then to be subject to the prescription of the action which grows from these contracts, as persons of age are. II. This prescription is not established as a penalty for the negligence of the creditor, which might be forgiven in a minor; but upon a simple presumption of payment, resulting from this that the payment of these debts is not commonly delayed so long: therefore this prescription operates equally in regard to minors and persons of age. III. As our custom does not except minors from this prescription, as it has taken care to do in regard to the prescription of thirty years, we ought not to except them.

§. V.

Of the foundation and of the effect of these prescriptions.

684. These prescriptions are founded solely upon the presumption of payment.

Hence it follows that the creditor is not so far not receivable as that he cannot defer to his debtor the oath, whether the sum by him demanded is due or not. This is formally decided by the ordinance of 1673. *tit.* 1, *art.* 10. The custom of Orleans has also a disposition to this effect. *art.* 265. In this, these prescriptions differ from other prescriptions, which, being established in the form of a penalty against the creditor, deprive him entirely of the action.

685. The debtor to whom the oath is deferred, is holden to swear that the sum which is demanded from him is not

due. On his failing to ſwear, the oath is deferred to the perſon demanding, and upon his oath, he ought to obtain judgment.

686. When the widow or the heirs of him to whom the delivery has been made, are ſued, they cannot be obliged to ſwear whether the thing be really due or not by the deceaſed debtor; becauſe the oath cannot be deferred to one upon what is not his own act; *arg.* L. 42, ff. *de regul, juris.* Paul eſtabliſhes a principle to this effect: *Heredi ejus cum quo contractum est, jusjurandum deferri non potest.* Paul, *sent.* 11, 1, 4. But although they cannot be obliged to ſwear preciſely that the ſum demanded is not due, the ordinance however permits the oath to be deferred whether they have not a knowledge that the ſum is due; this is expreſſed by the article 10, above cited. On their default to make this oath it ought to be deferred to the plaintiff. The ordinance likewiſe permits this oath to be deferred to tutors of minors, the heirs of the deceaſed.

687. If the widow who was in a community of property with her huſband, refuſed to take this oath, or even agreed that the ſum is due, ought judgment to be had againſt the heirs who ſhould offer on their part to affirm that they have no knowledge that it is due? To this queſtion we muſt anſwer, no; for the debt, by the death of the deceaſed, being divided between the widow and the heirs, the oath which is deferred to the widow and which on her refuſal is deferred to the plaintiff, relates only to the part of the debt which is due by the widow. This widow, on refuſing to ſwear, or even in acknowledging the debt, can only oblige herſelf; ſhe cannot bind the heirs: ſhe may, by her own act, cauſe the preſcription to ceaſe for the part which ſhe owed; but ſhe cannot cauſe it to ceaſe for the part due by the heirs.

It is the ſame thing, if one of the heirs acknowledged the debt: this acknowledgment would not oblige him, but for the part of it which he owed, and it would not oblige the other heirs, who took the oath that they had no knowledge of the debt.

688. Not only has the creditor the right to defer the oath notwithstanding the prescription; he may also, when the object does not exceed one hundred livres, be received to prove by witnesses, that the defendant has offered to pay the sum since the demand, or even before the demand, since the time that he has declared that he paid it. The reason is, that although the action which arises from the bargain be prescribed, that which arises from the promise which has been made to pay, when it is in any manner proved, is a new action which is not prescribed.

ARTICLE V.

Of several other kinds of prescriptions.

689. The demand of journeymen, for the payment of their daily wages, is prescribed by the time of forty days. *Orleans, art.* 264.

This prescription, as well as the preceding, is founded upon the sole presumption of payment; it is presumed that these persons who have need of their wages for their support, do not wait a long time in procuring payment, or at least in demanding it.

Therefore this prescription does not exclude the plaintiff from deferring the oath to the defendant, as in the case of prescriptions which have been before spoken of, nor from being received to prove that the defendant has promised to pay, when the price of the wages does not exceed one hundred livres.

It is asked whether the prescription for all the sums runs only from the day of the last day's work? In strictness it seems that we ought to say the prescription should run for the price of each day's work, from the day that each is finished; for as the journeyman has a right from this time to demand this day's work, his action for the price of this day's work has been from this time open, and consequently the prescription of it should run from this time. However we may maintain that it ought to run only from the day of the last day's work, especially if the journeyman was during this time supported by the hirer; for journeymen do not commonly demand their wages until their work is finished.

690. The demand of attorneys for their fees is prescribed by two years, counting from the day of the decease of their clients or of the revocation of their power; *Arret de reglem.* 28, *Mar.* 1692.

The second article establishes against attorneys another prescription; it expresses that they cannot in cases not determined, demand their costs, fees and charges for the proceedings had beyond six years immediately preceding, though they have always continued to act, unless they had them settled and adjusted by their clients, and this with an account of the sum to which they amount, when they exceed two thousand livres.

The law has only spoken of fees in cases not determined; in regard to those terminated by a final judgment, the prescription of two years ought to run from the day that the power of the attorney expired by the final judgment: as in cases not determined, it runs from the day it has ceased by the revocation, or by the decease of the party.

691. There is no law which limits the time of the action for fees of notaries and officers. It would be equitable to extend to these officers the prescription of six years established in regard to attorneys; but, this not being fixed by law, we should have great regard to circumstances.

There is another kind of prescription against attorneys and officers which results from the return which they have made of the papers of the suit to the parties: there results from this return a presumption of payment and it is commonly said at the bar, *papers returned, papers paid.*

Attorneys being obliged by the rules of the court, to have a journal upon which they are to enter the payments which are made to them by their clients, there results from the want of shewing this journal a plea in bar against the demand which they make for their fees. *Reg. de Cour,* 2, Aug. 1692.

692. The demand of a client for the restitution of the papers, with which an advocate or attorney has charged himself, is prescribed by five years from the day of the date of the final judgment or from the compromise; and by ten years, when the proceedings have not been terminated.

This prescription is of the same nature as the preceding, and is founded upon the presumption of the restitution of the papers after this lapse of time; therefore it does not exclude the decisory oath.

It is the same thing with that which operates in favor of counsellors of the court, their widows and heirs; they are discharged from their liability to account for papers of the suit, by the lapse of three years from the day of the judgment, when the suit has been determined, or *from* the day of the decease of the counsellor, or from his resignation, although the suit has not been determined.

We have no law in regard to inferior judges; but we cannot refuse to them the prescription of five years granted to advocates and attorneys.

693. All these prescriptions have for their sole foundation the presumption of payment, and they do not prevent the plaintiff from deferring the oath to the defendant, whether it be true, that he has paid, or that he does not retain the papers which are demanded from him.

There are other kinds of prescriptions against different kinds of actions, as that of ten years against all rescissory actions, that of five years for arrearages of annuities, that of a year against demands for redemption; that against actions *redhibitoriæ*, on account of a defect in the thing sold to take back or restore, of which the time is differently ruled by the custom and different usages of places. We shall speak of these prescriptions when we treat of the subjects to which they relate.

FOURTH PART.

Of the proof as well of obligations as of the payment of them.

694. HE who claims to be the creditor of any one is obliged to prove the act or agreement which has produced his claim, when it is contested: on the contrary when the obligation is proved, the debtor who claims to have discharged it, is obliged to prove the payment. There are two kinds of proofs, literal and testimonial, of which we will treat separately in the two first chapters. Confession and certain presumptions hold also the place of proofs, as also the oath: we shall treat of them in a third chapter.

CHAPTER THE FIRST.

Of literal proof.

695. Literal proof is that which results from instruments or writings. For example. The literal proof of the obligations which arise from agreements, as from a contract of sale or of hire, is that which results from the instruments or writings which include these agreements. The literal evidence of the obligation which a judgment produces, is the record which contains that judgment. The literal evidence of the payment of any obligation whatever, is the receipt which the creditor has given thereof.

These instruments are either authentic or private. We call authentic instruments, those which are taken by a public officer, as a notary or clerk of a court. Private instruments are those which are taken without the aid of a public officer.

These instruments are also original, or copies: we also distinguish titles primitive and recognitive. We will treat in a summary manner of these different instruments.

ARTICLE THE FIRST.

Of authentic original titles.

§. I.

What instruments are authentic.

696. Authentic inſtruments are thoſe which are taken by a public officer, with the requiſite ſolemnities.

It is neceſſary that the inſtrument ſhould be taken in the place where the officer has a character of public officer, and a right to act as ſuch. Therefore if a notary takes an inſtrument out of the diſtrict where he is notary, this would not be an authentic inſtrument.

By a particular practice of the courts of Paris, of Orleans and of Montpellier, notaries of theſe courts have the right to take inſtruments all over the kingdom. *Orleans, art.* 463.

697. Although there are ſome regulations which have denied to ſubaltern notaries to take inſtruments between other perſons than thoſe who are within the diſtrict in which they are eſtabliſhed, and for other property than that which is ſituated within their diſtrict, yet ſuch inſtruments are not the leſs authentic, theſe rules having been conſidered as fiſcal laws, and not having had effect.

698. If the notary or public officer was interdicted his office, when he took the inſtrument, the inſtrument would not be authentic.

It is neceſſary alſo for the authenticity of the inſtrument, that the formalities required ſhould have been obſerved; that the notary ſhould be himſelf accompanied by another notary or two witneſſes, that the inſtrument ſhould be upon ſtamped paper, that it ſhould be regiſtered.

699. When the inſtrument is not authentic, either by the incompetency, or the interdiction of the officer, or for want of form; if it is ſigned by the parties, it has at leaſt the ſame evidence againſt the party who has ſigned it, as an inſtrument under private ſignature. *Boiceau 4, part.* 2 *ch.* 4.

§. II.

How authentic instruments are evidence against the parties.

700. An authentic original inftrument is full evidence of itfelf of what is contained in the inftrument.

Neverthelefs, when this inftrument is produced without the diftrict of the public officer who has taken it, it is common to eftablifh the fignature of this officer, by a note or certificate at foot.

This certificate is an atteftation given by the judge of the place, by which this judge certifies that the officer who has taken and figned the inftrument, is truly a public officer, notary, &c.

The fignature of the public officer who has taken the inftrument gives full faith to whatever it includes, and to the fignatures of the parties who have fubfcribed it, fo that it is not neceffary confequently to prove it otherwife.

Neverthelefs, authentic inftruments may be ftated to have been forged; but until the plea of forgery has been fo adjudged, they are proof by provifo, and the judge fhould ordain the provifional execution of what they include. This is decided by the law 2, *Cod. ad l. Corn. de fals.* This decifion is a very wife one. Crime is not to be prefumed, and it would be very dangerous that debtors fhould have power to ftop during a long time the payment of lawful debts by a charge of forgery. It is in confequence of this principle that Dumoulin in *Cons. Par.* §. 1, *gl.* 4, *n.* 41, decides that homage made by the vaffal, although the record fhould be pleaded by the lord, to have been forged fhould procure a provifional replevy from feudal feizure.

§. III.

Of what things authentic instruments are evidence against the parties.

701. Authentic inftruments are evidence principally againft perfons who were parties, their heirs and thofe who are in their rights. They are full evidence againft thefe perfons as to every difpofition of the inftrument, that is to

say, of what the parties have had in view, and which was the object of the instrument.

702. They are full evidence as to whatever has been expressed by way of recital, when the recitals have a reference to the disposition. *Molin. in Cons. Par.* §. 8, *gl.* 1, *n.* 10. For example. If one by an instrument make acknowlegement of a rent due in these terms, "*he acknowleges that such a house by him possessed is charged towards Robert, now present, for so much yearly rent, of which the arrearages have been paid to this day, and he has therefore obliged himself to continue it to him;* these terms, *of which the arrearages have been paid,* although they be only by way of recital, and it be not expressed that Robert acknowleged to have received them, are however evidence as to the payment against Robert, a party to the instrument: because they have reference to the disposition of the instrument, and it ought to have been mentioned in the instrument how much was really due of the arrearages of this rent.

703. In regard to recitals in the instrument, which are entirely foreign to the disposition, they may indeed have the nature of half-proof; but they are not entire proof, even against the persons who have been parties to the instrument; *Molin, ibid.* For example. If in the contract of sale of a piece of land which Peter has made to me, it is recited that this piece of land comes to him from the estate of James; a third person, who as heir on the part of James should demand from me the restoration of his portion of this estate, could not, in order to ground his demand, prove by this single recital in my contract, that this piece of land was really of the estate of James, although I was a party to the instrument, in which this recital is; because it is entirely foreign to the disposition of the instrument, and I had not then any interest in opposing this recital.

§. IV.

Of what things instruments are evidence against third persons.

704. The instrument proves against a third person *rem*

ipsam, that is to ſay, that the agreement which it includes has intervened. *Molin, ibid. n.* 8.

For example, the inſtrument which includes the contract of ſale of an eſtate proves even againſt a third perſon, that there has really been a ſale of this eſtate contracted at the time expreſſed in the inſtrument.

Therefore if the lord of a manor has made an agreement with his ſteward, who has bound himſelf to account for all the feudal profits which ſhould ariſe during a certain time in his manor; the inſtrument containing the contract of ſale of an eſtate ſituated in the manor, is evidence againſt the ſteward, although he has not been party to the inſtrument, that there has been a ſale of this eſtate; *probat rem ipsam*, and conſequently the lord may demand from the ſteward an account of the profits, to which this ſale has given riſe, which the ſteward ought to have collected.

But the inſtrument is not evidence againſt a third perſon, who has not been a party to the inſtrument, of what is there recited. *Molin. ibid. n.* 10.

For example. If it is recited in the contract of ſale that the houſe of the ſeller has a right of view over the houſe adjoining, this recital will make no proof againſt the proprietor of the adjoining houſe, who is a third perſon, not a party to the inſtrument.

705. This rule undergoes an exception; for *in antiquis enunciativa probant*, even againſt third perſons, when theſe recitals are confirmed by long poſſeſſion. *Cravett. de antiq. temp. p.* 1, *cap.* 4, *n.* 20. For example. Although long uſage does not eſtabliſh a right of way or of view, &c. yet if my houſe has had for a long time paſt a view over the houſe adjoining, and in the old contracts of purchaſe by thoſe from whom I hold, it is recited that it has this right of view, theſe old contracts, confirmed by my poſſeſſion, will be evidence of my right of view againſt the proprietor of the neighbouring houſe, although he be a third perſon and his predeceſſors have never been parties to the contracts.

Likewiſe in our cuſtoms which do not admit of any

allodium without title, if in the old contracts of purchase which my anceftors have made of an eftate, it be recited to be allodial, this recital will be evidence againft the lord in whofe territory it is, if he has never been recognifed as lord of the eftate.

706. From this, that authentic inftruments prove *rem ipsam*, againft third perfons, ought we to conclude that the inventory of the papers of an eftate, made before a notary, in which it is faid, that there was a minute of an obligation for a certain fum made by A. B. for a loan, at a certain time and before a certain notary, is evidence of the debt againft the debtor who is a third perfon, and who was not prefent at the making of the inventory, without its being neceffary to produce the minute of the obligation? No; for from this, that the inventory proves *rem ipsam*, it follows only that there is a minute of the obligation; but it does not follow that the debt is due, becaufe the want of fhewing the minute of the obligation makes it prefumable either that there is fome defect in the minute which they do not fhew, that prevents it from being evidence of the debt; or that fince the inventory, it has been rendered up to the debtor, at the time of the payment which he has made of what is contained in the obligation.

Neverthelefs, if it appeared that fince the inventory, a fire had happened in the houfe where the titles were, which has confumed them, the mention of the minute of the obligation expreffed by the inventory would be evidence of the debt, as the law 57, *de adm. tut.*, feems to fuppofe: which would apply in the cafe in which the debtor fhould not alledge to have paid it, or perhaps in the cafe in which the time of payment, expreffed in the recital of the obligation, not being yet expired, the prefumption would be that the debt has not been difcharged: all this depends much upon circumftances and is left to the difcretion of the judge.

Article II.

Of private writings.

707. There are different kinds of private writings; in-

ftruments under private and ordinary fignatures, thofe derived from the public archives, the archives and rentals of a manor, journals of merchants, domeftic papers, writings not figned. Tallies have alfo fomerelation to private writings.

§. I.

Of instruments under private and ordinary signatures.

708. Inftruments under private and ordinary fignature, are the fame evidence againft thofe who have fubfcribed them, their heirs or fucceffors, as authentic inftruments. But there is this difference between thefe inftruments and authentic inftruments, that thefe do not require any acknowlegement; whereas the creditor cannot in virtue of an act under private fignature obtain any judgment againft him who has fubfcribed it, his heirs or fucceffors, unlefs he has previoufly holden him to acknowlege the inftrument and eftablifhed it on this acknowlegement. *See the edict of December* 1684.

There is in this refpect a difference between the perfon who has himfelf fubfcribed the inftrument, and his heirs or fucceffors. Thefe, being called upon to acknowlege the fignature of the deceafed of whom they are the heirs, may not know it, and are not obliged to acknowlege or deny it precifely; and upon the declaration which they make that they do not know it, the judge requires a verification: whereas the perfon who has himfelf fubfcribed the inftrument, not being ignorant of his proper fignature, ought to acknowlege it or to deny it precifely, and for want of his denying it, the judge pronounces the acknowlegement of the inftrument as fubfcribed by him.

709. In the confular jurifdictions when the defendant denies the verity of the fignature, the confular judges ought to remand it before the ordinary judge to be there proceeded upon to an acknowlegement; during which time the paper under private fignature would be no evidence. But there is this in particular in thefe jurifdictions, that

when the defendant has not yet contested the truth of the signature, the paper under private signature is evidence, and the plaintiff may without being obliged to procure the acknowlegement of it, obtain in virtue of this paper a judgment. *Declaration of the 15th May* 1703.

710. There is also something particular in regard to the notes and promises by which a person obliges himself to pay a sum for the loan of money or other thing; to wit, that when the promise is written in another hand than that of the person who has subscribed it, it is necessary, in order that it may be evidence against the person who has subscribed it, that this person should have written, besides his signature, with his own hand the sum which he is obliged to pay, which is usually done in these terms, *good for such a sum*. This has been ordained by the declaration of the king, 22d September, 1733, to avoid the surprise by which some persons are taken, who sign instruments at which they are present, without having read their contents.

But as commerce would be restrained, if all sorts of persons were bound to this formality of writing in their own hand the sum which they oblige themselves to pay, there being a great number of persons who know only how to sign their name, the law excepts from its disposition, traders, artisans, labourers and people of the country, against whom promises subscribed by them are evidence, although they contain only their signature.

711. When the sum written in the hand of the debtor out of the body of the note or promise, is less than the sum expressed in the body of the note, written in another hand; for example, if in the note it is said, *I acknowledge to owe to such a person the sum of three hundred livres*, and at the foot and out of the body of the promise it is written, in the hand of the debtor, *good for two hundred livres*, it is not to be doubted that the promise should be evidence only for the two hundred livres.

If the body of the note was written entirely in the hand of the debtor, as well as the words *good, &c.*; in the doubt whether the sum expressed in the body of the instrument, or that expressed at the foot, *good, &c.* is the sum truly due, we ought, *cæteris paribus*, to decide in favor of the liberation, according to this rule, *Semper in obscuris quod minimum est sequimur*; L. 9, ff. *de R. J.* Therefore, in the instance proposed, the promise would be good only for two hundred livres. But if the cause of the debt expressed in the body of the note makes it known that the sum expressed in the body of the note is that which is truly due, we must decide otherwise. For example. If the promise written in the hand of the debtor expresses, *I acknowledge that I owe to A. B. the sum of three hundred livres, for fifteen yards of cloth of Pagnon which he has sold me*, and it appears that this kind of cloth was worth twenty livres a yard, the promise would be good for three hundred livres, although it be said *good for two hundred livres.*

712. The same rules of decision are to be followed in the inverse case.

When the sum expressed in the body of the note is less than that expressed at foot, *good, &c.* as when it is said I acknowledge that I owe to A. B. two hundred livres, and at foot, *good for three hundred livres; cæteris paribus*, the presumption is for the sum of two hundred livres, unless the expression of the cause of the debt manifests that it is that of three hundred livres which is really due.

713. If a person is and acknowledges himself debtor and depositary of a certain sum according to a minute of the money annexed to the instrument, it is the sum to which the money expressed in the minute amounts, which is the sum due, although that expressed in the instrument be different: it is in this case an error of calculation.

714. Instruments under private signature are not evidence against the person who has subscribed them, when they are found in his possession.

For example. If there be found among my papers a note subscribed by me, by which I acknowledge to owe you one thousand livres which you have lent me, this note will be no evidence of the debt; for, it being in my possession, the presumption is either that I had written this note with a hope that you would lend me the money, and that, as the loan did not take place, the note has remained with me, or that, if the loan did tak eplace, I have repaid the money, and have taken up the note.

It is the same with regard to instruments of discharge, though more to be favored. For example. if there has been found among the papers of my creditor a receipt signed by him of a sum which I owed him, it would not be evidence of the payment; for the receipt being in his possession it will thence be concluded that he had written it beforehand, in hopes that I would pay him, and this not happening, the receipt has remained with him.

715. Instruments under private signature as well as those which are authentic, are not evidence against third persons, except that the thing contained in the instrument has really taken place; *probant rem ipsam:* but they have this inferiority to authentic instruments, that these having an established date, by the testimony of the public officer who has received the instrument, are evidence against third persons that the thing contained in the instrument took place at the time expressed by the instrument; whereas those under private signature being subject to be antedated, are not commonly evidence against third persons, that the thing which they contain took place, except from the day when they are alledged and produced to third persons.

Therefore, if I have seized the estate of my debtor, and the tenant who is in possession of the estate opposes the seizure, and pretends that the estate belongs to him; if, to prove it, he produces an instrument under private signature, by which it is said that my debtor has sold to him this estate, and this instrument has an anterior date, not only to my actual seizure but even to my claim, he will not thereby obtain the replevy which he demands: for this instrument, being under private signature, does not prove against me, a third person, that the sale which it mentions was made at the day expreffed by the inftrument; this inftrument has no date but from the day when it is produced againft me; and as it is not prefented to me till after the actual feizure, it does not prove that the eftate has been fold to him, except fince the actual feizure, a time when it was not in the power of the debtor to fell to the prejudice of my feizure.

If however the inftrument under private fignature had an eftablifhed date, *puta*, by the deceafe of one of the parties who had fubfcribed it, it would be evidence even againft third perfons that the thing contained in the inftrument had already taken place, at leaft at the time of the death of the party who fubfcribed it.

§. II.

Of private writings, derived from the public archives.

716. We call public archives a depofit of titles eftablifhed by public authority. *Archivum*, fays Dumoulin, *est quod publice autoritate potestatem habentis erigitur.*

Thefe depofits, being eftablifhed only to preferve true titles, they affure the truth of thofe which are derived therefrom. Therefore inftruments under private fignature, taken from the public archives, with the atteftation of the keeper of the archives that they have been taken therefrom, are evidence, although they have not been otherwife proved. *Molin. in Cons. Par.* §. 8, *gl.* 1, *n.* 26.

§. III.

Of the archives and rentals of manors.

717. One cannot make titles for himfelf: therefore, inftruments which are not taken by a public perfon, fuch as the rentals or regifters which the lord of a manor himfelf keeps of the rents and duties which are annually paid to him, cannot be evidence of the payment of thefe rents, nor confequently a fufficient ground for the demand which the lord would make to have them recognifed.

Neverthelefs, when thefe rentals are antient and uniform, they form a half-proof, which joined with other proof, such as would be that which results from the recognition of the proprietors of the adjoining lands, would sufficiently establish the demand of the lord.

718. These rentals and other manorial papers which are not authentic, are not evidence for the lord against others; but they are proof for others against him. Therefore if the lord has usurped from me the possession of an estate, I may establish my demand against him for its restoration, by his archives and rentals from which it would appear that he had received the rents for this estate from me and my father, to whom I should contend that he had granted them.

But when the tenant has made use of the lord's rentals against him, he may in his turn make use of them against the tenant; and in this case they are full proof in his favor. *Molin. ibid. n.* 20. For example, if in the instance above proposed, the tenant has made use of the rentals of the lord to prove that an estate of which the lord had usurped from him the possession, belonged to him, as having been granted to him by this lord, the lord, on his part, could in his turn make use of the same papers to prove that this estate is charged with all the incumbrances mentioned therein; and the said rentals would in this case in regard to this particular be full proof in favor of the lord.

Nevertheless, they could only prove, even in this case in favor of the lord, facts which have relation to those for which they are made use of against him. For example, the lord could not prove by these papers that another piece of land which I possess is holden also from him.

§. IV.

Of the books of merchants.

719. No one being able to make a title for himself, according to the principle which we have already established, it follows thence that the journals of merchants, upon which they enter, day by day, the merchandises which they sell to different persons, cannot be full and entire

proof of these articles, against the persons to whom they have been delivered.

Nevertheless, in favor of trade it is established, that when these books are well kept, written from day to day without any blank, the merchant having a reputation of probity and his demand being made within a year after the delivery, they are half-proof; and very often the judge may, upon the demand of merchants for the payment of the said articles, receive their oath as to the truth of the delivery, in order to supply what is wanting in the proof which results from their books.

This is the opinion of Dumoulin, *ad* L. 3, *Cod. de reb. cred. vol.* 3, *p.* 635, *col. of the edition of* 1681, where in speaking of the books of merchants having a reputation of probity, he says: *Rationes ejus, quamvis non plenam probationem, nec omnino semiplenam inducant, tamen inserunt aliquam præsumptionem ex qua possit ei deferri juramentum, ita ut per se rationes probent.*

This ought especially to take place between merchant and merchant.

720. Boiceau, *part.* 2, *ch.* 8, requires that what results from the books of a merchant should be confirmed by other evidence, as, for example, that the defendant was accustomed to supply himself at the store of the merchant and to buy of him on credit. Such a fact or some other similar, being acknowledged, or, in case of its being denied, proved by witnesses, according to the decision of this author, the oath of the merchant, respecting the delivery of the articles charged in his books, ought to be received as evidence.

721. We may further add that in order to defer the oath to a merchant against a common person upon the truth of the charges in his book, it is necessary that they should not amount to a sum too considerable, and that it should be entirely probable that the defendant had need of them.

For example. The delivery of the articles would not be

very probable, if it were charged upon the book of a merchant, that he had sold and delivered to me ten yards of black cloth within a year; because I have not need of more than one suit in the year, for which four yards would be sufficient.

722. In regard to such shop-keepers as are not of the body or company of merchants, but people of the lower class, Boiceau, *ibidem*, thinks that their books ought not to be evidence.

723. After having seen what proof the books of merchants are in their favor, it remains for us to see what proof they are against them. It is not to be doubted that they are complete proof against them, either of the bargains which they have made, or of the delivery which has been made, or of the sums which have been paid, to them.

This takes place even when the thing has been written by another hand than that of the merchant, provided it be established that the journal is that which the merchant has been accustomed to make use of; for this journal being in his possession, the presumption is that whatever is there written has been written with his consent. *Dumoulin, ad L. 3, Cod. de reb. cred.*

Dumoulin, *ibid.*, alledges as the first limitation of this rule, that in order that the journal of a merchant may be evidence against him of the sum which he has acknowledged to owe to any one, it is necessary commonly that the cause of the debt should be there expressed; for as there cannot be a debt without a cause which has produced it, and the writing alone does not make the debt, the demand of the debt cannot be well grounded, while there does not appear any cause.

But it is sufficient that one should appear, even by presumption and conjecture. Therefore if a merchant has written upon his book that he owed a certain sum to a certain merchant, although he has not expressed the cause, his book would be evidence againſt him in favor of this merchant; if this merchant is the ſame who has been accuſtomed to furniſh him with merchandiſes of his own trade: for in this caſe the preſumption is, that the cauſe of the debt is the delivery of theſe merchandiſes. *Dumoulin, ibid.*

The ſecond limitation which Dumoulin alledges is, that faith ſhould be given to the journal alone, and not to the looſe papers which might be found in the journal.

The third limitation which he alledges is, that the journal of a merchant is no evidence againſt him in my favor, if, willing to avail myſelf of it againſt him, I will not allow it againſt myſelf; for one ought not to take advantage of a paper which he himſelf rejects. *Molin. ibid. Nam fides scripturæ est indivisibilis. Doct. ad L. Si ex fals., 42, Cod. de trans.*

§. V.

Of the private papers of individuals.

724. After having treated of the journals of merchants, it is in order to ſpeak of thoſe of private perſons, who are not merchants.

It is not to be doubted that what we write upon our private papers cannot be evidence in our favor againſt any one who has not ſubſcribed them. *Exemplo perniciosum est, ut ei scripturæ credatur, qua unusquisque sibi adnotatione propria, debitorem constituit;* L. 7, *Cod. de probat.* But are they evidence againſt us? Boiceau, *part.* 2, *ch.* 8, *n.* 14, diſtinguiſhes the caſes in which what we have written ſhould go to bind us towards one, or to diſcharge our debtor.

In the firſt caſe, for example, if I have written upon my journal, or my memorandum-book that I have borrowed twenty piſtoles of Peter. Boiceau, *ibid.*, thinks that if this acknowlegement made upon my journal or memorandum-book is ſigned by me, it is complete evidence of the debt againſt me and my heirs; and that if it is not ſigned, it is only half-proof, which ought to be confirmed by ſome other evidence.

I find this distinction of Boiceau plausible, but for another reason than that he has alledged. When the entry which I have made upon my journal of the money borrowed is not signed, this entry appears only to have been made in order to preserve an account for myself, and not to serve the creditor for proof of the loan which he has made to me: this creditor having no note, the presumption is that he has rendered it up to me when I paid him, and that, finding myself safe by the return which he has been made me of my note, I have neglected to erase the entry and to make mention of the payment which I have made. But when I have signed this entry, my signature indicates that I have made it with an intention that it should serve the creditor for proof of his claim, it ought then to serve him for that purpose.

Although I have not signed the entry or memorandum, if I have otherwise declared or made known, that I made it in order that it might serve for proof of the loan, in case I should be surprised by death, as when I declared by this memorandum that he who had made me the loan was not willing to receive a note from me, the memorandum in that case, though not signed, ought to be evidence of the debt against me and my heirs.

When the entry, although signed, is erased, it is no longer any evidence in favor of the creditor; on the contrary the erasure is a proof that I have returned the sum, if the creditor has not besides some other evidence.

We pass to the second case, which is that in which what I have written upon my journal does not go to oblige me but on the contrary to discharge my debtor; as when I have written upon my journal the payments which he has made me. It is not to be doubted in this case that what I have written upon my journal, whether I have signed it or not, is full evidence against me in favor of my debtor; for the discharge is to be favored.

§. VI.

Of writings of private persons not signed.

725. There are three kinds of these writings; I. journals and memorandum-books; II. writings on loose papers, and which are not at the foot, in the margin or on the back of a signed instrument; III. those which are at the foot, in the margin, or on the back of a signed instrument.

We have spoken of the first kind in the preceding paragraph.

Those of the second kind tend either to oblige, or to discharge; in regard to those which go to discharge, such as receipts written in the hand of the creditor not signed, which are found with the debtor; although we have decided in the preceding paragraph that the receipts written upon the journal of the creditor are full evidence of the payment, without its being necessary that they should be signed, I do not think that we must also decide that receipts not signed, upon loose papers, although written entirely in the hand of the creditor and in the possession of the debtor, should likewise be full evidence of the payment. The reason of this difference is, that it is not common to sign receipts which are written upon a journal, whereas it is common for a creditor to sign the receipts which he gives to his debtor. Therefore when the receipt is not signed, we may believe that it has been given to the debtor before the payment, *puta*, for a simple form, that the debtor might examine whether he would approve of the manner in which it has been expressed, and the creditor has delayed to sign it until he should be paid. Yet if this discharge is dated, so that nothing is wanting but the signature; if it is quite a simple receipt and of which it was not necessary to make a form; lastly if no reason appear for which this receipt could come to the debtor before the payment; in this case I think we must presume that it was merely forgotten that the receipt was not signed, and that it should be evidence of payment, especially if the supplementary oath of the debtor be added thereto.

In regard to writings not signed, upon loose papers, which tend to oblige the person who has written them, such as a promissory note, an instrument of sale, &c.; although they are found in the hands of him towards whom the obligation was to be contracted, they are no evidence however against the person who has written them, that the obligation has really been contracted, and they pass only for simple projects which have not been executed.

726. It remains for us to speak of writings not signed which are at the foot, in the margin or on the back of a signed instrument. These writings tend either to a discharge or to a new obligation.

In regard to those which tend to a discharge, it is necessary also to distinguish the case in which the instrument at the foot or on the back of which they are, is and has never ceased to be in the possession of the creditor, from that in which it should be in the possession of the debtor. In the first case, as when at the foot or on the back of a promissory note signed by the debtor, and which is in the possession of the creditor, there are found receipts of sums received on account; these receipts, although neither signed nor dated, are full proof of payment not only when they are written in the hand of the creditor, but also in any other, even in that of the debtor; because it is more than probable that the creditor would not have left these receipts written upon the note which he had in his possession, if the payments had not been actually made to him.

Further: although the writings not signed which are at the foot or on the back of an instrument in the possession of the creditor, and which tend to the discharge of what is expressed by the instrument, should be cancelled, they would not cease to be evidence; for it ought not to be in the power of the creditor in whose possession the instrument is, much less ought it to be in that of his heirs, to destroy, by cancelling this writing, the proof of the payment which it contains.

727. These dispositions apply when the instrument is

in the hands of the creditor: *quid*, if the inftrument is in the hands of the debtor, *puta* if at the foot, on the back or in the margin of a bill of fale made double, which is in the hands of the purchafer, debtor of the price, receipts are found not figned? Thefe writings will be full evidence, if they be in the hand-writing of the creditor; thefe receipts, being on the inftrument itfelf that contains the obligation, are better evidence than receipts, not figned, written on a loofe fheet. It is the fame with regard to receipts, not figned, written in the hand of the creditor that might be at the foot of a preceding receipt figned: but if thefe writings are in another hand than that of the creditor, not being figned by him, they are not evidence; for it ought not to be in the power of the debtor to procure his difcharge from the debt, by caufing receipts to be written on the inftrument which is in his poffeffion, by any perfon he pleafes.

Receipts, though in the hand-writing of the creditor, upon the inftrument that is in the poffeffion of the debtor, are no evidence if cancelled; for it is obvious that the debtor in whofe poffeffion the inftrument is, would not have cancelled them if the payment had really been made. And there is room to believe that the creditor had written the receipt on overtures of payment being made and that he afterwards cancelled it, thefe overtures not having been carried into effect.

728. As to writings, not figned, that tend to oblige, when they exprefs a relation to the figned inftrument at the foot, on the back or in the margin of which they may be, they are evidence againft the debtor who wrote them. For example. If under a promiffory note figned by Peter, by which he acknowleges that James has lent him one thoufand livres, there fhould be written in the hand-writing of Peter, *further, I acknowledge that the said James has lent me two hundred livres more*, this writing although not figned will be evidence againft Peter; becaufe by thefe words *further, more*, it has a relation to the writing figned by him. *Boiceau*, 11, 2; & *Danty*, *ibid*.

Likewise, if at the foot of a bill of sale of a farm, subscribed by both parties, there is a postscript in the hand of the seller, though not signed, stating that the cattle on the farm are included in the sale, this postscript will be evidence against the seller.

If it were written in another hand, it is obvious it would not be evidence against him, if the instrument were produced by the purchaser; but if the postscript were at foot of the instrument which is in the hand of the seller, this postscript, although in another hand, would be evidence against the seller; for he would not have suffered this postscript to be written at the foot of the instrument, which was in his possession, if the contents of it had not been agreed upon by the parties.

729. When the writings not signed, being at the foot, on the back or in the margin of an instrument, have no relation to this instrument, they are as if they had been written on a loose sheet. See what has been said *supra*, *n*. 725.

§. VII.

Of tallies.

730. We call *a tally*, the two parts of a piece of wood cleft in two, which two persons make use of, to mark the quantities of things daily delivered by one to the other.

For this purpose each of them has one of these pieces of wood. The one which the person who makes the delivery, retains is properly called the *tally*; the other is called the *standard*.

When the delivery is made, the two pieces are joined together and a mark, denoting the quantity of the things delivered, is made on them with a knife. Such are the tallies of bakers.

These tallies stand in the place of writings, and are a kind of literal evidence of the quantity of the things delivered, when he to whom they were furnished produces the standard to join it with the tally.

ARTICLE III.

Of copies.

731. It is a rule common to all copies, that when the original exists they are not evidence, except of what is in the original, as notaries ought not, even under pretext of interpretation, to add, in the instruments they copy and engross, any thing to what is contained in the original.

Therefore there can hardly be a question upon the faith which is due to copies, when the original exists; for if one should be in doubt respecting their contents, recourse may be had to the original.

There may be more difficulty, when the original is lost, to know what credit should be given in this case to copies. It is necessary first to distinguish those which have been made by a public person, and those which have not been made by a public person. It is necessary further in regard to the first, to distinguish three kinds; I. those which have been made by the authority of the judge, the party being present or having been duly cited; II. those which have been made without the authority of the judge, but in presence of the parties: III. those which have been made not in the presence of the parties, and without their having been cited by the authority of the judge. We will treat of these three kinds in the three first paragraphs. The register of entries includes copies of the class of those which are made by a public officer. We shall treat of these in a fourth paragraph. We shall treat in a fifth of copies which have not been made by a public person; in the sixth, of the copies of copies.

§ I.

Of copies made by the authority of the judge, the party being present or having been duly cited.

752. He who would have a copy of this kind which may serve instead of the original, presents a petition to the judge, at the foot of which the judge orders that a copy be taken from the original of such instrument, at a certain place,

day and hour, and that the parties interested be cited to attend. In consequence of this order, which is signified to the parties, they are caused, by the same instrument, to be cited to attend at the place, day and hour appointed.

The copy which in consequence hereof is made from the original by a public officer whether in the presence of the parties or in their absence after they have been, as we have already said, cited to attend, is a copy which we call a copy in form. When the original is afterwards lost, it has the same faith against the parties who were there present or had been cited to attend, and against their heirs or successors, as the original itself would have had. *Molin in Cons. Par.* §. 8, *gl.* 1, *n.* 37.

733. Observe that when these copies are still recent, the recital which is there made of the order of the judge, and the citations given to the parties to be at the place, day and hour, at which the copy was to be taken, is not sufficient proof that these formalities have been observed. Therefore, in order that, in want of the original, the copy should be as entire evidence as the original would have been, it is necessary that he who makes use of it, should shew the order of the judge and the citations.

But when these copies are antient, this recital of the formalities observed, is a sufficient proof that they were observed, according to this rule, *Enunciativa in antiquis probant;* and it is not necessary to shew either the order of the judge or the citations.

In order that a copy may be reputed antient, with the effect to dispense with shewing the proceedings which are there recited, it is not necessary that it should have an antiquity of thirty or forty years; such as that which is requisite to supply what is wanting in instruments, to make them full evidence, and of which we shall speak *infra, n.* 757: it is sufficient that it have an antiquity of ten years. On this principle it is holden that after ten years the highest bidder, under a judgment which is attacked, is not obliged to shew the proceedings on which the judgment has intervened.

734. These copies in form, which, in regard to persons who were present or had been duly cited, have the same faith as the original, have in regard to other persons who neither were present nor had been cited, only the effect which those would have had without the party being present or having been cited, of which we will speak *infra*, §. 3. *Molin. ibid. d. n.* 37.

§. II.

Of copies taken in the presence of the parties, but without the authority of the judge.

735. These copies are not properly *copies in form*; since they are not made by the authority of the judge: yet they have the same effect between the parties who have been present, their heirs or successors, as copies in form, and they are between these parties, like copies in form, for want of the original, the same evidence which the original would be. They derive this authority from the agreement of the parties; for the parties by their presence when the copies were taken have impliedly agreed that they should, between themselves, hold the place of the original. These copies are not however always the same evidence as copies in form; for as they derive their force solely from the agreement of the parties, it follows thence that they cannot have the same force in regard to things of which it is not in the power of the parties to agree, and of which the parties have not the disposal.

Therefore if, without the authority of the judge, I have taken a copy, with the incumbent of a benefice, of a long lease, viz, from nine to a hundred years, of an estate depending on this benefice, and of other papers containing the formalities which ought to have accompanied it, and the successor demands from me this estate; the copies which I have taken in the presence of his predecessor, would not be against the successor the same evidence that the originals of the said papers would have been, which are since lost; nor that which copies in form would be: for the predecessor who had not the free disposal of the estates of his benefice, could not, to the prejudice of his successors, agree that the copies which I have taken were conformable to the original instruments which established the legality of the alienation of this estate.

§. III.

Of copies made not in the presence of the parties, and without their having been cited by the authority of the judge.

736. The copies which are made from the original, not in the presence of the party and without his having been cited, are not commonly entire proof against him, of what is contained in the original, when it is lost: this copy forms only an index or inchoate proof in writing, which may authorise the admission of testimonial proof, to supply what is wanting in this copy.

This decision takes place, whether this copy has been made without the order of the judge or in virtue of such order; for it is the same thing, whether there was an order of the judge on which the party was not cited, or whether there was none.

This decision applies, according to Dumoulin, even when the copy should be made by the same notary who received the original. For example. I have executed a power of attorney to Peter in the presence of Gomet, a notary, to sell my house to James. Peter sells my house to James in virtue of this power, of which the copy is inserted at the foot of the contract of sale; and this copy is signed by Gomet, who attests that he has copied it word for word from the original which he received. Afterwards I bring a suit against James to recover back the estate, and the original of the power which I have given to Peter to sell it to him being lost; there remains only this copy to be produced against me. This copy will not be full and entire proof against me, that I have given a power to sell my house. The reason is, that this copy proves indeed that there was an original from which it has been taken, but not having been taken in my presence, it does not prove against me that the original from which it has been taken and which is not shewn, had all the characters necessary in order to be evidence: it does not prove that my signature, which is said in this copy to be at the foot of the original, was truly my signature. It is true that it is the notary who received the original and who has seen me sign the original, that attests it; but, says Dumoulin, a notary cannot attest and make full evidence of things which he is not required by the parties to attest. *Non potest testari, nisi de eo de quo rogatur a partibus:* he can only attest what he sees and understands *propriis sensibus*, at the time he attests it. At the time that he made this copy he saw only an original, but he did not see me sign it; he was not required by me to attest that there was an original duly and truly signed by me, from which he has made the copy; since it is supposed to be made in my absence, and consequently he cannot give to this copy the credit of the original; *d.* §. 8, *gl.* 1, *n.* 48, 62, 63, 64, &c.

737. All we have said is liable to an exception in regard to antient copies; for antient copies of instruments, whether made by the notary who received the original or even by another person, are evidence against all, for want of the original; because they recite that there was an original in form, and *in antiquis enunciativa probant.* This is shewn by Dumoulin, *ibid. n.* 41, *Si exemplum esset antiquum & de instrumento antiquo, non enim sufficeret originale fuisse antiquum, si exemplum esset recens ..... tunc ratione antiquitatis puto quod plene probaret contra omnes quantum ipsum originale probaret: ratio, quia habet authenticum testimonium de autoritate & tenore originalis, cui antiquitas loco cæterarum probationum quarum copiam sustulit, autoritatem plene fidei supplet.*

A copy is commonly reputed antient when it is of more than thirty or forty years; for according to Dumoulin, *ibid. n.* 81, 82, excepting the case of rights relating to things which admit only of immemorial and centenary possess ion, in regard to which an inſtrument is not reputed antient till one hundred years have elapſed; in all other caſes inſtruments are reputed antient after thirty or forty years. They may, even at the end of ten years, according to this author, paſs for antient, *ad solemnitatem præsumendam, nisi agatur de gravi prejudicio alterius*; *ibid. n.* 83.

§. IV.

Of the register of entries.

738. The copy of a deed of gift, tranſcribed in the regiſter of entries, is not evidence of the gift; otherwiſe it would be in the power of a diſhoneſt perſon to forge a falſe deed which he would cauſe to be tranſcribed in the regiſter of entries, and to elude the proof which might be made of the forgery, by ſuppreſſing the original. But Boiceau, *part.* 1, *ch.* 11, thinks that this regiſter forms at leaſt an inchoate proof in writing, which ought to authoriſe teſtimonial evidence of the gift. Danty thinks that this deciſion is liable to much difficulty. In order that this proof might be admitted, I would at leaſt have two things concur; I. that it ſhould appear that the minutes of all the inſtruments paſſed by the notary, in the year in which it is pretended that the gift was made, are not to be found; for if there was only the minute of the pretended gift which could not be found, there would reſult a ſuſpicion from the ſuppreſſion of this inſtrument, which would create a doubt of the genuineneſs or of the form of this inſtrument, and prevent the admiſſion of proof by witneſſes. II. I think that it would be neceſſary that the donor ſhould offer to prove the gift by witneſſes who were preſent when the inſtrument was executed, or at leaſt who had heard the donor admit it; and it would not be ſufficient that the donee ſhould prove that the deed of gift has been ſeen in his hands; for the witneſſes who ſee the inſtrument, know not whether it be a true inſtrument and whether it be clothed with all the neceſſary formalities.

739. If the inſtrument had been regiſtered on the application of the donor, and he had ſubſcribed the regiſter, Boiceau holds that in this caſe the regiſter would be evi-

dence of the gift, for the same reason which has been given before, that judicial copies, made in presence of the parties, are as good evidence as the original itself, against the party who has been present.

§. V.

Of copies absolutely informal, which are not made by a public person.

740. Copies which are not made by a public person, are called absolutely informal: they are no evidence, however antient; they may at most give rise to very slight presumptions.

Nevertheless, if one had produced this informal copy to raise from it a presumption, the other party might use it against him; and it would be evidence against him, because in producing it himself, he is holden to have admitted the genuineness of it; for one ought only to produce papers which he believes to be genuine.

When a copy has been made indeed by a public person, as by a notary, but who did not cause himself to be assisted by witnesses or another notary, it is not admitted to have been made by a public person, and it is as absolutely informal as if it had been made by a private person; for a public person who does not act as a public person is not reputed to be such. *Persona publica*, says Dumoulin, *agens contra officium personæ publicæ, non est digna spectari ut persona publica.*

§. VI.

Of the copies of copies.

741. It is obvious that a copy made not from the original but from a preceding copy, although made *servato juris ordine*, can be no better evidence than the preceding copy from which it was made, and against those persons only against whom the preceding copy would have been evidence.

Sometimes indeed, although this second copy, made from the first, has been made *servato juris ordine*, it is not equally evidence against the same person as the preceding copy would have been. This happens when the person against whom it is offered had not the same reasons to dispute the original, when the first copy was made in his presence, as he has now to dispute it with regard to him who has obtained the second copy. Dumoulin, §. 8, *gl.* 1, *n.* 34, adduces this example. Peter, the servant of one of my relations of whom I am the heir, has caused, by virtue of an order of the judge, in presence of my attorney, an entire copy to be taken of the will of this relation; after which he causes himself to be paid by me a legacy of one hundred crowns which was given him by the will. This copy was taken from the original which was desposited with a notary. Afterwards James comes, who demands the payment of a legacy of ten thousand crowns given by the same will, and as the original has since become lost, he presents a petition to the judge to have a copy of it taken, in my presence, or on my being duly summoned, from that which Peter has caused to be taken from it. Dumoulin says that this copy made by James from that made by Peter is not an entire proof against me, such as would be, in favor of Peter, that made by Peter from the original; because, says he, *nova contradicendi causa subest.* I have reasons now to contradict and contest the original, which I had not when Peter caused his copy to be taken. The legacy which Peter, demanded from me was a small legacy of one hundred crowns; it was not worth the trouble of contesting the original of the will: therefore I may have neglected the means which I had then to contest it; but now, when James demands from me ten thousand crowns, I have great interest in examining whether the original of the will is regular. Therefore, because I have indeed been willing that the copy of Peter should pass for a regular copy of the will, it does not follow from this that I ought to acknowlege the same thing in regard to the copy of James, taken from that of Peter.

Article IV.

Of the distinction of titles into primitive and recognitive.

742. The primitive title, as by the name it is underſtood to be, is the firſt title which has been paſſed between the parties, between whom an obligation has been contracted, and which contains this obligation. For example. The primitive title of an annuity is the contract by which it has been conſtituted. The recognitive titles are thoſe which have been paſſed ſince by the debtors, their heirs or ſucceſſors.

743. Dumoulin, *d*, §. 8, *n.* 88., diſtinguiſhes two kinds of recognitive titles or *acknowledgments;* thoſe which are in the form which is called *ex certa scientia*, and thoſe which are in what is called *forma communi*.

The acknowledgments *ex certa scientia*, which are called alſo *in forma speciali & dispositiva*, *n.* 89, are thoſe in which the tenor of the primitive title, is related. Theſe acknowledgments have this in particular, that they are equivalent to the primitive title, in caſe it ſhould be deſtroyed, and prove the exiſtence of it againſt the perſon acknowledging, provided he has the diſpoſal of his rights, and againſt his heirs and ſucceſſors. They diſpenſe conſequently with the creditor's adducing the primitive title, in the caſe in which it is found to be loſt. *Molin. ibid. n.* 89.

The acknowledgments *in forma communi* are thoſe in which the tenor of the primitive title is not recited. Theſe acknowledgments ſerve only to confirm the primitive title, and to interrupt the preſcription; but they confirm the primitive title as far only as it is regular: they do not prove its exiſtence or diſpenſe with the creditor's producing it.

Nevertheleſs, if there were ſeveral acknowledgments conformable to each other, of which ſome were antient or even one only antient, and ſupported by poſſeſſion, they might be equivalent to the primitive title, and excuſe the creditor from producing it; which takes place eſpecially when the primitive title is very antient. *Ibid. n.* 90.

744. The acknowledgments of each kind have this in common, that they are relative to the primitive title; that the person acknowledging, by these acknowledgments, is not presumed to have intended to contract any new obligation, but only to acknowledge the old one which was contracted by the primitive title. Therefore if by the acknowledgment, he acknowledges himself bound to any more than, or different from, what is expressed in the primitive title, in producing the primitive title and shewing the error which has crept into the acknowledgment, he will be discharged therefrom.

This decision applies even when the error is found in a long series of acknowledgments; recourse must always be had to the primitive title when it is produced.

Hoc tantum interest, says Dumoulin, *ibid. n.* 88, *inter confirmationem in forma communi, & confirmationem ex certa scientia, quod illa (in forma communi) tanquam conditionalis & præsuppositiva non probat confirmatum; hoc (ex certa scientia) fidem de eo facit; non tamen illud in aliquo auget vel extendit, sed ad illud commensuratur, & ad ejus fines & limites restringitur, &c.* And further, §. 18, *gl.* 1, *n.* 19, he says in general of acknowledgments, *non interponuntur animo faciendæ novæ obligationis, sed solum animo recognoscendi; unde simplex titulus novus non est dispositorius.*

745. If the acknowledgments on the contrary are for less than is expressed in the primitive title; if there are several acknowledgments conformable to each other, and which are of thirty years, which is the time sufficient for the prescription to operate, or forty years, when the creditor is privileged; the creditor in setting forth the primitive title, could not claim more than is expressed in the acknowledgments, because the prescription has applied itself to the surplus.

Article V.

Of acquittances.

746. As instruments are passed for the proof of engagements, so they are passed also for the proof of payments. We

call these acquittances. An acquittance is evidence of what it contains, against the creditor who has given it, his heirs or successors, whether it he passed before a notary or under the private signature of the creditor.

There are also certain cases in which an acquittance is valid and is evidence without its having been passed before a notary, or being signed by the creditor. See these cases *supra*, *n.* 724, 725, 726, 727, 728. Acquittances either express the sum which has been paid, without expressing the cause of the debt; or they express the cause of the debt without expressing the sum paid; or they express neither the sum which has been paid nor the cause of the debt; or they express both.

The acquittances which express the sum which has been paid, although they do not express the cause of the debt, are not the less valid; as when they are thus. *I have received of A. B. one thousand livres, this day, &c.* and in this case when the creditor who has given it, had at the time of the acquittance several claims against the debtor to whom he has given it, this debtor may apply it to that which he has the most interest to discharge, as we have seen *supra*, *Part.* 3, *ch.* 1, *art.* 7.

747. The acquittances which express only the cause of the debt without expressing the sum which has been paid, are likewise valid; and they are evidence of the payment of all that was due for the cause expressed in the acquittance at the time it was given. For example. If it is thus, *I have received of A. B. what he owed me for the price of my wine of Saint-Denis, which I have sold him*; this acquittance is evidence of the payment of what he owed me for the price of my wine of this place, either of the whole, if he owed me the whole, or of what remained due. But this acquittance does not extend to what is due for other causes than that which is expressed, and it is not necessary that I should make an express reservation. For example. The acquittance which I have given you, such as is expressed in the

inſtance above put, only includes what you owe me for the price of my wine of Saint-Denis, and you cannot oppoſe it againſt my claims for the price of the wine of my other places, which I have alſo ſold you.

When the debt of which the cauſe is expreſſed in the acquittance, is a debt which conſiſts of arrearages of annuities or rents, it is evidence of the payment of all which has accrued until the laſt day of payment preceding the date of the acquittance; but it does not extend to what has accrued ſince. For example. You have rented a houſe which belonged to me, of which the rent is to be paid on St. John's, or if you owed me a rent payable yearly on St. John's; the acquittance which I ſhould give you in theſe terms *I have received from A. B. what he owed me for rent*; or indeed *what he owed me for arrearages of rent*, this 10th December 1760: this acquittance is valid for all the arrearages or rents accrued until St. John's day, 1760; but it does not extend to what has accrued ſince.

Quid, if the acquittance was not dated? The want of a date preventing one in this caſe from knowing when the acquittance was given, the debtor cannot prove by it what time has preceded the day of the acquittance and to what time he has paid. In this uncertainty, this acquittance does not prove any thing, except that the debtor has paid at leaſt one term and conſequently it cannot avail for more than the term. If he was the heir of the creditor who had given the acquittance, it would be good for all the payments due in the life time of the deceaſed; for it is not to be doubted that theſe have preceded the time of the acquittance, the heir not having had power to give it, except ſince his becoming heir and conſequently ſince the death of the deceaſed.

When the debt whereof the cauſe is expreſſed in the acquittance, is the debt of a ſum divided into ſeveral times of payment, as when my father-in law has promiſed me for the portion of his daughter, whom I have married, the ſum of twenty thouſand livres, payable in four yearly payments; the acquittance which I give him without expressing the sum in these terms, *I have received of my father-in law what he owed me for the portion of my wife*, ought likewise to comprehend only the payments which were due at the time of the acquittance and ought not to extend to those which were not then due: for although a sum whereof the time of payment is not yet come, is not the less due, in a very true sense, yet in common language, according to which the acquittance should be understood, these terms *what he owed* refer only to what could be demanded and of which the time of payment has arrived; it is in this sense that we commonly say, HE WHO HAS TIME, DOES NOT OWE. *Loysel.* Besides it is not to be presumed that a debtor pays before the time.

There would be much more difficulty if the acquittance was expressed in these terms; *I have received the portion of my wife*. These general and indefinite terms appear to comprehend the whole portion, and consequently even the parts whereof the time of payment had not yet arrived at the date of the acquittance.

748. When the acquittance expresses neither the sum which has been paid nor the cause of the debt which has been discharged, as when it is expressed in these terms, *I have received from A. B. what he owed me, &c.* this acquittance is a general one which comprehends all the different debts which were due at the time of the acquittance, to him who has given it, from him to whom it has been given. If among these debts there were some which were demandable at the time of the date of the acquittance, and others whereof the time of payment had not then arrived, the acquittance would not extend to these, for the reasons already deduced above.

A fortiori, the acquittance ought not to extend to the principal of annuities due by the debtor; it comprehends only the arrearages which had become due at the last term preceding the date of the acquittance.

We must also except from this acquittance the debts

of which the creditor who has given it, had not probably any knowlege. For example. If at the time of the acquittance you were on your own account my creditor of certain ſums, and of other ſums as heir of Peter, to whom you had already ſucceeded, but the inventory was not yet made; the general acquittance which you have given me in theſe terms, *I have received of A. B. what he owed me*, does not comprehend what I owed to the eſtate of Peter: for as, at the time of your acquittance, you had not any knowlege of the effects of the eſtate of Peter, although you had already ſucceeded to it, you ought not to be preſumed to have compriſed in this acquittance the debt which I owed you in your quality of heir of Peter, of which probably you had no knowledge.

If I owed you certain ſums on my own account, and others as a ſecurity for another perſon, do theſe terms of the acquittance which you have given me, *I have received of A. B. what he owed me*, comprehend the ſums which I owed you as a ſecurity? The reaſon to doubt is, that theſe terms, *what he owed me*, taken literally in their general import, ſeem to comprehend them; for I owe in reality what I owe as a ſecurity. Neverthelefs, I think it muſt be preſumed that you have intended by theſe terms *what he owed me*, only what I owed *proprio nomine*, and not what I owed you as a ſecurity; I. becauſe, being able to defend myſelf from paying what I owed you as a ſecurity, until after a diſcuſſion of the property of the principal debtor, I did not owe it in the manner and in the ſenſe which theſe words generally import, before the diſcuſſion and at the time of the acquittance; II. becauſe, having a recourſe againſt thoſe for whom I was a ſecurity for what I might have paid, it is not to be preſumed that in paying for them, I ſhould not have taken ſeparate acquittances for the ſum I paid for them, and that I ſhould have contented myſelf with ſo general an acquittance.

If among the ſums which I owed you at the time of the general acquittance which you gave me, there was a ſum mentioned in a note which remained with you, would it be compriſed in it? The reaſon to doubt ariſes from the note remaining with you, which you ought to have given to me, and which, if I had paid it, ought not to have remained with you. The reaſon to decide that it is compriſed in it, ariſes from the generality of the expreſſion *which he owed me*, which includes all the debts which I then owed you. It may have happened that, truſting to my general acquittance, I neglected taking up my note, which you might have miſlaid.

749. The fourth kind of acquittances is that in which the ſum that has been paid, and the cauſe of the debt that has been diſcharged, are expreſſed. This can hardly occaſion any difficulty. If the ſum paid exceeded that which was due for the cauſe expreſſed in the acquittance, the debtor, ſuppoſing he owed nothing elſe, would have a right to claim back this exceſs, *per condictionem indebiti*: if he were debtor for other cauſes he might apply this exceſs to that which he has the moſt intereſt to diſcharge.

The queſtion whether the acquittances of one or ſeveral years' arrearages creates a preſumption of the payment of thoſe of the preceding years, is treated of *infra*, *ch.* 3, §. 2, *art.* 2.

CHAPTER II.

Of oral or testimonial proof.

ORAL or teſtimonial proof is that which is made by the depoſition of witneſſes.

ARTICLE THE FIRST.

General principles upon the cases in which this proof is admitted.

750. The corruption of morals, and the frequent examples of the ſubornation of witneſſes, have rendered us much more cautious in admitting teſtimonial proof than the Romans were. To prevent this ſubornation of witneſſes,

the ordinance of Moulins, of the year 1566, *art.* 54, ordains that for all things exceeding the value of one hundred livres, written contracts ſhall be made, by which only ſhall be received all proof of the ſaid things, *without admitting* any proof by witneſſes, beſides what is contained in the ſaid contracts.

This law has been confirmed by the ordinance of 1667, *tit.* 20, *art.* 2, which is, thus expreſſed: "Inſtruments of "writing ſhall be paſſed before notaries or under private "ſignature for all things exceeding the value of one hun- "dred livres; and no proof by witneſſes ſhall be received "againſt or beſides the contents of theſe inſtruments, al- "though the ſum in queſtion be leſs than one hundred "livres."

In the following article the ordinance excepts the caſe of unforeſeen accidents, and the caſe in which there is an inchoate proof in writing.

There is alſo in the firſt article an exception in regard to what is obſerved in the Juriſdiction of Conſuls.

From this diſpoſition of the ordinance may be derived four general principles which decide the caſes in which teſtimonial proof ought to be admitted or rejected.

Theſe principles are, I. he who had it in his power to procure literal proof, is not admitted to bring teſtimonial proof, when the thing exceeds one hundred livres, if there is no inchoate proof in writing.

II. When there is an inſtrument in writing, thoſe who were parties, their heirs or ſucceſſors, cannot be admitted to teſtimonial proof contrary to or beſides this inſtrument, even when the thing ſhould not exceed one hundred livres; if they have no inchoate proof in writing.

III. One is admitted to teſtimonial proof of things of which literal proof could not be obtained, to whatever ſum they may amount.

IV. Likewiſe, when by an accidental and unforeſeen circumſtance, acknowledged by the parties or proved, the literal proof is loſt, one is admitted to teſtimonial proof, to whatever ſum the thing may amount.

Article II.

First principle. *He who had it in his power to procure written proof, is not admitted to testimonial proof for things which exceed one hundred livres.*

751. The ordinance of Moulins ſays," we ordain that "for all things exceeding the ſum or value of one hundred "livres, for a ſingle payment, there ſhall be written con- "tracts &c."

The ordinance of 1667, *tit.* 2 *art.* 2, ſays, "there ſhall "be inſtruments of writing for all things exceeding the value "of one hundred livres."

Although the ordinance of Moulins has not ſaid *for all agreements*, but has made uſe of the term *things*, which is a more general term than *agreements*, yet the commentators upon this ordinance think that it includes in its diſpoſition agreements only; becauſe this ordinance ſays there ſhall be *contracts* in writing, and this term *contracts* includes only agreements.

The ordinance of 1667 having avoided the uſe of this term *contracts*, and having ſaid, *there shall be instruments of writing for all things*, we ought not to think that its diſpoſition includes agreements only, but generally all things of which he who demands to offer proof, had the power to procure proof in writing. For example although the payment of a debt is not an agreement, yet the debtor who makes it, having had it in his power to take an acquittance in writing, is not admitted to prove it by witneſſes, when this payment exceeds one hundred livres.

752. It was doubted before the ordinance of 1667, whether a voluntary depoſit was compriſed in the law of Moulins, which ordains that there ſhall be an inſtrument of writing for all things exceeding one hundred livres, and excludes teſtimonial proof thereof. The reaſon to doubt was, that it is not common to take inſtruments of writing

for deposits; that he who requests his friend to take charge of the things which he confides to him to keep, does not commonly think proper to demand an acknowledgment from the depositary, who only receives the deposit to accommodate him. Notwithstanding these reasons, the ordinance of 1667, *tit.* 20, *art.* 2, has decided that a voluntary deposit was comprised in the general rule, and that proof of it by witnesses ought not to be admitted; because he who made the deposit, either ought not to have made it, which he was not obliged to do; or when he made it, he ought to have required an acknowledgment from the depositary: not having required this acknowledgment, he ought to run the risque of the faith of the depositary, and ought to blame himself alone for having too easily trusted him, if he prove unfaithful.

Some decisions before the ordinance of 1667, had also admitted testimonial proof of the loan to use; because this loan, like the deposit, is commonly made between friends without taking an acknowledgment of it in writing. But the ordinance of 1667 having declared that a voluntary deposit was comprised in the general law, which requires written proof, we ought, *a fortiori*, to conclude the same thing in regard to the loan for use; since confidence is placed as well in him with whom the deposit is made, as in him to whom the loan is made; and he who makes a deposit has more reason to fear offending his friend by demanding from him an acknowledgment of it, than he who makes the loan.

753. It has also been questioned whether the bargains made in fairs and markets ought to be comprised in the disposition of the ordinance. The reason to doubt was, that these bargains are commonly made verbally; that there is no notary present, when they are made, to reduce them to writing. Nevertheless it has been decided that these bargains ought to be comprised therein; because as there are notaries now established in the smallest towns, and consequently in all the places where fairs are holden, it is not difficult for the parties, when they make a bargain on credit,

to call in a notary to reduce it to writing, if they do not know how to write. This is the opinion of Boiceau, 1, 9.

Obſerve however that in regard to bargains made between merchant and merchant, whether in or out of fairs, the conſular judges who have cognizance of them, are not bound by the diſpoſition of the ordinance, and that they may, according to circumſtances, admit teſtimonial proof of them, although the object exceeds the ſum of one hundred livres. It appears by the debates upon the ordinance of 1667, that the conſular judges had maintained this cuſtom, notwithſtanding the ordinance of Moulins: that of 1667 expreſsly ſupports them in this by theſe terms at the end of the article 2. *without innovating at all in regard to what is obſerved in the juriſdiction of conſuls.*

754. When a perſon demands the damages which he claims to be due him, for the inexecution of a verbal agreement to do or not to do ſomething, and it is uncertain whether the value of theſe damages ought to amount to the ſum of one hundred livres, in order to be admitted to teſtimonial proof of the agreement, the inexecution of which gives riſe to the damages claimed, the plaintiff ſhould reſtrict the demand for the ſaid damages to a certain ſum which does not exceed that of one hundred livres. He ought even to reſtrict it at firſt: for if he had once demanded a greater ſum, having himſelf acknowledged that the object of the agreement exceeded one hundred livres, and that the agreement was conſequently comprifed in the diſpoſition of the ordinance, he could not, in reſtricting himſelf afterwards, be admitted to offer teſtimonial proof. We may derive, in favor of this deciſion, an argument from a caſe of December 17, 1638, reported by Bardet, 7. 46, in the inſtance in which a taylor, who had demanded the ſum of two hundred livres from a widow for clothes furniſhed to her huſband, was excluded from teſtimonial proof which he offered, that this widow had acknowledged the debt, although he reſtricted his claim to one hundred livres.

755. I demand of you ſixty livres, the ſum remaining

of the price of a thing which I pretend to have sold you for two hundred livres; you deny having purchased any thing from me. Ought I to be admitted to testimonial proof of this sale? Boiceau, 1, 18, decides in the affirmative. He cites laws which do not appear to me to apply. It is true indeed that when a question arises respecting the jurisdiction of the judge, which is limited to a certain sum, *quantum petatur quærendum est, non quantum debeatur;* L. 19, §. 1, ff. *de jurisdic.;* because the judge decides only upon what is demanded. But in this instance, to know whether the proof of the agreement ought to be permitted to the plaintiff, it is necessary to know whether it is an agreement for which the ordinance would require an instrument of writing. This is decided by the object of the agreement, which exceeded one hundred livres, and not by what remains due; he cannot therefore be admitted to prove it by witnesses, although there remains due only sixty livres. This is the opinion of the commentators upon Boiceau.

For the same reason, if, as heir of my father for a fourth part, I demand of you fifty livres for the fourth of two hundred livres which I pretend were lent you by my father, I shall not be admitted to the proof of the loan by witnesses.

756. But if, in either case, the plaintiff offered testimonial proof, not of the sale made for the price of two hundred livres, not of the loan of two hundred livres made by the deceased, but of the promise which the defendant made to him to pay him the sixty livres which remained due of the price of this sale, or the fifty livres which were due to him for his fourth part, I think he ought to be admitted to the proof: for this promise is a new agreement confirming the first; and the object of this new agreement not exceeding one hundred livres, nothing prevents testimonial proof from being admitted.

757. When several claims do not exceed each the sum of one hundred livres, but altogether do exceed it, ought testimonial proof of all these claims to be admitted? It would seem that it ought to be; for the ordinance having required

instruments of writing for the things only which exceed one hundred livres, it seems that the plaintiff ought not to be blamed for not procuring written proof, and that testimonial proof ought not to be refused. Neverthelefs the ordinance of 1667, *tit.* 20. *art.* 5, decides that it ought to be refused; for the intention of the ordinance, in rejecting this proof, having been that individuals should not be exposed to the risque of the subornation of witnesses for considerable sums exceeding one hundred livres, which might be demanded of them by knaves, it ought to be rejected, whether this sum be claimed for a single or for several causes; it being as easy to suborn witnesses to swear to several false claims, as to suborn them to swear to a single one. In regard to the objection, the answer is that the creditor is not obliged to procure literal proof while his claims do not exceed one hundred livres; but when to those which do not exceed this sum there is added a new one which makes the whole amount of all his claims more than one hundred livres, there ought to be an instrument of writing.

The ordinance makes an exception, which is when the claims or rights proceed from different persons. Therefore I may be received to prove a loan of sixty livres which I demand of you on my own account, and another of eighty livres which I demand of you as heir of my father, by whom I pretend that this sum has been lent you, although these sums exceed one hundred livres.

Article III.

SECOND PRINCIPLE. *That testimonial proof is not admitted contrary to a writing, nor besides what it contains.*

758. Literal proof is preferred in our law to testimonial: therefore the ordinance forbids the admission of testimonial proof contrary to what is contained in a writing. For example. If I have made to A. B. my note by which I have acknowlaged to owe him sixty-six livres which he has lent me and which I promise to return him in two years, I shall not be received to prove by witnesses that I have only received sixty and that the surplus was or interest which

he had required me to include in my note: for this proof would be contrary to what is contained in a writing. I muſt blame myſelf alone for having made or written this note.

759. The ordinance not only excludes the proof by witneſſes of what would be directly contrary to an inſtrument of writing; it does not permit the admiſſion of any thing beſides the contents of theſe inſtruments, neither of what ſhould be alledged to have been ſaid *at the time, before or since*: for as they have made an inſtrument of writing, the party muſt blame himſelf alone for not having then expreſſed what he now alledges.

For example. The debtor will not be received to prove by witneſſes that there has been granted him a certain time for the payment, if it is not expreſſed in the inſtrument; neither of the parties will be admitted to prove that a certain place was agreed upon for the payment, if the inſtrument does not expreſs it.

A fortiori, the creditor will not be admitted to prove by witneſſes that there is more due him than is expreſſed in the inſtrument.

760. It would be an endeavour to prove ſomething beſides the contents of an inſtrument, to demand what is contained in a poſtſcript or marginal note not ſigned, nor even marked by the parties, although written in the hand of the notary; for theſe poſtſcripts or marginal notes, not ſigned nor even marked, cannot be preſumed to make part of the inſtrument. *Puta*, if in the margin of a leaſe by which the tenant obliges himſelf to pay ſix hundred livres of rent every year, there was a marginal note, *six capons besides*, the leſſor would not be admitted to prove by witneſſes that the tenant agreed to pay him the ſaid capons. *Danty* 11, 4. *in fin.*

Quid, if the poſtſcript were written in the hand of the tenant? See *supra, n.* 728.

761. When there is an inſtrument of writing of a bargain, and the time and place where it has been made is not expreſſed, may theſe be proved by witneſſes? For ex- ficult for the parties, when they make a bargain on credit;

ample. When a debtor demands to be admitted to the benefit of insolvency, may the creditor, in order to prevent him, be admitted to prove by witnesses that the contract which makes the cause of his claim, and of which there is an instrument of writing, has been made in a fair, although this was not expressed in the instrument? Danty, 1. 9, *in fine*, decides that he may be admitted to this proof, and that this proof of the place where the bargain is made, is not a proof besides the contents of the instrument, the place and the time in which the bargain is made being only extrinsic circumstances of the agreement, and not making part of the agreement contained in the instrument. This decision is liable to some difficulty.

762. All testimonial proof contrary to the contents of an instrument being interdicted, a party would not be received to explain by witnesses who were present at the making of the instrument, nor even by the notaries who received it, what is therein contained, and to prove by them what was agreed upon at the time of the execution. *Domat, p. 1, t. 3, t. 6, §. 2, n. 7.*

763. This rejection of testimonial proof contrary to or besides the contents of an instrument applies without distinction, even when the thing should be under the value of one hundred livres: the ordinance of 1667, *t.* 20, *art.* 2, is formally explicit in regard to this.

764. May he who, by an instrument of writing, is debtor of a sum less than one hundred livres be admitted to prove by witnesses the payment of this debt or a part? It seems that he ought to be admitted, and that the disposition of the ordinance which rejects the proof by witnesses contrary to or besides the contents of the instrument does not here apply; for the debtor in demanding to prove this payment, does not demand to prove a thing contrary to the instrument which contains his obligation; he does not attack this instrument: he admits every thing therein contained. It is not therefore a proof which he offers contrary to the instrument, and which may be said to be excluded by the

ordinance. However I find that in practice, whether by a bad interpretation which has been given to the ordinance, or for some other reason, testimonial proof of the payment of a debt of which there is an instrument of writing, is refused.

765. Observe that the ordinance excludes proof by witnesses contrary to what is contained in the instrument, only because it was in the power of the parties to procure written proof. But if a party alledges against an instrument, facts of violence exercised against him to constrain him to make the instrument; facts of deceit by which he pretends that his consent or signature has been taken by surprise; and other like facts: as it was not in his power to have proof by writing of these facts, there is no doubt that he ought to be admitted to prove them by witnesses, although he should attack the instrument *civiliter*.

A fortiori, when there is room to attack it *criminaliter*; as when it is alledged that the instrument contains some enormous usury which deserves to be prosecuted in an extraordinary manner.

766. It remains to be observed that the rejection of testimonial proof against or besides the contents of the instrument, applies only to those who were parties, who ought to blame themselves alone for having admitted what is there comprised, and not having taken some instrument of defeasance or having omitted something which should have been inserted; but this cannot affect third persons in fraud of whom one should recite in these instruments things contrary to the truth of what has taken place: for no fault or neglect being imputable to these third persons, we ought not to refuse to them testimonial proof of the fraud which is made upon them; since it was not in their power to have any other.

Therefore a lord may be received to prove by witnesses, contrary to a contract of sale, that the estate was sold for a price more considerable, than that which has been expressed, with a view to diminish the profits which are due him. *Vice versa*, a perſon having a right of redemption, will be admitted to prove by witneſſes that the eſtate was ſold for a price leſs conſiderable than that which has been expreſſed, and that the price was enlarged in fraud of the right of redemption. We may adduce other examples of theſe frauds.

ARTICLE IV.

Of inchoate proof in writing.

767. The firſt kind of inchoate proof in writing is when one has againſt another, by an authentic inſtrument to which he was a party, or by a private writing, written or ſigned by him, proof, not indeed of the truth of the whole fact which is advanced, but of ſomething which leads to, or makes a part of it.

It is left to the diſcretion of the judge to determine the degree of the inchoate proof in writing, in order, on this degree of proof, to admit teſtimonial proof.

Boiceau adduces ſeveral examples of this inchoate proof in writing. Firſt example. You bring a ſuit againſt me for a piece of land of which I am in poſſeſſion. I plead that you ſold it to me and that I paid you the price of it. I have no other proof than a writing ſubſcribed by you, by which you promiſed to ſell it to me for a certain price. This writing does not prove the ſale, much leſs the payment of the price; but, joined to the poſſeſſion in which I am of the land, it conſtitutes, according to this author, an inchoate proof, ſufficient to admit me to teſtimonial proof of the ſale. *Boiceau*, 11, 10.

Danty, *ibid.*, obſerves that this deciſion ought to admit of an exception when the promiſe to ſell expreſſed that a contract of ſale ſhould be entered into before a notary; for the parties having declared it was their intention that an inſtrument of writing ſhould be executed before a notary, we ought not to believe that the ſale took place unleſs ſuch an inſtrument ſhould be produced.

I think that even in the caſe when the promiſe to ſell

did not express that a contract should be entered into before a notary, the judge ought to be very cautious in considering it as an inchoate proof of the sale, and that he ought not thereon to admit testimonial proof, if the land in question was of any considerable value; it not being presumable that a piece of land of any considerable value should be sold without an instrument of writing.

Second example. I demand of you fifty crowns for the price of certain merchandises which I have sold and delivered to you: I have no other proof than your note which expresses, *I promise to pay to A. B. the sum of one hundred and fifty livres for the price of certain merchandises which he is to deliver me.* This is not a complete proof of my claim, since the note does not prove that I have delivered these merchandises; but it is an inchoate proof, which ought to authorise the admission of testimonial proof of the delivery. *Boiceau, ibid. Danty.*

Third example. You have given me a power of attorney *ad resignandum*, of your office. Before I obtain a commission, you revoke it. I maintain that you sold me this office for a certain sum, which I have paid you; and that you cannot therefore revoke your power of attorney without restoring to me the price. I have no other proof of what I advance than the power *ad resignandum*, which you have given me. This power does not form a proof of the sale, still less of the payment of the price; but it is proof of a fact which relates to it, which may consequently pass for an inchoate proof, and which ought to authorise the admission of testimonial proof of the sale, and of the payment of the price. This is the opinion of Loyseau in his treatise on offices, I, 11, 61, cited by Danty, 11, 1, 14.

768. Fourth example. You have written me a letter by which you request me to pay to your son, the bearer of the letter, one hundred and fifty livres of which he has need in his studies. I bring a suit against you for the repayment of this sum. I have omitted to take a receipt from your son; but I have your letter, which he left with me:

this letter in my possession is not an entire proof that I have paid this sum according to your order; but it is an inchoate proof in writing, which ought to authorise the admission of proof by witnesses.

If the person to whom the letter was written was not willing to pay the money and your son applied to another, who paid him the money and kept the letter; this letter in the possession of a third person to whom it was not written, would be a less proof than in the preceding case; yet Danty, 11, 2, 11, judges it, even in this case, sufficient to admit this third person to proof by witnesses.

If the person to whom I wrote to you to pay this sum, was a person against whom I might claim it back; on your neglecting to take his receipt, you would not be admitted to testimonial proof against me: for granting that you have paid it, you cannot demand it from me, because you have neglected to take a receipt which is necessary to enable me to recover it back.

769. If I have lent a minor a sum of money and demand from him the repayment of it, contending that it has been employed to his advantage; the note which I have from him, proving the loan, ought not to be regarded as an inchoate proof sufficient to authorise the admission of proof by witnesses, that the minor has advantageously employed the money; for this would render it easy for usurers to lend money to minors, and to recover it back by false witnesses who should testify to the use. *Danty*, 11, 4, 3.

770. A second kind of inchoate proof in writing is when I have against another by an authentic writing, to which he was a party, or by a private writing signed by him, proof that he is my debtor, without having proof of the sum: this is an inchoate proof in writing, which ought to admit me to proof of the sum by witnesses.

First example. I demand of you the payment of one hundred crowns; I have your note, which expresses, *I promise to pay to A. B. the sum of one hundred . . . . . which he has lent me.* The word *crowns* has been omitted in the note. You pretend that you borrowed only one hundred sous, which you tender. Your note is an inchoate proof in writing, which ought to admit me to testimonial proof of the loan of one hundred crowns.

Nota, if I fail in making this proof, I can only demand the one hundred sous; according to the rule, *semper in obscuris quod minimum est sequimur.* Observe also that in order to be admitted to testimonial proof, there ought to be some probability in the amount of the sum which I pretend to have lent you; therefore, in the instance put, I would not be admitted to prove by witnesses that I lent you one hundred thousand livres.

Another example of an inchoate proof in writing. I demand of you one hundred pistoles which I claim to have given you in deposit. I have no receipt for this deposit; but I have your letter by which you acknowlege yourself my debtor, without expressing of what sum, in these terms, *I will satisfy you in regard to what you know.* This letter does not contain the proof of the deposit of one hundred pistoles; but it proves that you are my debtor, which is an inchoate proof in writing that ought to admit me to testimonial proof. *Case reported by Chassanee, and cited by Danty*, 11, 1, 14.

771. Private writings, not signed, form against him who has written them, a third kind of inchoate proof in writing of what they contain. For example. I demand of you thirty pistoles which I claim to have lent you: I produce a note in which you acknowleged the loan, written in your hand and dated, but not signed. This note does not suffice to prove the loan, but it may, according to circumstances, form an inchoate proof in writing, which ought to admit me to proof by witnesses.

A fortiori, a receipt written in the hand of the creditor, although not signed, in the possession of the debtor, is an inchoate proof in writing of the payment, which ought to admit the debtor to testimonial proof; proof of the discharge being still more to be favored.

Obferve however that in order that an acquittance, not figned, may be an inchoate proof in writing of the payment of the debt, it is neceffary that the debt in difcharge of which the payment is made, fhould be expreffed ; a vague receipt, not figned, makes no inchoate proof in writing; *Danty, ibid.*

In certain cafes indeed, an acquittance, not figned, may be entire proof; as when it is written on the journal of the creditor, or on the back of a promiffory note.

772. According to the principles we have juft eftablifhed, inchoate proof in writing ought to refult, either from a public inftrument in which he againft whom the proof is to be produced has been a party, or from a private inftrument figned by him, or at leaft written in his hand.

This inftrument written by him who demands to offer the proof, cannot avail him as an inchoate proof, becaufe one cannot make titles or evidence for himfelf.

It is neceffary however to except from this decifion the books of merchants, which, when they are *regular*, are inchoate proof in favor of thofe who wrote them, as we have obferved *supra, chap.* 1, *art.* 2, §. 4.

773. The writing of a third perfon cannot make the inchoate proof in *writing which the ordinance requires*; for this third perfon is only as a witnefs, and what he has declared in writing can only be equivalent to teftimonial proof. Hence arifes the decifion of the queftion whether the acknowledgment which a widow has made, by her inventory, of a debt of the community, ought to be regarded as an inchoate proof in writing againft the heirs of her hufband? I do not think it ought: for the widow can only be confidered as a witnefs in regard to the heirs of her hufband, for the part which is demanded from them; and confequently the acknowledgment which fhe makes by the inventory, is, in regard to the heirs, equivalent only to the depofition of a witnefs, and ought not, it feems, to form againft them an inchoate proof in writing. Yet Vrevin, *on*

article 54, of the ordinance of Moulins, reports a case in which in consequence of a similar acknowledgment by a widow, testimonial proof was admitted against the heirs. But this case was decided at a time when the disposition of the ordinance of Moulins was not yet fully acquiesced in: this ordinance was then regarded as contrary to the general law, and as one which could not be too much restricted.

It is the same of the acknowledgment which one of the heirs should make of the debt of the deceased; it would not serve as an inchoate proof against his co-heirs.

774. Hence arises also the decision of the question, whether an instrument received by an incompetent notary, makes an inchoate proof in writing, of what is therein contained, against the parties who are said by this instrument to have contracted, when this instrument is not signed by the parties, who did not know how to sign? I do not think it does; for this incompetent notary being a private person in the place where he acted, his act can only be equivalent to the deposition of a witness, when the parties have not subscribed it. If the parties had subscribed it, it would be equal to a private writing, as we have said, *supra*.

I think the same ought to be said when the instrument is defective for the want of some formality; as when the notary received it without causing himself to be assisted by witnesses: for the notary not having acted as a public person, his act cannot pass for the attestation of a public person, and is equivalent only to the simple deposition of a witness; *supra, n. 740, in fine*.

ARTICLE V.

THIRD PRINCIPLE. He who had it not in his power to procure literal proof, ought to be admitted to testimonial proof.

775. The ordinance of Moulins, confirmed by that of 1667, in requiring that instruments of writing should be drawn, did not intend to exact impossibilities, nor even to require things too difficult, and which might cramp and restrain the course of trade; therefore it has prohibited

teſtimonial proof to thoſe only who had it in their power eaſily to procure literal proof.

Whenever therefore it has not been in the power of the creditor to procure literal proof of the obligation which has been contracted towards him, teſtimonial proof of the fact which has produced it, cannot be refuſed him, to whatever ſum the object of this obligation may amount.

776. According to this principle, teſtimonial proof of torts and quaſi-torts can never be refuſed to him towards whom they have been committed, to whatever ſum the reparation claimed by him may amount; for it is evident that it could not have been in his power to procure any other proof.

777. For the ſame reaſon, every one is admitted to teſtimonial proof of the frauds which have been committed againſt him. For example. We ought to admit proof by witneſſes of ſecret pacts to convey the property of the anceſtor to a prohibited perſon, in fraud of his heirs; for it is evident that it is not in the power of the heirs to have proof in writing of this fraud.

778. It is the ſame of the obligation which ariſes from a quaſi contract: as this obligation is contracted without the act of him towards whom it is contracted, and as it was not in his power to procure literal proof, we cannot refuſe to him teſtimonial proof of the fact which has produced it.

For example. If a perſon, during my abſence, has tilled my lands, and ſold the produce, he ought to render me an account of what he has done. If he refuſes to do this, teſtimonial proof ought not to be denied me; for it was not in my power to procure any other proof.

779. There are alſo ſome agreements that are made under certain circumſtances which hardly admit of any inſtrument of writing being made when they take place, and of which therefore the ordinance of 1667 has permitted teſtimonial proof, to whatever ſum the object of them may amount.

Such are necessary deposits in case of fire, ruin, insurrection, shipwreck. The ordinance of 1667, *tit.* 20, *art.* 3, expressly excepts them from the disposition which excludes proof by witnesses above one hundred livres.

For example. If in the accident of fire, or of the ruin of a house which thereby falls to the ground, he who dwells in it hastily deposits in his neighbour's house the furniture which he has saved from the flames or from the ruin, and his neighbour denies the deposit, he will be admitted to proof by witnesses of the things he has deposited, to whatever sum their value may amount; for the haste in which he was obliged to make this deposit, did not permit him to procure proof in writing.

It is the same when, at the time of an insurrection or invasion, I remove by a back door my goods, which I give to the first person I meet, to save them from the pillage of the insurgents or enemies, who are ready to enter my house; or when a vessel is cast on shore, I hastily trust my goods to the first person that comes. In all such cases it is obvious that a written proof of such deposits could not be procured; therefore the ordinance of 1667 permits the proof by witnesses.

780. For a like reason, the ordinance on the same title, *art.* 4, admits testimonial proof of deposits made by travellers to the keeper of the inn in which they lodge. For instruments of writing are not taken for such deposits. An innkeeper would not have time to make an inventory of all the things which travellers that come to his house, at every hour of the day and night, deposit with him.

Article VI.

Fourth principle. He who has by accident lost the literal proof, ought to be admitted to testimonial proof.

781. The same reason that obliges us to admit testimonial proof, when literal proof was not to be procured, obliges us to admit testimonial proof, when, by an unforeseen accident, the papers which served for literal proof are lost.

For example. If, at a fire or in the pillage of my houfe, I have loft my papers, among which were notes from my debtor to whom I had lent money, or receipts of fums which I had paid to my creditor, whatever may be the amount of fuch notes or receipts, I ought to be admitted to prove by witneffes the fums which I have lent or paid; becaufe it is by an unforefeen accident without any fault of mine that I have loft the notes and receipts which formed my literal proof.

I may make this proof by witneffes, who depofe that they have feen in my hands before the fire the notes of my debtor or the receipts of my creditor, whofe hand-writing they know and the tenor of which they remember; or who may depofe that they have a knowledge of the debt or payment.

But in order that the judge may admit the proof, it is neceffary that the accident which has occafioned the lofs of the papers that conftitute the literal proof, fhould be apparent.

For example. In the above cafes it is neceffary that it fhould be admitted by the parties that my houfe was burnt or pillaged, or that I fhould be able to prove it, before I can be admitted to introduce teftimonial proof of the loans of money or payments of which I pretend to have loft the notes or receipts.

If he who requires to be admitted to teftimonial proof, alledges merely that he has loft his papers, without there being any apparent *vis major*, through which he loft them, he cannot be admitted to prove by witneffes that thefe papers once exifted: otherwife the ordinance which forbids the proof by witneffes, to prevent the fubornation of witneffes, would be illufory. For it would not be more difficult to one who wifhed to introduce proof by witneffes of a loan or a payment which he had not made, to fuborn witneffes who would depofe that they faw in his hands the obligations and receipts, than to fuborn thofe who would fay that they faw him count the money.

ARTICLE VII.

How testimonial proof is made.

782. When the creditor demands to make proof of the obligation which he contends the other party has contracted towards him, and likewise when a debtor offers proof of the payment which he pretends to have made of the sum that is demanded of him; if, according to the principles established in the preceding article, the proof is admissible, the judge gives an interlocutory judgment, by which he permits the party to make the testimonial proof he offers; saving to the other party the right of proving the contrary.

This judgment is called a judgment of inquest. In execution of this judgment the parties ought in the time, and according to the forms prescribed by the ordinance of 1667, *tit.* 22, produce their witnesses before the judge or a commissioner; and an instrument of writing is drawn out, including their depositions, which is called an inquest.

783. That the inquest may contain testimonial proof of the fact which the party undertook to prove, it is necessary that this fact should be attested by two witnesses at least, whose depositions are valid.

The testimony of one witness can make no proof, however worthy of credit he may be, and whatever may be his dignity; *etiamsi præclaræ curiæ honore præfulgeat*, L. 9, *Cod. de testib.* But a single witness makes a half-proof, which being supported by the oath of the party, may sometimes, in very small matters, complete the proof.

It is on this principle that our custom of Orleans, *art.* 156, decides that when one has suffered his cattle to feed on the land of another, and they have done injury thereto, the proof of the obligation resulting from the trespass, may be made by one witness and the oath of the plaintiff, provided he claim no more than twenty sous, if the trespass was committed in the day, and forty sous if it was done at night. *Articles* 160 & 161.

When one claims two different sums, to the proof of

which he is admitted, he ought to prove each ſum by the teſtimony of two witneſſes. If he had the depoſitions of two witneſſes, one of whom proved one ſum, and the other the other, each being proved by one witneſs only, neither would be ſufficiently proved.

It would be the ſame if a debtor had been admitted to the proof of two ſeveral payments. It would be requiſite that each payment ſhould be proved by two witneſſes.

Quid, if I have been admitted to the proof of a ſingle claim, and to prove it I introduced ſeveral witneſſes, each of whom depoſed to different facts proving this claim, and none of theſe facts were proved by more than one witneſs? Will the uniting of all theſe particular witneſſes to each fact be a complete proof of the claim? For example. If I have been admitted to prove that I lent you ten piſtoles, and a witneſs ſhould depoſe to have been preſent at the loan and ſeen me count the money; a ſecond to have heard you acknowledge the debt: will theſe two ſingle witneſſes to each fact be a complete evidence of the loan. *Cravett. de antiq. temporum, 17th vol. de tract. p. 175, n. 15, & seq.*, determines this queſtion in the affirmative. The reaſon is, that as the acknowledgment you have made of the loan, ſuppoſes the loan, the depoſition of the ſecond witneſs conſpires with that of the firſt to atteſt the loan. They both teſtify to have knowledge of the loan; the loan which is the only fact to the proof of which I have been admitted, is then atteſted by two witneſſes, and conſequently fully proved.

It would be the ſame, if neither of the witneſſes had been preſent at the loan and the firſt witneſs depoſed to an acknowledgment of the loan made by you in his preſence at a certain time, and the ſecond to an acknowledgment which you made in his preſence at another time, the loan would be fully proved by the teſtimony of two witneſſes; for they both join in depoſing that they have knowledge of this loan: the time within which you made the acknowledgment being indifferent as to the teſtimony which they give of the loan, it ought to be indifferent whether they depose to an acknowledgment made at the same time, or whether they depose to several acknowledgments made at different times; it suffices that they each depose that they have knowledge of the loan. It is indifferent in what manner they have this knowledge; it is indifferent whether it was the same acknowledgment made *in their presence*, *or different acknowledgments made in the presence* of each of them, which afforded them this knowledge.

784. Although two witnesses suffice to make the proof of a fact, yet as the party who has been admitted to offer the proof is not certain as to what the witnesses will depose, he may extend their number to ten, upon the same fact: the addition he should make of more than this number ought not to be taxed in the costs adjudged against the other party. *Ordinance* 1667, *tit.* 22, *art.* 21.

785. In order that a deposition may be valid, it is necessary, I. that it should not be defective in form; otherwise it is declared null, and the judge does not regard it. See, on these forms, *ordinance* 1667, *tit.* 22.

Observe that when the deposition of a witness has been declared null for the act of the judge, who has omitted some formalities required in the examination of witnesses, the party who produced this witness is admitted to have him examined anew; *tit.* 22, *art.* 86: but when the nullity proceeds from the party, who has omitted some requisite formalities in the execution of the inquest, he cannot have him re-examined.

In order that a deposition may be valid, it is necessary, II. that it should not have been rejected for any cause of challenge to the witness. We shall see in the following article what are the causes of challenge.

786. In order that a deposition may be valid, it is necessary, III. that it should contain nothing in itself which might render the truth of it suspicious. Therefore a deposition ought to be rejected when it contains contradictions, or things entirely improbable.

It is neceffary above all, in order that a depofition may be valid, that the witnefs who fays he has knowledge of the fact, fhould explain how he has this knowledge; L. 4, *Cod. de test.* Bartolus, *ad d.* L. For example. If I would prove that you have fold me a certain thing, it does not fuffice that the witnefs fhould fay in vague terms that he knows you fold me this thing; it is neceffary that he fhould explain how he has this knowledge, by faying, for example, that he was prefent at the bargain, or that he heard you fay you had made to me this fale; if he faid that he knew it from having heard a third perfon fay fo, his depofition would not be proof.

787. The proof which a party has made by the depofition of two or more witneffes who have attefted the fact by him advanced, is valid only when it is not deftroyed by the inqueft of the other party, who on his fide has produced witneffes attefting the contrary. For example. If in an action for flander, I introduced witneffes who faid that they were prefent at the quarrel, and that you fpoke the words, which I did not retort; and on your fide you introduced witneffes who faid that it was I who fpoke the words, which you did not retort, the inquefts in this cafe mutually deftroy each other; and there refults no proof from either fide.

But if my witneffes were in much greater number than yours; or indeed if mine were good citizens, of known probity, and yours were people of the loweft clafs; the proof which refults from my inqueft ought to prevail, and would not be deftroyed by yours; *arg.* L. 5, §. 2, ff. *de test. Numerus testium, dignitas & autoritas confirmat rei de qua quæritur fidem.*

ARTICLE VIII.

Of the qualification of witnesses, and of the challenges which may be made to them.

788. It is not required in witneffes who are produced to prove a fact, that they fhould have all the qualifications

requisite in those who are called to be present at the execution of instruments of writing, for the solemnity of the instrument. Women, aliens, monks professed are admitted to testify. The reason of this difference is, that one has a choice of persons whom he may call to witness the execution and solemnity of an instrument of writing; whereas he can produce those only, to prove a fact, who have knowledge of it.

The causes of challenge which may be made to a witness, in order to reject his deposition, may be reduced to four heads; the want of reason, want of reputation, suspicion of partiality, and suspicion of subornation.

Of the want of reason.

789. It is not to be doubted that the deposition of a child and that of an idiot ought to be rejected.

In regard to minors who approach the age of puberty, and who therefore begin to have some use of reason, their depositions ought not to be indiscriminately rejected. But this ought to be left to the prudence of the judge, who may admit the deposition of such persons when the circumstances are well and particularly stated, and the facts to which they testify are not above their judgment.

Those who contend that the depositions of minors under the age of puberty, should be indiscriminately rejected, ground themselves on the law 3, §. 5, ff. *de testibus*, which does not admit the deposition of these persons in the capital accusation of public violence; but I cannot think this law ought to be construed as a general decision and extended to civil suits.

Of the want of reputation.

790. The depositions of those who have become infamous by some judgment, ought to be rejected. The ordinance of 1667, *tit.* 23, *art.* 2, presupposes it.

Not only the loss of one's reputation, but the mere suspension of it, which results from a capias issued in a criminal suit against a person, ought to cause his deposition to be rejected. Becaufe in order that a witnefs may be worthy of credit, it is not fufficient that he fhould be free from crime, it is requifite that he fhould be free from all legal fufpicion.

It is the fame in the cafe of a fummons in a criminal fuit, when the crime for which it has iffued is fufceptible of an infamous punifhment.

The ordinance of 1667, above cited, confiders the capias, as well as judgment, as a ground of challenge againft a witnefs.

Of the suspicion of partiality.

791. The fufpicion of partiality is a good ground of challenge, which will caufe the depofition of the witnefs to be rejected: witneffes, to be worthy of credit, ought to be perfectly difinterefted.

It is on this ground that they reject the depofition, I. of thofe who have a perfonal intereft in the determination of the caufe, although they be not parties to it.

For example. If in confequence of an inchoate proof in writing, I have been admitted to teftimonial proof of the fale of a piece of land which I contend you fold to me, the depofition of the lord of the manor from whom it is holden ought to be rejected, becaufe he has an intereft in the determination of the caufe, on account of the profits he will be entitled to, if it be determined that there has been a fale.

792. II. On the fame principle they reject the depofition of thofe who are related by confanguinity or affinity to one of the parties or both, to the fourth degree in the collateral line inclufively. *Ord.* 1667, *tit.* 22, *art.* 11.

Note, that thefe relations of a party cannot teftify either for or againft him. Their fituation gives rife to a prefumption of friendfhip or enmity, inconfiftent with impartiality. *Sunt apud concordes excitamenta charitatis, inter iratos vero incitamenta odiorum.* This is the reafon given in the debates on the ordinance.

It appears by thefe debates that this article of the ordinance met with great oppofition, and was admitted againft the opinion of the first president and the other magistrates of the parliament. In the civil law parents and children only were excluded from testifying against each other. L. 6, *Cod. de test.* All the relations of the collateral line were admitted, except that in criminal cases, relations, as far as the degree of children of cousins-german, were not compellable to testify against their relations. L. 4, ff. *d. tit.*

793. III. On the same principle they reject most commonly the depositions of servants and domestics of either party. I have said, most commonly; for the ordinance not having absolutely denied the admission of these depositions, as it has those of relations, but having merely required that whenever the witness is a servant or domestic of the party, this should be mentioned in the caption of the deposition, it gives us to understand that it is left to the discretion of the judge to regard it as he thinks proper, and to admit or reject the deposition according to circumstances.

We call *servants*, those whom we have hired to render us all the services which we may command them to render us, although they are employed principally for a certain kind of service.

Thus there may be a servant without his being a domestic, such as a gardener or a game-keeper, which a gentleman residing in town keeps on his estate. Such persons are not properly his domestics, since they do not dwell with him, nor are supplied from his table; but they are his servants, since he has them on wages, and he may command them, when he is on his estate, to render him all the services they are capable of rendering.

In this these persons differ from those with whom we have made a bargain for them to do a certain piece of work for a certain sum; such are vine-dressers. These are not properly our servants, and we have no right to command them, nor to exact from them any other thing than the work which they engaged to do: therefore in practice the testimony of a vine-dresser of the party is admitted.

We call *domestics*, persons who dwell in our house and eat of our bread, whether these persons are at the same time our servants, such as lackeys, coachmen, cooks, waiting-men, stewards, &c., or whether these persons are not properly servants, provided we have however some authority over them, as apprentices, clerks to attorneys, &c.

The depositions of servants or domestics are especially rejected, when they are offered for and at the request of their masters. For this the law 6, ff. *de test.*, is cited: *Idonei non videntur esse testes, quibus imperari potest ut testes fiant.* This law is not received however as entirely applicable. It speaks of slaves and children of a family, who were subject to a power from which they could not withdraw; whereas our servants are free persons.

794. IV. It is on the same ground of a suspicion of partiality that we ought not to receive in a cause the testimony of the counsel or attorney of either of the parties; L. 25, ff. *de test.*

Their testimony would be suspected of partiality, if they were witnesses in favor of their client, and it would be indecent to permit them to be witnesses against him.

For the same reason a tutor, a curator who is a party in this quality for his ward, cannot be a witness either for or against him. Officers of a corporation cannot be witnesses for or against it.

But the relations, and even children of these persons who are parties only in their quality of tutors, curators, or officers of a corporation, and likewise their servants and domestics may be witnesses: for these persons are not properly parties, it is the minor, the corporation, that is a party by their intervention.

For the same reason when a corporation is a party, the members of this corporation ought not to be received to give testimony: this testimony would be suspected of partiality, if they were witnesses for their corporation, and it would be indecent to oblige them to be witnesses against it.

But as each member of a corporation, being a person distinct from the corporation, according to the rule, *universitas distat a singulis*, 7, §. 1, ff. *quod cuj. univ.*, cannot be deemed a party, nothing prevents the relations, servants and domestics of each of the members of the corporation from being admitted to give testimony in the causes in which the corporation is a party.

795. V. The suspicion of partiality commonly authorises also the rejection of the depositions of witnesses who have a suit depending with the party against whom they are offered. The reason is that suits are seldom carried on without acrimony, and that they commonly excite enmities between the parties.

As criminal suits, especially, cause great enmities, it is not to be doubted that the deposition of a witness ought to be rejected when he stands to the party against whom he is produced in the relation of prosecutor, or accused, in a criminal suit. This is conformable to the novel 9, *ch.* 7. With regard to civil suits, I think they ought not to be considered indiscriminately as sufficient causes of challenge. If the law had intended it, the intention would have been expressed, as it has been with regard to relationship. As it is silent, it is to be presumed that it was intended to leave it to the discretion of the judge to admit the challenge or not, according to circumstances. For example: he will admit the challenge, if the suit concerns the whole fortune of the party, *lis de omnibus bonis*. For the acrimony that results from a suit is greater in proportion to the magnitude of the interest. The challenge ought also to be admitted, though the sum in dispute be not considerable, if the suit attacks the honor or probity of the party. But when the suit is of little consequence, and the honor or probity of the parties are not concerned, and it only involves a mere question of law, I do not think it ought to be considered as a sufficient cause of challenge to the witness who is at law with the party against whom he is offered. Such suits are not of a nature to create enmities. Even were they to excite an acrimony, this would be a very ſlight one, and it would be to judge men very hard, that a ſlight acrimony in the witneſs would alter the truth of a teſtimony which he gives on oath.

The judge ought above all to inquire whether the ſuit brought againſt the witneſs, which is alledged as a cauſe of challenge, is not a ſuit which was probably inſtituted at the time the party foreſaw that the witneſs might be introduced againſt him, with a view to procure a cauſe of challenge. If this appears to be the caſe, the judge ought to over-rule the challenge.

If a ſuit depending between the witneſs and the party againſt whom he is offered, is often a good cauſe of challenge, *a fortiori*, it is a good challenge if the property of the witneſs ſhould be executed by the party; for ſuch execution is ſtill more likely to create enmity than the ſuit.

Of the suspicion of subornation.

796. The legal ſuſpicion of ſubornation is alſo a good cauſe of challenge, which ought to occaſion the depoſition to be rejected. There is room for this ſuſpicion, and the teſtimony is to be rejected, when it is proved that the party who introduced him made him ſome preſent or gave him to eat and drink in his own houſe, or at a tavern at his expence, ſince the judgment of inqueſt. But if the witneſs had eaten with the party without having his expences paid, there would be no ground for the challenge.

It is alſo a ſtrong preſumption of ſubornation, when it appears that the party who introduces the witneſs gave him his depoſition in writing. *See a case reported in the 5th vol. of the journal cited by M. Jousse, on the 1st art. of the 23d tit. of the ordinance of 1667.*

CHAPTER III.

Of confession, presumptions and oaths.

SECTION. THE FIRST.

Of confession.

CONFESSION is judicial or extra-judicial.

§ I.

Of judicial confession.

797. The judicial confeſſion is the acknowledgment which the party makes before the judge, being thereto interrogated, and which the judge directs to be recorded.

The confeſſions or acknowledgments which the parties make in the ſeveral ſtages of a ſuit, by their inſtruments of writing or pleas, may alſo paſs for a ſort of judicial confeſſion, when the attorney has authority from his client to make them, and he is preſumed to have ſuch authority as long as he is not diſavowed.

798. The judicial confeſſion made by a party capable of being a party in a ſuit, makes full proof of the fact which is confeſſed, and diſcharges the other from making proof of it. Therefore if a debtor, ſued for a debt, confeſſes to owe the thing or the ſum demanded, the creditor is diſcharged from making proof of the debt, and he may, on this confeſſion, move for judgment againſt the defendant. *Vice versa*, if the creditor who has made out his claim admits in court the payments which the debtor pretends to have made, theſe payments will be allowed and the defendant will be diſcharged from making proof of them.

799. Note, that when I have no other proof than your confeſſion, I cannot divide it. Suppoſe, for example, that I ſue you for two hundred livres which I contend I lent you. If on this demand you have admitted the loan in court, adding that you have repaid me the money, I cannot derive from your confeſſion a proof of the loan, without its making at the ſame time proof of the payment; for

I cannot avail myſelf of it againſt you without taking it as it is and entire. *Si quis confessionem adversarii allegat, vel depositionem testis, dictum cum sua quantitate approbare tenetur; Bruneman, ad* L. 28, ff. *de pact.*

800. The proof which reſults from the confeſſion againſt him who made it, is not ſuch as that he cannot deſtroy it by ſhewing the error which occaſioned it; and herein this proof is leſs than that which reſults from the preſumption *juris & de jure*, (of which we ſhall treat in the following ſections) which excludes all proof of the contrary.

If, for example, I brought a ſuit againſt you for two hundred livres which I contended to have lent to your father, of which I produced no other proof than a letter by which your father had entreated me to make him this loan, and in this ſuit you acknowledged to owe me the money; this confeſſion forms againſt you a proof of the debt; and whereas before this confeſſion you might have been diſcharged from my claim without proving any thing, by ſaying ſimply that you had no knowledge of the loan, which this letter by me produced does not ſufficiently prove; on the contrary, ſince your confeſſion, I have againſt you, by your confeſſion, a ſufficient proof whereon I may obtain a judgment againſt you for this ſum: unleſs on your part you bring proof that the loan was not made, and that it was through error that you admitted it. As if, for example, you produced my letter in anſwer to your father's, by which I ſaid that I could not make him the loan which he requeſted, and you declared that you had diſcovered this letter ſince your confeſſion; the error of your confeſſion, being proved by this letter, deſtroys this confeſſion and the proof which reſulted from it: for as a conſent given through error, is not a true conſent according to this rule of law, *non videntur qui errant consentire;* L. 116, §. 2, ff. *de R. J.;* ſo a confeſſion, occaſioned by error, is not a true confeſſion: *Non fatetur qui errat;* L. 2, *de confessis.*

Obſerve that the error of a confeſſion can be proved only by the proof of ſome fact which did not come to the knowledge of him who made it, until after he had made it, as in the inſtance above adduced; but he who has made a confeſſion cannot deſtroy it by alledging that it was an ignorance of law he was in when he made the confeſſion, and which induced him to make it; for it is his own fault not to have informed himſelf before: therefore the law 2, above cited, after having ſaid, *non fatetur qui errat*, adds, *nisi jus ignoravit*.

This diſtinction between error of law and error of fact, will appear by the following example. Suppoſe a minor, of ſufficient age to make a will, had bequeathed a conſiderable ſum to his preceptor. The heir, being ſued, acknowledged to owe to this preceptor the ſum expreſſed in the will. If afterwards the heir diſcovered a codicil revoking the legacy, his confeſſion, occaſioned by his ignorance of the codicil, which is an error of fact, will be deſtroyed: but if the legacy had not been revoked, and the heir alledged only that it was through error that he acknowledged to owe the ſum expreſſed in the will, becauſe he was then ignorant of the law which forbids minors to bequeath to their preceptors; this error which he alledges being an error of law, he will not be allowed to avail himſelf of it, and the proof reſulting from his confeſſion will remain.

It remains for us to obſerve that, when a defendant who has confeſſed to owe the ſum which is demanded from him wiſhes to prove the error of his confeſſion, if the proof of the facts, by which he would prove this error, require a long diſcuſſion, the plaintiff may obtain a proviſional judgment againſt him for the ſum which he has confeſſed to owe: for until he makes the proof of theſe facts, the proof which reſults from his confeſſion remains, and ought to entitle the plaintiff to proviſional judgment.

§. II.

Of extrajudicial confession.

801. Extrajudicial confeſſion is that which is made not in any judicial proceedings.

We do not intend to ſpeak of the confeſſion which the parties make of their obligations by the inſtrument of writing from which they ariſe, or by inſtruments of writing to recogniſe and confirm them, which are drawn expreſsly for this purpoſe. We have treated of the proof which reſults from theſe inſtruments, *supra, chap.* 1.

The confeſſions of the debt, of which we ſpeak here, are thoſe which the debtor makes, in a converſation or by letter, or which are accidentally on ſome inſtrument of writing which was not expreſsly made for this purpoſe. Dumoulin diſtinguiſhes between thoſe which my debtor has made to me, and thoſe which he has made to a third perſon not in my preſence.

When it is to me that the debtor has confeſſed the debt, and his confeſſion expreſſed the cauſe of the debt, this confeſſion makes a complete proof of the debt; but if it was made in a vague manner, and without expreſſing the cauſe, it forms, according to this author, only an imperfect proof, which muſt be completed by the ſuplementary oath which the judge ought to require me to make.

When the confeſſion was made to one who repreſented me, as to my tutor, curator, attorney &c, it is the ſame as if made to me.

When it has been made to a third perſon not in my preſence, it makes only an imperfect proof, which ought to be completed by the ſupplementary oath. Such are the diſtinctions made by Dumoulin *ad. L.* 3, *Cod. de reb. cred.*

Theſe principles of Dumoulin appear to me to require a further diſtinction. When my debtor who has acknowledged, out of court, to owe me a certain ſum, denies, on being ſued, that he contracted towards me the debt of this ſum, the confeſſion which he has before made, convicts him of a falſehood, and eſtabliſhes the debt for which I brought the ſuit, without his being allowed afterwards to alledge, except with proof, that he has paid this ſum, of which he firſt denied to have been the debtor.

But if my debtor, whom I have fued, had confeffed that he did owe me this fum, but maintains that fince he made this confeffion he has paid it to me; whether his confeffion was made to a third perfon or to myfelf, whether in a converfation or by letter, or in fome inftrument of writing which was not made to afford me a proof of the debt, it would not be any proof that the fum is ftill due me at this day.

In regard to what is faid by Dumoulin, that the confeffion made to a third perfon makes only an imperfect proof of the debt, it muft be obferved that there are certain cafes in which it ought to make a complete proof.

Guthierez, *de contr. jura*, *q.* 54, *n.* 5, adduces as an example the cafe in which the debtor, in making this acknowledgment to third perfons, fays he does it in difcharge of his confcience. For example. If a fick perfon calls in two perfons to whom, in the apprehenfion of his death, he declares that he owes me the fum of one hundred livres, which I have lent him without a note; fuch a confeffion, although made to third perfons, appears to me to make a complete proof of the debt.

When my debtor, in an inventory taken on the diffolution of a partnerfhip, includes in the lift of debts due by the partnerfhip, the debt for which he is bound towards me, this confeffion, although made not in my prefence, ought alfo, it appears to me, to be a complete proof of the debt.

As the extrajudicial confeffion which the debtor has made of the debt in the prefence and on the requeft of the creditor, makes a complete proof of the debt; *a fortiori*, the extra-judicial confeffion of the payment made by the creditor in the prefence and on the requeft of the debtor, makes an entire proof of the payment: for the difcharge being to be favored, it ought to be more eafy to be proved than the obligation. It is the fame if this acknowledgment was made by the creditor in the prefence of fome one who had requefted it on the part of the debtor; for it is as if he had made it in the presence of the debtor himself; *Guthierez, ibid.*

There are indeed some authors cited by Guthierez, who think that the extra-judicial confession of the payment made by the creditor, although in the presence of the debtor, makes a complete proof of the payment; but Guthierez thinks that it makes only an imperfect proof. This ought to depend much on circumstances.

802. He who wishes to establish his demand by the extra-judicial confession of the debt, or his defence by the confession which he pretends the plaintiff has made of the payment or release of the debt, ought to prove this confession. It may be proved either by some writing or by witnesses. If however the fact which I intend to prove by your extrajudicial confession, was a fact whereof testimonial proof was not admissible, I could not be admitted to testimonial proof of your confession. For example. If I demand of you the restitution of a certain book of a value exceeding one hundred livres, which I claim to have lent you, and I advance that you acknowleged the loan before witnesses, I shall not be admitted to prove this confession by witnesses; because it would be to admit me indirectly to testimonial proof of the loan of a thing exceeding one hundred livres, which the ordinance forbids.

803. In order that the confession may be a proof against him who has made it, it is necessary that he who made it should be capable of binding himself; the confession of a feme covert not authorised by her husband, or of a minor, would not be proof.

804. The confession is proof not only against him who has made it, but also against his heirs: yet if one had acknowledged to owe to a person to whom the law forbids one to give, this confession would not be proof of the debt against them, unless the causes of the debt were well stated and explained; *Qui non potest donare, non potest confiteri.*

805. An implied confession ought to have the same effect as an express confession. Therefore the payment which

a person makes, being an implied confession on his part that he owed the thing which he has paid, there results from this payment a proof against him, that the thing which he has paid, was really due.

If therefore he wishes to claim back this thing, as having paid it unduly, he who has received it, is not obliged to prove that it was really due; he has a sufficient proof of it, resulting from the implied confession included in the payment which has been made to him; it is incumbent on him who made the payment, to prove the error. This is the decision of the law 25, ff. *de probat.*

Yet Paul, from whom this law is taken, adduces two exceptions. The first is, that if he to whom the thing has been paid, being sued to restore it, first denied the payment which was made to him, and this payment has been afterwards proved, he ought to be obliged to prove that the thing which has been paid to him, was really due. The reason of this exception is that the presumption against the truth of the debt, resulting from the false denial of the payment which was made to him, destroys the presumption of the truth of this debt, which resulted from the payment.

Paul adduces a second exception in favor of minors, women, soldiers, &c. As these persons are easily deceived, he thinks it proper that he who has received from them something in payment, should be bound to prove that the thing was really due. This exception it appears to me ought not to be admitted indiscriminately; it ought to depend much on circumstances.

§. II.

Of presumptions.

806. A presumption may be defined a judgment which one makes or which the law makes upon the truth of a thing, by a consequence drawn from another thing. These consequences are founded on what happens commonly and in the order of things: *Præsumptio ex eo quod plerumque fit. Cujac. in parat. ad tit. cod. de probat. & præs.*

For example, the law presumes that a debt has been paid, when the creditor has returned the debtor his note; because the creditor does not commonly give up his note to the debtor till after the payment of the debt.

Alciat says that this term *presumptio*, presumption, is derived from *præ* and *sumere*; because SUMIT *pro vero, habet pro vero*, it causes a thing to be holden for true; PRÆ, *id est antequam aliunde probetur*, without its being necessary to make other proof.

Presumption differs from proof properly so called: this is evidence of a thing directly and of itself; presumption is evidence of it by a consequence derived from another thing. This will be illustrated by examples. The proof which is made by an instrument of writing expressing the receipt of a debt, is a *literal proof* of the payment of this debt: the proof which is made by the depositions of witnesses who saw the creditor receive from his debtor the money which was due him, is an *oral proof*; for the receipt and the depositions of the witnesses are evidence of this payment directly and of themselves. But the proof resulting from the receipts of the three last years' rent, that the rent of the preceding years is paid, is a presumption; because it is not directly and of themselves that these receipts are proof, but by a consequence which the law deduces from the payment of the three last years', that the rent of the preceding years has been paid, which consequence is grounded on this reason that it is common to pay the old rent before the new.

There are, on the subject of obligations, different kinds of presumptions. There are some which are established by law and are called *legal presumptions*; and others which are not established by any law, which are called *simple presumptions*. Among legal presumptions there are some which are presumptions *juris & de jure*; others which are simply *legal presumptions*, *presumptiones juris*.

§. I.

Of presumptions juris & de jure.

807. Presumptions *juris & de jure*, are those which are such proof as excludes all proof to the contrary. Alciat defines the presumptions *juris & de jure*, in this manner: *est dispositio legis aliquid præsumentis, & super præsumpto tanquam sibi comperto statuentis.* It is, says Menoch, *Tr. de præs. lib.* 1, 9, 3, called *præsumptio JURIS*, because *a lege introducta; ET DE JURE*, because *super tali præsumptione lex inducit firmum jus, & habet eam pro veritate.*

808. These presumptions *juris & de jure* are stronger than literal or oral proof, or even confession.

Literal proof, as well as oral, may be destroyed by contrary proof. It does not exclude him against whom it militates, from being heard against it and making, if he can, proof of the contrary.

For example. If the plaintiff, who pretends to be my creditor for the sum of one hundred livres, which he pretends to have lent me, produces an obligation executed before a notary, by which I acknowledge the loan, the literal proof which results from this obligation, may be destroyed by contrary proof, and it does not exclude me from making, if I can, proof of the contrary; *puta*, by bringing a writing by which the plaintiff acknowledged that I did not receive the money mentioned in the obligation.

It is the same with regard to the confession, although made *in jure*. We have seen in the preceding section that the proof that results from it may be destroyed by the proof which he who made it may introduce, that it was occasioned by error.

On the contrary, the presumptions *juris & de jure*, cannot be destroyed, and the party against whom they militate is not permitted to prove the contrary, as we shall see in the following sections.

The principal kind of presumptions *juris & de jure*, is that which arises from the authority of the thing judged, *rei judicatæ*; as it deserves to be treated minutely, we will treat of it *ex professo* in the next section.

The presumption that results from the litis-decisory oath is also a kind of presumption *juris & de jure*, of which we shall treat in the fourth section, in treating of oaths.

§. II.

Of legal presumptions.

809. Legal presumptions are also established on some law, or by deduction from some law or text of law, and are therefore called *præsumptiones juris.* They have the same strength as proof, and excuse the person in whose favor they operate, from adducing any to establish their claim or defence. But, and it is in this that they differ from presumptions *juris & de jure*, they do not exclude the party against whom they operate, from being admitted to make proof of the contrary; and if the party succeeds in making this proof, the presumption will be destroyed.

810. When two persons of the same province, the custom of which admits the community of property between husband and wife, contract marriage in it; there is a legal presumption that they have agreed there should be between them such a community of property as is customary in that province. The wife, who afterwards demands from the heirs of her husband her share of the property which he has acquired, need not make any proof of such an agreement.

The presumption is established by the disposition of the customs, which say that *husband and wife are one and in a community, &c.*; for this is as if it were said that it is presumed that they agreed to be one and in community, &c. It is grounded on this that it is common in such a province for persons who intermarry to agree to have a community of property. Hence the law has drawn this consequence, that the parties who intermarry, without expressing their intention, ought to be presumed to have agreed to a community. *Præsumptio enim ab eo quod plerumque fit.* This prefumption not being *juris & de jure*, it difpenfes indeed with proof of any agreement for a community, but it does not exclude the proof of the contrary, which may be made by producing a marriage fettlement with a claufe of exclufion of the community.

811. It is likewife a legal prefumption, that in our city of Orleans the walls are common between neighbours to the height of feven feet above the ground. *Custom of Orleans, art.* 234.

He therefore who would avail himfelf hereof, cannot be prevented by his neighbour, and he is not obliged to fhew any proof of his right, which is fufficiently founded upon the prefumption eftablifhed by the cuftom; but this prefumption may be deftroyed by proof which the neighbour may make by his titles, that the wall belonged to himfelf alone.

812. The law 3, *cod. de apoch. publ.*, contains alfo a legal prefumption. According to this law, the receipts of the taxes for three fucceffive years, form a prefumption of the payment of thofe of the preceding years. Although this law was made only in regard to taxes, the decifion has been extended to arrearages of rents, annuities, and other like annual debts: *nam ubi eadem ratio, idem jus statuendum est.* This decifion is founded upon this, that as it is common to demand the old debts before the new, the payment of the late arrearages feveral times repeated, ought to make a prefumption of the payment of the old. It is alfo founded upon this, that we ought to affift debtors, and not oblige them to keep their receipts two long, and in too great a number, for fear that they might fome of them be loft. *Perez, ad d. tit. cod.*

There are fome who would even fay that the receipt for a fingle year ought to make a prefumption of payment for all the preceding years; but this opinion does not appear to be well grounded.

This prefumption does not apply except when the arrearages of the preceding years are due to the fame perfon who has given the receipts for the three laſt, and by the ſame perſon to whom they have been given. It has alſo other exceptions. See what we have ſaid in our treatiſe on the contract of hire, *part* 3, *ch.* 1, *art* 3. This preſumption, not being *juris & de jure*, does not exclude the creditor againſt whom it operates from proving that the old arrearages are due him, and that ſince the receipts of the three laſt years the debtor has acknowleged theſe old arrearages.

813. The law 2, §. 1, ff. *de pact.*, furniſhes us alſo with an example of a legal preſumption. This law preſumes that a debt is diſcharged, when the creditor has returned the debtor his note. It is founded upon this that it is not common or probable that a creditor ſhould return the note before it is diſcharged. This preſumption, not being *juris & de jure*, does not exclude the creditor from proving that the debt has not been paid. We have treated of this preſumption *supra, n.* 572.

The preſumption of payment which reſults from this, that the note of the debtor is cancelled, *chirographum cancellatum*, is ſimilar to the foregoing: it is a legal preſumption; the law 24 ff. *de prob.*, ſuppoſes it. It is founded upon this, that it is a common ſign of payment that a note is found to be cancelled; it excuſes the debtor from bringing other proof of the payment. But this preſumption may be deſtroyed by a proof which the creditor might make that it was by miſtake that the note was cancelled and [illegible] not been really diſcharged; L. 24, ff. *de prob.* [illegible] the creditor ſhould produce a letter by which the [illegible] written to him in theſe terms, "I return you the note of "my deceaſed father, which you have ſent me cancelled, "depending upon the promiſe which I had made [illegible] "diſcharge it. I am ſorry I have not been able to keep "it, &c.

814. The preſumption of the payment or of the [illegible] of profits, which reſults from an admiſſion to homage made without reſervation, is another kind of legal preſumption.

it is eftablifhed upon the article 66 of our cuftom of Orleans, and is founded upon this, that it is common that the lord fhould make this refervation when he has not been paid the profits and does not intend to releafe them. This prefumption excufes the tenant from making other proof of the payment of the profits, and from producing any receipt; but it does not exclude the creditor from proving that the profits are due to him; *puta*, by letters in which the tenant had acknowleged them to be due.

We might alfo adduce feveral other examples; thofe we have already adduced are fufficient.

§. III.

Of the presumptions which are not established by law.

815. There are fome of thefe prefumptions which, without being eftablifhed by any law, are fufficiently ftrong to be the fame proof as legal prefumptions; faving to the party againft whom they operate, the right to prove the contrary. A common example. When a party difavows the attorney who has acted for him in a fuit, if the attorney who is difavowed has the writ in his poffeffion, and the officer who ferved it is not difavowed, this writ which he has in his poffeffion, forms a prefumption in favor of the attorney, which is equivalent to a proof of authority.

The prefumption is ftill ftronger if the attorney has alfo the titles of the party upon which the fuit is founded; and the prefumption which refults from thefe titles alfo prevents the party from being able to difavow the officer. Likewife when the attorney of the defendant holds the titles of his client which have ferved for the defence of the caufe, thefe titles furnifh a proof of authority, and that he has been employed.

Thefe prefumptions excufe indeed the attorney from bringing other proof of an authority; but they do not exclude the perfon difavowing, from making, if he can, proof that he did not employ the attorney. As if he fhould produce a letter of this attorney in thefe terms, "I have receiv-

"ed the titles which you have sent me in order to take the "advice of counsel; I shall do nothing without your orders;" such a letter, which establishes that the titles were only sent to him for the purpose of obtaining advice, and by which he submitted to wait for orders to bring suit, destroys the presumption of a power of attorney, which results from his holding the titles.

Observe in regard to officers, that the title in the possession of an officer makes indeed a presumption of his authority for the service of a writ which he has made in consequence of this title, or for a simple demand which he has made in virtue of it; but it is very dangerous to establish from this a presumption in favor of the seisures, executions and sales which he has made: for we see it happen every day, that officers, under color of a title which is delivered them to make a demand, make, contrary to the will of the creditor, seisures which ruin the debtor and sometimes the creditor, by the costs.

The other presumptions which we call simple, do not form singly and by themselves a proof; they serve only to confirm and complete the proof which results otherwise.

816. Sometimes the concurrence of several of these presumptions united together is equivalent to a proof. Papinian, in the law 26, ff. *de probat.*, adduces an example of this. A sister was charged towards her brother with the restitution of a trust. After the death of the brother it was a question whether this trust was still due by the sister to the estate of the brother. Papinian decides that we ought to presume that the brother had released it to his sister; and this presumption of the release he derives from three circumstances, I. the relation of brother and sister; II. that the brother had lived a long time without demanding the trust: III. that many accounts had been settled between the brother and sister upon the respective affairs which they had together, in none of which was there any mention of this. Each of these circumstances, taken separately, would form only a simple presumption, insufficient to induce a deci-

sion that the deceased had released the debt; but their concurrence has appeared to Papinian to form a sufficient proof of this release.

SECTION THE THIRD.

Of the authority of the thing judged, rei judicatæ.*

The particular kind of presumption *juris & de jure*, which results from the authority of the thing judged, has appeared to us to require to be treated of particularly, in this section.

We shall here see, I. what judgments have the authority of the thing judged; II. what judgments are null, and cannot consequently have this authority; III. what is the authority of the thing judged: IV. in regard to what things it applies; and, V. between what persons.

ARTICLE THE FIRST.

What judgments have the authority of the thing judged.

I. In order that a judgment may have the authority of the *thing judged*, and also in order that it may have the name, it is necessary that it should be a definitive judgment, which contains either a condemnation or a discharge from the suit. *RES JUDICATA dicitur quæ finem controversiarum pronuntiatione judicis accipit, quod vel condemnatione vel absolutione contingit*; L. 1. ff. *de re jud.*

A judgment which contains a provisional condemnation cannot therefore have either the name or the authority of the *thing judged*; for although it gives the party, who has obtained it, the right to constrain the party condemned, to pay provisionally the sum or the things expressed in the judgment, it does not put an end to the suit, and does not form a presumption *juris & de jure*, that this sum or

* *All this section has been added in this new edition; therefore we have discontinued the order of the numbers, and have put particular numbers here, in order that, in what follows this section, the numbers which are in the first edition may correspond in this.*

these things are due; since the party condemned, having provisionally satisfied the judgment, is received afterwards to prove that they are not due, and may consequently procure the judgment to be revoked. *A fortiori* the judgments or interlocutory orders which do not contain either a condemnation or a discharge from the suit, cannot have the authority of the *thing judged*. *Non vox omnis judicis, judicati continet autoritatem*; L. 1, *Cod. de sent. & interloc.*

2. The ordinance of 1667, *tit.* 27, *art.* 5, adduces three cases in which definitive judgments have the authority of the thing judged. It is there said: "The sentences "and judgments which ought to have the force of the thing "judged, are those rendered in the last resort, and from "which there is no appeal, or of which the appeal is not "receivable, either because the parties have formally ac-"quiesced, or have not appealed in time, or the appeal "has been declared to be lost."

We shall treat separately of these three cases.

§. I.

FIRST CASE. Of judgments rendered in the last resort, and of those from which there is no appeal.

3. The ordinance unites in one article, with judgments rendered in the last resort, those from which no appeal is yet taken; because while there is yet no appeal, they have, like those rendered in the last resort, in a manner, an authority of the *thing judged*, which gives to the party in whose favor they were given, the right to pursue them to execution, and forms a kind of presumption *juris & de jure*, which excludes the party against whom they were given, from pleading any thing against them, while there is no appeal; but this authority, and the presumption which results therefrom, are only momentary, and are destroyed as soon as an appeal is taken.

This applies, even when the judgment should be of the number of those which are to be provisionally executed notwithstanding the appeal; for this provisional execution gives to these judgments, pending the appeal, only the effect of provisional judgments, which, as we have seen *supra*, have not the authority of the *thing judged*.

4. In regard to judgments rendered in the last resort, such as those of supreme courts and in certain cases those of the presidial and consular judges, when they are definitive, they have the authority of the *thing judged*, stable and perpetual.

When the judgment in the last resort has been rendered on a contestation, it has this authority, as soon as it is rendered; but when it has been rendered by default, unless it was in the course of the docket, the party making default, against whom it has been rendered, is received to move that it may be set aside, within eight days from the day notice of the judgment is given to his attorney, or if he had appointed no attorney, from the day notice is given to himself in person or at his house. This motion destroys the effect of the judgment. Therefore it is only after the party making default has let the eighth day pass without making this motion, that the judgment by default acquires the authority of the *thing judged*, stable and perpetual.

5. Judgments of supreme courts and of those in the last resort, can never be attacked in the ordinary way of appeal, but the former may be, in certain cases, by the extraordinary method of *civil petition*. Presidial judgments rendered in the last resort may likewise be attacked, in the same cases, by the method of a *petition in opposition*, which is also an extraordinary way and which differs from the civil petition only in this that it does not require the same formalities which are requisite for the civil petition, such as those to deposit the fine, expressed in the article 16 of the last title of the ordinance of 1667, and to annex to the petition a consultation of senior lawyers, according to the article 13.

These petitions not arresting the execution of the judgments of supreme courts and judgments in the last resort, (*art.* 18,) and the party not being received to avail himself, against the judgment, of other pleas than those which are the ground of the civil petition, without being heard on any plea to the merits; *Art.* 31, 37., it follows that judgments which are thus situated, for which there is room for a civil petition, until they are reversed by this method, have, not the less, an authority of the thing judged, but which is not stable or perpetual; since it may be destroyed by the reversal of the judgment: they have this authority only when the party has suffered the time to elapse within which he might avail himself of this method, or when he has failed in attempting to do so; for in this case he is no longer receivable to make the petition. *Art.* 41.

6. The ordinance adduces several instances in which there is room for the civil petition; it distinguishes in this respect between persons of age and minors, between individuals and the church.

The causes for which individuals, although of age, are admitted to the civil petition, are related in the article 34, title 35. It is there said, *no other causes for the civil petition by persons of age, shall be admitted, than,* I. *personal fraud.*

Which is to say, when the party in whose favor the judgment has been rendered, has employed fraud and artifice to obtain it, *puta,* by suppressing material papers or using such as are forged, as will be said hereafter.

II. *If the forms by us ordained have not been observed;* this defect renders the judgment null.

III. *If it has been pronounced upon things not demanded or not contested, and if more has been adjudged than was demanded;* this is another defect which renders the judgment null and of which we shall speak in the following article.

IV. *If it has been omitted to pronounce upon any point in issue.*

V. *If there has been a contrariety of judgments in supreme courts or those of the last resort, between the same parties, on the same pleas and in the same courts or jurisdictions; saving, in case of a contrariety in different courts or jurisdictions, an application for relief to the grand council.*

VI. *If in the same judgment there are contradictory dispositions.*

VII. *If the judgment has been given upon forged papers.*

Obferve that it does not fuffice, to refcind a judgment by means of the civil petition, that the party in whofe favor it has been rendered, had produced forged papers; it is neceffary that it fhould appear that it was upon the ground of thefe papers that the judgment was rendered: *Causa judicati in irritum non devocatur; nisi probare poteris eum qui judicaverit, secutum ejus instrumenti fidem quod falsum esse constiterit, adversus te pronuntiasse;* L. 3, *Cod. si ex fals. instr.*

It is neceffary alfo that thefe papers fhould not have been already attacked for forgery in the fuit in which the judgment was rendered; for in this cafe the queftion upon the genuinenefs of the papers would be a queftion which had been already determined by this judgment, and which confequently could not be renewed, as has been well obferved by M. Jouffe, in his commentary upon this article.

Finally, although the party, who would feek relief by civil petition, had through error acknowleged the genuinenefs of the paper which he pretends he has fince difcovered to be forged, he ought not the lefs to be admitted to attack this paper as forged, and the judgment which has been rendered upon it. L. 11, ff. *de except.*

VIII. *Or upon offers or admissions which have been disavowed, and the disavowal judged valid.*

If my attorney has made offers or admiffions upon which I have been condemned, I may, if I pretend not to have given power to my attorney to make thefe offers, feek relief by civil petition againft the judgment: but in order to be admitted to this, it is neceffary that I fhould difavow my attorney, and that I fhould procure my difavowal to be declared valid againft him.

IX. *Or if there have been material papers lately recovered, and retained by the act of the party.*

This is an example of perſonal fraud in the party in whoſe favor the judgment has been rendered, which gives room for the civil petition, as has been ſaid *supra.*

The recovery of material papers is not alone a ſufficient cauſe for the civil petition, and to reſcind the judgment, as we ſhall ſee *infra, art.* 8: it is the ſuppreſſion of theſe papers made through the fraud of the party, which gives room for it.

7. When it is againſt minors, againſt the church or againſt corporations, that the judgment of a ſupreme court has been rendered, beſides the caſes that have been juſt mentioned, there is likewiſe another caſe in which there is ground for the civil petition, to wit, *if they were not defended, or were not validly defended;* art. 35.

Theſe terms ought to be interpreted by the original article 36, as firſt introduced, which is found in the debates on the ordinance, page 463. It is there ſaid, "The above "applies to eccleſiaſtics, to corporations and minors. And "beſides, we conſider it, in regard to them, as a further "ground for the civil petition, that they have not been defend- "ed; that is to ſay, that the judgments of ſupreme courts and "thoſe of the laſt reſort have been given by default; that they "have not been validly defended, in caſe the principal pleas "were omitted, although theſe judgments were given upon "a plea; ſo however that it appears that they have not been "defended or not validly defended, and that the omiſſion of "their principal pleas gave room for the judgment which "was rendered."

It appears by the debates on the ordinance, that the original article was approved of. Hence it follows that it was only *brevitatis & compendii studio* that it was omitted, and becauſe it was thought that all it contained was ſufficiently included in the generality of the terms, *if they have not been defended or not validly defended.*

Obſerve that the church is always preſumed not to have been ſufficiently defended, when the affair has not been communicated to the king's law officers: the article 34 makes this a ground for the civil petition.

Obſerve alſo that the church has theſe rights only when the matter in queſtion relates to the principal of its eſtate: *case decided 27th March*, 1703, *reported by Augeard, vol.* 2. When the matter relates only to its revenues, it is rather the cauſe of the incumbent than that of the church.

8. The party againſt whom the judgment has been rendered, when it is in one of the caſes above mentioned, ought to ſeek relief by civil petition, before the court which rendered the judgment, within ſix months from the time notice of the judgment is given him, after his coming of age; *art.* 5.

If the party dies within the ſaid time of ſix months, his heirs have a further time of ſix months from the day of a new notice which ſhall be given to them; and if they are minors, the time will run only from their coming of age.

The church, corporations, lay and eccleſiaſtic, and individuals abſent from the kingdom on public buſineſs, have a year from the time notice is given to them of the judgment; *art.* 7.

If the incumbent dies during the year, the ſucceſſor, otherwiſe than by reſignation, has a further time of a year from the day of a new notice of the judgment, which muſt be given to him; *art.* 9. In regard to the perſon in whoſe favor the reſignation is made, he has, for his civil petition upon the judgment rendered againſt the perſon reſigning, only the time which remained to the latter; it is not neceſſary to give him a new notice: he is preſumed to have been inſtructed by the perſon reſigning.

9. When one ſeeks relief on account of the judgment being rendered upon forged papers, or on account of papers being newly diſcovered, the time of ſix months or of a year, runs only from the diſcovery, *provided*, ſays the ordinance, *art.* 12, *there be proof in writing, and not otherwise.*

It does not ſuffice me then, in order to be admitted to

my civil petition, after the common time of fix months, to fay that I did not difcover the paper, or that the paper was forged, till lately; it is neceffary that I fhould have a proof in writing of the time of the difcovery.

For example. If, after feveral years, the party in whofe favor the judgment has been rendered againft me, dies, and it appears by the inventory made after his death, of his papers, that the material paper in the fuit, which had been fuppreffed, was found among his papers; this inventory is a proof in writing that the difcovery of this paper was made at the time of the inventory.

Likewife if the party in whofe favor the judgment has been rendered againft me upon a forged paper, produces, after feveral years, in another fuit, againft another perfon, the fame paper, and in the courfe of this fuit it be attacked as forged, the judgment which fhould declare it forged, will prove the time when it was difcovered to be forged.

10. The caufes for which one may obtain relief by petition againft the prefidial judgments rendered in the laft refort, are the fame with thofe for which one may have relief by civil petition againft judgments of fupreme courts. In regard to the time in which this relief muft be applied for, there is no other difference except that the time of feeking it againft judgments of fupreme courts, is fix months for individuals, and a year for the church, corporations, and perfons abfent *rei publicæ causa;* that of feeking relief againft prefidial judgments is only three months for individuals, and fix months for the church and fuch abfent perfons.

§. II.

Second case. *Of the judgments from which an appeal is no longer receivable.*

11. The ordinance adduces in the fecond place, among the judgments which have the force of the *thing judged*, and which confequently form the prefumption *juris & de jure*, of which we are treating, thofe from which the appeal is no longer receivable.

It adduces two caufes for which it is no longer receivable. The firft is when the parties againft whom the judgments have been rendered, have *formally acquiesced therein*.

The ordinance by this term *formally* does not intend it fhould be neceffary that the party, in order to be excluded from his appeal, fhould have acquiefced in the judgment in exprefs terms, and have executed an inftrument of acquiefcence; it only intended to fay that his acquiefcence fhould not be equivocal. Therefore if, for the payment of the fum to which he has been condemned, he has requefted a delay, whether at the time of the judgment, or fince, it is not to be doubted that he would no longer be received to appeal; the requefting of time being an equivocal proof of his acquiefcence in the judgment: *ad solutionem dilationem petentem acquievisse sententiæ manifestæ probatur;* L. *Cod. de re judic.* *A fortiori* ought he to be prefumed to have acquiefced when he has made a partial payment, whether of the fum expreffed in the judgment or of the cofts to which he has been condemned, except in the cafe in which the judgment is to be provifionally executed, he has paid it only from conftraint, protefting that he fo paid it without prejudice to the appeal by him taken or to be taken.

When the party who has acquiefced in the judgment, is entitled to relief againft his acquiefcence, whether on account of minority, or of fraud, or any other caufe, the authority of the thing judged, which the judgment had acquired by his acquiefcence therein, is not ftable and perpetual; it will be deftroyed when the party fhall have been relieved againft his acquiefcence.

12. The fecond caufe for which the appeal is no longer receivable, is when the party againft whom the judgment has been rendered, has let the time pafs in which the appeal ought to have been taken.

The principles of our law are indeed different, as to the time, from thofe of the civil law. According to the civil law, the party who thought himfelf injured by the judgment, could, the fame day that it was rendered, appeal from it *viva voce APUD ACTA*, that is to fay, in the clerk's office or at the bar. *Si apud acta quis appellaverit, satis erit si dicat, APPELLO*; L. 2, ff. *de appell.*

The appeal being a mode authorifed by the laws, the Roman judges were not offended that the party who refuſed to acquieſce in their judgments, ſhould appeal therefrom in their preſence, provided it was done in a reſpectful manner, without any injurious reflections upon the judge or the judgment. L. 8, ff. *de appell.*

When the party did not appeal on the day the judgment was rendered, the appeal was to be taken by a petition which the appellant preſented to the judge who gave the judgment. It was neceſſary that this petition ſhould contain the names of the appellant and of the appellee, the judgment appealed from, and the objections againſt this judgment. It prayed that the judge would pleaſe to grant the writ, called *apostoli*, by which he ſent up the caſe to the judge of appeals. The party had for this appeal only two days after the judgment, when he was party in his own name, or three days, when he was party only in the quality of attorney, tutor, curator or adminiſtrator. L. 5, §. 5, ff. *de app.*; L. 1, §. 11, 12, 13, ff. *quand. app.*

Theſe days were *effective*; that is to ſay, they were not counted when the judge did not hold his court; *d.* L. 1, §. 7, §. 9.

Juſtinian, in his novel 23, *ch.* 1, has enlarged this time; he grants for the appeal a delay of ten days, from the day of pronouncing the judgment.

Theſe principles of the civil law, although indeed oppoſed to ours, appear very wiſe and very proper to preſerve, by reſtraining ſuits, the tranquillity of the citizens. The king of Pruſſia has adopted them in his code; he grants, for the appeal from judgments, the delay only of ten days, expreſſed in the novel. The party injured by a judgment ſuffers no prejudice from this ſhort delay: from the time the cause was brought before the first judge, this party could have foreseen that he might lose his cause; and during all the while the suit continued, he has had time to deliberate upon the part which he might take in case he should be cast.

13. According to the principles of our law, the party who thinks himself injured by a judgment, when he has done no act of acquiescence in this judgment, and has not been summoned to take his appeal, has the time of ten years entire for his appeal, which time begins to run only from the day notice is given of the judgment. *Ordinance* 1667, *tit.* 27, *art.* 17.

Double time is granted, that is to say twenty years, to the church, to hospitals, colleges, universities, lazarettos, to take an appeal from the judgments which they pretend are injurious to their estates; and this time runs likewise from the day notice is given of the judgment; *ibid.*

However long these delays may be, I have heard lawyers in practice say that this disposition of the ordinance was not always observed in the parliament of Paris, and that they there sustained appeals after the time of these delays had expired.

The party in whose favor the judgment has been rendered, may abridge the delays by making a legal summons to the party against whom the judgment has been rendered, to take his appeal if he thinks proper; but this summons can only be made at the end of three years from the day notice is given of the judgment, if the judgment has been rendered against individuals, and at the end of six years, if against the church, hospitals, colleges, universities, lazarettos, on account of their estates. *Ordinance* 1667, *d. tit. art.* 12.

The effect of this summons is, that the party to whom it has been made, has for his appeal no more than six months from the day of the summons; *art.* 12.

If before the expiration of these delays of three years, of six years or of six months, the party against whom the judgment has been rendered dies, or when he is an incumbent, if he refigns his benefice, his heir or general legatee or undifputed fucceffor to the benefice, muft have for his appeal a further delay of a year, befides the whole time of delay which his predeceffor had, and it is neceffary at the end of this new delay of one year to make a fummons to him, even when one had already been made to the deceafed or to the predeceffor; and from the day of this fummons the heir or the fucceffor would have no more than fix months to be admitted to take his appeal; *art.* 12, 13, 14. Thefe delays do not run againft minors; *art.* 16: but they run againft perfons abfent from the kingdom, even in the fervice of the king.

§ III.

THIRD CASE. Of judgments, the appeal from which has been declared to be lost.

14. The ordinance adduces in the third place, among the judgments which have the force of the *thing judged*, thofe from which the appeal has been declared to be loft.

The appeal is loft when it has failed by a difcontinuance of the proceedings for three years, and a judgment has intervened declaring the difcontinuance.

This judgment, which declares the difcontinuance of the appeal, carries a confirmation of the judgment appealed from, and gives it the force of the *thing judged;* the appellant who has fuffered his appeal to be difcontinued, being no longer admitted to appeal anew.

This is liable to no difficulty when the tribunal where the appeal was depending, is a tribunal of the laft refort: it is not to be doubted in this cafe that the judgment of this tribunal, which declares the difcontinuance of the appeal, being a final judgment, gives the force of the *thing judged* to the judgment appealed from, which it has confirmed. When the tribunal where the appeal was depending is not a tribunal of the laft refort, the judgment of this tribunal, which fhould declare the difcontinuance of the appeal, not being a final judgment, the appellant against whom it has been rendered, may appeal from it. But upon this appeal, the judges ought only to examine the question whether the discontinuance which the judge has declared was properly acquired; and if it appears to them that it was, they ought, without enquiring further into the merits, to confirm the judgment. If, on the contrary, the discontinuance was not properly acquired, in pronouncing the error of the judgment by which it was declared to be acquired, they remand the parties to proceed upon the merits.

15. Appeals, although not contested, may be the subject of a discontinuance, as well as those which have been contested.

It is the first process before the judge of appeal, to proceed upon the appeal, which introduces and forms the appeal, even when it should not be followed by any other proceedings, not even by an appearance: this first process alone is presumed to form a suit subject to a discontinuance, which the party in whose favor the judgment has been rendered, may cause to be declared, at the end of three years after such process. This is expressed by the rule of the court, 28th *March*, 1692.

When the first process has been followed by further proceedings, the time of three years for the discontinuance is counted only from the last proceedings. This time runs even against minors, saving their recourse against their tutors. Bouchel, *biblioth. verbo per empt.*, adduces several cases to this effect.

This time may be interrupted in several ways; by the death or change of condition of one of the parties, by the death of one of the attorneys, &c.

16. Although this time should be expired, the discontinuance of the appeal is not acquired until a judgment has intervened which has so declared it; and if, after the time has expired and before the judgment has intervened, there has been some proceedings on the part of the party against whom the appeal has been taken, and he has not disavow-

ed his attorney, the difcontinuance will be faved and will not be pleadable until at the end of three years from the proceedings.

Article II.

Of judgments which are null and which cannot consequently have the authority of the thing judged.

17. There is a great difference between a judgment null and a judgment iniquitous. A null judgment is that which has been rendered contrary to judicial form, *sententia injusta:* a judgment is iniquitous, *sententia iniqua,* when the judge has judged wrong, *puta,* in condemning a party to pay what in truth he did not owe, or in difcharging him from paying what he did owe. A judgment, although iniquitous, when it has been rendered according to judicial form, may have the authority of the *thing judged,* if it is in one of the cafes of the preceding article, and however iniquitous it may be, it is holden to be equitable without admitting any proof to the contrary.

On the contrary, a judgment null, which has been rendered contrary to judicial form, cannot have the authority of the *thing judged,* unlefs the informality has been cured.

A judgment may be null either in regard to what it contains, or in regard to the perfons between whom it has been rendered, or in regard to the judge who rendered it, or by the unobfervance of fome judicial form.

§ I.

Of judgments which are null in regard to what they contain.

18. I. A judgment is null when the object of the condemnation which it pronounces, is uncertain. *Sententia debet esse certa.* For example. If a judgment were thus expreffed. *We have condemned the defendant to pay to the plaintiff all that he owes him;* it is evident that fuch a judgment would not have the authority of the *thing judged,* and would be abfolutely null: for what is due to the plaintiff, being neither explained by the judgment, nor by any inftrument to which it relates, the judgment contains nothing certain.

This is decided by the law 3, *Cod. de sent. quæ sine certa quant. Hæc sententia,* OMNEM DEBITI QUANTITATEM CUM USURIS COMPETENTIBUS SOLVE, *judicati actionem præstare non potest, quum ita demum, sine certa quantitate facta condemnatio autoritate rei judicatæ censeatur, si parte aliqua actorum certa sit quantitas comprehensa.*

19. It is not however neceſſary that the object of the condemnation ſhould be explained by the judgment, it ſuffices that it appear by ſome inſtrument to which the judgment relates. For example. A judgment which condemns to pay what is demanded, is valid and may have the authority of the *thing judged,* when what is demanded appears by the proceſs to which the judgment relates. *Quum Judex ait, Solve quod petitum est, valet sententia;* L. 59, §. 1, ff. *de re judic.*

20. Nor is it neceſſary that the object of the condemnation ſhould be any thing liquidated; it ſuffices that it is to be liquidated by the proper perſons; therefore a judgment which condemns the defendant to damages, or to an indemnity, is not the leſs entitled to have the authority of the *thing judged,* although theſe damages or this indemnity, not being yet liquidated, the object of the judgment ſhould not be any thing liquidated and certain: for it muſt become ſo by the eſtimation to be made by the proper perſons. This is what Alexander Severus decides: *Quamquam pecuniæ quantitas sententia non contineatur, sententia tamen rata est, quoniam* INDEMNITATEM *rei publicæ præstari jussit;* L. 2, *Cod. de sent. quæ sine cert. quant.*

21. II. A judgment is null when the object of the condemnation which it contains is ſomething impoſſible. *Paulus respondit impossibile præceptum judicis nullius esse momenti;* L. 3, ff. *Quæ sent. Idem respondit ab ea sententia cui pareri rerum natura non poterit sine causa appellari; d.* L. §. 1.

22. III. A judgment is null when it is expreſsly againſt the laws. *Si expressim sententia contra juris rigorem data sit ..... si* SPECIALITER, which is to ſay, expreſsly, *contra leges vel Senatus-consultum, vel constitutiones fuerit prolata;* L. 19

ff. *de appell. Quum contra sacras constitutiones judicatur, appellationis necessitas remittitur;* L. 1, §. 2, ff. *quæ sent. sine appell.*

Obferve that, for the judgment to be null, it is neceffary that it fhould have been pronounced exprefsly againft the law; it is neceffary that it fhould have been judged that the law was not to be obferved. But if it was only judged that the cafe in queftion was not within the law, although indeed it was within it, this judgment is not prefumed to impugn the law; it is not null, it is only iniquitous, and relief cannot confequently be had againft it but by the ufual way of appeal: this is fhewn by Calliftrat: *Quum prolatis constitutionibus contra eas pronuntiat judex, eo quod non existimat causam de qua judicat per eas juvari, non videtur contra constitutiones sententiam dedisse; ideoque ab ejusmodi sententia appellandum est; alioquin rei judicatæ stabitur;* L. 32, ff. *de re jud.*

Obferve alfo that the judgments which pronounce exprefsly againft the laws, were among the Romans null *de pleno jure*: with us it is neceffary to feek relief againft thefe judgments before the council of error, when there is no ground for the common method of appeal.

23. IV. A judgment is null when it contains oppofite difpofitions which imply contradiction. For example. Being fued to give up an eftate which you fold me, I have called you in to guaranty my poffeffion: the judgment difcharges me from the demand, and condemns you to return me the price of the eftate which I have paid you, and my damages for its detention. Thefe difpofitions are oppofite; for it is implied that I am difcharged from the demand and my guarantee condemned. This contradiction in the judgment renders it null; therefore the plaintiff who has been by this judgment difallowed his demand, may, if it is a judgment in the laft refort, have his relief by civil petition, on fetting forth that this judgment is contradictory and contains a difpofition oppofite to that of which he complains, which has difallowed his demand. If he has let the time for his appeal pafs, the judgment will acquire againft

him the force of the *thing judged:* but in regard to my guarantee, I think that although he ſhould not be entitled to relief by the method of civil petition, I cannot be admitted to purſue againſt him the execution of this judgment, becauſe the diſcharge which is here given from the demand made againſt me, for ever forbids the condemnation of my guarantee, and good faith does not permit that in retaining the thing, I ſhould demand to have the price returned.

24. V. A judgment is null when it has pronounced upon what has not been demanded, or when it has condemned a party to more than has been demanded from him; for the judge is appointed only to reſolve upon the demands which are brought before him, and he cannot conſequently render the judgment except upon what is the object of the demand. *Potestas judicis ultra id quod in judicium deductum est nequaquam potest excedere:* L. 18, ff. *com. div.*

25. As the judgment is null when it condemns the defendant to pay what has not been demanded from him, it is alſo null when it has diſcharged the defendant from a demand which he has admitted; for in each caſe he has judged upon what was not the object of the conteſtation ſubmitted to his judgment. The ordinance of 1667, *tit.* 35, *art.* 34, has comprehended both caſes in ſaying that there is ground for the civil petition, when the judgment has been pronounced upon things *not demanded or not contested.*

26. Theſe nullities in regard to this, that the judge has pronounced upon what was not ſubmitted to his judgment, are not ſuch *de pleno jure;* they muſt be oppoſed either by the common way of appeal, when the judgment is not a judgment in the laſt reſort; otherwiſe by civil petition, and when the party has let the time paſs without ſeeking relief againſt the judgment, theſe informalities are cured.

§. II.

Of the nullities of judgments, in regard to the parties between whom they have been rendered.

27. A judgment, to be valid, muſt be rendered between

parties capable of being parties to a fuit, *quæ habent legitimam ftandi in judicio perfonam.*

All the proceedings had by one incapable of being a party to a fuit, or againft him, are null *de pleno jure*, as well as the judgments which might be rendered upon thefe proceedings.

28. The perfons who are not capable of being parties to a fuit are, I. thofe who have loft their civil capacity whether by a condemnation to a capital punifhment, or by becoming monks profeffed. Neverthelefs monks profeffed, who have left their convent for a benefice, fuch as are regular canonical curates, are reputed capable of being parties, as well plaintiffs as defendants; for although their benefice does not reftore them to their civil capacity, yet as the adminiftration of the property and rights of their benefice is granted to them, as well as that of their falary, it is neceffary that they fhould be able to be parties to a fuit for what may concern the goods and rights of their benefice, and to actions which arife from the perfonal obligations which they have contracted or which may be contracted towards them.

29. Minors, who are under the power of tutors, are not capable of being parties to a fuit: the actions which belong to them cannot be brought except by their tutors in their quality of tutors, and the actions which may be had againft them, muft not be brought againft them, but againft their tutors in this quality.

When the minor has no tutor, he who has an action to bring againft him, muft prefent a petition to the judge where the minor refides, that he may be permitted to convoke the relations of the minor, to have a tutor provided for him, againft whom, after he has been appointed, he may bring his action.

When minors are emancipated, they may be themfelves parties to a fuit; but they cannot be without the affiftance of a curator who is for this purpofe appointed by the judge and who muft be a party in the caufe with them.

30. A feme covert cannot in the cuftomary provinces, be a party to a fuit, whether plaintiff or defendant, without being authorifed by her hufband, or, at his refufal, by the court. Therefore it is not fufficient for thofe who have an action to bring againft a feme-covert to bring it againft her alone; it is neceffary that they fhould bring it againft her hufband alfo.

Finally a feme-covert is prefumed fufficiently authorifed by her hufband, when her hufband is a party to the fuit with her, and in this the judicial acts are different from extrajudicial: for in order that a feme-covert may contract validly out of court, it does not fuffice that her hufband fhould be a party with her in the contract; it is neceffary that it fhould be in exprefs terms that he authorifes her: as we fhall fee in treating of the marital power, at the end of the treatife on the contract of marriage.

This rule, that a feme-covert cannot be a party to a fuit without being authorifed, receives fome exceptions: our cuftom of Orleans, *art.* 200, permits her to bring actions without her hufband on account of injuries done to her, and to defend thofe on account of injuries which fhe is charged to have committed.

31. It remains for us to obferve in regard to all perfons who are incapable of being parties to a fuit, that this incapacity does not take away the power of profecuting them, when they have committed a crime; and they may defend themfelves againft the profecution.

32. From this principle that, for a judgment to be valid, the parties ought to be capable of being parties to a fuit, this confequence was deduced, in the civil law, that the judgment rendered againft a party who was dead before the judgment, was null: for to be capable of being a party to a fuit it is neceffary to be living at the time: when one has ceafed to live he ceafes to have any capacity. It is upon this ground that Paul fays, *Eum qui in rebus human-*

is non fuit sententiæ datæ tempore, inefficaciter condemnatum videri; L. 1, ff. *quæ sent. sine app.*

In our law when the death of one of the parties does not happen till the suit is ready for judgment, that is to say, when there is no further proceedings to be had or counsel to be heard, the death of the party does not prevent the judge from giving the judgment, which is as valid as if it had been given in the life time of the party. This is the disposition of the article 1, of the title 26, ordinance 1667. The ordinance has in this respect disregarded the subtlety of the law, in order to avoid the useless delay and costs which a revival of the suit would in this case occasion.

When a party dies in the course of the proceedings and the attorney has notified his death in writing to the attorney of the other party, which is called an essoin *propter mortem*, the other party cannot from this time proceed any further, and no judgment can be rendered, until the suit has been revived by the heirs or other successors of the deceased, or, on their having been cited to come in and defend, a judgment has been rendered which declares the suit revived: the proceedings had after the essoin, until the revival of the suit, as well as the judgments which should be rendered, are null *de pleno jure*, *d. tit. art.* 182. While the death is not notified, the proceedings had by the other party, although since the decease, are valid; *art.* 3: and it is the same with the judgments which he should obtain.

33. It is also a nullity in a judgment which proceeds from the part of the party for or against whom it has been rendered, when he has proceeded for another without having the capacity to act for him.

For example. If in our custom of Orleans which between persons not noble, deprives the wife who has married a second time of the tutelage of her children, and does not suffer it to pass to her second husband, this second husband through an error, of which I have seen examples, brings a suit for the said children in the capacity of their step-father, or he defends a fuit for them, the judgment rendered upon this demand would be null from the defect of capacity in which this ftep-father had proceeded.

For the fame reafon, if a hufband, who may alone and without his wife bring perfonal actions for his wife and defend them, thinking through error, that it is the fame with regard to perfonal actions and thofe that concern the lands and real eftate of his wife, brings in his capacity of hufband fuch actions, or defends them, the judgment rendered for or againft him in this capacity will be null.

For the fame reafon, if a tutor after the time of his tutorfhip is expired continued to act for his ward, who had become of age, the proceedings and judgments rendered thereon would be null for the want of capacity.

But if, in the account which he has rendered to his minor, he has accounted for what was due by the debtors, he may in his own name, as having a ceffion of the rights of his minor, purfue the faid debtors.

34. When I have given a fpecial power to one to bring a fuit for me, the fuit muft be in my name: it would be an irregular proceeding to bring the fuit in the name of this attorney and in the capacity of attorney by my fpecial authority. Hence this maxim, that it is only the king, who pleads by attorney.

§. III.

Of judgments which are null on account of the judges who have rendered them, or for want of the obfervance of judicial forms.

35. A judgment may be null on account of the judge who has rendered it, when he was without the character; as if he had not been admitted to his office, had been interdicted, or was incompetent.

Obferve that the nullity which refults from thefe defects is not *de pleno jure;* it is neceffary to feek relief by way of appeal, to have it declared.

36. The unobfervance of fome formality alfo renders the judgment null; as when judgment has been rendered

by default against a person who was not present and had not appointed an attorney, before his default had been noted by the proper officer, or before the expiration of the usual time. Many other examples might be brought.

These nullities are not such *de pleno jure;* it is necessary to seek relief by way of appeal or opposition: and when it is a judgment of a supreme court or in the last resort, by civil or presidial petition; this kind of nullity being one of the causes which furnish ground for these petitions, as we have seen *supra, n.* 6.

ARTICLE III.

What is the authority of the thing judged.

37. The authority of the *thing judged* causes whatever is contained in the judgment to be presumed true and equitable; and this presumption, being *juris & de jure*, excludes all proof to the contrary. *Res judicata pro veritate accipitur;* L. 207, ff. *de R. J.*

For example. The party who has been condemned to pay a thing is presumed really to owe it; he in whose favor the judgment has been rendered may consequently, after having notified it to him, constrain him to pay it, by the seizure and sale of his real and personal property, without his being allowed to offer proof that he does not owe it.

Vice versa, when the judgment has been given against the plaintiff, the things which he had demanded are also presumed not to be due to him; so that he cannot afterwards be received to demand them: there arises from the judgment a plea which we call *exceptio rei judicatæ*, which renders him not receivable.

38. The authority of the *thing judged* excluding proof against what has been judged, the party against whom the judgment has been given is not admitted to prove that the judge has made an error, even of simple calculation. *Res judicatæ si sub. pretextu computationis instaurentur, nullus erit litium finis;* L. 2, *Cod. de re jud.*

Neverthelefs if the error of calculation appears on the

judgment, this error corrects itself. *Puta*, if the judgment were thus expressed, "We have declared James debtor to "Peter of the sum of fifty livres for a certain cause; also of "the sum of twentyfive livres for another cause; the said "sums making together the sum of one hundred livres, "which we have condemned James to pay to Peter:" the error of the calculation in this case in the judgment would correct itself, and Peter could not exact the sum of one hundred livres, but only that of seventy-five.

39. The authority of the *thing judged* excludes contrary proof, so that the party against whom the judgment has been given is not receivable to contest it, although he should bring material papers which he had only obtained since the judgment. *Sub specie novorum instrumentorum postea repertorum res judicatas restaurari exemplo grave est*; L. 4, *Cod. de re jud.*

This principle that the *things judged* cannot be re-examined on account of material papers recovered since the judgment, admitted, in the civil law, of an exception in the case in which the judgment had been rendered in a doubtful cause, for the decision of which the judge had deferred the supplementary oath to the party in favor of whom he rendered it: in this case the party who had failed, could, on account of material papers since discovered, be received to contest the judgment. L. 31, ff. *de jurejur.*

This exception to the principle ought not to apply in our law; for the ordinance of 1667, *tit.* 35, *art.* 34, admitting the party against whom the judgment has been rendered, to seek relief against it by civil petition, on account of material papers since discovered, only in the case in which it should appear that they have been detained by the act of the other party, it is a consequence that it cannot be admitted in other cases.

Article IV.

In regard to what things the authority of the thing judged applies.

40. The authority of the *thing judged* applies only to

what was the object of the judgment. Therefore in order that the party who has failed in the suit which he had brought against me, may be prevented from maintaining a new suit which he has since brought against me by the plea *rei judicatæ*, arising from the authority of the *thing judged*, which the judgment has that has discharged me from his suit, it is necessary that his new suit should have the same object which the first had from which the judgment has discharged me.

It is necessary, for this, that three things should concur, I. it is necessary that he should demand the same thing which was demanded in the first suit from which I am discharged; II. it is necessary that in the new suit he should demand this thing for the same cause for which he had demanded it in the first: III. it is necessary that he should demand it in the same capacity, and against me in the same capacity as in the first.

Quum quæritur hæc exceptio (rei judicatæ) noceat necne, inspiciendum est an idem corpus sit, quantitas eadem, idem jus; & an eadem causa petendi, & eadem conditio personarum; quæ nisi omnia concurrant, alia res est; L. 12; L. 13; L. 14, ff. *de except. rei jud.*

Finally, when these three things concur, in order that the exception *rei judicatæ*, may be allowed, it is not material whether it be *eodem an diverso genere judicii*, that the question determined by the judgment is renewed.

§. I.

What is required in the first place, ut sit eadem res.

41. This principle, that, in order that the exception *rei judicatæ* may be allowed, it is necessary that the thing demanded be the same thing which was demanded in the first suit from which a discharge has been had, ought not to be understood too literally. *Idem corpus in hac exceptione non utique omni pristina qualitate servata, nulla adjectione, diminutioneve facta, sed pinguius pro communi utilitate accipitur*; L. 14, V. *Idem corpus*, ff. *de except. rei jud.*

For example. Although the herd which I demand of you to-day be not compofed of the fame number of which it was compofed at the time of the firft fuit which I brought, and from which the judgment has difcharged you; I am, not the lefs, prefumed to demand the fame thing, and confequently am not receivable. *Si petiero gregem (& victus fuero), & vel aucto vel minuto numero gregis, iterum eumdem gregem petam, obstabit mihi exceptio;* L. 21, §. 1. ff. *d. t.*

42. I am likewife prefumed to demand the fame thing when I demand fome thing which makes a part of it. *Sed & si speciale corpus ex grege petam, si adfuit in eo grege, petò obstaturam exceptionem;* d. L. 21, §. 1.

This is fhewn by Ulpian. *Si quis, quum totum petisset, partem petat, exceptio rei judicatæ nocet; nam pars in toto est; eadem enim res accipitur, & si pars petatur ejus quod totum petitum est; nec interest utrum in corpore hoc quæratur, an in quantitate, vel in jure;* L. 7; ff. *de except. rei jud.*

43. I am alfo prefumed to demand the fame thing which I have demanded in my firft fuit from which the judgment has given a difcharge, when I demand a thing which has proceeded from it, and which did not belong to me, or was not due except in the manner in which that from which it proceeded, and which I demanded in my firft fuit, had belonged to me or had been due to me.

For example. If, in our colonies, I had fued you for the negro wench Catharine, which I claimed to have bought of you and for which I paid the price; and not having been able to prove this pretended purchafe, a difcharge was given from my demand by a judgment in the laft refort; I fhall not be admitted to demand of you, upon the fame foundation, the child which fhe has afterwards had: for as this child cannot be due to me otherwife than as the mother was due to me, this would renew the queftion which was determined by the judgment. *Si ancillam petiero* (add *& victus fuero*), *& post litem contestatam conceperit & pepererit, mox partum ejus petam, utrum idem petere videor? Et quidem ita definiri potest, toties eamdem rem agi quoties apud judicem* *posteriorem id quæritur quod apud priorem quæsitum est; in his igitur fere omnibus exceptio (rei judicatæ) nocet;* d. L. 7, §. 1.

44. For the same reason, if I have failed in my demand for a principal sum, I ought not to be admitted to demand the interest of this sum; for this interest cannot be due me, if the principal sum is not.

It is not the same in the inverse case: although I have failed in my suit for the interest of a sum, I am not the less receivable to demand this sum; for it does not follow, because the interest is not due, that the principal sum is not. *Si in judicio actum sit, usuræque solæ petitæ sint, non est verendum ne noceat exceptio rei judicatæ;* L. 23, ff. *d. tit.*

45. If I have failed in a suit which I have brought against you for a right of foot-way, which I claim to have over your land, and I bring a suit against you for a right of way with beasts of burden, which I claim to have over the same land, ought I to be presumed to demand the same thing which I demanded in my first suit, in which I failed, and may you therefore oppose to me the plea *rei judicatæ*?

The reason to doubt for the affirmative, is that the right which I now demand, appears to include that which I have demanded in my first suit and in which I failed; since whoever has a right of way with beasts of burden has also the right of foot-way, and, it having been judged that I had not the right of foot-way, it follows, *a fortiori*, that I have not that for beasts of burden. The reason to decide, on the contrary, that there is no ground for the exception *rei judicatæ*, is that as these rights of way are different kinds of rights, the demand, which has for its object one of these kinds of rights, has a different object from that of the demand which is for another kind; one cannot then say that I demand the same thing which I have already demanded nor consequently oppose to me the plea *rei judicatæ*. As to what is said against it, that as it has been judged that I had not the right of foot-way, it has been judged, *a fortiori*, that I had not the right of way with beasts of burden, I anſwer, that it has been judged that I had not the right of foot-way, nor, *a fortiori*, for beaſts of burden, on my claim for the mere right of foot-way, which it has been judged does not belong to me. But becauſe I have not the ſimple right of foot-way, it does not follow that I may not have another right of way with beaſts of burden, which was not in queſtion at the time of my firſt ſuit and which I now demand. This is decided by Ulpian: *Si quis iter petierit, deinde actum petat, puto fortius defendendum aliud videri tunc petitum, aliud nunc, & ideo exceptionem rei judicatæ cessare*; L. 11, §. 6, ff. *d. tit.*

We muſt decide otherwiſe when the right of way which I demand, is of the ſame kind which I had claimed in my firſt ſuit from which a diſcharge has been given, although I claim it more conſiderable than I did then. Africanus adduces this example: *Egi tecum jus mihi esse ædes meas usque ad decem pedes altius tollere; post ago jus mihi esse usque ad viginti pedes altius tollere; exceptio rei judicatæ procul dubio obstabit: sed & si rursus ita agam jus mihi esse ad alios decem pedes tollere, obstabit exceptio; quum aliter superior pars jure haberi non possit, quam si inferior quoque jure habeatur*; L. 26, ff. *de tit.*

§. II.

What is required in the second place, ut ſit eadem cauſa petendi.

46. In order that there may be ground for the exception *rei judicatæ*, it does not ſuffice that the thing which you demand of me ſhould be the ſame which you have demanded of me in your firſt ſuit from which I have been diſcharged; it is neceſſary that you ſhould demand it for the ſame cauſe for which you had before demanded it: *oportet ut sit eadem causa petendi.*

There is in this reſpect a difference to be obſerved between perſonal actions and actions real. Although I have failed in a perſonal action by which I demanded of you a thing which I claimed to be due me on a certain ground of obligation, this does not exclude me from demanding of you the fame thing which I claim to be due me, on another ground of obligation.

Finge. I have made with you a bargain, by which we agreed that for a certain work which I was to do for you, and which I have fince done, you fhould give me the fum of two hundred livres, or your horfe, at my choice. Afterwards you fold me your horfe for a certain price. I brought againft you the action *ex empto*, that you might be condemned to deliver me the horfe; and, not being able to prove the fale which you made to me, a judgment in the laft refort has been rendered againft me. This does not exclude me from demanding of you the fame horfe by the action *præscriptis verbis*, which arifes from the bargain which we made for the work I have fince done for you.

On the contrary, in actions real, if I have claimed a certain thing which you had in poffeffion and which I claimed as belonging to me, the judgment which has been given againft me, excludes me from bringing againft you a new fuit to conteft with you again the property of this thing, although I fhould pretend to prove that it belonged to me on another ground than that which I offered at the time of the firft fuit in which I failed.

The reafon of the difference is, that the fame thing may be due on feveral different grounds of obligation, and I have as many different claims for this thing and as many different actions againft my debtor, as there are different grounds of obligation from which they arife; which different actions include as many different queftions. The judgment againft me in one of thefe actions, has determined nothing upon the other actions which I may have and the queftions they may include; and it cannot confequently exclude me from bringing them.

The judgment in the action *ex empto*, which I brought againft you, in which it was judged that you did not owe me on the contract of fale the thing which I demanded of you, has not determined that you do not owe it to me on another contract, and does not therefore exclude me from demanding it of you in another action which arises from this other contract.

It is not the same with regard to the right of property. If one may have different claims for the same thing, he cannot, on the contrary, have more than one and the same right of property to the same thing: therefore when, by a judgment which has been brought against me in a suit for a certain thing, it has been judged that the property of this thing did not belong to me, I can no longer have other actions against you to recover this property: it would be to renew the same question which has been determined by the judgment; for this question was singly whether the thing belonged to me or not. It is of no consequence that I have omitted to offer any proof by which I could establish my right of property; it suffices that I had it in my power to offer it.

This is shewn by Paul: *Actiones in personam ab actionibus in rem in hoc differunt, quod cum eadem res ab eodem mihi debeatur, singulas obligationes singulæ causæ sequuntur, nec ulla earum alterius petitione vitiatur: at quum in rem ago, non expressa causa ex qua rem meam esse dico, omnes causæ una petitione apprehenduntur neque enim amplius quam semel res mea esse potest, sæpius autem deberi potest*; L. 14, §. 2, ff. *de exc. rei jud.*

Hence this rule of law, *Non ut ex pluribus causis deberi nobis idem potest, ita ex pluribus causis idem possit nostrum esse;* L. 159, ff. *de R. J.*

47. What we have just said in regard to the action real, applies only when it has been brought in a general manner and without restriction; but as to the suit which I brought, if I have restricted it to a certain ground whereon I claim to be the proprietor of the thing, the judgment by which it has been judged that I was not entitled on this ground, would not exclude me from claiming the same thing on another ground on which I pretend to be able to establish that it does belong to me.

For example. If being the person whom the law calls

to the fucceffion of my inteftate relation, I have oppofed his will as forged or inofficious, and thereupon claimed the inheritance againft the legatee who was in poffeffion, although I have failed in the charge of its being forged or inofficious, this will not exclude me from bringing a new fuit for the inheritance on other grounds: *Licet quis ex eis titulus prior inofficiosi testamenti causam habuisset, judicatæ rei præscriptio non obstaret eamdem hæreditatem ex alia causa vindicanti*; L. 3, *Cod. de petit. hæred. Add.* L. 47, ff. *de pe it. hæred.*

48. However general the firft demand for the thing may have been, the judgment which has difmiffed the fuit does not exclude me from making a new demand when I pretend to have become the proprietor of it by a title which has accrued fince the judgment; for this judgment, in determining that I was not then the proprietor of this thing, does not eftablifh that I have not being able to acquire the property of it fince. The queftion which muft make the object of the new demand, which is whether the title fallen fince the judgment has not given me the property of this thing, is a queftion different from that which made the object of the firft; for it is a principle that the plea *rei judicatæ* can only apply when the fame queftion is renewed which has been determined by the judgment rendered on the firft demand.

§. III.

Of the third requisite, ut fit eadem conditio perfonarum.

49. The third thing requifite for the exception *rei judicatæ*, is that he who demands from me the fame thing which he had already demanded in a former fuit which the judgment has difmiffed, fhould make this new demand againft me in the fame capacity in which he proceeded on the other demand. For example, If in my capacity of tutor of a minor, I have demanded of you a certain thing, the judgment which has difcharged you therefrom, does not exclude me from demanding of you in my own name the fame thing, and *vice versa*: for when I was a party to

the first suit in the capacity of tutor, I was not properly a party, it was my minor who was a party by my interposition. The new suit which I bring in my own name is not then between the same parties and it cannot consequently be excluded by the authority of the *thing judged* in the former suit; for this authority cannot apply except between the same parties between whom the judgment was rendered, as we shall see in the following article.

§. IV.

That it is not material whether it be eodem an diverso genere judicii.

50. Provided the three things which we have explained in the preceding paragraphs concur, it is not material for the exception *rei judicatæ*, that the question determined by a judgment which has the authority of the *thing judged*, should be renewed *eodem an diverso genere judicii. Generaliter, ut Julianus definit, exceptio rei judicatæ obstat, quoties inter easdem personas eadem quæstio revocatur, vel alio genere judicatæ;* L. 7, §. 4, ff. *de except. rei judic.*

Several examples of this principle may be adduced. *Finge.* You have brought against me the action *quanto minoris*, that I might be condemned to make an abatement in the price of a certain horse which I have sold you, pretending that the horse has a certain defect against which I warranted; it was determined that the horse had not this defect, or that it was a defect which I did not warrant against, and I was discharged from your demand. If afterwards you should bring against me the action *redhibitoria*, on account of the same horse and the same defect, that I might be condemned to take it back, I may oppose to you the plea *rei judicatæ*, which arises from the judgment discharging me from your demand; although this new action which you bring against me should be another kind of action and you pray different relief. The three things requisite for this exception concur. It is the same horse which was the object of your first action, in which the judgment was rendered, that makes the object of this; it is *eadem res*; it is alfo *eadem causa petendi*, for the queftion in this new action is, as upon the firft, whether I have warranted againft the defect you complain of; and this queftion is renewed *inter easdem personas*, which fuffices for the exception to apply. The difference of the action and relief fought does not prevent this new action from having the fame object as the firft, and being therefore *eadem res: Cum qui actionem mutat & experitur, dummodo de eadem re experiatur, etsi diverso genere actionis quam instituit, videtur de eadem re agere*; L. 5, ff. *d. tit.*

ARTICLE V.

Between what persons the authority of the thing judged *applies.*

51. The authority of the *thing judged* applies only between the fame parties between whom the judgment has been rendered; it gives no right either to or againft third perfons: *Res inter alios judicatæ neque emolumentum afferre his qui judicio non interfuerunt, neque præjudicium solent irrogare*; L. 2, *Cod. quib. res jud. non noc.*

Sæpe constitutum est res inter alios judicatas aliis non præjudicare; L. 63, *de re jud.*

In applying this principle it is neceffary to examine, firft, in regard to what perfons the *thing judged* is prefumed to be judged between the fame parties, fo that it may have the force of law between them; and in regard to what perfons on the contrary the *thing judged* is prefumed to be *res inter alios judicata*, from which no right can arife, either in their favor or againft them.

52. The thing is prefumed to be judged between the fame parties, not only in regard to perfons who have been parties by themfelves, but in regard to thofe who have been parties by their tutors, curators or other lawful adminiftrators, who have a capacity to bring and defend their actions.

For example. If the tutor of a minor, in his capacity of tutor, has brought a fuit againft me in which judgment was given in my favor, and this minor coming of age, brought a fuit againft me for the fame demand, I may caufe him to be declared not receivable, by the plea *rei judicatæ*;

for the judgment rendered againſt the tutor is reputed to be rendered againſt the minor who was the true party by the interpoſition of his tutor.

For the ſame reaſon, if the wardens of a certain pariſh in their capacity of wardens, have brought againſt me a ſuit in which judgment was given in my favor, and their ſucceſſors bring a new action for the ſame demand againſt me, I may cauſe them to be declared not receivable, by the plea *rei judicatæ*, for it was the pariſh that was party to the ſuit in which judgment was given in my favor, and it cannot be therefore that, by the interpoſition of the new wardens, a ſuit may be brought againſt me for the ſame demand, which was determined by a judgment in which they were party by the interpoſition of their predeceſſors.

53. The ſucceſſors of parties are preſumed to be the ſame parties with the perſons to whom they have ſucceeded; therefore the thing judged is, in regard to them, reputed to be between the ſame parties, and conſequently has in their favor or againſt them the ſame authority of the *thing judged* which it would have had for or againſt the party to whom they have ſucceeded.

For example: The judgment which has diſcharged me from your demand, gives to my heirs as well as to me the plea *rei judicatæ* againſt your heirs as well as againſt you, if they ſhould bring a ſuit for the ſame demand.

54. This cannot be doubtful in regard to the heirs and other general ſucceſſors who are *hæredum loco*. In actions real, he who has ſucceeded, although in regard to a ſingle claim, to one of the parties, for the thing which was the object of a ſuit, is alſo preſumed to be the ſame party. For example. When you have brought a ſuit for a certain eſtate againſt Peter, the judgment which has been given in favor of Peter, will give to him who has ſince purchaſed this eſtate from Peter, the plea *rei judicatæ* againſt a new ſuit for this eſtate, if brought againſt this purchaſer; becauſe in regard to this he is preſumed to be the ſame party with Peter to whom he has ſucceeded. L, 11, §. 3, ff, *de exc. jud.*

For the fame reafon, if I had brought a fuit againft the proprietor of a neighbouring eftate to make him deftroy a work by which I pretended that he had fent the waters of his land upon mine, and, fince the judgment rendered upon this fuit, he has fold his eftate or I mine, the judgment rendered between us will give to the purchafer the plea *rei judicatæ*, if a new fuit on account of this work is brought againft him; or will give this plea againft him, if he brings a new fuit; *de Leg.* §. 9.

55. The laws cited are in the cafe of a purchafer; it cannot be doubtful in regard to a purchafer that when a new fuit is brought againft him there is ground for the plea *rei judicatæ*, which the feller could have pleaded; for this action will affect the feller who is bound to warrant and defend the purchafer.

Although this action ceafes in regard to the fucceffors by a lucrative title without warranty, we muft decide however that they ought to be reputed to be the fame party with him to whom they have fucceeded in the eftate which was the object of the judgment, and that they may, like him, oppofe to the party againft whom this judgment has been rendered, the authority of the thing judged which refults therefrom. For example. If I have procured againft you a judgment that my eftate did not belong to you, or that it was not fubject to a certain right of way to which you pretended it was fubject, and you fhould bring againft him to whom I have fince paffed this eftate by gift, a new fuit, either to recover it or to fubject it to the fame right of way, the donee, as being in my right, may oppofe to you the plea *rei judicatæ*.

Why? For this reafon. When we make any agreement in regard to a thing which belongs to us, we are prefumed to ftipulate as well for all thofe who fucceed to us for this thing, who are comprifed under the term *assigns*, as for ourfelves; and confequently the right which refults from this agreement paffes to all our faid fucceffors or affigns, as we have feen *supra* in the beginning of this treatiſe, *n.* 67, 62. As, when we have a ſuit at law in regard to a certain thing which belongs to us, we are preſumed to act as well for all our aſſigns and ſucceſſors to this thing, as for ourſelves; and the right which reſults from the judgment which is rendered in this ſuit, muſt paſs to all our ſucceſſors and aſſigns.

56. In the ſame manner as the ſucceſſor may plead the judgment which has been rendered in favor of his predeceſſor, as we have juſt ſeen, ſo, *vice versa*, may the judgment rendered againſt the predeceſſor be pleaded againſt the ſucceſſor; provided however that he has ſucceeded to his predeceſſor ſince the ſuit upon which the judgment was rendered againſt his predeceſſor. *Finge.* Peter has brought againſt you a ſuit for a certain eſtate, in which judgment was given in your favor. Peter afterwards mortgages to me this eſtate. If I bring an action againſt you to compel you to give up the eſtate, and I offer to prove that Peter, my debtor, was the proprietor of it, and has validly mortgaged the ſame to me, you may oppoſe to me the exception *rei judicatæ*, reſulting from the judgment which you have obtained againſt Peter, my predeceſſor, which, in diſcharging you from his demand, has determined that it did not belong to him, and conſequently that he could not mortgage it to me.

It would be otherwiſe if Peter had mortgaged the eſtate before the ſuit which he had againſt you. You could not in this caſe oppoſe to me the judgment which you had obtained againſt him; for this judgment by which it has been determined that Peter was not then the proprietor of the eſtate, does not decide that he could not have been ſo before he mortgaged it to me; and on my proving that he was proprietor of it then, my action may be maintained againſt you, although he afterwards ceaſed to be the proprietor, and was not at the time of the ſuit between you and him; L. 11, §. 10, ff. *de except. rei jud.*; L. 3, ff. *de pign. & hyp.*

57. Although a judgment is preſumed to have been

rendered for or against the successor, when it was for or against his predecessor, the same cannot be said *vice-versa.*

Therefore neither the judgment rendered for or against the successor nor the plea *rei judicatæ* which results therefrom, can be pleaded by or against his predecessor. *Julianus scribit exceptionem rei judicatæ persona autoris ad emptorem transire solere; retro autem ab emptore ad autorem reverti non debere;* L. 9, §. 2, ff. *de except. rei jud.*

He adduces this example: *Si hæreditariam rem vendideris, ego eamdem ab emptore petiero & vicero; petenti tibi non opponam exceptionem.* AT SI EA RES JUDICATA NON SIT *inter me & eum cui vendidisti; d. §. item si victus fuero, tu adversus me exceptionem non habebis;* L. 10.

58. We have established that a judgment was, in regard to any one, presumed to be rendered between the same parties, whether he had been a party himself in the suit in which the judgment is had, or his predecessor had been a party to it. On the contrary in regard to those who have not been parties either by themselves, or by their predecessors, this judgment is *inter alios judicata,* which cannot be opposed to them by the party in favor of whom it has been rendered, nor by them to the party against whom it has been rendered. This applies although the question between them is the same with that which has been determined by this judgment, although it is decided on the same grounds, and depends even upon the same fact.

This will appear by the example which Paul adduces. I have entrusted a certain sum to a person who has left several heirs. Having demanded from one of the said heirs the restitution of this sum for the part for which he was bound, the judge who has not given sufficient attention to the proofs upon which I established this deposit, has given judgment for the defendant. If I demand from the other heirs the restitution of the parts of this sum for which they are bound, they cannot oppose to me the judgment in favor of their co-heir; because this judgment to which they were not parties is, in regard to them, *res inter alios judi-*

cata, which cannot give them any right, although the question is the same with that which has been determined against me by the judgment in favor of their co-heir, and it depends on the same fact, which is whether I really entrusted this sum to the deceased, and whether he has not returned it to me. *Si cum uno hærede depositi actum sit, tamen & cum cæteris hæredibus recte agetur; nec exceptio rei judicatæ eis proderit; nam etsi eadem quæstio in omnibus judiciis vertitur, tamen personarum mutatio cum quibus singulis suo nomine agitur, aliam atque aliam rem facit*; L. 22, ff. *de except. rei jud.*

This principle, that the authority of the *thing judged* does not apply in regard to persons who have not been parties and who are not the successors of one of the parties, is supported by another principle which we have established in the preceding article, that the authority of the *thing judged* applies only in regard to the same thing on which the judgment has determined.

For example in the instance above adduced, if the judgment which has been given in favor of one of the heirs of the debtor, in a suit by a creditor of the deceased for the part of the debt for which it was pretended he was bound, has not the authority of the *thing judged* in favor of the other heirs for the parts for which it is pretended they are bound; it is not merely because it is *res inter alios judicata;* it is also because what is claimed from them is not the same thing with that which was the object of the judgment rendered in favor of their co-heir: for the parts of the debt which are claimed from them are indeed parts of the same debt, but they are not the same part of this debt which was claimed from their co-heir. The judgment rendered in favor of their co-heir has determined only upon this part, and cannot consequently have the authority of the *thing judged*, in regard to the other parts which are claimed from them. This is the meaning of the law above cited. *Mutatio personarum cum quibus singulis suo nomine agitur, aliam atque aliam rem facit.*

Likewise, when a creditor has left several heirs, the debtor in whose favor judgment has been given in the suit brought by one of the heirs for his part, cannot oppose this judgment against the suits which the other heirs bring for their parts; this judgment being *res inter alios judicata*, and not being *eadem res*; for these parts which the other heirs claim, although parts of the same debt, are not the same part with that which was the object and subject of the judgment.

59. It is not the same when the thing due to several heirs or other persons, joint-owners, is something indivisible, such as a right of way. This thing not being susceptible of parts, each of them is creditor or joint-owner of the whole; therefore the judgment rendered in the suit which one of them has brought for this thing had for its object the same thing which was the object of that brought for it by the others; it is *eadem res*. We may also say that this judgment is not *inter alios judicata*, in regard to the other creditors or joint-owners of this thing; for the indivisibility of their right with his own, causes them to be regarded as being the same party with him. This judgment has then in regard to them the authority of the *thing judged*: when it has been rendered in favor of their co-owner or co-creditor, they may, as well as he, oppose it to the party against whom it has been rendered, and if it has been rendered against their co-owner or co-creditor, it may be opposed to them, as it has been to him.

Yet if the judgment had been rendered by collusion, the law permits them to renew the suit. *Si de communi servitute quis bene quidem deberi intendit, sed aliquo modo litem perdidit culpa sua, non est æquum hoc cæteris damno esse; sed si per collusionem cessit litem adversario, cæteris dandam esse actionem de dolo;* (which is to say, as is well explained in the commentary, *replicationem de dolo contra exceptionem rei judicatæ*); L. 19, ff. *si serv. vind.*

60. According to our usages, the judgment rendered against one of several creditors or joint-owners of an indi-

visible right, may indeed be opposed to the others; but, without its being necessary to alledge collusion, they may take an appeal, although he against whom it has been rendered has acquiesced in it: and if it is a judgment in the last resort, they may contest it.

Likewise among several debtors of an indivisible thing, the indivisibility of their obligation causes them all to be deemed but one and the same party, and consequently causes the judgment rendered for or against one of them to be considered as rendered for or against the others; saving to those who have not been parties by themselves, to seek relief against it by way of appeal or opposition, as it has been said *supra*.

61. The dependance of the obligation of a security on that of the principal debtor to which it has acceded, also causes the security to be deemed the same party with the principal debtor, in regard to all that is determined for or against the principal debtor.

Therefore if the principal debtor has been discharged from the demand of the creditor, provided it be not upon pleas personal to this principal debtor, the security who is afterwards sued may oppose to the creditor the exception *rei judicatæ: Si pro servo meo fidejusseris & mecum de peculio actum sit* (add *& judicatum sit nihil a servo meo deberi*), *si postea tecum eo nomine agatur, excipiendum est de re judicata;* L. 21, §. 4, *de except. rei jud.*

The creditor cannot in this case reply that it is *res inter alios judicata*; for it being of the essence of the contract of securitiship, that the obligation of the security should depend upon that of the principal debtor, that the security should only owe what the principal debtor owed, that the security may oppose all the exceptions *in rem* which could be by the principal debtor, it follows that whatever is judged in favor of the principal debtor is presumed to be judged in favor of the security, who must in this respect be deemed the same party with him.

Vice versa, when the judgment has been rendered against the principal debtor, the creditor may oppose it to the security, and demand that it may be executed against him; but the security is received to appeal from this judgment, or if it is rendered in the last resort, to contest it. *Admittuntur ad provocandum fidejussores pro eo pro quo intervenerunt;* L. 5, §. 1, *item fidejussores;* ff. *de appell.*

62. According to the principles of the civil law, the right of legatees depending upon that of the testamentary heir, the judgment rendered against this heir, which has declared the testament null, is not regarded in respect to these legatees as *res inter alios judicata*, and may be opposed to them: the right of these legatees depending upon that of the testamentary heir, causes them to be deemed, in a certain manner, the same party with the heir; but they are received to appeal; L. 5, §. ff. *de appell.*; or when the judgment is in the last resort, to contest it.

It is otherwise in regard to a judgment which upon the suit of a legatee, has declared the testament null; this judgment is, in regard to other legatees, *res inter alios judicata*, which cannot be opposed to them, and from which they have no need to appeal. L. 1, ff. *de except. rei jud.* The reason of the difference is, that the right of the legatees does not depend upon that of their co-legatee, against whom the judgment has been rendered; whereas it does depend upon the right of the testamentary heir; *Quum ab institutione hæredis pendeant omnia quæ testamento continentur.*

SECTION THE SECOND.

Of the oath.

8 7. There are three principal kinds of oaths which are used in civil proceedings; I. the oath which one party defers or refers to the other, to rest on it the decision of the cause, and which is for this reason called the decisory oath. II. the oath which the party must take who is examined upon interrogatories. III. The oath which the judge defers of his own accord to one of the parties either to decide the cause, or to fix or determine the amount of the damages; it is called *juramentum judiciale*.

ARTICLE THE FIRST.

Of the decisory oath.

818. The decisory oath is, as we have said, that which a party defers or refers to the other, to rest on it the decision of the cause.

§. I.

Upon what things the decisory oath may be deferred.

819. The decisory oath may be deferred upon any kind of contestation whatever, and in any kind of civil suit, in possessory as well as real actions, in actions *in personam* as well as *in rem.* *Jusjurandum & ad pecunias & ad omnes res locum habet;* L. 34, ff. *de jurejur.*

The oath cannot however be deferred except upon what is the proper act of the party to whom it is deferred; a party is not obliged to take it upon what is the proper act of another person of whom he is heir or in whose rights he is: for I cannot be ignorant of my own act, whereas I do not necessarily know what is the act of another to whom I have succeeded. *Hæredi ejus cum quo contractum est, jusjurandum deferri non potest; Paul, sent,* 11, 1. 4.

A person who demands from me the price of a thing which he pretends to have sold to the deceased whose heir I am, cannot then defer to me the oath upon the fact of the thing's being sold to the deceased; for this is not my act, it is the act of the deceased which I do not necessarily know. But the usage among us is, that in this case the oath may be deferred upon the question whether I have any knowledge that the deceased owed the sum demanded; for in this case the oath cannot be deferred upon the fact of the sale which is the act of the deceased, but it may be deferred upon the knowledge which it is pretended I have of the debt which is my proper act.

§. II.

In what case the decisory oath may be deferred.

820. The plaintiff may defer the oath to the defendant, whenever the plaintiff thinks he has not sufficient

proof of the fact which makes the ground of his demand. Likewise the defendant may defer the oath to the plaintiff when he has not proof of the fact, which makes the ground of the defence he must set up against the demand.

This oath may be deferred as well before as after the plea in chief, in an appeal as well as in an original suit.

It is a question which has been much controverted whether some inchoate proof is necessary for the plaintiff to be received to defer the oath; or whether he must be received although he has not the least inchoate proof of his demand? The glossary *ad* L. 3, *cod. de R. cred.*, Bartolus, Baldus, and several other authors cited by Mascardus, *de probat. concl.* 957, require some inchoate proof. The reasons which they allege for this opinion are, I. that it is a general principle of law that the defendant ought to have judgment when the demand against him is not proved, without being holden to any thing in order to obtain it. *Actore non probante, qui convenitur, & si nihil ipse præstet, obtinebit*; L. 4, *cod. de edend.* Therefore, say they, the defendant ought not to be holden, in order to obtain judgment against a demand of which there is no inchoate proof, to take the oath, and the plaintiff ought not to be received to defer it to him, since the law says he is not to be holden to any thing, *& si nihil ipse præstet.* II. It is a further principle of law that the plaintiff must furnish on his part proofs of his demand and it is not for the defendant to furnish them against himself. *Intelligitis quod intentionis vestræ proprias adferre debetis probationes, non adversus se ab adversariis adduci*; L. 7, *cod. de test.* Therefore, say they, the plaintiff who brings no proof of his demand ought not to be admitted to procure it by deferring the oath, to the defendant. III. They say that one ought not without any ground to be received to bring suit against another, and occasion him the embarrassment of taking an oath which scrupulous persons with difficulty take upon things of which they think they are most certain: they pretend to derive also some argument from the law 31, ff. *de jurej.*; from the laws 11, & 12, *cod de reb.*

cred. The contrary opinion, that the plaintiff has no need of any inchoate proof, to be received to defer the oath to the defendant, is more correct, and it has been embraced by Cujas *obs.* 22. 28, Dauren, Doneau, and by several others: it is also that of Vinnius, who has thoroughly treated of the question, *select. quæst.* 1, 42, and which we only copy here. The reasons upon which it is established are, I. that one ought not to exact from the plaintiff what the law which has established the use of the decisory oath has not required from him: the edict of the prætor which established this law does not at all require any inchoate proof of his demand. It says without distinction, *eum a quo jusjurandum petitur, jurare aut solvere cogam*; L. 34, §. 6, ff. *de jurej.* II. it may happen very often that a demand of which there is no inchoate proof, is not at the same time the less just. For example. I have lent a friend a sum of money without taking any receipt or note. The demand which I make of him for the restitution of this sum, is not the less just in itself, although I have no inchoate proof of the loan which is the ground of it. The judge ought not to neglect any means which present themselves to discover the truth, in order to render justice to whom it is due. I present him one of doing so, by deferring the oath to the defendant; for if he refuses to swear that I have not made him any loan or that he has returned it to me, his refusal to swear will be an implied avowal of the debt. The judge ought then to take this mode of discovering the truth and admit me to defer the oath to the defendant, although I have no inchoate proof of my demand; the refusal which I hope the defendant will make to swear, may be of itself a complete proof of the debt and of the wrong which he has done in refusing the payment. *Manifestæ turpitudinis & confessionis est, nolle jurare*; L. 28, ff. *de jurej.* III. This opinion is further established by formal texts of law. It is said in the law 12, *cod. de reb. cred.*, that this oath may be deferred even in the beginning of the suit, *in principio litis*, and consequently even before the plaintiff has furnished any proof. The law 35, ff. *de jurej*, is expressed in terms still more formal; it says the oath may be deferred, *omnibus aliis probationibus deficientibus.*

In regard to the reasons above alledged for the first opinion, they are very frivolous and it is easy to answer them. When it is said the defendant ought to have judgment in his favor on a demand which is not proved, without being holden to any thing in order to obtain it, *etiamsi nihil ipse præstet* this signifies nothing else than that, in order to obtain this judgment, he has no need to produce on his part any proof; but this does not at all signify that he shall not be holden to take the oath, when it is deferred to him, As to what is said in the law *7, cod. de test.*, that the defendant ought not to be obliged to furnish proof against himself, this applies only to what is said in the beginning of the law, that the defendant ought not to be obliged to produce witnesses or papers against himself: *Nimis grave est quod petitis, urgeri partem diversam ad exhibitionem per quos sibi negotium fiat:* but this has no application to the deferring of the oath; a party cannot complain that he has been treated with hardship, when by the oath which is deferred to him he is himself rendered a judge of his own cause. In regard to what has been said that it is an inconvenience that a person without any ground, without any inchoate proof, should have it in his power to put another to the trouble of taking an oath, I answer that we cannot obviate all inconveniences. The trouble of defending a suit is indeed greater than that of taking an oath, since one may put a ready end to the latter by doing as required. However a person may, without any ground, by bringing against me a suit entirely unsupported by proof, occasion me the trouble of defending it. Why may he not as well give me the trouble of taking the oath, by deferring it to me? The Romans had established a kind of remedy against these inconveniences by the oath which the parties were obliged to take before the trial of the cause, that it was with good faith that they carried on the suit, and by that which the party who deferred the oath was likewise obliged to take, that he deferred it *bona fide* with the sole view to discover the truth, and without any view to vex the party to whom he deferred it; which they called *juramentum de calumnia.* These oaths are not in use among us. In regard to the laws alledged for the first opinion, nothing results therefrom. A question is made in the law 31, only of the supplementary oath which is deferred by the judge, and not of the decisory oath. There results indeed from the law 12, that there may be a question among the parties whether the oath has been well or ill deferred; but this question concerns either the nature of the fact upon which it has been deferred, or the quality of the party who defers it, or of the party to whom it is deferred, and it does not at all relate to the plaintiff's having any inchoate proof, this being indifferent.

§. III.

Of the persons who may defer the oath, and to whom it may be deferred.

821. As the decision of the suit and the right of the parties are made to depend on this oath, it follows that it is only those who have the disposition of their rights, who may defer this oath, and to whom it may be deferred.

Therefore a minor cannot, without the authority of his tutor, defer this oath; L. 17, §. 1, ff. *de jurej.*; and it cannot be deferred to him; L. 34, §. 2, ff. *d. tit.*

According to this principle, an insolvent person cannot, in fraud of his creditors, defer the oath to his debtor upon what is due to him; for he cannot dispose of his rights in fraud of his creditors. Therefore his creditors, without having regard to the oath taken by this debtor of theirdebtor, may attach what he owed, and, by proving the debt, obtain a judgment against him as garnishee: L. 9, §. 5, ff. *d. tit.*

Some authors have maintained that he to whom the oath cannot be referred, because on something which is not his proper act, and of which he has no knowledge, is not to be received to defer the oath to his adversary, although it should be on the proper act of this adverse party. This is the opinion of Natta, *cons.* 35. It is founded upon the law 33, ff. *de jurej.*, where it is faid that he to whom the oath is deferred cannot complain that any wrong is done thereby, becaufe he may refer it. *De injuria queri non potest, quum possit jusjurandum referre.* Therefore, fays he, arguing *a contrario*, he to whom the oath is deferred, is not obliged to accept the condition when he cannot refer it. This confequence is badly drawn; for the reafon alledged in the law 34, *quum possit jusjurandum referre*, is but a further reafon why he to whom the oath is deferred cannot complain: the principal reafon which is alledged elfewhere, and which fuffices alone, is that no perfon can complain of being made a judge in his own caufe. The contrary opinion, which is that of Fachinæus, of Cravetta and other authors by him cited, is founded upon reafons more folid. We ought not to exact from him who defers the oath, what no law requires from him; there is no law which requires that he who defers the oath fhould be fuch a perfon as that it could be referred to him. On the contrary, the law 17, §. 2, exprefsly permits a tutor and a curator to defer the oath in the caufes which they bring in this capacity, although it cannot be referred to them; fince the caufe of the ward or of the perfon interdicted, is not the proper act of the tutor or curator.

An attorney cannot defer the oath, unlefs he has a fpecial power or is an attorney *universorum bonorum*, that is to fay, unlefs he has a general power to adminifter. L. 17, §. 3. The fyndic of a corporation cannot, without a fpecial power. L. 34, §. 1.

It cannot be deferred to thefe perfons, becaufe it would be to defer it to them upon fomething which is not their proper act. L. 34, §. 3, ff. *h. tit.*

§. IV.

Of the effect of the oath deferred, referred, taken or refused.

822. He to whom the oath has been deferred ought to take the oath or refer it to him who has deferred it: if he does neither he ought to lofe his caufe; *Manifestæ turpitu-*

dinis & confessionis est nolle jurare, nec jurisjurandum referre; L. 33, ff. *d. tit.*

If the thing upon which the oath has been deferred is not of the act of both parties, but only of him to whom it has been deferred, he will not have the choice to refer it, and will be holden absolutely to take the oath, on pain of losing his cause.

If the party takes the oath which has been deferred to him, there will result from this oath a presumption *juris & de jure*, of the truth of the thing upon which the oath has been deferred, against which no contrary proof can be received, according to what we have already observed in the second section.

If he refers the oath, the party to whom it is referred will be holden absolutely to take the oath, in default of which he ought to lose his cause: if he takes the oath, what he swears will likewise be holden to be proved without admitting any proof to the contrary. All this is included in the law 24, §. *fin.* ff. *de jurej.*

When it is to the defendant that the oath has been deferred or referred, the oath which he takes that he owes not what is demanded of him, gives him against the demand the exception *jurisjurandi*, which ought to entitle him to judgment and costs. This being grounded upon a presumption *juris & de jure*, it excludes the plaintiff from being heard in offering proof that the party has taken the oath *mala fide*, and has committed a perjury. This is illustrated by Julian: *Adversus exceptionem jurisjurandi, replicatio doli mali non debet dari, quum prætor id agere debet ne de jurejurando quæratur*; L. 15, ff. *de except.*

He would not be heard in this although he should offer to prove it by papers since recovered: in this the decisory oath deferred or referred by the party, has more force than the supplementary oath of which we shall treat *infra, art.* 3, Caius, in the law 31, ff. *de jurej.*, observes this difference.

When it was to the plaintiff that the oath was deferred or referred, the oath which he took that the thing demanded was due or belonged to him gave him, in the civil law, an action *in factum, ad instar* the action *judicati*; to obtain judgment for it. L. 8, *cod. de R. cred.*, upon which action the only question was whether the oath had been regularly taken, without admitting the party who had deferred or referred it to him to be heard on any plea to the merits: *In qua (actione) hoc solum quæritur an juraverit dari se oportere*; L. 9, §. 1, *de jurej. Dato jurejurando, non aliud quæritur quam an juratum sit, remissa quæstione an debeatur*; L. 5, §. 2, ff. *d. tit.*

Among us, the plaintiff who has taken this oath may have judgment on his demand with costs, without being holden to bring other proofs, and without the party who has deferred or referred the oath to him being heard to set up any defence.

This effect of the oath is a consequence of this principle of natural law: *Quid tam congruum fidei humanæ, quam ea quæ inter eos placuerunt servare?* L. 1, ff. *de pact.* In fact when one of the parties defers to the other the oath upon what is the object of the suit which they have between them, to rest upon it the decision, and the one to whom the oath is deferred accepts the condition and consequently takes the oath or declares himself ready to take it, there results therefrom an agreement by which these parties agree to be holden to what may be sworn; from which agreement arises an obligation that binds the party who has deferred the oath, to abide by what is sworn, which excludes him from being allowed to make any proof of the contrary.

As the agreement is not made and does not produce an obligation but by the concurrence of the will of two parties, it follows thence that he who has deferred the oath on his part may recall his offer of the oath while the party to whom he has deferred it has not yet accepted the condition, by taking the oath or at least by declaring himself ready to take it; L. 11, *cod de reb. cred. & jurej.* Observe that when he has recalled his offer he cannot defer the oath a second time.

When the party to whom I have deferred the oath has accepted the condition and declared that he was ready to take the oath, I cannot afterwards recall the offer of the oath; but I may discharge him from taking it and in this case the thing upon which he was ready to take it will be holden to be proved, in the same manner as if he had taken the oath L. 6; L. 9, §. 1, ff. *de jur.*

823. From the principle which we have established, that the decisory oath derives its effect from the agreement implied by the deferring of the oath, between him who has deferred it, and him to whom it has been deferred, it follows also that as an agreement has no effect but in regard to the thing which was the object of the agreement, and between the contracting parties and their heirs; *Animadvertendum est ne conventio in alia re facta, aut cum alia persona, in alia re aliave persona noceat*; L. 27, §. 4, ff. *de pact.*; so also the decisory oath cannot have effect but in regard to the same thing upon which the oath was deferred.

To know whether what is demanded is the same thing upon which the oath has been deferred and which has been determined by this oath, we may apply all the rules which we have established in the preceding section, *art.* 4, to know when what is demanded ought to be presumed to be the same thing with what has been decided by the judgment which has intervened between the parties.

The oath likewise ought not to have effect nor cause the fact upon which the party has sworn, to be holden to be proved, except in regard to him who has deferred to him the oath, and in regard to his heirs and others who succeed to his rights, but it has no effect in regard to third persons: *Jusjurandum alteri nec nocet, nec prodest*; L. 3, §. 3, ff. *de jurejur.*

Therefore if one of the heirs of a deceased person has sued me for his part of a sum which he pretends I owed to the deceased, and he has deferred to me the oath upon the existence of this debt, and I have sworn that I owed nothing to the deceased, this oath will indeed exclude this heir from demanding the sum; but it will not exclude his coheir from demanding his part, and if he brings proof that I really owed the sum to the deceased, I shall be condemned to pay him his part notwithstanding the oath which I have made that I owed nothing: for this oath has an effect only in regard to him who deferred it to me and not in regard to his co-heir.

824. Nevertheless if one of two creditors *in solidum* had deferred to me the oath and I had sworn that I owed nothing, this oath would also exclude his co-creditor; L. 28, ff. *de jurejur.*

There is for this a particular reason, which is that the payment of a debt *in solidum* to one of the creditors *in solidum*, discharges the debtor towards all the others; therefore the oath which the debtor has taken that he owed nothing, is equivalent to a payment which he might make to him who defers the oath; *Nam jusjurandum loco solutionis cedit;* L. 27: consequently it ought to discharge him towards all.

825. As the decisory oath is proof only against him who has deferred it, so it is proof only in favor of him to whom it has been deferred and who has taken the oath, or who has been discharged from taking it; L. 5, §. 3, ff. *de jurejur.*

Nevertheless if my debtor to whom I have deferred the oath, has sworn to owe me nothing, I can demand nothing from his securities; for my debtor who has taken the oath, has an interest that I should demand nothing from his securities, who might have recourse against him, if they were obliged to pay me any thing: and it is to demand of him indirectly, to demand of his securities; L. 28, §. 1, ff. *de jurejur.*

Quid, vice versa, if I had deferred the oath to the security and he had ſworn that there was nothing due? The law above cited decides that this oath would avail the principal debtor, becauſe it holds the place of payment, *d.* L. 27, and the payment made by the ſecurity diſcharges the principal debtor.

For the ſame reaſon the oath deferred to one of ſeveral debtors *in ſolidum* avails all the others.

Theſe deciſions apply, provided *de re & non de perſona jurantis juratum ſit*: for if the ſecurity has ſworn only that he did not contract the ſecuritiſhip, the principal debtor cannot derive an advantage from it; L. 28, §. 1, L. 42, §. 1, ff. *de jurijur.* Likewiſe if one of the debtors *in ſolidum* has ſworn that he did not contract the obligation, his codebtors cannot derive an advantage from it.

From the principle that the deciſory oath derives its effect and its authority from the agreement implied by the deferring of the oath, we may alſo derive this conſequence, that if the party who deferred it, has ſome juſt cauſe of relief againſt the agreement by which he deferred the oath to the other party, he may, in procuring himſelf to be relieved againſt this agreement, cauſe the oath to fail.

Fraud being a cauſe of reſtitution againſt all agreements; if I can prove that it was by a fraud on your part that you induced me to defer to you the oath, I may, upon appeal from the judgment in your favor in conſequence of your oath, or, if this judgment is in the laſt reſort, upon a civil petition againſt this judgment, obtain letters of reſciſſion, by which, without having regard to my having deferred to you the oath, nor to what has followed, the parties will be reſtored to the ſame ſtate in which they were before. We may adduce as an example of fraud, your withholding from me the evidence which eſtabliſhed the claim for a certain ſum that I had againſt you. If upon the ſuit which I have brought for this ſum, not having my evidence. I have deferred to you the oath upon the exiſtence of my claim; as it is in this caſe your withholding my evidence; and conſequently your fraud which has induced me to defer to you the oath, I may, if I come to have proof of this fraud, cause myself to be relieved against my deferring to you the oath, as having been induced to defer it to you through your fraud.

This decision is not contrary to the law 15, ff. *de except.*, above adduced, *n.* 822, which says, *adversus exceptionem jurisjurandi non debet dari replicatio doli mali:* for the fraud which is spoken of in this law, is no other than the perjury which he who has deferred you the oath pretended you had committed in falsely swearing not to owe the sum demanded. He who has deferred you the oath is not received to prove this perjury by adducing more decisive evidence, although since procured; because the oath operates a presumption *juris & de jure*, which causes what you have sworn to be deemed true and excludes all proof of the contrary. Therefore when you have sworn to owe nothing, there can no longer be room for the question *an debeatur;* L. 5, §. 2, ff. *de jurejur.* But as the oath has not this authority except as it has been validly made and validly deferred, *quæritur an juratum sit*, §. 2; and he who has deferred it, in order to prove that it has not been validly deferred, is received to prove your fraud, that is to say, the manœuvres which you have employed to induce him to defer it to you, such as your having stolen or withholden from him the evidence of his claim.

Minority being a cause of relief, minors who, by the interposition of their tutors or curators, have deferred the oath to the party with whom they were at law, may sometimes be admitted to relief; but they ought not to be indiscriminately. They ought not, when, not having at the time of deferring the oath sufficient proof of the fact on which they deferred it, they have only done, in deferring it, what a prudent person in the like case would have done. This is illustrated by Ulpian: *Si minor detulerit, & hoc ipso captum se dicat, adversus exceptionem jurisjurandi replicari debebit, ut Pomponius ait: Ego autem puto hanc replicationem non semper esse dandam, sed Prætorem debere cognoscere an captus sit, & sic in integrum restituere; nec enim utique qui minor est, statim se captum docuit;* L. 9, §. 4, ff. *de jurej.*

Article II.

Of the oath of the party who is examined on interrogatories.

826. When a party exhibits interrogatories upon which he obtains an order that the other party shall be examined by the judge, the oath which the party examined takes, is very different from the decisory oath. The decisory oath is proof for him who takes it, whereas, on the contrary, this is no proof in favor of him who takes it: the answers which the party interrogated makes, are proof only against him, and are none in his favor. The reason of this difference is, that he, who causes the party to be examined on interrogatories, does not do it with the intention to rest the decision of the question on what the party examined may swear, but he puts to him these interrogatories in order to derive for himself some proofs or presumptions from the admissions which the party examined may make, or from contradictions into which he may fall: *ut confitendo vel mentiendo se oneret;* L. 4, ff. *de interr. in jur. fac.*

827. Observe that he who would avail himself of the admissions which a party in his answers to the interrogatories has made, ought not to divide them but to take them entire. If, for example, not having any proof of the loan which I pretend to have made you, of a certain sum of money, I cause you to be examined on interrogatories and in your answers you confess the loan, but add that you have returned the sum, I cannot avail myself of the admission you have made of the loan, and set aside what you added that you returned the sum; but I must take your declaration entire. Therefore if I wished your admission to prove the loan I must admit it also to prove the payment, without your being obliged to make any proof of it, unless I should be able to prove that the payment could not have been made in the time and place in which you have said it was made. See on interrogatories, *Ordinance* 1667, *tit.* 10 & *comment.* by M. Jousse.

proof. The law 35, ff. *de jurej,* is expressed in terms still

ARTICLE III.

Of the oath called juramentum judiciale.

828. The oath called *juramentum judiciale* is that which the judge defers of his own accord to one of the parties.

There are two kinds; I. that which the judge defers for the decision of the cause; it is understood by the general name *juramentum judiciale*: we give it sometimes also the name of supplementary oath, *juramentum suppletorium*; II. that which the judge defers to fix and determine the amount of the judgment he ought to pronounce: this oath is called *juramentum in litem*.

§ I.

Of the oath which the judge defers for the decision of the cause.

829. The use of this oath is established upon the law 31. ff. *de jurej.*, where it is said: *Solent judices in dubiis causis exacto jurejurando secundum eum judicare qui juraverit*; and upon the law 3, *Cod. de reb. cred.*, in which it is said: *In bonæ fidei contractibus, necnon in cæteris causis, inopia probationum, per judicem jurejurando, causa cognita, rem decidi oportet.*

It results from these texts, that three things must concur in order that there may be room for this oath.

I. It is necessary that the claim or defence should not be fully proved: this results from these terms of the law 3, *Cod. de reb. cred.*, *inopia probationum*. When the demand is fully proved, the judge gives judgment against the defendant without having recourse to the oath, and likewise when the defence is fully proved he gives judgment for the defendant without having recourse to it.

II. It is necessary that the claim or defence, although not fully proved, should not however be altogether unsupported by proof: this is the meaning of these terms *in causis dubiis*, which the law 31 makes use of. It calls by this name those in which the claim or the defence is not fully supported for want of entire and complete proof, nor absolutely unsupported by some inchoate proof which there is: *In quibus, judex dubius est, ob minus plenas probationes allatas*, Vinnius *sel. quæst.* 1, 44.

III. It is necessary that the judge should enter into an investigation of the cause, in order to estimate whether he ought to defer the oath and to which of the parties he ought to defer it; this results from the terms of the law 31, *causa cognita.*

830. This investigation of the cause consists in the examination of the weight of the proof, of the nature of the fact and of the relation of the parties. When the proof of the fact on which depends the decision of the cause, and which makes the foundation of the claim or of the defence, is complete, the judge ought not to defer the oath, but he ought to give judgment in favor of him who has made the proof.

Nevertheless if the judge, for the information of his conscience, had deferred the oath in this case, and the fact upon which he had deferred it was the proper act of the party to whom it was deferred, so that he could not be ignorant of it, this party ought not to refuse to take the oath, and he would not be heard in an appeal from the judgment; for although the judge could and indeed ought, the proof appearing complete, to give judgment in his favor without exacting from him the oath, he has not however done him any wrong in exacting it, since it costs the party nothing to swear what he knows to be true: his refusal to swear to this fact lessens and destroys the proof which he had made of it.

831. When the plaintiff has no proof of the fact which makes the foundation of his claim, or when that which he has forms only a very light presumption, the judge ought not to defer to him the oath, however worthy of credit he might be, and he ought to give judgment for the defendant. Nevertheless if these proofs, however light they may be, raise some doubt in the mind of the judge, he may, for the information of his conscience, defer the oath to the defendant.

Likewise when, the claim being proved, the defence set up against the claim is only supported by proofs too light for the oath of the defendant to complete the proof of it, the judge may, if he thinks proper, for the information of his confcience, in giving judgment for the plaintiff require his oath.

I would not however advife the judges to ufe often this precaution, which ferves only to give occafion to an infinity of perjuries. When a man is honeft, he has no need to be conftrained by the folemnity of an oath not to claim what is not due to him, and not to deny what he ought to admit; and when he is not honeft, he has no fear of perjury.

During forty years, which I have paffed in the exercife of my profeffion, I have feen the oath deferred an infinity of times, and I have not feen it happen more than twice that a party had been reftrained by the oath from perfifting in what he had maintained.

832. When the proof of the fact which makes the foundation of the claim is already confiderable, although it be not entirely complete, the judge ought to decide by the oath of one of the parties: he may even in this cafe defer it to the plaintiff, in order to fupply by his oath what is wanting in the proof which he has made.

It is neceffary however to except from this rule caufes of great importance, fuch as marriage caufes, &c. In thofe caufes, what is wanting in the proof of the claim cannot be fupplied by the oath of the plaintiff, and the defendant ought always to have judgment, when it is not fully proved.

In common caufes, as that which is wanting in the proof which a plaintiff was obliged to make may be fuppli-ed by his oath, fo when, after the plaintiff has eftablifhed his claim, the decifion of the caufe depends upon the proof of the facts which make the ground of the defence of the defendant againft the claim, and the proof which the defend-ant is obliged to make is confiderable, without being en-tirely complete, the judge may defer the oath to the de-fendant in order to complete it.

The judge ought alfo in the choice of the party to whom he defers the oath, have regard to the quality of the parties, and consider which is most worthy of credit, or which ought to have most knowledge of of the fact; he ought to determine *inspectis personarum & causæ circumstantiis. cap. fin. X, jurej.*

833. Dumoulin, *ad l.* 3, *Cod. de reb. cred*, adduces for examples of an incomplete proof, yet sufficiently considerable to be completed by the oath of the plaintiff, I. that which results from an extrajudicial confession of the debtor, when it has been made not in the presence of the creditor, or when it has been made in the presence of the creditor, indeed, but without being particular and without expressing the cause of the debt.

The books of merchants are also in their favor an incomplete proof of the entries therein in regard to their trade and dealings, which may be completed by their oath, when they are persons of known probity; *supra*, *n.* 719. Some authors adduce, for an example of proof which may be completed by the oath of the plaintiff, the disposition of a single witness, when this witness is a man worthy of credit; but it appears by our law that it is only in very light matters that the disposition of a single witness joined to the oath of the defendant, can entitle him to judgment. See *supra*, *n.* 783.

834. Although in the suit below, the cause has been decided by the oath which was deferred to one of the parties, this does not prevent the judge of appeal from deferring it to the other party, if he thinks that the question ought to be decided by the oath of this party rather than by the oath of him to whom it has been deferred in the suit below. This we notice every day in practice.

835. A difference remains to be observed between the oath which is deferred by the judge and that which is deferred by a party; to wit, that that which is deferred by a party may be referred to him: whereas when it is deferred by the judge, the party to whom it is deferred must take the oath or lose his cause. Such is the practice of our court which is improperly charged with error by Faber. It suf-

fices, to justify it, to attend to the meaning of the word refer; for in order to say properly that I refer the oath to my adversary, it is necessary that he should have deferred it to me.

§. II.

Of the oath called juramentum in litem.

836. The oath called *juramentum in litem*, is that which the judge defers to a party, to fix and determine the amount of the judgment which he ought to pronounce in his favor.

The interpreters of the civil law distinguish two of them; that which they call *juramentum affectionis* and that which they call *juramentum veritatis*.

Juramentum affectionis was that which the judge deferred to me to estimate, not the intrinsic value of the thing belonging to me of which I was deprived by the fraud of the adverse party, but the affection which I had for this thing.

The judge gave judgment in this case for the sum in which I swore that I *bona fide* estimated my affection for this thing, and this estimation might surpass the intrinsic value of the thing.

It is of this oath that Ulpian says, *Non ab judice doli æstimatio ex eo quod interest fit, sed ex eo quod in litem juratur;* L. 64, ff. *de judic.* And further; *Res, ex contumacia, æstimatur ultra rei pretium;* L. 1, ff. *de in lit. jur.*

This *juramentum affectionis* is not used in our practice; we have only admitted the *juramentum veritatis*.

837. There is room for this oath whenever the plaintiff has established his claim for the restitution of certain things and there is only an uncertainty respecting the amount of the damages which ought to be given against the the defendant on default of making the restitution of the said things, whereof the value is known only by the plain-

tiff to whom they belong. The judge in this case, in order to determine the amount of the damages which he ought to give, takes the estimation which the plaintiff may make of the true value of the things, whereof he demands the restitution, after the plaintiff has previously sworn to make this estimation *bona fide*.

For example, if a traveller had given his portmanteau in deposit to an innkeeper, and it was there stolen; the deposit being proved and the traveller, who demands the restitution of it, having alone the knowledge of what was contained in the portmanteau, the judge in order to determine the amount of the damages he ought to give against the innkeeper on default of making the restitution required, cannot do otherwise than take the oath of the traveller upon the value of the things contained in the portmanteau.

838. Among the Romans, the judge often left the plaintiff an indefinite liberty upon the sum to which he might swear that he estimated the things whereof he demanded the restitution: *Jurare in infinitum licet*; L. 4, §. ff. *de in litem jur.*

It was however left to the prudence of the judge, when he should think it proper, to limit the sum above which the estimation could not be carried: *Judex potest præfinire certam summam usque ad quam juretur*; L. 5, §. 1, *d. tit.*

According to our usages, the judge, after having heard the parties, limits the sum to the amount of which the plaintiff ought to be believed on his oath upon the value of the things whereof he demands the restitution.

He ought to have regard, in fixing this sum, to the quality of the plaintiff, the greater or less probability which appears in his allegations; the nature of the cause ought also to be considered. In this estimation one ought much less to spare a defendant who should be convicted of being an accomplice in the theft which has been made of the things to be estimated, than him who was in fault only by imprudence and want of care.

Although the judge ſhould take, upon this eſtimation, the oath of the plaintiff, without limiting to him the ſum, he ought not to be ſo far bound to regard it, as not to be able to depart from it, if he found it exceſſive: *Et... juratum fuerit, licet judici absolvere, vel minoris condemnare*; L. 5, §. 2, ff. *d. tit.*

THE END.

ERRATA.

PAGE.	LINE.				
24,	26,	for	*could,*	read	*could not.*
97,	3,		*valuable,*		*invaluable.*
111,	6,		*of the,*		*the.*
123,	29,		*required,*		*acquired.*
168,			§. 4,		§. 1.
170,	last,	after	*shall,*	add	*see*
209,	3,	for	*he,*	read	*be.*
248,			§. II.		*Section the Second.*
295,			*Section the Second,*		*Section the Fourth.*

www.ingramcontent.com/pod-product-compliance
Lightning Source LLC
LaVergne TN
LVHW092115300926
849161LV00002B/140
9781886363625